An Introduction to Sociology

Feminist Perspectives

Third edition

Pamela Abbott, Claire Wallace and Melissa Tyler

Routledge
Taylor & Francis Group

LONDON AND NEW YORK

First published 1990
by Routledge
Second edition published 1997
This third edition published 2005
by Routledge
2 Park Square, Milton Park, Abingdon, Oxon OX14 4RN

Simultaneously published in the USA and Canada
by Routledge
270 Madison Ave, New York, NY 10016

Routledge is an imprint of the Taylor & Francis Group

© 1997, 2003 Pamela Abbott and Claire Wallace
© 2005 Pamela Abbott, Claire Wallace and Melissa Tyler

Typeset in Amasis and Univers by
Keystroke, Jacaranda Lodge, Wolverhampton
Printed and bound in Great Britain by
TJ International Ltd, Padstow, Cornwall

British Library Cataloguing in Publication Data
A catalogue record for this book is available from the British Library

Library of Congress Cataloging in Publication Data
A catalog record for this book has been requested

ISBN 0–415–31258–2 (hbk)
ISBN 0–415–31259–0 (pbk)

Contents

CONTENTS

Tables

Preface

In feminist terms the twentieth century began, in Britain at least, with the suffragettes and ended with the Spice Girls and the popular perception, as Germaine Greer wryly observed, that 'feminism has served its purpose and should now eff off' (1999, p. 5). During the intervening period, feminism achieved profound success, improving the social, political, cultural and economic position of women in a whole range of ways. At the same time, feminist theory, particularly in the last three decades or so, has made a significant contribution to rethinking many aspects of the ways in which we make sense of society. Yet, many post-feminists consider that feminism has now achieved its aims and is therefore no longer relevant (or welcome) politically or theoretically, given the diversity of womanhood; or that feminism has simply gone 'too far' towards benefiting women, resulting in a gender 'backlash'. Others claim that feminism has not gone far enough in addressing social inequalities, and that those gains that have been made have focused too specifically on the needs of middle-class, white professional women living in the West. In many respects therefore, feminism (including feminist sociology) is currently engaged in something of a 'stock-taking exercise', reflecting critically on questions such as how to address the diverse experiences of women whilst maintaining some notion of commonality, at the same time as examining the relevance of the feminist project at the beginning of the twenty-first century.

For us, the relevance of feminism as both a political and a theoretical commitment, and its centrality to sociology as a critical project, becomes immediately apparent when we step outside of these debates and locate feminism and its relationship to sociology within the broader social totality.

As Goran Therborn (2004, p. 17) notes in his discussion of patriarchy throughout the course of the twentieth century, 'in the beginning of our story all significant societies were clearly patriarchal'. However, in many societies, he argues, patriarchy was forced into retreat during the last century, a process he describes as *de-patriarchalization* (p. 73). In most countries, the legal rights of women and girls have been extended, and the expansion of education and paid work has increased women's autonomy in many respects. Dramatic socio-economic, political and cultural changes have undermined the authority of individual husbands and fathers, and of men's power over women as a group. Yet this process of 'de-patriarchalization' has by no means been even. As Therborn puts it, 'the most important feature of the twentieth-century change of patriarchy is not its universal tendency. It is the variation in outcome as well in timing' (p. 129). This means that there are many areas of the world where patriarchy is still well entrenched; South and West Asia, North and sub-Saharan Africa, are notable examples. As he puts it, in these areas of the world

> The entanglement of patriarchy and misogyny with caste and religion through rituals and rules of pollution and purity provides male domination with a deep social anchor, largely out of reach for a secular bureaucracy and its discourse of equal rights.
>
> (Therborn, 2004, p. 112)

Even in those Western societies shaped by a commitment to equality, it is no exaggeration to argue that the difference between men and women continues to shape almost every aspect of our lives. Jan Morris, who started life as a male journalist called James and became a woman when she was in her thirties, sums up some of the experiences of living as both a man and a woman in her book *Conundrum*:

> We are told that the social gap between the sexes is narrowing, but I can only report that having, in the second half of the twentieth century, experienced life in both roles, there seems to me no aspect of existence, no moment of the day, no contact, no arrangement, no response, which is not different for men and women.
>
> (Morris, 1997, p. 1)

But as feminists have argued, men and women's respective experiences of the social world are not only shaped by difference, but by a *hierarchical ordering of difference*, what feminists have called 'the gender order'. This means that most societies value men and masculinity more so than women and femininity; the relationship between men and women is not simply shaped by difference, but by inequality. The consequences of this are summed up by an Amnesty International briefing to the United Nations on the global nature of discrimination against women:

> In every corner of the world, women and girls continue to face horrifying violence, systematic discrimination and other serious human rights abuses. They are beaten and killed in their homes, attacked in their communities, raped and brutalized in war, turned away as refugees, denied the right to education and employment, and are excluded from public life and exploited – simply because of their gender.
>
> (Amnesty International, 2002, p. 3)

It is with an awareness of the extent to which, while the lives of many people (particularly those living in the West) have improved considerably in recent years, this is certainly not the case for the majority of the world's women, that we have approached this third edition of *An Introduction to Sociology: Feminist Perspectives*. In the decade or so since the first edition of the book, the debates within feminism and within sociology have clearly moved on considerably. When the second edition was published in 1997, it seemed that debates about postmodernism and media culture were beginning to displace more traditional, sociological preoccupations with work, family and stratification and also, to some extent, feminism itself. In the intervening years, feminist research has begun to reaffirm its commitment to these key areas of sociology, however, at the same time as incorporating new ways of thinking about established topics. Black and post-colonial perspectives have been brought to bear, for instance, on traditional sociological concerns with issues such as social class, the household and the sexual division of labour.

The original text embodied the argument that an appreciation of society from women's perspective leads to a recasting of traditional sociological distinctions between, for example, work and the family or between violent crime and sexuality. Now, the impact of feminist scholarship has led to a recasting and, to some extent, a transgression of former boundaries between disciplines, as well as within them. It has also problematised the idea of a single women's perspective, emphasising instead the diversity of women's experiences and viewpoints. Much of the material in the first and second editions remains relevant, but in this third edition we have taken account of the shifting parameters and interests of feminism, and of diverse groups of men and women. We have brought the empirical data up to date and included material on new debates and issues to which feminist perspectives have made a significant contribution.

Our own position is that while there are important differences in women's experi-ence, there are also important commonalities; while acknowledging the contributions postmodernist scholars have made to the study of gender, we would nevertheless argue that sociology as a critical discipline can help to elucidate women's position and that feminist sociology still has an important contribution to make – yet one that is by no means universally recognised. We use the term 'feminist' here to refer to those who see women as exploited, devalued and oppressed, who are committed to chang-ing this, and who consequently adopt a critical perspective towards dominant intellectual traditions, modes of social organisation and cultural belief systems that have ignored or justified women's oppression. Our position as feminist sociologists is problematic in this sense, as our critical perspective is sociological, but as feminists we are also critical of sociology itself, for the ways in which it has tended to ignore, marginalise and exclude both women, and feminist perspectives.

Sociologists have now – in the main – taken some of the feminist criticisms of malestream sociology on board, but feminist arguments still tend to be ignored or marginalised in many areas of sociological thought. Although feminism has had more of an impact in sociology than in many other disciplines, it is still the case that the reconceptualisation of the discipline, which, we would argue, is necessitated by acceptance of the feminist critique, has not taken place in many areas of the discipline, particularly in sociological theory. Despite the proliferation of feminist studies over the past thirty years or so in sociology, their impact has been uneven. In this sense, our book still stands as one of the only feminist commentaries, and as something of a corrective to the other introductory textbooks in sociology.

The first edition of the textbook was written from a British perspective – we were British sociologists who had spent our working lives in Britain and were reporting largely British research. However, the textbook has been used in many countries of the world and translated into several languages. Moreover, over the last ten years or so British sociology has begun to reflect on its own ethnocentrism. To take account of the wider readership and shifts in both sociological and feminist thought we have therefore sought to introduce a more comparative perspective to this third edition, by incorporating a broader range of international literature and empirical data, and by rethinking our own perspectives.

The result, intended for students and for the general reader interested in understanding the feminist contribution to sociology, provides an introduction to feminist perspectives in sociology that stands on its own or can be used in conjunction with more conventional introductory textbooks. For those readers who want to incorporate feminist perspectives into their sociological understanding we suggest reading the appropriate chapter in this book after reading the corresponding chapter of a conventional textbook. The chapters in this book do not have to be read in the order in which they are written. We would suggest reading Chapters 1 and 2 first, however, as these give a broad overview of both the feminist critique of malestream sociology, and of the range of theoretical perspectives that feminists have developed. After that, you can follow your own interests or read the relevant chapters in line with the sequencing of the syllabus that you are following.

Of course, we are not presenting this as a 'true' or universal account of social reality, nor do we see ourselves as neutral scientists merely recounting the work of others. Nor are we claiming that our coverage of sociological concepts, topics and debates is in any sense exhaustive. All knowledge is partial and provisional, and this applies as much to feminist as to malestream knowledge. Feminism is not one theoretical perspective within sociology, but a broad range of complex (and often contradictory) ideas. However, feminist knowledge has made an important contribution to sociology and has challenged the basic theoretical assumptions of malestream work, arguing that sociological theories, methods and explanations need to be reconceptualised. It is with developing and illustrating this argument that we are concerned in this book.

Feminism is not a unified movement. While all feminists are agreed that women are subordinated and that it is necessary to develop strategies to liberate them, there are fundamental disagreements about the causes of that oppression and the strategies for achieving liberation. There are even disagreements about what the feminist project is about and, indeed, what women are (or, as we shall explore throughout the book, if women as a category even exist). There are a large number of feminisms. In this book we have tried to describe some of the main theories of relevance to sociology, but this inevitably means that some feminist theories – such as psychoanalysis and feminist literary theory – which have made a great contribution to understanding women's experiences have been left out.

This problem of distinguishing between different feminist perspectives is not just an academic one, but also a personal one. We have to try to identify *ourselves* as well. In the last edition we described ourselves as Marxist feminists who had evolved into socialist feminists – feminists who saw class and gender as carrying equal weight in shaping our experiences of the social world, and also in how we make sense of those experiences. This affected our interpretation of the material used in the book. We have since then been influenced by the poststructuralist and postmodernist critique of modernism and its associated theories – including those of Marxism and socialism. We have also been influenced by the claim made by Black and post-colonial feminists that Western feminism has been ethnocentric in its account of women's lives. Our position would now be a rather more eclectic one; while still seeing the need to take a fundamentally critical perspective on society, on sociology and on the issue of sexual difference (the difference between men and women), we are inclined to work more from a diversity of theoretical perspectives, arguing that all of them contribute to our understanding of the social world. Although we are of course aware that some ideas are incompatible (structural-functionalism and postmodernism, for instance), we would also argue that it is understanding rather than purity of theory that is of crucial importance. This book is therefore centrally a contribution to documenting how feminist sociology can enable us to better understand our lives.

It is important that you, the reader, be aware of our position. We do not feel that it is possible for us to detach ourselves from our theoretical perspectives and become neutral reporters of other feminists' arguments and research findings. It is important that you are aware that we are not neutral, and that our view is that it is neither possible nor desirable for anyone to be neutral. This lack of neutrality is especially important for you, the reader, to keep in mind when we are evaluating the adequacy of work by other feminists and sociologists.

Whilst feminist perspectives have had a considerable impact on sociology in recent years, particularly in terms of the sociological consideration of topics such as the body, sexuality, culture and lifestyle, recent debates in which feminist theory has been engaged have tended to take place largely at academic conferences or in the pages of scholarly journals. In this third edition we have aimed to provide a summary of this recent scholarly activity, by integrating it into a revised and updated version of the existing framework, hoping that it will be both accessible and stimulating to a wide audience. Hence, this updated version is intended to be more comprehensive, not only in its coverage of sociological topics (this edition features two new chapters on sexuality and media culture) but also in the range of theoretical perspectives and comparative material included, much of it written by international feminists and sociologists. But we are also mindful of the extent to which many academics feel it is undesirable to encourage students at any level to rely solely on a single textbook. This third edition is thus intended to be more comprehensive and comparative in its coverage of the feminist contribution to sociology, yet at the same time, seeks to provide a guiding framework to stimulate and actively encourage further reading on specific topics in more depth. For this reason, we have also included annotated suggestions for further reading.

We hope you will enjoy reading the book and will learn from it. We have learned much from writing it and have enjoyed the process. Feminism and sociology are not academic subjects that are just to be learned, but ways of coming to understand the society in which we live and our position in it. We hope that this book will stimulate you to look at the world afresh and come to new insights.

Acknowledgements

We would like to acknowledge the help that various people including Roger Sapsford, Philip Hancock, Becky Probert, Laurie Cohen and Amal El-Sawad have given us in writing the book and in giving us the opportunity to discuss much of the material presented here. We are also grateful to Moira Taylor, Constance Sutherland and Adam Gilbert at Taylor & Francis for their assistance in its publication. Special thanks also go to Julie Collett at Loughborough University for her research assistance, and for her enthusiasm for the project. We would also like to thank our students at various universities, who inspired us to write and develop the book and who also helped with the discussion of its ideas. We alone, of course, remain responsible for the contents.

CHAPTER ONE

Introduction: feminism and the sociological imagination

Setting the agenda

Despite long-standing criticism for its malestream orientation and bias, sociology remains a relatively male-dominated discipline. This has fundamental implications for its theories, methods, research and teaching. While the majority of students studying the subject – as well as an increasing number of lecturers and researchers – are women, women are found in senior posts less often than men. Female students tend to be taught 'malestream' sociology and so are inducted into knowledge that plays a key role in justifying the relatively disadvantaged structural position of (the majority of) women, and in perpetuating the cultural inferiority of femininity. Similarly, what is perceived as 'mainstream' sociological research and theory tends to be that which male sociologists produce.

However, there has been some progress. Sociologists can no longer afford to ignore sexual difference (a term used here to refer to the difference between men and women as social subjects), and there is now some discussion within the discipline about the changes needed for its malestream bias to be overcome. There is a steady flow of books, journal articles and conference papers published by women writing from feminist perspectives in sociology, and most academic social science publishers have a Feminist, Gender Studies or Women's Studies list. However, much sociological research continues to focus on men and boys, and to ignore women and girls or to incorporate women but without modifying the theories that justified their subordinate status. There is still a tendency in the social sciences, albeit a declining one, to generalise from male samples to the whole population, or to overlook the ways in which sexual difference shapes the social world and our experiences of it, and for textbooks to 'add gender in' as an extra topic or chapter rather than fully incorporating research findings on women and gender into each substantive area. There is also a tendency for feminist thought to be seen as an addendum deserving one or two lectures, or something that can safely be left to women to teach as an optional course, rather than as a core element of the sociology curriculum.

The relative success of textbooks such as this indicates that there is a demand for an alternative approach, however; one that places feminist contributions to sociology at the heart of the discipline. It is now the case that in most Western countries few courses in sociology could be designed without at least some recognition of feminist perspectives, while journal articles and research designs are routinely required by their reviewers to problematise sexual difference, or to incorporate a perspective that at least takes account of the differences between men and women. Indeed, in these contexts, feminist perspectives are more developed and more influential in sociology than in most other social science disciplines. So, much progress has been made. Sociology nevertheless remains a relatively male-dominated academic discipline, and in many parts of the world a feminist perspective is marginalised, missing from the agenda completely, ridiculed or even treated with outright hostility.

Even within Western sociology, acceptance of the centrality of feminist perspectives has been far from universal. Indeed, a number of malestream responses to feminist contributions can be discerned involving, at one extreme, ghettoisation and, at the other, colonisation. By ghettoisation we mean the marginalisation of feminist sociology as something that female lecturers can do or that should be taught on Women's Studies courses. While differences between men and women may be accepted as important, gender is added on as another variable, along with class and race; the serious challenge posed by feminists to malestream theories is ignored, distanced or undermined. In the main, men do not teach on these courses – possibly because they are not seen as prestigious enough or likely to lead to promotion (Richardson and Robinson, 1994), or because sexual difference, and gender particularly, continues to be seen as a 'women's issue'. The relatively small number of male students taking courses on feminist theory or gender issues certainly seems testimony to this. Perhaps the most problematic, enduring and frustrating response feminist approaches to sociology have been met with in recent years, in this respect, has been one of apathy from male academics, male students and from female students as well.

At the other extreme, we find what might be regarded as colonisation – the development of Men's Studies, and the argument that men need to study men in a way analogous to the way in which women have claimed the need to study women. Victor Seidler (1994), for example, has argued that problematising masculinity is central to the development of social theory. In contrast, Dianne Richardson and Victoria Robinson (1994) suggest that the development of Men's Studies may actually enable men to avoid taking seriously the key issues about masculinity that feminists have highlighted. They point out that Men's Studies is concerned mainly with masculine subjectivity rather than with research that would provide a greater understanding of how men gain, maintain and use power to subordinate women. Indeed, Men's Studies is often conceived largely as a concern with liberating men (Seidler, 1994). As Jalna Hanmer has suggested,

> To conceive of the study of men to be about liberating men is to have little interest in any area of social analysis that seriously critiques men as men, as part of the problem, not just to women and each other but to society and our continuation as a species.

> (Hanmer, 1990, p. 29)

A related development in the last fifteen years or so has been the general trend, in the UK at least, to rename Women's Studies 'Gender Studies' or to develop new courses entitled Gender Studies instead. Indeed, some publishers have changed the name of their lists from Women's Studies to Gender Studies. What is interesting is that in many cases this has not changed the content of courses; rather the concern has been to recognise that feminist research and theorising is not just about women and for women, but must include an analysis of women in relation to men, and that if women are to be liberated both men and women must change. However, in some cases this change seemingly involves a failure to recognise the ways in which male-stream disciplines, including sociology, have been implicated in the subordination of women. Related to this, the move towards Gender Studies represents what might be regarded as a de-radicalisation of women's studies. The danger is that the key insights and challenges to malestream sociology made by feminists will be diluted. The central issue for feminists is not that sexual difference divides – that differences between men and women need to be taken seriously – but that the subordination and exploitation of women (albeit recognising differences and divisions *between* women) needs to be explained. In other words, an awareness needs to be maintained that the subjectivity of women has to be understood in a structural relationship with men – a relationship shaped by difference and inequality.

The feminist challenge to malestream sociology is one that requires a radical rethink of the content and methodology of the whole enterprise; one that recognises the need not simply to see society from the position of women as well as from the standpoint of men, but to see the world as fundamentally gendered. Indeed, it is the feminist challenge to sociology that has been instrumental in triggering the now almost taken-for-granted understanding that a variety of standpoints – gendered, racialised, sexualised, embodied, ageing, and so on – need to be recognised, and that we need not only to deconstruct 'human' into men and women, but also to deconstruct these categories in themselves.

Thus many of the criticisms we have made above apply as much, if not more, to questions of ethnicity, social class, disability and sexuality. Sociology is a discipline that has been and continues to be dominated by able-bodied, white males who are middle class by destination if not necessarily by origin. Women have come into the discipline and challenged the relatively blinkered view of malestream sociology, but they too have tended to be white, Western and largely middle class. Hence, many white feminist sociologists have been criticised for their ethnocentric view of gender relations, and for their failure to take adequate account of diversity amongst men and women in relation to social class, age, sexuality, disability and global power dynamics. Yet recognition of the sociological significance of these various forms of social identity, and crucially of the interrelationships between them, has emerged – we would argue – partly as a result of the space created by feminist research, theory and politics.

With this in mind, we examine in the various chapters that follow the contribution that feminists have made and are making to sociology, but aim to do so in a reflexive and constructive way. We aim to explore the society in which we live from a range of feminist perspectives. In doing so, we have not aimed to provide an exhaustive overview of the contributions of female sociologists – recognising, of course, that not all (pro) feminist sociologists are women and that not all female sociologists are feminists; nor have we sought to present a comprehensive summary of empirical research findings. Rather, we have selected material that enables us to demonstrate the contribution that feminism has made and is making to sociology, and also to reflect on areas where there is more to be done. We have tried therefore to include comparative material where possible, including some of our own research. In doing so we recognise that although some issues – such as women's oppression within the family – are important global concerns for feminist sociology, such issues are also contextual. This means that gender issues may well mean something different to women in different parts of the world, and in different sectors of the same society. In other words, the lived experience of structural similarities and differences is socially and culturally specific.

Hence, although domestic violence, for instance, is often triggered by the perception that a woman has 'failed' to fulfil her wifely duties, just what these wifely duties are can vary considerably throughout the world. In some countries a woman may be abused because her family has failed to supply a full dowry, whereas in other societies women are attacked for failing to cook or clean, or manage the housekeeping budget adequately. Many of the issues are the same; they are issues of power and control, shaped by sexual difference. In Eastern Europe and the former Soviet Union women were not liberated by their entry into paid employment, although many Western feminists drawing on a long tradition of liberal humanism had seen this as the road to independence. Hence, although our focus here, in terms of the research material we refer to in the book, is primarily on contemporary capitalist societies, we have attempted to take a broad, comparative and reflexive approach to understanding some of the similarities and differences in women's experiences and the sense which sociology might make of them on a global scale, whilst recognising that much more needs to be done – both politically and academically – in this respect.

As soon as we take the feminist criticisms of malestream sociology seriously we realise that we need to ask different questions and that in order to answer them we need to develop new concepts and theories; new ways of looking at and understanding the world sociologically. This is because the malestream legacy contemporary sociology has inherited from its 'founding fathers' in the main saw women's roles as natural and therefore did not investigate or problematise them; sociology was developed to understand the public world of men and, hence, is often inadequate for investigating the world that women inhabit and the relationships between men and women. Questions such as: Why is it usually women who care for young children? Why are there more male than female political leaders? Why do men rarely wear make-up, at least in Western societies, whereas women are often expected to do so? become key issues – sociological problems – requiring investigation and explanation. What is required, we would argue, is for sociology to be rethought or re-imagined, from a feminist perspective.

Gendering the sociological imagination

Sociology is about understanding the relationship between our own personal experiences and the social structures we inhabit (Mills, 1954). However, in the 1960s and 1970s women began to express the feeling that sociology did not relate to their experiences, because it examined the world primarily from the perspective of men. Indeed, existing theories and explanations could be challenged, they argued, if the perspective of women was taken into account. The realisation of this failure of sociology to speak to the experiences of women, and its consequent inability to theorise comprehensively, therefore led feminists to examine more closely why this was the case; why sociology, despite its claims to neutrality, had a malestream bias. Sociologist Dorothy Smith (1987) argued that this was because women's concerns and experiences were not seen as authentic, but subjective, while men's were seen as the basis for the production of 'true' knowledge. Consequently, sociological knowledge portrayed women as men saw them, not as they saw themselves. Sociology also played a key role in maintaining women's subordinate and exploited position. While sociology claimed to put forward a detached and impartial view of reality, in fact it articulated a view from the perspective of men, so that women became the objects rather than the subjects of the sociological imagination.

In this respect, it has been argued that women are relegated by sociology and within a whole range of other academic disciplines to a more 'natural' role than men, one defined by their biology and 'nature', while men are seen more in terms of 'culture' and 'civilisation', resulting in a relationship between 'cultured man' and 'natural woman'. Following Simone de Beauvoir (1988 [1949]), French feminists in particular have argued that, in this sense, women constitute the 'Other' against which culture, society, rationality, and so on are constructed. Thus women are seen as gendered but men are not (hence, sociology books, conferences and courses that focus on gender are often seen as being primarily for women, and not of interest or direct relevance to men). Men tend to be regarded as being part of universal rationality – those who analyse and understand the world from a (social) scientific perspective – and women are the ones who need explaining or 'bringing in'. Yet, arguments for the 'special' perspective and understanding of women often reinforce this point of view.

Some feminists have argued that women have a unique outlook on the social world, rooted in the 'special' nature of their experiences of the body, and particularly of motherhood, which are different from those of men. Such feminists have therefore concurred with other (more conservative) perspectives claiming that differences between men and women are ultimately rooted in biology. Others argue that such differences between men and women are largely socially constructed and should be overcome, or at least their impact on men's and women's lives ought to be minimised (see Chapters 2 and 3).

Our own position is somewhere in between these two extremes, in that we regard sexual difference as a socio-cultural construction. In our view, biological and physiological differences are often used as the basis for an ideology of sexual difference, one that serves to 'justify' and hence maintain women's inferior social position. We would argue that gendering is a process whereby biological differences are used *post hoc* to justify subordination and exploitation based on sexual difference, and are not the *basis* of the original differentiation. This is not a fixed process but is culturally and socially variable, so that ideologies of sexual difference need to be subjected to sociological analysis.

Ideologies of sexual difference

Feminists argue that malestream theories fail to meet the criteria for being accepted as adequate and valid knowledge because they do not take account of men's and women's different experiences of the social world. They in fact serve as an ideological justification for the subordinate position of women, rather than a critique or an explanation of it. By 'ideological' we mean a pattern of ideas (knowledge that is regarded as 'common sense') – both factual and evaluative – which purports to explain and legitimate the social structure and culture of a social group or society and which serves to justify social actions which are in accordance with that pattern of ideas. Ideology also shapes our everyday feelings, thoughts and actions. However, the knowledge provided by an ideology is partial or selective and sometimes provides contradictory descriptions and explanations of the social world. Ideologies, especially dominant ones, also serve to construct certain aspects of the social world as natural and universal and therefore unquestionable and unchangeable. Aspects of the social world that are created as natural and universal by an ideology are thereby protected from the charge of being socially produced.

There are a number of ideologies of sexual difference that do not necessarily present consistent accounts but cohere together to form a 'dominant ideology'. A dominant ideology is more easily able to present its ideas as natural and universal because it is produced and reproduced by those in positions of relative power. The exclusion of women from positions of power and from the production of knowledge has, feminists argue, meant that patriarchal ideology (male-dominated ideas) has been able to present itself as universal knowledge. However, feminists have challenged and continue to challenge patriarchal ideologies – that is, ideas that support male supremacy – arguing that they are partial and distorting. But because men are in positions of relative power (in politics or in the mass media, for instance) they are able to marginalise feminist ideologies.

Ideology as we are using the term, then, is made up of a set of common-sense beliefs or practical knowledge that form the basis for social action. For example, familial ideologies in capitalist societies tend to present the nuclear family – of mother, father and dependent children living as a household, with the man as economic provider and the woman as the primary carer in the domestic sphere – as a natural (biologically based) and universal institution. Alternative styles of living are represented as deviations because they try to change that which is believed to be inevitable. However, ideologies conceal the fact that they are socially constructed and benefit some groups more than others. The nuclear family, with a gendered division of labour, serves the interests of men as well as capitalist development, feminists have argued.

However, ideologies are not all encompassing; they can be opposed by sub-ordinate social groups and forces and become subject to contestation and change. Feminists challenge patriarchal ideologies by demonstrating their partial and distorted view of the world, or by undermining them. Think of internationally renowned pop star Madonna's various attempts to parody patriarchal representations of feminine sexuality as passive and servile, for instance, or of TV character Buffy the Vampire Slayer's physical strength and ingenuity. Whether we find these strategies convincing or not, they are part of the culture of feminist challenges to patriarchal ideology.

Patriarchal ideologies have the effect of disguising the actuality of male power. Men defined themselves as powerful because of their ability to master nature – to be dominant. Women, because of their biological role in reproduction, have traditionally been defined as being closer to nature than men, thus justifying their domination by men. Male ideology confirms and reinforces men's dominant status by devaluing women's work and reproductive functions while at the same time presenting male work as of social and economic importance. Masculinity ('man') is equated with the public sphere; to be a man is to be a person who does important things outside of the domestic sphere.

In some Eastern and Central European countries, women were expected to work in the public sphere in the same way as men throughout most of the twentieth century. However, this did not 'liberate' them in the way that Marxists and socialists assumed it would, partly because of the patriarchal division of labour that continued in the home and also because of patriarchal assumptions that pervaded the workplace and public life. Therefore it is not simply a question of changing laws and putting women in the same position as men. What is needed is an understanding of the structures of power and the way in which the sex/gender system, and ideologies of sexual difference, forms part of it. This means developing an understanding of the private as well as the public sphere from a range of feminist perspectives.

Feminists have challenged the notion that biology is destiny, emphasising instead, as Simone de Beauvoir put it, that 'one is not born but rather becomes, a woman' (1988, p. 295). They have argued that biological differences between men and women do not explain their social roles and that these need to be understood as socially constructed and in need of sociological explanation. While there may be anatomical differences between males and females, what is important is the way these differences are perceived and evaluated, the way boys and girls are socialised into what is seen as appropriate gender behaviour, and what behaviour is expected and valued. Parents, teachers and society in general both treat boys and girls differently and have different expectations as to how they should behave. The expected behaviour of boys and girls is both encouraged and reinforced by the adults with whom they come into contact and the institutions of which they are members. Thus television programmes and school reading schemes both show appropriate role models. Boys and girls who do not conform to the appropriate role model are both chastised and ridiculed by adults and by their peers. Boys who display what are seen as feminine traits are referred to as 'wimps', and girls who behave in masculine ways as 'tomboys'. While some girls may actually welcome being referred to as tomboys, boys often dislike being called 'sissies', which is seen as a term of derision both in terms of gender and sexuality; boys and young men tend to act to avoid any notion that they have what may be seen as female traits (see e.g. Willis, 1977).

However, historical and anthropological research suggests that what is seen as an appropriate role for men and women is specific to particular societies, or social strata within societies, at particular times (Oakley, 1972). Different societies have different images of what is appropriate behaviour for males and females, and these also differ over time. There are important differences in the ways in which gender roles are defined even within any given society either at different points in history or between social and ethnic groups. Female sexuality, for example, can be seen as a source of untrammelled libido at one point in time or by one social group, and as completely missing in other social groups or at other points in time. In the nineteenth century in Britain and the USA, for example, white women were seen as having no sexual desires at all, while Black women were seen as uncontrollably promiscuous (see hooks, 1992). While working-class women were required to work long hours in paid employment, middle-class women were excluded from paid employment on the grounds of their 'biological weakness'. Explanations based on biological differences or biological factors are therefore unconvincing. It is necessary for sociology to develop theories that are adequate both for explaining gender divisions and for taking account of gender differences.

The sex–gender distinction

Largely following Ann Oakley (1972), feminist explanations for inequalities based on sexual difference have tended to make a distinction between 'sex' and 'gender', one that parallels a more general sociological separation of the biological from the social; of 'nature' from 'nurture'. According to this distinction, while 'sex' refers to the biological differences between males and females and provides the (pre-social) basis for gender socialisation, 'gender' refers to the socio-cultural construction of roles appropriate to men and women, and to the qualities and characteristics ascribed to being masculine or feminine. To put it simply, biological sex is deemed to be an aspect of identity a person is born with, whereas (social and cultural) gender is an identity we learn and acquire through an ongoing (lifelong) process of socialisation. From this perspective, we are born as *human* beings (males and females) who become *social* beings (gendered subjects) in part through learning and acquiring a (socially acceptable) gender identity. Feminists such as Oakley have argued that socially acceptable gender roles for males and females are defined according to patriarchal ideology. In this respect, the family, peer groups, education, work, religious and cultural beliefs and practices, and particularly the mass media are all regarded as key agents of gender socialisation. Hence, feminist approaches to understanding gender roles as shaped by the 'sex–gender distinction' tend to emphasise the role of social structures in shaping gender socialisation and in constraining the identities into which men and women are socialised.

More recent approaches have tended to emphasise not merely the role of social structures in constricting men and women into a relatively narrow range of gender roles, but also their capacity to exercise agency – to challenge and resist gender socialisation and stereotypes. 'Agency' refers to the ability of individuals and groups to think, speak and act as knowing subjects who are able to engage and interact with the social world (including social structures) in a purposeful and meaningful way. In short, an approach that privileges agency highlights the extent to which gender is not simply something that is 'done to us' but rather something that we 'do' – an aspect of our identity and behaviour in which we play an active part. Influenced largely by post-structuralist and postmodernist perspectives some feminists developing this approach – one that has come to be known as a 'doing gender' perspective – have argued that, just as 'gender' is a social construct, so too is 'sex' – in other words, that sex is used as a justification for the subordination of a group, rather than providing any (pre-social) basis for social differentiation.

Judith Butler (1990) in particular argued that feminists need to begin to understand not simply the relationship between sex and gender as one that is shaped by a distinction between the natural and the social, but rather between sex, gender and sexuality, and that this relationship is far more complex than a simple nature–nurture distinction would suggest. Rather than biology (sex) providing the foundation for socially constructed gender, sexual difference (the differences between men and women as social subjects shaped by sex, gender and sexuality) ought to be understood as being shaped according to an ideological framework that Butler (1990) describes as a 'heterosexual matrix'. Drawing on de Beauvoir's (1988, p. 295) earlier contention that 'One . . . becomes, a woman', Butler argues that according to this matrix, males are socialised as masculine and (hetero)sexually dominant, whereas females are compelled to become feminine and (hetero)sexually passive. Butler (1993) also contends that according to this ideological framework, biology (in the form of bodies) is socially constructed in so far as the heterosexual matrix requires men and women to present and 'perform' their bodies in particular (gendered) ways. Hence, 'feminine', (hetero)sexual women are not supposed to develop their muscles, whereas 'masculine', (hetero)sexual men are often not permitted (in the West at least) to wear make-up. In order to challenge, resist and ultimately undermine the 'heterosexual matrix', Butler (1990) urges men and women to transgress these boundaries and to live outside of gender by making what she terms 'gender trouble'.

Postmodernist feminists also emphasise the differences between women, and resist dividing the world into simplistic categories from which interests are supposed to derive. Thus simple divisions between 'black' and 'white' or 'male' and 'female' are not sufficient – we need, they argue, to take into account the complex cross-cutting divisions based upon a variety of identities and differences. This means, however, as Susan Bordo (1990) argues, that an endless process of fragmentation starts to take place so that any coherent critique – including a discernibly feminist one – is impossible. We would agree with this viewpoint and in the chapters that follow attempt to explore some of the conceptual and theoretical insights of postmodern and poststructuralist feminist perspectives, whilst remaining committed to the project of a critical, feminist sociology.

The feminist critique of malestream sociology

Feminists from a range of theoretical perspectives have made a number of criticisms of malestream sociology. These are based primarily on the view that:

1. sociology has been mainly concerned with research on men, and by implication with theories and concepts that apply primarily to men's lives;
2. research findings based on all-male samples are generalised to the whole of the population;
3. areas and issues of concern to women are frequently overlooked or seen as unimportant;

4 when women are included in research they are often presented in a distorted and stereotypical way;

5 when sex and gender are included in research they have tended to be just 'added on', ignoring the extent to which the explanatory theories used are ones which have justified the subordination and exploitation of women.

In summary, this means that there is at best no recognition that women's structural position and consequent experiences are not the same as men's and that sexual difference is therefore an important explanatory variable; at worst women's experiences are deliberately ignored or distorted. Furthermore, the ways in which men dominate and subordinate women are either ignored or seen as natural. Ann Oakley (1982) has suggested that there are three explanations for this. These are that:

1 sociology has been biased from its origin;

2 sociology is predominantly a male profession; and

3 ideologies of sexual difference result in the world being constructed in particular ways and in assumptions being made about how we explain differences between men and women.

It is evident that these three factors are interrelated. Sexist assumptions were built into sociology from its origins and in many ways these still underline sociological theory and research. Sociology as a discipline developed in the nineteenth century, and early or 'classical' sociologists were primarily concerned with understanding political and economic changes relating to the development of industrial capitalism. These changes included the growth of factory production, new class divisions and relationships, the growth of a politically conscious (male) working class and the extension of political participation to more of the adult (male) population. A central aspect of this process for women was the increased separation of home from work, the separation of production from consumption and reproduction, and the development of an ideology that 'a woman's place is in the home'. Women became increasingly associated with the domestic (private) sphere of the home and with domestic relationships, and men with the public sphere of politics and the marketplace.

Most sociologists concentrated on the public sphere of government and the workplace and ignored the private sphere of the home and domestic relationships (see Engels, 1972 [1884] for a notable exception). This was at least in part because the division of labour between the public sphere (men) and the private sphere (women) was seen as natural – that is, as having a biological, essential basis. The biologist Charles Darwin indicated that

> The chief distinction in the intellectual powers of the two sexes is shown by man attaining to a higher eminence, in whatever he takes up, than woman can attain – whether requiring deep thought, reason, or imagination, or . . . the use of the senses and the hands.
>
> (Darwin, 1871)

This meant that there was no reason for sociology to explain sexual difference; it accepted biology as a pre-social given and therefore had no need to consider gender as an explanatory variable or to theorise the subordination and exploitation of women. Women were consequently 'hidden' from the sociological gaze, both theoretically and empirically.

Sociology has tended to ignore not just women, but the whole private sphere of domestic relationships; areas of interest to women were not theorised and researched in any sustained way until relatively recently. This means that sociology has failed to develop analytical tools that can be used to understand the public and the private sphere and the changing relationships between the two. While men have been seen as inhabiting both spheres and indeed as mediating between the two, women have tended until relatively recently to be seen primarily as inhabiting the private sphere, even when they have paid employment outside of the home. Consequently, explanations for men's attitudes and behaviour are generally based on their position in the public world (largely with reference to social class), while women's are explained largely by reference to their role in the private sphere as wives and mothers.

Towards a feminist sociology

The feminist challenge has meant that in many countries across the world, women's perspectives are seen as more important now than in the past. Sara Delamont (2003) points out that opening up new topics, as well as creating new intellectual spaces and definitions of 'knowledge', has been one of the main achievements of feminist sociology. We can identify some areas of sociology that have been reconstructed as a result of feminist contributions, some areas where there has been some impact, and some areas where feminist ideas have yet to be recognised:

1 *Areas of sociology which have been revived or reconstructed from feminist perspectives*: sexuality and the body; identity and difference; visual and cultural sociology.
2 *Areas of sociology where feminist perspectives have made a significant impact*: health and illness; the family and domestic labour; work, employment and organisation; education; crime and deviance; age and the life course; mass media and popular culture.
3 *Areas of sociology where feminist perspectives have not in the main been incorporated*: social class and stratification; political sociology; social and sociological theory.

Feminists are not agreed on what is required to fill the gaps in existing theory and research in sociology. We would suggest that there have been three broad responses:

1 integration
2 separatism
3 reconceptualisation.

We will deal with each of these in turn.

Integration

This position sees the main problem as being the sexist bias in malestream sociology. The task is seen as being to remove this bias by reforming existing ideas and practices in sociology, to bring women in (by providing courses or module options on the sociology of gender, or on 'gender issues', for instance) and thereby to fill in the existing gaps in our knowledge. The way forward is to carry out research that incorporates women in samples and to reform existing theories.

The major problem with this approach is that women are likely to continue to be marginalised. They will become merely an addition to the syllabus ('gender issues' is often regarded as 'women's issues', for instance, and frequently opted for only or primarily by female students) and lip-service will be paid to incorporating women into research samples. Moreover, it leaves the basis of the discipline untouched; it fails to challenge the assumption that the discipline is (or should strive to be) scientific, and does not take into account feminist criteria on what counts as knowledge. For example, this approach would leave unchallenged malestream assumptions about the division between the public and the private, about the primacy of paid work, about class being *the* fundamental division in society, and so on. Possibly most serious of all, it fails to recognise that gender is not just a variable of differentiation, but that men subordinate and exploit women and that sociology as a discipline has played a role in justifying that exploitation and in perpetuating gender ideology.

Separatism

This position – associated largely with women's studies – argues that what is needed is what Dorothy Smith (1987) described as a sociology *for* women *by* women. Feminists should not be concerned with trying to change the biases of existing sociology, but with developing a sociological knowledge which is specifically by and about women. Explicit recognition is given to the fact that the world is always seen from a particular position or site and that women's perceptions are different from men's. Furthermore, gender – or rather sexual difference – is seen as the primary division in society; all women are seen to share a common position because they are both exploited and dominated by men. Feminist scholarship should be concerned with developing theories and carrying out research on women that is of benefit to women. The strength of this approach, apart from its gynocentrism (or woman-centredness), is that it tends to be very multi- or even trans-disciplinary in its approach, drawing on feminist contributions in psychology, literary theory, history, media and cultural studies, and so on.

Its main problem, however, is that it tends to perpetuate the marginality of women. Rather than trying to overcomes women's marginalisation and exclusion from the discipline (and from the academy generally), a separatist approach tends to celebrate it. This means that malestream sociology is left to get on with the 'real' theorising and research and continue to ignore women and feminist perspectives. Furthermore, by ignoring men, important aspects of women's social reality continue to be ignored, including the ways in which men exploit, dominate and subordinate women in the public and the private spheres. Any analysis of women's oppression must reflect on – and attempt to challenge and resist – the role played in this by men and men's interests.

Reconceptualisation

This position also recognises the need for sociological research by women and for women, and the notion that women have different points of view from men, but also emphasises that it is essential that sociology is reconstructed to take account of men's and women's different experiences and of feminist perspectives. It recognises that it is necessary for women to carry out research on men and boys as well as women and girls and acknowledges that malestream sociological theories and research findings can have an impact on feminist sociology as well as vice versa.

However, it rejects the view that all that is needed is to integrate feminist sociology into existing sociological theory and research findings – that is, as it were, to fill in the gaps in our knowledge and to tinker with the edges of existing theories. Instead, it is seen as necessary to reconceptualise sociological theories; a total rethinking, rather than partial reform, is necessary. This is both because existing theories are sexist beyond reform by mere tinkering, and because feminist research actually challenges assumptions and generalisations made on the basis of malestream research. Feminist sociologists, for instance, have highlighted that Giddens's (1991, p. 219) understanding of the body as an integral element of the 'reflexive project of the self' seriously underestimates the extent to which women's bodies as projects continue to be more reflective of partriarchal norms and values than reflexive expressions of a self-determined individuality (Tyler and Abbott, 1998, p. 437). Similarly, the revised edition of Daniel Bell's (1999) *The Coming of Post-Industrial Society* includes merely 'a note on women' in the foreword, rather than a reassessment of the post-industrial thesis that takes account of sexual difference.

What is needed is a total and radical reformulation of sociology so that it is able to incorporate women adequately. In this sense, a feminist reconceptualisation of sociology urges us to think critically and reflexively about our assumptions about the nature of the social world, about the methods and methodologies we devise to understand that world, about the concepts and theories we draw upon, and about the perspectives we adopt in order to justify our knowledge and what we claim to be 'true'. Many feminists would argue that despite ongoing debates and criticisms, malestream sociology has tended to take the latter more seriously than the feminist contribution.

The major problem with this approach is that many malestream sociologists are resistant to the view that there is a need for a feminist reconceptualisation. Nevertheless, this is the position that we (the authors) advocate and have sought to pursue in our own work, and while we recognise that this is an uphill struggle we think that it is a necessary one if sociology as a discipline is to continue to provide any meaningful critique of the social world.

Conclusions

In this chapter we have argued that it is necessary for there to be a sociology from the position of women and that if this is to become an integral part of sociology then sociology itself needs to be reconceptualised. 'Filling in the gaps' by carrying out research on women and tinkering with existing theories is not sufficient. Looking at the world from a range of feminist perspectives means that we need to rethink sociology and to challenge existing theories and research findings. In the rest of this book we substantiate this, not only by explaining what feminist sociologists have found out but also by demonstrating how this requires a rethinking of existing sociological assumptions, methods, concepts and theories.

Finally, we want to point out that we have subtitled this book 'feminist perspectives', not '*the* feminist perspective' or even 'a feminist perspective'. This is because there are a number of feminist perspectives considered here, not just one. In male-stream sociology there are an increasingly complex range of competing theoretical approaches – Marxist, Weberian, symbolic interactionist, ethnomethodological, structural-functionalist and postmodernist, to name but a few of those most frequently encountered. Feminist sociologists are also divided among these schools of thought; what feminists have in common is a commitment to looking at the social world through the lens of sexual difference. We go on to examine the main feminist perspectives in the next chapter.

SUMMARY

What is needed is sociological theory and practice that recognises:

1 the importance of sexual difference (sex, gender and sexuality) as well as class, 'race', age, disability and other forms of differentiation;
2 that the world needs to be understood as being shaped by these forms of differentiation;
3 that social spheres such as the public and the private are not separate worlds, but have been socially (economically) structured as such. Instead, they are areas of mutual influence, and the relationship between the two changes and needs explaining; and
4 the existing assumptions, concepts and theories of sociology need to be reconsidered.

FURTHER READING

Beasley, C. (1999) *What is Feminism? An Introduction to Feminist Theory.* London: Sage. This introductory text outlines in a highly accessible way the complex and often conflicting ideas shaping contemporary feminism. Overall, it is a clear and concise guide to contemporary feminist ideas. Its main weakness is perhaps its brevity – it is very much an introductory outline. But in this sense, it provides a sound basis on which to explore the ideas introduced in more depth elsewhere.

Delamont, S. (2003) *Feminist Sociology.* London: Sage. This book is a lively and engaging exploration of the achievements of feminist sociology in theory, methods and empirical research. One of its main strengths is its consideration of the work of the 'founding mothers' of sociology, as well as the contemporary opportunities and challenges posed by postmodernism. Its focus is primarily Anglo-American, however.

Freedman, J. (2001) *Feminism.* Milton Keynes: Open University Press. This short book provides a comprehensive introduction to some of the major debates within contemporary feminism, focusing on the equality versus difference debate and considering a range of feminist perspectives.

Macionis, J. and Plummer, K. (2002) *Sociology: A Global Introduction.* Second edition. London: Prentice Hall. This is a comprehensive and engaging mainstream sociology text which takes a global perspective, and which also incorporates a consideration of feminist contributions and issues of sexual difference into every chapter.

Mills, C. Wright (1954) *The Sociological Imagination.* Harmondsworth: Penguin. This book is a sociological classic and is an excellent introduction to the idea of thinking sociologically, and to the concept of the sociological imagination – a way of thinking about the social world that links individual, personal experience to its broader social context, and vice versa.

CHAPTER TWO

Feminist sociological theory

A feminist sociology is one that is not just or necessarily *about* women but one that challenges and confronts the male supremacy that institutionalises women's inequality. The defining characteristic of feminism is the view that women's relative subordination must be questioned and challenged. This involves:

- *feminist research* (that attempts to document and describe the main social differences and inequalities between men and women);
- *feminist theory* (that attempts to explain and account for these differences and inequalities);
- *feminist politics* (that attempts to challenge and resist inequalities between men and women).

Throughout this book, we are concerned with each of these aspects of feminism but in this chapter particularly, our focus is on feminist theory.

Feminism proceeds from the view that women are oppressed and that for many women this oppression is primary, whereas for others it is part of a multiplicity of oppression. Women's freedom of action and expression is limited by the relative power of men – because men, in the main, tend to possess more economic, cultural and social resources than women. This is not to ignore the fact that there are differences between women and between men, and indeed that these differences themselves involve subordination and exploitation. Nor is it to suggest that differences are additive; we recognise, for example, that race and gender articulate to produce a unique subjectivity for Black women rather than simply 'layers' of oppression (see hooks, 1982). Nonetheless we would point out that the traditional emphasis in sociology on the state, economy and other public institutions as the main sources of oppression tend to ignore power inequalities in 'private' institutions such as the family and in personal relationships in both the public and the private sphere. Feminists have argued that 'the personal is political' – that is, that it is active agents who 'do the oppressing' and that it is necessary to give credence to women's concrete experiences of oppression – ones occurring in personal, everyday encounters – as well as those at the collective and institutional level. Feminist sociologists, then, are concerned to examine the relationship between individuals and the social structure, between women's everyday experiences and the structure of the society in which we live, between men's relative power in interpersonal relationships and the ways in which that power is institutionalised in a range of societies. Feminist sociologists are also concerned to understand the ways in which relationships between men and women, and between men and between women, are changing, and to reflect on the causes and consequences of some of these changes.

Feminist perspectives and sociology

In order to understand why sociology needs feminism it is necessary to understand what sociology is trying to do as a discipline. It is concerned with providing an understanding of the social; to enable us to understand the social world we inhabit, and our position within it – to develop and deploy the sociological imagination (see Chapter 1). Feminist sociological theory has pre-eminently been concerned with enabling women (and men) to understand the subordination and exploitation of women. Without taking account of the criticisms that feminists have made of traditional sociological theory and reformulating these theories to take account of feminist perspectives, sociology will continue to produce only limited accounts of the social world which, feminists have argued, are complicit in the subordination of women.

As feminists and sociologists we want a reformulated sociology, one infused by feminist ideas. However, one of the areas of sociology that has been most resistant to change has been theory – traditionally seen as a male preserve. Before we consider feminist theories and the ways they enable us to think about the social world as a whole (rather than just women's experiences of it), we want to consider what sociological theory *is* and what it means to 'think sociologically'. Theory is the basis not just of sociology, but of social science more generally. Theories shape the ways in which we make sense of the world – the questions we ask and the range of answers that we are prepared to accept. As John Scott (1995, p. xii) has pointed out, 'sociology is a theoretical enterprise' – it is about making sense of the world in which we live – yet, as we pointed out in Chapter 1, it is not just that the discipline has ignored sexual difference (the difference between men and women as social subjects), but rather that it has been complicit in justifying subordination and exploitation based on these differences. Theory is also the area that has been slowest to change – to take the feminist critique seriously.

While empirical sociology has by and large begun to recognise the need to incorporate differences between men and women into research designs, malestream theorists tend to remain relatively silent on sexual difference and on the contribution of feminist thought to sociology and social theory more generally. Rob Stones's (1998) *Key Sociological Thinkers* includes only three chapters (out of 21) on female (in this case, feminist) theorists, and only three chapters written by women. A similar text, *Profiles in Contemporary Social Theory* (Elliott and Turner, 2001) includes only five chapters (out of 34) on female theorists, and only nine chapters written by women. These omissions not only marginalise and devalue the contribution that female sociologists (both feminist and non-feminist) have made to sociological theory, they also perpetuate the myth that theory is 'difficult', and is something that only men can do well. They also reinforce the view that theory is an account of the thoughts of great men rather than an attempt to develop ideas that enable us to understand and influence the world in which we live. Furthermore, it demonstrates that male sociological theorists have not recognised the need to reformulate theory to take account of the critique made by feminist sociologists. It is in the area of theory, then, that we can perhaps see the greatest resistance within sociology to the challenge made by feminists to the phallocentrism (male centredness) of the discipline. However, as feminists, we remain committed to the development of a reformulated sociology that is able to theorise the social world adequately, for women as well as for men.

An invitation to feminist sociology

When we (the authors) first started sociology, we each of us found that we did not really understand what we were supposed to be learning, but we also felt that what we were doing was not just interesting but exciting. We were being asked to look at, make sense of, and ask questions about the society in which we lived, in ways that had not necessarily occurred to us before, and we found the tentative answers put forward by sociologists challenging – they made us think about society and social relations in new ways and provided a much clearer and much more interesting set of answers than we had come across before. We were being invited to grasp what Charles Wright Mills (1954) called 'the sociological imagination' (see Chapter 1). It was not easy to come to understand how to think sociologically, and indeed each of us is still learning, but we certainly came to a new perspective, a new way of thinking and, equally importantly, we began to ask 'new' questions about the social world.

Our concern in this chapter particularly, but in the book as a whole, is to explore what it means to 'think sociologically' from a range of feminist perspectives. In Chapter 13 we shall look at questions relating to the status of feminist knowledge, but the focus of this chapter is on the plurality of feminist perspectives – frameworks for understanding and making sense of social relations, which is the subject matter of sociology.

Sociology is of interest to us all because it is about subjects that concern us all in our everyday lives: media culture, crime, families, work, education, race relations, class, gender, political behaviour, and so on. These are issues of general concern, the frequent topics of newspaper articles and news broadcasts, the subjects of novels and plays. Sociologists, including feminist sociologists, explore these issues and try to provide answers to the kinds of questions we commonly ask, for example: How do images of 'perfect bodies' in the mass media – in advertising or in films, for instance – affect us? Why do some people commit crimes and not others? Why does getting married continue to be so popular, even in societies in which divorce is relatively common? Why do people do the jobs they do? Why do some people become political leaders and not others? We also ask these questions in relation to our own lives: Why do I feel conscious about my body size and shape? Why didn't I get that job? However, the questions feminist sociologists ask often take a different slant: Why are women more likely than men to develop an eating disorder? Why do so few women commit crime? Why do more women than men tend to experience poverty on divorce? Why are most secretaries women, most engineers men? Why are relatively few women involved in politics?

When we answer these questions we do not just look at 'the facts'; mere description can only tell us that something is the case, not *why* it is the case. When we try to say 'why', we are going beyond the facts; we are trying to explain them. Doing this, we are using and developing theories. In explaining to ourselves what is going on in our lives we often use 'common sense'; we justify our answers by saying that 'it stands to reason', or 'it is common sense' and 'everyone knows that'. We do not ask ourselves what our theory is and where it comes from, nor do we try to refute our own conclusions. Common-sense theories frequently 'blame the victim' – divorced women are living in poverty because they would rather live on state benefits than take a job; women make good secretaries because they have nimble fingers, and are naturally more obedient and diligent than men; women don't become political leaders because they are too 'soft' and not rational or competitive enough to cope with the responsibility. Of course, sociologists share some of these common-sense views – they are members of society whose experiences and expectations shape their own beliefs – but they try to go beyond them, to draw on their sociological knowledge and research to construct theories which provide a more sophisticated understanding of the social world as a complex totality, and which are not based merely on taken-for-granted assumptions and values, but instead seek to challenge them.

The insights of sociology

As feminist sociologists we do not want to reject sociology and the insights it provides us with; what we want to do is develop a feminist sociology. What defines sociology is not *what* it studies but *how*: the sociological perspective is a distinctive way of looking at the social world. It is concerned with the patterned regularities in social life and rejects the view that these can be explained adequately by reference to the biology or psychology of individuals. This is not to say that biological or psychological explanations are wrong, but that on their own they are inadequate. It is not possible, sociologists argue, to understand the social purely by reference to characteristics that are presumed to be inherent (pre-social) in the individual, nor by reference to the psychological qualities of individuals. Yet this is how we often explain things to ourselves. We perceive that it is 'natural' to grow up and fall in love, for example. In Western cultures, we grow up to assume that we will marry the person we fall in love with, or at least make them our long-term partner, whereas in communities in which arranged marriages are more common, the 'natural' assumption is that we will grow to love and respect the person we marry, or that marriage and love are separate but somewhat inevitable aspects of adult life. These assumptions, that we learn and acquire through processes of socialisation, mean that we come to perceive non-married adults – particularly women, for whom marriage and the family are often seen as the primary role – as having somehow 'failed' or deviated in this respect.

Sociologists challenge these seemingly common-sense assumptions about what is 'normal' and 'natural' as explanations and argue that they are inadequate because they do not take into account the ways in which the structures of society and our social interactions with others influence and shape us. Sociologists point out that we need to question these taken-for-granted explanations and then construct more adequate explanations – theories that help us to understand and make sense of what is going on, to look beneath the surface, to be sceptical and to have a questioning mind. What is necessary is to develop feminist sociological perspectives that enable women to become fully integrated into sociological understanding.

Once particular explanations have begun to dominate theoretical debates, other perspectives tend to challenge them and formulate alternative ideas, and so new theories evolve and begin to establish themselves. Hence, new ways of understanding and explaining the world tend to emerge from a critique of existing ideas. In this sense, sociological theory is always provisional and partial, because theory is never 'perfect' or 'total', and because the social world is constantly changing – if we had complete understanding we would have no more need for sociology. In the same way, if we knew the truth about everything in the natural world we would have no more need for biology or physics or chemistry, but we know that this isn't possible because, like the social world, the natural world is complex and constantly changing. We would suggest that while many substantive areas in sociology have recognised the need to take feminist critiques seriously, there has not been the same awareness of a need to reformulate sociological theory in the same way. Feminist theory has been seen as concerned with explaining the specific position of women, rather than as meta- or mainstream sociological theory. We would argue that it is much more than this, even if the position of women has been a central concern. Once the feminist critique of conventional sociology is taken seriously, and feminist theories are given careful consideration, it becomes evident that sociological theory as a whole needs to be reformulated.

In his book *The Sociological Imagination* C. Wright Mills (1954) provides one of the best accounts of what it is to grasp the sociological imagination, the relationship between biography and history, and to recognise the inadequacy of individualistic explanations. The sociological imagination should enable us to grasp that personal troubles are frequently social ills, that what we perceive as social problems can only be understood and explained fully when we examine social, political and economic factors – when we look for social explanations. Think, for instance, of women's position in the labour market and the systematic way in which women are concentrated in jobs that have a lower status and lower remuneration than men (see Chapter 9). This cannot be explained simply by reference to the characteristics of individual women; we have to consider *structural* factors that shape women's experiences. In this respect, we have to consider the relationship between structure (the constellation of social institutions, organisations and practices that shape our behaviour) and agency (the capacity of individuals to act) in shaping our experiences of, and positions within, the social world. Many women might choose to work part-time, for instance (and hence exercise agency), but they exercise that 'choice' within the context of structural constraints (a relative lack of availability of state-provided or funded childcare, inflexible working arrangements, ideologies of gender and so on).

Sociology, then, is about understanding the relationship between our own experiences and the social structures we inhabit. Students are often resistant to sociology because they feel that it denies that they and other people have 'free will' – that it takes away from people the responsibility for their actions and suggests that we are totally constrained by factors over which we have no control. Sociology is not the only subject in danger of reductionism and determinism; biological and psychological explanations can be equally reductionist. Biology and psychology tend to blame the 'victim's' biology (genetic make-up) or psychological constitution for social or psychological 'problems' (phenomena in need of explanation); sociologists tend to shift the blame to outside the individual, to external factors (as indeed do some psychological perspectives – behaviourism, for instance).

Thus there is a tension between acknowledging the power of social structures, and giving due allowance to individual variation in human behaviour. To grasp the full complexity of individual social behaviour and to discover the underlying patterns of similarity which may link them together requires a theory that can explain how the moral imperatives of 'society' are translated into the norms and standards that form the guidelines for people's lives. We are socially determined and yet determining; we are acted on and yet we act. This tension between agency (underpinning life choices) and structure (shaping life chances) is one of the issues that distinguishes different sociological and indeed feminist perspectives; some give more weight to structures emphasising the constraining effects of social structures on individuals and groups, and others give more weight to agency, stressing the ways in which we act on the world and in the process have the capacity to change it. Others have developed theories that attempt specifically to understand the relationship between these two aspects or dimensions of the social world, describing the dynamic relationship between structure and agency in terms of 'structuration' (see Giddens, 1991).

The historical context of sociology

To understand fully the sociological imagination and the contemporary theoretical debates in sociology and feminism, it is necessary to understand the historical development of sociology as a discipline. Although men and women have always asked questions about, and tried to understand and explain, society and social relations, sociology as a distinct discipline developed only in any coherent and purposeful way in the nineteenth century. It arose during a particular intellectual and social period in the history of European societies that has subsequently come to be known as 'modernity'. The changes that took place in European societies during the course of the nineteenth century, and which have since become more global, resulted in the social transformation of those societies. Three specific developments are crucial:

1 the *scientific revolution* which started in the sixteenth century;
2 the development of *Enlightenment thought* during the eighteenth century, culminating in the French Revolution; and
3 the *industrial revolution* which started in the late eighteenth century in England, and which provided the foundation for the development of modern capitalism.

Sociology is seen as a reaction to each of these developments, but also as a fundamental contributor to the ongoing social, economic, political and intellectual movements that developed as a result. In essence, sociology as an intellectual project – that is, as a set of concepts and ideas that sought to make sense of the ascendancy of science, the impact of the European Enlightenment and the development of capitalism – can be understood as part of a body of ideas that are thought of as 'modernist'. Modernist thought rejects religious doctrine as the guarantor of truth and replaces it with a commitment to rationality, reason and science – values that underpinned early (nineteenth-century, or post-Enlightenment) forms of sociology.

The scientific revolution made possible an unprecedented understanding and control of the natural world. Sociologists thought that the methodology of the natural sciences would make it possible to understand and control the social world also. Enlightenment thought led to the dominance of ideas of progress and of liberty and individualism. As well as the scientific method, sociologists took on the idea of progress but reacted against the emphasis on individualism, stressing the importance of the collectivity and the interrelationship and interdependence of members of society. The industrial revolution and the development and growth of industrial capitalism resulted in dramatic social and economic changes stemming largely from the separation of work and home (the public and the private) – urbanisation, new class relationships, paid employment, the economic dependence of women and children, and so on. Sociologists wanted to understand and explain these changes. In doing so, they also suggested ways in which societies could be reformed and the whole modernisation process could be 'mastered'.

Some sociologists and feminists argue that the late twentieth century witnessed a further transformation, into a 'post-modern' society, and that new postmodern theories, are necessary to make sense of what is happening as a result. The postmodern condition is seen as arising from a variety of social and cultural changes that took place in the latter part of the twentieth century – rapid technological change, shifting political concerns, globalisation, the creation of a knowledge society, and the rise of new social movements, for instance. Postmodernism rejects the ideas of the Enlightenment, of progress, of scientific truth and the possibility of universal, totalising theories (or 'metanarratives' – Lyotard, 1984) – theories such as Marxism which claim to explain everything and to have the *sole* explanation, often with reference to one particular determining factor, capitalism. Instead, postmodern theorists argue that there are no metanarratives, no notions of progress and no single history – there are different histories and multiple truths, rather than one foundational, universal truth. Many different and equally authoritative voices and orientations are possible in the post-modern world. Postmodernism therefore questions the foundationalism and absolutism of modernism – it challenges both positivistic and humanistic approaches to social science. Postmodernism rejects the declaration of difference between natural and social sciences – even Marxism, postmodernists point out, did not challenge the status of scientific knowledge but argued that social-scientific knowledge was equally as good as natural science, but different.

Feminists, too, have questioned many of the epistemological foundations of Western thought and argued that modernist knowledge, in the name of objectivity and truth, has subordinated and subjugated women. Some feminists have argued that feminism and postmodernism are therefore natural allies, as both have been critical of modernist thought – and there are a substantial number of feminists who identify themselves as postmodernist accordingly. However, others have indicated that total relativism and the abandonment of theory are as problematic for feminism as for sociology. Postmodernism, in their perception, challenges the very enterprise of both sociology and feminism – which is not just understanding what is going on but changing the social world, achieving progress by acting on the world on the basis of a 'truth' position.

Theory and theorising

In some ways, we are all theorists. Everybody thinks, everybody has ideas – not just experts and intellectuals. We all analyse and interpret in order to make sense of what is going on around us. Theories are how we try to explain, and make sense of, the social world. What is the difference, then, between our everyday, common-sense theories and sociological theory? Broadly speaking, in social science we tend to call an explanation a 'theory' if it is open-ended, open to new evidence, capable of modification and improvement, and clear about the way its concepts are formed. However, there is no absolute distinction in social science between science (knowledge based on disinterested explanation) and ideology (knowledge which reflects particular interests). Marxism, for instance, is both a theory and an ideology in so far as it tries to explain how society works, but also provides a guide for action. The same point applies to feminism and many of the others 'isms' within sociology.

All sociologists try to think theoretically, and social or sociological theories (including feminist ones) can be distinguished from our common-sense, everyday understandings and explanations in the following ways:

1 theory *attempts to be systematic* about explanations and ideas – it attempts to be *internally logical and coherent*;
2 it attempts to provide *adequate explanations* – that is, it tries to take account of competing explanations, different viewpoints, and so on and to *locate particular phenomena within a totality* – to see 'the whole picture';
3 it is *open to refutation and critique*.

A theoretical perspective is a lens through which the social world is 'seen', one that makes theorising (explaining and making sense of what is going on) possible. A theoretical perspective helps us to ask questions and to think about what we might need to answer those questions, directs us to the material ('evidence') we need and suggests how best to interpret and explain things. Sociology is always theoretical and sociologists adopt different theoretical perspectives.

From a narrow scientific view, *a theory* is a series of properties that describes a set of observations. Theories summarise and organise what we know about the world. A *theoretical perspective*, however,

1 *suggests the types of question we should be asking* and draws our attention to certain kinds of events rather than others (those we define as 'problems' – phenomena in need of explanation) – e.g. feminist sociologists ask the question 'Why do women tend to do more housework than men?';
2 *provides us with the concepts to use in our analysis* and accounts of our observations of social life – e.g. gender ideology, division of labour;

3 *provides us with ways of answering questions* in the form of orienting assumptions and guides to observation – e.g. feminist sociologists assume that the gendered division of labour is something that needs to be explained;
4 *helps us to interpret what we observe* – theory structures the process of perception – e.g. feminist sociologists explain the gendered division of labour as the outcome of patriarchal and/or capitalist processes;
5 involves value judgements about what social scientific knowledge is for and how it is to be applied to social life.

Thus sociological (and feminist) theories provide answers to 'how' and 'why' questions but they do not necessarily agree on the answers to these questions, or even what the questions themselves should be. Just as we can disagree on how something is to be explained in our day-to-day lives, so sociologists (and feminists) disagree when they are explaining the same thing. This is because 'facts do not speak for themselves'; they have to be explained, and it is theory that enables us to understand them.

Furthermore, what the facts are is not always self-evident. Take, for example, the question, 'What counts as crime?': this might seem self-evident at first, but on closer examination we realise that it is not. For example, is 'crime' all behaviour that breaks the law, or is it only that behaviour which is labelled as 'criminal' – and, if so, by whom? Even when the facts are straightforward, no amount of observation and data-gathering will explain them. For example, in Britain statistics on birth are probably almost totally reliable. It is very difficult not to register the birth of a baby. However, no amount of collecting and dissecting birth statistics will lead to an explanation of fluctuations in the birth rate. Description alone will explain neither the fluctuation or how it relates to other events and processes – e.g. the economic situation, the proportion of the population marrying, the infant mortality rate, and so on.

Sociologists (and feminists), then, develop theories that enable them to make sense of the social. Theories make sense of the facts – they interpret them for us. In sociology, theories are used to provide arguments about how society should be viewed and how the 'facts' should be apprehended and ordered. Facts alone cannot resolve theoretical disputes, because theories are explanations of the facts. Even when there is agreement as to what the facts are, they can be used to support different theories; two theories may be incompatible with each other and yet agree on what the available facts are.

Theories, then, direct us to what evidence to look for and then enable us to make sense of the facts that we have collected. This does not mean that facts and factual knowledge are not important for sociological understanding. It is important that sociological and feminist theories are open to refutation – that facts can refute our theories – and that theories take the facts fully into account. There is a complex relationship between fact and theory and disagreement over what is to count as a 'fact', as valid evidence or data. Theories guide us as to what counts as evidence. When we describe the relationship between two events as causal we are making a theoretical statement, not a factual one; we are explaining and interpreting, not describing.

Sociological and feminist theories are attempts to explain social life, and they comprise sets of logically connected ideas that can describe and explain social reality and be validated/refuted by evidence. Each of these approaches answers the questions

(1) 'What is the nature of social reality?' (answers to this question are what we call 'ontologies' – theories of existence or being) and (2) 'How can we know about it?' (answers to this question are what we call 'epistemologies' – theories of knowledge, see Chapter 13). When social scientists develop theories, their epistemology or theory of knowledge is often determined by the ontological position they take; that is, their understanding of the nature of reality. Broadly speaking, four ontological perspectives can be discerned within sociology. These are:

1 positivist
2 idealist
3 realist, and
4 postmodernist.

Positivism

A positivist approach sees continuity between the natural and social sciences, with society existing as an analytic reality. Social structures and social processes are seen as comparable to those of the natural world and can be studied by the same methods and according to the same values as are used in the natural sciences. The sociologist's task is to collect empirical evidence – social facts – and on the basis of this to explain and predict the social world. Sociologists construct theories that comprise general statements about relationships existing in the (real) social world. A positivist approach therefore emphasises that the sociologist should study the social world in much the same way as a geologist might examine rock formations, or a chemist might study chemical reactions – as neutral, impartial observers. For a positivist, then, values such as objectivity, reliability and validity are seen as crucial in making convincing claims to scientific knowledge.

Idealism

The idealist approach sees social life as the product of human consciousness (subjectivity) – of the meaning that human beings give to their conduct rather than as an external (objective) reality. The sociologist's task is to explain the ideas, beliefs and motives of social actors – to interpret the meaning of social events. Sociology's subject matter is the meaning of social-historical reality. This approach rejects the view that the methods of the natural sciences are appropriate for sociologists, emphasising for instance the extent to which the social world is complex and messy; that inanimate entities such as rocks and chemicals cannot attribute meaning to their experiences, nor can they exercise agency or engage in social interaction – all key concerns of the sociologist.

Realism

In contrast, the realist approach argues that there is an external (objective) social reality, but that it is not immediately (subjectively) apprehensible. The task of the sociologist is to uncover underlying social structures – the reality that underpins and explains particular events. Sociology is seen as an empirically based, rational and objective discipline, but realists make a distinction between explanation and prediction and see the primary object as explanation. Realist sociologists explain why something happens by showing how and by what means it occurs.

Postmodernism

A postmodernist approach argues that there are only interpretations – 'readings' – of social texts (phenomena capable of multiple meaning and interpretation), that there is an indeterminacy and heterogeneity of actual meanings and meaning-productions. Like the idealist approach it rejects the ideals of objectivity and neutral judgement and argues that such ideas are the creation of social beings rather than the (more or less adequate) representations of material reality. However, postmodernists reject the idea that in order to know about the social world we need to transcend our own position so as to achieve objective knowledge, emphasising instead that all knowledge is situated, partial and provisional; in other words, relative. Whereas modernists tend to argue that objective knowledge can be obtained, in principle at least – and that scientific knowledge is thereby objective as opposed to the everyday subjective knowledge of 'lay people', for postmodernists subjectivity cannot be transcended even in principle – there is no objective 'view from outside'. Furthermore, given the multiplicity of subject positions and the ways human beings make and continuously remake meaning in the world, so that there are endless 'points of view', claims to the discovery of universal, foundational 'truth' are seen as meaningless.

Sociologists (and feminists), then, disagree about what valid sociological knowledge is, and about how that knowledge can best be obtained and defended. Thus sociology and feminism are characterised by fierce and open debates about intractable and important questions. Students have traditionally been introduced to sociological theory via a 'schools of thought' approach, each perspective being seen as internally coherent and as rejecting the validity of other approaches. However, there has been a move more recently in sociology (largely since the impact of postmodernist thought on the discipline in the past decade or so) to accept that all theories, all understandings, all explanations are provisional and partial, and perhaps that they provide different (compatible rather than competing) versions of 'truth'. Although, as we noted above, some explanations continue to be seen as more important, more authoritative and therefore more 'truthful' than others – namely malestream rather than feminist theories.

In sum, sociologists and feminists do need a framework that enables them to make sense of the social world, to make it meaningful and intelligible. There is no one sociological or feminist perspective, but a set of interrelated theories all providing provisional and partial accounts. Some of them provide competing explanations, but others provide (compatible) understandings of different aspects of social reality and social processes and enable us to make some theoretical sense of what is going on in the social world, however we conceptualise it.

Feminist theory

There are a wide variety of feminist views regarding the relationship between feminism and malestream social, political and cultural theory. As Chris Beasley puts it:

> They range from a perspective which considers feminism and mainstream theory to be compatible and quite similar, to an approach which sees feminism as breaking down the very categories that are used in traditional theory. . . . However, the critique offered by feminism – that is, the viewpoint that there is something inadequate and unjust about traditional theory – is more straightforwardly encapsulated than what feminism offers as the alternative. What feminism actually offers, beyond its initial criticism of existing thought, is very diverse. And so the question remains, 'what *is* feminism?'
>
> (Beasley, 1999, pp. 14–15)

Feminism, like sociology, is a theory – a world view. However, it is not a unified one; feminists do not agree on the ways in which we can explain women's subordination or on how women can be emancipated, or even on what constitutes oppression. As Alison Jagger (1983, p. 353) has put it, 'there are many ways of being a feminist'. Indeed, by the close of the twentieth century, Western feminism could no longer be divided simply into the general categories of liberal, radical and Marxist traditions – if indeed, it ever could. 'Many other approaches, drawing upon an increasingly eclectic and sometimes rather inaccessible range of social and political theories, became a feature of academic feminism at least' (Beasley, 1999, p. 65).

Hence, there are now a large number of feminist perspectives, and feminist sociology draws on a wide range of disciplines, so that any attempt to classify feminist theories is fraught with problems. Also, the impact of postmodern thought on sociology means that theoretical perspectives that might previously have been regarded as incompatible (Marxist and radical feminisms, for instance) have in some ways begun to cross-fertilise. Similarly, the assumption that sociologists adhered to one particular theoretical perspective and so rejected all others out of hand has also been largely disregarded. Any system of classification is therefore arbitrary and incomplete. It is arbitrary because we force ideas into a category, one with which feminist theorists themselves may not identify, and describe a given position as if it were totally unified rather than representing a range of ideas that show some broad agreement, or that share certain concepts and influences in common. It is incomplete because our categories do not incorporate all feminisms (psychoanalytic and existentialist feminisms, for instance, have not been included here as, to date, their impact on sociological thought has been relatively limited).

Early second wave feminism (in the 1960s and 1970s) emphasised the role of structural and material factors in understanding women's oppression, whereas more recent approaches (largely since the 1980s) have shifted the feminist focus to symbolic and representational issues, addressing questions of power, knowledge and subjectivity. This has led some feminists to argue that the arts, humanities and philosophy have replaced sociology as the major arenas in which feminist theorising takes place. In part, we hope to counter this claim by demonstrating the breadth and depth of ideas that feminists have contributed to sociology in recent years, and by outlining the ways in which feminist thought has been shaped by an engagement with ongoing theoretical debates within the discipline. We are not therefore stressing the primacy of any one theoretical perspective, but try to show the strengths and weaknesses of each. The epistemological foundations of different feminist positions are explored more fully in Chapter 13.

We have identified seven feminist perspectives: liberal, Marxist, radical, dual-systems, postmodernist, critical, Black/post-colonial. We also consider post-feminism here (as both an empirical claim, and a theoretical disposition). All these perspectives address the question of what constitutes the oppression of women, how that oppression might be explained, and all suggest strategies for overcoming it. All argue that women are oppressed but they differ in their explanations of the 'cause' of this oppression and their suggested strategies for overcoming it. In brief, liberal feminism is concerned to uncover the immediate forms of discrimination against women and to fight for legal, educational and other reforms to overcome them. Marxist feminists argue that the family is a key site of women's oppression on a global scale and that the struggle for gender emancipation is an integral part of the struggle against capitalism. Radical feminists see male control of women (patriarchy) as the main problem and argue that women across the world must fight to free themselves from this control. Dual-systems feminists argue that women's oppression is both an aspect of capitalism and of patriarchal relations. An end to capitalism, they argue, will not lead automatically to the emancipation of woman (hence, gender inequalities in socialist or communist societies) – women also need to fight to free themselves from control by men. Postmodernist/poststructuralist theories argue that we need to deconstruct the binary oppositions through which women are constructed as socially inferior. They also argue that rationality, and therefore sociology, is a product of a masculine (phallocentric) attempt to objectify and control the world. Materialist/critical feminists argue that women as a social group are exploited and subordinated by men as a group, and that sexual difference (the social differences between men and women) provides merely the ideological justification rather than the foundation for this exploitation. Black and post-colonial feminists argue that a feminist perspective needs to take into account the impact of race and racism, as well as issues of global power relations, migration and colonialism in understanding women's oppression, and to be more reflexive about ethnocentrism within (white, mainstream) feminism.

Feminist theories differ, then, according to the ways in which they explain the subordination of women, and the different theories mean that feminists working from different perspectives tend to be interested in different aspects of the social world, to ask different questions and to come to different conclusions. This will become evident as you read this book, when we look at specific aspects of men's and women's lives. One key concern that unites these otherwise disparate perspectives is the meaning and significance of sexual difference: the difference between men and women as social subjects.

Feminist debates on sexual difference

As Chris Beasley (1999, p. 15) notes, 'sexual difference is inevitably of some importance in feminism given feminists' inclination to consider the subject of "women" – a grouping identified by sex differentiation'. Broadly speaking, sexual difference refers to the difference between men and women as social subjects, and not merely to biological differences between males and females, or to gender differences between masculinity and femininity, and is thought, by most feminists, to be one of the primary forms of social stratification. Seyla Benhabib (1992, p. 152) defines sexual difference as 'the social-historical, symbolic constitution and interpretation of the differences between men and women'. Chris Beasley outlines four approaches to understanding sexual difference within feminism. We would describe these as:

1 humanism
2 gynocentrism
3 postmodernism, and
4 critical feminism.

Humanism

Humanist feminists who emphasise not difference but 'sameness' argue that, as rational social beings, men and women are essentially the same and hence, are engaged in reworking what they regard as defective, ill-conceived, biased or ideological representations of women in social theory and society. These feminists argue that men and women are human beings, but that women have been denied many of the rights and responsibilities accorded to humanity, resulting in the restriction of women's potential. From this perspective, 'women are seen as capable of doing what men do, as capable of being "men" and are expected to enter the world of men' (Beasley, 1999, p. 15). This approach is described variously as equality, egalitarian or humanist feminism, and is associated most commonly with liberal feminism, but also with Marxist and socialist feminisms, and often with the work of feminists based in the UK and North America. For this reason, this approach is also often termed (perhaps oversimplistically) Anglo-American feminism.

Gynocentrism

Gynocentric (woman-centred) perspectives emphasise women's difference from men (or rather, the difference *between* men and women), and define their political agenda largely in relation to a celebration or valorisation of women's social and cultural constitution as different. 'Difference feminism' as it has come to be known involves reconceiving the relationship between men and women as 'different but complementary'. This involves valuing difference but, *crucially*, seeking to dismantle and undermine the hierarchy underlying the relationship between men and women in patriarchal societies. By contrast with views found in traditional, malestream thought, where women's difference from men is taken as indicative of inferiority, sexual difference is celebrated by those who champion gynocentric feminism. This celebration is most commonly associated with radical feminism.

Some feminists consider women's difference from men to render them ethically superior; to be somehow better than men – more caring or intuitive, for instance. This approach involves not so much a flattening, but rather a reversal of the traditional gender hierarchy that tends to characterise patriarchal societies. In other words,

> the hierarchical relationship between the sexes assumed to be associated with sexual difference in mainstream theory is turned upside down. The notion of women as better people is often (though not always) connected to a perception of women as *innately*, intrinsically pre-eminent.
>
> (Beasley, 1999, p. 18, original emphasis)

Women's inherent superiority is often deemed to be associated with their moral–ethical constitution, deriving from the life-giving potential of their bodies and/or their close connection with others (through, for instance, their emotional disposition, experience of socialisation, child bearing/rearing capacities, and so on). Such an approach is particularly associated with North American radical feminism of the 1970s, and its various antecedents such as Carol Gilligan's (1982) work on women and ethics.

Postmodernism

An increasing number of (relatively disparate) feminists writing largely since the 1980s (or whose work has been translated into English since then) have expressed concerns regarding any straightforward distinction between sameness and difference. They tend to emphasise men's and women's difference from each other, but in a less cele-bratory way than gynocentric feminists, acknowledging that some of these differences remain problematic. They are thus less inclined than the previous group to celebrate sexual difference but instead seek to reflect critically on how differences between men and women are constructed and maintained. This latter approach has come to be associated most commonly with (Western) European or Continental feminism, and has sought to deconstruct sexual difference, focusing on the ways in which differences between men and women (as well as amongst men, and amongst women) are socially constructed. In particular, this approach is characteristic of poststructuralist and postmodern feminism. (Again, however, this categorisation is somewhat simplistic, because the division of feminist thought into 'Anglo-American' and 'European' con-flates many complex diversities both within and between these bodies of work, as well as serving to exclude those writers whose work may fit somewhere in between.)

Critical feminism

Several feminist writers have also argued that men and women are not necessarily the same in an ontological sense; that is, they do not experience the same biological or social reality, but that they are allies engaged in many of the same political struggles. The issue of sexual difference (the question of whether men and women are the same, or different) is thus viewed through a political lens – men and women are seen to be essentially and/or socio-culturally different, but often occupying the same political or social position (in terms of social class or race and ethnicity, for instance). It is this similarity in political struggle or marginalisation that is seen to produce the similarities between men and women rather than some essential 'humanity'. Feminists adopting this critical perspective tend to perceive women as the same or as different from men in a range of ways, but all tend to be wary of any position that celebrates women's existence as a universal or essential group in the way that gynocentric feminists tend to. This way of thinking about sexual difference is the starting point for several theoretical perspectives within feminism, and is associated with Black and post-colonial feminists concerned with racism and ethnocentrism, and with feminist critical theory.

Feminists respond to the question 'Are men and women the same or different?' in a number of ways then, depending on whether a humanist, gynocentric, postmodernist or critical perspective is adopted. Each of these different ways of understanding sexual difference – of thinking about the nature of the social relationship between men and women, and of what it means to be a man or a woman in a patriarchal society – provide the basis for the various, and increasingly complex, theoretical perspectives that constitute contemporary feminist thought.

Feminist theoretical perspectives

Liberal/reformist feminist theory

In some ways liberal feminism is the most widely known form of feminist thought, and perhaps the easiest to understand in relation to the question of sexual difference – largely because of its associations with equal rights and equal opportunities. It is perhaps the most moderate or mainstream version of feminism in this respect, and is therefore also often referred to as reformist or equality feminism. It is also quint-essentially modernist, largely because of its commitment to humanism (a belief in the advancement of humanity by its own efforts), emancipation (freedom from un-necessary social, political or legal restrictions) and the creation of a just society (based for liberal feminists on a meritocracy in which power and reward are distributed solely on the basis of ability and effort, rather than gender privilege).

Liberal feminism has inherited from liberal political thought a conception of men and women as the same; this sameness is located, for liberal feminists, in men and women's equal (human) capacity for rational thought and action. As Beasley notes (1999, p. 52, original emphasis): 'liberal feminist political strategies reflect a conception of a *fundamentally sexually undifferentiated human nature* – that is, since women are much the same as men, women should be able to do what men do.'

Liberal feminists place great emphasis on the rights of individuals to compete in the public sphere (in the labour market, for instance) and also on what they see as the corresponding responsibilities of individuals to take part in public life (in politics for instance, or through financial contributions to social welfare). Liberal feminists emphasise that women's unequal position is a result of artificial barriers to women's full participation in the public sphere (beyond the home and the family), and hence their inability to fulfil their potential as human beings (as men's equals). One of the key political goals associated with liberal feminism is therefore equality of opportunity. Public citizenship and the attainment of equality with men in the public sphere are central to this approach.

> Liberal (equality) feminism, then, asks for equality in the sense of sameness of attainment, and therefore treatment, and justifies it via sameness, 'androgyny'. It says: *we deserve to be equal with you, for we are in fact the same.* We possess the same capabilities; but this fact has been hidden, or these abilities have, while still potentially ours, been socialized, educated 'out'.
>
> (Evans, 1995, p. 13, emphasis added)

Liberal feminism has therefore been concerned to argue for equal rights for women – for women to have the same citizenship rights as men. Equality feminists have fought against laws and practices that give rights to men and not women, or which are designed to 'protect' women. Recognising that mere formal equality is insufficient, they have also advocated the passing of laws to outlaw discrimination against women and to give women rights in the workplace such as maternity leave and pay, although the global impact of this has been variable.

Women, liberal feminists argue, are human beings; they have the same inalienable rights as men. A woman's sex is irrelevant to her rights; women are capable of full rationality and therefore are entitled to full human rights. However, women are denied equal rights with men, and as a group are not allowed some freedoms that men as a group are permitted to enjoy. Furthermore, while men are judged on merit as individuals, women tend to be judged on their accomplishments as females – that is, they are denied the same right as men to pursue their own interests.

In sociology, liberal or 'reformist' feminists have been concerned to demonstrate that the observable differences between the sexes are not innate but a result of socialisation or 'sex-role conditioning'. The ways in which boys and girls are treated differently, from about the moment of birth (or even before), arguably discourage women from developing their full potential as human beings. Feminist researchers have carried out research to demonstrate that women are discriminated against and treated differently from men, and argue that this explains women's subordinate position in society. To liberate women it is necessary to demonstrate that men and women are equal in potential, that women are fully human, that the differences between men and women in Western society are due to the different ways in which boys and girls are socialised and the different social expectations they face, together with discriminatory legislation.

Liberal feminism has certainly had a major impact on feminist theory and sociology particularly in Western societies – the publication of Betty Friedan's book

The Feminine Mystique in 1963 is cited by Judith Evans (1995) as the start of second wave feminism, for instance. However, it has been criticised on a number of grounds, particularly for its seemingly uncritical acceptance of male values as human values. This has led to accusations that liberal feminists suffer from a kind of 'penis envy' (Tong, 1998, p. 31). Indeed, Tong goes on to criticise liberal feminism on the grounds that it valorises a gender-neutral humanism over a gender-specific feminism. Sociological research from a reformist position does not tend to explore women's lived experiences, nor does it challenge the use of concepts and tools developed to explore society from the standpoint of men. Further, it does not really explain women's inequality (as it fails to take account of the structural origins and implications of the gender inequalities constraining women), it merely describes and challenges it. Liberal feminists place considerable emphasis on disadvantage being the sum total of individual (or collective) acts of discrimination. In this sense, their faith in legislation and education as the 'solutions' to gender discrimination ignores invisible, structural or cultural constraints that might defy such practices. Nor does liberal feminism adequately challenge malestream views of what the major issues are. It argues for the incorporation of women in research samples and for women to carry out research, but leaves intact the foundations of existing theoretical perspectives. However, research from this perspective has demonstrated the ways in which women are denied equal opportunities and are discriminated against, and has challenged the view that inequalities between men and women are adequately explained by biological sex differences.

Radical feminism

Unlike other versions of feminist theory radical feminism is not drawn directly from other bodies of malestream social, political or cultural theory – it is feminism in its 'purest' form, some might argue. It offers a challenge to, and a vehement rejection of, the humanism (and commitment to 'sameness') underpinning liberal feminism. Radical feminism is concerned with women's rights, rather than gender equality and emphasises (rather than seeks to overcome) the differences between men and women. In this respect, radical feminism is sometimes also referred to as gynocentrism (a woman-centred approach). Gynocentrism maintains the existence of a female or feminine nature that has been concealed and/or distorted throughout history; one that needs to be liberated and revalued.

Radical feminists argue that women's oppression is primary and fundamental. *Patriarchy*, an elaborate system of male domination which pervades all aspects of social and cultural life, is seen as trans-historical and global and is accorded particular explanatory power within radical feminism. Although the subject of considerable debate, the term patriarchy is widely used by radical feminists to refer to a society based on universal male supremacy and female subordination. All women are oppressed irrespective of historical, national, cultural, class or racial or ethnic differences. The notion that all women share an experience of oppression is intimately connected with a strong emphasis on sisterhood in radical feminism. The family is seen as a key instrument of the oppression of women, through sexual and maternal obligation, as is male control of women's bodies. One of the key concerns of radical feminists in this respect is the extent to which women themselves become so oppressed by patriarchal ideologies that they perpetuate men's control of women's bodies themselves. Radical feminists have cited cultural practices ranging from Chinese foot binding to wearing Wonderbras as examples of female collusion with patriarchal oppression. Radical feminists do not, on the whole, deny biological differences between men and women, but they challenge the meanings given to them. Women's oppression is seen as rooted either in men's control of women's biological capacity for motherhood or in the innate, biologically determined aggression of the male, as manifest in rape or in the ritual stoning of women accused of adultery, for instance.

The central tenet of radical feminism is that gender inequalities are the outcome of an autonomous system of patriarchy and are the primary form of social inequality. They argue that there has always been a sexual division of labour underpinning and reinforcing a system of male domination. Patriarchy is a universal system in which men dominate women. Radical feminists argue that no area of society is free from male definition, and consequently every aspect of women's lives currently accepted as 'natural' has to be questioned and alternative ways of living together as men and women must be found. Theory, they argue, is not a specialist area of academic activity, carried out by an intellectual elite, but is an integral aspect of feminist practice and politics. Theory arises out of practice and is continually measured against experience and continually reformulated. In practice, therefore, radical feminists have approached the dismantling of patriarchy through the pursuit of political action calling for change in gender relations, drawing political strength primarily from women's organisations. In contrast to liberal feminists, radical feminists tend to be very suspicious of government intervention, perceiving the state itself to be inherently patriarchal; dominated by men and men's interests (MacKinnon, 1987).

Radical feminists do, however, reject the view that women's subordination is anything to do with their biological inferiority. They reject the idea that the victim (woman) is to blame. Those who do argue for a biological explanation argue that *male* biology is to blame: men are naturally aggressive and use their aggression to control women (as, for example, in rape and domestic violence). Mary Daly (1978), in *Gyn/Ecology: The Metaethics of Radical Feminism*, documents the ways in which men have used aggression to control women. She cites Indian suttee, Chinese foot binding, African 'genital mutilation', European witch hunts and American gynaecology as examples of the ways in which men have systematically abused women and used violence against women's bodies to control them (and continue to do so). Some feminists such as Daly encourage women to create a new identity for themselves founded on 'true' femaleness, based on the biological nature of women which has been distorted by patriarchy. Women are encouraged to celebrate a new female creativity, based on sisterhood and self-identification. They reject androgyny because they argue that the most valuable qualities are those that are specific to women and, therefore, that women are morally superior to men. Also, because men dominate women even in the most intimate of relationships, women must live separately from men. The ideal, they argue, is for women to live free from patriarchy, which divides and mutilates them.

For radical feminists the subordination of women is the central concern, and their theories seek to uncover and eliminate the subordination of women by men. Men, it is argued, systematically dominate women in every sphere of life, and all relationships between men and women are institutionalised relationships of power and therefore an appropriate subject for political analysis. Thus radical feminists are concerned to reveal how male power is exercised and reinforced in all spheres of life, including 'personal' relationships such as child-rearing, housework and marriage and in all kinds of sexual practices including rape, prostitution, pornography, sexual harassment and sexual intercourse, and in the purchasing of so-called 'mail order' brides from developing countries or in practices of 'sex tourism' (see Chapter 8), for instance.

Radical feminists argue that women's culture, knowledge, and lived experience have all been denied by men – what is taken as 'truth' has been defined by men. Male science (including social science) has been used to legitimate the ideologies that define women as inferior, and women's role to be that of domestic labourers. Sociology is seen as part of this male-defined, distorting male culture. Radical feminists, then, do not want to participate in sociology – to bring women in – but to transform the way knowledge is produced so that women's subjective understandings are revalued. Much radical feminist research has been concerned with analysing male violence towards women and the ways in which this is hidden, marginalised or blamed on women by malestream social science imbued with patriarchal values. Radical feminists have also been concerned to uncover 'her-story', to recover for women their own cultural heritage and to reveal the ways in which women's knowledge and lived experience have been devalued and distorted.

Radical feminism has uncovered the ways in which even the most intimate and personal relationships are political – that is, are power relationships. They have also documented the universality of patriarchal relations. However, they have failed to adequately explain the ways in which women are subordinated and exploited by men in relation to either continuities or changes in patriarchy. They tend not to take sufficient account of the diverse forms that patriarchal relationships can take in different societies. They also tend to discount the ways in which men and women's experiences are shaped not simply by sexual difference, and patriarchal relations, but also by a whole range of other factors such as social class, nationality, race and ethnicity, sexuality, age, and so on (see Chapter 3) which problematise the concept of a 'universal sisterhood'.

Radical feminist biological explanations, while very different from those developed by malestream theorists, are equally reductionist and fail to take account of ideology and culture. Also they give the opportunity for socio-biological theories to be developed as a counter to feminist ones – theories that argue that women's role as presently constituted is naturally determined. However, not all radical feminists accept biological theories, arguing that they are developed to justify the subordination of women and that it is necessary to challenge the argument that there are two biologically determined sexes.

Marxist feminism

The third major feminist theoretical tradition we consider here derives from Marxism, and was particularly influential (often in dialogue with radical feminism) in the 1960s and 1970s. As Chris Beasley observes, however,

> while the impact of Marxism on feminist theory remains evident in a number of contemporary approaches (such as psychoanalytic and postmodern/post-structuralist feminisms, as well as those concerned with race and ethnicity), the Marxist feminist tradition is now waning,
>
> (Beasley, 1999, p. 58)

and has been largely superseded by feminist critical theory, that we consider below. Indeed, Curthoys (cited in Beasley, 1999, p. 59) asserts (perhaps prematurely, given that many feminists are still influenced by Marxism, even if they don't actually label themselves as Marxist feminists), that Marxist feminism 'more or less died at the end of the 1980s'.

Marxist feminism is sometimes also referred to as materialist feminism because of its emphasis on concrete, structural aspects of social organisation, particularly the role of the family and the sexual division of labour. As Kuhn and Wolpe (1978, p. 9) have put it; 'in this context, two interrelated issues are raised – the family and the sexual division of labour – whose crucial importance to a theorisation of the situation of women is constantly claimed.'

Marxist feminism developed out of feminist attempts to adapt Marxist theory so that it might provide an adequate explanation for the subordination and exploitation of women in capitalist societies. Marxist feminists recognise that Marxism is inadequate as it stands and needs to be developed in order to explain why women are excluded from the public sphere and are the main unpaid workers in the domestic sphere. They have also had to deal with the 'fact' that women did not become subordinated under capitalism but were subordinated already, and with the strong suspicion that the overthrow of the capitalist mode of production would not result in the emancipation of women – as has been demonstrated in Eastern European societies, for instance. However, while they recognise that the struggle between the sexes is not reducible to the class struggle, they tend to give primacy to the latter.

For Marxist feminists the defining feature of contemporary society is capitalism, within which women are subject to a special form of oppression, one that is mainly the effect of their exclusion from wage labour and of their role in the domestic sphere reproducing the capitalist relations of production. The main beneficiary of women's unpaid labour is capitalism, although men also benefit to some extent. Marxist feminists argue that women's role in the family benefits capitalism in three basic ways:

1 women perform *domestic labour on an unpaid basis*, and *provide care* for the current (and increasingly the previous) generation of workers;
2 women also *reproduce and socialise* the next generation of workers;
3 women *consume* the goods and services produced by capitalism.

A major problem that Marxist feminists confront is that Marx himself was not particularly concerned with the position of women in capitalist society. Marx rejected notions of morality, justice and equal rights as bourgeois ideas. He was concerned not with reform, but with developing a scientific account of the exploitation of the working class under capitalism, with a view to overthrowing that system.

The concepts Marx uses appear to be neutral, but they are in fact phallocentric; he fails to recognise that women are subject to a special form of oppression within capitalist societies and does not analyse gender differences and gender ideologies. Although he uses abstract categories such as 'labour power', his specific analyses suggest that he assumed a male waged labour force. He also adopted a naturalistic approach to the family, maintaining that women should provide care in the domestic sphere. The paid labour of women and children was seen by Marx as a threat to male workers – women and children, he argued, were used by capitalists to reduce the costs of production. Cheap female labour was or could be used to replace more expensive male labour. (Marx did not challenge the practice of paying women less than men.) This analysis ignores the fact that women have always made a contribution to the economic survival of the household and does not challenge the view that men should be paid more for their labour than women – presumably because men should be paid a family wage.

Marxist feminists want to retain the Marxist analysis of capitalist societies, integrating into it an explanation for the subordination of women. A starting point for the development of a Marxist feminist theory was the work of Engels, Marx's collaborator. In his analysis of the relationship between the origins of the family and the development of capitalism, Engels (1972 [1884]) argues that the bourgeois nuclear family was formed because of the needs of the capitalist system, and specifically because men wanted to pass on their property to their legitimate heirs. Engels argues that this meant men needed to control women in marriage so that they knew who their heirs were. Women's subordinate position was/is a form of oppression that serves the interests of capitalism. All women are oppressed, whether they are married to bourgeois or proletarian men.

Marxist feminists have adapted this line to develop a theory which attempts to provide an adequate account of the subordination of women as well as forms of class exploitation and which overcomes the theoretical marginalisation of women in conventional Marxist theory. They seek to analyse and explain the relationship between the subordination of women and other aspects of the organisation of the capitalist mode of production. The attempt to marry Marxism with feminism has been difficult, but Marxist feminists have argued that it is essential to recognise that the oppression of women is inextricably linked to the capitalist order. Given this, coupled with Marxism's sex-blindness, it is necessary to reformulate Marxist theory so that it provides an adequate explanation for the subordination of women, and of ethnic minorities and other exploited groups in capitalist societies as well. Such a theory, it is argued, will enable us to develop strategies that result in the emancipation of subordinated groups – something that the overthrow of the capitalist system would not automatically achieve by itself.

The major problem with Marxist feminist theory is that it places insufficient emphasis on the ways in which men oppress women, and the ways in which men benefit from their unpaid domestic labour. While Marxist feminists have recognised that it is necessary to understand the importance of patriarchal relationships and how these are intertwined with capitalism, they see them as relatively static and fail to recognise that there is no necessary and inevitable congruence between the interests of patriarchy and the interests of capital. Marxist feminism tends to reduce feminist (gendered) explanations to the categories of Marxist theory, then. It fails to take account of patriarchal relationships in societies other than capitalist ones, nor does it fully consider the specific location of women in post-colonial or developing societies. Much like radical feminism, it also tends to be relatively abstract and far removed from the everyday experiences of women in their relationships with men.

Dual-systems theory

Largely since the 1980s, and as a consequence of debates between radical and Marxist feminisms that took place a decade or so previously, socialist feminists began to develop a perspective that has come to be known as dual-systems theory. Socialist or dual-systems feminists argue that what is necessary is a dual analysis that articulates Marxist class theory with a feminist theory of patriarchy; a theory that takes account of what unites all women – oppression by men – as well as the class divisions between us. Dual-systems theory therefore attempts to maintain the materialist elements of Marxism, whilst incorporating a radical feminist emphasis on patriarchy and gender oppression into its perspective. While Marxist feminist theory continues to give primacy to class analysis, dual-systems feminists take as their concern the relationship of women to the economic system as well as the relationship of women to men. The key question for dual-systems feminists is the cause of male exploitation and domination of women. Dual-systems feminist Heidi Hartmann (1978) points out that the categories of Marxism are sex-blind and that patriarchal oppression preceded capitalism and undoubtedly succeeds it as well. In order to understand the sub-ordination of women in capitalist societies, she suggests, it is necessary to articulate Marxism with a critique of patriarchy – that is, to show the specific form that female exploitation takes in capitalist societies.

The form that patriarchy takes under capitalism is seen to be different from the form that it takes in other socio-economic systems. Patriarchy predates capitalism, but it takes new forms within distinct stages of capitalist development. In agricultural/developing societies men have to leave their home to work, and women work both in the home and in the fields. With industrialisation men tend to go out to work, and women are gradually excluded from much paid work (as Engels (1972) noted, the separation of the public and private spheres occurred following industrialisation in Europe). The confinement of women to the home is not unique to capitalist society, however; in most Islamic societies – industrial and pre-industrial – women are confined to the home, and upper-class women did not work in pre-industrial or industrial Europe.

However, the development of industrial capitalism did lead to changes. Women were excluded from certain types of paid work, especially skilled work, and lost certain legal rights they had previously held over property. Men also made gains: men had control over credit, and some men but few women had access to political arenas including Parliament. Men developed many new bases of power in the public sphere from which women were barred, and domestic ideologies became more dominant. The form that women's subordination takes in capitalist society is not an outcome of the logic of capitalism or patriarchy, but the result of a shift in the resources of male power consequent upon the development of capitalism. Men were in a position to develop new power bases as the domestic economy contracted and was replaced by capitalist production.

Dual-systems theory, then, attempts to develop an analysis that recognises two systems: the economic and the sex–gender. Patriarchy is seen as trans-historical – that is, men exercise power over women in all societies. However, an adequate feminist theory, dual-systems feminists argue, has to recognise that patriarchy takes a specific form in capitalist societies. The aim is to develop a theory of capitalist patriarchy that makes possible an understanding of the ways in which the capitalist system is structured by male domination.

Marxist theory presents the world from the position of the proletariat (working class); what is necessary, dual-systems feminists argue, is to develop a world view from the position of women. Traditional Marxist theory ignores women's labour outside of the market (domestic labour) and the gender-defined character of women's work within the market, and therefore obscures the systematic domination of women by men. Women, however, are controlled both by the ruling class and by men; male capitalists determine the conditions under which women sell their labour, and male workers receive monetary and other advantages from the fact that women's waged labour is remunerated at a lower rate than men's, and that women perform unpaid domestic labour. Also, men's sexual desires are taken as primary in the definition of women as sexual objects.

To understand women's oppression fully it is necessary to examine the sexual division of labour in the domestic sphere as well as in the labour market, and the relationship between the two. Women's reproductive labour limits their access to wage labour, but the limited range of wage labour available to women is what drives many of them into marriage. The ideology of marriage and motherhood as women's primary role serves to conceal this. The public/private distinction not only benefits capital but also men. The exclusion of women from the public sphere benefits men as well as capitalists, while women's unpaid domestic labour also benefits both men and capitalists.

Sylvia Walby (1990), emphasising the need for a dual analysis, argues that in capitalist society the key sites of patriarchal relations are to be found in domestic work, paid work, the state, culture, male violence and sexuality. Social relations in domestic work constitute the patriarchal mode of production, and this, she argues, is of particular significance in the determination of gender relations. However, when patriarchy is articulated with the capitalist mode of production, patriarchal relations in paid work are of central importance to the maintenance of the system. Walby also argues that throughout the course of the twentieth century, a shift from private to public patriarchy occurred in capitalist societies, partly because of the capitalist demand for labour and partly, somewhat ironically perhaps, as a result of feminist political activity. However, the interests of patriarchy and of capital are not necessarily the same; the main basis of the tension between the two lies in the exploitation of women's labour. It is in capital's interests, she argues, to recruit and exploit cheap female labour, labour which is cheaper than men's because of patriarchal structures and ideologies. This is resisted by patriarchy, which seeks to maintain the exploitation of women in the household. When men struggle to exclude women from competition for jobs, there is a strong cross-class patriarchal alliance. However, this cross-class alliance is weakened when it is in the interests of employers (capitalists) to recruit women, and then there is conflict between capitalism and patriarchy.

A way of reaching what Walby describes as a 'mutual accommodation' is for capital to recruit women to jobs defined as women's jobs – jobs which pay less than men's and which have a lower status. When this happens patriarchy fights to ensure that women are recruited only for women's work. Walby argues that the power of capital prevents this exclusionary strategy working in the long term and that segregation develops as an alternative at least in part because of the feminist movement – women demanding the right to have paid employment. Consequently, in Britain there has been a move from private patriarchy to a more public form, marked by a shift from exclusionary to segregation-based labour market strategies.

Despite its attempt to develop a more complex account of men and women's relative social and economic position than radical or Marxist feminism, dual-systems theory has been criticised for its lack of theoretical sophistication (for being unable, for instance, to articulate the nature of the 'duality' of capitalism and patriarchy). It has also been criticised because it tends to marginalise other categories of power (distinct from, but related to, class and gender) such as race and ethnicity, for instance, or to take account of global dynamics in shaping the relationship between patriarchy and capitalism.

Postmodern feminism

There has been a widespread debate within feminist theory and sociology more generally about the relationship between feminism and postmodernism. Within feminist thought, postmodernism tends to be viewed as either an unprecedented opportunity for women to resist their designation as the 'second sex' (de Beauvoir, 1988), or as a theoretical movement that is politically disabling, just as feminism is beginning to make a political and social impact (Nicholson, 1990). Many feminists have been critical of the ways in which modernist theory devalued their concerns. Their dissatisfaction with modernism's legacy therefore led many feminists to develop an interest in, and affinity with, postmodernism. In particular, postmodern feminists have

> mobilized the postmodern critique of the authority and status of science, truth, history, power, knowledge and subjectivity, bringing a transformative gender dimension to postmodern theory and developing new ways of understanding sexual difference.
>
> (Weedon, 1997, p. 171)

One of the main difficulties we face when considering the ideas of postmodern feminists is that the terms used to describe their work are often variable and confusing.

Broadly speaking, we use the term 'postmodern' here to refer to a range of ideas influenced largely by a particular group of (primarily male) French social theorists, including Jean Baudrillard, Jacques Derrida, Michel Foucault and Jean-Francois Lyotard. It is important to note, however, that the group of writers whose work we are discussing here tend not to apply the label 'postmodern' to their own writing – rather this is a term used in texts such as this one in an attempt to make sense of some of the commonalities and differences in their ideas. In this sense, Chris Beasley (1999, p. 89) goes as far as to assert that the term 'postmodernism' was actually 'made in America' and that 'the invention of the label . . . as a cultural remove . . . may well have overly encouraged misleading conceptions of it as a coherent intellectual phenomenon'. Such confusion is hardly surprising, given that if postmodern ideas share anything in common it tends to be a rejection of the notion of a foundational truth or essence, in favour of an emphasis on truth as constructed, partial and contingent. Nevertheless, in terms of their shared critique of modernist conceptions of the self, of knowledge and of language (as well as their overall impact on contemporary feminist thought), it makes sense to consider the contribution of postmodernism as a distinct and relatively coherent perspective.

Postmodern feminists argue that it is not simply that we live in a postmodern world – the postmodern condition – but that postmodernism is a style or mode of thinking that is more appropriate than modernist ideas to make sense of that world. Postmodern theory abandons explanatory goals and realism (a belief in the objective existence of an external reality) in favour of an extreme form of social consructionism or idealism, emphasising the discursive nature of reality. This means that, for post-modernists, there can no longer be any attempt to describe, analyse or explain reality in an objective or scientific way.

Postmodernism therefore challenges the explanatory (scientific) claims of approaches such as Marxism that propose an account of society as structured accord-ing to a determining principle (capitalism). Ironically, we might argue, any unity or common ground between otherwise disparate ideas lies in their shared antagonism to singular structural explanations, and their attraction to multiple determinants, diversity, plurality and indeterminacy. Postmodernists tends to stress the shifting, fragmented nature of meaning (and relatedly power) rather than its stability, and reject the idea that a stable relationship exists between an objective social reality and the language used to represent or describe it.

Among the key ideas that feminism and postmodernism share in common is a critique of the status of general, universalising theories or what postmodernists term 'metanarratives' (Lyotard, 1984). Feminism has criticised many of the metanarratives of Western thought (such as liberalism, Marxism, science and philosophy, for instance) for ignoring or trivialising sexual difference – for failing to regard difference as a fundamental aspect of human existence or for assuming that differences between men and women are natural, essential and pre-social (and not therefore the legitimate concerns of social theory). Postmodernist feminists are therefore inclined to connect modernist thinking with phallocentrism in (supposedly neutral) claims to knowledge. Claims to know the 'truth', they argue, are not neutral but gender-specific reflections of power (think, for instance, of the 'scientific' claim not uncommon in nineteenth-century Britain that formal education and over-development of the intellect would damage a woman's reproductive capacities). Postmodern feminists reject claims to knowledge based on absolute truth or universal meaning, arguing that knowledge is always contingent and contextual and is shaped by subjective interests. They emphasise, then, that there is not *one* truth but many, so that men and women literally 'know' the world differently yet neither version is more or less true than the other.

However, metanarratives have often played a crucial role in feminist political struggles. For example, Enlightenment ideas about human progress, emancipation and human rights have been fundamental to feminist theory and politics, in the fight for political representation and protective legislation, for instance. Hence, while some feminists have sought to produce their own metanarratives (Marxist feminist theories of capitalism, or radical feminist accounts of patriarchy, for instance), others have sought to deconstruct existing metanarratives (arguing that deconstruction in itself is a political activity), and to develop new (postmodern) theories that insist on specificity and no longer claim universal or 'meta' status.

Such approaches, however, have often been accused of relativism (the belief that all claims to truth are equally valid), and this is clearly problematic for feminism given its claim to 'know' that women are oppressed and that patriarchy is unjust. This means that some feminists see postmodernism as a threat to the integrity of feminism as it undermines the emancipatory potential of feminism as a political movement. Such feminists have emphasised that much of the feminist critique hinges on the claim that the oppression of women is 'irrational'. Hence, 'if we want to argue for changing, rather than merely deconstructing, some of the myths of femininity that have lingered for centuries, we need to admit to holding a rational position from which to argue this' (Nicholson, 1990, p. 39).

It is not only metanarratives that both feminism and postmodernism challenge. Another crucial area in which their respective concerns overlap is on the question of subjectivity – the nature and status of the social 'self'. Central to postmodern theory is the recognition that identity is multiple and provisional – race, sex, age, sexuality, and so on are constantly revised and renegotiated. By rejecting the idea of an essential core self constituting the person, postmodernism shifts attention away from the subject as a manifestation of her 'essence' to an emphasis on 'the subject in process' – never unitary or complete. In many ways, this aspect of postmodern feminist thought draws on de Beauvoir's (1988, p. 295) contention that 'One is not born but rather becomes, a woman' (see Chapter 1) in its emphasis on becoming gendered as an ongoing social process. However, rather than seeking to overcome women's Otherness in the way that de Beauvoir urged women to, some postmodern feminists tend to celebrate women's marginalisation from the malestream, arguing that this marginalisation enables women to challenge and undermine phallocentrism through the use of irony and parody (Butler, 1990).

So-called New French feminists (so-named in order to distinguish their work from de Beauvoir's earlier, more humanist approach), such as Hélène Cixous, Julia Kristeva and Luce Irigaray, tend to reject de Beauvoir's claim that women should try to overcome their femininity, arguing instead that we cannot reject what it means to be a woman because within the context of patriarchal discourse and power/ knowledge, women's ways of being are yet to be understood in their own terms. In other words, we can never really 'know' what it means to be a woman within a patriarchal (phallocentric) society because all knowledge – of both men and women – is patriarchal. This means that postmodern feminists challenge the positioning of woman as Other, and the privileging of men/masculinity over women/femininity, but not on the basis of any particular characteristics deemed to distinguish all women (in the way that some radical feminists do), arguing instead that there is nothing essential (or even stable) in the category 'woman'; it has no intrinsic qualities or universal content, and is yet to be 'known' from women's own perspective.

Some feminists who adopt a postmodern perspective reject the idea of substituting feminist theories for malestream ones, because they are sceptical about the possibility of true knowledge and argue instead that there is a multiplicity of truths. They argue for the need to deconstruct truth claims and analyse the power effects that claims to truth entail – to recognise, as Foucault (1980) argued, that knowledge is inextricably a part of power and vice versa. It is therefore necessary to focus on knowledge as opposed to truth, not only because there is no foundational truth, but because there is no reality 'out there' that can arbitrate between competing truth claims – proving that some ideas are true and others are false. There is no one truth, no privileged knowledge or producers of knowledge for postmodern feminists. All knowledge is historically and culturally specific, the product of particular discourses. The discourses that create knowledge also create power – the power that constitutes subjects as actors, and the mechanisms through which subjects are subjugated. The power of particular discourses depends on the extent to which their truth claims are successful – the extent to which the knowledge they produce is accepted as true, often because it is produced and disseminated by powerful actors (male sociologists and social theorists, for instance).

The work of postmodern theorists has been stimulating in raising new questions about social change and about the nature of feminism and sociology itself, and particularly so in encouraging a more reflexive approach to the development of feminist knowledge (see Chapter 13). Those feminists who argue for the development of a closer engagement between feminism and postmodernism emphasise that such an alliance would:

1 avoid the perpetuation of the modernist oppression and exclusion of women from social theory;
2 resolve some of the issues debated in contemporary feminist theory such as the nature of sexual difference;
3 contribute to debates on postmodernism in the social sciences and humanities more generally, by integrating a consideration of sexual difference into the development of theory ('a dimension lacking in many postmodern accounts', Hekman, 1990, p. 3).

Many such feminists believe that feminist notions of the self, knowledge, truth and language are too contradictory to those of the Enlightenment to be contained within its theoretical concepts and categories (Flax, 1997). Others have noted, however, that there is something of 'an uneasy alliance' (Benhabib, 1995) between feminism and postmodernism. On the one hand, because of its challenge to modernist, Enlightenment thought (the critique of metanarratives, of truth claims, and of a humanist conception of the self), feminism appears to be an intellectual ally of postmodernism; on the other hand, because of its commitment to emancipation and human progress, feminism can also be seen as a fundamentally modernist movement. As we noted earlier in this chapter, the historical origins of feminism lie in liberal humanism, a movement that is one of the primary objects of the postmodern critique. Although Marxist feminism represents in many respects a rejection of liberal feminism, it too has fundamentally modernist roots. As Hekman (1990) notes, from both traditions, feminism inherits a legacy that is thoroughly modernist. Yet, the contradiction between this legacy and many of the concerns and insights of contemporary, postmodernist feminism means that attempts to categorise feminist theory as either modernist or postmodernist continue to be problematic, for in many ways it is both *and* neither – modernism and postmodernism being categories of malestream rather than feminist thought.

Feminist critical theory

Several contemporary feminists are working towards attempting to reconcile the emancipatory impetus of feminism (and its modernist legacy) with the critical insights of postmodernism. It is at this theoretical juncture that perhaps some of the most interesting and insightful developments in contemporary feminist theory are taking place; in work that has come to be known as feminist critical theory.

Feminist critical theory has come to be associated with a body of ideas that draws together some of the conceptual insights of the poststructuralist critique of modernism, and subjects these to a revised Marxist approach to feminism. The latter draws from Marxism an emphasis on the appropriation of women's labour (both in terms of paid work and domestic labour) as an experience that many women share in common. Feminist critical theorists also take from Critical Theory (the body of writing associated primarily with the Frankfurt School – see Chapter 12) a concern with the role of culture in maintaining oppressive social relations – hence, they emphasise the need to understand *both* material and cultural forms of power in relation to sexual difference.

Whilst those writers who have broadly come to be associated with the development of feminist critical theory – Seyla Benhabib, Nancy Hartsock, Sandra Harding and Iris Marion Young, for instance – share in common with postmodernism the conception of subjectivity as a process, they tend to reject the corresponding emphasis post-modernism places on this process as discursive. Particularly controversial among feminists who are unsympathetic to the postmodern project is the view that subjectivity is merely an effect of discourse. They argue that such an approach effectively denies women a position from which to develop a critique of patriarchal power relations outside of this established discourse. Many such feminists argue that postmodernism, in contesting Enlightenment values such as emancipation and progress, expresses the claims and needs of white, relatively privileged Western men who have effectively had their Enlightenment and can now reflect critically on it. Nancy Hartsock, for instance, asks

> Why is it that just at the moment when so many of us who have been silenced begin to demand the right to name ourselves, to act as subjects rather than objects

of history, that just then the concept of subjecthood becomes problematic? Just when we are forming our own theories about the world, uncertainty emerges about whether the world can be theorized. Just when we are talking about the changes we want, ideas of progress and the possibility of systematically and rationally organizing human society become dubious and suspect?

(Hartsock, 1990, pp. 163–164)

Postmodernism is often criticised on the basis that it leads to pluralism, relativism and ultimately to a highly individualistic politics. To avoid this, feminist critical theorists have argued that feminism requires a general theory of oppression and liberation, yet one grounded in the lived experience of men and women. Feminist critical theory thus locates itself neither in the metanarratives of liberal, radical or Marxist feminisms, nor in the abandonment of theory associated with postmodernism. It is not based on an essentialist notion of the stable, rational subject of the Enlightenment, or on a postmodernist conception of the subject as the outcome of discourse, but somewhere between these two alternatives.

In relation to knowledge, feminist critical theorists do not argue for relativism and multiplicity, but for 'the necessarily always partial, historically specific and interested nature of theory and practice' (Weedon, 1997, p. 178). Thus, while feminist critical theorists reject essentialising or totalising theories in the form of metanarratives, they continue to use theory strategically – namely, in working towards understanding and transforming oppressive social relations.

As well as a critical engagement with postmodernism, many feminists associated with feminist critical theory draw (critically) on Marxism, arguing particularly that Marxist theory contains several features that can help feminists gain a better understanding of the social world. However, they have also rejected and questioned some fundamental categories of Marxist analysis. Hartsock (1998, p. 400) outlines these as follows:

1 feminists have raised questions about how labour is understood, and have highlighted the importance of non-waged labour;
2 feminists have challenged the centrality of class as the only foundation for social analysis;
3 feminist theory raises questions about Marxism as a theory of social evolution and progress, noting the persistence of patriarchal relations in non-capitalist societies;
4 feminist theory has questioned (in line with postmodernism), the Marxist claim to be a single theory that can explain all aspects of society, including its history and future.

Rethinking these basic categories of Marxist analysis, many feminists drawing on critical theory have argued, however, that 'in the context of a capitalism that has become truly global, and in which ever more of life is commodified, much of Marx's critique of capitalism remains very apt' (Hartsock, 1998, p. 401). Feminist critical theorists tend to share in common with Marxism the contention that relations of sexual difference are shaped primarily by the appropriation of labour, and also emphasise the idea (known as 'dialectics') that the social world is composed not of 'things' but of processes – a perspective which holds that social phenomena must be understood within the context of the social totality. This emphasis on the dialectical nature of social reality is believed by some feminists to provide a more complex and sophisticated understanding of the social world than is available from either liberal-humanism (modernism) or theories associated with postmodernism. It also has important implications for the ways in which power and knowledge are understood (see Chapter 13) within feminist critical theory, and for the ways in which the purpose and nature of feminism itself is defined.

Seyla Benhabib and Drucilla Cornell (1987, p. 1) outline what they term 'feminism as critique', which represents an attempt to link a conception of the social world (and our social identity) as dialectical, with a commitment to the idea that knowledge and power are 'situated'. This involves a theoretical shift in Marxist feminism, amounting to what they term 'the displacement of the paradigm of production'. The traditional Marxist category of production involves an active subject transforming, making and shaping an object (the product of labour). According to Benhabib and Cornell, this is inadequate to understand much of the labour that women perform (both in the home and in paid work) that involves not subject–object relations, but inter-subjective relations. They also argue that the Marxist emphasis on production as the structuring principle of society subsumes feminine categories and inter-subjective relations. For Benhabib and Cornell, this model (and the public/private distinction on which it depends) is detrimental to acknowledging the social significance of women's labour, and effectively trivialises women's social and economic role.

As well as their critique of the Marxist paradigm of production, Benhabib and Cornell reject the liberal-humanist conception of the 'self'. They argue that the liberal definition of the self as the bearer of certain rights and responsibilities is belied by the inequality, asymmetry and domination which permeates the *gendered* identity of this self. Feminist critical theory, or what they term 'feminism as critique' therefore involves a critique of the postmodernist rejection of metanarratives, the Marxist paradigm of production, and the liberal-humanist conception of the self.

In the main, feminist critical theorists are sceptical about the claims of postmodernism and argue that the project of modernity (with its core concepts of progress, humanity and liberation), despite its flaws, still contains considerable potential on which to ground an emancipatory, feminist politics. But they also argue that we must give more attention to gendered subjectivity, to the body and to language than has traditionally been the case in (modernist) feminist theory and to begin to understand the role of culture in perpetuating women's oppression. Feminist critical theorists also tend to reject the liberal-humanist (and also Marxist) conception of a core, essential self in favour of a view of the self as the outcome of process. Theorists such as Benhabib (1992, p. 213) argue that 'one of the main consequences of the androcentric [male-centred] conception of the universal subject has been to obscure the fact that men, too, are gendered beings'. They argue that it is not an essential self that women are alienated from (in the way that liberal, Marxist or radical feminists might), but from the *process* of becoming a subject (that, for instance, dominant images of feminine bodies in the mass media serve to define and constrain female embodiment within patriarchal and capitalist norms, rather than enabling women to identify subjectively with their 'lived', material bodies).

Feminist critical theorists emphasise that the relationship of feminism to modernism is one shaped by conflict and contradiction, but that, nevertheless, the future of feminist theory lies in a critical continuation of modernism, not a rejection of it. Hence, feminism is seen to constitute both a critique and a defence of modernist thinking.

Feminist critical theory also rejects the poststructuralist critique of metanarratives, arguing that feminism needs to develop a theoretical framework that both recognises the plurality of women's experiences and perspectives, whilst also emphasising the importance (politically and intellectually) of a commitment to solidarity, and to understanding shared experience; the latter is deemed to be based largely on the exploitation of women's labour. Feminist critical theorists are thus critical of the postmodernist demand for an abandonment of the search for any certain or stable foundation for knowledge, as this is thought to undermine, as Hartsock puts it, 'the very real political interests which underlie feminist theory, which are necessarily founded on the belief that a feminist perspective is superior to a non-feminist perspective' (1998, p. 403).

Feminist critical theorists believe, then, that it is possible for feminism to radically challenge the core beliefs of modernism, whilst retaining a commitment to its political impetus: 'to reshape its categories of analysis without severing ties with its emancipatory aspirations' (Benhabib, 1995, p. 32).

Black and post-colonial feminisms

While Marxist, dual-systems and feminist critical theorists have all argued that it is necessary to analyse and explain class, gender and racial subordination, Black and post-colonial feminists have been critical of the lack of centrality given to issues of ethnic difference, racialisation, colonialism and racism in feminist theory and research. Here the term Black (with a capital 'b') is used to refer to a group of people who have a subjective sense of belonging together not because of the colour of their skin, but because of a shared experience of marginalisation, oppression and racialisation. This political (rather than racial) use of the term has been criticised, however, particularly by post-colonial feminists who argue that it loses sight of important differences in the experience (and causes) of racism, thereby homogenising diverse identities and experiences. By 'post-colonial' we mean groups of people whose identity is shaped, at least in part, by a shared history or experience of subjection to colonial power, and often also to migration.

There has been a growing sociological interest in post-colonial studies in recent years. Many would argue that this in itself represents merely another form of colonisation. Others might argue, more optimistically perhaps, that this signifies the extent to which the discipline (partly as a result of the impact of feminism, post-modernism and post-colonialism) is becoming more reflexive. That is, more aware of the ways in which sociology itself has perpetuated inequalities in power and the marginalisation of particular groups of people. The sociological interest in post-colonialism seems to have been fuelled by a growing awareness of the Eurocentrism of the Enlightenment, and of the liberal traditions it engendered. The Enlightenment, according to this outlook, actually perpetrated the interests of the few – European, mostly white, men – in the name of a generic commitment to universal values such as rationality, liberation, democracy, equal rights, and so on.

Black and post-colonial feminists have argued that the universal claims of white feminists do not provide adequate theoretical explanations for the unique experiences and structural locations of Black and post-colonial women. They point out, for example, that the relationship between white women and white men is not the same as that between Black women and Black men. They do not deny that Black men oppress Black women in patriarchal ways but argue that capitalism and patriarchy do not distribute power evenly among Black and white men, so that there is often more solidarity (in terms of shared experiences and interests) between white males and females than there is between white males and Black males.

What the relatively disparate range of approaches to Black and post-colonial feminist theory share in common is a critique of white mainstream, academic feminism. As Beasley has put it,

> The only assertion that is consistently reiterated within the field is the *critique of feminism* as, at minimum, *inattentive to race and ethnicity*. More often feminism is seen as being exclusionary and (either implicitly or explicitly) racist/ethnocentrist.
>
> (Beasley, 1999, p. 104, original emphasis)

Broadly speaking, Black and post-colonial feminist theory has brought four particular 'charges' against mainstream, white feminism. These can be summed up as:

1 ethnocentrism,
2 the perpetuation of a 'victim ideology',
3 theoretical racism, and
4 cultural appropriation.

Ethnocentrism

Black and post-colonial feminists have argued that white feminism has ignored the existence and specific experiences of Black women, and has over-homogenised 'women's experience' derived from white perspectives and priorities. In particular, radical feminists' insistence that sexual oppression is the most fundamental form of power and their related view that women have more in common with each other than with any man is perceived as exemplifying authoritarian claims that Black and post-colonial feminists refute. Rather, as Beasley notes,

> Feminists concerned with race/ethnicity draw attention to the solidarity created between men and women who experience racism/ethnocentrism and, in asserting this commonality, they sometimes pose race/ethnicity as the more fundamental form of power.
>
> (Beasley, 1999, p. 111)

In this respect, white feminism is charged with being ethnocentric – based on the perspective, experiences and priorities of one particular ethnic or racial group, yet making statements about social reality that are claimed or assumed to be universal. The claim that Christopher Columbus 'discovered' America, or that Australia is a little over two hundred years old, is ethnocentric, for instance. Similarly, the feminist claim that the family is one of the key sites of women's oppression could be regarded as ethnocentric, because it fails to take account of the diversity of experiences of family life amongst women of different racial, ethnic and national identities. Women living in post-colonial and developing countries particularly have challenged the assumption that there is a generalisable, identifiable and collectively shared experience of womanhood.

The perpetuation of a 'victim ideology'

It is also argued by Black and post-colonial feminists that white, Western feminist theory has tended to see Black and post-colonial women as the helpless victims of racism (or simply of their racial, ethnic, cultural or religious identities), and so have failed to take account of the complex interaction between race and sexual difference in relation to cultural practices that are unfamiliar. In her book *The Whole Woman*, Germaine Greer (1999) discusses some of the complex issues underpinning feminist (and non-feminist) debates on clitoridectomy (referred to by radical feminists such as Mary Daly as 'genital mutilation' – see above). Greer outlines how when she discussed breast augmentation surgery with Somali women, many of whom had experienced clitoridectomy themselves, they were horrified at the lengths women in the West would go to mutilate their bodies in order to make themselves more sexually attractive to men. Greer argues that this indicates the level of ethnocentrism underpinning the 'victim ideologies' at work in Western feminist thought. Other examples we might cite are assumptions about dress codes and arranged marriages, for instance. As Jennifer Saul (2003, p. 266) notes in her discussion of Western judgements about Islamic women's 'veiling' (itself a homogenising term that refers to a range of garments and practices), veiling – although in many ways problematic – has historically been widely 'misunderstood and oversimplified' by Western feminists.

Theoretical racism

It is this lack of reflexivity that bell hooks (1982, 1984) is particularly critical of in her evaluation of white feminism. She accuses feminist theory of racism, and argues that in recent years a division has arisen in the 'type' of writing that feminists are expected to produce. She argues that Black and post-colonial women are expected to write 'from the heart' about their lived experiences, whereas white feminists are expected to write 'from the head' and to provide theory according to which Black women's experiences can be analysed and explained. hooks argues that this racial/epistemological division of feminism effectively reproduces the dichotomies of modernist, patriarchal thought that feminism is supposed to challenge, and according to which women's experiences were understood with reference to the systems of meaning produced by men.

Most Black and post-colonial feminists are highly critical, therefore, of the ways in which feminist empirical, theoretical and political claims have been based largely on the experiences of relatively affluent and privileged white, Western women. This 'false universalism', hooks argues, has been profoundly ethnocentric.

Furthermore, Black and post-colonial feminists have argued that the customary division of the history of feminism into 'waves' reflects the extent to which feminism has tended to be constructed and organised with reference to North American and European thought. Irene Gedalof (1999) in her book *Against Purity* has also developed a critique of the ways in which white, Western feminism has tended to conceptualise a focus solely (or even primarily) on gender as feminism in its 'purest' form. Her account of Indian feminist theory shows how Indian feminist ideas and politics have evolved alongside anti-colonial movements and within the context of Hindu/Muslim conflicts. Thus, writers such as hooks and Gedalof have argued that, however unintentionally, the 'grand narrative' of feminism becomes the story of Western feminist endeavours, and tends to relegate the experience of non-Western women to the margins of feminist theory.

Cultural appropriation

bell hooks (1992) has also been particularly critical of the ways in which, at the other extreme and especially within popular culture, the experiences and identities of (or rather attributed to) Black women have been appropriated by white women in the name of feminism. Writing in the early 1990s, hooks has been particularly critical of Madonna in this respect, but argues that much the same critique can be developed of feminist theory. This, she argues, effectively amounts to a cultural (and material) colonisation of Black and post-colonial women by white feminism. She also notes, in this respect, how white feminism has often served not only to leave intact but often to reinforce racist stereotypes of Black femininity. hooks (1992) argues, for instance, that white feminist perceptions of Madonna as subversive fail to acknowledge that her projection of aggressive sexual agency is scarcely of use to Black women who might wish to challenge racist representations of themselves as explicitly and overly sexual.

In common with postmodernist feminism, then, many Black and post-colonial feminists are committed to questioning universal assumptions about 'womanhood'. Both approaches are concerned with developing theory that avoids generalising from the experiences of white, Western heterosexual, middle-class women. Indeed, it may be argued that, as Chris Weedon (1997, p. 179) notes, 'by questioning all essences and relativising truth claims, postmodern feminisms create a space for political perspectives and interests that have hitherto been marginalised'. They also help guard against creating alternative generalising theories in their place.

However, Black feminists such as bell hooks in particular – in their commitment to racial as well as gender emancipation – do not abandon any sense of collective politics. Rather, they argue that some notion of a shared experience of womanhood remains politically necessary. In particular, bell hooks is concerned that postmodernism may mean that feminism becomes overly preoccupied intellectually with recognising and celebrating differences amongst women at the expense of maintaining a commitment to emancipatory politics.

This dilemma leaves feminism with something of a theoretical (and a political) problem – How can feminist theory base itself upon the uniqueness of women's experience of the social world, without reifying one particular definition or description of what that experience is; without succumbing, in other words, to universal claims about women's position? Postmodernism, Black and post-colonial feminisms all raise fundamental questions for feminist theory about the nature and role of feminism itself. The current stress on diversity amongst women complicates the question 'What is feminism?' and particularly 'Who is feminism trying to emancipate?' This complexity has led some feminists to argue that we now live in what should be regarded as a post-feminist era.

Postfeminism

Sarah Gamble sums up some of the issues raised by postfeminism when she notes that

> 'postfeminism' is a term that is very much in vogue these days. In the context of popular culture it's the Spice Girls, Madonna and the *Girlie Show*: women dressing like bimbos, yet claiming male privileges and attitudes. Meanwhile, those who wish to maintain an allegiance to more traditional forms of feminism circle around the neologism warily, unable to decide whether it represents a con trick engineered by the media or a valid movement.
>
> (Gamble, 2001, p. 43)

Indeed, as Gamble goes on to note, many feminist and sociological texts tend to barricade the term in inverted commas 'thus keeping both author and reader at a properly skeptical distance' (p. 43). For many feminists, postfeminism is best under-stood not as something that comes after feminism but rather as a regressive development – as a perspective that 'delivers us back' as Tania Modleski (1991) has put it. Perhaps the most clearly articulated discussion of postfeminism as a relapse can be found in Susan Faludi's (1991) *Backlash: The Undeclared War Against Women*. For Faludi, postfeminism – which she defines as an ironic, pseudo-intellectual critique of the feminist movement – is a backlash against the achievements of second wave feminism. She notes how, in a society in which we define ourselves largely with reference to media culture (see Chapter 12), women are easily persuaded that feminism is passé.

Although for some, postfeminism engenders scepticism, for others, it represents something much more liberatory and an opportunity to throw off the stifling shackles of an ethnocentric and anachronistic movement. Much of this latter approach coalesces around a liberal ideology of individualism and a rejection of what is perceived as a victim mentality within second wave feminism. In *The Morning After: Sex, Fear and Feminism*, for instance, Katie Roiphe (1993) argues that the feminist perpetuation of an image of women as victims of their gender and sexuality transports us back to the ideas of earlier generations that framed women as delicate and in need of protec-tion – ideas that both first and second wave feminism fought hard against. In a similar vein, Rene Denfeld's (1995) *The New Victorians* emphasises that the term 'feminism' has come to stand for an extremist movement that valorises what she calls 'the figure of the female victim'. She concludes that feminism is becoming a spent force – one that has lost credibility in the eyes of those whose real social and political inequality still needs to be addressed. As she puts it, 'trapped in a stagnant, alienating ideology, the only thing most of the feminist movement is heading toward is complete irrelevance' (cited in Gamble, 2001, p. 47).

In parallel with trends in the development of postmodern thought, perspectives on postfeminism can broadly be categorised as those that stress either post-feminism as a socio-cultural phenomenon, characterised by the emergence of an historical period 'after' feminism, and postfeminism as a theoretical perspective concerned to emphasise diversity rather than commonality of experience amongst women (and men), and therefore the extent to which a coherent feminist theory is no longer tenable. Indeed, the postmodernist claim that there is nothing stable or universal – definitive – in the category woman effectively implies that there can be no subject of feminism. As Beasley has noted in this respect, postmodernist feminism

> may be said to offer the greatest challenge to feminism yet given . . . feminists' concerns with the subject of 'woman', a concern which places centre stage women as a category or group identified by sex differentiation.
>
> (Beasley, 1999, p. 83)

Post-feminism as an historical period

The term post-feminism (with a hyphen) tends to be used largely by those who argue that the political demands of first and second wave feminism have now been met (enfranchisement, equal pay, sexual liberation, and so on) and that it is time for men and women to compete on a level playing field. Many such writers claim that to prolong feminism as a political project would be socially regressive and politically divisive (and that, as a result, men would become an oppressed minority). Hall and Rodriguez (2003, p. 878) have recently outlined four claims made by post-feminists. These are '(1) overall support for the women's movement has dramatically eroded because some women (2) are increasingly antifeminist, (3) believe the movement is irrelevant, and (4) have adopted a "no, but . . ." version of feminism'. Helen Wilkinson (1994) in her account of what she terms 'the genderquake' argues that

1 the cultural, political and economic enfranchisement of women is deep and irreversible (there has been a convergence of the values of men and women);
2 most of the jobs created in market societies in the last thirty years or so have been in so-called 'women's work' (non-manual, service sector work – see Chapter 9);
3 conversely, construction, manufacturing and the military (traditionally sectors of large male employment) have contracted;
4 the terms of the feminist debate have shifted – sociologists now acknowledge that men as well as women can be subject to discrimination, harassment and inter-personal violence;
5 feminist politics is severely lacking behind culture (most young women don't identify themselves as 'feminist', although they may have sympathy with many of the empirical, political and theoretical claims of feminism);
6 there are major generation gaps between women (many of the current generation now take for granted what previous generations struggled for);

7 a new agenda for feminism is needed if it is to survive in any useful form into the twenty-first century.

One of the most identifiable 'faces' of postfeminism as a period 'after' or opposed to feminism, particularly in the USA, is Naomi Wolf. In her book *Fire With Fire* (1993), Wolf argues that feminism has consistently failed to capitalise on its gains and to be more reflexive about how far it has come. For Wolf, power is there 'for the taking' and she urges women to be more proactive in this respect, and to reject the feminist perpetuation of a victim ideology. As Gamble (2001) notes, perhaps power really is there 'for the taking' if one is a white, middle-class, educated and relatively wealthy American; but what if you are Black, or poor, or subject to an oppressive political, military or religious regime? These are things that Wolf tends not to consider, an omission which we could argue highlights many of the problems associated with the claim that postfeminism is a socio-cultural phenomenon – a historical period after or opposed to feminism.

In her book *The Whole Woman*, Germaine Greer (1999) argues that the claim that we live in a post-feminist era is little more than a marketing strategy, for 'the most powerful entities on earth are not governments, but the multi-national corporations that see women as their territory'. The idea that (as Naomi Wolf emphasises) women can 'have it all', for Greer, serves merely to reinforce women's role as the world's foremost consumers of cosmetics, pharmaceuticals, clothing, cosmetic surgery and convenience foods. Greer also argues that the adoption of a post-feminist stance is a Western luxury – much like other consumer goods – one that only the world's most affluent women can indulge in, and that by taking power for themselves in the way that Naomi Wolf advocates, (male and female) champions of post-feminism merely perpetuate the oppression of others.

Postfeminism as a theoretical perspective

As Sarah Gamble (2001, p. 50) has argued, postfeminism is more convincing when it is developed as a theoretical approach (as opposed to an empirical claim): 'in this context, postfeminism becomes a pluralistic epistemology dedicated to disrupting universalizing patterns of thought, and [is] thus capable of being aligned with post-modernism, poststructuralism and postcolonialism.' As a theoretical perspective (as opposed to an empirical claim), postfeminism implies that given the diversity of womanhood it is problematic to assume that feminism is based on a unified subjectivity (as in the idea of a 'universal sisterhood', for instance), so that if there is no universal 'woman' as the subject of feminism, it is logical to argue that contemporary theories of sexual difference are 'postfeminist'. This raises the question of what we mean by 'post'. In terms of post-feminism as a political or historical phenomenon, the term tends to be used to signify a period that comes after (or instead of) feminism. In relation to postfeminism as a theoretical perspective, a shift in feminist thinking is implied, and particularly in the way in which 'woman' as the subject of feminism is conceptualised.

A notable example of this approach is Ann Brooks's (1997) *Postfeminisms: Feminism, Cultural Theory and Cultural Forms*. Brooks argues that feminism tends to base its claim to equality on an appeal to the liberal humanism of Enlightenment modernity, a claim that postfeminism seeks to destabilise, focusing instead on the ideological processes through which women were excluded from the (European) Enlightenment. According to Brooks, postfeminism signals the development of an exciting and dynamic intellectual debate within feminism – over equality and difference, commonality and diversity, for instance – one invigorated by the various contributions of postmodern, Black and post-colonial theorists.

Indeed many of those writers considered above tend to reject the label 'feminist' altogether, arguing that feminism is a political movement that is liberal-humanist in its orientation and which seeks to obtain a place for women as men's equals in a patriarchal culture. Instead of becoming feminists, Hélène Cixous argues, women should strive to disrupt the established gender order. Julia Kristeva similarly refutes the term feminist, and particularly a feminist conception of 'woman' which, she argues, has traditionally sought merely to replicate men's power within established patriarchal structures. She refers to liberal, Anglo-American feminism as 'bourgeois' and therefore not representative of the politics of the feminine.

In terms of the relationship between race, ethnicity and postfeminism, the influence of post-colonial theory is important to consider. On the one hand, while white feminism has claimed to have theorised the colonisation of all women who are subject to patriarchal oppression, feminists such as bell hooks (1982, 1984, 1990) and Gayatri Chakravorty Spivak (1987) have found this problematic in so far as it ignores specific cultural and material conditions experienced by Black and post-colonial women, in favour of an emphasis on the politics of 'universal sisterhood'. Postmodernism's emphasis on diversity – as this manifests itself in postfeminism as a theoretical disposition – is thus welcomed.

On the other hand, however, post-feminism as a political term (signifying an empirical-historical rather than theoretical shift) tends to be rejected by Black and post-colonial feminists as lacking concrete relevance to 'real' (material) conditions of marginality experienced by Black and post-colonial women; and therefore as being exclusionary and ethnocentric in its focus. bell hooks in particular has been critical of post-feminism for embracing the 'death of the subject' thesis in postmodernist thinking, just when Black and post-colonial feminists were beginning to claim a strong presence in feminist theory.

As well as debates on gender relations, postmodernism, and race and ethnicity, postfeminism is also implicated in feminist debates on the impact of recent developments in media and communication technologies (see Chapter 12). In her 'Cyborg Manifesto', Donna Haraway (1991) argues that there is nothing inherently female that binds all women together, there is not even such a state as being universally 'female' – itself, she argues, a category constructed within scientific discourse and other social practices that define patriarchy. Haraway argues that women should learn to embrace and control technology rather than (continue to) allow it to control them; hence her approach has been termed 'cyberfeminism' – a postfeminist (or third wave feminist) approach that celebrates the evolution of cyber-reality as an alternative gender order.

In a similar vein to Haraway, Sadie Plant (1997) has argued that women must embrace developments in media and communication technologies. Forms of communication such as hypertext, Plant claims, are non-linear and thus more 'female' in their orientation. She argues that in terms of communication, women can celebrate their femininity in a cyber-reality in which disembodied beings can conceive of gender identity as one option amongst many, and her work too has been referred to as 'postfeminist' or cyberfeminist. She maintains that the evolution of cybernetics marks a fundamental shift away from a linear (modernist) conception of development, and a return to a (pre-modern) cyclical reality 'now transformed into circuitry' (p. 507) that resonates more closely with women's experiences of reality. She contends that we are heading towards a post-human world in which the intentions of 'man' as the author of the human species are no longer the guiding force of global development; a (post-gendered) era in which cyberfeminism can flourish.

Not surprisingly, then, postmodern and cyberfeminists tend to regard identity politics (for instance, the radical feminist conception of a 'universal sisterhood') with some disdain. They insist that resistance to male power does not have to involve recourse to accepting what has traditionally been defined as 'womanhood', and thus refuse to valorise or celebrate (in the gynocentric way that some radical feminists do) any notion of an essential identity supposedly shared by all women. Hence, because of their rejection of any unitary, stable notion of the subject, and their related scepticism regarding emancipatory politics and metanarratives, some postmodern and cyber-feminists urge the abandonment of engagement with any form of identity politics or patriarchal discourse, and include feminism within that category. As Weedon notes in this respect, however,

> How . . . could women organize together and develop new positive identities if there were no essence of womanhood on the basis of which women could come together in the spirit of sisterhood? This question has become central to feminism.
> (Weedon, 1997, p. 170)

We would argue that the competing feminist theories considered here ask different questions and thereby provide different understandings of the social world, and of relations of sexual difference. Rather than argue that one is more adequate than the others, we would suggest that all feminist ideas contribute to our understanding and help us make sense of the social world; each adds something to the process of gendering the sociological imagination.

Conclusions

In this chapter we have argued that malestream sociology has failed to develop theories that can make sense of the social world for women. Furthermore, there has been a resistance to taking account of the critique of malestream theory that has been developed by feminist sociologists. We have indicated that feminists have developed a number of theoretical perspectives that provide a basis both for making sense of what is going on in the social world and for political action – for challenging and changing patriarchy in all its guises. These provide the basis for developing a sociology for women, one that provides an understanding of the social world that speaks to the experiences of women – a gendered 'sociological imagination'.

SUMMARY

1 Sociology as a discipline is concerned with enabling us to understand the social world we inhabit and our position within it – to grasp the sociological imagination.
2 Feminist sociologists wish to reformulate sociology so that it provides a sociological imagination for women as well as men, something that malestream sociology has failed to do as sociological theory remains largely male dominated.
3 Sociology is concerned to develop theories in order to provide answers to 'how' and 'why' questions.
4 Sociologists disagree both on what it is that is being explained and on how it can be explained. We outlined four theoretical positions on social reality – positivist, idealist, realist and postmodernist.
5 Sexual difference – the difference between men and women as social subjects – is central to feminist theory and feminists have devised four main ways in which sexual difference can be understood. These are – humanist, gynocentric, postmodernist and critical feminist.
6 There are a number of feminist theories, which differ in the ways in which they explain inequalities based on sexual difference, and on the emancipatory strategies they advocate. Those that have had the most significant impact on sociology to date include – liberal/reformist, Marxist, radical, dual-systems, postmodern, feminist critical theory and Black/post-colonial feminism.
7 Post-feminism is both an empirical claim and a theoretical disposition that, along with cyberfeminism, raises interesting and potentially problematic issues for feminism.

FURTHER READING

Evans, J. (1995) *Feminist Theory Today: An Introduction to Second Wave Feminism*. London: Sage. This book is a useful starting point – it is an accessible guide to a range of feminist perspectives and debates and is particularly useful for its outline of feminist perspectives on sexual difference.

Saul, J.M. (2003) *Feminism: Issues and Arguments*. Oxford: Oxford University Press. This is a stimulating book for anyone with an interest in feminist theory and particularly the philosophical issues underpinning feminist debates on identity and difference. It explores the politics of work and family, sexual harassment, pornography, abortion, issues relating to feminine appearance, feminism and language, science and also feminist debates on culture.

Tong, R. (1998) *Feminist Thought: A More Comprehensive Introduction*. Second edition. London: Routledge. This is a comprehensive and engaging outline of a range of feminist theoretical perspectives, focusing on their historical development and including close textual readings. It is a useful follow-on from any of the other more introductory texts.

CHAPTER THREE

Stratification and inequality

In all societies there are differences between people in terms of the amount of power and wealth they command. In this chapter we discuss various social and cultural divisions, considering the main forms of social stratification in the contemporary world and exploring how these might be explained from a feminist perspective. Focusing initially on gender and then social class, we also look at racial and ethnic divisions, as well as feminist contributions to sociological perspectives on disability. Finally, we examine global patterns of stratification and the ways in which these are shaped by sexual difference (the difference between men and women). This is not to say, however, that issues of identity, difference and inequality are not considered in subsequent chapters. What we are aiming to do here is merely map out a conceptual and empirical framework by exploring sociological and feminist perspectives on aspects of identity and difference that shape men's and women's experiences of the social world, and particularly of social stratification.

Sociologists use the term stratification to refer to a structure according to which individuals and groups are positioned within a social hierarchy in which some groups occupy more powerful and privileged positions than others – in a class, caste or gender system, for instance. Macionis and Plummer (2002) argue that social stratification is:

1 *a characteristic of society* – not simply a reflection of individual differences or competences;
2 *persistent over generations* (although some individuals do experience social mobility – see below);
3 *universal but variable* – stratification is a feature of all societies from the simplest to the most complex, but what counts as inequality varies between and also within societies;
4 *not simply material but also based on belief systems* – just as *what* constitutes inequality varies between societies, so do explanations of *why* people are unequal, as does the basis on which people might come to be thought of as inferior.

The basis of stratification – the division of people according to a hierarchical system – varies from society to society. Divisions may be based on sexual difference, social class, race and ethnicity, culture, disability, age, and so on. Feminist writer Iris Marion Young (1990a, pp. 49–59) has identified a number of social processes at work in the stratification of societies into hierarchical orders. These include:

1 *social exclusion and marginalisation* – a process by which 'a whole category of people is expelled from useful participation in social life';
2 *exploitation* – through which there is 'a transfer of the results of the labour of one social group to benefit another';
3 *powerlessness* – whereby 'people come to lack the authority, status and sense of self that many professionals tend to have';
4 *cultural imperialism* – involving 'the universalization of a dominant group's experience and culture, and its establishment as the norm';
5 *violence* – directed at members of a group simply because they belong to that group (examples of which might include violence against women, racial violence and homophobia).

Sociologists have tended to argue that in capitalist societies the primary form of stratification is based on social class. However, sociologists disagree about what constitutes class, and how it is determined. Some argue, for instance, that countries such as Britain and the US are increasingly 'classless'. Others emphasise that class is no longer defined by production (the occupational group to which we belong, or by our income) but by consumption (our spending patterns and the kind of lifestyle we adopt). Most sociologists maintain, however, that

> Capitalist industrial societies are still stratified, and theories of social class still provide us with essential insights into the manner in which established in-equalities in wealth and power associated with production and markets, access to educational and organisational resources and so on have systematically served to perpetuate these inequalities over time.
>
> (Crompton, 1993, p. 266)

However, class processes are not the only factors contributing to the reproduction and maintenance of social inequalities. As we have seen in Chapter 2, feminists argue that sexual difference is also a primary form of stratification, with men having more power and prestige than women in most societies. Racial and ethnic differences are likewise a primary determinant of stratification. One feature of Indian society, for instance, despite attempts by some Hindu reformers to outlaw it, is the caste structure. This is a system of stratification based on inherited or ascribed social status premised on the assumption that hierarchy is, at least in part, natural or pre-social – part of the divine intention for natural order. Social groups or 'castes' are defined primarily by birth, but also by marriage and occupation.

Today, caste barriers have largely broken down in urban areas of India, and 'untouchability' – the idea that some groups are too low to be categorised within the caste system – has been abolished by law. However, the *Jati* (modern caste) system continues to emphasise the importance of rituals of purity and impurity. Hence, members of the upper castes tend to consider the lower castes to be ritually 'unclean', and so marrying someone from a lower caste, for instance, whilst not officially out-lawed, might not be recognised or celebrated. Loyalty to a caste continues to provide a strong sense of belonging and constitutes a significant aspect of social identity and stratification in Indian society, particularly in rural areas.

Age is also a significant aspect of social stratification, with young people and elderly ones generally having less power than those in middle-aged groups. Although the proportion varies between countries, there are more women than men amongst the elder populations of most societies, with the largest differences being in Eastern European and Central Asian countries (see Chapter 5). Since women are more likely than men to become widowed or live alone, they are more vulnerable to social inequalities resulting from changes in population structure and inadequate social welfare provision. Also, since women are more likely to be disadvantaged in the labour market (see Chapter 9), to undertake informal and unpaid caring activities, and because they tend to lack social security and pension rights relative to men, they are more vulnerable to poverty than men in later life.

Patterns of global stratification are also important to consider. The division between the West (the advanced industrial societies) and the Rest, to use a distinction made by Stuart Hall (1992a), also involves a relationship of exploitation and subordination as post-colonial sociologists and feminists have argued.

It is also important to recognise therefore that while all societies are divided according to sexual difference, women are not a unified and homogeneous group and may experience inequalities based on sexual difference in a range of ways. They share a subject position (as women) but are differentiated by age, sexual preference, race, class, physicality and geopolitical status. As we noted in Chapter 2, white, Western, middle-class varieties of feminist theory and practice are increasingly coming to be challenged as ignoring the experiences of many women. Postmodernist and post-colonial feminists have highlighted the dangers of inappropriate generalisation, stressing the importance of acknowledging the many voices and experiences of women. Postfeminists have also argued that because womanhood is such a diverse experience and identity, it makes no sense to continue to speak of – and attempt to emancipate – women as a homogenous group.

While it is important to recognise the different interests of women situated in terms of class, race, age, and so on, other feminists (e.g. Doyal, 1995) have warned of the dangers of doing so, arguing that in rejecting general categories we may lose sight of the commonalities between women. Lesley Doyal points out that the body, for example, imposes real (material) constraints on women's lives and that 'this is evidenced by the fact that the fight for bodily self-determination has been a central feature of feminist politics across very different cultures' (p. 7). We would agree with this position, and argue that whilst it is important to recognise the diverse range of experiences and identities within womanhood and avoid making universalising or ethnocentric claims, feminism must also emphasise commonalities amongst women, particularly in terms of shared experiences of oppression, exploitation and marginalisation.

Gender-based stratification

The distinction between men and women, masculine and feminine, is a fundamental basis of social and cultural organisation and a primary form of stratification, feminists argue. Common sense suggests that becoming a man or a woman is a linear process of 'natural' development, but sociologists have long since argued otherwise, maintaining that differences between men and women are not ahistorical, absolute or universal but historically and culturally variable. Bob Connell (1995, 2002), for instance, has argued that in any given societies there are a range of masculinities and that only some of these become dominant – defining the most socially acceptable ways of being a man, and hence assuming the status of what he terms 'hegemonic masculinity'. Sociological perspectives on gender therefore aim to understand the key social differences between men and women and attempt to explain these with reference to social (rather than biological or psychological) differences. These differences are often referred to as the 'gender order' – the structure through which men and women, as well as forms of masculinity and femininity, are accorded different levels of power and status in any given society.

Gender inequalities

Gender differences are evident throughout the social world and are grounded in relations of power and inequality because in most societies men are accorded a dis-proportionate share of social, political, economic and cultural resources. Gender inequalities, much like the other forms of social stratification considered here, are both cultural and material – women are marginalised not only in cultural beliefs, representations and practices (in language, for instance – see Chapter 12), but are also oppressed and exploited through political, economic, social and physical forms of power. The following examples from current research give some indication of the nature and extent of gender discrimination and disadvantage across the world, or what sociologist Goran Therborn (2004, p. 107) calls 'the patriarchal burden of the twenty-first century'.

In contemporary India, two rapes and three kidnapping and abduction cases involving women are reported to the police every hour. Similarly, every hour at least four molestation and one sexual harassment cases are reported. A study conducted on behalf of UNICEF in Bangalore on the ways in which the police respond to reports of crimes against women and children found that most of the cases reported were not registered and instead, victims were often subject to police harassment in the name of 'counselling'. Cruelty to women by husbands and their relatives was also found to be occurring at a rate of six cases every hour. Another finding was that among the rape cases reported, 84 per cent of the offenders were known to the victims (*The Hindu*, 2 March 2004). One dowry death is reported in India every hour. Indeed, Therborn (2004, p. 173) notes that in the first half of the 1990s, dowry conflicts led to 5,000 registered killings of women each year in India, with a heavy concentration in the conservative northern states of Uttar Predesh and Harayana, and in the federal district of Delhi (see also Thakur, 1998).

In Australia, the first national survey of sexual harassment has recently found that more than one in four women have been harassed at work. Twenty years after the first laws against sexual harassment were introduced there, some 28 per cent of women aged 18–64 said they had been sexually harassed at work. The figure for men was found to be 7 per cent. The survey also found that less than a third of those harassed had reported the offence, and more than half said they lacked faith in the system. Almost half of all those who had been harassed said their harasser was a co-worker, but 35 per cent said it was a supervisor or boss. In half of the reported cases, the harassment had continued for more than six months (*The Age*, 25 March 2004).

A report by the UN (2004) entitled 'Millennium Development Goals: China's Progress' found that many Chinese women and girls face widespread discrimination and oppression in all spheres of life. The report estimates that 13 per cent of the country's 600 million women are illiterate, compared to only 5 per cent of men, and only 22 per cent of the country's government and public bodies are women. Women in China are 25 per cent more likely to commit suicide compared to men and women in the rest of the world, where on average 3.6 times more men kill themselves than women. The report recommends that China includes gender and discrimination issues in teacher training programmes and in school textbooks, and enforces measures to reduce incentives for pre-natal sex selection (*China News*, 26 March 2004). Indeed, the latter has become a particular social problem in China as official statistics suggest that in 2002, there were 117 boys born for every 100 girls (in 1982, the proportion of males to females was 108 to 100, closer to the worldwide ratio of 111.9 to 100). If this trend continues, there will be up to 40 million more men than women in China by 2020. Although the law prohibits doctors from revealing the results of ultrasound screening of embryos, in practice this is often ignored and abortion of female foetuses is not uncommon since the introduction of China's 'one child per couple' policy in 1979. Many baby girls are abandoned at hospitals and birth centres, and girls are over-represented in Chinese orphanages (United Press International, 8 March 2004).

Structuralist explanations

Feminist sociologists such as Sylvia Walby (1990) have argued that gender inequalities such as these are sustained through a range of social structures that subordinate women. The term 'patriarchy' has been used in this respect both to describe and to explain gender stratification. Patriarchy literally means 'rule of the father', and has traditionally been used in English-speaking societies to refer to a household headed by a male. As Beechey (1987) points out, its use in analysing gender inequalities is not new – the term patriarchy was deployed by early feminist writers such as Virginia Woolf and Vera Brittain, as well as by Weber to refer to a system of government in which men ruled societies through their position as heads of household. Sociologists such as Walby have used the term to refer to a much broader form of social organisation in which men dominate, oppress and exploit women in a whole range of social settings. As we noted in Chapter 2, for Walby, patriarchy in contemporary capitalist societies consists of six interrelated structures or systems. These are:

1 *paid employment* – in most societies women are likely to be paid less than men;
2 *household production* – women are largely responsible for domestic labour and childcare;
3 *the state* – women are much less likely than men to have direct access to political power or representation;
4 *violence* – women are much more likely than men to be the subject of physical, emotional and/or sexual abuse;

5 *sexuality* – women are more likely than men to be sexually commodified or objectified, and to be controlled through their sexuality;

6 *culture* – women more than men are under-represented or misrepresented in media and popular culture.

For Walby, these structures are dynamically interrelating in so far as changes in one of the components of patriarchy will cause changes in the others, and in the nature and extent of gender stratification. While some degree of patriarchy may be universal, there is of course significant variation in the relative power of men and women in different parts of the world. In Southeast Asian countries and those in the Middle East such as Saudi Arabia for instance, men's control over women in all of the six structures Walby identifies suggests that these are highly patriarchal societies. The least patriarchal societies appear to be Scandinavian ones such as Norway and Sweden, in which men and women seem to occupy much more equal positions within paid employment and household production (www.un.org).

The term 'patriarchy' and its use in feminist sociology has not been unproblematic, however, and it is fair to say that there remains some unease about its usefulness as a conceptual tool. This is not least because it is such a homogenising term that does not adequately enable us to understand the causal elements that make up patterns of gender inequalities. In this sense, Crompton and Sanderson (1990) see the concept as an 'imperfect but descriptive' tool.

Some sociologists have been particularly critical of the arbitrary exercise of dividing patriarchy up into the six structures outlined above, and have described the way in which Walby uses the term as 'abstract structuralism' that merges explanation with description (see Pollert, 1996). Others have noted that its use tends towards a biologically deterministic and ahistorical analysis of gender inequalities (Barrett, 1980; Rowbotham, 1981). Other criticisms have been levelled against its insensitivity to the experiences of women of different cultures, classes and ethnicities (hooks, 1984; Anthias and Yuval-Davis, 1993). In responding to these criticisms writers such as Walby (1997) and also Witz (1992) tend to take the view that the concept can have explanatory potential if used in a historically and culturally sensitive way.

Other sociologists who use the term have attempted to qualify its descriptive use by distinguishing, for instance, between 'post' and 'neo' forms of patriarchy. Therborn (2004), for example, argues that most Western societies underwent a process of 'de-patriarchalization' throughout the course of the twentieth century, coupled with a shift towards secularisation and democratisation. These societies, he argues, have effectively become post-patriarchal in so far as most adults are relatively autonomous from their parents and enjoy (at least formally) equal male–female social rights. He acknowledges however that although 'a post-patriarchal society gives men and women equal rights to act, . . . their relative income taps their ability to act' (p. 127). He also argues that there are several areas of the world – that he calls 'neo-patriarchal' – where patriarchy is still firmly entrenched: South, Central and West Asia; and Northern, sub-Saharan and West Africa. The latter, he argues, is 'the region of the world where the confrontations between modernist thrusts to de-patriarchalization and religiously grounded patriarchal counter-blasts have been most violent' (p. 112).

Poststructuralist explanations

Many sociologists and feminist theorists, particularly those influenced by post-modernism (see Chapter 2), have challenged structuralist approaches, such as Walby's, or 'institutional' perspectives, such as Therborn's, on the grounds that they tend merely to replace biological determinism with social determinism; emphasising an ontology (theory of existence) of gender as something that is imposed on us, or 'done' to us by patriarchal social structures. Instead of a structuralist approach to understanding gender stratification, such feminists highlight the extent to which power is embedded in everyday practices and relationships at every level of society and not simply in particular social structures. This more poststructuralist approach to gender emphasises the extent to which sexual difference is socially shaped and constantly renegotiated in a wide variety of social settings.

Whereas social interactionists such as Goffman have long since argued that social identities are merely performances, and that we perform different 'roles' according to our audience and script, feminists such as Judith Butler (1990) have argued that our gender identities are merely performative; that, as she puts it, 'there is no doer behind the deed' or actor behind the action. For those who adopt this perspective, sex and gender are much more fluid and flexible than the sex–gender distinction developed by Oakley (see Chapter 1), and the structuralist approaches to gender stratification developed by Walby and others, seem to suggest. Butler (2000), for instance, argues that there is a 'heterosexual matrix' – a sex–gender order – operating in contemporary societies that organises sexual difference as shown in Table 3.1:

Table 3.1 Sex–gender order

Sex	Gender	Sexuality
Male	Masculine	Heterosexual (active)
Female	Feminine	Heterosexual (passive)

Source: Butler, 2000

Butler argues that this heterosexual matrix serves to define what is 'natural' and 'normal' in any given society; the assumption being that a 'normal' male will be masculine and heterosexually active, and that a 'normal' female will be feminine and heterosexually passive. She argues that this matrix distorts the similarities and differences both between and amongst men and women, resulting in gender inequalities (such as those considered above) and the devaluation of femininity, and invites us to make what she calls 'gender trouble' (Butler, 2000) – to play with what is socially defined as normal in gender terms. From this perspective, gender is seen as something that we do, rather than an identity that is imposed on us by social structures – an experience that varies considerably according to age, ethnicity, sexuality, embodiment, social class, and so on.

Other feminists have been concerned, however, about the political implications of poststructuralist approaches to gender stratification, arguing that emphasising diversity amongst women, as well as advocating the need for irony and making 'gender trouble' (Butler, 2000), might result in undermining the category 'woman'. This is of concern because feminists are looking for their identity *as women* to be socially, economically and politically valued. Nevertheless, this 'doing gender' approach is particularly useful in emphasising that gender stratification cannot be adequately understood solely as a single hierarchical division between men and women. As Sue Lees (1993) points out, relationships between men and women are not static, but constantly changing; although gender remains an important element of stratification most feminists would argue. The opportunities available to men and women remain unequal in most societies, but are not fixed. Women are able to exercise agency, but this agency is constrained, we would argue, by structures and dominant discourses so that women's 'choices' are relatively limited. Many women might 'choose' to work part-time for instance (see Chapters 6 and 9), but this choice is exercised within a relatively narrow structural context and is shaped by factors such as the lack of state-funded/provided childcare in most societies.

Social class-based stratification

As we noted above, in all complex societies there is an unequal distribution of material and symbolic resources, resulting in economic and social inequality. Inequalities in contemporary Western societies are generally regarded, by malestream sociologists, as being based not primarily on sexual difference, but on social class – on production, distribution and exchange. In this respect, class-based stratification and inequality, as well as social mobility, continues to be a central theme particularly in British sociology.

Feminist sociologists in the UK and elsewhere have been strongly influenced by Joan Acker's (1973) critique of sociological research on class stratification. Following Acker, three particular issues have concerned feminist analyses of social class in the last thirty years or so. Sara Delamont frames these as three rhetorical questions:

> First, was it sensible to treat the household as the unit of analysis, with its class location treated as that of the male head? Second, were the very categories of occupation, which were used to group occupations together into classes, inherently sexist? Third, what empirical and theoretical insights would result if women were treated as having their own occupationally based class identity and therefore their own social mobility?
>
> (Delamont, 2003, pp. 52–53)

These feminist interests have developed alongside a series of debates in malestream sociology about the changing nature of social class and about the role of class analysis in sociology (see Savage, 2000) but, as we noted in Chapter 1, have had a relatively limited impact on the malestream core of the discipline.

Sociological analysis and social class

Debates surrounding whether the household should persist as the central unit of analysis came to prominence in the UK after the publication of the results of the Nuffield mobility study in 1980 (Goldthorpe *et al.*, 1980; Halsey *et al.*, 1980). This project had collected data on social mobility since 1972 based on an all-male sample in England and Wales. During the 1980s a debate took place between Goldthorpe and a range of sociologists critical of his methodology and the assumptions underpinning it (Goldthorpe, 1983, 1984; Stanworth, 1983). Goldthorpe remained confident that the male was the head of household and that his occupation determined the class position of the family, even in households in which women also engaged in paid work. As Delamont (2003) notes, however, there may be sociologically interesting differences between, for example, 'A household where the man was a doctor and the woman a secretary compared to a household where both adults were doctors, or one where the man was a routine clerical worker and the woman a doctor' (p. 53).

As well as methodological disputes, one of the main problems in developing a feminist-infused class analysis within sociology is that, as Rosemary Crompton (1993) has pointed out, there are a number of different ways in which the term 'class' is used, both by sociologists and in everyday discourse:

1 to refer to groups, ranked in a hierarchy, which are formally unequal and have legally defined rights;
2 to refer to groups ranked according to social standing or prestige;
3 to refer to structural inequalities – to the unequal resourcing of groups – which are the outcomes of competition for social resources in capitalist societies;
4 to refer to actual or potential social forces competing for control over scarce resources.

We could also argue that the term class also refers to the cultural values, dispositions and lifestyles attributed to those occupying distinct social positions. In this sense, class is used to refer not simply to economic resources but also to 'cultural capital' (Bourdieu, 1984) acquired through education, socialisation and participation in particular social networks. Of course, cultural and economic capital are closely related in so far as a person who is deemed to be socially and culturally skilled is more likely to succeed materially in a competitive, market society – in the labour market, for example. Sociologists make use of virtually all these meanings of the term in their research; a person's social class is regarded as a summary variable which tells us about attitudes and values, standards of living, levels of education, consumer behaviour, and so on. Sociological research has shown that social class is an important determinant of life chances in terms of education and health, for instance.

In Western sociology particularly, two main theories of social class dominate: those based on Marxist theory (emphasising the centrality of the economic), and those based on Weberian theory (emphasising the relationship between economic, social and political status). These are often referred to as neo-Marxist and neo-Weberian, to indicate that the basic ideas of Marx and Weber have been developed into theories of class divisions and relations in contemporary societies in which class systems are complex and dynamic. Both theories see classes as distinct groups, each class consisting of individuals with shared economic and social interests which are different from, and may be in conflict with, those of other classes. Members of a household are thought to share a common class position, and generally the male head of household's class position is seen to determine that of all the members of his household.

Marxist perspectives on class

In Marxist theory social class is determined by an individual or group's relationship to the means of production – that is, whether one owns and controls capital or sells one's labour power. Those who share a common relationship to the means of production – owners, labourers – share the same class position. Marx argued that members of the same class would come to realise that they shared common interests and that these were in opposition to those of other social classes. The resulting class conflict would lead to the overthrow of the existing mode of production and its replacement by a new one. Marx argued that eventually there would be a classless, post-capitalist society in which social groups no longer sought to exploit each other.

According to Marx there are two main classes in capitalist society, the bourgeoisie and the proletariat. The former are the owners of the means of production and exploit the labour of the latter, who have to sell their labour on the market and at market-determined rates in order to subsist. Exploitation comes about because capitalists pay workers less than the true value of their labour and thus make a profit – what Marx called 'surplus value'. The price of goods on the market (the exchange value) is made up of two elements: the costs of the raw materials, and the cost of labour. However, the worker is paid only for some of his or her labour – the amount s/he can demand as a wage; the remainder is retained as profit. Thus a worker produces surplus value that constitutes profit. However, only use value is produced when the producer consumes the product him or herself (as, for example, when a housewife provides a meal for a family, makes clothes for a child or grows vegetables for the table).

It is evident that for Marx, classes were predominantly made up of men, and that women were relatively marginal in his analysis. Further, Marx saw class exploitation as the key issue and other forms of exploitation such as gender and race as secondary or derivative.

Weberian perspectives on class

Neo-Weberian theories of social class are based on the view that class position is determined primarily by the labour market, which positions people in a multi-dimensional status hierarchy. Occupations that share a similar market position – that is, those in which employees have comparable conditions of employment – are said to be in the same social class. Weber argued that members of a social class would both seek to protect their advantages vis-à-vis other groups and try to enhance their share of rewards and resources. A class would exclude subordinate groups from securing its advantages by 'closure' of opportunities to others, which it defines as inferior and ineligible. Subordinate groups try to break through this closure and to access the advantages of higher groups.

Taking account of the extent to which class dynamics are fluid and complex, those following a neo-Weberian approach tend to focus on what they describe as 'socio-economic status' which, they argue, is shaped by a combination of class, status and power and so takes account not just of economic position but also occupation, wealth and income, status and lifestyle, consciousness and identity as well as a person's degree of political influence. Parkin (1979) and Murphy (1984) have argued that Weber's view of social stratification, and especially the concepts of socio-economic status, market position and social closure, can be used to develop an adequate explanation of gender inequalities. Examples of feminist approaches that have adopted a neo-Weberian perspective include Walby's (1990) analysis of the relationship between private and public patriarchy, and Witz's (1992) account of the relationship between professions and patriarchy. Men, it is argued in these approaches, have used strategies of social closure to exclude women from those occupations with the highest rewards and status.

Feminists such as Walby and Witz have challenged the conventional view that stratification theory should only be about explaining class (economic) inequalities, and have suggested that it should be equally (or more) concerned with inequalities based on sexual difference, and a range of other fundamental aspects of identity, a criticism that mainstream sociologists have gradually begun to take on board. Most sociology textbooks, journals and conferences now accept, then, that a range of factors and not simply social class differences shape social stratification, although analysis of class inequalities clearly remains central to sociology, particularly in the UK.

The class system in Britain

Broadly speaking, sociologists in the UK (and other similar societies) tend to identify three social classes – upper, middle and working. The upper class forms a very small proportion of the population in Britain – about 10 per cent – and has received relatively little sociological attention. It comprises the landed aristocracy and those who live on income derived from the ownership of land, business, property, etc. – what Marxists refer to as the bourgeoisie. Top civil servants, the heads of the armed forces and members of the government may also be classified as upper class. The middle class comprises professional and managerial workers – for example, teachers, doctors, university lecturers, the clergy, factory managers, clerks, civil servants, and so on. The working class is made up of service personnel and manual workers – e.g. waitresses, cooks, car mechanics, bricklayers, dustmen, and so on.

The division between manual and non-manual workers was seen as an important class divide by Weber, who saw the skills that individuals brought to the market as a key determinant of the rewards they receive for their work. Those with scarce skills could command higher pay and superior conditions of work. However, with universal schooling and the routinisation of clerical and service work the significance of the manual/non-manual divide has been eroded as the pay and work conditions of (male) routine non-manual workers have declined relative to those of skilled manual workers.

While there are a variety of social class scales used by sociologists and others in the UK and elsewhere, probably the most significant official measure in Britain, one that provides a relatively straightforward way of classifying social groups by occupation, is the National Statistics Socio-economic Classification (NS-SEC). Announced in 1998 and introduced for the 2001 UK Census, this scheme replaced the Registrar General's scale. The Registrar General's scale (used in the UK since the 1911 Census) provided a relatively straightforward classification of occupational categories, and was widely used throughout the twentieth century (this scale should not be confused with the social grading – ABC1-scale used by market researchers which uses letters to label 'classes'). It ranked occupations of similar social standing from professionals to unskilled manual workers. The six categories in this scale are shown in Table 3.2. The revised NS-SEC scheme ranks labour market position not simply according to occupation but also job security, promotion prospects and work autonomy. It divides the population into eight social classes, as shown in Table 3.3.

Table 3.2 Registrar General's scale

Class	Name of class	Examples
1	Professional	Solicitors, accountants
2	Managerial and technical	Managers, teachers, nurses
3a	Skilled non-manual	Secretaries, sales assistants
3b	Skilled manual	Bricklayers, electricians
4	Semi-skilled	Bus drivers, fitters
5	Unskilled manual	Pub/bar staff, cleaners

Table 3.3 National Statistics Socio-economic Classification (NS-SEC)

Class	Name	Examples
1	Higher professional or managerial	High court judge
1.1	Large employers and senior managers	Senior police officer
1.2	Higher professional	Solicitor, social worker
2	Lower managerial and professional	Nurse, journalist
3	Intermediate	Secretary, administrator
4	Small employers and self-employed	Publican, farmer, taxi driver
5	Lower supervisory, craft and technical	Printer, plumber, butcher
6	Semi-routine	Shop assistant, hairdresser
7	Routine occupations	Courier, labourer, waiter
8	Long-term unemployed	(or never worked)

Although the Registrar General's scale was widely used it was replaced for several reasons, including:

1 *socio-economic changes* concentrating an increasing proportion of the population in classes 3a and 3b;
2 *increasing variation* in earnings and social status *within categories*; and
3 *the classification of women* according to the occupation of their nearest male relative (male 'head of household').

This latter point in particular had been the subject of ongoing criticism from feminist social scientists concerned to understand the relationship between women and social class which, they argued, was obscured by the routine classification of women according to the social class of their (male) 'head of household'.

Women and social class

Prior to 2001, feminists in the UK had continually challenged the long-standing practice by which many women were thought to have a derived class position, determined by the occupational experiences of the man with whom they lived. Ann and Robin Oakley (1979) pointed out that the instructions generally given to survey interviewers were that if a man is living in the household it will be his occupation that determines the household's class. This was not just a coding device; it amounted to a theoretical statement that women's experiences, loyalties and social actions are determined by the occupational position of the man with whom they live, and not by their own experiences. Acker (1973) suggests that there were five shortcomings to this conventional approach:

1 the assumption that the family is the rational unit of analysis, with complete class equivalence within it;
2 that the social position of the family is determined by the occupation of the head of the household;
3 that the male is necessarily the head of the household;
4 that women not living with a man nonetheless determine their own class;
5 the assumption that inequalities between men and women are inherent and inevitable.

Feminists argued not just that the classification of women by the class of male heads of household was sexist, but that the basic assumptions on which this position rested were false. Sheila Allen (1982) for instance pointed out that a wife does not acquire her husband's education on marriage, nor does she automatically acquire a socially or politically powerful background or network (which even if she does can often be lost on divorce or widowhood).

Feminists have argued that the incorporation of women into research on social class necessitates at the very least a modification of existing theories and conclusions, if not a complete rethinking of them (see Crompton and Mann, 1986; Abbott and

Sapsford, 1987). Elizabeth Garnsey (1978) argues that taking the household as the unit of analysis obscures inequalities between women and men within it and also the different market and work situations they face outside of it. Women tend to be at the bottom within each occupational class (see Chapter 9), and this pervasive inequality needs to be seen as central to the study of social stratification. The participation of women in the labour market affects the nature of that market for men. Women are disproportionately concentrated in low-paid, low-status jobs, and this affects the range of jobs available for men. The sex-typing of jobs as 'female' has resulted, historically, in them losing status and economic reward – as in the case of clerical work – or being created as lowly paid, low-status jobs – as, for example, speech therapy in Britain (Crompton and Sanderson, 1990). It is just not the case, as David Lockwood has argued, that 'it is the position of an occupation within some hierarchy of authority that is decisive for its status and not the sex of the person who happens to be in it' (1986, p. 21). The ways in which female wage labour and domestic labour are combined and interact with each other and with the capitalist system also have complex consequences for class structure and class consciousness.

There is considerable evidence to suggest that women's social class position cannot be ignored or treated as derivative from the social class position of husbands, partners or fathers; not only does this fail to explain their social and political behaviour, it often leads to mistaken conclusions about the social mobility of men and the structure of class-based stratification for both genders. For example, the social mobility of men and the openness of the occupational structure to upward mobility cannot be fully understood without taking the mobility and occupational distribution of women into account. Women's preparedness to 'have a job' rather than following a career is certainly important in explaining male mobility; few 'dual income' families actually have two partners following careers – more often the male has a career and the woman fits her work into the demands of that career. Janet Finch (1983) has demonstrated the importance of a wife's unpaid labour for many men in enabling them to follow their occupations, and Tony Chapman (2003) has suggested that most upward mobility depends on the wife being able to take on the 'higher' lifestyle.

The study of women's social class convinces us at least of the importance of studying family members in their own right and not making common-sense assumptions about shared household norms and interests or shared experience of the social world. It may be, contingently, that there are considerable shared interests and a considerable amount of shared experience. It may be that social class is a more important principle of stratification than gender in our society. That this is the case must be demonstrated, however, not taken for granted in the untheorised way which has been typical of much malestream sociological (and governmental) research on social class, yet it is only relatively recently that sociologists and demographers have begun to accept this.

Race, ethnicity and stratification

Class and gender stratification interact then in complex ways that much sociological research has ignored or overlooked. This same point can be made about the interaction between sexual difference and racialised forms of stratification; that is, that they have been largely overlooked sociologically. Racialised men and women are those subject to racial differentiation and racism. Feminists such as Kum-Kum Bhavnani define racism as

> a system of domination and subordination based on spurious biological notions that human beings can be fitted into racially distinct groups. It is identified as a 'natural' process and is seen to be a logical consequence of the differentiation of human beings into 'races'. Given that there is no sound evidence from the natural and biological sciences to justify the assumption that the human species can be divided up into separate 'races', both 'race' and racism come to be economic, political, ideological and social expressions. In other words, 'race' is not a social category which is empirically defined; rather, it is created, reproduced and challenged through economic, political and ideological institutions.
>
> (Bhavnani, 1993, p. 27)

Bhavnani goes on to outline four ways in which processes that have resulted in the marginalisation of women apply also to racialised groups. These are:

1 *erasure* – the process by which experiences are removed or 'hidden' from history;
2 *denial* – the process by which differences between men and women, white and black, heterosexual and homosexual, young and old, working class and middle class are not acknowledged;
3 *invisibility* – the outcome when differences are not considered as something worthy of research, for example, survey findings are not analysed in terms of the racial identity, or gender, or sexual orientation, or age of the respondent (these are not considered important or relevant variables, and thus differences are rendered invisible);
4 *tokenism* – when racial groups (or gender, or class) are analysed separately, but the need to modify or reformulate the analysis to take full account of difference is not recognised.

It would be problematic if feminists, while criticising the marginalisation of women, did not acknowledge also the social processes that have marginalised racialised groups (see Chapter 2). Many sociologists have argued that the position of racialised men and women, in the UK and elsewhere, needs to be understood with reference to patterns of colonialism and migration, as this enables us to begin to locate racial inequalities within their social, economic and political context (see Braham *et al.*, 1992; Solomos, 2003).

For instance, in the period after the Second World War the UK government encouraged workers from post-colonial societies to migrate to Britain to fill job vacancies, initially in the service of post-war economic recovery and subsequently during a period of economic expansion. The initial immigration in the early 1950s was mainly from the Caribbean, and Asian immigrants (largely from India and Pakistan) came in the late 1950s and early 1960s. Immigrants were expected to come and fill the growing number of job vacancies and to take on the low-paid, low-skilled jobs that indigenous workers were reluctant to accept. These immigrant workers were often met with hostility by the latter, who (urged on by racist ideologies and stereotypes – in the mass media, for instance) regarded them as inferior and as a threat to a British 'way of life'. They were often seen as being in competition for housing, educational and health services and blamed for the deteriorating state of the inner cities, particularly from the 1970s on. Both the mass media and politicians clearly played a major role in shaping racist ideas in this respect. While many migrant workers had thought that coming to Britain would be like coming home, returning to the 'mother' country, many experienced considerable hostility, a low standard of living, poor educational facilities for their children and eventual unemployment (particularly since the 1970s) fuelled largely by a hostile political and media culture.

Sociological perspectives on racial inequality

The status of racialised groups has often been 'explained' by reference to biological factors – for example, that Black or Asian people are inherently less intelligent than white people, a proposition to which the work of psychologists such as Eysenck (1971) and Jensen (1973) has given some scientific credibility. An alternative explanation is one that focuses on norms and values – the idea that immigrant groups do not share the values of white society and that this explains why they do not 'get on'. Recent debates on the disproportionate representation of Black families amongst the so-called 'underclass' in Europe and the USA have often conflated both of these (biological and cultural) explanations in this respect, intimating for instance that because single parenthood is supposedly more socially acceptable in some ethnic groups than others, Black families are more likely to fall into cycles of deprivation. Similarly, racial prejudice has been 'explained' in terms of the blind and irrational prejudice against 'outsiders' of bigoted individuals or the inability of groups to cope with the 'unusual' cultural character of a different racial group – that is, the group's way of life, including language, religion, family customs, clothes, and so on. All these 'common-sense' explanations tend to present non-white people as 'deviant' or as 'strangers' and seek to explain reactions to this status. This leads to a tendency to study the characteristics of ethnic minority groups themselves and to make a problem out of these very characteristics rather than problematising racist structures and ideologies.

Such approaches to understanding racial disadvantage, sociologists argue, are dependent upon the perpetuation of racial stereotypes (often relating to sexuality, criminality and so on) and are not really explanations for racial inequalities, in a sociological sense. Rather, biological or cultural 'explanations' are merely self-confirming prejudices – dominant ideologies that position particular groups of people as inferior thus 'confirming' their inferiority. In this sense, such approaches tend to individualise or essentialise what sociologists would argue are social, structural inequalities.

More sociological approaches to understanding racial stratification attempt to analyse the institutional structures within society as a whole – and this includes white, Western sociology – which has often presented 'the problem' in terms of difference rather than in terms of racism (e.g. CCCS (Centre for Contemporary Cultural Studies),

1982; Anthias and Yuval-Davis, 1993). Two major theories of race and ethnicity have emerged in sociology – neo-Marxist and neo-Weberian.

Neo-Marxist perspectives on racial inequalities

Marxists argue that racial disadvantage can be explained by reference to the class structure of capitalism. Racialised groups are an integral part of the proletariat, the working class, who are exploited by capitalists. Racial prejudice can be explained by reference to Britain's colonial past and the development of ideologies during the nineteenth century that justified British and European exploitation of the Black and Asian inhabitants of colonial societies by suggesting that they were inferior. Patterns of migration into the UK in the 1950s and 1960s must be seen in the context of the needs of industrial capitalism. Migrant workers came to a country where ideologies of racial inferiority/superiority already existed. As the economic situation changed and a shortage of jobs arose, prejudice intensified the already relatively disadvantaged position of Black and Asian men and women. Furthermore, Marxists argue that the ruling class is able to exploit the ideologies of racial prejudice to maintain its position of dominance. Thus conflict between Black, Asian and white working-class people is based on white people blaming Black and Asian people for their bad housing, lack of hospital resources, etc., while the Black and Asian population blame their plight on the prejudice of white people with whom they come into contact. This, it is argued, deflects attention away from the 'real' – structural – causes of racial inequalities, the economic exploitation of the working class as a whole. Racism therefore helps to sustain what Marxists term 'false consciousness', in this respect preventing various factions of the working class from recognising their own, shared exploitation.

Marxist approaches to understanding racial disadvantage have been criticised for being overly simplistic, however – for failing to acknowledge or explain why it is that not all ethnic groups share the same structural position (in the UK for instance, Black men and women are relatively disadvantaged compared to most Asian groups in terms of key social indicators such as employment, housing and health). This has led many sociologists to argue that Black people experience an additional layer of disadvantage that somehow differentiates them from the rest of the working class. Those who adopt this approach tend to be associated with more of a Weberian than a Marxist analysis of racial inequalities.

Neo-Weberian perspectives on racial inequalities

Neo-Weberian sociologists tend to reject a Marxist theory of racial divisions. They argue that racial disadvantage arises out of competition between groups for scarce resources – such as housing, employment and education. Hence, Weberian sociologists emphasise that structural disadvantage is compounded by racism. Because a person's status and life chances are determined by their 'market capacity' – a person's ability to sell his or her labour power – racism (combined with practices of 'closure') devalues the market capacity of certain ethnic groups (Carter, 2003). In Britain and elsewhere the white indigenous population has used social closure against racialised groups, especially those from former colonial societies and their descendants, to perpetuate their structurally disadvantaged position.

Feminist perspectives on racial inequalities

Black feminists have criticised both Marxist and Weberian theories of racial and ethnic disadvantage for failing to take adequate account of gender differences, and for not realising that the experiences of racialised women, and the ways in which they are exploited, are different from the case of racialised men. In the UK, for instance, many Black women often experience subordination and exploitation as women, as members of the working class and on the basis of their race or ethnicity. Sociologists have been concerned to reject biological and psychological explanations for the subordinate and inferior position of Black and Asian women in Britain and elsewhere. Instead they have explored the social and structural aspects of social inequalities and examined how Black and Asian women become socially constructed as subordinate. They have considered differences in power, both in social and in economic terms, and examined the ways in which patriarchal and racist ideologies have come to construct some women as inferior, and to justify their unequal social status, often by framing Black and Asian women as 'dependents'. Women immigrants have not come to Britain just as the dependents of men, however. In the 1980s, they made up about a quarter of the immigrant labour force in Britain and over 40 per cent of all migrants (Phizacklea, 1983). Yet as Sheila Allen and Carole Walkowitz (1987) have argued, racialised and ethnic minority women tend to be concentrated in arduous and poorly paid work and experience relatively high rates of unemployment as well as being engaged in unregistered home-based work.

Black and Asian women are disadvantaged in housing, in employment, in the health service and in the criminal justice process. Black families are more likely to be seen as inadequate or incapable of caring for their children, and Black women are over-represented in the prison population. In employment, Black and Asian women may be concentrated in the same occupational categories as white women, but this may conceal the fact that they are more likely to be in lower-status and lower-paid work *within* those categories (Abbott and Tyler, 1995).

Sociologists have argued that this situation is not just a result of individual prejudices, but of 'institutional racism'. This was defined in the Macpherson Report (1999), published at the end of the inquiry into the Metropolitan Police's investigation into the murder of Stephen Lawrence, as

> the collective failure of an organization to provide an appropriate and professional service to people because of their colour, culture or ethnic origin. It can be seen or detected in processes, attitudes and behaviour which amount to discrimination through unwitting prejudice, ignorance, thoughtlessness, and racist stereotyping which disadvantage minority ethnic people.
>
> (Macpherson Report, 1999, p. 1)

Examples of institutional racism would be the ways in which successive Immigration Acts have excluded Black immigrants while still permitting white immigration. (Although Britain now restricts immigration of white non-EU nationals, for a considerable period of time it did not.)

Black and post-colonial feminists have argued that both malestream and white feminist models of oppression are inadequate for understanding the experiences of racialised women. By setting up theories of women's oppression as applying to all women they have contributed to 'institutionalised racism' (see Chapter 2). Black feminists have pointed out how women from post-colonial societies, and particularly Southeast Asian ones, are often perceived as dominated and oppressed by their own cultures. Assimilation into Western mores is therefore portrayed (ethnocentrically) as a form of liberation, allowing women to rebel against their families, wear Western clothes, cut their hair, and so on. Similarly, Western feminists have argued that for white women the nuclear family is a central site of oppression, partly because of the way in which familial ideology situates women in the private sphere (Walby, 1990). Some Black feminists, on the other hand, have argued that the family – threatened by slavery, indentured labour and migration – is often something to be defended, a source of support and resistance to racism (Brah, 1986).

Some feminists have questioned whether the whole notion of 'patriarchy' – and analyses such as Walby's (1990) that describe a shift from private to public patriarchy – is applicable to the experiences of Black women (and men). Black men never possessed 'patriarchal power' over women in the way that white men did. However, many Black feminists have argued not for the rejection of the concept of patriarchy but for an analysis that recognises the specific situation of racialised men and women in patriarchal societies. For example, Floya Anthias and Nira Yuval-Davis (1993) point out how women are exploited as unpaid workers in family businesses in some ethnic minority groups. Often (male) entrepreneurs have set up businesses as a way of avoiding exclusion and disadvantage, but they then exploit the upaid labour of their own family members or the lowly paid labour of other women from ethnic minority groups.

What is evident is that it is very difficult to make sociological generalisations about all racialised groups, which have very different histories and traditions. While many Black and Asian women came to Britain and other European societies explicitly as workers, some came to join families but later became workers.

In sum, sociological studies of racialised groups have tended to ignore the diverse experiences of men and women, and the sociology of gender has proceeded relatively separately from the sociology of race and ethnicity. White feminist accounts of women's oppression have tended to be relatively ignorant of the distinctive experiences of racialised men and women. The sources of oppression of white women – for example, the nuclear family – are not necessarily the same for Black and Asian women. Racialised women (and men) are oppressed not only by sexual difference, but by the intersections of class, race and ethnicity.

Disability and stratification

Many sociologists concerned with disability and impairment have argued that disabled people are also relatively overlooked sociologically and that, despite the recent resurgence of sociological interest in the body, disabled people have often had only a token presence in sociological analysis. One seemingly plausible explanation for this is that disabled people are only a small minority of the population of most societies and have, therefore, like many other minorities before them, simply escaped sociological notice. However, there are two basic problems with this seemingly 'common-sense' assumption. First, research suggests that disabled people are not a statistical minority – in the UK approximately 6.8 million adults are disabled (www.nso.gov). These figures, of course, cannot be accepted uncritically (any more than any other official statistics can) and, if anything, they are likely to be an underestimate, but they do give an indication of the extent to which disabled people have been ignored. Second, sociologists have never simply played a 'numbers game', taking an interest only in large groups. Being a minority activity or group has never stopped sociologists from taking a research interest in say crime or suicide, for instance, any more than large numbers prevented women from being relatively ignored sociologically until recently.

Other reasons for the sociological neglect of disability might include the under-representation of disabled people in academia (and in the labour market generally) – so it might be that few sociologists are themselves disabled. Related to this, disability provokes a range of emotional responses in the non-disabled and avoidance – that is, not studying disability – is perhaps one way in which sociologists have dealt with this. However, perhaps the most likely explanation for the sociological neglect of disability is the way in which it has traditionally been perceived as an individual, often medical, 'problem' rather than a social issue.

A sociology of disability *is* beginning to establish itself, however, based largely on a social model that has its roots in political campaigns against medicalisation, discrimination, inequality and welfare dependency (Oliver, 1983). This social model rejects both a bio-medical approach to disability that frames impairment in terms of a deficient or defective body in need of 'cure' and an individualised, welfare model that defines disability largely in terms of personal tragedy, and a person in need of 'care'.

The social model of disability

Underpinning the social model of disability is a focus on the ways in which disabled people confront both the aesthetic norms and structural configurations of 'able bodied society' and are disadvantaged as a result. Whereas a medical model of disability assumes that the degree of impairment determines the degree of disability, a social model focuses on the ways in which social factors (including physical, organisational and attitudinal arrangements) determine the degree to which a particular impairment is disabling. The development of this latter approach has led to a sociological concern with the ways in which bodies – and hence, disabilities – are socially constructed

(Barnes *et al.*, 1999). This sociological approach has also highlighted the extent to which disabled people are disproportionately affected by poverty and social exclusion because not only are they relatively disadvantaged in the labour market, disabled people may also have to meet the 'extra costs' of impairment (Barnes *et al.*, 1999).

Research evidence suggests that disability has a considerable impact on an individual's labour market position. In the UK, for instance, there were 6.8 million people of working age with a disability, of whom just under 50 per cent were economically active. This compares, according to *Social Trends* 2001, to an economic activity rate for the whole working age population of 78 per cent (www.nso.gov). Disabled men are more likely than disabled women to be in employment, as Table 3.4 indicates.

Table 3.4 Economic activity status of disabled people by sex, UK, 2001 (%)

	Males	Females	All
All in employment	49.1	44.6	46.9
Full time	43.5	22.9	33.8
Part time	5.6	21.6	13.1
Unemployed	5.1	3.2	4.2
Less than one year	3.1	2.3	2.7
One year or more	2.0	0.9	1.5
Economically inactive	45.8	52.2	48.8
All disabled people (=100%) (millions)	*3.6*	*3.2*	*6.8*

Source: www.nso.gov

Recent decades have been witness to a politicisation of disability, which has been transformed from a medical or individual problem into a civil rights issue, so that in many societies disabled people have collectively organised themselves into a social movement. Much like women, Black and gay people, disabled people have self-consciously organised themselves into a movement demanding emancipation from social oppression and exclusion. As Kevin Paterson and Bill Hughes have put it,

> Disabled people are (and have been throughout modernity) depicted as dependent individuals waiting patiently or petulantly for care, cure or charity. The elimination of this infantilizing portrayal of disability is a central tenet of the disabled people's movement. Rather than accept the injunction to 'pass as normal', the movement has adopted the Gay Rights concept of 'pride' in difference and the practice of 'coming out'. . . . 'Coming out' transforms the ideology of the disabled body as deficit into a statement of collective muscularity. Indeed, the concepts of political 'movement' and 'activist' challenge the notion of the 'dependent invalid'. They symbolize agency and autonomy.
>
> (Paterson and Hughes, 2000, p. 31)

The social model on which the disability movement is grounded is based largely on a sociological distinction between (physical) impairment and (social) disablement, one that in many ways parallels other distinctions in sociology – between race and ethnicity, sex and gender, for instance. Since much of the discrimination and exclusion of disabled people has been justified, ideologically, on grounds of physical difference the disability movement has tended to ignore or underplay the 'impaired' body and to focus instead on the structural aspects of a disabling society. Michael Oliver (1983, 1990) in particular has claimed that disability is socially produced in an analysis that distinguishes between (pre-social) physical impairment and socially constituted disability. This dualistic view of disability and impairment (much like sex and gender, race and ethnicity) facilitated a de-biologisation and a politicisation of disability that parallels the feminist attack on 'biology as destiny' in the sex–gender distinction (see Chapter 1).

A major strength of this approach is that it could be used to challenge dominant medical or charitable models of disability and the portrayal of disabled people as victims of their bodies. However, just as various binary oppositions have been subject to criticism in recent years, particularly by those who have argued that seemingly pre-social, biological categories such as 'sex' and 'race' are actually socially constructed (see Butler, 1990 and also Guillaumin, 1995), so too has the distinction between impairment and disability. Paterson and Hughes (2000, p. 40) in particular have problematised the way in which 'the social model of disability denies the embodied experiences of pain and affliction that are an integral part of the lives of many people with impairments'. In doing so, their account also highlights that debates about how the experience of disability varies with respect to class, gender, race and sexuality need to be opened up within sociology, and some of the areas of overlap between disability studies and feminist sociology need to be more clearly articulated.

Disability, identity and difference

Several writers, such as Morris (1991), Begum (1992) and Abu-Habib (1997) have emphasised the need for a greater exploration of issues relating to the gendered and racial aspects of disability. Barbara Fawcett (2000) has observed that, although there are some notable exceptions, issues of gender, race and sexuality are only just starting to feature strongly in writing on disability. She highlights the difficulties associated with viewing disabled people and women as homogenous, unified groups rather than as diverse associations. Some writers such as Morris (1996) and Crow (1996) argue that we should explore differences in the lived experience of disability as these are shaped by gender, age, race, sexuality and impairment. Others such as Finkelstein (1993) and Oliver (1990) are wary of the consequences of fragmenting the disability movement in this way, because of the implications this might have for its political unity and also for the coherence of the social model as a credible alternative to bio-medical and welfare-based approaches. In this sense, Fawcett (2000) notes the ways in which the debate over 'projected homogeneity' in disability studies parallels that taking place within contemporary feminism that has, as we noted in Chapter 2, been struggling with questions of difference and sameness for some time.

Indeed, it is largely within this political and theoretical context that feminist perspectives on disability have begun to draw attention to the social construction of disabled bodies *as gendered*. As Fawcett puts it,

Within the UK, the social model of disability and disability rights campaigns based on the social model of disability have only relatively recently begun to grapple with issues of diversity and difference between and amongst various groupings in relation to gender and also impairment, 'race', class, age, sexuality and varying dimensions of social division.

(Fawcett, 2000, p. 36)

Feminist perspectives on disability

Early formulations of the social model of disability have been subject to critical amendment by disabled women, who have argued that differences between men and women who are disabled have been neglected (Lloyd, 2001). Disabled women activists have, however, been equally critical of the failure of mainstream feminism to recognise disabled women's perspectives. Lloyd has proposed the development of 'a model of disability which understands the concerns of disabled women as central to both feminism and disability politics' (p. 715), highlighting the importance of developing a disabled perspective on some of the complex issues on the feminist agenda such as sexuality and reproduction, for instance. Feminist perspectives in particular have emphasised the ways in which gender shapes the lived experience of disability both for men and women who are disabled, but also for those who are carers of, or assistants to, disabled people, by far the majority of whom are women. Sociologists have argued that not only is the majority of this caring work unpaid; it is also largely unrecognised. Morris (1991, 1996), however, draws attention to the way in which homogeneity is also assumed in this respect, often by malestream sociologists and members of the disability movement, and highlights differences between disabled people and in the nature of caring relationships. She further criticises feminists such as Gillian Dalley (1988) who unproblematically refer to able-bodied women as 'carers' and (ungendered) disabled people as those who are cared for. Morris insists that disabled men and women 'care' too and emphasises the ways in which caring relationships are often reciprocal and inter-dependent, and are shaped by a range of factors including (but not limited to) disability.

Feminist writers on disability have argued for the social model to be recon-ceptualised to take into account not just material inequalities and the way in which we think about relationships of inter-dependency, but also issues relating to cultural representations and practices such as language and media culture. Abberley (1997), for instance, emphasises the importance for disability studies of feminist deconstruction which, although rejected by many feminists, she argues has considerable political potential for developing a critique of value-laden concepts such as 'birth defect' or 'invalidity', as well as more fundamental binary distinctions between impairment and disability (see Paterson and Hughes, 2000, and the previous section).

Feminists have also drawn attention to the way in which disabled people are effectively denied sexual agency and have argued that this is especially the case with regard to (both disabled and non-disabled) women who tend to be socially constructed, in gendered terms, as sexually passive. Notable exceptions to this are works such as *Passion in Plenitude*, which was commissioned (in 1991) by the Council for the Disabled in the Netherlands, and is developed by Gon Buurman (1997) in her account of the embodied experiences of disabled women that displays their struggles, but also their powers and pleasures, photographically.

Another aspect of disability that feminists have argued is fundamentally gendered is pregnancy and childbirth, and feminists have highlighted issues relating to reproductive technologies and genetic screening that sociology (including feminist sociology) has yet to address with reference to the relationship between gender and disability in any sustained way (Lloyd, 2001). Julie Kent (2000), for instance, makes only passing reference to disability in her discussion of social perspectives on pregnancy and childbirth.

Although feminism has begun to make a significant contribution to disability studies, there still remains much work to be done – empirically, theoretically and, of course, politically. In this respect, Barbara Fawcett (2000) outlines four main ways in which feminist insights could be incorporated into disability studies. These are:

1 *deconstructive analysis* (that problematises disability in terms of its discourse);
2 *a critique of binary oppositions* (between the 'natural' and the 'social');
3 *issues of unity* (identifying ways of valuing diversity without losing sight of political and intellectual coherence); and
4 *the place of experience* (in maintaining a communal voice campaigning for change).

In sum, much like race and ethnicity, writing about disability in sociology has been both contentious and relatively neglected. Questions relating to the relationship between disability and gender have only recently begun to be addressed sociologically. Sociologists tend to work with a social model of disability that challenges the biomedical assumptions of a medical model as well as the framing of disability in terms of 'personal tragedy' and charity. That this model is dependent upon a problematic distinction between (pre-social) impairment and (social) disability has also been noted, however. Feminists have drawn attention to the ways in which disabled people and women alike are seen to comprise undifferentiated, unitary groups and have argued that this can be both beneficial in political terms but problematic in so far as it fails to take account of diversity in lived experience and other aspects of identity. Feminists have also highlighted the ways in which disabled women in particular are denied sexual agency, as well as drawing attention to some of the ways in which disability is gendered both for disabled men and women, but also for those who are carers of, or assistants to, disabled people.

Global stratification

Just as the relatively disadvantaged position of disabled people has been sustained through their being defined as 'Other' – different from the norm – so too has the marginal position of non-Western people. 'The Rest' is a term developed by sociologist Stuart Hall (1992a) to refer to countries outside of the 'core' of Western industrialised nations; they are also often referred to as the 'developing nations', or 'underdeveloped', 'less developed', or 'non-industrial nations', or as 'the Third World'. They include areas such as Latin America, much of Southeast Asia and most of sub-Saharan, West and East Africa. Hall coined the term 'The West and the Rest' then to distinguish between Western industrialised nations and developing countries. The term 'the Rest' in this sense consciously lumps together a large variety of cultures and countries and so reflects the way in which they are positioned both economically and politically within Western (colonial) ideology. In doing so, the distinction between the West and the Rest provides a useful framework for understanding the relative position of countries existing in a state of economic dependence upon the West; a state that has been created by the imperialistic economic policies of capitalist countries and by multinational corporations in their desire to create global 'empires'.

In 'the Rest' there is a large pool of cheap labour available and prepared to work for relatively low wages – far less than workers in Britain. This potential labour pool has been exploited by Western capitalism in two ways: first, Western firms have moved production to developing countries, and second, Western governments and corporations have encouraged immigration from developing countries to remedy labour shortages in their own economies. In developing countries taxation is generally very low as there is no welfare state, no pension and no social security system for the majority of people. Employers can get away with production processes which are much more dangerous to people and the environment than would be allowed in the West – and therefore cheaper – since the industrial safety and environmental protection legislation is less stringently enforced than in Western nations. It is important to recognise that not only are women from developing or post-colonial societies exploited and racialised by capitalism, but that women in the West often benefit (albeit indirectly) from the exploitation of women in 'the Rest'. As Macionis and Plummer (2002, p. 212) have put it: 'in rich societies, the work women do is typically unrecognized, undervalued and underpaid; women receive less income for their efforts than men do. In low-income countries, this pattern is even more pronounced.'

While the situation of 'the Rest' generally receives little attention in the West, the position of women particularly receives even less. However, gender serves to structure social relationships in all societies, and just as Western economic and cultural relations have penetrated Third World countries, destroying traditional ways of life and creating dependent economies, so Western notions of femininity and the family have likewise been imposed upon other models of gender and rendered them 'peculiar', 'heathen', 'unliberated' or sexually exotic. On the other hand, the adoption of Western lifestyles and gender roles is often seen as evidence of 'progress'. This has created considerable conflict and contradictions for many women living in developing countries, or in cultures that have been subject to rapid social change brought about by recent developments in media and communication technologies (such as advertising, the internet and satellite television, for instance – see Chapter 12), particularly in societies where there are clear tensions between traditional norms and values and more commercial, Western influences.

Sociology has tended to concentrate on explaining why the poorer countries of the world have not industrialised in the same way as the richer nations. Some theories have tended to stress the lack of motivation or the inappropriate attitudes of 'the Rest', or suggest that they lack the economic foundation on which to build, or that they have been systematically exploited and underdeveloped by Western countries. Less attention has been paid to the role of women in 'the Rest' and what happens to them as countries attempt to industrialise and develop. Many women working in agriculture or industrial production in their own countries are exploited both by the men of their own country and by Western capitalists, as women (and their children) are seen as a source of cheap and docile labour, to be used to provide goods for Western markets.

Seager and Olsen (1986) suggest that we need to understand the ordinary lives of women and to recognise their common everyday experiences:

> They are the providers of food, fuel, water and often the whole family income – the sustainers and developers of their families, communities and countries . . . the fate of women is a critical determinant of the fate of whole societies.
>
> (Margaret Snyder, UN Voluntary Fund for Women, quoted in Seager and Olsen, 1986, p. 7)

Third World women are, in many ways, worse off than their male counterparts – they have less power, less authority, do more work for less money and have more responsibility than men. They are also more vulnerable to extreme forms of exploitation such as sex tourism (see Chapter 8). In most societies women shoulder the primary responsibility for housework, nursing children and meeting the needs of their families, and in many countries women are also responsible for farming. According to the United Nations women constitute half the world's population but do nearly two-thirds of the world's work, receive 10 per cent of the world's income and own less than 1 per cent of the property. Women are therefore disproportionately the poorest of the world's poor – the UN estimates that more than 500 million of the 800 million people living in absolute poverty and whose lives are at risk as a result are women (www.un.org).

Women who are displaced or are refugees are particularly at risk from extreme poverty and famine. Refugees are people who flee their own country for political or economic reasons, or to avoid war and oppression. They usually experience not only extreme material hardship but also a well-founded fear of persecution. In leaving behind their 'home' they have not only to abandon their possessions but also leave behind their families and social networks. Kushner and Knox (1999) have described the twentieth century as 'the century of the refugee' noting how at the end of the century the majority of the world's people were not where they were at the beginning.

Central and Eastern Europe is a particularly interesting example in this respect, with a population of more than 550 million. In 1989, there were only nine independent countries across the region – today that figure has increased to twenty-seven. The establishment of so many nations in such a relatively short time has been a factor contributing to a tremendous increase in migration since the 1990s. Migration patterns vary considerably within Central and Eastern Europe, and indeed elsewhere, and men and women tend not to experience the same patterns – women have traditionally travelled shorter distances than men (often within the same province), men have generally tended to migrate longer distances, often across national or regional boundaries in search of work. Although research evidence suggests that women are increasingly migrating internationally as autonomous economic actors, many migrant women continue to have limited access to economic and social welfare programmes because of their status as dependents. Migrant women commonly face double discrimination in the labour market (being both female and foreign), and generally earn less as migrant workers than native born women and men, and migrant men.

In contrast to refugees, displaced people are those who find themselves homeless in their own land. This may be due to civil war, or to environmental disaster. An estimated 50 million people across the world live off land that is rapidly deteriorating (Macionis and Plummer, 2002), and as time progresses they will no longer be able to live and work off the land they inhabit and so become displaced.

Refugees and particularly asylum seekers are always controversial groups and, with the expansion of the European Union in 2004, debate in Europe has begun to coalesce around issues such as humanitarian need and national identity. Refugees effectively 'test' the willingness of governments and societies to provide asylum on humanitarian grounds. They are also vulnerable to human trafficking and commercial exploitation by gaining illegal entry into countries by effectively selling themselves as workers – an industry that, at the beginning of the twenty-first century, the UN estimates to be one of the largest and most profitable in the world and in which women are disproportionately exploited (see Chapter 8). Many of the women and girls involved in trafficking are believed to be subject to sexual harassment and violence, and to be forced into prostitution; a minority are thought to be engaged as domestic help, usually with very low (or no) pay and no contractual security (www.un.org).

Development is usually assumed to be 'a good thing' despite the enormous human costs. One area of interest to feminists has been the effects of socio-economic development on women. Susan Tiano (1987) has suggested that there are three competing perspectives on the impact that economic development has had on women:

1 the *integration thesis*, which argues that development results in female liberation and sexual equality as women become more centrally involved in economic and public life;
2 the *marginalisation thesis*, which holds that with capitalist development women become increasingly excluded from production roles and confined to the private sphere of the home – losing in the process their control over resources and becoming economically dependent on men; and
3 the *exploitation thesis*, which argues that modernisation results in the creation of a low-paid female labour force – women become more central to industrial production (particularly in the provision of services) but are exploited because they are seen as a secondary labour force.

In order to understand the impact of economic change on women it is necessary to have some understanding of women's lives in pre-/non-industrial societies. However, there is considerable controversy over the position of women in such societies. There is some agreement among anthropologists that gender inequalities were less prominent in hunting and gathering societies and in simple horticultural societies than in peasant-based agrarian ones. However, cultural factors, especially religion, are also important. Furthermore, the effect that economic change has on women also depends on class, as well as ethnic status. What is clear is that as a society undergoes economic change, so does the nature of work and so does the distinction between men and women. There is an increase in the sexual division of labour, and this occurs in a way that seems to perpetuate female subordination. In countries where men and women both tend to engage in paid work, employment is segregated into industrial sectors and women are typically in lower-paid work than men, and in work that is defined as less skilled than the work men do (see Chapter 9).

Industrialisation in developing countries often also means that women become more closely associated with the domestic sphere, and in many areas they lose the land they farmed to produce food for their family to men who produce crops for cash. Thus women's economic dependency is increased. Often these changes are actively encouraged by aid agencies and Western employers, who work with Western ideologies of the family and the sexual division of labour (see Chapter 6). Thus, in parts of Africa where women generally farmed to produce food for their families, aid agencies have trained primarily men in farming techniques and have encouraged them to produce cash crops. In the process women have often lost control of their land or been edged out into more marginal land, which they till with no access to modern farming technology. The very low pay of women employed in manufacturing can similarly be said to be based on the assumption that women either have only themselves to support or are partly supported by a man. Rae Lesser Blumberg (1981) suggests three reasons why economic development results in the marginalisation of women:

1   there is an increase in women's real workload;
2   there is a decrease in women's resource base; and
3   there is a decrease in women's well-being and their opportunities as people.

As men are drawn into the cities to participate in the cash economy, women often have less control over resources. Men are less likely to help out as they are freed, by the demands of regular paid work, from traditional male domestic responsibilities. However, women are often expected to continue to grow crops, to feed the family and carry out all the domestic work. There is also some evidence to suggest that gender ideologies mean that women's marginalisation is perpetuated even within development programmes. Kathleen O'Reilly's (2004) study of women's participation in an Indian drinking water programme found that even those women employed by the project as fieldworkers were largely marginalised as a consequence of gender ideology.

The impact of economic change on agriculture varies between regions. In sub-Saharan Africa and some parts of Southeast Asia and Central America the 'slash and burn' technique has traditionally been used. Men cleared the land while women did most of the cultivation. Women had a central role in food production and therefore some influence on decision-making (Blumberg, 1981). European settlers, however, brought in the idea that farming is men's work and that crops should be produced for the market, thus marginalising women. Women were also excluded from agricultural education; in Africa less than 5 per cent of trained agricultural personnel are women (www.un.org).

In India the 'Green Revolution' – the introduction of modern farming methods – began in 1964 (Beyres *et al.*, 1983), the goal being for India to become self-sufficient in the production of food grains. The changes this brought about had a considerable impact on women's roles. In India prior to the Green Revolution women were economically dependent on men in all classes, although the dependency varied in form and intensity between classes. As Neerja Chowdhary (1998, cited in Kurian, 2001) notes in her essay on women in Indian politics, the achievement of post-colonial independence in India certainly did not lead to a marked improvement in the political participation or socio-economic position of women across the country. Indeed, in land-owning and peasant households it was always men who owned the land and the means of production. In the dominant classes the dependency of women was further intensified by purdah (the concealment of women), which made it difficult for them to move outside their own homes, preventing their participation in the public sphere. Peasant women did work the land owned by their husbands, but only the wives of poor peasants and landless labourers worked for wages. In all households women would have been responsible for all domestic duties, including the processing of grain and looking after livestock.

The introduction of new technology has not affected all parts of India alike, but where it has been introduced it has tended to result in a decline in employment for women. In rich peasant households women have been withdrawn from direct participation in farm work – labour has been hired to do the work previously done by women. This has reinforced women's economic dependence on men. In poor peasant and landless labourer households women have not voluntarily withdrawn from labour – their wages are essential for survival – but in many cases they have been squeezed out of employment by the introduction of both new technology and Western gender ideologies. Hence, male labour is employed to use the new machinery.

A relatively small proportion of women in less developed countries are employed in factory or office work, but they tend to be employed in 'female' jobs. Most production in Third World countries is mass production for corporations based in developed countries who have located (or 'outsourced') some manufacturing (and increasingly administrative work) in the Rest but control it from the West. The work exported is generally standardised and repetitive, calling for little technical knowledge; it is labour-intensive and often uses assembly-line operations that would be difficult and/or costly to mechanise still further. The aim is to exploit a suitable labour force – that is, one that is lower in costs of employment and/or higher in productivity. The wages in non-western factories and offices are often as little as a tenth of those in the developed countries, and working hours up to 50 per cent higher, while productivity is as high as that of the West or higher.

Female labour is cheaper than male labour, female productivity tends to be higher than that of men, and because of gender ideology women are thought to be 'naturally' better than men at some tasks – sewing, for instance. Western owners do not have to bear the cost of training the female workforce. The work is seen as unskilled, not because it does not require skill, but because girls are assumed to have already learned the necessary skills in the home. Much of the relocated or outsourced work is there-fore defined as women's work or becomes seen as such because of the perceived advantages of female labour.

The poverty found in much of the world as a result of global stratification is a complex problem, reflecting limited industrial technology, rapid population growth, traditional cultural patterns, internal social stratification, male domination and global power relations – particularly those shaped by the demands of capitalist societies and multinational corporations that have exploited the labour and the economies of developing and post-colonial countries. Gender inequalities appear to be most pronounced in the world's poorest countries, and among refugees and asylum seekers. Whilst economic development may give women opportunities to attend school, to reduce birth rates and to work outside of the home and hence to weaken traditional male power bases, this process of 'modernisation' also carries risks to women.

Investigating the lives of women in poor, rural areas of Bangladesh, Sultana Alam (1985) noted three ways in which 'development' may impede women's emancipation. First, as economic opportunities draw men out of rural areas and into cities, women and children (often abandoned entirely) must fend for themselves. Second, the declining strength of the family and the neighbourhood as rural communities are eroded means that women are often left with little social support. The same applies to women who have been left alone or with children as a result of divorce or death of their husband. In the past, Alam argues, other households would have traditionally taken in a woman who had been left alone. Rather than enhance women's autonomy, a developing culture of 'individualism' has eroded women's social support and worsened their vulnerability to poverty. Third, economic development combined with the growing influence of Western media and consumer culture has undermined women's traditional roles as wives, mothers and daughters and framed women in increasingly sexual and aesthetic terms – terms defined and imposed by the West. This culture, Alam notes, has been detrimental to Bangladeshi women in a range of ways including increasing prostitution and the spread of sexually transmitted diseases, as well as older women being abandoned by their spouses in favour of younger sexual partners and left with little means of supporting themselves or their children.

'Modernisation' does not, then, impact on men and women in the same way. In the long term, evidence does suggest that development may bring about a more equal relationship between men and women, but in the short term, the social and economic position of women may decline as women are forced to deal with new social problems that were virtually unknown in more traditional societies.

The subordination and exploitation experienced by women in developing and post-colonial societies is based not only on ideologies of women's role but also on ideologies of racial inferiority developed to justify the West's exploitation of 'the Rest'. Nevertheless, all women's lives are structured by expectations of role-appropriate behaviour, the idea that women are – and should be – dependent on men, and the notion that women's primary fulfilment comes from marriage and caring for a husband and children. These assumptions are crucial to understanding women's subordination and exploitation – why women lack control over resources. This is equally as true in the West as in 'the Rest'.

Conclusions

We recognise that men's and women's experiences are structured by a range of factors such as class, race, disability, and so on, and that racialised women suffer discrimination, exploitation and subordination, are 'othered', because they are Black as well as because they are women, for instance. While middle-class women are relatively privileged compared to their working-class sisters, this does not prevent them from becoming poor if they become a head of a lone-parent family, or from suffering relative poverty in later life. Subordination and exploitation are also shaped by global power relations which are based not only on ideologies of women's role, but also on ideologies of racial inferiority developed to justify the West's colonisation and exploitation of 'the Rest'. Nevertheless, all women's lives are structured by social and cultural expectations of role-appropriate behaviour, the idea that women are – or should be – dependent on or subordinate to men, and the notion that women's fulfilment derives largely from marriage and motherhood. These assumptions are important to understanding women's subordination and exploitation – why women lack control over resources, and to understanding not only the differences between men and women, but also amongst women.

SUMMARY

1 Men and women experience stratification in different ways, shaped by sexual difference, social class, race and ethnicity, disability, global power relations, and so on.
2 Women are disproportionately represented amongst the world's poorest groups.
3 Women are generally worse paid and suffer worse conditions of employment compared with men, the world over.
4 'Development' has often worsened the situation of women because:

   (a) Western ideas of sexual difference are imposed through the introduction of new forms of socio-economic organisation and through aid programmes;
   (b) women are primarily responsible for subsistence and household needs – maintaining the family economy and bearing and raising children – whereas men working as migrant labour may have to leave home altogether;
   (c) where women are engaged in production their wages are generally lower.

FURTHER READING

Anthias, F. and Yuval-Davis, N. (1993) *Racialised Boundaries*. London: Routledge. This book is a critical focus on a relatively neglected aspect of sociology – namely, the relationship between race, ethnicity and sexual difference. It focuses on issues of identity and difference as these are shaped by racialised boundaries and patterns of migration.

Cohen, R. and Kennedy, P. (2000) *Global Sociology*. London: Palgrave. This book takes a specifically sociological perspective on globalisation which explicitly challenges the 'West and the Rest' stance of many malestream sociology texts. It highlights gender, race and class inequalities and focuses on how these are shaped by processes of development and globalisation. It also considers gender politics in relation to themes such as migration, sustainability and new social movements.

Jackson, S. and Scott, S. (2001) *Gender: A Sociological Reader*. London: Routledge. This reader offers an overview of sociological work on gender written over the last thirty years or so. It includes both empirical and theoretical work from a range of perspectives and each section addresses intersections between gender, class, race and sexuality.

Savage, M. (2000) *Class Analysis and Social Transformation*. Buckingham: Open University Press. This is a comprehensive and engaging summary of sociological debates on social class in the last twenty years or so, focusing particularly on issues of lifestyle and consumption-based approaches to class. It focuses primarily on the UK, however.

Thomas, C. (1999) *Female Forms: Experiencing and Understanding Disability*. Milton Keynes: Open University Press. This book explores important debates within disability studies and links these to medical sociology and feminist perspectives. It offers an accessible review of a range of contemporary debates and theoretical approaches. In particular, it focuses on the experiences of disabled women, as told by themselves, and attempts to make sense of these (collective and individual) experiences with reference to feminist and sociological ideas, and debates within disability studies.

CHAPTER FOUR

Education

The sociology of education has been concerned primarily with examining class inequalities in educational achievement, and especially the relative failure of working-class children in obtaining educational qualifications. Until recently, sociologists have overlooked other important dimensions of educational differentiation – for example, gender and racial differences in achievement. Feminists have argued that girls are not only disadvantaged in the educational system, but that it is there that they learn to be subordinate and to accept dominant ideologies of femininity and masculinity. Girls are gendered; they come to see themselves as less important than boys. Despite the wide publicity given to the fact that on average girls in the UK now show a higher level of achievement than boys in formal education, the vast majority of boys and a significant number of girls still hold the view that it is better to be male than female (Reay, 2002). Specifically, school creates girls as 'no good' at mathematics, science and technology. Girls are apparently channelled into particular subjects that are seen as suitable for them and thus have their opportunities in the labour market severely reduced as a consequence. Girls also become specific *sorts* of female. Being and becoming, practising and doing femininity are very different things for women of different classes and ethnicities (Skeggs, 1997) – ethnicity and class articulate with gender to place girls and women in hierarchies of power.

What needs to be explained is how girls come to accept this. Feminist studies undertaken in the UK in the 1970s and 1980s concentrated on how girls came to be channelled into certain subject areas in spite of the equal opportunities legislation (the Equal Opportunities Act 1975). With the introduction of the National Curriculum following the 1988 Educational Reform Act, boys and girls now have to follow the same curriculum. Nevertheless, the most recent research indicates that subtle processes are still at work that result in girls making choices that tend to propel them into 'female' jobs and prepare them for subordinate roles in a patriarchal society, both at work and in the domestic sphere (EOC, 2004). Furthermore, the most recent research indicates that, despite anti-sexist work in schools and initiatives to encourage girls into science and engineering, the situation has changed only marginally and patchily. These processes are mediated by class and race, and girls do resist them. However, the majority of girls end up in 'female' jobs – that is, jobs that are seen as 'not for men', such as the 'female' semi-professions, routine non-manual work or 'female' service work (see Chapter 9). They come to see themselves as having chosen these jobs, often *because* they are women's jobs; indeed, as more women move into an occupation it comes increasingly to be seen as feminine and thus 'not for men'. Many girls continue to see their destiny as marriage and motherhood, and while most envisage this as being combined with a career or paid employment, others do not; for some Muslim girls, for example, the norms of their community mean that it is unlikely they will engage in paid employment after marriage. It is not just what happens in school that prepares girls for their (subordinate) adult roles, but their experiences at home and with their peer group and the opportunities that are available to them in the labour market (see Lees, 1993; Bates, 1993; Reay, 2002). Mothers continue to play an important role in influencing the educational success or otherwise of their daughters. However, for working-class girls, even being 'pro-school' and having a supportive mother with high aspirations for her daughter is no guarantee of high educational achievement (Lucey and Reay, 2000).

Sue Lees (1993) has suggested four strategies that girls adopt in secondary school – strategies that indicate the complex ways in which class, race and gender articulate in structuring girls' schooling. These involve:

1 *Girls who are pro-school and academically or work oriented.* They are oriented to academic success and occupational careers and are typically white girls from middle-class homes with strong parental support. (Subsequent work confirms this. They have strong support from parents and the school and are able to envisage a range of possible future career paths (Laurie *et al.*, 1999). High examination success characterises the majority of middle-class girls' educational experiences, and anything else is seen as failure (Walkerdine *et al.*, 2001). The examination success of pro-school working-class girls is nowhere near as good, however. The middle-class girls typically follow from GCSE to A levels to university, while working-class girls have more disrupted, fragmented and chequered educational careers.)

2 *Girls who are anti-school but pro-work.* These girls reject or feel rejected by the school but nevertheless are academically and/or career oriented. This is a typical response of able Black Caribbean girls, who reject the racist attitudes of school and teachers but have a strong commitment to academic success and an occupational career.

3 *Girls who are pro-school but anti-work.* These girls value school life as a place to have contact with friends and resist the attempt of teachers to harass them into working. Resistance was expressed, in Lees's research, both by disruptive classroom behaviour and by flouting the school regulations concerning dress, make-up and jewellery. Girls in this group often argued that academic work was not worth worrying about because they would only have part-time work, to fit in with family responsibilities, while others indicated that appearance was more important for girls in obtaining employment than academic qualifications. Some girls in this group also indicated that the behaviour of boys had prevented them from learning and that girls who resisted the boys were denigrated by other girls as well as by boys.

4 *Girls who are anti-school and anti-work.* These girls do not see school as a focus for their social life and reject education and any orientation to an employment career. The majority of these are anxious to leave school and get a job and are already looking forward to marriage, motherhood and domestic labour. These girls regard low-paid routine work as preferable to school and are deterred from an employment career by their expectation that their major role will be raising children.

In Lees's research these girls indicated that girls who did not accept the inevitability of a future as mothers and domestic labourers were deluding themselves.

There is strong evidence that in schools girls acquire appropriate femininity. Not only do the majority strive to avoid labels such as 'slag' or 'lezzie'; they also strive to take on an appropriate feminine identity, within the double bind of being a normal pupil and 'compulsory heterosexuality' (Hey, 1997). White middle-class girls have to strike a delicate balance in the relationship between their femininity and their academic success, while working-class girls neither have the 'right' femininity as measured against the bourgeois ideal, nor achieve academic success (Skeggs, 1997; Dwyer, 1999).

Feminist research has demonstrated that schooling is centrally important in the processes by which girls come to take on a complex identity that is feminised, racialised and located within a class system. Schooling is an integral part of the patriarchal system within which women take on subordinate positions – a system that structurally disadvantages women. This happens irrespective of the attitudes and values of individual teachers or the policies of individual schools or local educational authorities (see Jordan, 1995). Although anti-sexist policies can mitigate the impact, they cannot eliminate it. Indeed, the within-school processes interact in complex ways with the influences of the home, the peer group, the labour market and wider social and cultural forces. These combine to 'produce' girls who are prepared to positively choose and take on women's jobs in a segregated labour market. While middle-class and Black Caribbean girls tend to see their future in terms of an employed career and marriage, working-class girls see it in terms of child care and domestic labour, possibly combined with part-time paid work. The evidence from labour market participation would suggest that Chinese and non-Muslim Asian girls, similarly, anticipate combining a career with marriage, while Muslim Asian women tend to withdraw from the labour market permanently on marriage.

Girls' educational achievements

In recent years there has been a moral panic about girls' 'over-achievement' in the education system (Abbott, 2000), a success that is seen as a challenge to male hegemony (Abbott and Wallace, 1992) and which has been cited by those who claim we now live in a post-feminist society as evidence of a 'genderquake' (Wilkinson, 1994). Frequently in the reporting of these issues no recognition is given to the huge investment over the last thirty years or so in improving girls' educational achievement and, in particular, encouraging girls to continue into higher education. Rather than celebrating girls' success in catching up with and in some areas overtaking boys, or expressing concern that girls are still not taking science, engineering and technology degrees, concern is expressed about their 'apparent' success in education. Beyond this, the widespread publicity given to concern about 'failing boys' does not acknowledge that the educational performance of both boys and girls has improved, but with middle-class girls' performance improving at a faster rate than that of boys, enabling the girls to catch up.

Girls now generally do better than boys in school, as measured by passes in school examinations (GCSE and GCE A levels in England and Wales; Standard and Higher grades in Scotland); as girls and women have been granted more equal access to education so they have caught up with boys and men at each level, and at some levels they are now overtaking them. Young women obtain better results in 16+ examinations than boys, and they are overtaking them at GCE A level as well (Table 4.1). In 2000/1, 40.6 per cent of young women obtained two or more A levels or three or more SCE Highers, compared with 32.1 per cent of young men. This shows not only the gap in achievement between young men and women but also the overall improvement among young people in gaining credentials; ten years earlier, 31.4 per cent of females and 27.8 per cent of males obtained *one* A level or more.

Table 4.1 Obtainment of 2+ A level passes or 3+ SCE Highers by sex, UK, 2000/1 (%)

	Boys	Girls	Total
England	32.7	40.7	36.6
Wales	31.5	38.8	35.1
Northern Ireland	30.6	45.4	37.8
Scotland	32.8	45.2	38.9
Total UK	32.1	40.6	36.2

Source: www.nso.org

Female enrolments are fast catching up with male enrolments in higher education too. Although the numbers in higher education in general have grown during the 1980s and 1990s, the biggest growth has been amongst women; there are now two-and-a-half times more women in the system than in 1970/1 (see Table 4.2). Indeed, in terms of applications to university in 2001/2, there were more female applicants than male ones. Even in postgraduate education, numbers of women going onto further degrees have increased dramatically since 1980. In 1970/1 there were twice as many male postgraduate students as female, but by 1992/3 there were only 11 per cent more (CSO, 1995). Figures for 1994/5 (Department for Education, May 1995) indicated that for the first time there were more full-time female students on first degrees than male ones – 324.1 thousand compared with 320.6 thousand. Male students continue to dominate engineering and technology degree courses, as well as computer sciences; whereas women are over-represented in social, economic and political studies, in languages and in education. (Men still outnumber women as full-time postgraduate students – 43.1 thousand compared to 35.8 thousand – and on non-degree full-time programmes – 58.6 thousand compared with 56.3 thousand.)

A study by Kim Thomas (1990) looked at how different subjects in higher education are gendered. She compared undergraduates in Physics and English/Communications Studies and looked at the different experiences of men and women in each subject area. She found that sciences were seen as embodying hard, incontrovertible and necessary knowledge leading to more serious, well-rewarded and prestigious careers. Scientists saw themselves in a 'subject hierarchy' above 'vague and wishy-washy' subjects such as humanities. The minority of women who studied such 'hard' sciences were very

Table 4.2 Full- and part-time enrolments in higher education by sex, UK, 1970/1–1992/3

	Males No. (000)	Females No. (000)	(%) Females
1970/1	416	205	49
1980/1	524	303	58
1985/6	563	386	68.5
1992/3	759	685	90
2000/1	469.5	550.5	

Source: EOC, 2004.

determined to succeed but nevertheless felt marginalised in the male-dominated and competitive world of sciences. They were likely to see their career goals as conflicting with family goals if they were to marry. They were never seen as totally successful within physics and were often nonconformist in their behaviour within the science establishment. By comparison, only a small number of students of English were men but although this was seen as a more vague, indeterminate and 'feminine' subject in the hierarchy of university values, men who behaved in an assertive, individualistic way with strong opinions were able to do very well. Here it was the men who tended to be less conformist. Thomas concludes that subjects were gendered in very particular ways and that masculinity and femininity took different forms within them.

Women tend to become qualified in different subjects from men. Specifically, there is evidence that women come to reject science, engineering and technology, and indeed see themselves as lacking the ability to do these subjects at degree level, despite the fact that women now outnumber men in these subjects at school. In 2001, 38 per cent of physics first-year undergraduates, 43 per cent in chemistry, 39 per cent in mathematics, 20 per cent in computing and 14 per cent in engineering were female (DTI: www.set14women.gov.uk).

Therefore, the expansion of higher education has particularly benefited women, but women tend to be found in very particular sectors of education. It would seem that removing the barriers from female participation in education means that women start to do better at all levels of the education system. It has taken some years for women to catch up at the higher levels, however. They are now doing so, but studies have tended to show that they do not necessarily end up in the most prestigious academic positions (these are still heavily dominated by men). Therefore academia is still very much a male-dominated domain with women holding fewer chairs or senior positions. Nor does a higher proportion of women obtaining degree-level qualifications mean that there has been a significant increase in the proportion of women in the high-status jobs traditionally dominated by men. In higher education, female academic staff are concentrated in a narrower range of subject areas than men. The most gender-segregated subject is engineering and technology: 88 per cent of full-time academic staff and no less than 97 per cent of full-time professors in this subject area are men (EOC, 2004). More generally, a much higher proportion of male than female academic staff are in higher grades: 90 per cent of professors and 78 per cent of senior lecturers and research fellows in the UK are male (EOC, 2004). By contrast, the majority of entry grade lecturers and research assistants are women.

In schools, 84 per cent of full-time primary and nursery teachers are women; however, almost half (47 per cent) of full-time teachers in secondary schools are men. In both the nursery/primary and secondary sectors, the female proportion of teachers has been gradually increasing since the mid-1990s (EOC, 2004), but women remain under-represented in the higher levels of the teaching profession; for example, in England, seven out of ten secondary school head teachers are male (EOC, 2004).

Women's jobs in the white-collar and service sector are the ones most likely to need qualifications; highly qualified women tend to end up in the female semi-professions (see Chapter 9). Indeed, some of the growth in women's higher education is accounted for by the fact that semi-professions such as nursing and primary school teaching have gone over to graduate-level initial qualifications.

It is also necessary to look at what happens to non-academic girls. Here it is evident that their main education is preparation for 'women's jobs'. Their aspirations are shaped not just by educational failure but also by the expectations of their future roles in the family. Many parents, teachers and employers ask: 'What is the point of girls striving for success at school when they will only get married and become dependants of men?' as do some girls themselves (Lees, 1993). Such expectations filter through to girls, and domestic roles are seen as the alternative to academic success for them. In reality they are likely to spend much of their lives in paid employment (see Chapter 9), so this experience in the education system leaves them ready to accept lower-paid, lower-status jobs without promotion prospects. However, there has been something of a shift in attitudes. Research by Sue Sharpe (1995) suggests that while in the past young women saw marriage and motherhood as an inevitability and the latter as necessitating a break in their working life, they now expect to have jobs, babies *and* a husband. Rather than marriage and motherhood being seen as an alternative career, it is seen as a parallel career. However, Sue Lees (1993) argues that while academic girls expect careers, non-academic girls anticipate part-time employment taken to 'fit in' with child care and domestic responsibilities. Mirza (1992) found that the Black girls she interviewed anticipated a career, but this was in marked contrast to the Irish girls in her study, who saw their futures as homemakers, childcarers and part-time workers. For these girls domestic fulfilment and commitment to the full-time labour market were seen to be incompatible.

In order to understand women's situation in the education system it is necessary to understand how gender interacts with race and ethnicity. What is evident is that Asian and Black Caribbean women tend to have fewer academic qualifications than white women. However, Black Caribbean women are more likely than Black Caribbean men to have obtained GCSE grades A–C, to have vocational qualifications (a large percentage in nursing), and their performance is improving relative to their white peers. Furthermore, African-American women are also likely to be the higher achievers in continuing education in the US (Mickelson, 1992; UN, 2003). The way in which women perform relative to men in the educational system varies according to ethnicity (as does the value of having or not having educational qualifications).

It is also important to recognise that, despite the moral panic about girls out-performing boys in gaining educational credentials, social class and race/ethnicity are much more powerful determinants of educational success.

Gender [is] a less problematic issue than the significant disadvantage of 'race' and the even greater inequality of class . . . in 1997 the gap between boys and girls attaining five or more higher-grade passes was nine percentage points. The difference between managerial/professional and unskilled manual was 49 percentage points . . . the data highlights a particular disadvantage experienced by Pakistani/Bangladeshi and Black Caribbean pupils. Here girls attain rather higher than their male peers but the gender gap within their groups is insufficient to close the pronounced inequality of attainment associated with their ethnic group as a whole.

(Gilbourn and Mirza, 2000, pp. 23–24)

Thus education is a gendered, class-based and racialised experience for girls and boys, young men and young women. A result of the Macpherson Report (1999) was the recognition that Britain is an institutionally racist society and this includes the education system and the ways in which schools reproduce racialised inequalities. It is important to recognise that educational success and failure are the outcome of the complex articulation of class, gender and ethnicity. Beyond this, while girls from all ethnic and racial groups outperform boys from the same group, there is wide variation between groups. Taking the main minority ethnic groups in the UK, the highest-achieving group at 16+ is Chinese girls, followed by Chinese boys, while the lowest-performing are Black Caribbean girls and boys. The percentage point difference between Chinese girls and Black Caribbean girls in terms of achieving 5 or more GCSEs at grades A*–C is 38.9, and the difference for boys is 45.8 (Table 4.3). In general, from the earliest key stage assessments in primary schools, Chinese and Indian children have the highest levels of achievement and Black Caribbean, Black African, Pakistani and Bangladeshi the lowest levels of achievement. The differences in achievement between boys and girls from the same ethnic background are generally similar.

The history of girls' education in Britain

In Britain, middle-class Victorian girls were inculcated from an early age with ideas of self-sacrifice and service while boys were encouraged to be independent. Middle-class Victorian boys and girls were separated at puberty, and girls were generally forced to cease any vigorous exercise, to dress in a more feminine way and to curtail educational activity. This was because it was assumed that women were inherently weak and needed to reserve all their energies for their natural function of bearing children. At this time boys entered the all-male world of work or the public school; they were encouraged to increase their physical and intellectual activities and to become more active and independent. Thus middle-class young people had a prolonged period of education, but while boys went to boarding school or into employment young women were kept at home and prepared for domesticity.

Schooling for working-class children, by contrast, was not made compulsory until 1880, although the state permitted local school boards to build schools for them, by an Act of Parliament passed in 1870, and had required that factory children be

Table 4.3 Achievements at GCSE/GNVQ by ethnicity and sex, UK, 2003

| | 5 or more A*–C | | | | | |
| | Number of 15-year-olds | | | % achieving | | |
	Boys	Girls	Total	Boys	Girls	Total
White	*239,854*	*232,149*	*472,003*	*46.2*	*56.7*	*51.3*
White British	233,151	225,855	459,006	46.1	56.6	51.3
Irish	1,093	1,111	2,204	58.4	61.8	60.1
Travellers of Irish heritage	97	64	161	43.3	39.1	41.6
Gypsy/Roma	90	138	228	24.4	22.5	23.2
Any other white background	5,423	4,981	10,404	46.3	58.2	52.0
Mixed	*4,869*	*5,320*	*10,189*	*42.7*	*55.4*	*49.3*
White and Black Caribbean	1,778	1,959	3,737	32.3	46.8	39.9
White and Black African	390	410	800	39.5	55.1	47.5
White and Asian	878	915	1,793	60.9	68.6	64.7
Any other mixed background	1,823	2,036	3,859	44.9	57.7	51.6
Asian	*18,620*	*17,391*	*36,011*	*47.1*	*59.0*	*52.8*
Indian	7,151	6,899	14,050	60.3	70.3	65.2
Pakistani	7,162	6,329	13,491	35.7	48.1	41.5
Bangladeshi	2,741	2,689	5,430	38.5	52.6	45.5
Any other Asian background	1,566	1,474	3,040	53.8	64.6	59.0
Black	*9,208*	*9,737*	*18,945*	*29.1*	*43.1*	*36.3*
Black Caribbean	4,159	4,403	8,562	25.1	40.3	32.9
Black African	3,790	4,145	7,935	34.1	46.8	40.7
Any other Black background	1,259	1,189	2,448	27.2	40.3	33.6
Chinese	*1,082*	*967*	*2,049*	*70.9*	*79.2*	*74.8*
Any other ethnic group	*2,330*	*1,948*	*4,278*	*41.3*	*51.2*	*45.8*
Unclassified	17,439	15,170	32,609	43.1	52.2	47.4
All pupils	*293,402*	*282,682*	*576,084*	*45.5*	*56.1*	*50.7*

Source: www.nso.org

educated for two hours per day by an Act in 1834. The main aim of education for working-class children was seen as teaching them to be obedient, punctual, clean and deferential to authority – to compensate for what were seen as the deficiencies of the working-class family. Literacy skills were taught, but there was more concern with moral education and discipline. While boys were taught gardening and carpentry, girls were instructed in needlework, cooking and other domestic skills. The aim was to produce a skilled and docile male workforce and more domesticated wives, mothers and domestic servants. However, education was regarded as less necessary for girls than for boys by parents and employers. Truancy was treated with greater leniency when committed by girls since it was felt that if they were at home helping their mother this was probably a useful education for them (Dyhouse, 1981).

Generally it has been argued that schooling was made compulsory for economic and political reasons, but Anna Davin (1979) has argued that in fact since women were not able to vote it is difficult to see why they were included in mass education at all. The explanation, she argues, is that this was a way of furthering the ideology of domesticity, since education was the way in which the middle-class model of the family could be imposed upon the working class (see Chapter 6). Education was designed, then, to prepare girls for mothering, so that they would bring up a healthy, properly socialised future generation. During the slow process of introducing education for girls in the nineteenth century, two alternative models of female education emerged. In the first model, based on the traditional view and embodied in the work of Miss Beale at Cheltenham Ladies' College, girls were equipped for their role in life as wives, mothers and companions to middle-class men. An education was supposed to make them more attractive to a potential partner by training them in domesticity and the feminine arts. This helped to foster the nineteenth-century ideology of middle-class domesticity. The second model was developed by Frances Buss at the North London Collegiate School. Miss Buss argued that girls often had to earn a living if they did not get married, and the usual career for a middle-class spinster was as a governess. The girls of Miss Buss received the same academic education as boys. However, girls were barred from higher education; Oxford did not allow women to become full members of the University until 1920 and Cambridge not until 1947. After feminist campaigns in the nineteenth century, they were finally admitted to special women's colleges – such as Girton at Cambridge. Some colleges gave them the equivalent education to what was available at the men's colleges, but in others they received a different, less academically demanding intellectual diet.

The emphasis on differentiated curricula for boys and girls continued into the twentieth century. In the debates over education in the 1920s and 1930s, arguments concerning biological differences between boys and girls were used to strengthen the view that their curricula should be different. The 1927 Haddow Report accepted the evidence from teachers that girls were more passive, emotional, intuitive, lethargic and preferred arts subjects, despite alternative evidence from academic experts that natural differences in mental/physical capacity and educability were small and not relevant to the design of the curriculum. The 1943 Norwood Report accepted the view that while a boy's destiny was to have a job and be academically successful, a girl's was marriage and motherhood, and for this she did not need academic success.

The 1944 Education Act was the first formal recognition of the concept of equality of educational opportunity – that ability should determine the type of education that a child received. However, boys were (and are) admitted to the selective grammar schools on the basis of a poorer academic performance in the 11+ examination than was required of girls. If selection were accurately tied to ability at that age, then 30 per cent more girls than boys would have gone to grammar schools (Weiner, 1986). As far as less academic girls were concerned, official reports continued to emphasise the importance of education for motherhood. The 1959 Crowther Report argued that the curriculum for 'less able' girls should take account of their 'natural' domestic specialisation, and the influential Newsom Report, *Half our Future* (1963), argued that:

we are trying to educate girls into becoming imitation men and as a result we are wasting and frustrating their qualities of womanhood at great expense to the community. . . . In addition to their needs as an individual, girls should be educated in terms of their main function – which is to make for themselves, their children and their husbands a secure and suitable home and to be mothers.

Two models of girls' education continued to exist in the early post-war period. A small minority of middle-class girls received a grammar school education, while for the majority of so-called 'non-academic' girls the emphasis was still on education for domesticity.

In the 1960s and 1970s there was a general move to comprehensive, co-educational schools, and this is the way in which most children are now educated. The comprehensive schools were introduced as a response to research that had demonstrated that the school system advantaged children who had fathers in non-manual occupations. However, subsequent research, both immediately following the reforms and more recently, indicated that comprehensive schools did not necessarily overcome class inequalities (Ford, 1969; Abrahams, 1995; Hargreaves, 1996), and feminists have questioned whether the strategy benefited girls.

for sociologists [the comprehensive system] has failed because it has not broken the cycle of social and economic reproduction, for feminists it has failed because it contributes to the continuing oppression of women, and for members of ethnic minorities it has failed because it does little more than perpetuate the institutional racism they confront elsewhere.

(Ball, 1988, p. 24)

In secondary co-educational schools the choices made by boys and girls become even more sex-stereotyped – girls were even less likely to take science subjects than in the single-sex girls' schools. Furthermore, it has been reported that girls are academically less successful in co-educational schools (NUT, 1980; Harding, 1980; Kelly, 1982). It seems that in mixed classes girls were less able to develop an 'ethic of success', were less likely to have female teachers and heads as role models, and were more likely to come under the influence of stereotyped images of femininity which are antithetical to academic attainment (Shaw, 1976). Consequently, some feminists have argued for a return to single-sex schooling. Indeed, some studies have indicated that women-only education may be in the best interests of women at all levels (Coats, 1994). Other research has questioned the extent to which anti-sexist strategies have had any impact and challenged the view that a compulsory National Curriculum reduces subject stereotyping (Arnot, 1989). The EOC has noted for instance that

Children develop ideas about the roles of men and women even before they start school and these are often reinforced by many different influences including parents, teachers and the media. As a result, subject and career choices may be shaped from an early age.

(EOC, 2004, p. 1)

Although the introduction of the National Curriculum removed many of the gender inequalities in subject take-up which previously existed, the EOC goes on to note, however, that

> Decisions remain strongly influenced by gender and as optional vocational subjects are introduced into schools, choices made generally reflect the traditional pattern of the labour market. Few people choose subjects or jobs which they associate with the opposite sex either at school or college or in the training and careers that follow. In this way certain pathways through employment are immediately closed down.
>
> (EOC, 2004, p. 1)

Once educational equality was codified in the Sex Discrimination Act 1975 and the Race Relations Act 1976, the concept of equality of educational opportunity had been broadened to include race and gender as well as class. More recently there have been debates about the situation of lesbian, gay, bi- and trans-sexual people in education as well (Garber, 1994).

However, feminists have argued that processes within the school, the gendered labour market and the pressures on women to take up domestic roles, albeit combined with paid employment, mean that ensuring that boys and girls have the same curricular choice, or even an identical curriculum, will make little difference to patterns of inequality and that this is because of factors quite apart from whether boys and girls, working class and middle class, are educated together in the same classroom. Miles and Middleton (1990) point out that equal access to a common curriculum does not guarantee equal treatment in the classroom and wider society. Hilary Burgess (1990) concludes that co-educational schools are really boys' schools and that girls have to 'fit in'.

Explaining girls' continued disadvantage

Christine Skelton has pointed out that girls' educational experience is different from and unequal to that of boys:

> Whether the focus of research has been on female pupils, teachers/lecturers or students in further and higher education, the findings have all illustrated how females *receive* and *perceive* different messages about their aptitudes and abilities from those of males, which has implications for their place in the family and the labour market.
>
> (Skelton, 1993, p. 324)

Sandra Acker (1994) has indicated that feminists are not solely or mainly concerned with issues of achievement. She suggests that it is now indisputable that girls perform as well as, if not better than, boys in formal schooling. The debate is more complex, however. It is about differential curricula, the avoidance by girls of science and technology, sexual harassment, the career prospects of women teachers and lecturers, the unequal treatment by teachers of boys and girls, and the weaving of gender differentials into the very fabric of school life. Acker suggests that there is a 'hidden curriculum' of gender differentiation that continues to operate and influence school processes despite the apparent gender neutrality of the official curriculum.

First, the academic hierarchy remains very firmly masculine (David and Woodward, 1998). As noted above, the higher up the academic ladder we go, the more dominated it becomes by men. Primary and infant schools are more likely to have women teachers and women heads. At the other end of the spectrum, there are far fewer women professors than male ones and hardly any female vice-chancellors or college principals. In Scotland, for example, there are nineteen institutions of higher education and only one female principal. Women are concentrated at the bottom rungs of the professional ladder within colleges, and this applies equally to any level of the educational system at which we choose to look. The proportion of female primary head teachers has actually declined since the 1960s, while the proportion has remained constant for men (Evetts, 1990). Furthermore, female teachers in secondary schools are less likely to teach science and technology – shortage subjects, the teachers of which are often given allowances to encourage them not to move (Acker, 1994). Female teachers are therefore concentrated in posts as classroom teachers and less frequently found in promoted posts. Teaching provides a job for female teachers but the potential of a career for men. This means that the role models which boys and girls have available are ones suggesting that men occupy positions of prestige and power, thereby reinforcing roles found elsewhere in society.

Second, feminists have demonstrated that teachers have stereotyped attitudes to boys and girls and that the school reinforces rather than challenges gender divisions in the wider world. Ann-Marie Wolpe (1988) has argued that girls are encouraged to behave in a feminine way, and teachers see it as part of their duty to inculcate properly feminine standards of behaviour; she has argued that in order to bring about change in girls' education it will be necessary to review and restructure the whole educational system systematically. Girls' disruptive behaviour tends to be interpreted more negatively than boys', and when little girls 'talk rough' they are scolded or excluded. Teachers refer to such girls as 'real bitches', 'a bad influence' and 'little cows' (Reay, 2002). Michelle Stanworth (1983) found, in her study of a humanities department in a further education college, that in an A level class there was a tendency for both boys and girls to underestimate girls' academic performance and to regard the boys as more capable and more intelligent. Male teachers, when asked what they thought their pupils would be doing in future, tended to see even the most able female pupils' futures in terms of marriage, children and domesticity. When careers for girls were mentioned they tended to be sex-stereotypical – personal assistants and secretaries – even when these were not what the girls themselves wanted. However, the male pupils were seen as having careers ahead of them, with marriage hardly mentioned. This expectation of the teachers was in turn reflected in the expectations of pupils. Stanworth found that teachers seemed to be heavily influenced by the verbal contributions that pupils made in the class when making judgements about their academic ability, as were the pupils when making judgements about each other. The teachers agreed with the opinion of boys that they were more able than the girls and based this judgement on verbal contributions in the class, as the boys rarely had access to the girls' marks. This was despite the fact that some of the girls consistently got better marks for the written work than did the boys. Boys continue to dominate classroom space and teachers' attention (Francis, 2000) and to belittle girls' contributions (Skelton, 2002).

Sue Lees (1993) argues that there is an increasing body of evidence that mixed comprehensive education has increased sexism in schools. She indicates that teachers do little to challenge the sexual harassment that girls experience from boys, while Sandra Acker (1994) argues that many teachers do not challenge the view that boys and girls are naturally different and that girls' destiny is domesticity and motherhood. Margaret Goddard-Spear (1989) suggests that teachers think boys are more intelligent that girls. Her research demonstrated that teachers grade boys' science work more highly than girls'. She asked a group of secondary school science teachers to grade a sample of written science work. The sex of the pupil was altered, and half the work was presented as boys' work and half as girls'. The most generous marking was by female teachers of work presented as being by boys, and the most severe by male teachers of work presented as being by girls. Valerie Walkerdine (1990) suggests that teachers know that girls are more able academically than boys, but they continue to undermine girls' achievements. Male expertise and male values continue to be presented in the curriculum as normal and dominant (Paechter, 1998).

Third, textbooks embody various assumptions about gender identities. Children's reading schemes have been shown to present boys and girls, men and women in gender-stereotyped roles. Science textbooks are more likely to portray men than women, and where women are portrayed it is again likely to be in a stereotyped way. Research in the late 1980s and 1990s suggested that, despite some attempts to produce reading schemes that are gender and race 'fair', racist and sexist schemes continue to be used (Skelton, 1993). Reading material and texts across the curriculum tend to portray boys and girls, men and women in stereotypical ways or, in some subjects, to ignore the contribution of women (Skelton, 1993; Abrahams, 1995). Michelle Commeyras and Donna Alvermann (1996) have demonstrated the ways in which 'textual inscriptions can define or relegate women and men to particular gendered positions and how the positioning serves to perpetuate imbalances in classroom talk about texts' (p. 31). They go on to point out that despite thirty years of feminist historical writing this has had little impact on secondary school textbooks. School textbooks and history curricula, with their emphasis on factual knowledge of key people and political development in Britain, perpetuate bias and influence students' interpretation of and attitude towards women in general by marginalising and ignoring their role. Indeed, they point out that the inclusion of one unit of non-European history in the primary National Curriculum and one at secondary level led critics to claim that too much attention was being paid to gender and race issues. Peterson and Lach (1990) have indicated that despite thirty years of concern about gender stereotypes in children's literature little has changed. However, Jackie Bradshaw and her colleagues (1995) argue that educational software manufacturers have made considerable efforts to exclude obvious gender bias from their products for primary schools. They point out, though, that there is a problem when packages are being used to deliver a content which is already gender-biased, and they found that gender-neutral characters were often seen as male:

The evidence for gender assignment is overwhelming, with 'male as norm' as the dominant strategy. Simply stripping images of obviously sex-stereotypical features does not rob them of their ability to carry gendered meaning. . . . Our findings have potentially serious implications for girls, since the overwhelmingly male identification at the initial stage may make it more difficult for girls to identify directly with the images on the screen. The schema they bring with them already worked against seeing 'neutral' characters and gave rise to a tendency to translate sexual ambiguity into maleness. These readings may be one factor in the complex process whereby from an early age girls learn that computers are associated with maleness.

(Bradshaw *et al.*, 1995)

Fourth, although most schools are now co-educational, gender differentiation is nevertheless reflected in the organisation of the school. The outcome of gender differentiation is that, while girls, especially in primary school, are the 'model' pupils, both they and boys come to see boys as more important and to accept that it is boys/men who must be prioritised and who ultimately have authority.

Gender is routinely used in schools to divide children into groups for activities – for example, boys do football and girls do netball. Although in some schools girls may do football, boys rarely opt for netball, and mixed team games are uncommon after primary school. Segregation by sex is an administrative device that continues to be used in the majority of schools and by teachers in the classroom. Registers, record cards and cloakrooms are often divided on the basis of sex, and in primary schools children are frequently 'lined up' as girls and boys and given separate activities. Teachers consider separating children by sex as a routine and efficient means of organisation.

However, organisation by gender is only one of the features of school life that differentiates between boys and girls and reproduces ideas of 'femaleness' and 'maleness'. The very organisation of the school continues to reinforce gender. Staffing structures provide a model of male 'superiority', with the majority of authority positions occupied by men. Head teachers, heads of department, science teachers and the school caretaker are normally men, while classroom teachers (especially in primary school), auxiliaries, dinner attendants and school secretaries are women – 'women teach and men manage'. Hilary Burgess (1990) has argued that the organisation of the primary school mirrors paternal and maternal roles and reinforces the model of women as maternal and natural carers controlled by the paternal male authority figure. Primary classroom teachers are overwhelmingly female, while school management (head teachers) are frequently male. Child-centred primary education increases the identification of a class of children with a teacher as 'my children' (see also Reay, 2002).

However, despite the child-centredness of primary schooling, feminists have argued that boys are advantaged – it is not so much child-centred as boy-centred (Skelton, 1993). Katherine Clarricoates (1980) has demonstrated, from her observation study of a primary classroom, that the key to understanding the way in which teachers organise and structure classroom life is to recognise that their central concern is to maintain control. Discipline is an important factor for teachers – both because it is necessary for them to carry out their teaching role and because of the expectations of their colleagues. The outcome is that boys receive more contact with teachers than girls because boys need more controlling. Teachers actually select material in lessons that will gain the attention of boys; this is both to help in the control of boys and to encourage them to work because girls score higher on tests. Not only the teachers but also the girls and boys recognise that certain subjects are 'boys' things' and others 'girls' things'. All of these are based on masculinist assumptions, which result in boys identifying with science and girls seeing it as a 'boys' subject'.

Maarit Lindroos (1995), in a study in Finland, has argued that the ways in which primary teachers interact with pupils produces different discursive spaces for boys and girls. She suggests that girls are interrupted more often than boys by teachers, as well as the teacher offering more space for the rest of the class to interrupt girls. The ways in which teachers enable girls to make contributions in class also serves to marginalise them, with teachers frequently interrupting them to make their points for them. She points out that:

> The boys did almost the same amount of talking as the teacher and used the longest terms. . . . The teacher talked with the boys instead of the girls, who were just an 'addition' or something timid and in need of assistance.
>
> (Lindroos, 1995, p. 155)

She suggests that the outcome is that the boys are accorded authority while the girls are encouraged to be co-operative.

Research in secondary schools has also demonstrated boys' domination of the classroom and teacher time (Lees, 1993). At secondary school level it is also argued that girls and boys develop subject preferences that prepare them for their future roles. Until the introduction of the National Curriculum the choices that girls made in the secondary school, as well as parental and teacher expectations (Kelly, 1982) and the ways in which the timetable and subject choices were organised, prepared girls for 'female' jobs and domesticity. Traditional careers advice and teachers' attitudes tended to mean that girls did not choose science subjects; it is often suggested that girls are uneasy in handling science equipment and that they lack the familiarity with it that boys often have. The introduction of the National Curriculum has meant that boys and girls have to follow broadly the same curriculum until they are 16, science and technology being compulsory in the primary as well as the secondary school. However, this may have unintended consequences if the intent was to encourage girls to develop more positive attitudes towards science and technology. To the extent that science and technology are seen as masculine subjects, and teachers are likely to reinforce the view that they are (Skelton, 1993), their explicit introduction into the primary curriculum may well ensure that these perceptions are developed at a younger age. The Association for Science Education found that there was little difference in the background knowledge that girls and boys brought to secondary schools but a significant difference in attitudes and interest, with boys already focused on physical sciences and girls on biological sciences. The report concludes:

> Teachers' own attitudes to science will be transmitted to their pupils in day-to-day classroom interactions. If women and men primary teachers display differing

levels of confidence and enthusiasm in teaching biological and physical sciences/ technology themes, then the early introduction of these subjects may reinforce rather than challenge the traditional gender bias.

(ASE Educational Research Committee, 1990, p. 4)

The most recent statistics on the relative success of boys and girls at GCSE and A level show that more boys opt to take single science subjects (except biology) than girls, with boys tending to outperform girls in the specific science subjects (except biology) and IT, while the mathematical performance of boys and girls is relatively equal. (Girls outperform boys in combined science awards with the exception of SCE Scottish Standard science – www.eoc.org.)

The statistical evidence on girls taking science subjects at school and in higher education indicates that, despite a number of initiatives designed to encourage girls into science and engineering, there was little change between the early 1980s and the 1990s. While girls marginally outperformed boys in biology, chemistry, physics, mathematics and IT at A level, the numbers taking the subjects were lower apart from in biology. Of A level biology candidates 60 per cent in 2001/2, were young women but only 23 per cent of physics candidates were.

In higher education more men apply for places on science, engineering and technology courses (SET) than women, more accept a place if it is offered, and more obtain the qualification. However, the number of female SET candidates is increasing; between 1992 and 2002 the number of female SET graduates went up by 55 per cent, compared with a 29 per cent increase among males. However, only a third of SET graduates were female. There are striking differences between SET subjects, however. While one in five SET undergraduates is female, females account for 43 per cent of chemistry undergraduates, 39 per cent of mathematics, 20 per cent of computer science and only 14 per cent of engineering undergraduates. By way of contrast, humanities and social science subjects at degree level, such as languages, education, media studies, sociology and business studies, are female-dominated, as are the degrees leading to careers in nursing and the professions allied to medicine, while the proportion of female medical students is also now over 50 per cent. More girls stay in full-time education after the age of 16 than boys, although boys are more likely to have day release from an employer – reflecting the small number of girls who are taken on as apprentices.

Why do girls and young women do so well within the education system? One answer is that achievement and conformity at school contradict certain codes of masculinity, especially working-class masculinity (Willis, 1977). Additionally, the greater surveillance of girls and young women by parents also pushes them into doing homework. Girls are denied the freedom to 'go out' in the evenings that is extended to boys, and they tend to spend at least some of the time doing their homework. This differential policing of boys and girls and the ways in which it encourages girls to do homework is particularly evident in the fact that girls meet the deadlines for GCSE coursework which boys often miss (Warrington and Younger, 2000). However, some girls are disadvantaged and have difficulty in producing coursework or indeed in doing homework because of the large amount of domestic labour and childcare that they are expected to perform at home (Lees, 1993; Bates,

1993). Boys are generally not expected to contribute to the same extent – and, indeed, girls may be expected to perform domestic labour for their brothers (Bates, 1993; Lees, 1993) – although some of the boys Sue Lees interviewed in London did help with housework and thought that it was right that they should be asked to do so. Some research has suggested that Asian girls may be particularly disadvantaged by the amount of domestic labour they are required to perform, and other research (Bates, 1993) has indicated that girls may be expected to take time off school for housework and childcare. In many developing and post-colonial countries girls are kept away from school to help their mothers with childcare and other female tasks, including agriculture, and are frequently unable to complete even primary education (see next section).

Subject preferences can also be seen to influence the skill-based (vocational) further education courses that young men and women take. Female-dominated areas include nursery nursing, arts and crafts, family care, personal care, hairdressing, beauty therapy and health care, while male-dominated areas are sports and recreational studies, construction, manufacturing and production, oil, mining, plastics and chemicals and transport. Business studies is also predominantly female. In 2001/2, 54 per cent of young people studying Foundation Modern Apprenticeships were women, but only 3 per cent of these were on manufacturing apprenticeships, 1 per cent on construction and 3 per cent on motor industry apprenticeships. In contrast, 97 per cent of those in childcare, 94 per cent of those in hairdressing and 89 per cent of those in health and social care were women. A similar gender split is found on Advanced Modern Apprenticeships. In terms of achieving a vocational qualification, 95 per cent of those obtaining one in engineering or construction and property are men, while 61 per cent of those gaining one in information technology, 75 per cent in education, training and lecturing, 56 per cent in art and crafts and 90 per cent in healthcare, medicine and health and safety are women.

Judy Wajcman (1994) has indicated that the proportion of women taking computer courses in higher education has declined in the last twenty years, while at the same time information technology has become widely used in schools. She argues that access to computing at home and in schools is dominated by boys, that computing has become sex-stereotyped. She concludes that 'the absence of technical confidence or competence does indeed become part of the female gender identity as well as being a sexual stereotype'. The evaluation of projects such as *Girls in Science and Technology* (Kelly, 1987), *Women in Science and Engineering* and the *Technical and Vocational Education Initiative* (Skelton, 1993) indicate that encouragement is insufficient to attract girls to science and technology (see also Warrington and Younger, 2000.) As Jackson concludes:

> When we started there was a feeling that these poor unfortunate girls did not know the delights of a scientific (or engineering) career, and if only we gave them the information they would all be converted. What we increasingly discovered is all the obstacles: peer pressures in schools, parental attitudes in some cases, inability to get to the apparatus because the boys grabbed it. Now I think we need to look at the training of teachers and the education of boys and men.
>
> (Jackson, in Gold, 1990, p. 42)

Other researchers have suggested that science and technology teachers see girls as deficient, as lacking the necessary aptitude to do science and technology (Versey, 1990). However, the accumulating evidence is that the 'ability' to do science and technology has more to do with the differential opportunities that girls and boys have to tinker and play with construction toys (Sharpe, 1995) and the gender stereotyping of subjects as boys' and girls' areas (EOC, 2004). Volman and Van Ecke (1995) suggest that the problem needs to be reconceptualised – away from seeing girls as the problem and towards seeing science and technology as the problem. The attitudes of girls to science and technology do not reflect misunderstanding or prejudice, but social realities. They conclude:

> By starting from the assumption that girls are the problem researchers have been led into looking at them as an object. They have concentrated on explaining the 'behaviour' of girls. We think that approaching girls as agents, who can be asked what they think and feel, makes more sense if we want to understand how they experience mathematics, science and technology, different ways of teaching them and how and why they are compatible or not with being a girl. We think that this can help to avoid falling into the trap of concluding that education does not really make a difference and that it is only misunderstanding of girls themselves that they do not like mathematics, science and technology.
>
> (Volman and Van Ecke, 1995, p. 292)

There are also different kinds of classroom interaction associated with the different genders. Detailed analysis of the moment-to-moment interaction in the classroom indicates that boys talk more and are allowed to dominate the classroom interaction, and this continues even when teachers are consciously trying to overcome it (Spender, 1982). Skelton (2002) has suggested that teachers typically work to interest boys for the sake of maintaining order. Goddard-Spear (1989) argues that boys are perceived as more active learners than girls, dominate teachers' time and are regarded more highly by teachers. Feminist researchers have pointed to the importance of language in the classroom. They have drawn attention to the tendency of girls to take a back seat in the classroom and to be more hesitant in making contributions than boys. Girls are often reluctant to speak in class, and diminished in the discussion which takes place. The classroom becomes seen as a man's world and girls are marginalised. Furthermore, teachers often use sexist remarks and sexist language in controlling girls. Katherine Clarricoates noted that:

> If boys get out of hand they are regarded as 'boisterous', 'rough', 'aggressive', 'assertive', 'rowdy', 'adventurous', etc. For girls the adjectives used were 'funny', 'bitchy', 'giggly', 'catty', 'silly'. It is obvious that the terms applied to boys imply positive masculine behaviour, whereas the categories applied to girls are more derogatory.
>
> (Clarricoates, 1980, p. 161)

Sue Lees's 1993 research indicates that the situation has changed little and, despite the fact that they object to boys' domination of the classroom and their disruptive and sexist behaviour, in the end the girls have to put up with it. Indeed, Jackson and Salisbury (1996) suggest that teachers do little to challenge the disruptive, dominating behaviour of boys in the classroom – although they point out that it is not *all* boys who behave in this way.

Taken together, these indirect forms of socialisation are sometimes called 'the hidden curriculum'. While the overt message may be that the expectation of girls and boys is the same, this is subverted by a different message underlying the curriculum.

In sum, until recently girls were disadvantaged in the educational system because they were not provided with an education equivalent to that of boys. Although there now appears to be more equality in terms of co-education and equal access, in practice girls are still disadvantaged in that they are channelled into particular subject areas and their participation is not taken seriously. This is on account of the 'hidden curriculum' which in the case of girls includes such factors as the organisation of the school, the expectations of teachers, the content of textbooks, the gender balance in the academic hierarchy and the way in which classroom interaction takes place. For both academic and non-academic girls the consequence is that their career and job opportunities are limited. Several competing models exist as to how girls should be educated. The first model argues that they should be equipped for their lives as wives and mothers. The second argues that they should compete on equal terms with men by receiving the same education as boys. The third model argues that girls should be educated separately as a way of better enhancing their academic performance.

Global inequalities in literacy and education

Research suggests that enrolment in various levels of education has generally improved more for girls than for boys in post-colonial and developing societies; the gender gap in education is closing in many regions of the world. Nevertheless, in many areas the gap in educational opportunities between boys and girls remains wide. In 22 African and 9 Asian countries, enrolment for girls is less than 80 per cent of that for boys according to the United Nations (2003) *World Youth Report*. According to this Report, the divide is greatest in Southeast Asia and sub-Saharan Africa, particularly for secondary education; in these regions fewer than 40 per cent of secondary school students are female.

Also, literary rates around the world have been increasing, although it remains the case that by far the majority of the world's illiterate population are women. Thought to be a result of both cultural and economic factors, inequalities in illiteracy rates between males and females are also at their most extreme in Southeast Asian and sub-Saharan as well as West African countries. Improvements in girls' literacy rates are occurring in these regions only very slowly. In the 1970s, girls were 1.8 times more likely than boys to be illiterate; by 2000 the ratio had dropped only slightly to 1.6 times (United Nations, 2003). In 2000, Africa and Asia had the highest illiteracy rates in the world amongst 15–24-year-old girls, at 29 and 19 per cent respectively. However, while high, these figures represent a major improvement over the past generation or so; in 1970 the illiteracy rate for girls was 72 per cent in Africa and just over 50 per cent in Asia. The level of development in a country has come to be regarded as a major

107

determinant of its level of literacy, particularly for women; although the situation in developing countries has been steadily improving in this respect, the gap between developing and Western societies remains marked.

Girls outnumber boys in schools only in regions where overall access to basic education is high – such as in Southern Africa, Latin America and East Asia. Larger gaps are noted in regions of the world with lower overall levels of education. Educational access is notably lower in rural areas for both boys and girls, but particularly so for girls. In Niger, for instance, there are 80 girls for every 100 boys in schools in cities, but in rural areas the corresponding ratio is only 41 to 100 (United Nations, 2003). These differences are thought to reflect family expectations of future returns from their educational investments. The Report concludes that

> Faced with a choice, some parents elect to educate sons because there are more and better-paying jobs for men than for women. Some parents invest less in girls' education because economic returns will go to their future husbands' families after marriage. Disparities in educational access also reflect the lower value parents place on education compared with household activities for girls; some girls are kept or taken out of school to work at home.
>
> (United Nations, 2003, p. 255)

Also, some parents may well be unwilling to send girls to school if the school is some distance away, or if the teachers or other pupils are male. In Pakistan, for instance, where schools are segregated by sex, a large proportion of girls living in rural areas do not have a school within one kilometre of their home.

Studies have repeatedly shown that investment in educating girls and women raises every index of progress towards economic sustainability and development. Despite this, the UN estimates that two-thirds of the 300 million children without access to education are girls, and two-thirds of the 880 million illiterate adults are women. Although the educational gap has begun to narrow at primary level, female representation decreases at secondary level and beyond in many parts of the world.

A related factor is that fertility affects levels of educational attainment and vice versa. Various determining factors appear to relate to the young women themselves as well as to cultural, economic and family considerations (such as a pregnant mother's decision to withdraw her daughter from school to help at home or to supplement the household income through paid work). A study in Bangladesh found that children in small families stayed in school longer because they were not called upon to care for younger siblings at home (cited in United Nations, 2003). (See Therborn, 2004 for a discussion of similar issues in parts of West Asia and North Africa.)

Literacy and educational attainment among young women also positively correlate with reduced child mortality; the more educated women are, the less likely they are to have larger families, particularly at a relatively young age. In Kenya, for instance, 11 per cent of children born to women with no formal education will die by the age of 5, compared to 7 per cent of children born to women with a primary school education, and 6 per cent of women with a secondary school education. Botswana, Kenya and Zimbabwe, with the highest levels of female education in sub-Saharan Africa record the lowest levels of child mortality (United Nations, 2003).

Feminist perspectives on education

Liberal feminist perspectives

Liberal feminist perspectives have been very influential in education, and indeed it was campaigns by liberal feminists that created opportunities for girls within the educational system. They argue that girls should have an equal chance to be educated in the same way as boys and that this will lead to equal opportunities elsewhere. They measure their 'success' in terms of the higher achievements of girls: better examination results and a higher proportion of girls entering higher education. However, these are only successes when seen from a middle-class perspective, and although more girls may be in the educational system this does not mean that they enter jobs as 'good' as those of boys (see Chapter 9). They simply enter feminine jobs at a higher level. Moreover, dominant expectations of femininity also follow them through the educational system. Hence, radical and Marxist feminists argue that equality of opportunity is not enough and more fundamental changes need to be sought.

Radical feminist analyses of schooling

Dale Spender (1982) has argued that knowledge taught within the educational system is not neutral but rather that it reflects masculine assumptions about the world – for example, about the role of 'objective' interpretations rather than subjective, intuitive ideas, and about controlling nature through science rather than trying to live with it, and about the importance of political leaders as opposed to ordinary people. The school system, likewise, sets up teachers as 'experts' who pass on knowledge to others and who have authority over others, who determine what is a 'right' answer and what is a 'wrong' one. This also reflects a masculine view of the world – boys and girls learn that the 'great' artists, scientists, writers and sociologists were men. Men are portrayed as superior to women in all areas of knowledge, and women rarely find their experiences reflected in this knowledge. Knowledge, in this model, is packaged into discrete 'subjects' which become either masculine or feminine, and students are not encouraged to see the connections between them or to question these classifications. The importance of competitive striving for success in an individualistic way, which is embodied in the education system, is for radical feminists an example of a male approach to the world. Other ways in which patriarchy is reproduced in schools include the ways in which boys come to dominate the classroom and teachers' time and the ways in which girls are sexually harassed in schools (Lees, 1993). The outcome of these processes is not so much that boys have the chance to reduce girls' possibilities for success, but rather that girls come to accept male power as inevitable. Teachers do not challenge the domination of boys in the classroom and their sexual harassment of girls. Girls withdraw and police themselves (Measor and Sikes, 1992) and develop strategies for coping.

Radical feminists have tended to focus on within-school processes and ignore the wider structural factors. By focusing on girls' experience they have ignored the experience of many boys who do not dominate or sexually abuse (Wolpe, 1988), and they probably underestimate the extent of girls' resistance (Measor and Sikes, 1992). Sue Lees (1993) does quote in her research examples of boys who objected to the sexual harassment of girls by boys and to the disruptive behaviour of (some) boys in the classroom. A further problem with radical feminist approaches is their reliance on 'patriarchy' which, as we noted in Chapter 3, some feminists have argued conflates description with explanation (Pollert, 1996).

Marxist and socialist feminist perspectives

Marxist and socialist ('dual-systems') feminists both argue that gender inequalities in education need to be seen in the wider context of a capitalist society. The school in capitalist society is the major ideological state apparatus that ensures that the relations of production are reproduced – that is, that the next generation of workers graduate not only with skills appropriate to the position they will take in the labour market but also with appropriate attitudes. Thus it is necessary to understand how schools provide different experiences for girls and boys so that gender as well as class relations are reproduced. This takes place through cultural reproduction – including the way in which those girls who develop anti-school attitudes and values and overtly resist the authority of the school nevertheless end up accepting low-paid 'women's' jobs.

Michelle Barrett (1980) has suggested that in relation to education three key questions need to be answered:

1   How is education related to the reproduction of the gender divisions of labour in capitalist societies?
2   What is the relationship between class and gender in schooling?
3   What role does education play in preparing men and women for a particular social order – one structured by class and gender?

In answering these questions Marxist and socialist feminists have adapted the Marxist theory of social class to analyse the question of gender relationships by examining patriarchal and class relationships within capitalist society. The aim is to provide an analysis of the role of education in creating a sharply sex-segregated, racialised labour force and to explain the processes involved in this. To do so they have adapted theories of social reproduction such as those developed by Bowles and Gintis (1976) and of cultural reproduction such as that developed by Willis (1977). In the process they have challenged the political neutrality of education, arguing that its structures and ideologies are already linked to the needs of the capitalist labour market and dominant class interests.

Bowles and Gintis (1976) analysed the way in which the school acts as a selection and allocation device for the social reproduction of the class structure. The major function of the education system, they suggest, is to produce a stratified and con-forming workforce. Experiences at school prepare pupils for the labour market; for example, pupil/teacher relationships and the hierarchy of authority in the school prepare pupils for supervisor/manager/worker relationships. Different forms of education provided by different streams in the school system prepare children for different levels of occupation. Middle-class pupils are encouraged to develop the autonomy necessary for middle-class jobs, and working-class children are prepared for their subordinate position in the divison of labour. Thus for Bowles and Gintis the school reproduces the relations of production.

In England, Paul Willis examined the way in which class divisions are culturally reproduced. He asked not just why working-class boys finish up in working-class jobs, but why they see them as desirable jobs to take on. In other words, he argued that working-class boys were not forced into unskilled manual work but positively opted for it – seeing it as 'real men's work'. His study focused mainly on a group of twelve 'lads' in a school in Birmingham who constituted a small 'subculture'. It was evident that the lads experienced school not as a process of enlightenment but as a source of oppression. They reacted against teachers' authority by escaping from supervision and doing the things they valued most: smoking, drinking, swearing and wearing their own variation on the school uniform. While the teachers saw these lads as trouble-makers, the lads themselves were effectively driven by their experiences in the school to embrace male working-class culture. The lads were proud of their actions and saw those who conformed to school as passive and absurd 'ear 'oles'. The lads looked forward to starting work, their subcultural values and expectations reflecting those of the factory subculture.

Feminists have argued, in the same way, that school reproduces gender divisions; it prepares girls not only for their place in the workforce but also for the sexual division of labour. Ann-Marie Wolpe (1988) argues that the family and the school prepare women for low-paid work in the secondary labour market and for domesticity. Michelle Barrett (1980) has pointed out that women have a dual relationship to the class struc-ture. The education and training women receive by virtue of their class background prepares them for the places they will occupy in the labour market, but this is mod-erated by the expectation that all women will take on domestic labour and childcare and become economically dependent on a man. Thus working-class girls are prepared for low-paid secondary sector jobs, while middle-class girls are prepared for semi-professional 'female' jobs (see Chapter 9). Research by Bates (1993) indicates that despite Equal Opportunities legislation and educational reforms the situation remains largely unchanged.

Marxist feminists have criticised Marxist models of work-role reproduction for not including any account of the reproduction of gender roles. They have examined the experiences of female working-class pupils in order to understand the ways in which they interpret and mediate the structures and ideologies transmitted by the school. The aim has been to understand how working-class girls come to have a particular definition of femininity which is constructed and negotiated in a competitive education system in which they 'lose out'. It is argued that the particular version of schooling that working-class girls get puts them in a position where they freely choose their own subordination – that is, they choose marriage and domesticity. The form of resistance that working-class girls develop is different from that of working-class boys. Girls form a subcultural ideology of love and romance – an exaggeration of the feminine stereotype. Some girls experience school as dull and boring, and their hopes for the future focus on romance, marriage and motherhood. Their ambitions are not focused on achievement and qualifications but on leaving school, 'getting a man' and setting up a home of their own. Girls also signify in other ways their opposition to a school system which aims to control expressions of femininity in the interests of discipline and management. Girls use their sexuality to control the classroom; flirting with male teachers, for example, can be used to undermine the teachers' authority and control. Refusal to wear school uniform, or adapting it to the current fashion, wearing costume jewellery or certain kinds of shoes, are all forms of the same strategy.

Black feminist perspectives on education

Black feminists have been critical of the way in which educational theories are assumed to apply to Black as well as white women (see e.g. Bryan *et al.*, 1985; Amos and Parmar, 1981; Mirza, 1992; Phoenix, 2002). They argue that racism is as much if not more a central aspect of their experience than sexism. The differences between Black women, especially between Black Caribbean and Asian girls, who have very different cultural backgrounds, complicates this argument. Indeed, the cultures of Asian girls also vary considerably depending on the country from which their families came and the religion of their family. However, Valerie Amos and Pratkha Parmar (1981) argue that all Black women share a history of subordination and of being treated as second-class citizens. They suggest that Black culture is blamed for the problems of Black people – that is, the relative educational failure of Black children is said to be because of their religion, their language, their communities, rather than being seen as a result of a racist society. In particular, Black Caribbean pupils (and especially boys) are blamed for their supposedly uncontrollable behaviour. Gilbourn (1995) argues that teachers have a general view that Black pupils are a disciplinary problem and that this takes on a reality for Black children, who are disciplined more frequently and more severely than white children – not always with justification. He quotes one teacher pointing out how an individual girl's behaviour becomes a generalised view. Following on from talking about one girl, the teacher suggested 'I think there is a problem with Black Caribbean girls in this school . . . I am not sure how to handle them, how to cope. You try hard not to sound racist but some of them are very lively' (p. 183).

In Britain, to understand the experience of Black girls in school it is necessary to understand the racist, class and sex/gender system of which school is a part. Black girls experience racism in school not only from white pupils and some white teachers, but also from a racist and Eurocentric curriculum. Thus Bryan *et al.* quote the experiences of a number of Black girls:

> School became a nightmare for me. They poked and pulled at me. 'Is your hair knitted, then?' 'Do you live in trees?'

> I remember my early school days as being a very unhappy time. . . . There was a time when this teacher pulled me up in front of the class and said I was dirty and that she was going to make sure that my neck was cleaned – and she proceeded to do it, with Vim.

> My memories of school are of being laughed at and everyone calling me golliwog.
> (Bryan *et al.*, 1985, pp. 62–63)

They point out that the curriculum is racist and Eurocentric and Gilbourn (1995) suggests that the National Curriculum has exacerbated this. Not only do the reading books present women in sex-stereotyped roles; the majority of children and adults in reading schemes are white. History is taught from the perspective of white Britain. English books are selected on 'literary merit', which is judged from a white perspective. Black people are often portrayed as inferior:

> You will be getting deep into a story and suddenly it will bite you – a reference to black people as savages or something. It was so offensive. . . . Sometimes you would sit in class and wait, all tensed up, for the next derogatory remark to come tripping off the teacher's tongue: Oh yes it was a 'black' day today, or some kid had 'blackened' the school's reputation.
>
> (Bryan *et al.*, 1985, p. 65)

While few educationalists overtly accept the view that Black children are genetically less intelligent than white children, nevertheless teachers often expect less of them and Black children consistently underachieve at school. On the other hand, Black Caribbeans are expected to do well at games and are encouraged in this area of the curriculum. The result is that a substantial proportion of Black women underachieve at school and a relatively high proportion leave with few qualifications and are propelled into the very same jobs that their mothers or grandmothers were encouraged to come to Britain to take up in the 1950s and 1960s – dirty, low-paid jobs in the secondary labour market (Gilbourn, 1995).

However, as with white working-class girls, some Black girls do resist racism and ethnocentrism. Mary Fuller (1980) has argued that some Black Caribbean schoolgirls' anger and frustration at the way they are treated at school leads them to a positive self-image – a positive embracing of being Black and female. They aim to achieve good educational qualifications, get decent jobs and move out of the subordinate position that their parents are in. Gaining educational qualifications gives them a sense of their own worth. However, this does not necessarily result in conformity to the norms of the school. They conformed to the ideal of the 'good pupil' only in so far as they did their school work. Apart from this their behaviour was designed to exasperate the teachers. In the classroom they gave the appearance of inattention, boredom and indifference; they expressed opposition to what they regarded as boring and trivial features of school by, for example, reading magazines or doing homework in class. They accepted the relevance of the school only in terms of academic benefit; they were able to exploit the school system without becoming subordinate to it.

Mirza (1992) has suggested that Black girls' academic achievement is due to their ambitions for themselves and their willingness to work hard despite a lack of encouragement from teachers. She points out that the ambitions of Black girls are not reflected in the jobs in which they end up. This is due to the location of the schools they attend, the racialised and sexualised labour market and the careers advice rather than to Black girls' expectations of marriage and motherhood. The Black girls she interviewed were committed to paid employment but made choices on the basis of realistic assessments of their abilities and the opportunities available to them.

Masculinity and education

The sociology of education in the 1960s and 1970s was gender-blind – either no consideration was given to the different experiences of boys and girls in the education system, or research focused exclusively on boys, or girls' experience was interpreted through the boys' eyes. This meant that boys were constructed as the norm and girls as different from the norm. Thus sociology failed to challenge the commonly held view that if men/boys were not naturally superior to girls/women, they necessarily became so, both because of their role as breadwinners and also because boys/men needed to be constructed by the work and other demands placed on them (Abbott and Wallace, 1992).

Feminist sociology was concerned with studying the experiences of girls/women and challenging assumptions of male 'natural' superiority in education. In doing so they studied not girls/women in isolation but the relationship between men and women, highlighting the ways in which patriarchal power structured masculine and feminine identities. In the 1980s and 1990s two male perspectives developed which were concerned with understanding the construction of masculinity. The first, associated with 'men's studies', was concerned with men's rights and argued that it was necessary to study men in the same way as feminists had studied women – to bring men in. This perspective ignored both the fact that much research had been by men and about men and that feminist research had been concerned with the relationship between men and women. Some researchers from this perspective have been concerned to argue that schools are 'anti-boy'/'pro-girl' (e.g. Moir and Moir, 1999) – a position rejected by feminists. The alternative position is the study of men in the terms devised by feminists – 'pro-feminist' studies.

A recent set of studies has considered how masculinity is constructed through schooling. Taking their lead from feminist studies of schools that have explored how femininity is constructed and perpetuated through education, these studies have considered masculinity as problematic. Beverley Skeggs (1995), for example, argues that masculinity is part of a set of codes and expectations found within the school system. Mairtin Mac an Ghaill (1994), in an empirical study of how masculinity is created within a school setting, found that the male peer group (with which the male teachers colluded) encouraged an atmosphere of hostility, homophobia and misogyny – in other words, male peer groups were created out of a resentment of gay men and hostility towards women. He suggests that rather than such peer groups being supportive, they tended to ridicule and intimidate boys who did not conform. In this way masculine culture and peer groups within the school served to create and police the boundaries of masculinity and ensure a heterosexual dominance. The 'normal' form of sex was intercourse with women, although women were discussed in an extremely insensitive way and the young men did not actually want to spend any time with women.

Ashwin: You have to prove yourself all the time. And it's different things to different groups. Like, everyone can look at a street gang and say, oh yeah, all their behaviour is about being hard. But in the top sets it's the same way, getting the best marks and all that. That would be seen as 'poofter' stuff to the gang but it is acceptable to the top set lot. But it's still about beating other people, doing better than them, and you're shamed if the girls get better marks. That would be real slack. You have to prove to them that you're better than them and the other boys.

(Mac an Ghaill, 1994, p. 93)

Other studies have suggested that harassment of women pupils and women teachers is a routine part of school life so that confrontational heterosexual norms were once again established – by the informal culture as well as the formal one. Mac an Ghaill indicates that there were indeed a number of codes of masculinity and that the middle-class and white boys subscribed to different ones than the Black boys and working-class boys. He explains this phenomenon by arguing that masculinity is in fact a *fragile* construct. Hence it has to be vigorously reinforced in these various brutalising ways which tend to perpetuate a certain kind of domineering manhood. Feminist studies in the classroom have shown, similarly, how formal and informal cultures, including the culture of masculinity, work together to produce and manage 'girls'. Ellen Jordan (1995), for example, has explored the ways in which boys in primary schools operate with a definition of masculinity that has femininity as the subordinate term, and boys therefore 'need' to dominate girls in order to demonstrate that they are masculine, while Kehily (2002) points out that boys strive to avoid being labelled 'gay' in the context of compulsory heterosexuality in schools.

Conclusions

This chapter has tried to show the persistent inequalities existing in education and provide some explanations for them. Although women's performance in education is very high and they are already outperforming men in many fields and levels of education, women nevertheless do *not* get better jobs and careers afterwards. The relationship between education and the labour market means that a set of assumptions and constructions of masculinity and femininity tend to affect both, and that there is continuity between sexism and disadvantage in education and sexism and disadvantage in the labour market. Future domestic roles play a part in depressing young women's expectations and career or education prospects, even though, for contemporary young women, childcare responsibilities necessitate only a short break – if any – in an employment career, and marriage in most societies is no longer seen as a reason for giving up paid employment.

SUMMARY

1 Although young women are more likely to be qualified than young men, they find themselves in parts of the labour market – notably the service sector – where wages are lower and prospects bleaker as their role in paid work is assumed to be secondary to marriage and motherhood and, for many girls and young women, their orientation to education comes to reflect these expectations.

2 Vocational education and training tends to reinforce gender inequalities by emphasising particular kinds of masculinity or femininity, in spite of a formal commitment to equal opportunities.

3 Women's careers are conditioned by the expectation of marriage and motherhood, even though in contemporary Britain, childcare is less likely to lead to a significant career break than in the past. Contemporary young women expect to have everything – an interesting job, children and marriage – rather than choosing between a career and motherhood as in the past but this is not necessarily a global pattern.

FURTHER READING

Brine, J. (1999) *Under Educating Women: Globalizing Inequality*. Buckingham: Open University Press. This wide-ranging book considers the global dynamics shaping gender, racial and class-based aspects of education. It rejects a 'deterministic' reading of global inequalities in education and explores many of the collaborative and conflicting interests shaping girls' and young women's experiences of education. It also considers opportunities for change and resistance.

Coffey, A. (2001) *Education and Social Change*. Buckingham: Open University Press. This text is a sociological analysis of contemporary education policy and practice, focusing on the social, political and economic context of changes and continuities in education in Britain in recent decades.

Francis, B. and Skelton, C. (eds) (2002) *Investigating Gender: Contemporary Perspectives on Education*. Buckingham: Open University Press. This book addresses empirical and theoretical issues relating to gender and education, and provides a useful introduction to the diverse areas of research within the field. It incorporates a range of contributions from various perspectives and provides an excellent overview of recent developments and debates.

Jones, K. (2002) *British Education 1944–2001*. Cambridge: Polity. This book offers a comprehensive introduction to the development of the British education system over the last fifty years, taking account of the relationship between social institutions such as the school, the workplace and the family.

CHAPTER FIVE

The life course

Age is usually seen as a natural or biological status, yet historical and cross-cultural research shows that the way in which different societies divide up the life course is highly variable, as is the behaviour associated with different age groups. Feminists have argued that age status is of particular importance to women, who are more often defined in terms of ascribed biological characteristics than social achievements, and whose identity is frequently defined according to their social role as someone's wife or mother. Feminists have also argued that men and women are ascribed, and experience, the life course differently so that because women are defined largely in terms of reproductive capacity and sexual attractiveness, women are thought to be 'old' at a relatively younger age than men (Friedan, 1993). Thus age-status transitions serve to define different kinds of femininity and what it means to be a woman, even though the categories ascribed may not correspond to the lived experience of many women. In this chapter we look at various aspects of the life course including childhood, youth, adulthood (often defined for women largely in terms of marriage and mother-hood), middle age and old age, and consider how these are shaped by various aspects of identity, including sexual difference (the difference between men and women – see Chapter 2). There is now a burgeoning sociological literature focusing on each of these aspects of the life course, addressing issues such as age stratification, variations in the meaning and experience of childhood, ageing and particularly the implications of an ageing population in many parts of the world.

As Macionis and Plummer (2002, p. 322) note, 'age divisions are found across all societies as a major means of differentiating people'. Although all societies seem to have some system of age stratification, whereby there is an unequal distribution of social, political and economic resources between different groups at different stages in the life course, the nature and extent of these inequalities as well as the categorisation of groups varies considerably between societies and across different historical periods. Sociologists have argued that, however they are defined, attached to each stage of the life course are a series of expectations governing social behaviour.

Childhood

Today, most countries in the world define childhood as a time of relative freedom from the social, political and economic burdens of the adult world. Children are denied many of the rights enjoyed by adults but, by the same token, in many societies are absolved of adult responsibilities such as the need to earn a living, to provide care for elderly or dependent relatives, or to go to war. This is not the case in all parts of the world, however, or throughout all historical periods. The social meaning and experience of childhood varies considerably. Until about a century ago, children in Europe and the US bore many of the burdens of adulthood. Likewise, if we look at the position of children in a range of contemporary developing and post-colonial societies, we find many examples of children taking on the responsibilities and concerns we would associate with adult life in the West. Childhood is therefore 'a very different experience across cultures and indeed even within one culture according to the class, gender and ethnicity of the child' (Macionis and Plummer, 2002, p. 323).

Some social scientists have argued that even in the West, the idea that 'irresponsible' children are protected by 'responsible' adults is a myth as, in an age of high divorce rates, working parents and an increasing level of exposure to 'adult' media culture, children are no longer protected from the adult world. Smart *et al.* (2001) have argued in this respect that while family life in societies such as the UK is being transformed by high rates of divorce, the idea that such changes have given rise to a deteriorating quality of life for children is misguided. They argue that rather than witnessing the end of the family and of 'protected' childhood, the emergence of 'post-divorce' and single-parent families has given rise to new experiences of childhood. However, in addition to the pressures of consumer culture and of the 'branding' of childhood (Quart, 2003), children are thought to be hurried through their childhood by some (Elkind, 1981; Winn, 1983). Others have argued that the 'hurried' or 'branded' child thesis overlooks the fact that children in relatively disadvantaged groups have always assumed adult responsibilities sooner than others (Lynott and Logue, 1993).

Global experiences of childhood

Macionis and Plummer consider several examples that illustrate the global diversity of childhood in contemporary societies, including child labour, child marriage, children and war, illness and mortality. As they note, work is commonplace for many children in low-income nations and societies across the world. High-income societies are rich enough that many people – including children – do not have to work. Many of the goods consumed by children and young adults living in these societies (branded trainers and clothing, for instance) are produced by child labourers living in less privileged parts of the world, however. Indeed, the United Nations estimates that large numbers of the world's children work in conditions that are detrimental to their physical health or psychological well-being, including dangerous industrial activities such as mining; illegal activities such as prostitution, pornography or drug trafficking; or work in extreme conditions of heat or cold, or in jobs that involve exposure to hazardous substances or chemicals (www.un.org). Many of the world's children are employed by organisations that supply branded goods to corporations that are household names in the West; particularly given the increasing popularity of 'outsourcing' manufacturing work to countries with cheaper labour costs (see Chapter 3), a global division of child labour is reinforced.

Research by Russian sociologists (Barkhatov *et al.*, 2002) has highlighted that 'street children' have begun to be recognised as a prominent social problem in post-communist Russia:

> Over the last ten years, as the country struggled with sweeping economic decline and a shift in values, it has also had to cope with a side effect of this massive transformation: homeless and neglected children. Away from home, deprived of shelter and parental care, these children are becoming a new cheap workforce and easy prey for the rampant criminal world.
>
> (Barkhatov *et al.*, 2002, p. 5)

The report found that children aged under 13 comprise about 50–60 per cent of the total number of street children, and that approximately a quarter to one-third of these are involved in prostitution or in the production of pornography. The researchers estimate that most working street children in Russia are boys; the same is true of children involved in criminal activities. Girls on the other hand are over-represented in underage prostitution and some 100,000 girls and young women in Russia are thought to be working as street prostitutes, as call girls, or as prostitutes in parlours or bars and clubs. Barkhatov *et al.* (2002) are particularly critical of the prevailing public attitude towards child prostitution, according to which 'social stigma falls upon adolescent girls compelled to engage in the sex trade, but not upon their respectable adult clients' (p. 10).

When asked about their reasons for working, twice as many girls as boys answered that they 'worked to survive'. The answer 'I am forced to work under threat' was received four times as often from girls as from boys, and the majority of those who said they worked to assist their parents were girls. By contrast, reasons such as the desire to have more pocket money, food or an expensive consumer item were more common among boys than girls. Many street children, especially young girls involved in prostitution, worked under an adult 'master' – about 47.6 per cent of girls and one-fifth (21.8) per cent of the boys were found to be working under the patronage or paid protection of adults.

As well as undertaking paid work outside of the home, many children across the world get married and consequently are required to perform domestic labour, and to engage in a sexual relationship, from a relatively young age. Often for economic or cultural reasons, early marriages (relative to Western norms) are pervasive in parts of Africa, and South and East Asia (Therborn, 2004). In some countries, half of all girls under the age of 18 are married. Countries with relatively high percentages of girls aged 15 to 19 years who are already married include the Democratic Republic of Congo (74 per cent), Niger (70 per cent), Afghanistan (54 per cent) and Bangladesh (51 per cent) (UNICEF, 2001). As Macionis and Plummer note, 'poverty is one of the major factors underpinning child marriage', which has several serious implications for the girls and young women involved:

> Child marriage may serve as a major life restriction, and can have a serious impact on *health*. It can cut off *educational opportunities*. And for girls in particular (and the rate of child marriage is very much higher for girls) it will almost certainly mean

premature pregnancy – with higher rates of *maternal mortality* and a lifetime of
domestic and sexual subservience.

(Macionis and Plummer, 2002, p. 323, emphasis added)

According to a UNICEF (2001) report on child marriage, domestic violence is common
in adult–child marriages. Early marriage is also linked to child prostitution it seems,
as many women and children flee violent spouses and, being unable to return to
their parental home, have little option but to turn to the sex industry in order to sustain
themselves (Therborn, 2004).

Child marriages are still very common in many regions of the world where
decades of sex determination tests followed by female foeticide have resulted in a
bride shortage (Therborn, 2004). As Calvert and Calvert (2001, p. 242) have noted, in
some parts of India 'even villages that lack running water typically have a doctor who
performs high-tech amniocentesis or ultrasound to determine the sex of a foetus'.
Therborn (2004) reports that given their traditional preference for boys, many Indian
families living in rural communities, and particularly in some of the more conservative
states such as Madhya Pradesh, often view sex determination tests and abortion of
females as a means of family planning. While the tests are illegal across India, the
law is frequently flouted and clinics offering them abound. India has a long history of
female infanticide; baby girls are poisoned, suffocated, drowned, starved or simply
abandoned and left to die. Girls are considered a liability because of the expensive
dowries that have to be paid at their weddings, but boys are an asset. Even the most
ineligible comes at a premium – commanding a dowry that can extend over several
years to a steady demand on the girl's family for money and other goods. Refusal
to comply may lead to 'bride burning'. Rather than increasing their value or importance,
a shortage of women means that, on the contrary, young brides are often subject to
domestic violence and abuse, and are forcibly detained in their homes to cook, keep
house and, above all else, produce male offspring (Therborn, 2004).

About half of the world's refugee population are thought to be children (www.
amnesty.org) and, as they are often thought of as the next generation of 'the enemy',
children are often one of the main targets of war. Female children and young women
in particular are also at risk from rape and other forms of sexual violence – violating
and impregnating 'their' women being a tactic commonly deployed in war. Children
(both male and female) are also recruited or coerced into being soldiers.

For many children around the world, their early years are marked by sickness
and morbidity, and in countries with high levels of infant and child mortality, loss of
siblings as well. In countries such as Botswana and South Africa, it is estimated
that one half of today's 15-year-olds will die of AIDS related illnesses (www.who.org).
But, as Macionis and Plummer (2002, p. 325) also point out, 'many of the children in
sub-Saharan Africa find their parents dying of HIV/AIDS and this makes for large
numbers of what have been called "AIDS orphans"'.

Globally, girls have a greater chance of surviving childhood than do boys, except
where gender inequalities are at their most extreme. As Therborn notes, in parts of the
world such as

Bangladesh, Nepal and Pakistan female life expectancy at birth is slightly lower
than that of males; in India as a whole, the female advantage is only one year. But

in the big Indian states of the north, Uttar Pradesh, Bihar and Orissa, female life expectancy is also shorter than male. This is an abnormal pattern indicating mistreatment of females. Among the rich countries women tend to live 5–7 years longer than men; in China and Indonesia the female advantage is 4 years, in Egypt 3 years, in Saudi Arabia 2.5 years and in Iran 2 years. The only social area in the world resembling South Asia in sapping the superior biological strength of the female sex is sub-Saharan Africa, particularly in the AIDS-ravaged southern part, but also including Nigeria and other West African countries.

(Therborn, 2004, pp. 110–111)

The gap between children from poor households and those from economically secure settings is also more pronounced for girls. Boys from poor households are 4.3 times more likely to die and girls from poor households are 4.8 times more likely to die than their respective counterparts from financially secure households (United Nations, 2003). This greater vulnerability most likely reflects the lower probability of girls receiving adequate medical care, or of being absolved of their everyday responsibilities when they are ill. In poorer households, these responsibilities may include a significant (or sole) contribution to domestic tasks such as cooking, cleaning and washing, or providing care for younger or older family members.

A study conducted at a family health centre in Bangladesh, for instance, found that boys were seen more than twice as often by doctors as girls. In India and Latin America girls are often immunised later than boys or not at all. In some places, boys tend to be given more and better food than girls. Breastfeeding and weaning practices are also thought to favour boys in many developing countries. Hence, 'surveys of girls' and young women's health show that, globally speaking, childhood is a period of relative inequality' (United Nations, 2003, p. 25).

The changing status of childhood in Western societies

It is generally argued that in pre-industrial, Western societies there were no distinctive phases of childhood and adolescence; rather, from the age of about 7 children became part of adult society, expected to undertake work roles and contribute to the maintenance of the family (Heywood, 2001). Children were punished for crimes in the same way as adults, being deemed morally responsible for their actions. By the nineteenth century they had come to have a 'special' status, as the idea of childhood as a distinct phase in the life course spread from the middle classes to the working classes. Nevertheless, children of this age were still usually prosecuted in the same way as adults. In nineteenth-century Britain for instance,

On one day alone in February 1814 at the Old Bailey sessions, five children were condemned to death: Fowler aged 12 and Wolfe aged 12 for burglary in a dwelling; Morris aged eight, Solomons aged nine and Burrell aged 11 for burglary and stealing a pair of shoes.

(Pinchbeck and Hewitt, 1973, quoted in Muncie, 1984, p. 33)

In pre-industrial Britain, working-class children in particular, whether they remained at home or went into service, had little freedom. At the age of 6 or 7 years they were sent away to work in other households as servants or apprentices and this continued until they were able to marry, usually in their late twenties. The rising middle class frequently sent their sons to be apprenticed, and from the sixteenth century increasingly to boarding school, although the main growth of these came in the nineteenth century. Middle-class girls were mainly kept at home, while the small number of girls' boarding schools trained girls for domesticity and marriage. Girls were controlled either by their fathers or by their masters. Wages were nominal, and many girls would have been expected to send money home to their parents.

In early nineteenth-century Britain working-class children provided cheap labour in the factories. However, from the 1830s, Factory Acts limited the age from which children could be employed (to 10 years) and the hours that young people could work, effectively making children under the age of 10 economically dependent on their parents. However, young people continued to work in paid employment well into the1800s; young girls were frequently sold into prostitution, and the use of children as chimney sweeps was not outlawed until late in the nineteenth century. Families were often dependent on the wages of their young, and this situation continued up to the First World War and beyond. Girls would also have been expected to help their mothers with domestic tasks and to help in the care of younger siblings.

Welfare reformers were instrumental in creating an ideal of childhood through their campaigns to save children from hard labour, from prostitution and vice, and from other forms of exploitation by adults. In doing so, the concept of an ideal, sheltered and innocent childhood was constructed with children, and later adolescents, being segregated into schools and penal institutions separate from adults where they could be reformed and 'saved'. Campaigns to help young people were also based upon the idea that their leisure time could be used productively in clubs and organisations and that this along with special institutions for the young could prevent them from developing bad working habits and falling into crime and sinful activities. Child welfare reformers, whose activities were later institutionalised in social policy, therefore helped to impose the middle-class notion of a sheltered and innocent youth onto other sections of the population.

By the twentieth century, childhood had become identified by psychologists and the medical profession as a crucial period of language and identity formation. As the welfare state developed, children were singled out as particular objects of welfare intervention, needing special diet, dental and medical assistance. The expanding social services were concerned with the moral and social welfare of children, and the education system began to concern itself not only with their erudition but increasingly with their well-being more generally. Associated with this was the development of various experts and professions specialising in the care, treatment and nurturance of children and later of adolescents in Britain and other Western societies.

Other trends served to change the status of childhood still further. The decline in infant mortality and in the birth rate after the Second World War meant that families were able to invest more in their children in the reasonable certainty that they would survive (Gittens, 1985). Under these circumstances, children became objects of fun and pleasure for adults, a sort of household luxury. Children became the main purpose and focus of family life, so that rather than supporting families through their work, they began to be seen as the dependants of families for whom other consumption priorities should be sacrificed.

The separation of home from the workplace resulted in the (spatial and social) segregation of women and children. The home in middle-class households was supposed to represent a haven from the fierce competition of the marketplace and the public world, in which men were supposed to seek solace and comfort, but in which women and children were cloistered and sheltered. This middle-class, sheltered view of home and childhood later spread to the working class.

Also from the late nineteenth century children began to be recognised as having rights of their own. Various legislative measures were designed to protect the child from his or her own family and from exploitation or neglect by other adults. However, the welfare of children was also linked to their social control, and the 1908 Children's Act was intended both to protect children from becoming criminal adults and to separate them in 'reformatories'. 'Problem' children were to be both protected and reformed. The young offender was handled differently from adult criminals, tried in 'juvenile courts', and schools were supposed to monitor the progress of children in order to identify 'problem' cases. This was partly because it began to be argued that disturbed children would become delinquent adolescents. Hence, childhood came to be associated with developmental and psychological stages which had to be correctly negotiated, if necessary with professional help (Sapsford, 1993).

In the course of the twentieth century, Western societies developed a view of childhood as something cloistered and innocent. Hockey and James (1993, 2002) indicate that this view is associated with a subordinate and dependent status in an age-structured society. Children came to be subject to a process whereby authority remains in the hands of adults. In addition, this sheltering is associated with innocence so that childhood is supposed to represent a happy part of a person's life. The global-isation of childhood (through mass-mediated fundraising activities and charitable events, such as Children in Need in the UK, for instance) means that children in other parts of the world are often presented primarily as victims of war, famine or other hazards in contrast to the safe and happy world of Western childhood. The Western model of childhood is therefore taken to be the ideal and the norm.

Female and male children are marked as different with different clothes and toys, and are subject to different kinds of socialisation from birth, or even earlier. Until the last few decades in Britain (and many other Western societies) young boys and girls led institutionally segregated lives, having different schools, different curricula, different youth clubs, and so on. Many of these institutional differences have been eroded along with a move towards co-education in schools (see Chapter 4), but in other respects girls and boys continue to be treated differently, and girls are often subject to more control and surveillance than boys of the same age. Girls are often sheltered more than boys from the real or imaginary dangers of the outside world or from sexual threats. This sexualisation of adult contact with children means that children are segregated more strongly from the adult world than previously, as a result of recent public anxiety about their protection and of media coverage of child abuse and abduction cases. Girls are seldom allowed to walk alone or spend much time on their own, autonomously, outside of adult surveillance.

However, this vigilance and anxiety on the part of adult protectors detracts attention from the fact that children are most likely to be physically or sexually attacked by the adults who are supposed to be protecting them. The tremendous psychological anxiety roused by child sex abuse means that gullible or negligent social workers or Satanic rituals are more easily blamed than loving parents. However, legislative changes (in the UK and elsewhere) and the setting up of telephone 'childlines' for the victims of sexual abuse have resulted in more sustained intervention to protect children from adults, as well as a renewed debate about the status of childhood.

Reports of bullying and also of young boys raping girls their own age or older women have also renewed debates on the question of what childhood is. These issues have raised public anxiety and debate about the age at which children could be said to be responsible for their actions, as well as denting their image as 'innocent'. Much of this debate illustrates the profound ambiguities in relation to childhood in Western cultures. Children are supposed to have sheltered, innocent lives but are victims of their own violent impulses and the sexually predatory actions of those who are supposed to protect them. Many have more autonomy and wealth inside the home than previously and less autonomous freedom of movement outside of it, yet many have access to global media and communication networks from their own bedrooms via television and the internet. *Young People, New Media*, a report published by the London School of Economics following research into young people's engagement with media culture found that two-thirds of children have a TV in their bedrooms, for instance (Livingston and Bovill, 1999).

Childhood in contemporary Britain

While the proportion of children in the population in many European societies such as Britain is reducing, the 2001 Census of England and Wales revealed that children still make up a substantial number of people in the UK – some 11.7 million. Nearly one in four (22.9 per cent) of these live in single-parent families, 91.2 per cent of which are headed by their mother. Overall, almost a third of households contain dependent children, and one in nine have children under the age of 5. More than one in ten dependent children live in a step-family. The majority, though, live with both natural parents (65 per cent). Many children live in 'workless' households; over two million (17.6 per cent) live in households where there are no adults in paid work.

In Muslim households in the UK this is even higher, with more than a third of children living in households in which no adult undertakes paid work. Muslim children also experience much more overcrowding (more than two in five – 41.7 per cent – compared with an average of 12.3 per cent) and one in eight Muslim children live in a household with no central heating compared with an average of 5.9 per cent (one in 16). High-rise housing may not be suitable for families with very young children, but over 58,000 children under 2 years old live in homes two or more storeys above ground level, and over 11,000 in the fifth floor or above (www.statistics.gov.uk).

Sociological perspectives on childhood

Until recently, children and childhood have been relatively neglected sociologically – for example, children were seldom questioned in sociological surveys, presumably on the assumption that they are incapable of making rational responses in the same way as adults (Lewis and Lindsay, 1999). But children have also been thought to have a 'privileged' status (in the West at least), representing the future hopes and aspirations of a society or social group and as such are accorded particular help and protection. As we noted above, this has not always been the case, however.

In recent years, a burgeoning sociological literature on childhood has begun to evolve, much of which has been concerned with the ambiguous status and changing experience of childhood (James and Prout, 1997). Sociological thinking about children has tended to reject biological or psychological definitions of childhood and, instead, emphasises that childhood does not exist in any essential or universal form, but is the outcome of the meanings attached to particular social roles, and largely focuses on the social construction of childhood (James *et al.*, 1998).

Traditionally, sociology has treated adults and children as theoretically different kinds of person – with adults seen as complete, stable and self-controlling, and children seen as incomplete, changeable and in need of (adult) control and supervision. Recent approaches, influenced largely by postmodern ideas, have problematised this assumption, however. Sociologists such as Nick Lee (2001) and Steven Miles (2000) have argued that because children are now 'growing up in an age of uncertainty' (Lee, 2001), childhood can no longer be regarded as a movement towards personal completion and stability. Rather, careers, intimate relationships, identities, and so on are all increasingly provisional; bringing into question the traditional sociological division between the mature adult and the immature child. Social processes such as globalisation and, in particular, the role of consumer culture and the mass media have been seen to be highly influential in shaping the contemporary experience of childhood in this respect (Miles, 2000).

Feminists have argued that sociological research on childhood has often placed considerable emphasis on childhood as a socially and culturally homogenous experience and consequently have paid comparatively little attention to the ways in which childhood is shaped by social class, race and ethnicity, disability, global power relations, and gender (Russell and Tyler, 2002). Berry Mayall (2002) has argued that much like a sociology for women, feminists should begin to develop a sociology *for* (rather than *of* childhood); one driven by a political concern to overcome the oppressive social relations that shape inequalities in childhood, both between adults and children and between children themselves.

Feminist research on childhood has highlighted the relationship between gender, childhood and consumer culture, in terms of the increasing market recognition of 'tweenies', as well as the role of 'pester power' and 'branding' in shaping the Western experience of childhood (Quart, 2003). Children, it appears, are now a major source of purchasing power and some sociologists have argued that childhood has become subject to intense 'branding' by global corporations. According to Walls Monitor (a marketing organisation that specialises in researching the demographics of the 5 to 16-year-old age group in the UK and the USA), there was a 38 per cent rise in pocket

125

money between 1993 and 1998, with 28 per cent of this being between 1997 and 1998. This corresponds with market research in the UK and the USA indicating that pre-teen girls are twice as likely as any other demographic group to visit a shopping centre at a weekend. As recent research on gender, childhood and consumer culture has highlighted,

> the commercial perception seems to be that women are never too young to be self-conscious about their bodily appearance and to define their identity in relation to a relatively narrow set of social and cultural reference points.
>
> (Russell and Tyler, 2002, p. 628)

Indeed, research by Russell and Tyler (2002) focusing on a UK-based chain of retail outlets called *Girl Heaven* (aimed primarily at 3–13-year-old girls) has emphasised that in the context of consumer culture 'the opportunity for girls to play with their femininity is reduced to the purchasing of a series of products and make-overs that not only separates them from themselves and each other, but crucially from the process, the social experience, of becoming feminine' (p. 631).

Adolescence

Just as childhood is a socially and historically variable phenomenon, so is adolescence, although it too is usually assumed to be biologically defined. 'Adolescence' is some-times portrayed as a phase in which people have to make difficult psychological adjustments to the physical changes in their bodies. For girls and young women it is particularly associated with the onset of puberty and with becoming physically capable of bearing children. Many girls, particularly those living in Western societies, experience adolescence as a period of increasing sexualisation, according to which they come to be defined largely in terms of their sexual availability and reproductive capacity.

Young women and sexuality

Throughout history, young women have been scrutinised with regard to their attitudes, behaviour and general conduct in relation to sexuality. The setting and monitoring of cultural and moral standards, often involving the policing of young women's sexuality, is conducted in private, in public and through the mass media. Moral panics are often constructed in Western cultures over women's sexuality. For example, young single mothers have frequently been identified as a problem group and are often discussed in an effort to find ways to alleviate the problems they are thought to represent and cause. Inner-city disturbances and increasing crime rates have often been attributed to the growing proportion of young single mothers for instance (Furlong and Cartmel, 1997; Griffin, 1997). This policing of young women's sexuality is clearly not unique to Western societies. In Turkey in the late 1990s, for instance, school authorities sent girls suspected of being sexually active for virginity tests; if found not to be virgins, the girls were expelled from school (including young women the age of student nurses). Only in 2002 was this practice outlawed by the Turkish Ministry of Education (Ilkkaracan, 2002).

In many societies across the world, young women have little or no 'youth' and in this sense it might be argued that adolescence as a distinct phase in the life course is something of a Western privilege. As Therborn (2004, p. 215) notes, 'most girls do not have any youth in South Asia, and not very much in Indonesia, Central and West Asia/North Africa either'. For example, one in every ten births worldwide is to a teenage mother, but in some countries the proportion is considerably higher. Early pregnancy carries a higher risk of death or serious illness. The United Nations reports that in developing societies, girls aged 10 to 14 years are five times more likely to die in pregnancy or childbirth than are women between the ages of 20 and 24. At least one in ten abortions worldwide occurs among women aged 15 to 19 years, meaning that at least 4.4 million adolescent women undergo the procedure every year; 40 per cent of which are thought to be performed under unsafe conditions (United Nations, 2003). In Argentina and Chile, more than one-third of maternal deaths among adolescents are the direct result of unsafe abortions. In Peru, one-third of the women hospitalised as a result of complications during abortions are aged 15–24 years, and the World Health Organization estimates that in sub-Saharan Africa up to 70 per cent of women hospitalised because of abortion complications are under 20 years of age (www.who.org). In a Ugandan study, almost 60 per cent of abortion-related deaths were among adolescents (cited in United Nations, 2003, p. 253). Also, as we noted above, many girls and young women in developing, post-colonial or post-communist societies are forced into prostitution or 'sex tourism' (see Chapter 8).

Young people in Britain

In legal terms the status of adolescence is ambiguous. In Britain, young people are seen as responsible for their criminal activities from the age of 10. However, a young woman cannot give consent to sexual intercourse with a man until she is 16, although a doctor may give her advice on contraception and provide contraceptives before she reaches that age. Gail Hawkes (1995) has argued however that the covert regulatory practices adopted by 'family planning' professionals towards those whose lifestyles they deem 'irresponsible' often serve to discriminate against young girls on grounds of gender, race and class ideology. Young men and women may marry at the age of 16 but need their parents' consent. A young man used to be liable to conscription into the armed forces at the age of 16, but the age of voting for Members of Parliament is 18, and this is also the minimum age for standing for election. The legal point of transition from childhood to adulthood is 18 years – reduced from 21 in 1970.

In Western societies, it seems that (as noted above) kids are 'getting older younger' (Quart, 2003) at the same time as youth is getting longer and longer. This phenomenon is described in Alissa Quart's (2003) critique of the 'branding' of girls and young women as adult women who like to 'hang out', and who construct their social identities and friendship networks primarily in terms of consumer culture. The protracted period of growing up which follows childhood is extending. As the years in full-time education increase (often through statutory changes but also as a result of more young people choosing to stay on at school), as the number and range of vocational and technical education courses increases, so young people spend longer and longer charting a course through the complex maze of opportunities and possibilities. The numbers going into higher education in Britain have increased too (see Chapter 4).

The fact that young people are increasingly found in education and training rather than at work has changed our view of youth in Britain and other Western societies. To put it starkly, in 1945 80 per cent of 14-year-olds were at work in Britain. Now 80 per cent of 14–18-year-olds are in full-time education. We would now think that people of this age are 'too young' to work, but (as we noted above) this is by no means a universal view.

The general tendency in state and welfare legislation is to recognise young people as independent actors – to give them more autonomy and decision-making power. However, this is also a contradictory process since efforts to cut welfare expenditure have meant that benefits have also been taken away from young people on the assumption that they should be more dependent upon their families. This process of increasing autonomy is reflected in the cultural and social experiences of young people as part of a process of 'individualisation'. This means that although young people may be dependent upon their parents for longer and longer periods of time, they have more autonomy and space within the home for longer periods.

Adolescence, youth culture and social change

The lifestyle and behaviours of girls and young women have begun to change in this context; smoking and drinking have become more common, as have drug use and involvement in crime (although women are still thought to be less criminal than men – see Chapter 10). Women have also become more sexually active at a younger age, although the average age of teenage sexual initiation varies considerably.

In the period after the Second World War, with increased affluence in the 1950s and 1960s, considerable attention was paid to youth culture in sociology. Young people were portrayed as 'affluent consumers' who were able to stimulate the culture industries (particularly producers of pop music, magazines and fashion) with their new found spending power (Wallace, 1989). Media, political and sociological attention tended to focus attention on specific 'problem' groups such as muggers, football hooligans and drug-takers. These groups of young people were seen as deviant, as holding antisocial values and as challenging adult society. In the 1950s it was the 'Teds', in the 1960s the 'Mods' and 'Rockers', followed by the 'punks' in the 1970s. During the 1960s the 'hippies' – a more middle-class subculture – and the student movement rejected middle-class ideas of the protestant work ethic and 'respectability' in a consumer society. The problems with these groups were portrayed as problems of 'the youth of today' in general. In this way the idea of adolescence as a universal phenomenon was reinforced (see Chapter 12).

However, Marxist sociologists at the Centre for Contemporary Cultural Studies (e.g. Hall and Jefferson, 1976), analysing these subcultures, argued that they were not examples of 'universal' problems of youth but rather of particular class formations.

Thus the Teds and Skinheads were examples of working-class youth subcultures and the hippies of a middle-class one, rather than a reflection of the behaviour, attitudes and values of all young people. Feminist researchers were particularly critical, however, of the relative neglect of women in sociological research on youth sub-cultures (see Chapter 12). The 'subculture' literature does not take young women into account, they argued; it focuses entirely on male subcultural activity. McRobbie and Garber (1976) wondered whether this was because young women are really not active in subcultures, or because they are rendered 'invisible' by male researchers. They addressed this issue by arguing that young women are not present in male subcultures, except as girlfriends and hangers-on, because they have their own cultural forms of expression based upon the retreat from male-defined situations into an alternative culture of 'femininity' based around the young women's bedrooms and being a 'fan' of popular cult heroes or music groups. These feminine cultures tend to be negatively defined in the sociological literature:

> They are marginal to work because they are central to the subordinate and complementary sphere of femininity. Similarly, marginality of girls in the active, male-focused leisure subcultures of working-class youth may tell us less about the strongly present position of girls in the 'complementary' but more passive subcultures of the fan-club.
>
> (McRobbie and Garber, 1976, p. 211)

The behaviour of teenage women is at least in part an outcome of the ways in which they are treated differently from boys. Because young women are seen as more in need of care and protection, parents 'police' their daughters' leisure more strictly than that of their sons. This is linked to the dominant ideological definition of 'appropriate' behaviour for women. Sue Lees (1986) has also shown how boys control young women in the public sphere through the threat of labelling them as sexually promiscuous. It is expected that boys will 'sow their wild oats', but similar behaviour attracts censure in young women and is likely to lead to derogatory labels (see Chapter 8). Indeed, this sexual labelling has less to do with the actual sexual practices than with the extent to which young women's behaviour deviates from the popular ideas of femininity – for instance by the use of swear words or loud behaviour. To remain desirable – a 'nice girl' – young women must suppress any real sexual desire and conform to gendered expectations of romantic love, sexual passivity and monogamy. This double standard serves to constrain the private and the public lives of young women to ensure conformity based on a model of sexuality which ultimately takes its form from the ideology of the nuclear family, feminists have argued.

Feminist sociologists showed that ideas of 'masculinity' and 'femininity' which had been taken for granted as natural were in fact social in origin: these roles had to be learned by young people. Feminist critics such as McRobbie and Garber argued that young women did not 'rebel' in the way that young men did, but rather used romantic fantasy as a source of escapism. Other studies such as those of Sue Lees (1986), Christine Griffin (1985) and Claire Wallace (1987), by contrast, have argued that the ideology of romantic love plays a more complex role in the lives of young women. In many respects young women are not deceived by the images of life portrayed in women's literature but have very realistic ideas of what married life might hold in store for them. Second, they argue that young women do have access to a number of strategies of resistance, which flout the 'nice girl' stereotype. Third, these studies have emphasised the importance which jobs hold for young women, as a source of status and independence both outside and within the family. Marriage and motherhood are not their only goal in life. For example a re-study of the original 1980s sample carried out in London by Sue Sharpe in the 1990s (Sharpe, 1995) found that in contrast to the earlier study, the young women she interviewed no longer saw marriage and motherhood as their only goal in life. More recent studies of young women have tended to emphasise the variety of feminine identities available to them and the ways in which they can switch between these, manipulate them or change them as it suits them. These studies, in line with more postmodern feminist perspectives, have therefore tended to emphasise the ways in which feminine identities are chosen rather than predetermined.

Yet, on a more global level, the United Nations *World Youth Report* (2003) on the situation of adolescent girls and young women emphasises the prevalence of negative attitudes towards women; exclusion and discrimination; relatively limited access to social resources such as health, education and employment (particularly in terms of maternal health); and the extent to which girls and young women continue to be subject to violence. The report found that

> The status of men is higher than that of women in developed societies because women's unpaid household labour is still not seen as an essential and valid contribution to the industrial economy. In other societies, girls and young women are viewed mainly as 'reproductive labourers'. They have fewer rights to political and economic participation than do boys and young men, and they perform essential work for which they are neither paid nor fully recognized. They still live mostly in the private sphere, as the public sphere remains largely a male domain.
>
> (United Nations, 2003, p. 249)

Gender differences in literacy and education

Participation in various levels of education has generally improved for girls more so than boys so that the gender gap in education appears to be closing in many parts of the world (see Chapter 4). However, as we noted in Chapter 4, in 22 African and 9 Asian countries, enrolment in education for girls is less than 80 per cent of that for boys (United Nations, 2003). The divide appears to be greatest in South Asia and in sub-Saharan Africa, particularly for secondary education, in which less than 40 per cent of secondary schoolchildren are female. Similarly, Africa and Asia have the highest rates of illiteracy among 15–24-year-old girls, at 29 and 19 per cent respectively. In fact, globally, female illiteracy rates are decreasing only very slowly – Wallace and Kovatcheva (1998) estimate that in the 1970s girls were 1.8 times more likely to be illiterate than boys, and by the end of the 1990s the ratio had dropped only slightly to 1.6 times. The figures for Africa and Asia, however, while relatively high, do represent a considerable improvement; the United Nations reports that in 1970 the illiteracy rate for girls was 71.1 per cent in Africa and 50.3 per cent in Asia.

Yet, although the situation in developing countries has been steadily improving, the gap between rich and poor nations remains significant in terms of girls' and young women's literacy rates and educational opportunities. In all countries, young women are over-concentrated in particular educational disciplines and sectors that tend to lead to lower-paid jobs and a narrow range of occupational opportunities (see Chapters 4 and 9). Life chances for adolescent girls vary considerably in different parts of the world but a general pattern seems to be that girls (as a group) are disadvantaged relative to boys in terms of education and literacy. What is clear from recent sociological research, however, is that girls and young women often construct their identities with reference to other agents of socialisation, particularly (in both Western and developing societies) the mass media and consumer culture.

Young women and consumer culture

There is now a growing body of sociological literature that explores the relationship between young women and consumer culture (McRobbie, 1994, 1996; Lury, 1995; Radner, 1995) much of which emphasises that shopping occupies a pivotal place both in shaping and manifesting this relationship (Ganetz, 1995; Falk and Campbell, 1997). Much of this material has tended to draw attention to the social significance of themes such as 'girlie culture' and particularly 'girl power'; to the ability of girls and young women to challenge, resist, parody and ultimately undermine hegemonic representations of what it means to be a young woman through various aspects of consumer culture, and particularly shopping as a quintessentially 'girlie' pastime. The term 'girl' is clearly a market of status in this respect, denoting both a positioning within childhood or adolescence, but also a relatively passive designation within a gender, class and racial hierarchy, one that the popular cultural theme of 'girl power' (associated largely with the all-female pop group the Spice Girls) attempted to re-articulate (see Chapter 12).

Feminist analyses have tended to highlight the role of a concern with appearance and the body – and the social construction of femininity largely in terms of how girls and young women look – in shaping the relationship between gender and consumer culture. Much of this work has focused on the extent to which the presentation of a feminine body is maintained through the pursuit of social and cultural norms simultaneously governing women's behaviour and appearance, as reflected in discourses on beauty and cosmetics (Wolf, 1990), fashion (Young, 1990a), sport and exercise (Bartky, 1990), as well as cosmetic surgery which, research suggests, increasing numbers of girls and young women are undertaking (Davis, 1995). Such approaches emphasise that femininity constitutes a mechanism for controlling young women's behaviour through appearance – through an emphasis on an ideal standard of femininity, but also through the definition of femininity itself largely in terms of aesthetics (Russell and Tyler, 2002).

Other (more postmodern) feminist perspectives on gender identity and consumer culture have focused instead on the importance of celebrating, rather than developing a critique of, women's relationship to consumer culture (Nava, 1992; McRobbie, 1994; Ganetz, 1995). Angela McRobbie (1994, pp. 175–178), for instance, argued for 'a reappraisal of the pleasures of femininity'. This approach tends to focus on young women as creative consumers, as the subjects of consumer culture rather than as the passive objects of marketing ideology. Such approaches emphasise that women are able to resist, challenge and re-appropriate consumer goods in order to fashion their own identities. Considerable emphasis is placed on young women's ability to subvert patriarchal norms, enabling a degree of resistance to prescriptive definitions of what it means to be (and to look) feminine. Mica Nava (1992) highlights the ways in which young women are able to use consumer culture for their own style creation, premised on the conviction that, far from being objects of the male gaze, 'the possibility of aestheticizing the body has been primarily a *privilege* of women ever since the romantic period' (p. 73). From this perspective, consumer culture is seen as a 'creative space' in which girls and young women are able to develop their potential for symbolic creativity and self-expression (Ganetz, 1995, p. 88).

Adulthood

Adulthood is largely associated with taking up full status in society – with having sexual relationships, getting married, having children, holding a full-time job and living in an independent household. Again, this is not a universal view, however – the concept of adulthood varies historically and geographically and, much like the social meaning and experience of childhood and adolescence, is shaped by a range of factors including gender, social class, race and ethnicity, disability and global power relations. In most Western societies, adulthood is associated with citizenship status – the right to vote, to take out loans or to enter a legal contract. In some societies, such as in India, a woman comes to be seen as an adult only when she gives birth to a son. In most Western societies the transition to adulthood is not usually marked by 'rites of passage' as in traditional, non-Western societies, but there are ritual markers associated with the process. These can take three forms: private markers (such as first menstruation, first sex, first alcoholic drink); public markers (such as marriage or graduation, eighteenth or twenty-first birthday parties); official markers (such as the right to vote).

Adulthood and sexual difference

These rituals take place in different ways and often have a different meaning for women than for men. Entering adult society usually takes place a few years earlier for young women than for young men since they generally marry earlier, have sex earlier, and so on. For young women (particularly those in developing or post-colonial societies) such life transitions are often accelerated and this is particularly the case also for working-class women, while for middle-class young women life transitions are often more protracted. This also varies across Western cultures – for example, in Germany or Denmark young people generally get married and start households later than is the case in Britain.

These life-status transitions also have different meanings for different sexes. While the beginning of sexual activity can be a source of great pleasure and pride for young men, for young women it can be difficult territory to negotiate – a complex series of bargains and transactions, sometimes involving coercion or physical violence, or concerns about not being seen as a frigid 'drag' on the one hand or as a promiscuous 'slag' on the other (Cowie and Lees, 1985; Halson, 1991; Holland *et al.*, 1994). Marriage too has different meanings for men and for women, as do childbirth and parenthood, since women have the main responsibility for these and often have to interrupt their careers to care for children. Increasing numbers of women in Western societies are raising children without a male partner for at least some period of time – as we noted above, the majority (90 per cent) of lone-parent families are headed by women (see Chapter 6).

Adulthood and the body

Although the bodies of both men and women change as they progress through the life course, women's lives are often perceived as more intimately tied to their biology and reproductive cycles than men's. As men are perceived as universally rational beings who are defined in relation to their performance and action in the labour market and public life, their reproductive functions and bodies are seldom referred to and tend to be seen as relatively unproblematic. Women's bodies and reproductive functions, on the other hand, are constantly discussed and are often seen as in some ways determining their lives (Ussher, 1989).

Ussher argues that in the nineteenth century women were seen as prey to their wombs through hysteria, an illness thought to be caused directly by emanations from the womb, and to their peculiar disposition to illnesses such as neurasthenia which required them to take constant rest and special diets. However, even at the beginning of the twenty-first century, women are still seen as victims of various biological processes. If we begin with menstruation, women are frequently seen as victims of 'raging hormones' either because their 'periods' are just beginning, because they have 'premenstrual tension' or because their hormone levels are declining, in the case of menopause. In each condition women are often thought to suffer from temporary indisposition bordering on insanity. Thus premenstrual tension is often given as the reason for moodiness or inconsistency at work.

On account of these biological 'problems', women's life course is more likely to be subject to medical intervention or to be seen as a kind of disease (see Chapter 7). Women are often recommended hormone replacement therapy or hysterectomies as a solution to menopausal problems. Women are given hormone treatment or special diets for premenstrual tension or irregular menstruation. The fact that many problems associated with such life changes can also be traced to social and psychological issues is overlooked in the enthusiasm to find medical explanations and 'cures'. For example, Ussher (1989) found that premenstrual symptoms were very varied and there was no one pattern or experience of them for women. For some women it was a pleasurable and for some women a miserable experience. Some women did not even notice it. Experience of menstrual tension depended to a great extent on what other things were taking place in a woman's life. Nevertheless this 'problem' is frequently subject to medical diagnosis and intervention.

Nelly Oudshoorn (1994) points to the ways in which science has constructed the hormonally controlled female body and the ways in which medical science has come to manufacture and mass-produce drugs (especially the contraceptive pill) in order to control sex and the female body. The introduction of the 'hormonally controlled' body concept, the idea that hormonal treatment can cure many of the problems from which women suffer – 'female problems' or 'women's troubles' – has resulted in the notion that control can be exercised over women through their bodies from menstruation to menopause. 'Women's problems' – premenstrual tension, unwanted pregnancy, hot flushes, and so on – can be controlled by medication. The natural female body can be controlled by male scientific knowledge, and in the process women's lives come even more closely under the scrutiny of (patriarchal) medical science. This, of course, reinforces the notion that women are different from and inferior to men and in need of male (rational, scientific) control.

> Imagine what might have happened in a world with different cultural and moral attitudes towards gender and responsibilities for family planning and children. It is not beyond imagination that we would have ended up with a male contraceptive pill, a medical treatment for male menopause and a classification system of multiple sexes.
>
> (Oudshoorn, 1994, p. 151)

Ageing itself is a problematic process for women in a society which defines them primarily in terms of the body, and which values physical attractiveness as the defining feature of femininity. Losing this attractiveness is often a major source of anxiety, and women are constantly exhorted through advertising to control their bodies with the help of creams or potions, dieting, exercise or even plastic surgery. Although men are also increasingly purchasing such goods and services, it is to women's anxieties that most of the advertising is directed.

Women who have passed the menopause are seen as having no use anymore for their reproductive functions and therefore as uninterested in sex. Doctors are more likely to recommend hysterectomies for them, and sex is often seen as of no more importance to them. In medical textbooks their ovaries and reproductive organs are seen as 'shrivelled' or 'senile', metaphors which imply that they are used up and useless. Men's organs, on the contrary, are never described like this, although they too undergo physiological changes with age. The removal of sexual organs is never recommended for older men in the same way that hysterectomy is for older women, as though they had no use for such organs (Martin, 1987).

Women are classified as 'premenstrual' in their youth, as 'pre-menopausal' in their thirties, 'menopausal' in their forties and 'post-menopausal' in their fifties, as though the experiences of their reproductive organs define their lives and can be used as a classificatory system for women generally. The menopause is seen as a loss of function, a decline of some kind. However, women have more recently tried to redefine this life phase and to see it instead as a new beginning, a new period of growth in their lives. Far from it being associated with a loss of sexual activity, some women report that sexual desire becomes stronger (Ussher, 1989).

Women and motherhood

Similarly, women who have children find themselves defined in terms of their roles as mothers and carers (see Chapters 6 and 7). Once pregnant, their bodies are the subject of continuous examination and supervision by medical experts, and the experience of birth itself is increasingly one controlled by technology and remote expertise rather than by the woman herself, although considerable efforts have been made in many societies recently to reclaim childbirth for women, in midwife-led 'birthing centres' for instance. It still remains the case, however, that the time and location of the birth is chosen frequently by doctors rather than by the woman herself.

On the other hand, childless women are often seen as frustrated mothers, as somehow incomplete; condemned to a marginal life. Having children is seen as women's ultimate goal, irrespective of whatever else they may have achieved in life, so that the lack of children often has to be explained by some 'problem' – the woman's psychological inadequacies, biological 'failure', or her lack of feminine qualities or more often that she is a 'career woman' and therefore not maternal. Now that women are able more easily to have careers, they are often described as selfish for committing themselves to a career instead of having children. Men are not seen as suffering from such problems, whether or not they father children.

These essentialist theories of femininity can be seen as ideologies and discourses which construct women's lives in particular ways – ways which are derogatory and which see them as biologically controlled. This also helps to provide legitimation for medical control and intervention in women's lives – their problems (which can have many sources) are explained and treated in terms of their biology. This reinforces the idea raised in Chapter 1 that men do the analysing and it is women as the 'Other' who need explaining. What needs 'explaining' is why their bodies are different from men's, which are seen as the norm. These biological discourses surrounding women's bodies help to prevent women's sexuality or reproductive cycles from being seen in any other way. Although they are presented as 'scientific', they in fact reflect a male view of the world (Sayers, 1986).

Ageing

Broadly speaking, sociologists have developed three distinct perspectives on ageing. Functionalist analyses, drawing on the ideas of Talcott Parsons, argue that as ageing disrupts the social order, society's response is to disengage older people by gradually transferring their roles and status to the next generation so that social tasks are performed with minimal interruption. Much like the 'sick role' whereby ill people are defined as 'sick' and hence absolved of their normal social responsibilities (see Chapter 7), older people are granted greater freedom so that what might otherwise be thought of as socially unacceptable or deviant behaviour is defined as harmless eccentricity (Cumming and Henry, 1961). A functionalist perspective on ageing, also known as 'disengagement theory', emphasises that social order is maintained through disengaging people as they age, from their social roles and responsibilities, and transferring these to the next generation.

Sociologists have largely rejected disengagement theory in recent years. As Macionis and Plummer (2002, p. 336) outline, this is due to its four main weaknesses. First, large numbers of people cannot disengage from paid work because of financial insecurity. Second, many elderly people do not wish to disengage from their established social roles. Third, there is no evidence that the benefits of disengagement outweigh its costs – in an ageing society, high levels of disengagement may be socially dysfunctional – a point we return to below. Fourth, disengagement theory defines elderly people as passive 'victims' of the ageing process, and recent sociological research has emphasised that this is not the case.

This latter point is addressed most clearly by those who adopt a symbolic interactionist perspective on ageing which, as Macionis and Plummer note, is almost a 'mirror image' of a functionalist approach. This is because, instead of disengagement, an interactionist understanding of ageing focuses on the ways in which older people actively construct the meaning and experience of being 'old'. Also known as 'activity theory', interactionist perspectives propose that what it means to be old is socially constructed through the meanings that are attached, including those attached by elderly people themselves, to later life. As Macionis and Plummer note,

> Activity theory thus shifts the focus of analysis from the needs of society (as stated in disengagement theory) to the needs of the elderly themselves. This second approach also highlights social diversity among elderly people.
>
> (Macionis and Plummer, 2002, p. 336)

Again, this latter point in particular is developed by the third main sociological perspective on ageing – what has come to be known as 'critical gerontology'. Critical gerontologists emphasise the relationship between ageing and inequality (Atchley, 1982; Phillipson, 1982). Drawing on ideas and concepts derived from Marxism, they highlight how different age categories compete for social and economic resources, and how this contributes to age stratification. In most Western societies, middle-aged people have the largest share of social power and status, while elderly people (and children) have less and hence are at greater risk of social deprivation and poverty. In a bid to keep down wages, employers often dispense with older workers in favour of younger (and hence cheaper) employees. Critical or neo-Marxist gerontologists have argued, therefore, that age stratification is central to the maintenance of capitalist societies. Because capitalism has an overriding concern with profit, those social groups defined as unproductive come to be regarded as second-class citizens. Highlighting what conflict theorists call 'structured dependency' – the process through which some people receive a limited share of social, political and economic resources as a consequence of the relations of production (Vincent, 1996) – critical gerontologists draw attention also to social diversity in later life.

Feminist perspectives on ageing

Feminists have emphasised that age stratification is compounded by gender inequalities, so that female children and the elderly are doubly disadvantaged (Arber and Ginn, 1995). They have also highlighted the ways in which inequalities experienced throughout the life course – in education, the labour market, the family and the household, for instance, as well as in politics – further exacerbate women's disadvantage in later life, increasing women's vulnerability to poverty, to abuse and also to social isolation and deprivation. This is particularly the case as women are disproportionately represented among the increasing numbers of elderly people.

An increasing proportion of the Western world consists of elderly people. It is estimated that in Britain, the population of pensionable age will have exceeded the number of children by 2007 (www.nso.gov.uk). People live longer and birth rates in many parts of the world have been falling. This is an issue for older women because the majority of elderly people are women. The proportion of people aged over 65 has grown both in absolute terms and as a proportion of the population of most Western societies, including the UK. This shift in the age structure of the population will have marked implications for society as a whole, and for patterns of social organisation. Women outnumber men in the elderly population, and this discrepancy increases with advancing age: at ages 70–74 there are roughly four women for every three men; at 80–84 there are two women for every man, and by 95 the ratio becomes three to one (Walker and Maltby, 1997).

Ageing populations

The ageing population is often referred to as a 'demographic time bomb' because the number of dependent children relative to productive age groups (the dependency ratio) is increasing. Changes predicted for the twenty-first century suggest a dramatic increase in the dependency ratio, often attributed to rising longevity as a result of rising living standards, and advances in medical technology and provision. One key area of concern is the health care system, and the increasing demands likely to be made on it. Other social issues and implications of an ageing population include:

- *an increased incidence of various forms of disability*, and a growing need for health and social services, and financial support;
- *the need to rethink retirement*, in relation to the changing shape of the life course, new patterns of work and leisure in later life, and changing incomes of the elderly;
- *an increasing prevalence of poverty*, as a result of greater strain on finances for some groups in old age as a result of living longer;
- *changes in the family*, and a need to rethink familial roles and expectations as the 'young old' look after the 'old old', and developments such as assisted conception mean that older people may have children;
- *psycho-social issues* such as problems of isolation and bereavement, raising the need for new meanings of later life and the need for communities of support;
- *political issues* such as the rise of the 'grey vote' and pressure groups. A new politics of ageing may begin to emerge;

- *cultural representations of the elderly* need to be rethought as ageing becomes recognised as an increasingly varied social experience;
- *the concept of community* needs to address social phenomena such as the development of retirement colonies (such as lesbian and gay communities in Palm Springs, or gated communities in Florida and other parts of the USA).

(Macionis and Plummer, 2002, p. 328)

Just as the earlier stages of the life course are socially constructed, so too are the later stages, sociologists have argued. Class differences are often important in retirement for instance. Working-class retirement may often lack an 'active concept of retirement', whereas middle-class retirement, with better resources, has led to an expanding consumer market and culture aimed at attracting the 'grey pound' (Blaikie, 1999; Hockey and James, 2002). Social variations in the meaning and experience of old age can be illustrated by looking at how older people are differently treated at different points in history and in different cultures. Among the Venda-speaking people in Africa, elderly people have a particular authority because of their perceived proximity to the spirit world: grey hair is seen as a positive sign of status rather than a negative one (Hockey and James, 1993). In most societies older men have more status and power than older women.

In our own society, the treatment of later life can be shown to have varied considerably too over time. Giarchi (2000), for example, identifies three main historical periods – pre-modern, high modern (or Fordist) and postmodern or post-Fordist periods. In the pre-modern era ageing was seen as negative, but it was not seen as being attached to any particular chronological age – rather, it was seen as a general deterioration, but also a sign of wisdom and authority. Although the old body occasioned disgust, the old woman's body excited particular disgust because beauty and love were associated with younger bodies. Erasmus (1466–1536), for example, wrote of older women: 'these broken-down women, these walking corpses, stinking bodies. They display their flaccid, disgusting breasts and sometimes they try to stimulate their lovers' vigour with quavering yelps' (cited in Giarchi, 2000).

In the modern period, associated with industrial capitalism, a number of transformations took place.

- First, *old age was medicalised* – it came to be seen as a medical condition requiring medical intervention and control, despite the fact that most elderly people are healthy.
- Second, *the body came to be seen as a machine*, one where the parts were wearing out or breaking down. The broken-down, unproductive body was one to be discarded or no longer used in the industrial process – it was relegated to a different area of life. (Women, of course, are seen to have unproductive bodies when they have been through the menopause; at a younger age than men they are seen as past being productive workers.)
- Third, there was *the development of the welfare state*, which sections off old age according to legal norms of retirement (between 60 and 70 in most European countries – although in some societies such as the USA there is no formal age of retirement) and entitlements to pensions and other benefits. In most countries

women are compelled to retire earlier, despite the fact that they are most likely to live longer than men and therefore for women the period of retirement can be relatively long. The vast array of care systems associated with the development of the welfare state serves further to relegate older people to being burdens, in need of assistance and a drain on the productive population. However, many of the carers are themselves older women over the age of retirement, as are those employed in the care system. Both the carers and the cared-for are often women in later life.

• Other *cultural changes* included the change in the nature of family life, with elderly people increasingly disengaged from the family (50 per cent of women over the age of 60 live alone). The shift towards youthful fashions and the pre-eminence of the ability to participate in consumer culture tends to marginalise older people who have lower incomes (Giarchi, 2000).

The result has been a tendency to 'infantilise' the elderly – to treat them in the same way as children: as having less authority, less status, as being unable to make decisions for themselves, and as being people who are not suited for sexual activity. This latter point is particularly gendered; while older women are often seen as sexually redundant, older men are often seen as justified in their sexual libido as long as it is with younger women.

Giarchi (2000) goes on to identify a third phase of post-modernisation in which the life course is deconstructed and rigid demarcations of age begin to disappear as life gets longer, and early as well as later retirement becomes more common. During this phase (in relatively privileged sectors of affluent, Western societies), alternative, pluralistic significations of age emerge with older people associated with a range of activities including continuing education. However, the continuity of ideas associated with modernity and Fordism tends to slow down the liberating potentialities of this postmodern age, Giarchi argues.

The increasing numbers of elderly people and their changing position has led to a questioning of the position of the elderly and the formation of pressure groups such as the 'Grey Panthers' to defend their interests. In the words of Grey Panthers' leader Margaret Kuhn: 'Our oppressive, paternalistic society wants to keep the elderly out of the way, playing bingo and shuffleboard. . . . We are not mellowed, sweet people. We're outraged' (quoted in Giarchi, 2000). Consequently, many older people (particularly those from relatively privileged social groups in Western societies) are challenging the notion that they are dependent and lonely, that they are in ill-health or that they are mentally confused or demented. Arber and Ginn (1991) argue that an increased political consciousness may be developing amongst older people around such issues. Many of the diseases of old age can be traced to environmental problems such as pollution rather than old age per se and affect only some old people just as they affect some younger people.

There is great variation in the experience of ageing however; while for many people retirement may be a period in the life course marked by increased leisure and freedom, for others it is one of deprivation and exclusion. This is particularly the case in terms of the ways in which ageing is shaped by sexual difference (the difference between men and women). The situation of women in later life in fact magnifies their inequalities at earlier stages of the life course. This is linked to factors such as gender,

139

class, race and how old they are (see the Black Report, 1978; Whitehead, 1987). Since the Second World War, there has been a dramatic rise in the proportion of older people living alone throughout most Western societies. In most countries, the older population is predominantly female, largely as a result of sex differences in mortality. In the UK, the National Health Service and Community Care Act 1990 (implemented in 1993) was intended to reaffirm the objective of allowing older people to remain in their own homes for as long as possible, and hence to reduce the number of people in residential or institutional care. Other European countries such as Sweden and the Netherlands have also implemented explicit policy objectives to reduce the use of institutional care and in the US, a decline in the 'institutionalisation' of older people has been attributed, in part, to increased use of home care and the development of new housing schemes, including 'assisted living' units (Tomassini *et al.*, 2004). However, in the UK, over half of people living in communal establishments are women living in residential care and nursing homes, and the majority of these women (87 per cent) are over state pension age. According to the 2001 Census, there were two and a half times as many women in residential care and nursing homes as men in 2001 (www.statistics.gov.uk).

Poverty is particularly a problem for older women. First, they are likely to live longer than older men and to find themselves in the category of the very elderly, who are generally poorer. Second, due to their interrupted careers in the labour market and their positions, which are generally in lower-paid, lower-status jobs, they are less likely to benefit from occupational pension schemes (Groves, 1992; Walker, 1992). Older women are more likely than men to be living alone – nearly half of Britain's 3.1 million one-person households are one-pensioner only and three-quarters of these are occupied by a woman living alone (in younger age groups, male occupants outnumber women by three to two). Single-person households are least likely to have amenities such as central heating or sole use of a bath/shower and toilet. More than one in eight single-person pensioner households do not have central heating, and over 21,000 pensioner households do not have sole use of a bath/shower and toilet. The experience of old age is also shaped by disability; according to the Census 2001, 60.4 per cent of pensioner-only households contain someone with a mobility limiting long-term illness or disability (www.statistics.gov.uk).

Older people are more likely to be living in poverty than other age groups, and older women are especially vulnerable to poverty in all societies (Storey-Gibson, 1985).

> In addition to sex-based inequalities in income and household resources, older women in general are more disadvantaged than men. . . . They are three times more likely than older men to be living alone, and only half as likely to have a spouse. Older women report more illness and long-standing health problems and consult their GPs more frequently than men. . . . Older women are also more likely than older men to suffer from psychological problems such as loneliness and anxiety and to have lower levels of morale or life satisfaction.
>
> (Walker, 1992, p. 181)

In Western societies, men more than women have traditionally experienced the transition to retirement. As more women are undertaking paid work outside of the home, however, this pattern is changing, although sociologists have argued that women do not 'retire' in the same way as men, and that when a male partner retires a woman's workload may actually be increased (Arber and Ginn, 1995).

As many societies place such a strong emphasis on youth, the elderly (and especially elderly women) may encounter discrimination and ageism. Much like other forms of discrimination, ageism can be direct (denying a person a job because he or she is deemed to be 'too old' for instance), or more subtle and covert but no less pervasive (like when people speak to the elderly with a condescending tone, as if they were children). In her book *The Fountain of Age*, liberal feminist Betty Friedan (1993) argued that ageism is central to Western cultures, and that women in particular are subject to it, as they are often thought to be 'too old' at a younger age than men. Friedan argued that older women are notably absent in the mass media; only a small percentage of television programmes feature characters who are over 60. In addition, when older characters are portrayed, they are often represented in negative terms so that being old is perceived largely as a time of 'disease, deterioration and decline'.

In sum, the experience of ageing is shaped by numerous transitions some of which might be particularly problematic for individuals, such as those brought on by physical decline. Other problems – such as poverty, social isolation and ageism – are social. While the meaning of ageing varies historically and socially, for many people (particularly women) growing old is an experience of increasing social disadvantage and isolation. Feminists have argued that later life compounds many of the forms of oppression experienced by women throughout the life course.

Conclusions

This chapter has examined the life course in relation to a range of male–female dynamics and relationships involved in childhood, adolescence, adulthood and ageing. It has considered a range of issues relating to sexuality and motherhood, the labour market, education, consumer culture, the body and the consequences of an ageing society. It has also considered these various issues in terms of social stratification and inequalities, and the politics and economics of global power relations, and how these shape the social meaning and experience of being a child, an adolescent, an adult or an older person. The various inequalities considered here are not superficial, but are embedded within social structures and cultural values, as well as in the relationship between production and reproduction, and between family responsibilities and paid work.

In some parts of the world, improved social opportunities for girls and young women have built up expectations of greater equality in both working and family life, which may be frustrated by lived experiences of the labour market and of male behaviour. This requires young women in the West to somehow resolve the conflict between the often incompatible goals of a competitive labour market and motherhood. In societies such as the UK, gender is of less significance in determining a person's life chances than in developing or post-colonial societies. Even within these more affluent societies, young women of lower socio-economic status or of particular ethnic or national origins still tend to have relatively limited opportunities.

Inequalities between men and women undermine development and prospects for reducing poverty; studies show that societies in which discrimination against girls and women is greatest experience more poverty, slower economic development and a lower quality of life than do less oppressive societies. As the United Nations report on the situation of girls and young women concludes:

> The world is witnessing significant changes, many of which are increasing the level of vulnerability among girls and young women. Depression, eating disorders, suicide attempts and other psychological problems have all become more common in developed countries, threatening girls and young women who are in the process of establishing adult female identities. Girls and young women in developing countries are vulnerable to the health risks that emerge in connection with inadequate food and medical services.
>
> (United Nations, 2003, p. 266)

In many cultures, boys are valued more than girls from birth or even earlier, and this pattern continues throughout the life course. Many adolescent girls and adult women as well as older women continue to be defined according to patriarchal norms which construct femininity largely in terms of the needs of men. Sociological research emphasises that women's lives are often defined in terms of age stages, which are seen as 'natural'. At each stage of the life course women are often thought to be controlled by their biology, and particularly their hormones. Feminists have challenged this and argued that life stages for women are *socially* constructed, as they are for men. Malestream theories have either not challenged biological explanations for women or have constructed the 'scientific' knowledge which sustains the view that women are controlled by their biology. Feminists have argued that men have used this knowledge to reinforce their power over women, in medicine and health care, for instance; knowledge about women (including social scientific knowledge) constructed by men has been used to control and subordinate them.

In various parts of the world, a pattern of life course convergence is occurring between men and women. In some Western societies, in particular, this convergence is taking place with regard to educational experiences and attainment, work and career opportunities, and lifestyles. However, those girls and young women and older women who are exposed to a relatively poor quality of life tend to experience high levels of vulnerability to poverty, violence and abuse; in Western societies, immigrant and ethnic minority women are the worst affected; in other parts of the world, women from a range of social backgrounds continue to be subject to a range of inequalities and forms of oppression throughout the life course.

SUMMARY

1 Key stages in the life course – childhood, adolescence, adulthood and ageing – are socially, culturally and historically variable, and are shaped by a range of other aspects of identity including social class, disability, global power relations and sexual difference.

2 Throughout the life course women experience a range of inequalities and forms of oppression.

3 Women are more often defined in relation to their bodies, and their physical attributes, than men.

4 Old age is particularly a problem for women because the majority of the elderly are women and the majority of the poor elderly are women.

5 The numbers of elderly, especially elderly women, are increasing.

6 On the one hand, the crisis of the welfare systems in Europe means that there may be less scope for caring for the elderly in future and there are concerns about how to pay their pensions; however, there are also 'postmodernising' tendencies which could lead to the liberation of elderly people.

FURTHER READING

Arber, S. and Ginn, J. (eds) (1995) *Connecting Gender and Ageing: A Sociological Approach.* Buckingham: Open University Press. This book focuses specifically on the gendered meaning and experience of ageing, considering the effects of ageing on men and women's social roles, relationships and identities.

Hockey, J. and James, A. (2002) *Social Identities Across The Life Course.* London: Palgrave. This text draws on sociological, anthropological and social policy perspectives on the life course. It also considers postmodern perspectives on self and identity in relation to childhood, youth, adulthood and ageing, focusing on themes such as sexuality, consumer culture and the body.

James, A., Jenks, C. and Prout, A. (1998) *Theorising Childhood.* Cambridge: Polity. This is a key text in the developing 'sociology of childhood' literature that outlines sociological perspectives on childhood, as well as considering variations in the meaning and experience of being a child.

United Nations (2003) *World Youth Report.* Vienna: United Nations. (www.un.org/esa/socdev/unyin/wyr/index.html). This report focuses on the situation of young men and women in terms of global power relations, and includes a detailed study specifically of girls and young women.

CHAPTER SIX

The family and the household

The family is a concept that is familiar to all of us in some form or another. Most people regard themselves as members of one or more families and the family forms to which we belong can be very diverse. What we think of as a family can vary enormously in terms of co-residence, economic relations, roles and responsibilities, sexual orientation and reproduction; the family is clearly a dynamic social phenomenon – one that varies historically, geographically and culturally.

Yet, in market societies at least, we are constantly bombarded with images of a particular type of family – what anthropologist Edmund Leach (1967) called 'the cereal-packet family' – consisting of a breadwinner husband and his children, all being cared for by a smiling wife. We come to think of this as the normal, natural and inevitable family form. In fact only one in twenty households in contemporary Britain consists of a father in paid employment, a dependent wife and two children.

In order to understand something of the complexity of domestic life we need to distinguish 'the family' – a group of relatives – from 'the household' – a more technical term used to describe people living in one home, who may or may not be related. The nuclear family (in the form of the cereal-packet family) is often the unit which is assumed in advertising, housing and social policy, and it is to this that we shall mainly be referring here. However, it is important to emphasise from the outset that this is an ideal – an ideal which does not necessarily fit the reality, and one which is not descriptively neutral but value-laden. Dianne Gittens, in challenging the view that the family is a universal institution which performs essential functions for individuals and societies, has pointed out that:

> Social recognition of mating and of parenthood is obviously intimately bound up with social definitions and customs of marriage. It is often assumed that, in spite of a variety of marriage customs and laws, marriage as a binding relationship between a man and a woman is universal. Yet it is estimated that only ten per cent of all marriages in the world are actually monogamous; polygyny and polyandry are common in many societies, just as serial monogamy is becoming increasingly common in our own. Marriage is not always a heterosexual relationship. The Nuer . . . practise a custom known as 'ghost marriages' whereby when an unmarried or childless man dies, a relation of his then marries a woman 'to his name' and the resulting children of this union are regarded as the dead man's children and bear his name.
>
> (Gittens, 1992, p. 69)

Sociologists have tended to assume that the modern Western, largely white and middle-class idea of the family is what is, if not actually the norm, then what *should* be the norm, elsewhere as here. In this type of family there is assumed to be a gendered division of labour such that the man takes on the major responsibility for earning a wage and the woman for caring, even if she also works outside of the home. This view of the family is one that is widely shared as an ideal. Hence, although other family forms such as single-parent families, same-sex partnerships, extended families or re-formed families are increasingly common not just in the UK but in many societies, they are not necessarily seen as normal or desirable. Indeed, families in which no father is present to exercise control are often seen, in Western societies at least, as the cause of social problems such as crime, juvenile delinquency and welfare dependency in later life.

Sociological perspectives on the family

In sociology the family has traditionally been seen as a social institution formed on the basis of kinship – a social bond based on blood, marriage or adoption that unites individuals into close social groups and networks. More recently, sociologists such as David Morgan (1999) have begun to argue that the family is best understood as a set of practices (as opposed to an institution) so that rather than thinking of the family as something we are 'in' it is more appropriately thought of as something that we 'do'; this reflects the view that our social experiences are shaped not just by social structures but also by agency – our capacity to act (see Chapter 1). Throughout the world, families tend to form on the basis of marriage. Embedded within the English language is evidence of an enduring cultural belief that (heterosexual) marriage is the most appropriate context for procreation – indeed, as Macionis and Plummer (2002) note, the word 'matrimony' in Latin means 'the condition of motherhoood'. Traditionally children born out of wedlock have been referred to as 'illegitimate'. The cultural association of the family with marriage and childbearing, at least in many Western societies has begun to weaken (in reality if not in familial ideology), however, and an increasingly diverse range of lived experiences of the family and procreation now exist.

In Sweden, for instance, more than 20 per cent of adults live alone, and a large proportion of adults (some 25 per cent) live together outside of marriage. Half of all Swedish children (compared to about one in three in Europe as a whole) are born to unmarried parents. Average household size in Sweden is the smallest in the world – 2.2 persons (Macionis and Plummer, 2002). Yet even in Sweden (which also has the highest number of women in the labour force –77 per cent, as opposed to 59 per cent in Europe generally) – as a glance through the idealised images of family life in the IKEA catalogue (supposedly now read by more people the world over than the Bible) suggests – the family remains central to Swedish society, albeit in a more diverse range of forms than in previous generations, or in more conservative societies. Let us look now at what sense sociologists have made of the family as a social institution.

Functionalist perspectives

Sociologists have claimed that the family is a central and necessary institution in society. Structural-functionalist sociologists, largely following the work of Talcott Parsons, have argued that the family performs a variety of functions. Parsons and Bales (1955), for instance, argued that the family:

1 *Is the primary agent of socialisation* – ideally, parents teach their children to be well-integrated and contributing members of society although, of course, socialisation continues throughout the life course.
2 *Regulates sexual activity* – in the interests of maintaining kinship patterns and property rights. Hence, one relatively universal sexual norm is the 'incest taboo', although precisely which kin fall within its boundaries varies.
3 *Maintains social placement* – some aspects of identity are pronounced at birth – sex, race, and so on – others are prescribed – gender, ethnicity, religion – and are learned and acquired largely through the family (see 1, above). The family therefore maintains social position, inheritance rights and social transmission.
4 *Provides material and emotional security* – the family, for many, is a key site of physical protection, emotional support and financial assistance, as signified by many English language sayings such as 'home is where the heart is', or the belief that the family is 'a heaven in a heartless world', that 'blood is thicker than water', and so on.

Functionalist perspectives have tended to assume that the co-resident nuclear family, with a gendered division of labour, is the one most suited to the needs of industrial society. In doing so, they have tended to assume that within this context, familial relations are relatively consensual and harmonious. For Parsons and Bales (1955) the family is the 'backbone of society' – an institution that serves the interests of society as a whole.

Conflict perspectives

More critical (conflict) theories have drawn attention to the ways in which inequalities are perpetuated within, and because of, the family. Marxists have challenged the 'rosy' picture painted by functionalist sociologists to the extent that they have suggested that the family meets the needs not of society as a whole but specifically of capitalism, and so serves the interests primarily of the ruling class. Marxists have emphasised that the nuclear family serves the interests of capitalism by reproducing the workforce and also by consuming the goods and services produced by capitalist economies (see Chapter 2).

However, both approaches have tended to take the domestic division of labour for granted. This is largely because both Marxist and functionalist theories of the family have tended to look at the relationships between the family and society and have not examined relationships *within* the family, nor have they considered how these internal relationships both structure and are structured by external social, economic and power relations shaped by sexual difference (the difference between men and women as social subjects – see Chapter 2). Hence, the domestic sphere has tended (until relatively recently) to be regarded as a largely private arena – not only outside of public concern, but also beyond (or beneath) the concerns of sociologists. Feminist sociologists, by contrast, have highlighted the position of women in families and argued that the family is one of the main ways in which women are oppressed.

The symmetrical family

One of the most influential sociological studies of the family was undertaken in Britain by Willmott and Young in the 1960s (Young and Willmott, 1973), building on previous studies they had carried out in London into families in the 1950s (Willmott and Young, 1957). Their research was undertaken in a period when rehousing policies and increased affluence meant that most young people, when they married, could set up home independently, and more geographical mobility meant they often did so at some distance from their kin. It was argued, partly as a consequence of this and partly because more married women (including those with children) were undertaking paid employment, that the division of labour between men and women in the domestic sphere was changing; Willmott and Young predicted that men would take on more domestic work and women would be more likely to work outside the home. They argued that the family would become more democratic, with both partners sharing decision-making and financial resources. It was suggested that rather than having segregated conjugal roles, where husbands and wives did different jobs within the house and had separate activities and friends, husbands and wives were increasingly spending their spare time together and had friends in common. The main conclusion of the Willmott and Young studies was that the British family was becoming increasingly symmetrical – that is, the roles of husbands and wives were becoming more alike and would eventually become identical. Willmott and Young were careful to argue that this was the *emergent* family form – the way that the family was developing, not the way that it was already – but argued that in Britain there was a definite progression in this direction.

Feminist approaches to the family

Feminists have challenged the view that the family is becoming more egalitarian and symmetrical arguing, by contrast, that the family is a site of inequality in which women are subordinated. Feminists have argued that this is largely because of women's position as wives and mothers, and because socialisation processes in the family, during which children internalise patriarchal ideas and transmit them to their own children, perpetuate male domination and female subordination.

Feminists argue that women's position in the family as wife/mother results in a position of subordination to men/fathers, at least in part because of economic dependency, but also because of widely shared ideologies of the family. While Marxist feminists stress that women's exploitation in the family serves the interests of capitalism, radical feminists stress that it serves the interests of men, who benefit from

147

the unpaid labour of women in a system of patriarchy. They are agreed, however, that the family oppresses women and that women are exploited and subordinated within it. Thus feminists have questioned not only sociological assumptions concerning the family, but common-sense ones as well. Sociologists Christine Delphy and Diana Leonard (1992) have argued that the family is an economic system in which men benefit from the work of women (and in many countries and cultures, the work of children too). Family members effectively work for the (male) head of household they argue, and so men benefit both from women's work in the labour market and their (unpaid) work in the home.

Barrie Thorne (1982) has argued that four themes are central to the feminist challenge to the conventional sociology of the family:

1 *Assumptions concerning the structure and functioning of the family.* Feminists challenge an ideology that sees the co-resident nuclear family with a gendered division of labour as the only natural and legitimate form. Feminists argue against the view that any specific family form is natural – that is, based on biological imperatives.
2 *Feminists have sought to claim the family as an area for analysis;* a move which challenges the gender-based categories of analysis in malestream sociology (see Chapter 1).
3 *Feminists argue that different members of families experience family life in different ways.* They argue that women's experiences of motherhood and family life have demonstrated that families embody power relationships that can and do result in conflict, violence and the inequitable distribution of work and resources.
4 *Feminists question the assumption that the family should be thought of as a private sphere.* While women and children (particularly in very traditional societies) are often cut off from outside contact on religious or cultural grounds, feminists argue that the form the family takes in most societies is heavily influenced by economic and social policies and the family is (and should be) permeable to outside intervention.

It is argued that common-sense beliefs about the nature of the family deny women the opportunity to participate in wider society and gain equality with men. It is in this way, also, that we can explain women's exclusion from the labour market or their relative disadvantage within it, as well as their relative marginalisation in youth cultures, political life and other areas of social life discussed elsewhere in this book.

Industrialisation and the origins of the family wage

Feminists have examined the history of family life and changes in the way in which the family is organised, particularly in industrialised societies. There is some disagreement amongst feminists as to whether or not women have always been subordinated and exploited in the family, or whether their subordination is a result of the growth and development of capitalism. Radical feminists argue that patriarchy (the domination of women by men) in the patriarchal mode of production (the family) existed long before the development of capitalism. Marxist feminists argue that the economic dependency of women on men, which enables them to be dominated and exploited in the family, is a result of the growth of industrial capitalism. Dual-systems feminists suggest that the ideology of patriarchy predates capitalism but that the way in which women are exploited and subordinated in industrialised societies is a result of the interaction of this ideology with the material relations of production (the way in which goods and services are produced and the relationship between the workers and the owners of the means of production) in capitalist society. Feminist critical theorists have highlighted the ways in which women's role in the family problematises the Marxist category of 'production' emphasising the work involved in reproduction. Most recently, Black and post-colonial feminists have criticised Western feminism for its ethnocentric analysis of women's experience of the family.

For women in industrialised societies the greatest change that has occurred in the family since the seventeenth century has been the institutionalisation of the 'house-wife and mother' role. As Engels (1972) argued in his book *The Origin of the Family, Private Property and the State* (originally published in 1884), before industrialisation the product of labour was regarded as the joint property of the family, and not seen as the property of individuals to be divided up. Every member of the family worked to produce what the family needed – there was no distinction between production and consumption. With industrialisation the home became separated from the place of work – consumption from production. Gradually women became associated with the domestic sphere, the care of the home and children, and men with the public sphere, earning a wage and participating in politics. These changes were gradual and affected different classes at different times.

Most middle-class women in Britain accepted the housewife role by the beginning of the nineteenth century, and the number of working-class women in officially recog-nised paid employment (as recorded by the Census) declined rapidly after 1850. Roberts's (1982) research demonstrates that by 1900 the majority of working-class women thought that ideally a wife should stay at home to care for her husband and children, although there were regional variations.

The changes brought about by the industrial revolution altered not so much the type of work that women did as the context in which that work was carried out. Women became economically dependent on the wages of their husbands and no longer had direct control over economic resources. The legal subordination of women to men continued; women had limited rights in property, and the ability of women to participate in public life was relatively restricted. Until 1884 a married woman had no right to her own property in Britain – this passed from her father to her husband – nor did she have any right to custody of or access to her children. It was not until the passage of the Marital Causes Act of 1928 that women could divorce their husbands on the same grounds as their husbands could divorce them, and not until 1882 that an Act was passed instituting maintenance for women from the husband in case of legal separation, and even then only on the grounds that he had committed aggravated assault on her.

The industrial revolution resulted in the growth of towns and cities, in a vast increase in population (particularly in urban areas), in the development of new and better modes of transport (roads, canals and railways), and in new class relationships shaped by the emergence of a working class (factory workers), a middle class (clerks, administrators and professionals) and an upper class (the owners of factories and productive land). Changes in the relationships between men and women, husbands and wives, parents and children took place in the context of these developments as well as newly established social, economic and political structures.

In the pre-industrial period middle-class women helped their men in productive roles. A notable example in Britain was the Birmingham-based Cadbury family. Before the nineteenth century they all lived above the chocolate shop and the wives and daughters were actually involved in the running of the business. However, when with the growth of the town the Cadburys moved to the suburb, the men went to work at the shop and the women stayed at home. Mrs Cadbury and her daughters undertook domestic tasks and the supervision of domestic servants, and the daughters were instructed in feminine graces. The women particularly became involved in religious and philanthropic activities. The Cadburys wanted to have a different kind of home life. With increased affluence they no longer needed the labour of the female members of the family and could afford to bring in labour. They also valued the newly emerging domestic ideal – the home as a retreat from work and a view of women as delicate and needing protection from the world of work as a place of danger and sin. The Cadburys did not *have* to move from the shop, but for other middle-class families new methods of production meant that the factory was separated from the home, and the home, the domestic sphere, came to be seen as the rightful (ideal) place for a woman.

For the working classes the changes were very different. In pre-industrial Britain the family had been a unit of production. There had been a division of labour by gender, and men were generally seen as having a dominant role, but women were not regarded as the economic dependents of men. In the early stages of industrialisation, men, women and children all worked together in the factories. Men generally managed to secure for themselves the jobs that were seen as the most skilled and, hence, the most highly paid. Gradually during the course of the nineteenth century women and children were excluded from factory jobs and became increasingly dependent on men economically. The working class came to share the domestic ideals of the middle class and to see a non-working wife as the ideal – a wife who could care properly for her husband and children and provide a home for them. The reasons why this happened are complex, and feminists do not agree on them precisely, but two factors do emerge as very important:

1   *Middle-class philanthropists attempted to shape working-class life to fit their ideas of what family life was like*, and put pressure on government to implement reforms that reinforced these conceptions. The 1834 Poor Law assumed that a woman was dependent on a man, for instance. 'Protective' factory legislation restricted the hours women and children could work, lessening their worth as employees. Women were assumed to be responsible for caring for their husbands and children, and middle-class women set out to teach working-class women how to do this, as well as to 'protect' them from the labour market.

2   From the mid-nineteenth century sections of *the male working class* (through the trade union movement) *began to argue that a man should be paid sufficient to support a wife and children*, so excluding the necessity of his wife or children taking paid employment. Most feminists argue that the '*family wage*' principle reinforced the

exclusion of women from paid employment and their economic dependence on men, thus giving men power over their wives. Hence, women perform domestic and other duties in exchange for being maintained by their husbands.

Michele Barrett and Mary McIntosh (1980) argue that women were disadvantaged by the growing idea that a man should earn a family wage, and that both capitalists and the organised male working class benefited. Capitalists benefited because women at home caring for their husbands and children helped to reproduce and maintain a fit and active workforce, and working-class men gained the unpaid services of their wives. It also enabled men to have economic and social power in the home. They argue that this ideology of the family wage is still powerful and is a major aspect of inequality for women – not only because married men are supposed to support wives and children, but because men are thought to be entitled to earn a 'family wage' while women are not. This justifies the low pay that attaches to 'women's work' (see Chapter 9), restricts women's choices and reduces their economic status within marriage.

In the former Communist societies of Central and Eastern Europe, industrialisation also resulted in the exclusion of women from paid employment (Voronina, 1994). However, Communist governments introduced equal rights legislation, and the majority of women came to have full-time employment. Being engaged in full-time employment, however, did not liberate women from domestic work (Khotkina, 1994), and indeed the hours of domestic labour put in by women in Communist societies probably exceeded those of their sisters in Western Europe (Einhorn, 1993). Zoya Khotkina (1994) has suggested that while there was equality according to the constitution, there was patriarchy in real, everyday life. Women were (and are) not only expected to carry out the majority of domestic labour but are also restricted in their work opportunities (Voronina, 1994).

Diversity in family forms and practices

While the 'ideal family' form (consisting of an economically dependent caring female, children, and an economically active male) may be the moral or ideological norm in a range of societies, in reality there is a wide variety of living arrangements and kinship systems throughout the world (Therborn, 2004). Even within contemporary Britain there is a considerable diversity of family forms and ways of organising roles within the family. Sociologist Judith Stacey has argued that what we mean by 'the family' now refers to such a broad range of experiences that it makes sense to talk about a 'postmodern family condition':

> The postmodern family condition is not a new model of family life equivalent to that of the modern family; it is not the next stage in an orderly progression of stages in family history; rather the postmodern family condition signals the moment in history when our belief in a logical progression of stages has broken down. . . . The postmodern family condition incorporates both experimental and nostalgic dimensions as it lurches forward and backward into an uncertain future.
>
> (Stacey, 1996, p. 8)

151

However we conceptualise or explain it, as research in the UK and elsewhere suggests, more and more households do not conform to conventional norms or to the 'ideal' nuclear family at the centre of familial ideology. Changes in household size and composition, in marriage and cohabitation, in divorce, in parenting and in working patterns all suggest the existence of an increasingly diverse range of family forms, in Western societies at least.

Household size and composition

Substantial changes have taken place in recent years in the size and composition of households and families in many societies. The size of households has decreased substantially since the 1970s, largely due to falling fertility rates, increasing divorce rates, patterns of migration, increased life expectancy (with many elderly people – especially women, see Chapter 5 – living alone), and changes in family forms such as an increasing proportion of single-person households, cohabiting couples and lone-parent families. According to the 2002 General Household Survey *Living in Britain*, 30 per cent of UK households (6.5 million) consist of only one person – up from 26 per cent in 1991. Nearly half of these (3.1 million) are one-pensioner only households, three-quarters of which are occupied by a woman living alone. Single-person households (particularly those consisting of women) are least likely to have amenities such as central heating or sole use of a bath/shower and toilet. More than one in eight single person households do not have central heating (www.statistics.gov.uk). This means that, largely due to the cumulative effect of disadvantage throughout the life course (see Chapter 5), elderly women particularly living in single-person households are at risk from poverty and social deprivation.

Cohabitation and marriage

Marriage, as Therborn (2004, p. 131) puts it, 'is a socio-sexual institution, a part of the wider institutional complex of the family' so much so that there is what he calls a 'rule of universal marriage' in most human societies. As he goes on to note, however, 'marriage has often been a messy business'. Since the 1960s, 'we have been witnessing a dramatic change in the landscape of human coupling' such that it has become what he describes as 'a variegated phenomenon within and between Western societies' (p. 193). More couples are cohabiting (living together without formal marriage) than ever before in Western societies, and cohabitation has become a normal prelude to marriage for almost all young people, as well as an alternative to it for many (Therborn, 2004). Cohabitation has increased dramatically over the past twenty years or so in Britain and elsewhere (Table 6.1). As with marriage, women tend to cohabit at a younger age than men (women aged between 16 and 24 are twice as likely as men to cohabit), while men over 25 are more likely than women of the same age to cohabit.

In some respects marriage is more popular than ever, however, and contrary to what many may believe, in Western Europe about as many people are married today as a hundred years ago (Table 6.2). This means, therefore, that the majority of adult

Table 6.1 Cohabitation by sex and relationship type, UK, 2002 (%)

	Single	Widowed	Divorced	Separated
Men				
Cohabiting	22	18	34	22
Not cohabiting	78	82	66	78
All men	100	100	100	100
Women				
Cohabiting	29	8	30	12
Not cohabiting	71	92	70	88
All women	100	100	100	100

(source: www.statistics.gov.uk)

Table 6.2 Western European women never married by the age of 45–49, c.1900 and 2000 (% of age group)

	1900	2000
Austria	13	17
Belgium	17	12
Denmark	13	16
Finland	15	18
France	12	14
Germany	10	13
Ireland	17	13
Italy	11	6
Netherlands	14	12
Norway	18	14
Portugal	20	4
Spain	10	13
Sweden	19	27
Switzerland	17	20
UK	17	8
Unweighted average	*15*	*14*

Source: Therborn, 2004, p. 182.

women in most European societies are married (Table 6.3). There are both gender and class differences in marital age, with working-class couples marrying on average at a younger age than middle-class ones. In 2002, the average age for a woman to marry for the first time was 28, and for a man 30. People are also increasingly marrying more than once, and the percentage of remarriage has risen as the divorce rate has increased – in 2002, 18 per cent of all marriages in the UK were remarriages for both parties (www.statistics.gov.uk).

Remarriage often creates what Macionis and Plummer (2002, p. 451) call 'blended families' composed of children and some combination of biological parents and step-parents (who may become adoptive parents). In the UK, however, the majority of stepfamilies consist of a couple with one or more children from the previous

Table 6.3 Family status of women in the EU, 1996 (% of all women aged 16 and older)

	Single	Married	Cohabiting	Divorced	Widowed
Austria	23	48	4	10	16
Belgium	18	61	6	7	9
Denmark	22	43	17	7	12
Finland	21	42	10	13	14
France	22	43	12	11	13
E. Germany	16	62	4	7	11
W. Germany	19	55	2	8	17
Greece	19	65	0	2	14
Ireland	32	51	3	2	13
Italy	37	49	2	2	10
Netherlands	22	54	7	8	9
Portugal	24	59	1	4	13
Spain	28	57	2	2	12
Sweden	27	41	15	7	10
UK	23	54	4	8	12
Average	*24*	*52*	*5*	*6*	*13*

Source: Therborn, 2004, p. 203.

relationship of the woman only. This reflects the tendency for many children to stay with their mother following divorce. In less than one in ten stepfamilies in the UK, the children are from the father's previous relationship (www.nso.gov.uk).

Divorce

The number of divorces in the UK nearly trebled between 1961 and 1971, doubled between 1971 and 1981 but increased by only 11 per cent between 1981 and 1991 (www.nso.gov.uk). The rise in the divorce rate correlates with legal changes that have extended the grounds for divorce and made it easier to obtain one. The majority of divorced people subsequently remarry or cohabit.

The most common reason in the UK for a woman to be granted a divorce is the 'unreasonable behaviour' of her husband, whereas for a man it is on grounds of 'two years separation with consent' (www.nso.gov.uk). Most divorces in Britain are granted to women (70 per cent in 2002). Various explanations have been put forward for the relatively high divorce rates in societies such as the UK. Divorce is legally easier to accomplish than was the case for previous generations. Demographic changes mean that in the past the early death of a spouse probably ended as many marriages after a few years as divorce does now (Macionis and Plummer, 2002). Ideologies of individualism are increasing and so more men and women expect choice, control and equality over their lives (Beck and Beck-Gernsheim, 1995). Ideologies of romantic love mean that partners are more likely than in the past to dissolve one relationship in favour of another when sexual passion subsides. Many contemporary marriages are stressful, particularly given the increasing likelihood that even in families with young children both men and women are likely to work outside of the home. Divorce is more socially acceptable (and no longer carries the negative social stigma that it did, say, a century ago, particularly in more secular societies), and some women are now (relatively) less financially dependent on men.

However, because mothers usually gain custody of children following divorce, but fathers typically earn more income, the well-being of children often depends on fathers making court-ordered child-support payments – so a woman who has divorced her husband on grounds of his 'unreasonable behaviour' is likely to remain financially dependent on him, particularly if she has children, and it could be argued that this is another example of the way in which the ideological concept of the 'family wage' serves to disadvantage women.

Birth outside of marriage

More people are having children without being married in most Western societies including the UK. Whereas only 6 per cent of all live births in 1961 were outside of marriage, by 1991 32 per cent of live births were outside marriage. By 2001, 40 per cent of all births in the UK were outside of marriage, although 64 per cent of these births were registered jointly by parents living at the same address.

Lone parents

As Table 6.4 illustrates, the number of women who are lone parents has also increased substantially in recent years. In fact, the number of households headed by a female lone parent in the UK has more than trebled in the last three decades. Lone-parent families (originating from separation and divorce, from birth outside of marriage, and in very small proportions from widowhood), have become increasingly common across many Western countries. As we noted above in the case of divorce, women in most countries

Table 6.4 Family type and marital status of lone mothers, UK, 1971–2001 (%)

Family type	1971	1981	1991	2001
Married/cohabiting	92	87	81	75
Lone mother	7	11	18	22
Single	1	2	6	10
Widowed	2	2	1	1
Divorced	2	4	6	7
Separated	2	2	4	4
Lone father	1	2	1	3
All lone parents	8	13	19	25
All	100	100	100	100

Source: http://www.statistics.gov.uk

are more likely than men to be given custody of their children. Because of the relative disadvantage faced by women when they become the sole supporter of a family (as a result of various factors including the impact of the family wage, as well as their limited access to resources such as childcare and employment opportunities), large numbers of women and their children are vulnerable to poverty. UNICEF argues that this is particularly the case for women who experience motherhood at a relatively young age – in European countries less than 4 per cent of all live births are to women under 20, in other parts of the world this figure is much higher. In Central and Eastern European countries such as Moldova and the Ukraine, for instance, teen births are about 18 per cent of the total (www.unece.org).

Working mothers

In the UK, working-age women with dependent children are less likely than those without to be economically active: 68 per cent in the UK, compared with 76 per cent. The age of the youngest child affects the economic activity of mothers; 55 per cent of working-age women with children under 5 are in the labour force. Conversely, men with dependent children are more likely than those without to be in the labour force. The age of their children has no impact – around 93 per cent of men with dependent children are in the labour force regardless of the age of their youngest child. Women are more likely than men to work part-time (www.nso.gov.uk), particularly if they have dependent children. Nearly 40 per cent of women with dependent children work part-time compared with 23 per cent of those without. Only 4 per cent of men with dependent children and 9 per cent of men without work part-time.

Women, regardless of their working status, tend to spend more time caring for their children than men. In 2003, women living in a couple and working full-time spent on average nearly four and a half hours on childcare and other activities with their children on a weekday (the figure for men was three and a half hours). Both men and women working full time spent just over six and a half hours a day with their children at weekends, suggesting a greater degree of equality in parenting than previously. Nevertheless, men and women tend to spend time with children in different ways. Women spend around two hours a day at weekends on housework while with their children, compared to one hour and twenty minutes spent by men. In contrast, men spend around one hour and twenty minutes watching TV in the company of their children, compared with around fifty minutes by women (Labour Force Survey, Spring 2003, cited in EOC, 2004).

Many people have argued that the trends cited here are evidence of the break-down of the family. However, these contemporary patterns tend to be of a form that mirrors the conventional nuclear family, including its sexual fidelity (Therborn, 2004). A large proportion of children may now be born outside marriage, but the majority of parents who have children outside of marriage do tend to marry subsequently. Traditional roles of motherhood tend to have remained relatively constant, and indeed children born to single women are now more likely to be brought up by their biological mothers than to be given up for adoption as in the past. The result of increasing divorce and increasing birth outside marriage, however, is that more children grow up for at least part of their childhood in lone-parent families, and these are almost invariably headed by women.

Equality, choice and diversity have become key features of many contemporary family forms – gay and lesbian registered partnerships are now formally recognised and socially accepted in many Western societies, for instance – but so too has the risk of poverty and deprivation, particularly in single-parent households headed by women. Such diversity has considerably challenged the idea that there is one 'ideal' family form. Some sociologists have argued that even if we wanted this to be the case, the world has become too complex for this to be possible. As Beck and Beck-Gernsheim argue in *The Normal Chaos of Love*, society has become focused very much on the individual and his/her lifestyle choices so that

> it is no longer possible to pronounce in some binding way what family, marriage, parenthood, sexuality or love mean, what they should be or could be; rather they vary in substance, expectations, norms and morality from individual to individual and from relationship to relationship.
>
> (Beck and Beck-Gernsheim, 1995, p. 5)

Familial ideology

Despite (or perhaps because of) such diversity in family forms and dramatic changes in the ways in which the family is configured, particularly in contemporary Western societies, however, what sociologists call 'familial ideology' – dominant ideas about how roles and responsibilities within families should be organised – persists. Veronica Beechey suggested that two assumptions underlie familial ideology. These are that:

> the co-resident nuclear family . . . is normatively desirable, [and that] . . . the form of sexual division of labour in which the woman is the housewife and mother and primarily located within the private world of the family, and the man is wage-earner and bread-winner and primarily located in the 'public' world of paid work, is also normatively desirable.
>
> (Beechey, 1986, p. 99)

She suggests that familial ideology rests on the assumption that the family is biologically determined and that particular family forms are somehow 'natural'. The patriarchal family form is therefore reproduced by social and legal institutions in Western societies because it is assumed that this is both how people *do* live their lives and how they *should* live their lives. For example, these assumptions about families underlie patterns of schooling, labour markets and ways in which the social security system is organised, as well as the type of housing that tends to be provided in both the private and the public sector. Their force is three-fold:

1 to set up the role of housewife and mother as a normal and natural lifestyle for women;

2 to declare it a lifestyle that is inherently satisfying for women and one with which they ought to be satisfied;

3 to place on women as individuals any blame for the lifestyle's failure to satisfy them.

In other words, like any ideology the familial ideology has the effect of converting the interests of a dominant group into the self-perceived interests of a subordinated one and making the dominated group responsible for any consequent failures – in this case by individualising a set of discontents which might otherwise be thought to have their base in collectively organised structural pressures rather than in individual failures. The association of female single parents with juvenile delinquency, a decline in the work ethic, welfare dependency and the emergence of an 'underclass' are examples of this.

Boys and girls, men and women take it for granted that men are strong and tough and should be 'breadwinners' and that women are submissive and gentle and should care for men and children. Even when men and women's own experiences do not live up to this ideal they still tend to see it as how things ought to be. It is also assumed that this type of family best serves the interests of its individual members and of society generally. Feminists question the assumption that a particular set of living arrangements is natural and universal and that this way of life necessarily best serves the interests of women and society as a whole; they highlight instead various aspects of gendered experiences of family life that serve to oppress and exploit women, arguing variously that this oppression is in the interests of men, of capitalism, or of both. In particular, feminists have considered themes such as gendered power relations and economic inequalities within the family, violence within families, the domestic division of labour, and men and women's different experiences of parenting.

Gendered experiences of family life

To understand the feminist critique of the family it is necessary to examine the disjuncture between ideologies of domesticity and women's lived experiences as wives and mothers. Betty Friedan (1963) referred to the pressures experienced by middle-class American mothers in the 1960s as 'the problem that has no name', while Liz Stanley and Sue Wise (1983) have argued that many women distinguish between the family as an 'institution' and their own family. The former is seen as desirable, while the latter is often experienced as problematic.

Many girls grow up expecting and wanting to get married, seeing their wedding day as the most important of their lives; the mass media and popular culture clearly plays an important role in perpetuating ideals of 'dream weddings' and 'marital bliss'. The reality is often very different from the dream, however – particularly for those women who become subject to domestic abuse and violence. Jessie Bernard (1973) suggested that in heterosexual couplings there is 'her' marriage and 'his' marriage, two different realities, and that men tend to benefit more from marriage than women do. Married women are more likely than single women or than single men to suffer from mental illness, while married men are the least likely to do so. Single women are often thought to be in need of the protection of a man. Media culture often perpetuates the idea that there is something 'wrong' with an unmarried adult woman, and this is an additional pressure towards marriage. Men, on the other hand, gain both economic and social advantages from marriage – they are cared for, they enjoy the 'unpaid' domestic labour of their wives, and often 'unpaid' help with their employed role as well, or in family businesses. Many women 'help' their employed husbands by entertaining colleagues and clients, by doing unpaid clerical work (by acting as a telephone answering service, for instance), and in some cases a wife is seen as essential or nearly essential for a man to be able to carry out his work role (Finch, 1983). Most wives are expected to organise their lives around the demands of their husbands' jobs – preparing meals and other activities to fit in with their partners' working hours – and to tailor what they do to his 'needs'.

Domestic labour is estimated to be worth quite a lot if it had to be paid for at market rates. In 1987 the Legal and General Life Assurance Company estimated that a 'dependent' wife was worth £19,253 a year in earnings (quoted in *The Sunday Times*, 29 March 1987). The Company located on a computer the 'average' wife, a 37-year-old mother of two named Rosalind Harris. Her work was found to start at 7 a.m. on Monday when she began to prepare the breakfast and to end at 9 p.m. that day (a 14-hour working day). During the week she worked as a shopper, a window-cleaner, a nurse, a driver, a cleaner, a cook and a childminder. Her total working week was of 92 hours' duration. (This excludes periods 'on call', when the children were in bed.)

Feminists have suggested a number of reasons why the reality of married life might be different from the rhetoric. Ann Oakley (1982) has suggested that women experience four areas of conflict in family life:

1. The *sexual division of labour* means that women are expected to be responsible for domestic work and childcare. This means that women become economically dependent on men and have no (or limited) access to money that they see as their own.
2. Conflict arises over the *different emotional needs of men and women*. Women are expected to deal with the frustrations and anger of husbands and children but often have no one to whom they can turn themselves (research suggests that women undertake a large amount of 'emotion work' within the family).
3. *Economic and physical differences in power* between husbands and wives mean that women can experience lack of control over financial resources, an inability to engage in social activities and even physical violence from their husbands.
4. *Male control of sexuality and fertility* means that men's needs are assumed to be the more important. Women are expected to 'please' their husbands, to give in to their sexual demands, and to have and to care for their children.

Indeed, it could be argued that married women do not have a separate identity either in their own eyes or the eyes of others. Married women generally put the needs of their families before their own, and they are often identified primarily with their husbands or children. In Britain, married women generally take their husband's name and often become seen as an appendage of their husbands or children, being 'John Smith's wife' and 'Jean and Billy Smith's mother' – having no separate social identity of their own.

This identification with the family often carries over into paid employment (see Chapter 9). Men, on the other hand, tend to take their main identity from their employment. Wives are frequently asked what their husbands do for a living, as if that were a major source of their identity, and seldom what they do themselves.

Ideas about women's role are reinforced by media culture, which constructs and represents women in a relatively narrow range of roles, often with an emphasis on that of wife and mother. This is especially noticeable in advertising and popular soap operas (see Chapter 12). What is equally important is the range of roles that women are *not* portrayed in, or which are seen as exceptional for women. Even in television programmes such as *The X Files* and *Buffy the Vampire Slayer* the 'tough' women not only have male bosses or leaders but are frequently portrayed in domestic and caring roles as well. Similarly, children's books and reading schemes have often been shown to portray men and women, boys and girls in typically segregated masculine and feminine roles (see Chapter 4).

Power relations and money

The choices about who works in the family and who stays at home to care for children and the household are based on an ideology of appropriate gender roles (see Chapter 1). However, this is reinforced by labour market factors; men can generally earn more than women, so that it is often the case that men have the paid employment and women care for the children. This traps women in a situation of financial dependency. Employment, taken to fit in with domestic responsibilities, rarely pays sufficient to give a woman financial independence, and most women do not feel they are entitled to control the spending of the 'family wage'. Even where it is the norm for married women to have full-time paid employment, the horizontal and vertical segregation of the labour market (see Chapter 9) means that wives generally earn considerably less than their husbands.

The family wage is supposed to be large enough to support a man, his wife and his children. A man's need to earn a family wage is used in wage bargaining by trade unions, and a wife's earnings are often seen as supplementary – money with which to buy luxuries. Hunt (1980) found that the husband's money was often spent on the essentials and the wife's on 'extras', so it was the man's employment that was seen as essential and the wife's as something that could be given up if necessary. However, not all married men with a family earn a 'family wage' – the number of families living in poverty would undoubtedly increase if it were not for married women's earnings – and many men and some women without family responsibilities do earn one, and considerably more.

It is important to keep in mind that the 'family wage' is not paid to the family as a unit, but to the (male) wage earner. How this money is distributed within the family depends on power relations between men and women, and on who is seen as having the right to decide how and where the money is spent. This highlights the problems of using the family as a unit of class analysis in malestream sociological research, and of attributing a class position to women based on that of the male head of household (see Chapter 3).

Jan Pahl (1980) has described several different ways in which husbands and wives manage their household income. In some cases the husband hands over the wage packet and the wife gives him back his 'pocket money'; in others the husband gives the wife 'housekeeping money'; in a third type of case resources are pooled and spending decisions made jointly. Increasingly in dual-income households men and women's earnings are retained separately. Furthermore, research shows that resources are not shared equally within families. Graham (1984) and Pahl (1983) found that women with children whose marriages have broken down have sometimes found that they are better off on state benefits than they were when they lived with their husbands.

Women tend to put their husbands and children first and their own needs last. When money is tight, women are often the ones who tend to go without food, clothes and other necessities. Women rarely have personal spending money in the way that men do, and often feel that if they spend housekeeping money on themselves they are depriving their children. It is generally men and children who have the primary use of household goods such as computers. In households with one car it is usually men who have the main use of it; even if the woman can drive it tends to be the man who does, particularly on family journeys. In cases where the car or computer is a 'perk' of the job, the wife may feel she has no direct claim over it in any case.

Many women may accept their relative lack of control because they are not the main breadwinners. Obviously women's lack of power over financial resources relates not just to ideologies concerning appropriate roles for men and women but also to the realities of who is seen as earning the money and who is seen to be 'not working'. Women's domestic labour is not seen as 'real' work because it does not bring in money, and women are not paid for it. Hence, in exchange for their domestic labour, husbands effectively maintain married women. However, it is men's control over financial resources that (at least in part) gives them relative power in marriage and makes it difficult for a wife to leave her husband even if he is mentally or physically violent to her, or if she is just unhappy in her marriage. Again this is compounded by the kind of job that she would be able to get if she left, and if she has children.

Women's financial dependence within the family appears to be compounded by factors such as arranged marriage and also by cultural beliefs about the role of women in developing and post-colonial societies, particularly in Asian and African societies where the norm is for a married woman to move in with her husband's family.

Arranged marriage and patriarchal family forms

In many parts of the world, the principle and practice of arranged marriage has been both widely challenged and defended on grounds of cultural diversity. As Goran Therborn (2004) notes,

> In a global perspective, one of the most powerful expressions of patriarchy . . . is paternal and/or parental power over children's marriage. A marriage is one of life's most important decisions, and therefore one where the difference between autonomy and heteronomy weighs most heavily. All available evidence indicates that the autonomy of marriage has increased during the twentieth century.

Nevertheless, parents still have a major say regarding their children's marriage, in at least half, probably more, of the populations of Asia, in many parts of Africa, in pockets of Europe – not only among recent immigrants – and also among Indian peoples of the Americas. Parents also play a significant part in the marital life of many adult children through post-marital household patterns.

(Therborn, 2004, p. 107)

For many women, this means that their relative freedom within marriage and the family is limited. However, as Gerami and Lehnerer (2001) note in their research on the family, numerous forms of resistance to what they describe as 'patriarchal fundamentalism' can be identified, not only in terms of organised collective efforts, but also through individual women's agency. Using a series of narrative interviews, they discuss four strategies used by Iranian women to negotiate patriarchal family practices (such as parental household living arrangements) and arranged marriages. The women in their research exercised agency by responding to the various demands of the family and the state through collaboration, acquiescence, co-optation and subversion. Their narratives show how some women negotiated the economic hardship and gender oppression brought on by the Iranian revolution, and how these negotiations affected women's role within the family when filtered through the cultural norms of Islamic fundamentalism in ways that problematise the 'victim' narratives that often characterise Western feminist discussions of fundamentalism, particularly in relation to marriage, the family and the household. However, most women in their research remained financially dependent on their own or their husband's families, and some reported being subject to violence and intimidation within the home (see also Saul, 2003).

Violence within families

While the ideal family may serve as a haven in a heartless world; the reality is that for many women and children, and for some men as well, the family can be an extremely dangerous and violent place. Research suggests that a woman is more likely to be killed, injured or physically attacked in her own home, by someone she is related to (either biologically or through marriage or cohabitation) than in any other social context (Macionis and Plummer, 2002). Russian sociologist Galina Sillaste (2004) reports that some 15,000 Russian women die annually as a result of violence within the home. US government statistics report similarly that almost 30 per cent of women who are murdered (as opposed to only 3 per cent of men), are killed by partners or ex-partners.

Although most US states and European countries had passed marital rape legislation by the mid-1990s, in 2001 only 30 countries worldwide recognised what is increasingly referred to as 'non-consensual sex within marriage' (Macionis and Plummer, 2002). In many countries, then, a man cannot be charged with raping his wife, even if they are separated. As Therborn (2004) notes, in many parts of the world, husbands still control not only all major family decisions but also whether their wives may leave the house or not: 'Nor have special gender sacrifice and institutionalized violence against girls and women disappeared. While violence against women has become an issue in Africa and Asia, wife-beating is still legitimate in many social milieux' (p. 107). Also significant is the extent to which not only men but also women internalise the belief that violence against women is acceptable. In a recent study in Egypt, for instance, 90 per cent of women thought that beating a wife was justified if she 'answered back', 70 per cent if she 'refuses sex', and 64 per cent when she 'talks to other men'. Of the married women questioned, over half had been beaten by their husbands in the past year (Zanaty-el *et al.*, 1996).

One of the most obvious questions to ask, particularly in relatively egalitarian, Western societies, is 'Why does a woman subject to violence within the home not just leave?' Feminist research suggests that most physically, emotionally and sexually abused women – especially those with children – have few options, particularly because of their relative financial dependence on men. Some women may blame themselves for their partner's violence; others, perhaps raised in violent families themselves, may have learned to view violence as a normal part of family life (Leonard, 1982). Some sociologists have noted that, in addition to (and largely because of) their role in providing an emotional safety valve for men and children, many women may perform 'emotion work' on themselves and so convince themselves that their family life is really a happy one; this means that they tend to 'reproduce their own false consciousness' (Duncombe and Marsden, 1995, p. 150).

In the past, violence within the family tended to be regarded by the state as a largely private matter, but now even without separation or divorce, a woman can obtain court protection from a violent partner or relative. Anti-stalking legislation (such as the 1997 Harassment Act in the UK) is now in place in many countries. Communities across Europe and other parts of the world have established shelters and refuges for women and children driven out of their homes by violence. The first women's refuge in the UK was set up in Chiswick, East London in 1972 by Erin Pizzey and today almost every large town and city in Britain has a women's refuge or shelter. On the one hand, the spread of such refuges illustrates the persistence of violence within the home; on the other hand, it is testimony to the extent to which feminist campaigners have shifted social attitudes so that family violence is now seen very much as a social (as opposed to an individual) problem. As radical feminists have long since argued, 'the personal is political'. Nevertheless, it remains the case that violence within the home is closer to the reality of domestic life than the 'cereal-packet' ideal for many women and children. It also remains the case that, although by far the majority of (reported) domestic violence is perpetrated by men, patriarchal ideology often means that when men do become the victims of abuse they are often not believed or even ridiculed. This highlights a contentious point within feminism – the extent to which men can also become subject to patriarchal ideology and oppression.

The domestic division of labour

To understand the division of labour within the family we need to examine not just who does what, but who is seen as responsible for ensuring that a particular job is carried out, and to challenge the common-sense assumption that there is an equitable division of labour between 'man the breadwinner' and 'woman the carer'. We also need to consider that what constitutes women's 'rights' in this respect varies culturally. As one young woman from the high-caste Rajputs in the conservative Indian state of Uttar Pradesh describes:

> I can talk to my husband even in the presence of others, but my mother could not talk to her husband when we were very young children. . . . Although, so far, I have never eaten in the presence of my husband, I can talk to my husband any time I want. . . . My mother could not serve meals to her own husband [because of pollution norms]. . . . Now I can serve my husband myself.
>
> (cited in Minturn, 1993, p. 84)

For this woman, being able to serve her husband food was a measure of progress in terms of gender equality, whereas women in the West have tended to argue that 'serving' husbands has been one of the primary causes of women's relative disadvantage both within and outside of the family.

Imbalances in the domestic division of labour come about partly because women, in Western societies at least, increasingly undertake paid employment as well as being responsible for the home, and partly because (in these societies and elsewhere) doing housework, cooking and caring for children often requires far more hours of work and responsibility than paid labour does. Domestic labour is physically and emotionally demanding work, but is rarely recognised as such (even by women themselves), feminists have argued. Feminists often point out that it is women who are generally responsible for the necessary, repetitive jobs that have to be done on a regular basis, while men often do those that are creative and can be done when convenient. Often this division is based on what men and women are thought to be naturally good at. Women are often thought to be naturally good at cleaning, sewing, washing up, shopping, washing, caring for children, cooking, and so on.

Ann Oakley (1974a, 1974b) was the first feminist sociologist to examine the division of labour in the household sociologically, and to look at domestic labour as work. She challenged the view that women have a private domain of their own – a domain which they rule and where they make the decisions. In fact, she argued that as men spend more time in the home, take more interest in their children and have more joint activities with their wives, so women's domestic power is diminished. Writing in the 1970s, David Young and Peter Willmott (1973) suggested that men and women in Britain now share childcare, domestic tasks, and the 'breadwinner' role and make decisions jointly, but Ann Oakley (1982) has argued that even when conjugal roles are shared, men are generally said to be 'helping' their wives. Women are often held responsible if essential tasks are not carried out, and men will often 'make do' for meals if their wives are absent, or wives feel obliged to make provision in their absence. This means that women tend to assume what Doucet (2001) has described as the 'emotional responsibility' for domestic labour. Stephen Edgell (1980) argued that wives are often left to make the more minor decisions, about meals or purchasing children's clothes, while the major decisions such as moving house tend to be made more by men. However, even in the more minor areas of decision-making a husband's wishes may be paramount. Pauline Hunt (1980) has suggested that women usually prepare meals that are the ones their husbands or children like and often discount their own preferences. Research in a number of other countries suggests a very similar picture (see e.g. Einhorn, 1993; Voronina, 1994; Khotkina, 1994).

Even when they have paid employment women continue to do most of the domestic work – to take on what feminist sociologists have called 'the dual role'. In recent years, feminists have recognised that many women actually undertake a 'triple shift' – not only working outside of the home, as well as taking responsibility for the performance of domestic labour, but also providing care and assistance to elderly or dependent family members as well. In the UK, by far the majority of those people providing (unpaid) care or assistance to another person are women (see Chapter 7).

While it is evident that men are not sharing domestic (or caring) work equally with their wives or partners, even if their wives or partners are in full-time employment, it is even more clear that they are not taking on shared responsibility for tasks. The jobs men seem to do more often than women – 'do-it-yourself', for example – are those that tend to have a lasting, tangible output, while women are often responsible for the day-to-day repetitive, never-ending jobs. This division of labour is often considered to be 'natural' by both men and women. It is also apparent that the amount of time women spend performing domestic labour and other household tasks has not declined substantially, even with the introduction and increasing ownership of consumer durables such as so-called 'labour saving devices'. Sociologists Ruth Madigan and Moira Munro (1996) have argued, for instance, that the term 'home' carries a heavy ideological weight that permeates domestic consumption and labour. As they put it, 'questions of style, design and tastefulness evidently cause anxiety, but they are largely subsumed by familial values (a relaxed, comfortable haven) and also by the desire to maintain "respectability" through maintaining high house-keeping standards' (p. 41). This latter point also applies particularly to caring for children.

Parenting

Many feminists argue that having children perpetuates women's subordination and exploitation. In *The Second Sex*, Simone de Beauvoir (1988 [1949]) argued that mother-hood was one of the mainstays of women's subordination. It is this more than any other role that is seen as the basis upon which men subordinate women, with women thereby placed under the control and protection of men. Ideologies of parenting are clearly gendered – think of the different cultural connotations of the phrases 'she mothered him' and 'he fathered a child'. (In English at least) the former suggests a role that involves nurturing and nourishing, the latter purely a reproductive (biological) act. The idealisation of motherhood means than men are often excluded from the care of newborn and very young children – even when they might want to be involved. In an attempt to counter this, Scandinavian countries such as Sweden and Norway have introduced one-month paternity leave and a range of policy initiatives designed to encourage men to play a more active role in childcare.

Radical feminist Shulamith Firestone (1974) has argued that women will be able to free themselves from men's control only when they are freed from the burden of reproduction. Not all feminists accept this biological argument as an adequate explanation for the subordination and exploitation of women, however. Many feminists have pointed out that there is a need to distinguish between the biological capacity to have children and the social role of parenting. It is assumed in many societies that because women have children they will look after them. But, as Miriam David (1985) has pointed out: 'Motherhood is a social concept, fatherhood barely recognised. To father a child [as noted above] refers only to the act of procreation' (p. 32). Not only is motherhood a social construction, it is also a historically and culturally specific concept, in terms of its being seen as a woman's chief vocation and primary identity. In Britain, it developed among the middle classes during the industrial revolution as part of the new ideology of domesticity and womanhood. By the end of the nineteenth century a woman's primary duty was seen as having and caring for her children.

Motherhood is often thought of as a *vocation* for women. Indeed, in the former Communist states it is increasingly argued that women ought to remain at home and care for their children as a patriotic act. This is because demographic research in Russia suggests that the country's population is currently shrinking by about 1 million people annually and the Russian birth rate has lowered to only 2.6 children per household (Therborn, 2004). The media subtext is that women are to blame for Russia's shrinking population.

In most societies motherhood is regarded as something that women are naturally good at and derive great emotional satisfaction from. Women are seen as responsible for the care and control of their children. When something goes wrong – when children develop health or social problems, for instance, the mother is often blamed; she is seen as inadequate or negligent. In the early part of the twentieth century in Britain women were blamed for high infant mortality rates and the poor health of their children. While there was considerable evidence that the real underlying causes were poor housing, poverty and appalling environmental conditions, women were blamed for not being hygienic in the home and for not providing adequate nutrition. In the period after the Second World War the popular theories of psychoanalysts such as Winnicott and Bowlby led to an emphasis on the need for mothers to care for their pre-school children full-time. Mothers who did not do so were in danger of raising delinquents and badly adjusted children, it was argued. These ideas continue to have widespread popular appeal despite considerable evidence that it is the quality of care and not the quantity nor the biological identity of the person giving it that is important, and that young children benefit from forming attachments to a variety of adults and children. Interestingly, upper-class parents who employ nannies and who send their children away to boarding schools at a young age are rarely accused of neglecting them in the same way as working-class or single-parent mothers who have to work outside of the home are.

The ideal of motherhood as a full-time vocation has shaped our thinking about women and mothering. Women's primary identity is often defined as wife and mother – a vocation that is thought to enable them to fulfil their emotional needs. However, as we noted above, feminists have pointed out that there is a wide gap between the ideal and the reality. Parenting is hard work – children require constant care and attention – and is generally carried out in isolation. Ann Oakley (1974a) found that the housewives in her study enjoyed caring for their children more than the other aspects of their work. Nevertheless, many of them felt isolated and missed the company of other adults during the day. Oakley suggested that, given the disjuncture between the ideal and the reality of mothering, we should not be surprised at how many women experience post-natal depression, but rather at how few do so.

Research by Brown and Harris (1978) found that women at home with pre-school children were at highest risk from clinical depression, largely because 'they are the buffer and absorber of stresses of the other members of the family'. They suggested that women often coped by turning the stress in on themselves. Hilary Graham (1984) has argued similarly that working-class mothers with young children smoke cigarettes as a way of coping – sitting down with a cigarette is the one peaceful time they have. Despite all this evidence the myth persists that motherhood is a universally satisfying and fulfilling role for women. Helen Roberts (1985) found that general practitioners could not understand why the married women who came to them reporting depressive symptoms were dissatisfied. They could not see that a married woman with a good husband, lovely children and a nice home could be unhappy.

Gendered assumptions about women's natural roles structure women's lives, not only in families, but in education and the world of work. Women are seen as 'natural' carers because of their role as actual or potential mothers (see Chapter 9). Employment opportunities are often limited because employers assume that motherhood is more central to women's lives than a career. This affects all women, and indeed the limited job opportunities and the low pay that women receive may actually push women into marriage and motherhood (Walby, 1986, 1990). Ann Oakley (1974a) found that many of the housewives she interviewed reported that when they got married they wanted to have children in order to escape from boring jobs. (Interestingly, many of them found being a housewife even more boring and could not wait to get back to work!) It could also be argued that because most women have to get married, to have access to a living wage, having children is the price they have to pay. Other women may, on the other hand, regard marriage as the price they have to pay to have children.

Because motherhood is presented as a natural and desirable role for women, abortion of unwanted pregnancy is often seen as unnatural and even horrific. Contraceptive use is relatively widespread in most Western societies but in transitional or developing societies (in Central and Eastern Europe, or in sub-Saharan and West Africa, for instance) access to contraception is limited and the number of unwanted pregnancies, particularly amongst young women, is still large (www.un.org). Abortion rates are the highest in the world in these societies and in the early 1990s, the number of abortions was equal to (or in some areas higher than) the number of live births. During the 1990s, as contraceptive measures became more easily available, the number of abortions began to decrease in most countries. In Kazakhstan, for example, the abortion rate decreased from 60.7 to 32 per thousand between 1990 and 1999, largely as a result of reproductive health promotion campaigns (www.unece.org). Feminists have campaigned for many years in Britain and the USA to defend their right to abortion, but it is still relatively difficult for married women to get abortions, since it is often thought that they should want to have children.

Similarly, women who become commercial surrogate mothers are often thought of either as exploited victims, or as heartless and unnatural profit-seekers. In her discussion of surrogate motherhood, Rosemary Tong noted that when a woman consents to become a commercial surrogate mother, such apparently 'free' choices must be understood within their economic context. As she puts it,

> Most surrogate mothers, like prostitutes, are much poorer than the people to whom they sell their services. Unable to get a decent job, a woman may be driven to sell her body if it is the only thing she has that anyone seems to value enough to buy. But to say that a woman 'chooses' to do this . . . is to say that when a woman is forced to choose between being poor and being exploited, she may choose being exploited as the lesser of two evils.
>
> (Tong, 1997, pp. 200–201)

One interesting development in recent years, in Western societies particularly, is the trend towards having children later in life, or not at all. In the UK for instance, the average (mean) age of women giving birth in 2002 was 29.3 years (and 27.3 years for women at first birth). Fertility rates for women in London and the south-east of England are currently higher among women in their early thirties than in their twenties (www.statistics.gov.uk). Much like those women who terminate unwanted pregnancies, women who choose not to have children often tend to be regarded in largely negative terms – as unnatural, defective, selfish or tragic. Ironically, those women who postpone having children until they have begun to establish a career for themselves (as increasing numbers of women in the West are doing) and then find their fertility has declined tend to be seen as 'doubly deviant'. In this context, and partly as a result of developments in medical technologies in recent years, various forms of assisted reproduction are increasingly used by women to have children when their own fertility has declined or has precluded them from becoming pregnant naturally, to have children on their own, to have children in lesbian partnerships, or to assist others (gay couples, for instance), in having their own children. (For a feminist discussion of some of the issues surrounding motherhood and assisted reproduction see Wallbank, 2001.)

Conclusions

Feminists have argued that family ideology has constructed the bourgeois nuclear family as natural and inevitable. While some feminists have located the cause of women's subordination in the family, others have argued that wider social and economic processes and structures influence women's decisions to get married and have children. Women's experiences of family life are mediated by their differing locations within patriarchal, racist and capitalist society, and within global power relations. In spite of social and economic changes in the last thirty or so years, gender divisions remain pervasive features of families – women continue to be responsible for the greater part of domestic labour and in the main are at least partially economically dependent on their male partners.

That said, dramatic changes have taken place in the family and the household in recent decades in many parts of the world. Such transformations have generated considerable controversy, with advocates of traditional 'family values' opposing supporters of new family forms and diverse ways of living together. Sociologist Judith

Stacey has advocated a rejection of traditional family forms and values, arguing that the family perpetuates and enhances various kinds of social inequality. Families, she argues, play a key role in maintaining a range of social divisions and inequalities based on social class (transferring wealth as well as cultural capital from one generation to another), gender (many families are patriarchal and so subject women and children to men's authority), and sexuality (familial ideology perpetuates the idea that hetero-sexuality is both normal and natural – see Chapter 8). Stacey therefore celebrates what she argues are signs that the traditional family (the 'cereal-packet' norm) is beginning to break down and regards this as a measure of social progress.

Whatever position one takes on the family, and the likely implications of recent trends in its formation, change seems certain to continue as the family has always been, as we noted at the outset of this chapter, a dynamic social phenomenon. Macionis and Plummer (2002, pp. 457–458) make five predictions about the future of family life. These are:

1   divorce rates are likely to remain high;
2   family life will be highly variable;
3   men are likely to play a more active role in parenting;
4   economic changes will continue to reform marriage and the family;
5   the importance of new reproductive technologies will increase.

SUMMARY

1   Whereas malestream sociologists have emphasised the ways in which the family serves the interests of society as a whole (functionalists) or of capitalism (Marxists), feminists have argued that the family is one of the key sites of oppression for women, whether it is capitalism, men as a class or both that benefit from this.

2   Feminists have looked at various factors associated with women's position within the family: marriage, violence within the family, the domestic division of labour, women's relative economic dependency and the gender relations of parenting.

3   Women experience a wide variety of household arrangements and feminists have been concerned to endorse these. However, there is also a strong familial ideology that is reinforced through state legislation, media culture and institutional structures. This ideology represents the patriarchal nuclear family as the natural and normal way to live.

4   There is some evidence, however, that the strength of this familial ideology is beginning to weaken and that an increasingly diverse range of family forms is beginning to emerge in a range of societies.

FURTHER READING

Silva, E. and Smart, C. (eds) *The New Family?* London: Sage. This edited collection, featuring both theoretical and empirical contributions by contemporary sociologists adopting a range of perspectives, focuses on recent changes in the family. It develops a critique of familial ideologies, and highlights the discrepancy between policies based on how families should function, and how they are experienced. Gender inequalities in family life are a theme throughout.

Therborn, G. (2004) *Between Sex and Power: Family in the World, 1900–2000.* London: Routledge. Written from a pro-feminist perspective, this comprehensive book surveys the ways in which the family changed during the course of the twentieth century. It is effectively a global history and sociology of the family focusing on the rights and powers of men as fathers and husbands; on marriage, cohabitation and extra-marital sexuality, and on reproduction. It considers, theoretically and empirically, how the major family systems of the world have formed and developed, and concludes by predicting what changes the family might experience during the course of the twenty-first century.

 Wallbank, J.A. (2001) *Challenging Motherhood(s)* London: Prentice Hall. This book critically examines contemporary social and legal constructions of motherhood with reference to a critique of the discussion of families in Western, and particularly British, sociology. A number of themes are considered, including the regulation of family life, gendered issues of child support, and particularly political and media representations of single parents. It also considers discourses on motherhood, reflecting on the ways in which these have developed according to a particular set of Western ideals as to what motherhood could or should entail. It also reflects on the capacity of women to challenge dominant discourses.

CHAPTER SEVEN

Health, illness and caring

Health is an issue of central concern to women. Women form the majority of health care workers; are responsible, in the family, for the health of others, and are the major consumers of formal health care. However, until the development of feminist sociology little attention was paid to gender as a key variable in understanding health. Feminists have reopened the history of women healers, explored the roles that women play in the health care system, analysed the ways in which health inequalities affect women, pointed to the ways in which medical power is used to control women and the ways in which doctors have taken away control over pregnancy and childbirth from women and medicalised what women have perceived as a natural process. More recently, feminists have focused on the informal health care work done by women, pointing out that much of the caring work women do in the domestic sphere is concerned with promoting the health of household members. Women also play a key role in the lay referral system – the system in which decisions are made about whether to visit the doctor or not, or what other action should be taken. In the process of highlighting the key role that women play as unpaid health care workers, feminists have also drawn attention to the ways in which conflicts develop between informal and paid providers, and the extent to which paid providers are unaware of the needs of the unpaid carer. The unpaid carer is often invisible, the focus of attention being the patient, so that the needs of a woman caring, for example, for 24 hours a day, seven days a week for an ill or disabled relative are often ignored (see e.g. Lewis, 2003). A key point here is that the paid providers are themselves often women, yet because they work within the dominant medical paradigm they fail to identify with the unpaid carers and assume that women are ready, willing and able to provide the constant care demanded of them. Indeed, it may be argued that woman are 'coerced' into caring. The implementation of the National Health Service and Community Care Act 1990 in Britain reinforced this view of women as carers, with its emphasis on the role of informal care.

Furthermore the increased emphasis on care in the community means that resources are being concentrated on those who would otherwise have to be taken into residential care. Beyond this, developments in medical technology and the early discharge of patients from hospital can all add to the demands made on lay carers, the majority of whom are women, many of them giving up paid employment or at least some part of their earning capacity in order to be carers. The rhetoric may emphasise supporting informal carers, but the reality is often that the resources are not available (Ackers and Abbott, 1996; Land, 2003; Baldock, 2003).

The multiple roles that women play affect their physical and mental well-being. Women and men have different health care needs; men are more likely to have accidents while they are young, but only women give birth to children. Most research into work and ill health has focused on male-dominated occupations; little attention has been paid to the health hazards of work roles where women predominate, and even less to those of the housewife.. Similarly, research into health inequalities has focused on differences between social classes or between deprived and non-deprived households; little attention has been paid to differences in the health experiences of women and men, nor has account been taken of the ways in which resources are distributed within households, often meaning that some members are deprived while others are not. Indeed, poor women with young children bear a particularly heavy burden (Lahelma *et al.*, 2002; Bradshaw, 2003; Graham, 1993) and this has adverse consequences for their health. Jennie Popay and Jill Jones (1990) have reported on the poor health of mothers bringing up children alone, compared with those in two-parent families. There is evidence to suggest that when resources are limited women do without in order to ensure that their husbands and children are adequately provided for, while Brown and Harris (1978) suggested that women at home with young children are more likely than others to suffer from clinical depression.

One reason why gendered inequalities *within* families tend to be overlooked may be that there are dilemmas in dealing with them. As Lesley Doyal (2000) points out, if health resources are limited, giving more to women must be at the expense of men and attacking women's greater morbidity will entail greater morbidity (or perhaps even mortality) for men. Similar considerations apply to material resources as a whole: 'Men on the edge of poverty, for example, might be dragged down below subsistence if their income had to be shared equally with their wives' (p. 937). It is not immediately evident what incentive men would have for co-operating with this kind of rearrangement, other than a sense of equity.

The discourse of health assumes that women will care for the members of their family when they are unwell and takes for granted, as natural, the health care work that women do in the domestic sphere. It also assumes that mothers will prioritise the needs of their children, putting their needs and care above their own needs – that women will, if necessary, sacrifice themselves for their children. (Full-time carers do this even without knowing: women who have full-time employment as well as domestic 'duties', in advanced industrial societies, report better physical and mental health than do full-time domestic carers.) The discourse also, paradoxically, defines as health care only the formal health care provision supplied by the state and private paid medicine. Health care is seen as provided by doctors, nurses, health visitors, and so on; the health care provided by women in the home is not defined as such; rather it is seen as an integral aspect of their caring role in the family (see e.g. Land, 2003).

Women and medicine

During the course of the nineteenth and twentieth centuries, scientific medicine came to dominate health care in the Western world and doctors have achieved a high social status and considerable power. In Britain the National Health Service provides health care free at point of delivery to all citizens, and we generally regard this as 'a good thing'. We regard medicine as something good that has improved the health of the nation and alleviates pain and suffering. We tend to argue that what we want is more: more hospitals, more doctors, more nurses, more research, and so on; then there would be an improvement in health. Historically, however, improvement in health has often come from raised living standards, changes in behaviour and general public health reforms rather than from specific advances in medical knowledge. Jane Lewis (1980), for example, suggests that the decline in the maternal mortality rate in Britain in the 1930s and 1940s was as much due to improvement in the diet of pregnant women as to medical advances. Today, a decline in female deaths from lung cancer, for example, is much more likely to come from women stopping smoking, and indeed from the elimination of pressures in women's lives that led them to smoke, than from advances in treatment. This is not to deny that medical advances improve health in some instances and reduce mortality (death) and morbidity (illness), but to point out that preventive measures are often more effective than curative ones and indeed are less costly in the long run.

Western scientific medicine is said to be objective and value-free, and doctors are seen as medical scientists who are objective about their patients in much the same way as any other scientists are about their subject matter. Medical science progresses via the scientific method (the experiment and specifically the randomised controlled trial), resulting in the acquisition of certain, objective and unchallengeable facts and an autonomous and value-free body of knowledge. However, there are problems with this view of science, which sociologists have challenged in general and specifically with respect to medicine. Sociologists argue that all scientific activity is inevitably influenced by the society in which it is carried out and that the scientist often plays a major role in explaining and ultimately justifying various aspects of the way in which a society is organised.

Furthermore, feminists regard medical knowledge as highly gendered and part of the means by which gender divisions in society are maintained – modern medicine acts as a form of patriarchal control over women. Medicine not only reflects discriminatory views of women but serves to reproduce these views by actively stereotyping and controlling women who deviate from them. The way in which women were seen as weak and in need of constant rest by the medical profession in the nineteenth century, thus justifying, for instance, their exclusion from higher education, is one example. More recently the US radical feminist Mary Daly has argued that modern medicine has actually exercised more control over women as a 'backlash' response to the rise of feminism. She argues that there is:

> every reason to see the mutilation and destruction of women by doctors specialising in unnecessary radical mastectomies and hysterectomies, carcinogenic hormone therapy, psychosurgery, spirit-killing psychiatry and other forms of psychotherapy as directly related to the rise of radical feminism in the twentieth century.
>
> (Daly, 1978, p. 228)

Women often experience the health care system as paternalistic, and their own experiences and knowledge are ignored or downgraded. This has been especially highlighted in the area of pregnancy and childbirth and it is also true with respect to contraception. In terms of women's informal caring roles, their own knowledge and understanding of the patient is frequently dismissed as irrelevant. Often, feminists argue, medical intervention does more harm than good, and in other cases it offers palliation rather than a cure. In childbirth, for example, it has been suggested that many procedures that became routinised, such as routine episiotomy, are of dubious benefit to mother or child. More recently there has been considerable debate about the prescribing of hormone replacement therapy (HRT) for menopausal women, which has become seen as a panacea for menopausal problems. In medical literature the menopause has been transformed from a natural, non-problematic event to a deficiency disease – 'curable' by HRT (Foster, 1995). While there is considerable clinical and patient evidence that HRT alleviates physical menopausal symptoms, there is less evidence that it assists with psychological problems. Claims have also been made that HRT reduces the possibility of older women having heart disease, strokes and osteoporosis, but less emphasis has been placed on the possible long-term and serious side effects – increased risk of both endometrial and breast cancer; and even less on the immediate ones – fluid retention, weight gain, breast tenderness, abdominal cramps, irritability, nausea and vomiting (Kahn and Holt, 1989). Peggy Foster (1995) concludes that:

> it is perfectly logical to support the prescribing of HRT as a treatment for the more severe physical symptoms of the menopause while opposing its growing use as a panacea for all the problems women associate with ageing, including losing their looks.
>
> (Foster, 1995, p. 82)

Similarly, the giving of tranquillisers to housewives with depression only renders the intolerable more tolerable; it does nothing to alleviate the underlying causes of depression.

Women and health inequalities

Gender inequalities in health care provision and the ways in which the specific health care needs of women are ignored have been highlighted by feminists – including the ways in which the focus on explaining male mortality has obscured the millions of premature deaths that women experience simply because they are women (for example, through domestic violence, botched abortions, dowry deaths and as a result of the inequitable distribution of resources between men and women – see Freedman and Maine, 1993). So also have the ways in which medical intervention is used as much to increase the power and prestige of medical men as to improve the health of women, and the questionable benefits of much medical intervention to its receivers. Marxist feminists have highlighted inequalities in health care and the ways in which the health care system serves the needs of a capitalist society. A 'cultural critique' has questioned the view that medicine, as a science, is value-free and objective, that doctors as professionals are knowledgeable and concerned with meeting the health care needs of clients, that medical intervention is always of benefit to clients and that the dramatic reductions in ill health and general improvements in health achieved in industrial countries in the last hundred years are due to advances in medical knowledge. The concern that feminists have expressed, then, is not just that women's health needs are ignored, nor that medicine is sexist, but that modern medicine itself may be less valuable than is claimed. The actual technical competence of doctors and of modern medicine needs to be scrutinised. It is argued that doctors exhibit massive ignorance on such subjects as birth control, menstruation, breastfeeding, the management of childbirth, the menopause, vaginal infections, and so on. (See e.g. Foster, 1995; Doyal, 1995)

The publication of the Black Report (1978) on health inequalities in Britain stimulated investigations into the existence, extent and causes of health inequalities. It was of course recognised that health inequalities between northern and southern regions were due to poverty and deprivation. What the Black Report revealed was that within an affluent society, with a national health service providing free medical care, there were still large and systematic differences in mortality between social classes. Sociologists have developed materialist and structuralist accounts to explain these. They have argued that the major causes of health inequalities are material inequalities – that the reason why the working class have higher mortality (death) rates and higher levels of morbidity (illness) is material deprivation. More recently, they have been concerned with exploring the pathways that link material circumstances to health outcomes. Three broad positions have emerged:

1 *A structuralist explanation* arguing that health (or rather, mortality) outcomes are mainly the direct result of the impact of material conditions and in particular of the unequal access to resources related to welfare regimes.
2 *An 'action theory' approach* that identifies social capital as a major intervening variable, with a particular emphasis on psychosocial responses to inequality and lack of social cohesion and social support.
3 *A 'healthy lifestyles' approach* arguing that culturally shared practices formed by socialisation and experience and shaped by material circumstances result in materially deprived groups leading unhealthy lifestyles.

(For a further discussion see Abbott, 2004.)

However, the priority in such research has been on investigating men's health (and in particular mortality) and the work hazards of male-dominated occupations. Little attention has been paid to the health hazards of women's paid and unpaid work. Research into causes of coronary heart disease, for example, primarily focuses on men, who are more likely to die prematurely than women, yet more women die of diseases of the circulatory system in the UK than men – 409.5 per hundred thousand population for women in 2001 compared with 394.8 for men. Researchers have been concerned about the dramatic increase in male mortality in mid-life, from heart disease and external causes, while in the former Soviet Union following the collapse of communism in 1991, they have ignored (or naturalised) the poor health of women (Abbott, 2004).

Although it is recognised that men and women do have different health experiences, little account has been taken of the sex/gender system in examining the pattern of health and illness. Thus research has failed to explain why it is that although men die on average at a younger age than women, women appear to suffer more ill health than men. Men die at a relatively younger age from the illness they contract or from the injuries they suffer, while women live on.

There are social class differences between women in terms of life expectancy. Women married to men employed in semi- or unskilled jobs are 70 per cent more likely to die prematurely than those whose husbands are in a professional or managerial occupation. Furthermore, women in social classes IV and V have higher mortality rates than men in social classes I and II, despite the overall tendency for women to live longer than men. The main influence on women's self-assessed health remains the degree of affluence or poverty of her household living circumstances (Arber, 1997) rather than class position as determined by her own occupation. The class differences in health relate not just to immediate experience but to experience over the life course; deprivation in childhood affects adult health. Class is inscribed in our bodies and accounts for the socio-economic gradients in health (Graham, 2002).

There is strong evidence that in Western countries women's multiple roles (often married, with children and paid employment) protects women's health (Lahelma *et al.*, 2002). While household economic circumstances are the main determinant of self-reported health in post-Soviet societies, there is no evidence that multiple roles have any positive or negative effect on it (Abbott, 2004).

The gendered health pattern is found in all societies – women on average live longer than men and there are social class differences between women, although the male–female gap in life expectancy does vary significantly between countries. Of particular interest in this respect has been the significant growth in the male–female mortality gap in the former USSR, with Russia now having the largest male–female gap in life expectancy in the world, of about fourteen years. This is in sharp contrast to some of the countries of Southeast Asia, as well as parts of sub-Saharan and West Africa, where the gap is much smaller or even eliminated altogether, mainly due to the low value placed on female children (see Chapter 5). However, studies in Britain have indicated that women rate their own health as worse than men rate theirs (Whitehead, 1987) and the same has been found in post-Soviet societies (Abbott, 2004). Thus, despite their longer life expectancy, women report more illness and disease than men. However, there is considerable debate about whether women have poorer health than men across the life course or whether the excess in women's poor health is related to their longer life expectancy. Analysis of UK data suggests that it is only for the oldest age groups that there is an excess of poor physical health among females, although women across the life course report poorer socio-psychological health than men, and similar analyses have been made for other Western countries. However, in the former USSR, women do report poor physical and psychological health across the life course (Abbott, 2004).

Women of all social classes consult their general practitioners more often than do men, consume more drugs and medicines than men, occupy acute hospital beds slightly more often and are admitted to psychiatric units more often than men (Kane, 1991). Female consultation rates with GPs for depression are three times those of men

(Royal College of General Practitioners, 1990). One in twenty women aged between 25 and 74 seeks help from her GP for emotional problems, compared with one in fifty men in Britain. Across a number of developed countries women are twice as likely as men to be prescribed tranquillisers (Ashton, 1991) and women report significantly higher levels of psychosocial problems than men in Russia and other Eastern European and Central Asian countries (Abbott, 2004). Again there are social class differences. Women married to men in the lowest social classes suffer three times more long-standing illness than do those in the highest social classes.

However, it is not the case that we can determine the relative health experience of different groups from the amount that they consult doctors or make use of the health services. Women of the lowest social classes, for example, make more use of the health services than the more affluent, but not to the extent that their much greater health problems would suggest that they should (LeGrand, 1982). Preventive services are used least by the women who suffer most from the problems that these services are intended to forestall (Doyal, 1987). A good example here is screening for cervical cancer. Although women married to men in social class V are four times more likely to die of cancer of the cervix than women married to men in social class I, they make much less use of the screening facilities than middle-class women; the difference in death rate between working-class and middle-class women is not fully explained by differential use of the preventive services. There is also a marked social class gradient in the use of services connected with fertility control. Women married to men in middle-class occupations are much more likely than women married to manual workers to attend family planning clinics or discuss fertility control with general practitioners. Inequalities are also evident with regard to abortion. While working-class and Black women argue that they are often pressured into having an abortion, other women point out how difficult it is to get one – especially on the NHS. In fact, in the UK most abortions are performed outside of the NHS.

It is necessary to consider, if women's greater use of health services suggests that women are sicker than men, why working-class women make less use of preventive services than middle-class ones, and why working-class women make less use of the health services than their health problems would suggest they need. Some feminists have suggested that women's life experiences mean that they suffer more ill health than men. Others have argued that this is an artefact – that women's greater use of health services is due to factors other than that they are suffering more ill health than men. It should be noted, however – as we have already pointed out – that women report poorer physical and psychosocial health than men overall, and there is no evidence that women are more likely to report trivial conditions than men (Adamson *et al.*, 2003). Explanations that stress the different life experiences of women are:

1   *the biological* – that women suffer more problems as a result of their reproductive functions than do men (Kane, 1991);
2   that the *isolation* of women in unpaid domestic labour seems to be linked with a higher incidence of depression among women (Brown and Harris, 1978; Ussher, 1989); and
3   *lifestyle* – that women have healthier lifestyles than men, and in particular that they eat a healthier diet, drink less alcohol and are less likely to 'binge drink' than men.

Peggy Foster has pointed out that the biological and feminist models of women's need for health care both assume that it is women who rely on health care providers. She argues that:

> any dependency relationship between women and health care providers is at least partly the other way round . . . all those employed in the manufacturing and delivery of health care need women to consume their work as much as, if not more than, women need the type of products and services provided.
>
> (Foster, 1995, p. 3)

Those that stress the artefactual nature of the difference suggest:

1 that women often visit the doctor on behalf of others, especially children (Graham, 1984);
2 that female socialisation in Western cultures makes it more acceptable for women to adopt the 'sick role', or that male socialisation makes men less likely to adopt it;
3 that women are subject to the 'medicalisation' of normal childbirth (Lesson and Gray, 1978; Oakley, 1980);
4 that women live longer than men (the ratio of women to men aged 75+ is 2:1, and increasing), and older people tend to have more health problems than younger ones.

Other research suggests that consultation rates are a poor guide to the amount of illness suffered in the community, and that women are more likely than men to 'suffer in silence'. Scambler and Scambler (1984) found that women do not necessarily visit the doctor when they are unwell. Helen Roberts (1985) found that women differed in the extent to which they visited the doctor and divided them into the frequent attenders and the infrequent attenders. She did not find that the latter group suffered less ill health than the former, but rather that they differed in their views as to when the doctor should be consulted. The infrequent attenders argued that the doctor should only be visited when this was essential, the frequent attenders that the doctor should be visited when one was unwell, before things became too bad. Both groups were concerned with not wasting the doctor's time, but while the former group argued that this meant only going when it was essential, the latter argued that the doctor should be visited at the first signs of illness to prevent a lot of time having to be spent treating a serious illness.

Scambler and Scambler found that women differentiated between illness that required a visit to the doctor and illness where alternative methods were indicated. Thus women often experience suffering but do not regard themselves as ill. A similar situation was noted some sixty years ago in the Workers' Health Enquiry into the lives of working-class women:

> many women replied 'yes' to the question, 'Do you usually feel fit and well?' In answer to the next question, 'What ailments do you suffer from?', the same women listed a whole series of problems including anaemia, headaches, constipation, rheumatism, prolapse of the womb, bad teeth and varicose veins.
>
> (Spring-Rice, 1981 [1939], p. 69)

178

As is the case today, certain 'ailments' had to be suffered, but the women were 'well enough to carry on'. Women's domestic and caring roles mean that they cannot be ill because they have to care for their families. Williams (1987) found in Aberdeen that fatigue or weakness did not constitute 'illness', and 'fit' meant being able to work. Jocelyn Cornwell (1984), in her study in Bethnal Green, also found that women regarded themselves as 'not ill' if they could 'carry on'. Pill and Stott (1986) suggest, from their study of 204 women in Cardiff, that working-class women have a low expectation of health and that the women were not accustomed to thinking particularly about their health. Women are also the ones who decide when their husbands and children are ill and may adopt the sick role (Locker, 1981).

It is also important to consider why working-class women make less use of health services than middle-class women when we take into account the health needs of both groups; and make less use of preventive services. There has been a tendency to blame the working-class woman, to suggest that she is less able to perceive the benefit of the services offered, especially preventive ones. However, feminists have suggested that it is necessary to turn the question around and ask what is wrong with the way the services are provided. They argue that often the provision does not meet the needs of the woman, that there are no arrangements to care for the young children they often have to bring with them, that working-class women find it difficult to communicate with middle-class professionals, and that the women are aware that the main causes of their ill health (children, housing, lack of money, and so on) lie outside the province of the medical profession and also outside their own control (Pill and Stott, 1986; Blaxter, 1985; Cornwell, 1984). While working-class and Black women experience the greatest control from health professionals – at the extreme, being pressured into having unwanted abortions or being prescribed Depo-Provera (a long-term birth control measure with serious side effects, banned in the US) without informed consent – feminists argue that all women are controlled by medical ideology. A key example here would be the way in which male doctors have come to control pregnancy and childbirth (see e.g. Oakley, 1980, 1984a).

Radical feminists emphasise the ways in which male medical ideology is used to control women, and feminists in the US in particular have strongly attacked the exploitative nature of the American health care system. Marxist feminists, meanwhile, have been concerned to point to health inequalities between women from different social classes and ethnic groups and the ways in which the state controls the health care system to meet the needs of capitalist society. Lesley Doyal (1987) suggested that the NHS was a powerful mechanism of social control both because it appeared to be a major move to meet the needs of the working class and because it served the interests of the capitalist class by ensuring a healthy workforce (although she was also critical of the male doctors' patriarchal, sexist attitudes towards their female patients). However, despite over fifty years of the NHS the inequalities in health between women from different social classes persist, and while the health of all women has improved, relative inequalities have remained the same – or even increased to some extent. Indeed, it could be argued that the NHS has failed to meet the specific needs of women because the ways in which services are provided do not enable women to make full use of them. Lack of facilities for caring for young children, the timing of appointments, the centralisation of provision and the attitudes of the profession have all been cited as reasons why services have not been used.

Iatrogenic medicine

Some medical intervention, it is suggested, is iatrogenic – that is, it causes more harm than good; the treatment actually causes more symptoms and side effects than the original illness. We have already mentioned the side effects of hormone replacement therapy, prescribed for menopausal women. Another good example is the use of a particular drug to treat arthritis. Some patients who were prescribed the drug, which relieves the pain of arthritis, ended up with poor health as a result of the so-called 'side effects' of the drug, such as an inability to tolerate daylight. However, with women's health there is greater concern because some drugs or treatments that are prescribed on a routine basis, not to treat illness but to prevent unwanted pregnancies, have been found to be iatrogenic. The 'coil', for example, has been found to cause extensive menstrual bleeding and low back pain in some women. However, the main cause for concern has been the contraceptive pill, the most reliable method of contraception available to most women.

The pill was introduced into the US in 1960 and has subsequently been used by millions of women throughout the world. It was seen as an effective, modern and scientifically respectable method for controlling fertility and was freely prescribed by doctors to women of childbearing age. However, by the mid-1960s it began to be suspected that there was a link between the pill and cancer of the cervix and circulatory (heart) diseases. Attempts to assess the validity of this suspicion uncovered serious deficiencies in the testing of contraceptive drugs. It was found that they had not been tested on women for the whole period of the reproductive cycle, so that the possible effects of taking the pill for twenty or thirty years were unknown. A study by the Royal College of General Practitioners in 1974 found that the risk of dying from circulatory disease was five times greater for women taking the oral contraceptive pill than for others. Women who were over 35 years old who had been taking the pill for five or more years and who smoked were found to be at the greatest risk. The pill has also been found to have a number of side effects – depression, a loss of libido (sex drive), headaches, nausea and excessive weight gain – but there has been little research into these. Furthermore, the subjective experiences and feelings of women have often been dismissed as irrelevant or 'not real' by medical men. Indeed, research indicates that GPs strongly prefer the pill, especially for young women, and the medical profession seem to have few doubts about its safety (Reid, 1985) and feel that women are unnecessarily worried about it (Tindall, 1987). Similarly, there is medical confidence in Depo-Provera and the IUD (see Wilson, 1985; Guillebaud and Low, 1987; and an editorial in *The Lancet*, 28 March 1992). However, in the United States most drug companies ceased researching, developing and manufacturing contraceptive drugs nearly fifteen years ago because of the escalating costs of testing the product and the high price of the insurance needed to protect them against lawsuits from those damaged by their products (Lincoln and Kaeser, 1988).

It has by now, and as a result of availability of such devices as the pill and the coil, become generally accepted that it should be women who take the responsibility for birth control precautions, and it is women who suffer the serious consequences if contraception fails. (This has changed to some small extent, however, with the AIDS risk and the emphasis on using condoms and barrier cream. However, these are less effective as a prevention of pregnancy than they are in preventing the spread of HIV and other infections.)

It seems unlikely that what are often referred to as the 'side effects' of female contraception would be so readily ignored if men were the users. It would be interesting to know how many men would be prepared to use the intra-penile device (IPD) described by Dr Sophie Merkin:

The newest development in male contraception was unveiled recently at the American Women's Center. Dr Sophie Merkin of the Merkin Clinic announced the preliminary findings of a study conducted on 763 unsuspecting male under-graduates at a large mid-Western university. In her report, Dr Merkin stated that the new contraceptive – the IPD – was a breakthrough in male contraception. It will be marketed under the trade name Umbrelly.

The IPD (intra-penile device) resembles a tightly rolled umbrella which is inserted through the head of the penis and pushed into the scrotum with a plunger-like device. Occasionally there is a perforation of the scrotum, but this is disregarded as the male has few nerve-endings in this area of his body. The underside of the umbrella contains a spermicidal jelly, hence the name Umbrelly.

Experiments on 1000 white whales from the continental shelf (whose sexual apparatus is said to be closest to man's) proved the IPD to be 100% effective in preventing the production of sperm and eminently satisfactory to the female whale since it does not interfere with her rutting pleasure.

Dr Merkin declared the Umbrelly to be statistically safe for the human male. She reported that of the 763 undergraduates tested with the device only two died of scrotal infection, only twenty developed swelling of the testicles and only thirteen were too depressed to have an erection. She stated that common complaints ranged from cramping and bleeding to acute abdominal pains. She emphasised that these symptoms were merely indications that the man's body had not yet adjusted to the device. Hopefully the symptoms would disappear within a year. One complication caused by the IPD and briefly mentioned by Dr Merkin was the incidence of massive scrotal infection necessitating the surgical removal of the testicles. 'But this is a rare case,' said Dr Merkin, 'too rare to be statistically important.' She and other distinguished members of the Women's College of Surgeons agreed that the benefits far out-weighed the risk to any individual man.

(From *Outcome* magazine, the *East Bay Men's Center newsletter*, and *The Periodical Lunch* published by Andrew Rock, Ann Arbor, Michigan, USA)

This is of course a spoof – no such device has actually been invented. The account was published to illustrate the fact that most men would not be expected to suffer what many women experience with an IUD, such as heavy bleeding, backache and vaginal infections. Indeed, any development at all in this direction is highly unlikely, given that little attempt has been made to develop and market new methods of contraception for men (Bruce, 1987).

While it may be true that women choose what method of contraception to use, their choice is limited by what is available. Modern methods do enable a woman to have control over her own fertility, rather than relying on her partner or risking having an abortion after conception, but her choice is limited by decisions that have already been made by drug company executives, doctors, researchers and others about which methods will be developed and made available. Further, given that most methods have their own problems, the choice is often a negative one. Women choose the method that affects them least – so one may choose the pill because the IUD caused excessive bleeding, while another may make the reverse decision because the pill resulted in excessive weight gain. Medical control of many of the newer methods of birth control means that women are dependent on their doctors for advice, and doctors are generally inadequately trained in this area. Most women will have to make a judgement based on what their doctors tell them, and doctors often become resentful if female patients question their advice or reveal that they are knowledgeable in the area. Doctors frequently expect patients to accept that they know best. Yet they rarely talk to their female patients about birth control in detail and are inclined to dismiss subjective experience and base their advice on what they regard as sound scientific judgement. (A further restriction of women's ability to choose which method of contraception to use is the preference of their partners. Pollack (1985), for example, found that many men preferred their partners to use the pill rather than spoil their pleasure and use a condom.)

Nevertheless, doctors' non-medical values do influence the decisions they make about sterilisation and abortion, for example (and about the issue of less drastic means of contraception – see Hawkes, 1995). While white middle-class women have been demanding the right to choose to be sterilised or to have an abortion, working-class and Black women have pointed out that they have often been pressurised into having an abortion or being sterilised against their inclinations. On the other hand, Rose Shapiro has suggested that:

> The need of family planning organisations and doctors to prevent pregnancy is so powerful that it manifests itself almost as an irrational fear. The impression given is that accidental pregnancy is the worst thing that could ever happen to women and that abortion is an absolute disaster.
>
> (Shapiro, 1987, p. 41)

However, in other parts of the world abortion has been the main or only form of contraception available to women. Lesley Doyal (1995) indicates that, worldwide, abortion ranks fourth after female sterilisation, IUDs and contraceptive pills as a method of contraception. In Russia and other transitional societies abortion has been seen as the main form of contraception (United Nations, 2003).

While many women have undoubtedly benefited from the development of modern forms of contraception and these have enabled women to avoid unwanted pregnancies, they have nevertheless extended medical and social control over women. The worldwide market for contraceptive pills and devices is worth billions of dollars, and it is in the interests of multinational companies to encourage the medical profession to prescribe and women to use high-tech contraception. Women's ability to control their own fertility has been restricted and heavily controlled by the medical profession and the multinational pharmaceutical companies.

Gender, power and medicine

The way in which medical men 'construct' women is a powerful element in their control of their female patients. While in the nineteenth century medical men argued that women were physically frail, in the twentieth century they suggested that they are mentally weak and easily dissatisfied with their domestic roles. Medical images of women are of course reinforced by the ways in which medical education is carried out and the contents of what is taught. Female medical students (and feminist doctors – see Eisner, 1986) have argued that sexism is rampant in medical training and that women are often treated as objects of ridicule by (male) lecturers. Men are seen as the norm against which women – and particularly women's bodies (see Chapter 5) – are seen as abnormal.

Medical images of women

Analysis of medical textbooks shows that they include 'facts' about women that are little more than prejudices. They stress the superiority of doctors' objective knowledge and clinical experience over women's own subjective perceptions – even when women's own experience is under examination. Little attention is paid in the medical curriculum to problems specifically suffered by women except those relating to pregnancy and childbirth; thus common female problems such as cystitis (bladder infection) or vaginal infections are not taken seriously and there has been little basic research into female incontinence and osteoporosis. Even the menstrual cycle has not been extensively researched (Koblinsky *et al.*, 1993). Gynaecologists and obstetricians are considered to be experts on women, yet it is a male specialism (see Chapter 9). They exercise great power vis-à-vis women and are in a position to define 'normal femininity' and 'normal sexuality'. Not only are they often given little training on female sexuality, but an analysis by Scully and Bart (1978) of the major gynaecology textbooks suggests that what they are taught is out of date. They found that myths about female sexuality continued to be stated as facts even after major surveys had revealed them as myths. Lesley Doyal (1995) points out, furthermore, that when health problems do affect both men and women, possible gender differences are never explored. For example, coronary heart disease, more common among women than men, has been researched in the main on male-only samples.

Doctors tend to see women's medical problems as emotional and mental rather than physical. Susan Penfold and Gillian Walker (1984) reviewed a number of cases where women received a psychiatric diagnosis but were subsequently found to have a physiological problem. Furthermore, women's depression is assumed to arise because of their inherent weakness – because they cannot cope with the demands of a family, the isolation of domestic labour, combined with paid work, caring responsibilities, and so on. However, the research of Brown and Harris (1978) has suggested that depression in women relates primarily to their life circumstances, while the American feminist Jessie Bernard (1973) has argued that being a housewife makes women sick because they become depressed and suggested that paid employment protects women from depression. (However, Arber *et al.* (1985) have suggested that married women under the age of 40 with children may suffer more physical illness if they have full-time paid employment.) Maggie Eisner has referred to the attitude of male general practitioners and suggested that it is because women have to cope with their families' problems that they turn to the GP for emotional support:

> A speaker said that women ask their GPs for more emotional support than men do, implying that women, being weaker than men, have greater need for such support. I pointed out that the women spend a lot of their time and energy giving emotional support to many people in their lives and often have no one but the GP to turn to for their own emotional support.
>
> (Eisner, 1986, p. 121)

Scully and Bart (1978) suggest that doctors 'blame' women's emotional and hysterical behaviour on the female reproductive tract, and this was certainly the case in the nineteenth century. Nineteenth-century doctors argued that women were controlled by their biology. Women, it was argued, were entirely under the control of their reproductive organs, and so doctors could provide a 'scientific' explanation for this truth – namely that a malfunctioning uterus could result in the spread of disease throughout the body (hysteria). Some Victorian doctors thought that women did not have sexual feelings, while men had strong sexual urges. Instead of sexual urges, women were said to be endowed with a strong maternal instinct (see Chapter 8), and their most important duty in life was motherhood.

The upper-class woman in particular was portrayed as frail and sickly – her delicate nervous system was seen as needing protection as much as her sickly body. Middle-class women were encouraged to have long periods of rest – especially at times of menstruation. It was thought especially dangerous for women to engage in intellectual activity. Higher education was seen as a special danger, and women were excluded from universities on the grounds that they were a risk both to their health and to their femininity. It was claimed that a woman who developed 'masculine' intellectual qualities would necessarily fail to develop her 'female' qualities, endangering both her fertility and her capacity for motherhood. While middle- and upper-class women were encouraged to be idle, working-class women were expected to work, but the work assigned to them was hard manual labour. Thus the inherent inferiority of women was used to justify the two very different lifestyles enjoyed by middle- and working-class women in Victorian England.

The cult of frailty among upper-class and upper-middle-class Victorian women was strengthened by the view that a man should be able to support a leisured life; to be able to afford domestic servants was a status symbol. Some Victorian wives rebelled, but the majority did not because they were totally dependent on their husbands/fathers. The boredom and confinement of upper-class women resulted in a cult of hypochondria, and especially hysteria. Doctors argued that it arose from a morbid condition of the uterus, which began at puberty and ended with the menopause.

Medical intervention was said to be necessary to establish personal and social control. 'Cures' included hysterectomies, clitorectomies, ovarectomies and other forms of genital mutilation. While most women were not 'treated' surgically, they did consult medical men and came to define themselves as inherently sick – a view that was reinforced by the view that hysteria was a contagious disease and isolation from other women was considered essential to successful treatment.

The portrayal of women, and especially upper-class and middle-class ones, as inherently sick created more work for medical men, which enhanced the status and income of those who were doctors to wealthy women. It also underpinned doctors' campaigns against midwifery, as they claimed that all women's complaints, includ-ing pregnancy, were diseases and demanded the care of a doctor. It was thus in the financial interests of doctors, as well as sustaining their claim to exclusive right to treat the sick, to maintain the view that women were not only weaker than men but also inherently sick. It also justified the exclusion of women from the public spheres of education, business and politics and reinforced the view that a woman's role was in the domestic sphere and that women's fulfilment came from motherhood. This view is still evident in the ways in which women are often treated during pregnancy and childbirth by the medical profession to this day.

Women, medicine and reproduction

As Lesley Doyal has pointed out,

> If women are to maximise their health and their autonomy they must be able to determine the nature of their reproductive lives ... they must be able to control their own fertility without risking unpleasant or dangerous side effects and they must be able to pass safely through pregnancy and childbirth.
>
> (Doyal, 1995, p. 93)

Medicine is involved in three areas of reproduction:

1 contraception – the prevention of unwanted pregnancy;
2 pregnancy and childbirth; and
3 reproductive technologies designed to enable women who could not otherwise do so to become pregnant.

While feminists have been critical of medical intervention in these areas, it is nevertheless important to recognise that there have been positive aspects to this intervention. In the nineteenth and early twentieth centuries women did face extreme hazard in childbirth, and many, including upper-class women, had severe complications and long-term ill health as a result of pregnancy and childbirth, including prolapse of the uterus and irreparable pelvic tears. Medical advances have made pregnancy and childbirth a much less hazardous process for both the mother and the child. Medicine cannot take all the credit – improved diet, hygienic conditions and a general rise in the standard of living have all played an important role in reducing maternal and infant mortality and morbidity. Nonetheless, credit is due.

However, medical dominance in these areas of women's lives means that women are controlled to a large extent by medical men, and they rely on doctors for advice and information. For example, pregnant women are treated 'as if' something is going to go wrong – women are required to make regular ante-natal visits and are often subject to medical pressure to have their babies in hospital, where doctors control the management of labour and childbirth. As Ann Oakley (1987) argues, motherhood has become a medicalised domain.

The key point is not that medical intervention has played no role in making pregnancy and childbirth safer, but that doctors have taken over total control of the management of pregnant women, so that women are unable to make informed decisions about their lives. This came out clearly in the case of Wendy Savage, the consultant obstetrician who was suspended on a charge of incompetence (of which she was eventually cleared) after a campaign by her male colleagues, who objected to the ways in which she practised (see Savage, 1986). During the campaign to clear her and the subsequent inquiry it became evident that the key issues surrounded how pregnancy and childbirth were to be managed. Savage argued that women should be allowed to make informed choices during pregnancy and childbirth, that ante-natal care should be provided in clinics near women's homes and that they should be allowed to give birth at home if they wanted to do so. The role of the doctor was to assist women, not to control them and make decisions for them.

Feminists have argued not only that women often do not feel in control during pregnancy and childbirth, but also that there is little evidence to support the view that technological intervention in childbirth is beneficial for mother and/or child. Ann Oakley (1982), reporting on research carried out in 1975, found that 69 per cent of first-time mothers did not feel in control of themselves and what was going on in labour. She also quotes research carried out in Wales, finding that the increased use of induction (artificial starting of labour) did not reduce perinatal mortality (death of the baby in the first two months of life), but did increase the number of low birth-weight babies. Induction carries risks to both maternal and foetal health – for example, the tearing of the perineum in the mother and an increased likelihood of a forceps-assisted birth with its associated risks. There has also been an increase in the use of Caesarean section without clear evidence that this has improved the health of babies or mothers. Other routine procedures such as foetal heart monitoring and routine episiotomy (cutting the perineum to prevent tearing) are also of doubtful benefit.

Feminists have suggested that women and doctors have very different views about pregnancy and childbirth. During pregnancy, they suggest, the mother is seen by doctors as a life-support system for the foetus, and the emphasis is on the needs and health of the baby rather than those of the mother. Doctors regard themselves as the experts on childbirth and pregnancy. Medical practice is based on the assumption that doctors have access to a scientific body of knowledge about childbirth, but doctors deal mainly with illness and they tend to treat pregnancy as if it were a sickness. This means that they are more interested in the pathological than the normal, in using technology, and in women taking medical advice.

Graham and Oakley (1981) argue that while doctors see pregnancy as a medical problem, women see it as a natural phenomenon. While for the doctor pregnancy and childbirth are medical events starting with diagnosis and ending with discharge from medical supervision, for women they are parts of a process which has to be integrated with other social roles. They are accompanied by a change in status, to mother, with the obligations that this imposes permanently and comprehensively on a woman's life. While for medical men the success of pregnancy and childbirth is measured by low perinatal and maternal mortality rates and low incidence of certain kinds of morbidity, and a 'successful' outcome is a healthy mother and baby in the immediate post-birth period, for the mother success is measured by a healthy baby, a satisfactory personal experience of labour and delivery, the establishment of a satisfactory relationship with the baby and integrating the demands of motherhood into her lifestyle. While the doctor sees himself as the expert, possessing superior knowledge and therefore in control, the mother sees herself as knowledgeable about pregnancy, as perceptive about the sensations of her body and its needs. However, the mothers in Graham and Oakley's research felt they were not in control. Pregnant women spoke of problems in communicating with their doctors, of not being able to ask questions, and of being treated as ignorant. They also disliked being seen by different doctors at each visit and complained that they felt like battery hens – as just one unimportant item in a factory production system.

While feminists have argued that doctors have medicalised childbirth and in the process taken away control from women, they have also pointed to medical control in other areas of reproduction. Doctors control the most effective means of birth control – the pill, the coil, the cap and sterilisation. Women have to seek medical advice to be able to use these methods of controlling their fertility. The 1968 Abortion Reform law made abortion on medical grounds legal and more freely available, but the decision as to whether a woman can have an abortion is made by doctors. Doctors also control the new reproductive technologies concerned with helping women to conceive and have children. Doctors often refuse sterilisation or abortion to young married women while single women and women from ethnic minority groups are positively encouraged to have abortions. Doctors also decide which women should have access to reproductive technology, and the decision is often based on moral rather than medical judgement. (Many health authorities in the UK routinely refer applications for NHS assistance with reproduction to their Ethics Committees when these are from lesbian couples, but not necessarily from heterosexual ones, for instance.) Also, access to reproductive technology and abortion is mediated by ability to pay; NHS provision is greatly outstripped by demand, so many women are forced to turn to private practitioners. This option, however, is available only to those with money. Scientific and medical advances in the area of reproduction have on the one hand given women the possibility of deciding if, when and under what conditions they will have children. On the other hand, however, the dominance of so much of reproductive technology by the medical profession and the state has permitted doctors to have even greater control over women's lives.

The development of *in vitro* fertilisation in the late 1970s, which was seen as a 'miracle cure', has led feminists more recently to turn their attention to what are commonly described as the 'new' reproductive technologies – the medicalisation of infertility. These include not only technologies that make it possible to extend parenthood to people who have been unable to realise their wish to have a child, but also techniques that can be used to diagnose genetic or chromosomal abnormalities *in utero* and which at the same time enable the sex of the child to be determined. Feminists and disability activists have raised concerns about the ethical issues raised by these developments (Hughes, 2000). Traditionally, childlessness has been seen as a punishment or a sign of divine disfavour – the stigma of being barren. IVF offers infertile couples hope (although many of those treated do not conceive). However, medicalised reproductive genetics treat the body as a machine and there is a disjuncture between women exercising agency and the medical imperative to produce a perfect baby (Ettore, 2002).

While some feminists have been concerned about the availability of the services on the NHS and the ways in which access to them is controlled by the medical profession, others have raised questions about the impact that they will have on women's lives. Access to infertility treatment is restricted and a majority of infertile women who undergo techniques such as IVF still do not have a child – 90 per cent of treated women do not have a baby. Some have suggested that the new technologies will be used by men to control and exploit women even further. Amniocentesis, it is argued, will be and has been used to determine the sex of the unborn foetus and force women to have an abortion if the foetus is not of the desired sex – generally male – while it is very difficult for a single woman to get IVF treatment, reinforcing the patriarchal ideology of the heterosexual nuclear family. (Indeed, there is evidence that new technologies are used to determine sex in India, where male children are valued over female ones – see Therborn, 2004.)

Other feminists (e.g. Michele Stanworth, 1987) have suggested a more cautious approach. While recognising the strong desire of some women to have children and the ways in which they will be assisted by the new technologies, Stanworth suggests that insufficient attention has been paid to questions of safety, women's health and their ability to make informed decisions. Also, it is necessary to recognise that there is a range of reproductive technologies – not just the various 'new' techniques that have been the focus of public attention. While many of these techniques are flawed and their safety questionable, nevertheless they provide an indisputable resource on which women draw according to their priorities. What is necessary is for women to be better informed about these technologies so that they can make better informed decisions. While science may be seen as helping women, the control over it is often not in their hands, but those of doctors.

These issues can be illustrated by reference to ultrasound – a method of enabling doctors and patients to see an image of the foetus on the screen. Doctors use it to detect abnormalities and to date conception exactly (women's knowledge of when they became pregnant is regarded as unreliable, and some women cannot give an exact date for the first day of their last period, which is used to date conception). Women gain great benefit from seeing their own baby in this way (Petchesky, 1987), but, Ann Oakley (1987) has pointed out that it is not entirely certain that the procedure is completely safe – it may cause some risk to the health of the mother and/or the foetus.

Women, health and domestic violence

The ambivalent attitude that feminists adopt to the medical profession and medical interventions has been highlighted in the attention given to domestic violence as a health problem. Feminist research on domestic violence has highlighted it as a serious problem and indicated that it is probably the single most common cause of injury to women, although health professionals, at least in Britain, appear not to recognise it as such. Doctors tend to treat the physical injuries and not their cause – the abusive relationship (Pahl, 1995). Doctors do not see domestic violence as an area for medical intervention, as Mildred Dealey Payclaw has suggested: 'Physicians will often say, "I'm not a law enforcement officer, and I'm not a social worker. I'm here to treat the body, and she needs to see a psychiatrist"' (quoted in *Journal of the American Medical Association*, 1990).

The issue, as Jan Pahl indicates, is 'What can health service professionals do to help women?' (1995, p. 127). She suggests that health professionals must respect women's accounts, know the relevant information to enable them to help women, keep careful records of injuries and give the time to help women. In the US, Needs Assessment Profiles have been developed for use with women whom doctors or other health care workers suspect of having been abused (Jezierski, 1992; Lazzaro and McFarlane, 1991; Flitcraft *et al.*, 1992).

> If abuse is to be prevented, the cycle of violence interrupted and the health and well being of women provided, nurses in all settings must take the initiative in assessing all women for abuse during each visit [for ante-natal care] and offering education, counselling and referral.
>
> (Lazzaro and McFarlane, 1991, p. 28)

However, while health professionals may be able to provide immediate treatment, the long-term help they can provide is limited, given that the long-term solution to domestic abuse is giving more power to women, individually and collectively:

> Violence against women is the product of the subordination of women. Short-term measures may have short-term effects . . . but it is certain that no long-term measures will be successful unless there is a fundamental change in the social and economic structures that maintain the subordination of women within marriage and in wider societies.
>
> (United Nations, 1989, p. 108)

The danger is that health professionals medicalise domestic violence, lay the blame for the violence on the woman victim and ignore the perpetrator of violence and the context in which the violence took place. Thus on the one hand feminists recognise that health professionals are in a powerful position to provide help and support for women who are abused by their partners, while on the other hand they are wary of the extent to which professionals will be able to move outside patriarchal assumptions about the family and the causes of domestic violence.

Women as providers of health care

Women form the majority of health care workers, both formal and informal. Over 75 per cent of all employed health care workers in the UK are women. Women are concentrated in the lower-paid, lower-status jobs. While 90 per cent of nurses are female, only 25 per cent of doctors are. Also, the majority of cleaners and kitchen staff are women. Black women tend to be in the lowest-paid, lowest-status jobs. Thus there is horizontal and vertical occupational segregation in the health service. The majority of doctors are men in Western medicine and the occupation is gender-segregated and gender-stratified (see Chapter 9), with male doctors tending to specialise in the more prestigious areas (Lorber and Moore, 2002).

Women are also the major providers of unpaid health care in the home. Even excluding those caring for dependent children, about 75 per cent of adults caring for an elderly or disabled relative in the home are women (see Arber and Ginn, 1991). Much health education is directed at women, who are assumed to care for other relatives in the household. Health visiting was developed in the early part of this century specifically as a way of educating mothers in how to look after their babies and young children. Girls' education at school has been seen as part of the process of training them for motherhood. Mothers have been blamed for the poor health of their husbands and children, and maternal education has been seen as a way of improving the nation's health. Often the poor material and economic circumstances under which women are caring for their families have been ignored and the blame for the poor health of children has been placed on the ignorance of mothers rather than on poverty.

Women as healers, men as professionals

Feminists have rediscovered the historical role of women as healers, showing that until the eighteenth century healing was mainly women's work, but that since then men have come to play a dominant role in medicine. However, long before this men had tried to prevent women practising medicine, and from the eighteenth century they challenged their right to practise midwifery autonomously.

While there is evidence that women practised medicine in medieval Europe (Verslusyen, 1980), a law was passed in England in 1421 preventing this practice. Pressure for this law came from male doctors, and in this they were supported by the Christian belief that women were inferior and had an evil nature (Daly, 1978). However, health care given by women, as today, extended far beyond professional work. Women cared for the sick members of their families and community and played a central role in childbirth, which until the seventeenth century was seen as the exclusive concern of women. Women learned about helping the sick and assisting women in childbirth from other women in the community who had acquired the necessary skills and expertise. Thus, while women were barred from formal institutions of learning, they learned from each other (Ehrenreich and English, 1979). Indeed, the poor had little access to formal medical care until the nineteenth century, with the growth of the voluntary hospitals, and the available evidence suggests that women continued to rely on informal knowledge, and on each other, in areas such as birth control and abortion until well into the twentieth century.

A key question that has concerned feminists is how men came to usurp women's traditional role as healers. It seems unlikely that this happened because men's skills and knowledge were superior, as there is little evidence that qualified doctors had effective treatments to apply before this century, although the claims made by male medical men that they had superior skills may have been believed by some patients. Also, the ability to afford the high fees charged by physicians may have been a way of achieving and maintaining a high status in middle-class society.

Ehrenreich and English (1979) have suggested a link between the campaigns against witches that occurred in Europe between the fourteenth and seventeenth centuries and the suppression of female healing. They argue that women healers were singled out to be executed as witches and that thousands of women peasant healers were seen as part of a subversive social movement threatening the (male) authority of Church, Crown, the aristocracy and the few university-trained physicians. However, there is no clear evidence that all or even most women healers were regarded as witches during this period, and indeed there is considerable evidence that unqualified women healers continued to practise in England after the witch-hunts had ceased.

Other feminists have argued that the changes that accompanied the industrial revolution were a major factor in men achieving control and dominance in medical practice. Alice Clark (1982 [1919]) argued that the displacement of women healers by qualified medical guilds (the precursors of the Royal Colleges) was part of the process whereby skilled workers in general moved out of the family into the marketplace and excluded the unskilled and unqualified from practice. Margaret Verslusyen (1980) also points to the development of hospitals. Before the eighteenth century medical men treated only the wealthy, in their own homes. By the end of the eighteenth century hospitals had begun to be built in the growing towns. These hospitals were built with charitable money donated by the wealthy for the exclusive use of working-class patients. In them, medical men began to treat 'charity' patients who were their 'inferiors'. Doctors were therefore able to develop and test new ideas on these patients. At the same time the growth of the middle class meant that there was an increase in the number of fee-paying patients for doctors to treat at home. The growth in clientele and the claims to new scientific knowledge provided a base from which qualified doctors pressed for the banning of their unqualified female rivals.

Anne Witz's (1992) neo-Weberian analysis has argued that the ways in which medical men struggled to establish and sustain a sexually segregated division of labour provides an example of *social closure* and *demarcation* (and that they were aided in applying this closure by the state) – closure in that women were excluded from practising medicine, and demarcation in that doctors defined what was medical work, and therefore the preserve of medical men, and what was ancillary and could be carried out by female nurses and midwives. In 1858 the Medical Act established the exclusive male prerogative. The Act defined a person who could practise medicine as one who was a qualified medical practitioner by virtue of possessing a British university degree or a licentiate membership or fellowship of one of the medical corporations. The Act did not exclude women in itself, but women were not allowed in practice to go to universities or become members of medical corporations.

The exclusion of women from medical practice was challenged by women who conducted a protracted struggle to gain admittance to the medical profession. The first qualified female medical practitioner to practise in Britain was Elizabeth Blackwell, who qualified at a US medical school in 1849. Elizabeth Garrett (Anderson) qualified in 1865 with the Society of Apothecaries, the only medical corporation that did not explicitly exclude women. However, the Society immediately changed its rules so that the same could not happen again.

Women campaigned to be allowed to qualify as doctors on the basis of equal rights claims – a common demand of feminists in the nineteenth century and based on the dominant liberal political philosophy. Women also argued that women and children should have the right to be treated by a woman doctor. They had to gain the support of male Members of Parliament to introduce legislation. In 1875 an 'Enabling Bill' was passed, permitting universities and medical corporations to admit women, but this did not force them to do so. (In 1899 an Act of Parliament removed all the remaining legal barriers to women training as doctors, so that they had in theory to be admitted to training, but the de facto barriers remained.) In the late 1870s, Sophia Jex-Blake and other women established the London School of Medicine for Women. However, even when women were admitted to medical training and became qualified medical practitioners, they tended to confine their practice almost exclusively to women and children, working in hospitals or in dispensaries they established themselves, or as medical missionaries.

While women won the right to train as doctors and practise medicine, it continued to be a male-dominated profession. There has been a steady increase in the number of women training as doctors and in the proportion of female to male medical students; nevertheless the high-status jobs continue to go to men (see Chapter 9). Female general practitioners argue that they are frequently expected to look after women and children, yet they want to deal with the full range of patients and medical complaints dealt with by general practitioners.

Nurses, midwives and medical men

A key feature of health care is the dominance and control that doctors exercise over paramedical workers, including midwives and nurses, a position that is sustained through state support (Johnson, 1972; Larkin, 1983). Nursing was established as a profession supplementary to medicine (Gamarnikow, 1978), and the Midwifery Act of 1903, which required that only registered midwives be permitted to practise, placed them finally under medical control. Jeff Hearn (1982) has argued that the process of professionalisation is a process of male assumption of control over female tasks. Thus as male doctors acquire the status of a profession they not only exclude female healers from practising but gain control over other female workers, who take on a subordinate role in the medical division of labour.

Women healers retained control over childbirth for a much longer period than they did over healing generally, but even in midwifery they began from the 1660s to have their dominant role challenged by male midwives (obstetricians). It is possible that the origins of male midwifery relate to the invention of the obstetric forceps, or more simply that it was just another example of males attempting to take over a field previously dominated by females. However, there was opposition to male midwifery (1) from the general public, who thought it indecent, (2) from female midwives because of the threat to their livelihood, and (3) from established medical men who saw midwifery as degrading women's work and not part of medicine at all.

The invention of the obstetric forceps was certainly an important 'breakthrough'; prior to their invention, an obstetric delay (slow birth) resulted in the death of the mother and/or the child. The use of them was restricted to barber-surgeons and therefore to men, and the number of cases helped was small and the risk of infection and death as a result of their use was enormous. The growth of the lying-in hospitals where male midwives delivered women also played a role in raising the status of male midwifery, especially as women were excluded from the scientific knowledge they claimed to have. Probably more important was the fact that from the seventeenth century a fashion gradually developed for the wealthy to use male midwives, giving support to the male midwives' claim that their knowledge was superior to that of female midwives. This was supported by the argument that only the male midwives could do surgery if complications should arise.

It was in the late nineteenth century that medical doctors accepted that midwifery should be undertaken and controlled by men. During the nineteenth century the Colleges of Physicians and Surgeons both argued against doctors' involvement in midwifery, but by 1850 lectures in midwifery were being given in British medical schools and by 1866 proficiency in it was necessary for qualification as a medical practitioner. The claim by doctors to control childbirth was made on the basis that medical men had superior knowledge. By 1880:

> a great advance had been made in the science and art of midwifery. This was due chiefly to the introduction of male practitioners, many of whom were men of learning and devoted to anatomy, the groundwork of obstetrics.
>
> (Spencer, 1927, p. 175)

This claim was not justified on medical grounds. In the nineteenth century a quarter of women giving birth in hospital died of puerperal fever, and those delivered at home were more likely to be infected if they were attended by a male doctor rather than a female midwife. (Puerperal fever is an infection transmitted by doctors from other areas, and especially from dead bodies, to women in childbirth.) Nevertheless medical men were determined to gain control of midwifery and to determine the role of female midwives – to establish the division of labour between themselves and female midwives. Thus they set out to demarcate what areas were rightfully theirs at the same time as defending the medical prerogative. The struggle between medical men and female midwives since the seventeenth century had begun to establish a distinction between assistance at childbirth and intervention in childbirth – one between normal and abnormal childbirth. Only male doctors (qualified medical practitioners) were allowed to use forceps and to intervene surgically.

The Midwifery Registration Act of 1903 resulted in the registration and education of midwives coming under the control of medical men, and a doctor had to be called in if anything went wrong with a delivery. A major reason why doctors did not usurp the role of midwives was that they realised that there was no way in which they could meet the demand – in the late nineteenth century, seven out of every nine births were attended by female midwives. Also, many doctors did not want to attend poor women.

Doctors thus deskilled midwives, and while female midwives continued to attend poor women in childbirth, doctors attended the wealthy. Medical domination of childbirth continues in the early twenty-first century, and indeed it could be argued that it has increased, because the majority of births are in hospital under the (official) control of a consultant, and because of the increased use of medical technology. While most women are actually delivered by a (female) midwife, the ultimate control remains in the hands of the (generally male) obstetrician.

Nurses, too, play a subordinate role in the medical division of labour. Nursing has always been and continues to be a predominantly female province. Most nursing is of course done by women, as unpaid carers in the domestic sphere. However, nursing in the public sphere is also predominantly a female occupation. While caring for the sick was undertaken in a variety of institutions in the past, it was not until the middle of the nineteenth century that nursing emerged as a separate occupation. Prior to that, nursing in hospitals was seen as a form of domestic work that required little specific training and was usually undertaken by married women, doing little different for their patients than they did for their families at home. The demarcation between nurses and patients was blurred – able-bodied convalescent patients were expected to help the nurses with the domestic work on the wards. Florence Nightingale suggested that in the mid-nineteenth century nursing was mainly done by those 'who were too old, too weak, too drunken, too dirty, too sordid or too bad to do anything else' (quoted in Abel-Smith, 1960, p. 53). The argument that nurses needed training and the recognition by doctors that bedside medicine meant that patients needed monitoring developed before Florence Nightingale's reforms. However, she did attempt to develop nursing as a profession and to recruit middle-class women, who received a training. These reforms took place in the voluntary hospitals, and it was not until late in the nineteenth century that nurses in workhouse hospitals were trained.

While Florence Nightingale recognised the need for trained nurses, she trained them in obedience, so that in the division of labour between nurses and doctors, nurses were seen and saw themselves as the subordinates of doctors and as under medical control. Nor did Nightingale challenge the link between womanhood and nursing. Eve Gamarnikow (1978) has pointed out that in the Nightingale model nurses were still responsible for the cleaning of the wards as well as the care of the patients. She suggests that the relationship between doctor and nurse paralleled the relationship between the Victorian husband and wife in the family. The nurse looked after the physical and emotional environment, while the doctor decided what the really important work was and how it should be done. Thus the good nurse was the good mother, concerned with caring for her patients (family).

During the twentieth and early twenty-first centuries, while nurses no longer see themselves as handmaidens of doctors, they have remained trapped in their status as subordinate to doctors; their role is to care while that of doctors is to cure. In 1918 the Nursing Register was introduced, and the Nurses Act 1943 established state-enrolled nurses as well as state-registered ones, but neither kind is recognised as independent practitioners. Ann Oakley (1984b) confessed:

> In a fifteen-year career as a sociologist studying medical services, I confess that I have been particularly blind to the contribution made by nurses to health care.

Indeed, over a period of some months spent observing in a large London hospital I hardly noticed nurses at all. I took their presence for granted (much as, I imagine, the doctors and patients did).

(Oakley, 1984b, p. 24)

Nursing in the early twenty-first century is seen predominantly as a lowly paid female occupation, but there are clear ethnic and class divisions in nursing. The greater emphasis on community care for frail elderly people has also resulted in home helps taking on personal care work, creating even greater divisions between women who perform paid caring work and those who supervise it (Abbott, 1995). Working-class women and women from ethnic minorities are concentrated in the assistant grades and white middle-class women in the registered grade in the prestigious teaching hospitals. Furthermore, more men are entering nursing, and the new managerial structures introduced in the 1970s have resulted in a disproportionately large number of men appointed to management posts (Evans, 2004). Although men have been able to become general nurses only since 1943, they have increasingly moved into senior posts in what was once, as far as the nursing of physical illness was concerned, an all-woman and woman-managed occupation. (The situation is much the same in other Western countries – see e.g. Lorber and Moore, 2002. Interestingly, medicine is a female-dominated occupation in Russia – but it is also poorly remunerated and carries low status.)

Women, motherhood and 'informal' care

Women are seen as primarily responsible for maintaining the health of their families, and as informal, unpaid carers they play a major role in caring for the sick, the disabled, the elderly and other dependent groups. Hilary Graham (1987) argues that women are providers of informal health care in the domestic economy and that this role is shaped by the sexual division of labour such that men are seen as providers and women as carers, and by the spatial division of labour, where the local community is seen as the setting for routine medical care and centrally located institutions of medicine for the application of specialist medical skills. Graham suggests that there are three aspects to women's health work:

- *providing* for health;
- *teaching* for health; and
- *mediating* professional help in times of crisis.

Thus she argues that much routine domestic labour and caring is about health maintenance, while women are seen as responsible for the health education of their children and are generally the ones who decide whether it is necessary to consult a doctor.

The welfare state was built on the assumption that the traditional nuclear family was the norm and that women would care and provide for the members of this family. As is pointed out in Chapter 6, more recent policies of community care are built on the assumption that women are prepared to care for dependent members of their families (including the wider, extended family). Health promotion campaigns are also often directed at women, assuming that it is their role to care for and look after the health of their men and children.

Women are also blamed when their families are seen as unhealthy. They are seen as responsible for bringing up healthy children and maintaining the health of their men for the nation. Health visitors, social workers and other professional state employees 'police' the family to ensure that women are carrying out their task adequately. Since the early twentieth century motherhood has been a medical domain not just in terms of ante-natal care and delivery, but in terms of bringing up healthy children. When in the early twentieth century considerable concern was expressed about the poor health of the working class, made visible in public by the poor state of men volunteering to enlist in the army at the time of the Boer War, the blame was placed on negligent mothers. It was argued that women should put caring for their families first, should give up paid employment and be trained in domestic skills and childcare. The government advocated the employment by local authorities of trained health visitors under the control of the district medical officers, building on the voluntary movement that had developed in the nineteenth century which visited the houses of working-class families with young children. Scant attention was paid to the poverty and appalling conditions in which working-class women were struggling to bring up their children and the poor health experienced by most of these women. The available evidence suggests that, then as now, women put the needs and demands of their families first and gave little consideration to their own needs.

While it is rarely given official recognition, and the tendency is to see paid health workers as the primary providers of health care, women provide most health care within the confines of the family. The unpaid, rarely recognised health care work of women in the domestic sphere is extensive. The welfare state is built on the assumption that women will perform this work and that women naturally want to care for their partners and their children.

While feminists are correct in arguing that male medical men have usurped women's role as healers in the public sphere, women continue to have the major role in the private sphere. However, women are under medical dominance and control in the medical division of labour, whether they are paid workers in the public sphere or unpaid workers in the domestic one.

Conclusions

Women play a dominant role in health care systems, both as providers of care and as patients. Women have the major responsibility, in the domestic sphere, for providing informal health care for husbands, children and other dependents. Within the formal health care system women predominate, but they are concentrated in the least prestigious and powerful jobs – as nurses, junior doctors, care assistants and domestics. Black women are found disproportionately in the least prestigious jobs – that is, those that are poorly paid, often part-time, and insecure. Medical knowledge has played a powerful role in constructing popular images of women as 'inferior' to men and as controlled by their bodies.

SUMMARY

1 Women are some of the main workers in the health services. The medical services are highly segregated by gender, with employment such as nursing associated with feminine roles – caring, nurturing, domestic work, and so on being associated with female workers while high-status posts associated with specific expertise such as consultancies are associated with male professionals.

2 Women are the main consumers of health services because:

- they are responsible for the health of the family and are likely to see the doctor on the family's behalf;
- women are themselves more likely to suffer from a variety of ailments;
- women live longer than men.

3 Western medicine is defined according to masculine models of health and illness. It has not been concerned with the well-being of the individual but rather with curing disease.

4 Women are more likely to be the informal carers and the ones responsible for health care outside of the formal services – for example, treating the illnesses of family members.

FURTHER READING

Annandale, E. and Hunt, K. (eds) (2000) *Gender Inequalities in Health*. Buckingham: Open University Press. This edited collection is extremely comprehensive and reflects on recent feminist work on gender inequalities in health and health care. It also develops an agenda for future research. It incorporates contributions from a range of perspectives, and from academics who have been central to the development of a gendered analysis of health.

Barry, A-M. and Yuill, C. (2002) *Understanding Health: A Sociological Introduction*. London: Sage. This book is a comprehensive and accessible introduction to the sociology of health and illness. It develops a critique of the 'medical model' and explores the social context of health and health care, the role of the health care professions, and also organisational constraints on health care delivery. Each chapter considers a range of thematic issues and theoretical debates in relation to gender and other aspects of identity and inequality.

Doyal, L. (ed.) (1998) *Women and Health Services: An Agenda for Change*. Buckingham: Open University Press. This practice-oriented book addresses gender inequalities in health care, focusing on the extent to which women's health concerns have moved up the health service agenda in recent years. Its focus is primarily on Britain, however.

CHAPTER EIGHT

Sexuality

Sexuality is generally taken to refer to the social experience and expression of physical bodily desires, real or imagined, by or for others or for oneself. It encompasses erotic desires, identities and practices. Seemingly one of the most private, intimate aspects of our lives, sociologists have argued that sexuality is fundamentally social and political. This is because sexuality is experienced and expressed within relations of power and exchange and what we think of as sexual varies historically and culturally as well as in different social contexts. Sociologists have therefore argued that no human sexual behaviour or practice can be divorced from the social and political circumstances in which it takes place, and the social relations within which it is embedded. This means that even individual sex acts (such as masturbation or other forms of auto-eroticism) are social acts because the way in which we think about and make sense of them is shaped by a range of social values, attitudes, norms and sanctions. Yet sexuality remains something of a neglected topic in sociology when compared to say social class or the mass media, brought onto the sociological agenda only relatively recently. Largely as a result of the contribution of feminist sociologists and political activists sexuality has now begun to emerge as a legitimate focus of sociological concern. Indeed, that New Right movements in many Western societies have mobilised considerable political energies through their emphasis on the sanctity of the family, hostility to gay and lesbian sexuality and to 'sexual deviance' of various kinds is, as Jeff Weeks (1991, p. 12) has noted, something of a 'back-handed compliment to the success of feminism'.

Sexuality has been one of the main concerns of feminist theory and politics not least because feminists regard men's control of women's sexuality as one of the key mechanisms through which patriarchy is maintained. Feminists have drawn attention to the social control of women's sexuality through religious, state and medical regulatory practices. In particular, feminists have emphasised the role of sexuality in reinforcing patriarchal power relations, highlighting issues such as pornography, sexual violence, clitoridectomy, prostitution and 'compulsory heterosexuality' (Rich, 1980) – the social compulsion to be heterosexual. Feminists have also made a significant contribution to theorising sexuality and the sexual body. They have also highlighted the relative neglect of issues of sexual identity in the social model of disability (Lloyd, 2001). Many have argued that the so-called 'sexual revolution' has merely been a means of increasing and legitimating a male right of sexual access to women. Others have highlighted, however, the ways in which sexuality can be a means of challenging and resisting women's oppression. Feminist contributions have also drawn attention to the ways in which so-called scientific perspectives (including those developed by social scientists) have served to perpetuate women's sexual oppression.

Broadly speaking, social scientific approaches have tended to conceptualise sexuality in one of two ways: as either a biological or psychological essence and therefore as pre-social, or as a social construct – a product of the meanings attributed to certain forms of social and physical interaction. Both approaches are premised on the conviction that sexuality has a biological, psychological or social essence; that is, that sexuality constitutes a relatively stable aspect of our biology, psyche or social identity. More recently, and particularly since the influence of postmodernism and poststructuralist ideas, sexuality has come to be regarded as a 'performative' aspect of identity devoid of biological or social essence, but rather constantly enacted and negotiated within the context of power relations and language.

Essentialist perspectives on sexuality

Essentialist perspectives on sexuality are based on the view that sexuality is a biological or psychological essence. Until relatively recently, they have tended to dominate social scientific, as well as legal, moral, religious and medical, discourse on sexuality and sexual relations. A pre-social or essentialist theory of sexuality is grounded in four basic assumptions. These are that sexuality:

- is a basic human drive or force that exists prior to social life;
- is determined by the biological or psychological make-up of human beings;
- resides or exists within the human body; and
- functions throughout our lives essentially as a 'property' of the individual.

From this perspective, human beings are deemed to have a fixed, stable and biologically or psychologically determined sexual identity. It has subsequently become enshrined in five basic assumptions underpinning the legal definition of sexual intercourse in most Western societies:

- sex is natural;
- what is natural is heterosexual;
- genital sex is primary and determining;
- 'true' sexual intercourse is phallocentric; and
- sex is something that ideally takes place within marriage, or at least in a long-term relationship.

Such positivist approaches take for granted the social classification of certain kinds of behaviour as sexual, and within that category certain forms as natural and normal, while others are seen as unnatural or deviant. The concern has often been to explain why sexually deviant behaviour occurs. Anti-positivist or social constructionist approaches (that we consider below) are concerned by contrast to illuminate the socio-historical processes through which certain kinds of sexuality come to be constructed (as normal and natural) and to explore the power relations involved.

In the twentieth century, at least in Western societies, psychoanalytic theories of sexuality gradually became more influential than biological ones. Associated most notably with the work of Sigmund Freud, the conception of sexuality as a basic human drive came to underpin the development, in the early twentieth century, of sexology – the 'science' of sex. In a simplified form, psychoanalytic approaches emphasise that adult identity, including sexuality, is largely determined by childhood experience. Thus, what are seen as abnormal forms of sexual behaviour are thought to be the result of experiences in early childhood, or of arrested libidinal development. Thus, lesbianism is characterised in terms of 'mother fixation', and gay men are seen as coming from homes in which the mother was a strong influence whilst the father was a submissive or absent figure. Many aspects of these theories have a strong 'common-sense' appeal, and are reflected in political debates and social policies concerning, for instance, single parenthood or fostering and adoption by gay and lesbian couples.

Sociologists have made a number of critical points about biological and psychoanalytic theories of sexuality. First, the extent to which there is a biological basis to sexuality remains open to debate. Second, research by social psychologists has found no common factor in the upbringing of homosexuals different from that of heterosexuals, nor any consistent personality differences between the two groups. Third, positivist approaches tend to assume that adult sexuality is fixed and stable, and easily categorised: that people are either homosexual or heterosexual (or bisexual).

Sexology evolved as a body of specialist knowledge collated and disseminated by 'experts' such as Havelock Ellis and Alfred Kinsey, as well as William Masters and Virginia Johnson who proclaimed themselves to be devoted to establishing scientific proof of what is normal and natural in terms of sexual identity and behaviour. Though, on the one hand, it could be argued that sexology was potentially a radical social movement that freed sexuality from its close association with religious and moral doctrine, focusing instead on the 'scientific' study of sexuality (religious moralism and authoritarian codes were deemed to be dissolved in the light of scientific reason), on the other hand, sexology lent scientific credibility to essentialist and, feminists have argued, highly patriarchal, definitions of 'normal' sexuality. 'Normal' sexuality came to be defined as heterosexual (penetrative), monogamous and procreative (a development that had important legal implications). Sexology tended to be highly gendered, and defined women largely as sexually passive and men as naturally sexually active, with a high sex drive. Feminists have argued that this 'scientific' insight served to reinforce and perpetuate a sexual double standard between men and women.

During the decades after the First World War in Britain, sex and the nature of male and female sexual desire was being opened up to scientific scrutiny by doctors, sexologists, psychologists and members of other, relatively new professions, such as psychoanalysis and psychotherapy. Their ideas were also being popularised through the publication of marriage manuals and advice literature by a number of authors, of whom perhaps the most influential was Marie Stopes. Her most famous book *Married Love* was first published in 1918 and by 1930 has been through eighteen editions (seven in its first year), sold 690,000 copies and had been translated into ten languages. The book's successors included *Wise Parenthood, Radiant Motherhood* and *Enduring Passions.*

200

Stopes was unequivocal in her message that both men and women should marry as early as possible. She painted a highly idealised picture of lifelong sexually satisfying unions between loving partners – a goal which, she believed, was achievable by every 'normal' person. While the idealisation of marriage was not in itself new, Stopes's emphasis on the importance of sexual satisfaction not only for men but also for women, and on mutual pleasure and marital harmony, was something of a revelation in the public imagination. It has been argued by feminists such as Susan Kingsley Kent (1993) that the advice given by Stopes and others in the inter-war years marks a shift in gender relations, towards an unprecedented emphasis on mutual sexual pleasure for men and women. Where her advice is particularly problematic in feminist terms is in Stopes's insistence that sexual satisfaction was normal, beneficial and indeed essential for married men and women, while at the same time denying its benefits to single people. Yet it is also clear why she adopted this position. Given that her principal object was to promote birth control she had to protect herself against accustations (from members of the Church for instance) that her work was licensing immorality and vice. As June Rose (1992) notes, *Married Love* would surely have been banned if there had been any explicit suggestion that single people might benefit from its contents. That sex outside of marriage was so inherently problematic for Stopes illustrates both the hegemonic position marriage occupied in the early part of the twentieth century, as well as the strain this institution was under. However, it was not until the pill was made widely available and acts decriminalising abortion and homosexuality were passed in the late 1960s that the connections between sex and marriage began to lose their hegemonic grip (see Chapter 5). Yet even today, as the popularity of TV shows such as *Men Behaving Badly* in the UK, and the best-selling novel and film *Bridget Jones's Diary* testify, the sexual relationships of single men and women are still seen as problematic set against an ever more illusory happily married norm.

Margaret Jackson (1987) has emphasised that the development of sexology meant that those aspects of female sexuality and heterosexuality that feminists viewed as social and political were reaffirmed as fundamentally natural, and by constructing a 'scientific' model on that basis, sexuality was effectively removed from the political arena. Hence, by consigning sexuality to the sphere of the natural, the exclusive preserve of the (largely male) scientist, sexologists 'helped to protect it from feminist challenge' (p. 56). Jackson argues that a scientific model of sexuality has the effect of universalising male sexual supremacy, so that:

> Male sexuality has been universalized and now serves as the model of *human* sexuality. Furthermore, by equating human sexual desire with a coital imperative, i.e. a biological drive to copulate, 'sex' is ultimately reduced to a reproductive function, with the obvious implication that the only really 'natural' form of sexual relationship is heterosexual.
>
> (Jackson, 1987, p. 73)

As she goes on to note, the word 'impotent' means powerless, and carries the implication that a man who is unable to penetrate a woman is also unable to exercise power over her; his penis is (or should be) a 'tool' of male power. The scientific model of sexuality constructed by sexologists is therefore one which both reflects male supremacist values and promotes the interests of men by defining sex in male terms and thus facilitating the sexual–political control of women by men within the institution of heterosexuality and by means of specific heterosexual practices.

(Jackson, 1987, p. 74)

The increasing sexualisation of Western women since the nineteenth century, and other women before and subsequently, should not be seen as liberating, Jackson concludes, but rather as an attempt to eroticise women's oppression, one legitimated by discourses of science and modernity, and particularly by what has been described as 'modernist sexuality'.

Modernist sexuality

Sociologist Gail Hawkes (1996) has argued that a 'modernist sexuality' underpinned sexology, and a much broader series of social processes involving the 'modernization' of sexuality. For Hawkes, modernist sexuality was shaped largely by three factors:

1 the association of sexuality with 'nature';
2 the 'scientific' classification of sexual subjectivities, or the emergence of 'sexual types'; and
3 the primacy of heterosexuality.

A persistent presence in the construction of healthy, moral and natural sexuality was (and remains, sociologists have argued), the privileging of heterosexuality. As a consequence of this 'modernization' process, Hawkes argues,

those manifestations of desire which were deemed to have negative consequences for the maintenance of the patriarchal bourgeois hegemony – women's sexual autonomy, same-sex desire, expressions of youthful sexuality and auto-eroticism – were marginalized and even outlawed.

(Hawkes, 1996, p. 3)

This effectively meant that the central position of heterosexuality was both retained and strengthened as 'what was once ordained by God was affirmed by the men of science' (p. 72). In this respect, sexological research also lent scientific credibility to pre-modern, largely religious or superstitious links between gender and sexuality, providing 'evidence' of women's innate sexual passivity and men's naturally higher sex drive. As Holland et al. have put it,

In medical and common-sense thought, men have uncontrollable sexual urges which are not shared by women. 'Normal sex' then entails active men satisfying passive women in the satisfaction of their own 'natural' desires. Women's sexuality is defined as finding fulfillment in meeting men's needs.

(Holland et al., 1994, p. 29)

Feminists have argued that much of the sexological research carried out in the early to mid-twentieth century was far from scientific, but rather represented patriarchal interests in the production of 'evidence' that served to give credibility to the maintenance of a sexual double standard, to the sexual objectification of women and to the marginalisation of gay, lesbian and celibate sexualities (Jackson, 1987). Sheila Jeffreys (1985) has argued that the category 'lesbian' was introduced in the late nineteenth century in order to control and marginalise both sexual and social intimacy between women.

An essentialist perspective has also shaped our thinking about the relationship between sexuality, race and class. In lending 'scientific' credibility to the idea that working-class and Black people are sexually rampant and immoral, for instance, and less able to control their sexual 'urges'. The influence of racism adds another dimension to the way in which Black and Asian women's sexuality has been understood in essentialist terms. Black women, particularly African and African–Caribbean women have been seen in racist ideology as 'bursting' with an uncontrollable and insatiable sexuality, rendering them in need of 'civilization' by white men (hooks, 1992). Asian women have simultaneously been seen as passive victims, and as exotic and sexual beings. Black women's sexuality has often been constructed in terms of their 'nature' therefore, involving, as Jean Carabine (1992) has put it, normative values about sexuality that are also replicated and reasserted in social policies through ideologies of racism, heterosexuality, familialism and motherhood.

It has to be said then that most of our contemporary understanding of sexuality comes from the work of biologists, medical researchers and sexologists, rather than sociologists, who have tended to focus on hormones, brain structures, drives and instincts. Hence, most of the research on sexuality has been concerned with laying out the biological foundations of sexuality. As Macionis and Plummer (2002, p. 306) note, this is also true of our common-sense understanding, as most people tend to assume that sex is just 'natural'. But, recall from Chapter 1, sociologists tend to challenge common-sense assumptions and taken-for-granted views of the social world, and focus instead on the ways in which what might appear to be natural and pre-social is actually socially constructed and shaped by power relations. Sociologists therefore link sexuality to broader patterns of social stratification and inequality (see Chapter 3).

Sociological perspectives on sexuality

More sociological approaches to sexuality began to develop in the 1960s and tended to shift away from the conceptualisation of sexuality as a biological or psychological essence, focusing instead on the ways in which sexuality is socially constructed (Gagnon and Simon, 1973; Caplan, 1987; Weeks, 1991). William Simon and John Gagnon were arguably the founders of what has become known as the social constructionist approach to sexuality. Both worked at the Kinsey Institute for Sexual Behaviour in the 1960s, and both felt the need to turn to more sociological theories to explain the findings of their empirical research. Drawing on a drama metaphor, they developed the idea of a sexual script to understand the social rules, regulations and roles that serve as a guide to sexual behaviour. They outline three major forms of sexual script:

1 *Personal scripts* are those in our heads – telling us, for instance, what turns us on.
2 *Interactive scripts* are those which emerge from sexual relations – between partners or groups, for instance, and which tell us what role to play.
3 *Historical–cultural scripts* are those which exist in culture and society, and which tell us what is expected of us sexually in any given society.

Jeff Weeks (1986) provides a historical account of the social construction of sexuality in Western societies, identifying three key moments in the evolution of the West's preoccupation with sexual orientation and, particularly, the stigmatisation of homosexuality. The first, he argues, occurred in the first century AD which witnessed a growing disapproval of the indulgence of sex purely for pleasure. The second was in the twelfth century, which saw the triumph of the specifically Christian tradition of sex and marriage, and the belief that the only morally acceptable form of sexual relations was intercourse between a married couple for purposes of reproduction. The third began in the eighteenth century, which produced the explicit construction of heterosexual sex as 'normal' and the consequent categorisation of other forms of sexuality as deviant or perverse (see also Hawkes, 1996).

Underpinning a social constructionist approach is the idea that sexuality is not a fixed entity but rather a complex, interactive aspect of identity and experience, one shaped largely by interaction between individuals and the wider social, economic, and political context. This social constructionist approach has been concerned primarily with the ways in which what we deem to be 'sexual' is not a pre-social, biological essence but rather an, albeit relatively stable, product of the shared meanings attributed to certain forms of behaviour. Professional norms governing the de-sexualisation of gynaecological examinations, for instance, are indicative of the ways in which sexuality is socially constructed through the meanings that come to be associated with particular modes of social interaction. This approach rejects then, the essentialist contention that sexuality is a pre-social given, emphasising instead its social construction. This perspective also highlights the extent to which 'we . . . cannot think about sexuality without taking into account gender' (Weeks, 1986, p. 45).

What sociological perspectives also tend to emphasise is that all cultures have mechanisms to organise sexuality, and no society allows a total 'free for all'. As Macionis and Plummer (2002, p. 307) put it, 'human sexualities are patterned through law, religion and a range of social institutions such as kinship and family systems and economic and social organisation'. Nevertheless, there is considerable variation in the nature and extent of these controls: some religions such as Islam, for instance, seek to regulate sexuality very strictly. According to the classical Hanafi school of Islamic jurisprudence, for example, a wife may only be granted a divorce on grounds of her husband's impotence (Therborn, 2004).

In her account of women's sexuality and social policy, Jean Carabine (1992) emphasised the role of social policy in perpetuating a heterosexual norm. She argues that heterosexuality is a central ideological theme running through social policy in Western societies and intermeshing with ideologies of the family and motherhood.

Other feminist and pro-feminist sociologists have linked heterosexual hegemony to the concept of citizenship, arguing that gay men and lesbian women and other sexual 'minorities' have historically been denied the citizenship status and rights accorded particularly to heterosexual men (Evans, 1993; Richardson, 1998).

Closely linked to the idea that sexuality is socially constructed according to a system of rules and regulations is the concept of a 'hierarchy of sex'. Developed by feminist sociologist Gayle Rubin (1984) the concept of a sexual hierarchy captures the extent to which societies come to classify sexuality according to a system of stratification so that some forms are valued (and hence, come to be located in what she calls our ideational 'comfort zones') while others are not. Rubin devised this hierarchy in the early 1980s and it is interesting to consider some of the ways in which it might have changed since then (see Table 8.1).

Table 8.1 Rubin's hierarchy of sex

'Good' sex	Areas of contest	'Bad' sex
Normal	Unmarried heterosexual couples	Abnormal
Natural	Promiscuous heterosexuals	Unnatural
Healthy	Masturbation	Sick
Holy	Long-term, stable lesbian and gay couples	Sinful
Heterosexual	Promiscuous gay men	'Way out'
Married		Transvestites
Monogamous		Transsexuals
Reproductive		Fetishists/SM
At home		Commercial sex Cross-generational

Source: Rubin, 1984.

What sociological approaches also emphasise is not only the social construction of sexuality, but the social context of its enactment. As Macionis and Plummer have put it,

> We often tend to use sex for social ends, not just biological goals such as reproduction. Far from sex being just biological, we come to use it for many reasons: as an expression of love, as a means to establish bonding, as a way of being clear about our manliness or womanliness, or indeed our maturity. It can be used to show our aggression (as in rape) or to fill up our boredom or as a kind of hobby. It can be used as play, as performance, as power and as a form of work.
> (Macionis and Plummer, 2002, p. 309)

What both essentialist and sociological perspectives on sexuality share in common, nevertheless, is the conviction that sexuality is a relatively stable social identity, one maintained in a (biologically or socially) constant and continuous way throughout our lives, through either a (biological/psychological) developmental process or a process of socialisation and stratification through which we are deemed to acquire a relatively stable, 'true' sexual identity. Both approaches, feminists have argued, also tend to give insufficient attention to power relations in shaping, respectively, the social expression or social construction of sexuality. A more specific concern with the relationship between the social context of sexuality and power relations underpins a third approach to sexuality that can be discerned in more recent sociological literature.

Postmodern sexualities

The contention that sexuality is merely a 'performance' devoid of biological or social essence has been influenced largely by poststructuralism, and particularly the work of Michel Foucault (1979) and its development in Judith Butler's (1990) writing on gender and sexuality. It has also been influenced by the empirical contention that we live in a post- or late modern era in which social identity has come to be shaped by a proliferation of lifestyle choices (Giddens, 1992). The idea that sexuality is performative is based on the view that sexuality is an aspect of identity – a mode of being – that exists only in the way it is presented and performed at any given moment; in other words, it is thought to have no stable biological or social essence outside of its performance.

Postmodern perspectives tend to see society and social identity (including sexuality) as the outcome of discourse. They emphasise that those with more power – heterosexuals, for instance – are able to define those with less power – homosexuals – as abnormal, unnatural, and so on. Discourses on homosexuality, for instance, have tended to define it as an illness (it was not until 1973 that the American Psychiatric Association removed homosexuality from its list of psychological disorders, and then only to relabel it as a 'disturbance' in sexual orientation). Similarly, gay men have often been constructed in homophobic discourse as effeminate, over-sexed, promiscuous, disease-spreading child molesters, while lesbian women have been labelled as butch, man-hating and aggressive. Many gay men and women do of course come to perceive themselves in accordance with such discourses, and so internalise the negative labels applied to them. Research conducted by the London Lesbian and Gay Research Project in 1984, based on a sample of 416 adults aged under 21 who identified themselves as gay, lesbian or bisexual, found that one in five had attempted suicide.

Equally, however, dominant discourses may be challenged and resisted. Indeed, a variety of gay and lesbian resistance movements have developed in the West since the late 1960s. In Britain, for instance, 'Stonewall' established in 1989, has pursued a policy of working through legitimate political channels to bring about social and legislative changes and to advocate the rights of gay and lesbian people, whilst 'Outrage', founded in 1990, has tended to favour direct action and a less conciliatory approach. The gay and lesbian rights movement has also helped to shift academic interest in homosexuality away from studying 'causes and cures' towards the study of homophobia. Narrowly defined, this term refers to a fear of homosexuality, but is now more commonly associated with hostility towards gay men and lesbian women.

As we noted in Chapter 2, Michel Foucault was interested in how specific ways of thinking, talking and writing about the world – what he called discourses – structure our sense of self, our perception of the social world, and of other people. He argued that subjectivity is the outcome of dominant discourses circulating in society at any given time. These discourses shape the social meanings people attach to their own and others' identities and actions – what they 'know' to exist in the social world. Discourses aren't simply ways of knowing in Foucault's terms, though, but define how the world should be categorised and organised; in other words they do not merely describe to us how the world *is*, but also shape our thinking about how it *ought* to be. In *The History of Sexuality*, Foucault (1979) argued that measures to control populations introduced in Western societies since the eighteenth century (what he calls 'bio-power') meant that, inevitably, sexuality and sexual relations came under the influence of dominant social and political discourses of the time. The discourse that consequently developed around homosexuality, for instance, defined it as a perversion.

Although Foucault (1979) himself paid little attention to gender, and regarded the regulation of women's sexuality as only one aspect of its subjection to social control, feminists have found much in his work useful, particularly the contention that sexuality is socially constructed and reconstructed through discourse, and in complex and often contradictory ways. Indeed Foucault's rejection of a 'repressive hypothesis' – the contention that an essential sexuality has been contained and controlled by various religious, social, moral and medical forces – in favour of an analysis which focuses on the ways in which sexuality is constructed in and through power relations has been seen by some feminists as politically liberating, allowing as it does for sexuality to be reconstructed and negotiated on feminist rather than patriarchal terms.

For Butler (1990), far from constituting innate dispositions or relatively stable social categories, sexualities are created and lived through their performance. Butler (1990) illustrates this point with reference to the drag queen, deemed (by the audience) to have a 'true' gender and sexual identity underneath his 'act'. But she argues that what is assumed to be the drag queen's 'true' identity is as much of a performance as that enacted in drag and contends that, in effect, we are all 'on stage' because there is no true self beneath the various identities we perform in different contexts. This perspective emphasises that heterosexuality is not normal or natural, as many biological essentialists and social constructionists might argue, but is merely one performance amongst many possible alternatives. As Butler (1990, p. 31) put it, 'gay is to straight not as copy is to original, but as copy is to copy'. This contention poses two main challenges to heterosexual hegemony. First, it exposes the mechanisms through which heterosexuality is socially constructed as normal and natural, and second, it severs ascribed connections between sex, gender and sexuality (Butler, 1990) emphasising that heterosexuality is only *naturalised* as an 'original'. As Meyer (1994, pp. 2–3) puts it, 'queer does not serve to label a new kind of sexual subject but . . . instead a concept of self which is performative, improvisational, discontinuous, and processual, constituted by repetitive and stylized acts'.

What has come to be known as queer theory, based on a reappropriation of the derogatory term in homophobic discourse, has been particularly significant to the idea that sexuality is performative, emphasising that although Western societies have developed a range of crude categories to contain sexuality, these can never be all-encompassing because of the diverse range of sexual practices, desires and identities that exist. In a challenge to dominant classifications (of straight, gay, lesbian, and so on), Eve Kosofsky Sedgwick (1990) proposes a range of sexual configurations and categories, based on the following ideas:

- even identical genital acts can mean very different things to different people;
- some people spend a lot of time thinking about sex, others little;
- some people like to have sex a lot, others little or not at all;
- many people have their richest mental/emotional involvement with sexual acts that they don't do, or even that they don't *want* to do;
- for some people the possibility of bad sex is aversive enough to make them avoid sex all together, for others this isn't the case;
- some people like spontaneous, unstructured sex, others like sex to be highly scripted, others like sex to seem spontaneous when it is nonetheless totally predictable;
- some people's sexual orientation is shaped by auto-erotic pleasures, for others auto-eroticism is secondary or non-existent;
- some people's sexuality is firmly embedded within a sex–gender matrix, for others it is not.

Characteristic of queer theory, Kosofsky Sedgwick's ideas about sexual identification suggest a mapping of sexuality that does not rely on established categories of homo/hetero/bisexual but instead draws attention to the ways in which these sexual identities are merely performances or roles.

This 'performative' perspective on sexuality, one inspired largely by post-structuralism, is characterised then by a rejection of what is viewed as the essentialism of those approaches considered above that conceptualise sexuality as either biologically determined or socially constructed. Instead, a more postmodern approach is premised on the view that the modernisation of sex (its so-called 'liberation' from the confines of religious and moral teaching, and its location within science) outlined by Gail Hawkes (1996) effectively equates to its 'naturalization' and categorisation in a way that is far from liberatory (Foucault, 1979). The postmodernisation of sex is understood, in William Simon's (1996, p. 30) work for instance, as 'the de-naturalization of sex' involving, in many societies, the dissolution of traditional social structures, the ascendance of secularism over religion, and the relatively recent separation of sexuality from procreation.

Sexuality in the post- or late modern era is understood in terms of a proliferation of lifestyle choices, which are no longer perceived as expressions of an essential or even relatively stable or consistent disposition. Developing the idea of a 'sexual script' (Gagnon and Simon, 1973), Simon (1996) suggests that contemporary sexualities are best understood as dramas, and that heterosexuality constitutes a particular sexual genre – a relatively formulaic performance. He argues that following the emergence of a post-modern society, sexuality has become more fluid, fragmented and diffuse than previously, largely due to the proliferation of lifestyle choices.

This approach involves a rejection of the credibility of so-called scientific studies of sexuality. This perspective also rejects the idea that acquiring a sexual identity is the result of successful completion of a developmental or socialisation process, one that moves through certain key stages. Rather, postmodernists such as Plummer (1996,

p. xv) have argued that in terms of contemporary experiences and identities, 'a supermarket of sexual possibilities pervades'. In this sense, one particular signifier of a possible shift towards a post-modern, performative sexuality that is often cited is that 'heterosexuality has ceased to be a fixed terrain'. Technological innovations in contraception of course greatly facilitated a disassociation of sexuality and procreation. As we noted in Chapter 7, the pill became available in the US in 1960, and in Europe in 1964, quickly followed by IUDs which became available in the late 1960s.

As Therborn (2004) notes, more than anything else, the sexual revolution has brought about a normalisation of long periods of pre-marital sex and a plurality of sexual partners over a lifetime, in a statistical as well as (to a lesser extent, perhaps), in a moral sense. Therborn's (2004) account also emphasises, however, that the effects of sexual revolution have been far from universal. The extreme rigidity and control in South Asia and in West and North Africa, for instance, seems on the whole to have loosened in recent decades, but changes in sexual norms as dramatic as those in northwestern Europe and the US are hard to detect in other parts of the world, he argues. Post-modern perspectives on sexuality are therefore influenced by the idea that fixed points of reference that determined sexual norms and ethics during the modern era – religious, scientific, heterosexual, monogamous (see Hawkes, 1996) – were radically challenged in many Western societies in the latter half of the twentieth century, giving way to a proliferation of sexual choices and identities (Giddens, 1992). Anthony Giddens in particular argues that late modernity has released sexuality from the confines of a single (heterosexual) hegemony and replaced it with 'sexual pluralism' – a sexual identity defined and structured by individual lifestyle choices and relative gender equality. This means, he contends, that behaviours previously thought to be 'perverse' have become an acceptable part of sexual diversity or what he calls 'plastic sexuality' – sexuality for pleasure rather than reproduction. The latter is closely linked to his idea of the 'pure relationship' – sexual relationships enhanced by more open communication and a greater degree of equality than previous generations have experienced, and hence a broader range of emotional and sexual experiences. As sociologist Zygmunt Bauman (1998, p. 24, original emphasis) has put it 'in its postmodern rendition, sexual activity is focused narrowly on its orgasmic effect; for all practical intents and purposes, postmodern sex *is about orgasm*'.

However, as Plummer also notes, poststructuralist and post-modern approaches to sexuality can ultimately be politically disabling not only because they under-emphasise the material factors that constrain our sexual 'performances' or lifestyle choices, but also because (like postmodernism more generally – see Chapter 2) they tend to abandon the pursuit of progress towards sexual liberation or enlight-enment entirely. They may also be misguided empirically; as the figures in Table 8.2 indicate, even in the UK many people still consider homosexual relations, sex outside of marriage and sexual relations under the age of consent to be socially unacceptable.

In its study of social attitudes towards sexual relations, *Social Trends* (1998) found, perhaps not unsurprisingly, that younger people are more likely than older ones to have tolerant attitudes towards same sex sexual relations. The survey found that almost two-thirds of people aged 65 and over thought sexual relations between two adults of

Table 8.2 Attitudes to sexual relations, 1998

	1 Always wrong	2 Mostly wrong	3 Sometimes wrong	4 Rarely wrong	5 Not at all wrong	Other	Total %
A man and a woman having sexual relations before marriage	8	8	12	10	58	5	100
A married person having sexual relations with someone other than their spouse	52	29	13	1	2	4	100
A boy and a girl having sexual relations aged under 16	56	24	11	3	3	3	100
Sexual relations between two adults of the same sex	39	12	11	8	23	8	100

Source: *Social Trends* 30, 1998.

Note: People aged 18 and over were asked whether they thought different types of sexual relations were wrong, on a five-point scale: 1 = always wrong, 2 = mostly wrong, 3 = sometimes wrong, 4 = rarely wrong, 5 = not at all wrong. 'Other' includes those who did not reply, those who replied 'don't know', and those responding 'depends' or 'varies'.

the same sex were always wrong compared with less than a fifth of people aged 18–24. Overall, almost two in five people thought such relationships were always wrong, with about one in five thinking they were not wrong at all. Four in five people thought it always or mostly wrong for a married person to have sexual relations with someone other than their spouse, and a similar proportion thought that sex between a boy and a girl aged under 16 was always or mostly wrong.

Feminist perspectives on sexuality

Largely following Ann Oakley's (1972) distinction between sex, gender and sexuality, feminists have argued that although gender and sexuality are conceptually distinct, they are so closely interrelated in terms of our lived experience that we cannot understand one without reference to the other. Indeed, as Jackson and Scott (1996, p. 3) have put it, 'it is the relationship between the two which makes sexuality a crucial issue for feminists'. Furthermore, feminists have argued that sexuality is embedded within power relations shaped, at least in part, by gender as well as other aspects of identity such as social class, race and ethnicity, global power relations, age, disability, and so on, 'so that we each live our sexuality from different locations within society', as Jackson and Scott have put it (1996, p. 3). Feminists have criticised so-called scientific approaches to sexuality, arguing that they are largely contradictory in defining women as both asexual and saturated with sexuality (Poovey, 1989).

Radical feminists in particular have emphasised that, in the main, it is men who abuse, harass and rape women. It is men who buy and use pornography and it is men who buy commercial sex. It is men who become sex offenders and killers. For radical feminists women's subordination is perpetuated primarily through men's control of women's bodies and sexuality. One of the strongest theoretical elaborations of the role of sexuality in maintaining women's oppression was developed by Catharine MacKinnon (1982), who argued that just as the exploitation of labour is at the heart of class relations, so sexual exploitation is fundamental to what she calls the 'sex class system'. In particular, MacKinnon (1987) has argued that pornography is the foundation of male dominance because it portrays women in dehumanising ways – as the subservient playthings of men – and that this shapes how men (as a group) see women (as a group), and how women see themselves and each other. A related charge is that pornography promotes and incites sexual violence. Radical feminists argue that pornography, like many forms of male sexuality, degrades and abuses women, that it is primarily about the eroticisation of men's power over women, and that it is an ideology that promotes violence against women. As Rebecca Huntley has noted,

> radical feminists reserve a special kind of hatred for . . . fetish pornography focused on physical deformity, for example involving amputees and the physically disabled, [which] is singled out and attacked as the worst kind of pornographic material. Possibly because pornography that features 'atypical' bodies emphasizes the fact that pornography is so clearly about 'the body' as a sexual object. In the same way, pornography that involves pregnant women is equally reviled.
>
> (Huntley, 2000, p. 352)

More libertarian feminists argue that any form of censorship is socially undesirable and ultimately works against women's interests, and that censorship would also restrict the availability of feminist and lesbian erotica. Other feminists argue that the pornography debate, and the preoccupation with sexuality more generally, deflects attention from other important feminist issues.

It is not difficult therefore to understand why sexuality has been so central to feminist theory and politics, for as Jackson and Scott note,

> Historically, enormous efforts, from chastity belts to property laws, have been made to control female sexuality and to tie women to individual men through monogamous heterosexual relationships. The double standard of morality has entitled men to sexual freedoms denied to women. It has also divided women themselves into two categories: the respectable Madonna and the rebarbative whore. Women's sexuality has been policed and regulated in a way which men's has not: it is the woman prostitute who is stigmatized and punished, not her male clients. Heterosexual activity has always been risky for women, associated as it is with loss of 'reputation', with unwanted pregnancy and with diseases which threaten fertility. Women have also been vulnerable to male sexual violence and coercion, yet held responsible for both their own and their assailants' behaviour.
>
> (Jackson and Scott, 1996, p. 3)

All this provided the impetus for the feminist critique of the sexual objectification of women in beauty contests such as Miss World, in pornography, and through the commodification of women in prostitution, as well as the subjection of women to sexual violence since the 1970s. Indeed, feminists have sought to emphasise the relationship between women's sexual objectification and their vulnerability to sexual violence – some by arguing that there is a direct connection (that 'pornography is the theory, rape is the practice'), others by arguing that 'pornography contributes to the cultural construction of a particular form of masculinity and sexual desire which make rape possible and which script the possibilities for its enactment' (Jackson and Scott, 1996, p. 23). Much of this critique has contributed to a fundamental criticism of heterosexual practice and ultimately of the institution of heterosexuality itself.

Feminists such as Sheila Jeffreys (1990) have emphasised the co-option of women into heterosexuality as a manifestation of patriarchal power, along with a series of social assumptions about what it means to 'have sex' being defined largely in patriarchal, heterosexual terms. Jeffreys's critique of the assumption that the sexual revolution was a milestone in the struggle for women's sexual freedom emphasises that many aspects of so-called sexual liberation should actually be seen as directly opposed to feminism, involving, rather than an increase in sexual freedom for women, an eroticisation of women's oppression. Sexologists, she argues, 'have been the high priests who have organized the worship of male power' (p. 1) and in doing so have affirmed the institutional status of heterosexuality.

In her account of heterosexuality and lesbian existence, Adrienne Rich (1980) similarly focused on the institutionalisation of 'compulsory heterosexuality', arguing that what was assumed to be either a natural drive or a social choice was imposed on women. Sociologists have subsequently used this concept to describe the ways in which heterosexism and homophobia have been institutionalised in law, education, religion and language. There are more than 70 countries across the world that criminalise homosexual acts and some of these – Iran, Afghanistan and Saudi Arabia, for instance – have the death penalty for gay sex (Amnesty International, 2001).

Feminists have seen heterosexuality as an institution through which men appropriate women's bodies and their labour. Some, particularly those who came to identify as 'political lesbians' in the 1970s, argued that romantic attachments with men led only to exploitation. The feminist critique of heterosexuality meant that for many feminists 'lesbianism began to be seen as both a viable alternative and a form of resistance to patriarchal domination' (Jackson and Scott, 1996, p. 12). It was tensions between these radical, 'separatist' women and other feminists which Jackson and Scott (1996) argue proved to be particularly disruptive for feminist politics at the end of the 1970s, and which in part 'made a unified women's movement increasingly difficult to sustain' (p. 14). Indeed, debates on heterosexuality and lesbianism have been a major source of tension within feminist theory and politics. Some, as Jackson and Scott outline, have been the destructive cause of major rifts within the women's movement, others have been more productive in forcing feminists to theorise women's diverse sexual experiences and attitudes more adequately.

Women's sexual experiences and attitudes

In her first and most well-known work, *Married Love* (1918), Marie Stopes emphasised the need for a woman to be aroused as a preliminary to sex, and for satisfactory orgasm for both parties. As Lesley Hall (2000) noted in her account of women's attitudes to sex throughout the course of the twentieth century, Stopes practically became a brand name for a new genre of woman-centred sexual advice, but she was not the only woman writing in this field. The female doctor Isabel Hutton also indicated the importance of female orgasm in her book *The Hygiene of Marriage* (published in 1923) as well as the need for preliminary arousal for women's enjoyment of sex (cited in Hall, 2000). Another doctor, Helena Wright (1930), produced a short guide to sex for women, *The Sex Factor in Marriage* in 1930, with a sequel *More About The Sex Factor in Marriage* in 1947. She too placed supreme importance on women's right to sexual arousal and satisfaction. Wright was adamant that a penile–vaginal model of sex was inadequate for many women, and strongly advocated women familiarising themselves with their genitalia and exploring ways of stimulating themselves. In her later work (Wright, 1947), she described how many women remained ignorant of the idea that they too could derive pleasure from sexual relations within marriage, reporting one female patient who, when asked about the happiness or otherwise of her sex life, asked 'Why doctor, what is there to enjoy?' This attitude was also reported by other writers on women and sexuality such as Slater and Woodside (1951, p. 5) who found that 'husbands are valued in an inverse relation to sexuality: "he's very good, he doesn't bother me much"'. Among the women Slater and Woodside interviewed, sex was seen as a duty to be undertaken with endurance, but from which they did not expect to derive any particular pleasure.

Later work, such as Chesser's *The Sexual, Marital and Family Relationships of the Englishwoman* published in 1956, found that when women did experience sexual pleasure they found it difficult to articulate. As he puts it, 'many women have difficulty in describing their sexual sensations, in defining the nature of their sexual pleasures, and are confused as to the definition of their genital experiences' (p. 421, quoted in Hall, 2000, p. 4). He also found that many women felt ashamed to admit that they did not experience orgasm. Clearly, the increased importance given to mutual sexual gratification in marriage brought about its own problems and pressures. In fact, this was the situation that had prompted Wright to expand upon her previous work, conceding that although a certain degree of improvement had resulted from the wider dissemination of sexual guidance to women, it ought to be conceded that ignorance had to an extent given way to performance anxiety. Hence, 'lacking direct information about sex and marriage, and with misleading ideas gleaned from romances, films and popular music', many women were embittered to discover that their own experiences of sexual relations within marriage were rather different from the ideal (Hall, 2000, p. 6).

Shere Hite's initial report in 1976 in many ways only substantiated the insights of these earlier writers – Hite actually cites Helena Wright's work on the need for women to familiarise themselves with their own bodies and sexual potential (Hite, 1976). In her recently updated report, Hite (2000) emphasises the continuing dominance of a penetrative model of 'real' sex, and the gap between women's own sexual feelings and experiences of sexual pleasure within heterosexual relations, and media images of women as sexual beings that, she argues, are defined largely in terms of male sexual fantasies.

The kinds of issues explored in Hite's second report have also been considered by feminist researchers, particularly those focusing on young women and sexual health promotion. In *Ruling Passions*, Sue Lees (1997), for instance, argues that to speak of a woman's 'reputation' still invokes her sexual experiences, and this remains central to the way in which she is judged both in everyday life (in education, for example) and by courts, and welfare and law enforcement agencies. Her recent research on adolescent girls found that the fear of being labelled a 'slag' or a 'slut' (by both boys and other girls) is still a potent force that serves to contain and control young women's sexual self-presentation and behaviour (see Chapter 5 for a discussion of her earlier research – Lees, 1986, 1993). Within sex education, Lees points out, girls are not presented as desiring subjects or initiators of sexual encounters but rather as sexual victims, having to defend themselves against the threat of disease, pregnancy and being 'used'.

Similar conclusions were reached in *The Male in the Head: Young People, Heterosexuality and Power*, based on interviews with young women in London and Manchester by the Women, Risk and Aids Project (Holland *et al.*, 1998). Here Holland and her colleagues comment on the continuing lack of sexual agency amongst young women, concluding from their findings that an active female sexual desire is almost inconceivable to the young men and women who took part in their research. Rather, they found that even girls who were conscious of their own sexual desires were under considerable pressures to contain these, and to focus instead on developing stable heterosexual relationships. Drawing on Foucault's (1979) analysis of sexuality as the outcome of discourse considered above, their account emphasises the extent to which

> Adopting different languages of sex and love is a crucial mechanism in the constitution of gender within heterosexuality. The choices that young people make about the language they use and the discourses they invoke are shaped and constrained by existing power relations and have powerful effects. Although young people may be aware of and resist these processes as individuals, they are nevertheless complicit in collectivities that reproduce these divisions.
>
> (Holland *et al.*, 1998, p. 89)

In particular, for instance, they note that 'metaphors of battle and conquest are central to the way young men talk about their experiences in the male peer group' (p. 87), whereas an emphasis on relationships and romance characterises young women's use of language in their discussions of sexual encounters. Similar research carried out in New Zealand by Jackson and Cram (2003) highlights that although young women's discussions of sexual relationships and experiences suggest various ways in which the double standard is disrupted, ultimately these are individual rather than collective acts of resistance, and so the sexual double standard remains relatively stable. They argue that despite significant changes in the social landscape over recent decades, young women's negotiations of heterosexuality remain dominated by the sexual double standard according to which an active, desiring sexuality is positively regarded in men, but denigrated and regulated by negative labelling in women.

Hence, research on women's experiences of sexuality and their attitudes to sex has identified some obvious changes since the publication of Marie Stopes's *Married Love*. It is no longer assumed amongst most ethnic groups that a woman will be a virgin when she marries, or that her future husband will have been her only sexual partner. Many women cohabit in lesbian or heterosexual relationships rather than marry, or remain single. Birth control is more widely available and reliable than previously, as is abortion, though sexually transmitted diseases and sexual violence remain important issues, as do prostitution and pornography. Sexual reputation, and the fear of losing it, are still powerful constraints affecting not only social relationships but also encounters with judicial and welfare systems. This latter theme is emphasised by Gail Hawkes (1995) in her discussion of young women and 'family planning' in the UK, which emphasises the regulatory content of family planning practice, directed particularly at young women 'whose lifestyles are deemed "irresponsible", and who are, therefore, considered as illegitimate family planners' (p. 257).

Sexuality and power relations

As Therborn (2004, p. 1) has noted, sex and power are intimately related: 'sex may lead to power, through the conduit of seduction. Power is also a basis for obtaining sex, whether by force or lubricated with money and what it can buy.'

Sexuality and oppression

Many feminists have developed critical analyses of sexual violence, pornography and prostitution which have emphasised the ways in which the sexual appropriation of women serves as a mechanism of social control. One key theme that has emerged from much of this work is the link between heterosexual power relations and sexual violence, so much so that some feminists such as Liz Kelly (1988) have argued that sexual violence is best understood as a continuum, ranging from the myriad forms of sexism women encounter everyday, through to the murder of women and girls by men at the other extreme. She describes as 'pressurized sex' sexual relations that women are expected to have with men, even when they do not really want to. As Jackson and Scott (1996, pp. 17–18) have noted, 'within dominant cultural discourses, men are cast as the active initiators of sexual activity and women as passive recipients of male advances; men's desires are seen as uncontrollable urges which women are paradoxically expected both to satisfy and to restrain'.

Sexual violence has been a major concern of feminists, and a key site of feminist political activism. While sexual violence might appear to be an issue around which all feminists could unite, since all women regardless of sexual orientation, social class, race, disability or age can be subject to violence, the various intersections of oppression mean that women's actual experiences of violence and the threat of violence might vary considerably. As Jackson and Scott note with regard to the relationship between race and sexual violence, for instance,

> Sexual violence has very specific meanings for black women, since routine sexual exploitation, coercion and brutality towards women have been very much a part of the history of slavery and colonialism. This renders it inseparable from racism: enslaved and colonized women have been subject to specific racialized forms of patriarchal oppression and sexualized forms of racial oppression. This is complicated by the ways in which black masculinity under colonial and slave regimes has been constructed as a threat to white women.
>
> (Jackson and Scott, 1996, p. 18)

bell hooks (1982) has argued that white feminists have tended to see the rape of women slaves as merely an historical incidence of sexual violence, and hence have failed to acknowledge the extent to which the abuse of Black women continues to be framed by the legacy of colonial discourses and power relations, manifest, for example, in terms of exaggerated fears of the rape of white women by Black men, in overtly sexualised images of Black men and women, and in racist and sexist ideologies about inter-ethnic sexual relations, all of which, she argues, amount to a continued devaluation and sexualisation of Black womanhood.

Emphasising that rape should be understood in terms of power relations rather than sexual relations, feminists have focused on sexual violence as an enactment of male power. The regularity with which women are subject to male sexual violence has led some feminists to emphasise the eroticisation of women's oppression in popular and media culture, and to argue that rape and sexual violence are extreme manifestations of much broader cultural phenomena.

Pornography is another central issue for feminists in this respect, and one that is complicated by a range of perspectives. Some feminists see pornography as centrally implicated in women's oppression and campaign against it, others argue vehemently against feminism aligning itself with any form of censorship or moral conservatism, while others maintain that the production of feminist pornography potentially amounts to a politics of subversion (McIntosh, 1992). Others highlight the material aspects of pornography, emphasising that pornography entails more than just representations since it involves the employment of real women as models and actors and in a whole range of associated occupations such as stripping, dancing and hostessing. Indeed, from this latter perspective (one with which we, the authors, would agree), prostitution and pornography are both most appropriately understood as part of a 'sex industry' and with reference to the concept of commercial sex, or 'sex work'. These terms emphasise that commercial sex involves not just prostitution, but also the production and consumption of pornography, as well as other areas less commonly researched to date, such as telephone sex work, 'call girl' or escort services, as well as work in lap and pole dancing clubs (Weitzer, 2000). The increasing prevalence of these more peripheral forms of sex work, particularly given developments in communication technologies such as telephone call centres and the internet, has meant that what Karen Sharpe (1998) has described as the 'problem of prostitution' – namely, how to regulate it – remains a perpetual issue. Some feminists argue that only fundamental social reorganisation will address the demand for commercial sex, others adopt a more reformist approach and maintain that prostitution should be decriminalised. One of the most commonly proposed strategies in this respect is that prostitutes should be put in state-registered brothels. However, as Sharpe notes, radical feminists in particular argue that such a strategy would simply 'signify the state's validation of the use of women's bodies as commodities' (p. 160). Others have argued that the decriminalisation of soliciting could create a 'sexual free for all' for men (Wilson, 1983, p. 224).

Feminist anti-prostitution activists and feminists such as Kathleen Barry (1995) have argued that prostitution has undergone a process of industrialisation in many parts of the world since the 1960s. Through this process prostituted men, women and children have come under the control of big business in the Western world, as prostitution has been legalised and normalised. The International Labour Organization report on prostitution in Southeast Asia entitled *The Sex Sector* (Lim, 1998) suggests that prostitution is so important economically to the countries of Southeast Asia that there is a strong argument for recognising and legitimising it:

> The scale of prostitution has been enlarged to an extent where we can justifiably speak of a commercial sex sector that is integrated into the economic, social and political life of these countries. The sex business has assumed the dimensions of an industry and has directly or indirectly contributed in no small measure to employment, national income and economic growth.
>
> (Lim, 1998, p. vi)

One of the most fundamental divisions between different groups of feminist theorists and activists concerned with prostitution has focused on the distinction between 'forced' and 'free' prostitution, and is based upon the notion that adult women may exercise the free will of an individual and 'choose' prostitution or 'consent' to it. Scambler and Scambler's (1997) *Rethinking Prostitution* is a collection of essays by academics, activists and members of the English Collective of Prostitutes that advocates thinking about prostitution as sex work and which considers some of these issues. Without wishing to assert that 'all engagement in sex work is a function of free and informed choice', the editors hold that the starting point for any feminist-oriented analysis of prostitution should be 'the respectful attribution of agency' (p. xv).

Anti-prostitution activists such as Sheila Jeffreys (1997, 1998) are critical of the concept of 'choice', however, pointing out that economic coercion makes a nonsense of any idea of free choice, as do other constraining circumstances that act upon women's lives, such as gender ideologies. Feminists such as Jeffreys argue that 'women are not free agents, operating on a level playing field upon which they rationally choose prostitution over other occupations for the advantages it offers' (Jeffreys, 1998, p. 69). Rather, women's choices are already shaped by established patterns of gender inequality – what Carole Pateman (1988) calls the 'sexual contract' – that restrict women's ability to exercise agency in this respect. Hence, anti-prostitution feminists opposed to the concept of free choice prostitution emphasise that women constitute an oppressed sex class whose subordination has historically been symbolised in their exchange as sexual and reproductive servants between men (Dworkin, 1981). In Sheila Jeffrey's words, 'the argument of "choice" is used by those determined studiously to ignore these facts of the material power difference between men and women, those committed to rampant individualism' (1998, p. 69).

For Jeffreys, 'men's prostitution behaviour is the problem' (1998, p. 70), and particularly the idea that men's prostitution use is based on an inevitable and unstoppable male sexual desire, perhaps a biological necessity, which is best channelled into 'harmless' outlets. This ideology reflects the 'biological essences' model of sexuality considered above, and is one that feminists such as Jeffreys have been particularly critical of, arguing that

> in fact, men's prostitution abuse is not 'natural' behaviour but the result of the idea that such sexual abuse of women and children is vital for health, enjoyed by women, a right of manhood. The idea of prostitution abusers that it is reasonable, or even their birthright, to insert their penises in the bodies of other less powerful human beings who can be paid to tolerate it, is a learnt idea.
>
> (Jeffreys, 1998, p. 70)

Jeffreys points out that prostitution tourism depends upon pro-prostitution abuse attitudes formed in the West. As she puts it,

> Affluent cultures in the west and in the east which teach boys and men that the sexual use of women and children, irrespective of their pleasure or personhood, is a natural right of their masculinity, produces sex tourists and prostitution abusers.
>
> (Jeffreys, 1998, p. 70)

Also focusing on sex tourism in Latin America, the Caribbean, India, Thailand and South Africa, Julia O'Connell Davidson (1998) describes three types of sex tourist:

1 *'Macho lads in pornutopia'* who are socialised to believe that 'true' masculinity involves exercising control over other men, over women and over their bodies: 'this is partly because sexual access to prostitutes is extremely cheap, partly because there is an extensive array of commoditised sex on offer and partly because their racism allows them to reduce "Other" women and children to nothing more than their sex' (p. 25).
2 *'Women-haters'* who are socialised to believe that the human male has a natural, biological need to penetrate women, so that 'some men imagine themselves as victims of a biological compulsion to have sex' (p. 26). Such men therefore think of women as controlling a resource (their female bodies) that is vital to men's physical and psychological well-being. Again, racism plays a key role in disinhibiting such men.
3 *'Situational prostitute users'* who are not prostitute users in their home countries, but become sex tourists 'partly because they don't recognize informal sector prostitution as prostitution, and partly because they too buy into highly sexualized forms of racism' (p. 29).

Crucially, in sex tourism gender ideologies are compounded by racism routinely used by the travel industry, which often conflates the 'exotic' and the 'erotic' in its advertising.

Anti-pornography campaigners tend to focus largely on the degradation and exploitation of women involved in all aspects of the sex industry. Others are wary of seeing women only as victims of commercial sex, and are more concerned with recognising and reforming the working conditions of sex workers (Alexander, 1988). These are clearly complex issues given the wide variety of forms that sex work takes in different social, economic and geographical contexts as well as across a variety of media forms. The increasing prevalence of live sex shows broadcast on websites for instance problematises the traditional distinction between pornography and prostitution (one that feminists have tended to be critical of). Taking account of these various complexities, Jackson and Scott (1996, p. 24) argue that 'a feminist perspective should encompass both the economic relations which shape women's position within the sex industry and the patriarchal relations which make this particular form of exploitation possible'. Of course, the economics of prostitution are shaped not only by local labour markets but also by the global division of labour and by post-colonial power relations. Hence, within sex tourism post-colonial women are constructed as exotically docile and hospitable. In the local context in which women are recruited, research suggests that poverty is a major motivating factor for entry into sex work.

Feminist anti-pornography campaigner Andrea Dworkin (1981) has also drawn attention to the etymological connections between pornography and prostitution, reminding us that the term 'pornography' refers to the 'graphic depiction of women as vile whores', who exist only to serve men's sexual needs. She argues that the whore can only figure in male imagination under patriarchal domination, according to which women are reduced to the status of sex objects.

Of course, both prostitution and pornography provide employment for women and raise general questions about the relative position of women in the labour market, as well as the circumstances in which these particular groups of women work. Women's involvement in the sex industry is directly related to their lack of economic opportunities elsewhere, and to their vulnerability to poverty and social exclusion. What makes these issues particularly problematic for feminists is that their objection to pornography and prostitution has often placed feminist activists in an alliance with the moral Right, and particularly with defenders of the patriarchal family and of women's sexual passivity. Judith Walkowitz (1980) has shown, for instance, that feminist campaigners since the nineteenth century have often found their arguments hijacked by moral conservatives who have sought to 'protect' women rather than promote women's sexual rights. In contrast, a feminist critique of commercial sex has been concerned primarily with the sexual objectification of women's bodies and with the working conditions of women employed in the sex industry.

Though prostitution is an economic exchange, feminists have argued that it differs from other forms of employment in significant ways. Although the sex industry is a thriving economy in many countries across the world, it is not a 'mainstream' sector of the labour market and, in general, governments and other funding agencies have been interested in prostitution only as a problem of social control or public health. In sociology, this has often meant that prostitution has been studied not as a form of economic exchange, but as a public health risk, with the empirical focus being primarily on street prostitution (its most visible and seemingly uncontrollable form). As a result, the available body of empirical evidence on prostitution has tended to reflect a concern with the characteristics and practices of individual prostitutes (their health, psyche, sexual history, criminality and drug use, for instance), and a relative neglect of the social and organisational aspects of prostitution, power relations within the sex industry as a whole, and within client–prostitute relations, as well as a neglect of questions about the demand for prostitution. As Julia O'Connell Davidson (1997, p. 777) has put it, 'this represents a very real problem for all those who are engaged in theoretical, political or policy debate on prostitution'. Feminist research has begun to address this, however, and several ethnographic studies have been undertaken in recent years that have focused on various forms of prostitution, looking at the work experiences of prostitutes themselves.

This research has highlighted that prostitutes often work in dangerous and degrading conditions, with little or no protection from the state or their employer, or from the medical profession. Although much criticised on grounds of its unproblematic association of prostitution with HIV/AIDS, drug abuse and public health issues (Adkins, 1997; O'Connell Davidson, 1997), in their account of street prostitution, based on three years' research involving interviews with prostitutes and their clients, as well as observational research in a red light area, McKeganey and Barnard (1996, p. 70), for instance, document the risks to women as they negotiate with clients and also their vulnerability to violence. As one of the contributors to their research put it, 'if you lose your wits about you in this business you're done for'. Whittaker and Hart (1996) have also carried out research highlighting the extent to which sex workers operating in flats have to employ protective strategies such as co-working with 'maids' to protect themselves against the threat of violence from clients.

Research also suggests a strong degree of mutual support amongst prostitutes themselves. Downe (1999), for instance, highlights how sex workers in Costa Rica use humour as a way of resisting and coping with pain, humiliation and the fear of violence by re-framing traumatic experiences. Sanders (2004) identified a similar culture of coping through professional banter in her study of prostitution in the UK. Crucial to the discourse and identity of the prostitutes in Sanders's study was a sense of themselves as professional sex workers:

> They adopt the stereotypical image of the 'happy hooker' and the aesthetic characteristics of 'the prostitute', conforming to culturally prescribed norms of femininity as a strategy to attract and maintain a regular client base. Usually this entails adapting physical appearance, dress code, make-up and hairstyle as well as observable personality traits to conform to male expectations. A small number of interviewees considered cosmetic facial surgery and breast implants as capital investments for the role of sex provider.
>
> (Sanders, 2004, p. 282)

Sanders emphasises in particular the importance of solidarity amongst women working in the sex industry:

> Debbie and Louise have been working for 20 years, much of that together. During the 12 visits I made to their premises they would be laughing, joking and fooling around. They explained their behaviour was not a reflection of how they enjoy sex

work but out of necessity: 'If we didn't laugh so much we would just cry' (Louise). They were adamant that the only reason they survived prostitution is their friendship, solidarity and strength in coping together. 'We learned to laugh a long time ago, to make it less real and to stop us from hating to have to come here' (Debbie).

(Sanders, 2004, p. 284)

On a more global level, feminist groups have highlighted the vulnerability of women and children to sex trafficking, particularly in Central and Eastern European states (Therborn, 2004). The fact that trafficking is not only illegal, however, but also often connected to organised networks of violence and corruption means that access to research evidence is limited, if not impossible. The UN estimates that trafficked individuals are the commodities of a multi-billion dollar global industry dominated by highly organised (male-dominated) criminal networks, and that economic hardship, obstacles to migration and armed conflict in many of the world's developing and transitional countries have resulted in a considerable rise in the number of cases involving trafficking (www.unece.org). While trafficking routes vary over time, the direction remains relatively constant, namely from poorer countries to relatively wealthy ones. Doezema (2002) has argued in her critique of the UN Trafficking Protocol that current notions of 'consent', reflected in the ambiguity of the Protocol, are inadequate to serve as the basis for political strategies to protect the rights of sex workers and migrants because they purport views of female sexuality as 'both more virtuous and more dangerous than men's' (p. 20) and because they fail to take account of the material circumstances within which women may provide 'consent'.

Sex trafficking and tourism have become a particular problem for women and girls in Southeast Asia. Macionis and Plummer (2002, p. 297) report for instance that Bangkok is emerging as the sex-tourism capital of the world, and that almost half of the estimated 800,000 prostitutes in Thailand are under 18. In some cases, they note, parents sell female infants into the sex trade who are then raised by agents until they are able to work as prostitutes, to solicit in sex bars or to work in live sex shows. Agents provide girls with clothes and housing but (much like the old Geisha system of debt bondage) at a price that far exceeds their earnings, so that women are effectively sex slaves. Drawing on research by Kempadoo and Doezema (1998) and O'Connell Davidson (1998), Macionis and Plummer estimate that the number of girls and women involved is rapidly increasing: some 8 per cent of the female population of Thailand are thought to be employed in the sex industry, about 40 per cent of whom are estimated to be HIV positive. In addition, concubinage is still thought to be a widespread social phenomenon amongst the upper-middle classes of Southeast Asia, especially in Thailand.

Much of the Western research on prostitution in Southeast Asia, however, tends to replicate many of the earlier problems associated with defining prostitutes themselves as the problem. As Siriporn Skrobanek (of the Foundation for Women in Bangkok) puts it,

Women in Thailand are viewed as 'the other women', whose status is perceived as lower than that of women in the West. . . . But since there are two sides in a commercial transaction between foreign visitors and Thai women, why is only one party to the deal (Thai women and their society) the target of investigation, while the other party (the sex tourists) goes unexamined?

(quoted in Seabrook, 1996, p. vii)

Sexuality, pleasure and resistance

As well as sexuality as a site of oppression and exploitation for women, feminists have also emphasised the extent to which sexuality can be a cultural resource through which gender oppression can be challenged and resisted. Holland *et al.* (1994, p. 34) for instance have argued that sexuality constitutes an intimate yet social space within which men's power can be subverted and resisted and that 'if women can recognize and capture this space, they can negotiate relationships with men which upset the gender hierarchy and so are potentially socially destabilizing'. From this perspective, which emphasises not power *over* sexuality but rather the power *of* sexuality, sexuality is viewed as a site of hegemonic struggle on which gender relations can be contested. It is also viewed as the site of pleasure, and feminists such as Anne Koedt (1972), in her influential discussion of sexuality from a radical feminist perspective, have empha- sised women's right to derive pleasure from sexuality. Amber Hollibaugh (1989) has similarly argued that feminists must give equal attention to sexual danger and sexual pleasure, suggesting that there is a need to develop a feminist language of sexual pleasure that recognises that power in sex can be a source of both pleasure and resistance to gender oppression.

Research has highlighted several ways in which sexuality can be used as a way of challenging and resisting patriarchal oppression and heterosexual hegemony. We consider three examples here:

1 *female promiscuity* as a challenge to dominant ideas about women's sexual passivity and to patriarchal control of women's sexuality;
2 *camp* as a potential way of resisting and parodying hegemonic masculinity and what Judith Butler (1990) describes as 'the heterosexual matrix' – the idea that 'normal' men are masculine and sexually dominant and that 'normal' women are feminine and sexually servile, and that a particular configuration of the relationship between sex, gender and sexuality is natural – and the gender order; and finally,
3 the emergence of so-called *gay villages* – distinct social (and commercial) spaces in urban areas that potentially represent a challenge to the marginalisation and exclusion of gay and lesbian people, and the social dominance of 'compulsory heterosexuality' (Rich, 1980).

Female promiscuity

One interesting example of hegemonic struggle over gender relations often cited by feminists is female promiscuity. Because of the sexual double standard, reinforced by 'scientific' perspectives on sexuality as a biological essence, outlined above, women have traditionally been thought of as naturally sexually passive, whereas men have tended to be regarded as naturally sexually active. Female promiscuity – taking part in multiple and frequent sexual relationships – has tended to be regarded, particularly in medical and moral discourse, as a psychiatric disorder amongst young women. Promiscuity amongst young girls has often been cited as an argument against widespread sex education in schools; and in social work and protective social welfare discourse promiscuous women have often been described as being in moral danger, or as being 'out of control'. Medical practitioners frequently cite female promiscuity as a cause of the spread of herpes, cervical cancer and also (to a lesser extent) HIV.

In this sense, some feminists have argued that promiscuity might be regarded as a liberatory strategy used against the restriction and prescriptions of 'normal' femininity. In her book *Promiscuities*, for instance, Naomi Wolf (1997) argues that promiscuity can be 'a source of pleasure and strength, not of shame and vulnerability'. Other feminists, however, have argued that this perspective is a relatively narrow ethnocentric one that fails to take account of the experiences of Black and Asian women who have tended to be sexualised, racialised and gendered simultaneously within colonial ideologies and power relations (hooks, 1992). Others have argued further, that cultural representations of women as primarily sexual merely reinforce rather than subvert established patriarchal perceptions of women as sex objects, perceptions that are often used to justify sexual harassment and violence against women. Others have argued that a cultural focus on women as sex objects – in advertising or pop music videos, for instance – merely serves to perpetuate patriarchal stereotypes about both male and female sexuality.

Camp

In every culture, sexual relations are bound by formal and informal social rules concerning both with whom a person may have sexual relations, and how those relationships should be conducted. Homosexuality, in most Western cultures, as Jeff Weeks (1986) has pointed out, 'carries a heavy legacy of taboo'. But this is not the case in every culture, nor has it been true of all historical periods. In ancient Greece, for instance, love between two males was thought to be a 'higher' form of intimacy than that between a man and a woman. Nevertheless, as we have already noted, in many contemporary societies, homosexuality is not only stigmatised but criminalised (in many African countries, for instance). Many countries' legal codes do not make provision for lesbianism, but in some countries (such as Pakistan) it too is illegal. Some countries – such as China – have only relatively recently officially acknowledged the existence of gay and lesbian sexualities. The law in most European societies is more tolerant, however, with recent legislation in the UK equalising the age of consent and introducing legal protection against discrimination on grounds of sexual orientation. That said, many gay men and lesbian women still conceal their sexuality for fear of hostility, particularly in the workplace, for instance (Hall, 1989; Adkins, 2000). Some feminists, such as Judith Butler (1990), have argued that one of the ways in which homophobia and heterosexual hegemony is undermined is by parodying it in an ironic way: by making what she calls 'gender trouble', invoking, for instance, a 'camp' performance of gender.

In her 'Notes on Camp', Susan Sontag (1984, p. 275) argued that 'the essence of camp is its love of the unnatural: of the artifice and exaggeration'. Of the many themes she identifies as definitive of camp – often associated with the culture of gay masculinity – Sontag emphasises that camp is 'a sensibility that, among other things, converts the serious into the frivolous' (1984, p. 276). Camp, then, is playful and anti-serious and suggests a 'spilling over' of an irrepressible, uncontrolled sensibility that contemporary feminists such as Butler (1990) have argued represents a form of cultural resistance to gender and sexual power relations. This view echoes Sontag's earlier claim that camp can be understood as a kind of cultural defence mechanism, one that celebrates rather than berates exclusion from the cultural and sexual mainstream. Seen from this angle, camp has a radical and transgressive potential, Butler argues. As cultural theorist Richard Dyer (1992, p. 136) has put it: 'Identity and togetherness, fun and wit, self-protection and thorns in the flesh of straight society – these are the pluses of camp.' Camp also denies any essential sex, gender or sexuality. Rather, like postmodernist approaches to sexuality (and feminism – see Chapter 2), and particularly queer theory, it emphasises that all three are performances and not essences.

As a cultural phenomenon, camp has been criticised, however, particularly by gay rights activists for its politics, or rather lack thereof. Dyer (1992) comments that camp finds sexual politics in the form of the CHE (campaign for homosexual equality) and GLF (gay liberation front) simply 'too dull'. As Melly (1984, cited in Meyer, 1994, p. 22) has also noted, for many gay activists, camp tends to be viewed largely as an artefact of the 'closet' – the idea that homosexuality should be concealed; as an anachronistic embarrassment that fuels gay stereotypes and affirms heteronormative cultural perceptions of the gay community. Camp has therefore been interpreted as a sign of both oppression, and of the acceptance of cultural repression, but also as a cultural style that represents a mode of resistance to that oppression.

Gay spaces and villages

Another example of possible resistance to sexual oppression can be identified in the existence of virtual sexual communities on the internet (Hanmer, 2003), as well as gay 'villages' in major towns and cities across the world – New York, Sydney and Manchester being some of the most notable examples, that have been interpreted by sociologists as an attempt to claim a 'space' for resistance. While these spaces are geographical and social they are also of course largely commercial, and property developers, retailers and leisure industry entrepreneurs have certainly not been slow in the past decade or so to attract what has come to be known as the 'pink pound' or dollar. As feminist writer Susan Bordo (1993, p. 196) puts it, 'consumer capitalism depends on the continual production of novelty, of fresh images to stimulate desire, and it frequently drops into marginalized neighbourhoods in order to find them'. Heterosexual attraction to so-called gay villages might therefore be thought of as a form of what Suzanne Moore (1988) has described as 'gender tourism', as straight 'tourists' are able to take 'package trips' into gay culture and social spaces, but crucially, as she notes, not necessarily into gay sex or politics. The effect, therefore, is more commercial and cultural than political.

Manchester's gay village is an interesting case in point, in this respect, because its development in recent years illustrates some of the ways in which sexuality is shaped by what feminists and other sociologists following Foucault have argued is an interplay of power and resistance. As feminist writer Beatrix Campbell recently noted,

> When Greater Manchester's former chief constable, James Anderton, accused the city's gay population in 1987 of 'swirling around in a human cesspit of their own making', little did he know he would come to be regarded as one of the instigators of Britain's gayest city, and perhaps the most successful gay village in Europe. The roll call would also have to include Margaret Thatcher, whose notorious Section 28 [a clause in the Local Government Act passed in Britain in 1988] . . . galvanized a spectacular coalition, ranging from theatre impresarios to librarians, to defend the right to a gay life. Neither could have anticipated how their crusades would conjure up a queer constituency.
>
> (Campbell, 2004, p. 30)

In the 1980s, the area around Canal Street in Manchester was still a heavily policed red-light district, in which raids on gay nightclubs were commonplace. The effect, as Campbell notes in her article 'Village People', was to activate the gay community in Manchester, which forged an alliance with the city council which, in turn, gave support to gay businesses. 'The ghost of Anderton was finally laid to rest', she notes, when the current chief constable led his gay colleagues' contingent at EuroPride in 2003, a 10-day Mardi Gras in the thriving gay village. 'Now the place is so successful that it simultaneously welcomes and dreads hordes of straight invaders' (p. 30).

One of the main problems has in many ways been shaped by gender politics. Manchester's gay village quickly began to attract large groups of straight women (many of them on hen nights) who felt safe and free from harassment there. However, these groups of women were predictably followed in quick succession by large groups of heterosexual 'lads' and corporate breweries, resulting in what Campbell describes as a 'straightening of the village' in commercial and cultural terms. Conscious of exploitation of the Village rather than investment in it, however, the established gay community began to withdraw its custom from the straight, corporate bars and this appears to have resulted in their withdrawal from the area and, as Campbell concludes, quoting one of its main supporters, 'the village is going gayer again'.

Each of these examples emphasises the complex and often contradictory power relations that shape the relationship between gender and sexuality, one shaped by power and resistance, as well as structure and agency. This is also the case with regard to the ways in which sexuality is shaped by race and ethnicity.

Race, ethnicity and sexuality

Many Black feminists have argued that feminist debates on sexuality have often proceeded without reference to divisions amongst women not related to sexual orientation. Black feminists have been critical of white feminist tendencies to homogenise women as a category, and also for their failure to challenge stereotypical social constructions of Black and Asian women's sexuality. Feminists such as Patricia Hill Collins and bell hooks have argued that paying attention to the intersections between gender, sexuality and race reveals that sexual relationships with men may have different meanings for Black and for white women.

Black and Asian women are often perceived as sexually exotic by white men. This imagery is frequently mobilised in advertising for a whole range of products and services from ice cream (Nayak, 1997) to airlines. Post-colonial women are often seen as more submissive, obedient and hyper-feminine than Western women. Thus for racialised women, their sexuality is often shaped by racist assumptions. Hence, 'the racism which is often a feature of pornography is not accidental, but is the product of the double objectification of black women as objects to be used by their white masters' (Jackson and Scott, 1996, p. 22). Feminists such as Patricia Hill Collins (1990) have therefore argued that an analysis of racism is central to a feminist understanding of pornography and prostitution because racism does not simply compound sexism but rather makes certain forms of sexual objectification possible. In particular, she argues, biological theories of race and colonial ideologies underpin the depiction of Black women in terms of an animalistic sexuality.

Anoop Nayak (1997) has recently explored some of these stereotypes in his analysis of images of race and sexuality in advertisements for Häagen-Dazs ice cream. He argues that in the body images that dominate these advertisements, Black bodies are seen as a source of sexual desire and satisfaction – as 'the exotic promise of an extra-intense experience' (p. 52). Here, and elsewhere in media and popular culture he argues, 'black sexuality is constructed as threatening, dangerous and in need of control' (p. 52). Not only do the ads he considers mark out visible, racial binary oppositions between black and white, they then seek to 'blend' these through implications of inter-racial sex. Here, sexualised Black female bodies function as what bell hooks (1990, p. 57) describes as 'playing fields where racism and sexuality converge'. In her paper entitled 'Selling Hot Pussy', hooks has argued that media cultural portrayals of Black women's sexuality are no longer premised on the white supremacist assertion that 'blondes have more fun' but rather on equally racist and sexist contentions that, as she puts it,

> The 'real fun' is to be had by bringing to the surface all those 'nasty' unconscious fantasies and longings about contact with the Other embedded in the secret (but not so secret) deep structure of white supremacy.
>
> (hooks, 1992, pp. 21–22)

Sexuality and HIV/AIDS

Many of the debates considered here have taken place against a backdrop of increasing concern about HIV and AIDS and therefore about the potential dangers attached to certain sexual practices, and often also attributed to particular sexual identities and desires. As Sara Delamont (2003, p. 55) notes, 'the HIV/AIDS panic produced another impetus propelling sexuality into the sociological mainstream'. Fear of the risk of HIV transmission might seem to close down the potential for sexual pleasure, but some feminists have argued that safer sex could be better sex, especially in a heterosexual context. While 'safe sex' in health promotion discourse has tended to mean pene-trative sex with a condom, feminists such as Ros Coward (1987) have sought to promote a broader range of sexual practices arguing, for instance, that for heterosexual women safer sex (which de-privileges penetrative sex) possibly enhances rather than restricts the potential for sexual pleasure and more egalitarian sexual relations. However, as Jackson and Scott (1996, p. 19) note, the balance of power in (hetero)-sexual relationships, 'along with wider cultural discourses and the sexual scripts which men and women draw on, militate against women negotiating safer sex'. Research highlights, for example, the extent to which young women continue to experience problems in negotiating condom use when they have sex with men, and the ways in which their efforts to practise safe sex are often undermined by gender power relations which reaffirm male sexual 'needs' at the expense of women's pleasure and safety, relating largely to the difficulties women have in articulating their own sexual needs and desires within heterosexual encounters (Holland *et al.*, 1990). Jackie West (1999) has argued, for instance, that young women remain inhibited in their exploration of sexuality not only by heterosexual morality and their transitional status, but also by gendered power relations that limit social acceptance of their sexual needs and desires.

Other feminists, however, such as Fiona Stewart (1999) have argued that a possible shift in definitions and practices of heterosexuality is currently taking place, suggesting that modes of feminine heterosexuality that position young women as relatively passive and helpless may be changing. Her research, carried out in Australia, highlights several factors as indicative of this shift, including: young women's initiation of sex, their planned loss of virginity, the stating of conditional terms of relation-ships, their participation in casual sex, their efforts to ensure their own sexual pleasure is catered for, their refusal of unwanted sex and their insistence of condom use. She argues that 'in each of these areas, the conventional gendered imperatives are challenged and the gendering of masculine and feminine behaviour becomes less certain' (1999, p. 277). Her research reveals, she concludes 'a clear rejection of passive, traditional femininity' and a capacity to renegotiate 'the status quo of hegemonic or institutional heterosexuality'.

Empowering women, especially in post-colonial and developing countries, is clearly crucial in HIV/AIDS prevention, and vice versa, and has been cited as one of the most important strategies in slowing down the AIDS pandemic in sub-Saharan and West Africa (Therborn, 2004). However, the different contexts in which young women are exhorted to embark on HIV/AIDS risk reduction behaviours and the difficulties involved have been relatively neglected in research and policy terms. Augustine Ankomah (1999) has highlighted the relative powerlessness of young women in premarital sexual exchange relationships in urban Ghana for instance, where many sexual encounters are contracted for material purposes. Ankomah argues that women often engage in ad hoc 'sexual exchange' – where sexual services are performed for economic purposes – for financial reasons, and that it is only by improving women's economic status and addressing contemporary societal norms which support sexual exchange that women's vulnerability can be alleviated.

Conclusions

Sexuality has been a central political and theoretical issue for feminists, and also a source of major divisions. The question of whether heterosexual sex is oppressive to women, and whether heterosexuality is a tenable practice for feminists remains a source of contention. Feminists have emphasised that heterosexuality does not have the same meaning for all men and women, and this raises a number of questions about the pleasures and powers of sexuality.

In this chapter, we have looked at three broad ways of conceptualising the relationship between sexuality and the social. Generally speaking, these three perspectives themselves represent something of a sociological history of sexuality, although it is important to note that although a social constructionist and then poststructuralist approach have largely superseded a biological essences model in terms of the development of sociological ideas, the contention that sexuality is a pre-social, biological entity remains relatively dominant not only in the social sciences, but more generally in medical, religious, moral, legal and media discourse on sexuality. In this respect, one of the points that feminists have highlighted is that the distinction between the biological and the social is far from unproblematic.

The idea of the family as the natural and normal site where sexual relations take place has tended to privilege heterosexual relationships and to render deviant any sexual relations that take place outside of this context. Although more people now accept premarital sexual relations as normal, this also means that courting has become sexualised and the 'norm' of sex between a man and a woman, sanctified by romantic love, has been reinforced. In Victorian England women were not supposed to enjoy sex at all and it was only men who were thought to have an uncontrollable sex drive which impelled them to visit the many prostitutes who patrolled the streets. From the 1920s 'sexologists' started to argue that sexual satisfaction was important for both partners, and this became incorporated into ideas of what an ideal marriage should be – a satisfying sexual partnership. However, this companionate sexuality was defined according to masculine norms: women should enjoy penetrative sex with men; if they did not then they were 'frigid'. Furthermore, this whole discourse reinforced the idea that heterosexuality was the natural, biologically determined human relationship.

Sexuality more generally, however, continues to be defined in male terms. Women's bodies, conveying sexual promise, are presented as desirable and are used to sell anything from cigarettes to spare parts for cars. We are constantly presented with the idea of woman as sexually passive. Men are presented as sexually active and predatory, at the mercy of their 'uncontrollable lust' which can be satisfied only by penetrating women, whether the women are willing or not. Radical feminists have argued that unwanted sexual advances by men could be construed as a form of rape and that our society condones and indeed institutionalises rape. The sexual abuse of women and girls in the home is likewise a product of the presentation of men as having uncontrollable sexual appetites and women as victims of this, since most of the abusers are men and most of the victims are female.

Also, as Jackson and Scott note, feminist debates on sexuality have been framed largely by the 'special' status accorded to sexual relations in Western societies:

Sexuality is conventionally singled out as a 'special' area of life: it has been variously romanticized and tabooed, seen as a threat to civilization or the route to social revolution, as a source of degradation and a means to personal growth. ... Sexuality may be feared as a source of dirt, disease and degradation, but it is equally revered as a gateway to ecstasy, enlightenment and emancipation.

(Jackson and Scott, 1996, p. 26)

We would agree with their conclusion, in this respect and argue that feminism needs to reflect critically on this 'cultural obsession' with sex, including the ways in which it shapes feminist perspectives on sexuality, not least in terms of their essentialism and ethnocentrism.

SUMMARY

1 Sociologists have argued that although sexuality is perhaps one of the most intimate aspects of our lives, it is also social and political (embedded within power relations), and that what we think of as sexual varies historically, socially and culturally.

2 Three broad perspectives on sexuality can be identified in the social sciences: essentialist, sociological and postmodernist.

3 Feminists have argued that sexuality is one of the key sites on which patriarchal power relations are maintained; they have also argued that sexuality can be a source of power for men and women to challenge and resist patriarchal ideology and compulsory heterosexuality. Three examples of 'sexuality as resistance' were considered: female promiscuity, camp and the evolution of gay villages.

4 Black and post-colonial feminists have argued that white, Western feminists have neglected racial and ethnic difference among women, and have failed to challenge racist stereotypes regarding Black and Asian women's sexuality.

FURTHER READING

Giddens, A. (1992) *The Transformation of Intimacy: Sexuality, Love and Eroticism in Modern Societies.* Cambridge: Polity. This controversial text attempts to reflect on the meaning and impact of the so-called 'sexual revolution' in Western societies, and considers connections between sexuality and other aspects of social identity such as gender. Giddens argues that the transformation of intimacy, in which he contends women have played a major part, holds out the possibility of a radical democratisation of the personal sphere.

Hawkes, G. (1996) *A Sociology of Sex and Sexuality.* Buckingham: Open University Press. This book offers a historical and sociological analysis of ideas about the expressions of sexual desire, incorporating both primary and secondary historical and theoretical material. The major focus of the book is on sexuality and modernity.

Jackson, S. and Scott, S. (eds) (1996) *Feminism and Sexuality: A Reader*. Edinburgh: Edinburgh University Press. This reader is a comprehensive and engaging selection of feminist contributions to sexual theory and politics. It begins with an excellent overview of feminist debates and tensions, and then considers feminist perspectives on essentialism and social constructionism, sexual identities and categories, issues of power and pleasure and commercial sex. It contains a range of classic and contemporary readings from a broad spectrum of feminist perspectives.

Weeks, J. (1986) *Sexuality*. London: Routledge. This book is an excellent starting point as it is a short guide to the concept of sexuality, and to the political and theoretical debates that have shaped its academic study particularly within sociology. It also considers the contribution of feminist theory and politics.

CHAPTER NINE

Work and organisation

Sociologists tend to divide people's lives into 'work' (paid employment), 'leisure' (the time when people choose what they want to do) and 'obligation time' (periods of sleep, eating and other necessary activities). Feminists have pointed out that this model reflects a male view of the world and does not necessarily fit the experiences of the majority of women. This is partly because unremunerated domestic labour is not recognised as work – it is 'hidden' labour – and partly because many women participate in few leisure activities outside of the home. This is because, as we noted in Chapter 6, women and girls have the major responsibility for domestic labour. Whilst men do more paid work than women, they also have more leisure time. It is not only the organisation of work that is gendered but also the cultural values with which paid work and domestic labour are associated; paid work and the workplace are largely seen as men's domain, the household as women's. Rosemary Pringle sums up some of these issues when she points out that,

> Though home and private life may be romanticized, they are generally held to represent the 'feminine' world of the personal and the emotional, the concrete and the particular, of the domestic and the sexual. The public world of work sets itself up as the opposite of all these things: it is rational, abstract, ordered, concerned with general principles, and of course, masculine. . . . For men, home and work are both opposite and complementary. . . . [For women] home is not a respite from work but another workplace. For some women work is actually a respite from home!
>
> (Pringle, 1989, pp. 214–215)

Most of the classical sociological studies of paid work were of men – of coal miners, affluent assembly line workers, male clerks, or salesmen for instance – and, until relatively recently, the findings of these studies formed the empirical data on which sociological theories about all workers' attitudes and experiences were based. Even when women were included in samples, it was (and sometimes still is) assumed that their attitudes and behaviours differed little from men's, or married women were seen as working for 'pin money'; paid employment being seen as relatively secondary to their domestic roles.

A growing body of feminist and pro-feminist research has challenged these assumptions, however, and has provided sociologists with a more detailed under-standing of the relationship between gender, work and organisation, and particularly of how men's and women's experiences of work differ. Feminists have argued that domestic labour is work and should be regarded as such. They have also maintained that the majority of women do not undertake paid employment for 'pin money' but out of necessity, and that paid work is seen as meeting important emotional and identity needs by many women. This does not mean that women's experiences of paid employment are the same as men's, however, and feminists have highlighted a range of ways in which work is gendered.

In the UK, for instance, 46 per cent of people in the labour market are women. However, 44 per cent of women and only 10 per cent of men in employment work part-time. Average hourly earnings for women working full-time are 18 per cent lower, and for women working part-time are 40 per cent lower, than for men working full-time. Of mothers of under fives, 52 per cent are in employment, compared with 91 per cent of fathers of under fives. There are 4.5 children aged under 8 for each registered place with a childminder, in full day care or in out of school clubs. Modern apprentices in hairdressing and in early years care and education are mainly women, while those in construction, engineering and plumbing are mainly men. Women are by far the majority in administrative and secretarial (80 per cent) and personal service jobs (84 per cent), while men hold most skilled trades (92 per cent) and process, plant and machine operative jobs (85 per cent) (EOC, 2004). Feminist sociologists have sought to explain these patterns with reference to a range of concepts, particularly the sexual division of labour.

Gender ideology and the sexual division of labour

All societies seem to have a division of labour based on sex – work that is seen as women's work and work that is seen as men's work; labour is gendered. However, the nature of the work that is done by men or women varies from society to society and changes historically. Clearly, the sexual division of labour is embedded not only in relations of sexual difference (in the relationship between men and women), but also within racial and ethnic differences, in global power relations, in systems of age stratification, in social class, and so on. In almost all societies the care of babies and young children is seen as women's work, but in many societies men take on the task of caring for young boys, in others older children generally look after young ones, and in others older women tend to care for the children. Cooking is mainly seen as women's work, except the preparation of feasts and ceremonial meals which is frequently seen as men's work. In many but not all societies hunting and fishing are regarded as men's work (and in some societies as men's leisure activities), but women frequently under-take planting and harvesting either alone or alongside men. In many societies women are responsible for the care of livestock. Ann Oakley (1982) has suggested that the sexual division of labour is socially constructed, and not based on natural biological differences. Jobs become identified as men's work or women's work; *then* it is argued that men and women do these jobs because of natural biological differences.

In Western societies, following industrialisation, work became separated from the home, and work done in the public sphere – paid work – became more highly valued than unpaid work in the domestic sphere. Women became seen as those who were 'naturally' good at domestic work and caring, and men as the providers – those in paid employment in the public sphere. Male trade unionists, employers and the state were able to restrict women's paid employment and exclude them from certain occupations. Consequently, men were able to define the conditions and rules of the game, so that for women to succeed in the male-dominated world of paid work, it became necessary for them to play by the same rules. Often, for instance, in order to have a career, to be seen as worthy of employment, training or promotion, women have to be prepared to work full-time and to have no breaks in their career for having and raising a family. Even then, women are likely to be excluded from many aspects of the culture of the workplace and from its more informal aspects. Women in paid work also tend to maintain responsibility for domestic labour and so carry out a 'double shift'. For those women who also provide care for an elderly or dependent relative, this might be increased to a 'triple shift' (see Chapter 5). Research suggests that one in six people in the UK are currently caring for an elderly or dependent person and that women are more likely than men to provide care; of those, 26 per cent also have dependent children (EOC, 2004). Hence, both the structure and the culture of paid work can serve to disadvantage women. Feminists have long since highlighted the importance of women undertaking paid work as a means of achieving some degree of independence. Women are often refused training, however, or are recruited on the assumption that they will take extended career breaks (because their main role is as wives and mothers) in a labour market that continues to define continuous, full-time employment as the norm. In manual work, 'skill' is socially constructed in gender terms, so that jobs that involve tasks associated with masculine expertise – such as driving – are seen as more skilled than jobs deemed to involve feminine dexterity – such as sewing, for instance.

Both men and women often believe that work is less important for women than for men and that men should have higher wages and more secure employment because of their responsibility for supporting the family. Men are seen as 'breadwinners' whereas women are seen as domestic carers. Feminists have argued that there is no inherent, pre-social reason why this should be the case. It would be quite possible for men and women to be seen as equally responsible for the economic support of the household and for the necessary domestic labour and childcare. Indeed, there is a gap between the ideology that 'a woman's place is in the home' and the reality for many women who have paid employment. However, this ideology still has real consequences for many women, particularly married women with children; most assume, as do their husbands, employers and the state, that even if they have paid employment they are still solely or primarily responsible for childcare and domestic labour. This ideology is so pervasive, so much a part of taken-for-granted assumptions, that it is rarely questioned or challenged (even though it might be parodied in TV advertisements or situation comedies).

Gender ideology has important consequences for the type of work that many women with children seek and are offered. It influences the type of occupations that young women enter on leaving full-time education, not only because of their own aspirations but also what career advisers, their parents, school and employers see as suitable for them (see Chapter 4). While it is the case in many of the former Communist societies that married women had full-time employment, they were nevertheless still expected to do the bulk of unpaid domestic labour and were generally in jobs paid at a lower rate than men's (see Einhorn, 1993; Khotkina, 1994; Voronina, 1994).

Employers clearly have views of what is appropriate work for women, and women often share these views. Many 'female' occupations are clearly regarded as using the 'natural' abilities women require in the domestic sphere – caring for young children, nursing, preparing and serving food, and so on. Much of the growth in part-time work in many Western societies is dependent on the needs of women with domestic responsibilities to take on paid employment even if the pay is low and the conditions of employment relatively poor. Feminists have argued that many of the assumptions underpinning the sexual division of labour are not only grounded in structural inequalities that disadvantage women, but also cultural assumptions about women's 'nature' and ways of life which are empirically unsustainable. Not all women marry. Not all women who marry have children. Not all women with children are married. Many (including some married women, and women who have children) have a lifelong commitment to paid work. Many women work out of economic necessity; their families would be in poverty without their additional income.

Industrialisation and the gendered organisation of work

An analysis of some of the historical aspects of gender and work reveals a complex relationship between work in the home and in the labour market. In pre-industrial societies there was no clear separation between work and the home; economic production was not concentrated in factories, offices and other places of employment. Most people worked in or near their home. Nor was there a gendered separation between productive work and unproductive work. All work was seen as contributing to the maintenance of the household, although some tasks were seen as men's and some as women's. However, with the industrial revolution, paid employment became separated from the home – in factories, offices, and so on. Production and consumption, productive and unproductive (domestic) work became separated, and gradually men became associated with the former and women the latter. Women were largely excluded from paid work, and it became seen as 'natural' for women, or at least married women, to stay at home and care for their children and husbands. (Many nineteenth-century and some early twentieth-century feminists accepted this and argued for women having a choice – the choice between paid employment and marriage.) What aroused concern in the nineteenth century was not whether or not women should work – women's work in the domestic sphere and the home caused relatively little concern. It was the public appearance of wage-earning working women that produced hostile comments. Working wives and mothers in particular were regarded as un-natural, immoral and negligent homemakers and parents, in all but the poorest of families. They were also accused of taking work from men.

This concern was underpinned by a developing domestic ideology which was formed among the middle classes in the late eighteenth and early nineteenth centuries, and which gradually spread to all classes and to both sexes (see Chapter 6). This ideology maintained that the world was divided up into two separate spheres – the public and the private. Men should be involved in the public sphere of work and politics, making money and supporting their families (Davidoff *et al.*, 1976). Women should stay at home in the domestic sphere, caring for their children and husbands and dependent on their husbands for financial support.

Although many single and even married working-class women had to work, by the end of the nineteenth century they would not have expected to be lifelong workers and generally shared the domestic ideal of the middle classes. Married women believed that their primary commitment was to their families and worked only when it was essential for the maintenance of the family; while 25 per cent of married women worked according to the 1851 Census, this had fallen to 10 per cent by 1901. However, poverty did drive many married women into paid work, and it is estimated that in the period 1890 to 1940, when the Census recorded 10 per cent of married women as working, 40 per cent worked at some time during their married lives. It is also probable that the Census underestimated women's employment, partly because of the nature of it – e.g. domestic service, taking in washing – and partly because of the increased status of a man who earned enough to support his wife and children, so that men might have been reluctant to record their wives as working on their Census return forms. However, female participation in the labour market was quite high because the majority of single women worked and they comprised as many as one in four women at some points in the nineteenth century. In 1871, 31 per cent of women aged over 10 years were in employment, and in 1931, 34 per cent of women over 14 were in employment. (The school leaving age was 10 in 1871 and 14 by 1931.)

Industrialisation had two main consequences for the gendered organisation of work. First, there was a *bifurcation of social spheres*, which separated the public world of work from the private arena of the family and the household. The effect of gender ideology was to designate the former the realm of men, the latter the world of women. Second, gender ideology also established *patterns of labour market segmentation* which concentrated those women who did engage in paid work in a relatively narrow range of occupations, and at the lowest levels of the occupational hierarchies. By the end of the nineteenth century women had become segregated into a small range of low-paid, low-status occupations. The low pay of women at this point in time is partly explained by the comparative youth of female workers, as most women gave up employment on marriage (this was a formal requirement of many occupations, such as teaching). The male trade unions kept women out of higher-paid jobs and fought for a family wage for men – that is, one sufficient for the support of a non-working wife and children. Patriarchal trade union practices, particularly those concerned with the maintenance of a 'family wage', therefore served to close down labour market opportunities for women (Witz, 1992). Even when women did the same work as men they did not receive equal pay. Equal pay for male and female teachers, for instance, was not fully implemented until 1962. The state also played a role in 'creating' occupational segmentation and making men more desirable as employees. Restrictive legislation, supposedly introduced to protect women, also excluded them from certain occupations and restricted the hours they could work. The Mines Act of 1884 for instance forbade women to work underground, but women were still able to work above ground as pit-brow girls. The protection afforded by legislation did not extend to housework, or to domestic servants however, or to preventing women doing dirty and dangerous work (in agriculture, for example).

Most men saw working women and especially married women as a threat to their own paid employment and status as breadwinners. They argued that there was only a limited amount of paid employment, and if women were allowed to work then some families would be left without an income. Women were also thought to lower the level of wages for both men and women, because they could be paid less than men. Consequently, it was argued that women should be excluded from paid employment or confined to low-status, low-paid jobs – 'women's work'. But women's work is not just work that is seen as fit only for women; it also involves jobs that women are thought to be naturally skilled at, such as cooking, cleaning and sewing. Hence, gender ideology segregates the labour market not only by pushing women out of certain types of work, but also by pulling them into others (particularly low-paid, low-skilled 'service' work).

Most trade unions have historically been dominated by men, and continue to be so. Consequently, they have tended to be concerned with protecting men's wages and working conditions. Until relatively recently, women were prevented or discouraged from joining a trade union, and in any case trade unions were seen by many women as not concerned with representing their interests. Thus it could be said that protective legislation was designed as much to protect male workers from female competition as to protect women from the rigours of work. Not all women accepted this uncritically, however.

By the early twentieth century women at all levels fought for the right to participate equally with men in paid employment. Women, for example, fought for the right to go to university and qualify as medical doctors. Women formed their own trade unions and fought against the conditions of their employment. A notable example of this is the so-called Match Girls' Strike. However, on the whole, men, the trade unions and the state succeeded in creating a segregated labour market, and the domestic ideology was generally accepted by the end of the nineteenth century by men and women in all social classes. Although women worked in large numbers during the First World War, they accepted that after the war men should have priority in the labour market. Many employers, including banks and the government, operated a marriage bar, so that women had to give up employment on marriage; the marriage bar on female teachers was not removed until the 1944 Education Act. Since the Second World War increasing numbers of women have taken on paid employment, especially married women (both despite and perhaps also because of, post-war domestic ideology and consumer culture).

However, despite equal pay and equal opportunities legislation, a segregated labour market still persists and domestic ideology is pervasive in the UK and in other Western societies. Furthermore, women are still expected to take on the 'double burden' of paid work and responsibility for domestic labour (see Chapter 6).

The gendered division of domestic labour

Feminists have argued that understanding women's role as unpaid domestic workers is crucial to understanding their social position more generally, and particularly their role in the labour market. However, it is only relatively recently that housework has become a topic of serious academic concern. Functionalist sociologists argued that it was necessary for women to undertake the physical and mental servicing of men and children in complex industrial societies, and that it was socially functional for men and women to divide the roles of homemaker and breadwinner according to gendered dispositions. Marxists argued similarly that this was necessary in capitalist societies; women were responsible for the reproduction of labour power and for consuming the goods and services produced by the capitalist economy. While Marxists and functionalists both argued that domestic labour was a private 'labour of love', Marxists pointed out the ways in which it ensured that there was a continuing supply of well-serviced workers to meet the demands of capitalism.

The view that domestic labour is the responsibility of women is also widely held by many people – although this may be changing slowly. A comparative study of Europe (Deshormes LaValle, 1987) found that 41 per cent of those interviewed said that men and women should have equal roles in the home and in paid employment, and 47 per cent of married men said they would prefer a working wife. Of course, wanting a wife in paid employment does not necessarily indicate a willingness to share in domestic labour. Despite an increased participation of men in domestic work, women retain the responsibility for most work in the home (see Chapter 6).

Feminists have examined what housewives actually do and developed theories that explain the relationship of housework to the social structure and the economy in general. Most feminists agree that housework is hard, physically demanding work and that the notion of being 'just a housewife' has developed because housework is hidden from public view and done out of affection and duty rather than for payment. Crucially, feminists have examined the sexual division of labour in the domestic sphere and have defined women's unpaid activity within the home as work. Research by Hannah Gavron (1966), Ann Oakley (1974a, b), Jan Pahl (1980) and others rigorously analysed what work was done in the domestic sphere, for whom, to whose benefit and at whose cost.

This research found that the majority of 'housewives' were women. Housework is usually seen as women's work and it is assumed that women will do it if they live in the household. The general assumption, this research found, is that women have a natural aptitude for domestic tasks, while men do not. Furthermore, Oakley (1974a) argued that the refusal to acknowledge that housework is work is both a reflection and a cause of women's generally low social status. She points out that housework is largely underrated, unrecognised, unpaid work that is not regarded as 'real' work. However, domestic labour involves long hours of work: in 1971, in Oakley's sample, women did 77 hours a week on average. The lowest was 48 hours, done by a woman who also had a full-time job, and the highest was 105 hours (Oakley, 1974a).

Domestic labour is seen by feminists, then, as real work. Feminists also argue that the demands of housework and the economic and personal conditions under which it is performed mitigate against the formation of a sense of solidarity amongst women. Domestic labour is a solitary activity, and women are bound to housework by ties of love and identification. Women like to feel reasonably good about their domestic work; in the absence of clear standards or the praise of employers, women tend to use other women as the standard against which to measure their own performance in a competitive way. Housework consequently tends to divide women rather than unite them.

As feminists have also argued, it has significant consequences for women's role in the labour market.

Explaining the domestic division of labour

Feminists argue that all men derive benefit from the expectation that women will perform domestic labour. Gender ideology reinforces the belief that men work to earn a living, and expect not only an income from their employment but personal service from a wife (or mother) at a cost to themselves of less than the market value of the goods and services provided. Christine Delphy (1984), from a materialist (Marxist-derived) perspective, argues that gender inequalities are a result of the ways in which husbands appropriate their wives' labour. The wife does not receive an equitable return for the domestic labour and childcare she provides. Delphy argues not only that domestic labour is work just as much as factory labour is work, but also that it is provided in a distinct 'mode of production' – the domestic mode. In the domestic mode of production the husband appropriates the labour power of his wife; in return for the economic support provided by husbands, women are expected to provide domestic services. The marriage contract is a labour contract she argues, the terms of which only become fully apparent when it is alleged that the wife has failed to fulfil her side of the bargain.

According to radical feminists men benefit from the unpaid labour of women in the domestic sphere, and therefore have a vital interest in maintaining the sexual division of labour. Consequently, men resist equal opportunities legislation, support policies that protect men's privileged position in the labour market and 'allow' their wives to work – but still expect them to be responsible for housework and childcare. The main beneficiaries of the domestic division of labour, sustained by patriarchal ideology, are therefore men (both individually and as a group). Marxist feminists argue that it is the capitalist system that benefits from the unpaid domestic labour of women. Not only does women's domestic labour reproduce the relations of production, but it also contributes to the maintenance of tolerable living standards for men and may reduce political pressure for radical change. Women expend considerable effort and energy stretching the household income and maintaining the household's standard of living, sustained and encouraged by ideologies of 'domestic science' and 'good housekeeping'.

There are a number of problems with feminist perspectives on domestic labour, however. The major problem with Marxist theories is that they fail to take account of men's interest in perpetuating women's role as domestic labourers. Marxist theories are also not able to account for why in non-capitalist societies it is still the case that women are primarily responsible for the performance of domestic labour. Also, domestic ideology and the domestic division of labour predates capitalism. Radical feminists, on the other hand, tend to ignore the benefits that capitalism derives from women's domestic labour, and their accounts tend to be descriptive rather than explanatory; reducing 'patriarchy' to both a description of, and an explanation for, the domestic division of labour (see Pollert, 1996). Radical feminist perspectives are also relatively static, and unable to account for social changes in the ways in which domestic responsibilities are shared and organised. Although substantial change has been slow to occur, it is the case, for instance, that in many societies, the gendered division of domestic labour is becoming more equitable; particularly in countries such as Sweden and Denmark where large numbers of women work full-time and where provision of childcare is at a relatively high level. Also, radical feminist approaches tend to assume that it is only men who benefit from the unpaid labour of women, but other groups (and society in general) also benefit, particularly from women's unpaid caring work.

Caring and support work

Many women are expected to care not only for their husbands and children but also for other dependents, and in a voluntary capacity for people generally in the community. Women are also frequently seen as necessary to their husbands' work role. As Janet Finch (1983) has demonstrated, this extends beyond the wives of managers and businessmen who are expected to entertain on behalf of their husbands. Men in many occupations 'need' a wife, and the employer benefits from this labour. Finch also notes that in many professional occupations, women often support or substitute for their husbands in the more peripheral aspects of their work (in the case of clergymen, politicians, and so on). Goffee and Scase (1985) have suggested that wives play a vital role in helping self-employed husbands, who are often heavily dependent on the (unpaid) clerical and administrative work undertaken by their wives. Wives are often forced to abandon their own careers to underwrite the efforts of the 'self-made' man. Furthermore, given the long hours self-employed men often work, many wives are left to cope single-handedly with the children and domestic responsibilities. Sallie Westwood and Parminder Bhachu (1988) have pointed to the importance of the labour (unpaid) of female relations in Black and Asian business communities in the UK, although they also emphasise that setting up a business may be a joint strategy of husband and wife.

Women are also expected to care for elderly or dependent relatives (see Chapters 6 and 7). As we noted in Chapter 3, however, some feminists have developed a critique of the concept of 'care' arguing that it detracts from the reciprocal nature of many caring relationships. Other feminists have noted that policies of 'community care' (as opposed to care in institutions) that have been advocated by successive governments since the 1950s have a hidden agenda for women. Such policies, which often involve closing down or not providing large-scale residential care, have frequently assumed that women are prepared to take on the responsibility of caring. As we noted in Chapters 6 and 7, research suggests that by far the majority of those people providing care for elderly or dependent relatives, particularly those committed to providing care on a long-term basis are women. While it is generally suggested that 'the family' should care where possible, in practice this has often meant that it is the women in families who provide care. It is generally assumed that caring is part of a woman's role and that women are natural carers.

Sally Baldwin and Julie Twigg (1991, p. 124) summarise the key findings of feminist research on caring work and indicate that the work on 'informal' care demonstrates:

- that care of non-spousal dependent people falls primarily to women;
- that it is unshared to a significant extent by relatives, statutory or voluntary agencies;
- that it creates burdens and material costs which are a source of significant inequalities between men and women;
- that many women nevertheless accept the role of informal carer and indeed derive satisfaction from doing so;
- that the reasons for this state of affairs are deeply bound up with the construction of male and female identity, and possibly also with culturally defined rules about gender appropriate behaviours.

When women (or men) are responsible for the performance of domestic labour or are providers of care on an unpaid (and often unrecognised) basis, this has serious consequences for their role in the labour market. What is at stake is not just the loss of potential earnings or social status, or even the amount of labour required (although the hours and commitment involved in some caring roles are considerably more than those of a full-time job), but the fact that many women are 'trapped' in the domestic sphere. Janet Finch and Dulcie Groves (1980) have argued that ideologies of domesticity and policies of community care are incompatible with equal opportunities for women because domestic and caring roles are in themselves full-time commitments. Processes of labour market segmentation mean that many women cannot earn as much as their husbands, making it economically unviable for men to give up work, or for many women to earn enough to pay for childcare, and domiciliary or respite care. Feminists have emphasised then that women's role in the domestic sphere has serious consequences for gender relations in the labour market.

Feminists have also drawn attention to another aspect of domestic labour; one which is regarded as work and which is remunerated, albeit often at a relatively low rate, and which involves middle-class men and women employing other (usually) women to carry out their domestic work. Research suggests that cleaning and other domestic work in private households is often performed by working-class women, by older women, or by Black or Asian women (Ehrenreich and Hochschild, 2003). Bridget Anderson (2000) in her study of migrant domestic workers in five European cities found that such work not only brought low pay and long hours, but could amount to a form of 'slavery'. Women from poor countries would often be asked to complete an impossible list of tasks; they were expected to care for children and families, to have very little time away from the home where they worked, and were treated in a range of subservient ways. Often, they found it difficult to break away from the middle-class family that 'bought' them and to enter the mainstream labour market.

Men, women and the labour market

There was a steady increase in women's rate of participation in the labour market in most Western societies during the course of the twentieth century. Familial ideology may see a woman's primary role as that of wife and mother, but the majority of women (including married women) in most societies have paid employment for the majority of the years during which they are employable. As we noted above, however, with the process of industrialisation the labour market became, and remains, highly gender segmented.

Occupational segmentation

Feminists have pointed out that the labour market is segmented both horizontally and vertically. *Horizontal segmentation* means that women are segmented across the labour market into a relatively narrow range of occupations. *Vertical segmentation* refers to the way in which, within these categories, women tend to be concentrated in relatively low-paid, low-status occupations. Both types of segmentation combine to concentrate women in the lowest strata of a narrow range of jobs, particularly non-manual, low-skilled service sector work in which women (across all ethnic groups) tend to be over-represented. Feminists have also argued that within horizontal patterns of segmentation, *occupational segmentation* means that men and women are often concentrated in different occupations within the same sector, and within those occupations tend to perform different functions (even within the same job) – *functional segmentation*. In her study of secretarial work, Rosemary Pringle (1989, 1993) has also described a process of *cultural segmentation* in which, even when men and women do the same job, that job is perceived or performed differently depending on the cultural connotations of gender. In her study women who worked as secretaries were often thought of as 'office wives' who could be expected to type, make tea, collect dry cleaning and remember birthdays and anniversaries and so on on behalf of their boss. The men who worked as secretaries (and only relatively small numbers of men do), tended to be thought of (and perform the job) as 'personal assistants' or 'diary managers'.

Furthermore, the work that women do is less likely to be seen as skilled than the work that men do (Phillips and Taylor, 1980), partly because women are thought to possess the attributes necessary to perform it as a result either of their feminine nature or their gendered experience of socialisation. Feminists have argued that some types of 'women's work' are *essentialised*, that is socially constructed according to the skills associated with women's biological role as actual or potential mothers – e.g. nursing, primary schoolteaching; or according to women's bodies – women are thought to be naturally good at sewing or typing because of their 'nimble fingers' for instance. Many of these jobs are also imbued with racist or ethnocentric assumptions – airlines which advertise routes to the Far East for instance often emphasise the 'natural' servility and attentiveness of Malaysian or Thai air 'hostesses' (assumptions that manifest themselves also in sex tourism – see Chapter 8). Other types of work are *feminised*, that is defined according to the characteristics women are thought to have acquired socially, as a result of their gendered experience of socialisation and education for instance, or as a result of their social roles. Examples of feminised work might include secretarial work in which women are thought to be capable of organising, managing and multi-tasking – effectively working as 'office wives' – on behalf of their boss (Pringle, 1989). Feminist research has also highlighted that certain types of work are *sexualised*, that is defined according to an ideology of heterosexuality and the idea that a certain level of sexual interaction and banter with male customers and colleagues should be expected or encouraged as part of the work role. Lisa Adkins's (1995) study of the hospitality

241

industry in Britain and Diane Kirkby's (1997) study of Australian barmaids are both examples of work in sexualised occupations. The latter emphasises how the sexualisation of barmaids

> has been part of that culture of enjoyment that has mystified and obscured the skills demanded of the workers while simultaneously rendering their workplace a space for sexualised encounters they have had both to repel and attract.
>
> (Kirkby, 1997, p. 205)

As the figures in Table 9.1 indicate, men and women in the UK continue to be concentrated in a relatively narrow range of occupational sectors, a pattern that is common across many societies. From these figures we can discern that women are concentrated in a narrower range of occupations than men, and particularly those involving semi-skilled or unskilled non-manual work in the service sector, or in caring work. Women are by far the majority of cleaners and domestic workers, retail cashiers and checkout operators, general office assistants and clerks, primary and nursery schoolteachers, care assistants, hairdressers, nurses and receptionists. Men are spread across a broader range of occupations, and are the majority of drivers, security guards, software professionals, ICT managers, police officers, marketing and sales managers, and IT technicians. They are also the majority of medical and legal professionals, although this gap is narrowing. Men are notably under-represented in caring work, and are concentrated in jobs deemed to involve a high level of training and skill, and also in areas of work that involve exercising authority over others. Most of the jobs in which men are concentrated are carried out either on a full-time basis, or in areas of work that involve shift work (which often carry a premium rate of pay), whereas many of the occupations in which women are employed are associated with relatively low pay; they are relatively low status, often do not involve employer investment in training or have clear promotion structures, and are often carried out on a part-time basis.

As well as being concentrated in a relatively narrow range of service sector occupations, women are also over-represented in part-time work. Vertical segmentation means that women are also under-represented in the most senior levels of particular occupations. In the UK, women currently make up only 36 per cent of senior public appointments, 23 per cent of top management posts in the Civil Service, 12 per cent of university vice-chancellors, 7 per cent of senior police officers, and 1 per cent of senior officers in the armed forces (EOC, 2004).

Gendered patterns of work

The increased labour market participation of women does not mean that women's experiences of work are the same as men's, or that their working patterns are the same. Employed mothers are concentrated in an even narrower range of occupations and sectors of the labour market than women in general; a pattern that is consistent across many countries throughout the world. The type of work, the hours that women work and the return that they receive for their labour all differ from men's. Even where women are employed in the same occupation as men and have equal pay, their

Table 9.1 Occupational segmentation of employees and self-employed (aged 16 and over), UK, 2003

Selected occupations	Women No. (000)	% of occupation	Men No. (000)	% of occupation
Taxi/cab drivers	14	8	168	92
Security guards	18	12	134	88
Software professionals	38	14	241	86
ICT* managers	40	16	207	84
Police officers up to sergeant	34	22	123	78
Marketing and sales managers	122	25	359	75
IT operations technicians	36	32	77	68
Medical practitioners	60	39	95	61
Solicitors, lawyers, judges and coroners	49	42	69	58
Shelf fillers	73	48	80	52
Chefs and cooks	115	49	117	51
Secondary teachers	197	55	161	45
Sales assistants	905	73	343	27
Waiters and waitresses	143	73	54	27
Cleaners and domestic workers	469	79	121	21
Retail cashiers and checkout operators	238	82	52	18
General office assistants and clerks	495	83	102	17
Primary and nursery schoolteachers	289	86	48	14
Care assistants and home carers	480	88	66	12
Hairdressers and barbers	133	89	17	11
Nurses	418	89	50	11
Receptionists	255	96	12	4

Source: Labour Force Survey, cited in EOC, 2004.

Note: * Information and Communication Technology.

experiences may differ greatly from men's. However, women and men are frequently concentrated in different jobs, often with men supervising or controlling women. Women often work part-time (44 per cent of all working women in the UK work on a part-time basis), while the vast majority of men work full-time (90 per cent). Men tend to work part-time either early or late in their working lives: 46 per cent of men who work part-time in the UK are aged 16–24 and 28 per cent are aged 55 or over, whereas women work part-time at all ages: 49 per cent of women part-time workers are aged 35–54 (EOC, 2004). As the figures in Table 9.2 indicate, women are over-represented among part-time workers throughout all age groups.

As a result of their concentration in part-time work, women often do not enjoy the same conditions of employment as men, or even the protection of employment legislation. Women who work part-time are often not only without fringe benefits;

Table 9.2 Part-time employees (aged 16 and over), UK, 2003 (% of full-time employees)

Age group	Women No. (000)	%	Men No. (000)	%
16–24	790	45	534	29
25–34	861	33	115	4
35–44	1,408	47	86	3
45–54	1,067	42	106	4
55–64	758	56	199	13
65 and over	123	89	123	69
All ages	5,007	44	1,163	10

Source: EOC, 2004.

they also lack seniority and are unlikely to be promoted, and this is often the case for part-time professional and managerial employees as well as those further down the occupational hierarchy. In addition, women are more likely than men to be doing 'homework' – producing industrial goods at home – on piece-rates that often work out at extremely low wages. It is thought that there is anything up to half a million homeworkers in Britain, although it is impossible to estimate precise numbers because much of this work is subcontracted or concealed.

Women's labour market participation is clearly affected by their domestic responsibilities. It is not so much marriage as having dependent children that conditions gendered patterns of work; in all ethnic and occupational groups, having children has a considerable impact on women's labour market position. Many women with young children tend to withdraw temporarily from the labour market, returning to part-time work when the children reach school age and to work full-time when the children are older. Yet not only do a high proportion of women return to paid employment after having children, but many return between births, and the time that women are taking out of the labour market for childbirth and childrearing is decreasing. Women are spending an increased proportion of their lives in employment, though relatively few have continuous full-time careers because of their domestic responsibilities.

Table 9.3 Male and female employees working full- or part-time, UK, 2003 (%)

	Full-time	Part-time	All
Single men	87	13	100
Married men	94	6	100
No children	92	8	100
With child 0–4*	97	3	100
With child 5+*	97	3	100
Single women	67	33	100
Married women	48	52	100
No children	58	42	100
With child 0–4*	32	68	100
With child 5+*	42	58	100

Source: EOC, 2004.

Note: * age of youngest child.

In the UK, women whose youngest child is aged under 5 have lower rates of full-time working than other women. About a third (32 per cent) of women with a child aged 0–4 work full-time, compared with 42 per cent of women with older children, and 58 per cent of women without dependent children (see Table 9.3).

Research suggests that there are significant gender differences in men's and women's reasons for working part-time (see Table 9.4). The most common reasons given by women are related to their family or domestic situation. In total, 54 per cent of female part-time employees told the Labour Force Survey in Spring 2003 (cited in EOC, 2004) that they wanted to spend more time with their family, had domestic commitments which prevented them from working full-time, or felt there were insufficient childcare facilities available to them. Only 5 per cent of male part-time employees stated that their reason for working part-time was related to their family or domestic situation. Instead, the most common response was that they worked part-time because they were also studying (44 per cent). The next most common reasons were that they couldn't find a full-time job (17 per cent) or that they had no need to work full-time (14 per cent). Another way of viewing these figures is to take each response in turn and calculate what percentage of respondents giving that reply were women (the last column in the table shows these percentages) (EOC, 2004). Although more than four-fifths (82 per cent) of part-time employees were women, almost all (98 per cent) of those citing family or domestic reasons were women, whilst only 55 per cent of those working part-time because they were students were women. Women also comprised fewer than two-thirds of those working part-time because they were ill or disabled (60 per cent), or who could not find a full-time job (63 per cent).

Table 9.4 Part-time employees (aged 16 and over) by reason for working part-time, UK, 2003

Reason	Women No. (000)	% of all women	Men No. (000)	% of all men	Women as a % of all
Studying	602	12	499	44	55
Ill or disabled	67	1	44	4	60
Unable to find full-time job	319	6	189	17	63
Did not want full-time, of which:					
No need to work full-time	536	11	158	14	77
Family or domestic reasons	2,679	54	55	5	98
Other reasons	802	16	181	16	82
All part-time employees	5,005	100	1,125*	100	82

Source: EOC, 2004.

Note: * discrepancy in total is due to rounding.

Similarly, the majority of those who job share and engage in term-time working are women. 'Job-sharing' is a type of part-time work in which a full-time job is usually divided between two people. The job-sharers work at different times, although there may be a changeover period. Term-time workers work during the school or college term and take (usually a combination of) paid or unpaid leave during the school holidays, although their pay may be spread evenly over the year. Many more women than men job-share or have term-time working arrangements in the UK. Overall, 91 per cent of job-sharers and 84 per cent of term-time workers are women (EOC, 2004). However, only a small proportion of women who work (1.6 per cent and 8.2 per cent respectively) either job-share or have a term-time working arrangement. The comparable figures for men are much lower. Only 1.4 per cent of male employees in the UK have a term-time working arrangement and 0.2 per cent currently job-share (EOC, 2004).

The pattern of women's paid employment across the life course is changing in all European societies, but there are clear differences between countries. Denmark and Portugal are the two countries where female participation most nearly matches the 'Inverted U' curve – that is, the majority of women do not take 'career breaks' – although participation rates are higher in Denmark. In France, the UK, Germany and the Netherlands, the activity pattern of women most clearly resembles the 'M-shaped' curve, with a high proportion of women having a career break, although the Netherlands has a higher rate of participation among women aged 40–50 than the other three countries. In other countries such as Italy, Spain, Greece, Ireland and Belgium, despite an increase in female economic activity rates, there continues to be a peak in female employment at about age 25 and a decline thereafter.

Although the availability of childcare (and out-of-school care for those of primary-school age) is a factor in explaining women's varied participation in paid employment, it is not by itself a sufficient explanation. Ireland and the Netherlands, for example, have significantly more places for pre-school children in publicly funded care than the UK, but much lower employment rates for women aged 25–49; 45 and 58 per cent respectively (compared with 73 per cent in the UK in 1992) – see Maruani (1992). However, it is clear that the availability of childcare is a significant factor in enabling women to participate in the labour market. In France, for example, the almost universal availability of pre-school publicly funded childcare, combined with long school hours, has meant that large numbers of French mothers work full-time. By contrast, in Britain the relatively low level of pre-school provision and a short school day accounts, in part at least, for both the continuing 'M-shaped' pattern of the female activity-rate curve and for the high level of part-time employment of women with children. It is also likely that the provision or not of childcare by the state interacts with cultural attitudes to whether married women or women with children should participate in paid employment. The low employment rate of married women in Ireland, for instance, would seem to be heavily influenced by cultural factors and gender ideology. A combination of structural and cultural factors also explains the persistence of the gender pay gap.

The gender pay gap

The gender pay gap (the disparity between men's and women's earnings) has not narrowed significantly in Britain since the introduction of the Equal Pay Act in 1970 (and its subsequent amendment in 1980 to include 'equal pay for work of equal worth'). There has been virtually no change in the full-time gender pay gap since the mid-1990s (EOC, 2004). Women working full-time in Britain earned 81 per cent of the average full-time earnings of men in 2003 – this meant that the pay gap in hourly earnings was

Table 9.5 Gender pay gap, 2003 (%)

	Hourly	Weekly	Annually
Women f/t and men p/t	18.8	25.4	27.8
Women p/t and men p/t	15.9	13.0	19.9
Women p/t and men f/t	41.1	72.0	72.3
All women and all men	23.9	41.4	43.8

Source: EOC, 2004.

19 per cent (see Table 9.5). Women working part-time earned only 59 per cent of the average hourly earnings of men who worked full-time. This average gender pay gap of 41 per cent has hardly changed since 1975 (EOC, 2004).

The gender pay gap is even wider in weekly earnings (25 per cent), and even more so annually (28 per cent). This is because men tend to work longer hours than women on average, and are more likely to receive additional payments such as shift pay and bonuses. Men are also more likely to work overtime than women. The pay gap is particularly wide for managers and administrators (30 per cent) and in sales occupations (28 per cent), and narrowest in clerical and secretarial occupations (2 per cent). There is, however, clear evidence that even when they are in the same occupations and are working similar hours, women earn less than men; that there is a 'gender premium'. The gender pay gap for all employees is higher for those with dependent children (31 per cent) than without (18 per cent). It is also higher amongst disabled women who have lower than average earnings of men, regardless of working full- or part-time.

The gap between men's and women's pay increases with age, and this is partly because men's average pay does not peak until they are in their fifties, whereas pay for women peaks in their thirties (EOC, 2004). Young women tend to be better qualified than older ones, which is part of the explanation also, although there is a wide gender pay gap at every qualification level, including for graduates. Indeed, there is a considerable difference between the average annual earnings of female and male graduates in the youngest age group (20–24); EOC research has shown that in 2002–3, earnings of men in the age group were on average 15 per cent higher than those of women (EOC, 2004).

The gender earnings gap seems to be compounded in later life. Some 61 per cent of male employees but only 53 per cent of women are members of one or more occupational, personal or stakeholder pension schemes. Women are less likely to make regular contributions to a pension than men; of those aged 25–59 in work in 2003, 44 per cent of men but only 26 per cent of women had made pension contributions in each of the previous ten years (EOC, 2004). This, combined with an ageing population (see Chapter 5), means that women are potentially at an increasing risk of poverty in later life, as women's disadvantaged labour market position throughout their working lives is reflected in later life.

A research review by the Equal Opportunities Commission in the UK (EOC, 2001) highlights women's concentration in a narrow range of occupations and in part-time work as two of the main factors contributing to the persistence of the gender pay gap.

The report also emphasises that compared with other industrialised countries, women in the UK suffer high earnings losses over the life course, particularly those who leave work to raise children: 'the high penalty reflects relatively weak maternity and parental leave entitlement and limited childcare provision. This restricts opportunities for continuity of employment, especially for low paid and low skilled mothers' (p. 5).

Women's orientations to work

Whereas most feminists argue that the major factors explaining women's position in the labour market and gendered patterns of work are structurally determined, Catherine Hakim (1995, 1996) has argued that insufficient attention has been given to women's orientation to paid employment, and to their work commitment. In exploring gendered patterns of labour market participation, she argues that there are three groups of women:

1 *Home-centred women* (accounting for between 15 and 30 per cent of women) who prefer not to work and whose main priority is children and family.
2 *Adaptive women* (accounting for between 40 and 80 per cent) who are a diverse group including women who want to combine work and family, and those who want to have paid employment but are not committed to a career.
3 *Work-centred women* (accounting for between 10 and 30 per cent of women) who are mainly childless, and whose main priority is their career.

She develops what she calls 'preference theory', arguing that women can now choose whether to have a career or not. She argues that the majority of women who combine domesticity with employment (the 'uncommitted') seek part-time work even knowing that it is concentrated in the lower grades and is less well remunerated than other work. In contrast to feminist sociologists who have argued that women's employment patterns are the outcome of structural factors that limit women's choices, the exclusionary tactics used by men, or gendered ideologies, Hakim argues that women positively choose low-paid, low-status part-time work that fits in with their domestic and familial roles, which they themselves see as a priority.

However, Crompton and Le Feuvre (1996) argue that there is little empirical evidence to support the view that there are such clear categories of women as far as work commitment is concerned. They conclude this from their study of women in banking and pharmacy employment in Britain and France and suggest that there is no evidence, even when these professional women work part-time, to suggest that they are not committed to their paid employment. Martin and Roberts (1984) in an earlier study reported that although many women found it difficult to cope with the often conflicting demands of work and home, this didn't mean that they were any less committed to either. More central, in their study, was the relationship between type of work, employment conditions and orientation to work. A further critique of Hakim's account is provided by Walsh (1999), in a study of part-time female workers in Australia. Walsh argues that women who work part-time are not homogenous in terms of their characteristics or orientations to work, and that there are a variety of reasons for women seeking part-time work. Whilst a majority of women in her sample were content with their work circumstances, a substantial proportion wanted to return to full-time work as soon as it was practical. She questions Hakim's view that the majority of female employees are not committed to a career and suggests that commitment to the labour market varies between groups and over the life course. Rosemary Crompton (1986) emphasised this latter point in her earlier discussion of service work, which highlighted the role of the life course in shaping women's orientation to work.

Finally, it is essential to remember that when women 'choose' to combine their commitments to unremunerated work with paid employment, the choices they make and their orientation to both are the outcome of a relatively narrow range of choices and the socially constructed expectations of women's roles and responsibilities. They are also shaped by material factors such as social class inequalities, and racial and ethnic power relations, as well as issues such as disability. For example, highly qualified women in managerial and professional occupations can often earn enough to pay for high-quality childcare and domestic help, and avoid the criticisms often directed at working wives and mothers, while other women cannot; their orientation to work is only part of the explanation for why this latter group of women may work part-time or not at all. More sociological explanations for women's working patterns and orientations to work have emphasised, then, the importance of exploring the ways in which structure and agency interrelate in order to understand the social construction (and restriction) of 'choice'.

Gender and unemployment

According to the Labour Force Survey (cited in EOC, 2004), 4 per cent of economically active women (women who are aged 16 and over and available for work), and 6 per cent of economically active men in the UK are unemployed. Traditionally in sociology, unemployment has not been thought to pose a problem for women, or at least for the majority of married women. This is because it is argued that women's wages are marginal, not essential to the family, that women's main identity and status is derived from their role as wives and mothers, and that women can 'return' to their primary domestic role. Women's unemployment is also 'hidden' in so far as a high proportion of women seeking employment are not registered as unemployed.

However, feminist research has challenged this view and has argued that work and work identities are central to many women's lives and that the money women earn is essential. Angela Coyle (1984), in a study of 76 women who were made redundant, found that only three (two of whom were pregnant and one near retirement age), took the opportunity to stop work. All the others sought alternative employment – and found work that was less skilled, had poor working conditions and was less well paid than their previous posts. The women said that they worked because a male wage was inadequate for the needs of their household, and because they valued the independence they gained from paid employment and having their own income. She concludes that paid work was seen as central to the lives of these women, and that redundancy was viewed as an unwelcome interruption to their working lives.

Reasons for non-employment vary considerably by gender. In the UK, the main reason given in the 2001 Census for women not being economically active was that they were engaged in non-remunerated work (looking after a family or home). The main reason for men was that they had been made redundant, were in full-time education or training, or that a temporary job had come to an end. Only 4 per cent of men were looking after a family or home (www.nso.org). Non-employment is also, of course, connected to other factors such as level of qualification, disability and ethnicity.

At the same time as the participation rate for women (albeit mainly in part-time jobs) has been going up in many societies, it has been declining for men. This is partly a result of high male unemployment rates, especially in Europe, and also because of an increase in the number of men, especially in their fifties and sixties, on long-term sick leave, taking early retirement or being made redundant. It is predicted that the gender gap in employment activity (with more women's jobs being created than men's) will continue to grow (Macionis and Plummer, 2002).

There are also gender differences in the activities that men and women undertake whilst unemployed, as well as the ways in which they seek new jobs. Surveys from several European countries, for instance, indicate that women find it more difficult than men to find a new job after being unemployed, and that they are more likely to rely on government services while men use more efficient methods such as personal contacts and networks (www.unece.org). The informal aspects of work seem to disadvantage women, then, both when they are in work and when they are unemployed, as many feminist studies of the workplace have revealed.

Feminist studies of the workplace

Many of the 'classic' feminist studies of work focused on factory workers (attempting to redress the neglect of women in malestream sociological studies of work), but have subsequently tended to focus more on sectors of the labour market in which women are over-represented, principally care work and work in the service sector. These studies have highlighted a range of ways in which gender shapes men's and women's experiences of paid work.

Feminist studies of factory work

Studies by Anna Pollert (1981) and Sallie Westwood (1984) show women and men working in separate occupations, with men employed in jobs classified as skilled and women doing work classified as semi- or unskilled, and earning substantially less than men. They all agree that 'skill' is socially constructed in such a way that it is seen as a characteristic of men's work and not of the work that women do. Ruth Cavendish (1982), describing a London factory, notes that the complex skills expected of women on the assembly line actually took longer to acquire than those of the male skilled workers. She provides a graphic account of what it is like to do unskilled factory work. The factory in which she worked employed around 1,800 people, of whom 800 worked on the factory floor. Virtually all the women were migrant workers – 70 per cent were Irish, 20 per cent African–Caribbean and 10 per cent Asian (mostly from Gujarat in

India). She notes that the men enjoyed significantly better working conditions than the women – their jobs enabled them to stop for an occasional cigarette, to move around and to slow down without financial penalty, while the women were tied to the line. Male-dominated trade unions and management worked together to protect the interests of male workers. Men and men's interests effectively controlled the women, who were frequently supervised by men.

All the women were semi-skilled assemblers with very few exceptions. Men, on the other hand, were spread throughout the grades and were divided from each other by differences of skill and pay. Even in the machine shop where men and women worked together on the same job the men were paid at a higher rate than the women on the grounds that they could lift the heavy coils of metal and the women could not. While young men were trained as charge hands, the young women were not; the latter lacked the possibilities for promotion that were open to the former.

The women were controlled by the assembly line and the bonus system. The views of the women workers were not sought when new designs and new machinery were introduced. The women had no chance to move or think while they were working and no time for a quick break, and if they could not keep up with the line they were dismissed. At work, the women were controlled and patronised by the men, but other women were generally supportive and friendly. The most important things in the women's lives appeared to be their family and home; the single women looked for-ward to marriage and domesticity. All the women shared a general interest in a 'cult of domesticity'.

Anna Pollert (1981), in her study of a tobacco factory in Bristol, found similarly that women's work in the factory was routine, repetitive, low-grade work that would not be done by men. The women thought that they should be paid less than the men because they were committed to marriage and having children, whereas the men had families to support. The women also thought that their work was inferior to the men's – less skilled and less important to the production process. Also, the women thought that if they were paid the same as men they would price themselves out of paid work.

The women accepted their relatively low pay therefore, partly because they compared it with the wages of other female jobs. While they rejected the idea that their place was in the home, they thought of themselves as dependent on men and conceived of their pay as secondary to a man's – even though two-thirds of the workforce were young, single women. They saw marriage and a family as their 'career' and thought of themselves as at the bottom of the labour market both in class and gender terms. The unmarried girls looked to marriage as an escape from low-status, monotonous work (even though they worked alongside married women for whom this had proved not to be the case). Val, one of Pollert's informants, expressed this well:

Get married [laugh]. Anything's better than working here. Well, most women get married, don't they? Not all of them work all their lives like a man. Put it this way, I don't want to work when I'm married. I don't really believe in married women working. Well. 'Cos there's not much work anyway, and they ought to make room for people what have got to lead their own lives.

(Pollert, 1981, p. 101)

251

Heterosexual romance permeated the talk of the women on the shop floor. Appearance, courting and marriage dominated the conversation and work was seen as temporary. Among the married women, who all did the 'double shift' (worked as both housewives and in paid employment), their main identity was as housewives.

Feminist studies of care work

Personal care work, such as that of care assistants and 'home helps', is predominantly performed by women; indeed, these jobs have generally been created as women's jobs and are assumed to require the 'natural' abilities of women. Women working as home helps, nursing auxiliaries, care assistants, and so on are employed in the female 'peripheral' labour market – low-status jobs with poor and insecure conditions of employment. They are often supervised and controlled by other female workers who have more secure employment in the 'core' labour market (Abbott, 1995).

Their client group is mainly elderly people (of which there are increasing numbers in most Western societies – see Chapter 5). Care workers often work across intimate bodily boundaries, and their work can be repetitive and emotionally draining, as well as physically demanding. While many of the women undertaking this kind of work are positive about it (Abbott, 1995), feminists have tended to see it as exploitative and therefore to see the women who do it as exploited victims of capitalist, patriarchal social structures. Yet, Hilary Graham (1991) has pointed out that feminists have tended, unintentionally, to take on policy-makers' definitions of care and to equate it with work carried out in the domestic home, for relatives and family, involving obligations of love and kinship. This, as she points out, has meant that they have ignored class and racial factors that impact on care and care work and the ways in which paid domestic labour in the private home results in a blurring of the boundaries between the domestic and the public spheres. Feminists have also tended to ignore paid care work in residential settings and the ways in which the structuring of work in these settings and the meanings given to it also blurs the public/private distinction in ways that merely transpose assumptions about women's caring role in the home to their employment in the public sphere.

Care work in both the private and the public sphere is principally women's work. It is not just that it is mainly women who undertake it, but that it is seen as naturally women's work (the skills involved are those that are culturally associated with women and hence are often not recognised). Drawing on Bourdieu's idea that certain forms of 'cultural capital' are needed for certain occupations, Beverley Skeggs (1997) has argued that for those women who want to work in occupations that involve caring, femininity can be an asset in the labour market. However, this means that caring work is often not remunerated as skilled work (see Abbott, 1995). It is also seen as work that is 'fit' only for women to carry out, largely because it involves both physical and emotional labour, as well as a concern with hygiene and health; in other words, it often involves intimate contact with other people's bodies. This designation of caring work as 'women's work' applies to much of the work that women do, both in the home and in the labour market and, feminists have argued, is central to understanding the relationship between the work that women do in both spheres. This applies particularly to women's work in the service sector, and in clerical work.

Feminist studies of clerical work

In clerical work, women are often found in relatively low-paid jobs, with few career prospects and benefits. Women are frequently recruited on the basis that they will not be promoted, while men are recruited on the assumption that they will. Once in employment, women are less likely than men to be offered structured work experiences and the opportunity to study that would enable them to seek promotion and to be seen as promotable. A study by Kate Boyer (2004) has found for instance that the financial services sector works to create what she describes as 'a system in which men flow through and women function at fixed points' (p. 201). As clerical work has declined in status and the tasks it involves have become standardised, fragmented and rationalised, so increasingly women have been recruited to office work. The deskilling of office work is mediated for men by the possibility of promotion. While women are recruited to the lowest grades, paid at lower rates and replaced by other young women when they leave to have children, men, it is assumed, will be mobile out of clerical work.

One of the major debates on social class in malestream sociology since the Second World War has been whether or not clerical workers have been proletarianised – that is, whether the pay, conditions of employment and nature of clerical work have become comparable to manual workers. British sociologists, following a Weberian analysis of class (see Chapter 3), have looked at the market situation, working conditions and status of male clerical workers and argued that they are middle class because they enjoy superior working conditions, are socially accepted as middle class and do not identify themselves as working class (see Lockwood, 1958; Goldthorpe *et al.*, 1969). Braverman (1974) however, argued that clerical workers have been proletarianised and that the feminisation of clerical work is part of this process. Reviving the debate, Crompton and Jones (1984) argued that while female clerical work is proletarian, men's is not – primarily, they suggest, because male clerical workers have the possibility of upward mobility out of clerical work. They suggest that this situation may change as more women seek and are seen as potential candidates for promotion. However, the view that female clerical workers are proletarian holds only if they are compared with male manual workers. Martin and Roberts (1984) and Heath and Britten (1984) argued that female clerical workers enjoy pay and conditions of work more comparable to women in professional and managerial work than to women employed in manual work, where few are in work defined as skilled.

One of the most important sociological studies of clerical work is Rosemary Pringle's (1989) *Secretaries Talk*, based on interviews with almost five hundred office workers from a range of workplaces in Australia. Her analysis focused on the boss–secretary relationship, and highlights the ways in which this relationship is shaped by gender power relations. Adopting a largely Foucaldian perspective, Pringle examines the ways in which secretaries negotiate these power structures, shaped by gender and class, charting the changing roles and identities available to secretaries – from 'office wife' to 'sexy secretary' and 'career woman', and also the way these roles reflect technological change. She concludes that, although a variety of strategies of power and resistance are open to them, 'gender and sexuality continue to be extremely significant in the construction of secretaries' (p. 26).

Feminist studies of service work

Gendered patterns of occupational segmentation, at least in Western societies, mean that by far the majority of women who engage in paid work are employed in the service sector, largely in routine, non-manual interactive service work or 'women's work'. Feminist studies of service work have identified a range of occupations in which the skills, attributes and aesthetics associated with women are commodified – in nursing (James, 1989), in waitressing and bar work (Hall, 1993a, b; Adkins, 1995), in the airline industry (Hochschild, 1983; Tyler and Abbott, 1998; Tyler and Taylor, 1998; Williams, 2003) and in the betting and gaming industry (Filby, 1992), for instance. Elaine Hall's (1993a, b) study of waitressing, for example, highlights the performance of gendered service styles and that 'waiting on tables is defined as typical "women's work" because women perform it and because the work activities are considered as feminine' (1993a, p. 329). Her study found that men are expected to adopt a 'formal' style when they wait on tables, whereas women are expected to be more 'familial', and that these differences in expectations can be attributed to the gendered construction of the jobs themselves. What she describes as positional gender stratification within the occupation itself was shaped largely by three factors: the gendered meanings of waiting, the gendering of job titles, and the gendering of uniforms. Combined, these factors meant that being feminine was conflated with 'giving good service' (1993b, p. 452).

Mike Filby's (1992) ethnographic study of three betting shops also highlighted the relationship between gender and sexuality in shaping the work experiences of women in service occupations, and particularly the ways in which this relationship is shaped by employer and customer expectations. Filby argues that perceptions of good service were shaped largely by whether or not customers were satisfied with 'the figures, the personality and the bums' of female workers. He also highlights that both management and customers expected female workers to engage in sexual banter with customers as part of their work role so that 'the line between selling the service and selling sexuality in such activity is very thin' (p. 37). In this respect, he concludes that: 'This study . . . indicates how much the operation of workplaces and the production of goods and services depend on tacit skills and assumed capacities of sexualized, gendered individuals' (p. 38).

A more explicit focus on the relationship between masculinity and femininity underpinned Gareth Morgan and David Knights's (1991) study of 'selling as a gendered occupation' (p. 183) in a medium-sized insurance company. Their research highlights that women were largely excluded from the job of field sales representative partly because of 'protective paternalism' (sales reps have to travel around by themselves, and visit prospective clients), partly because women were thought not to be suited to the 'loneliness of selling', and partly because they were thought to be less resilient than men; 'too sympathetic' and 'not hungry enough' as some of the men in their research put it. Also, managers were conscious of an 'esprit de corps' amongst the sales force based on shared gender identity and thought that women might disrupt this. The role of sales rep, they found, was constructed largely according to a particular vocabulary associated with masculine characteristics; a masculine discourse that emphasised aggression and high performance as the defining features of the job, qualities that the (male) managers and (male) sales reps and (they assumed) potential customers, would not associate with women. Hence, 'for all these reasons, . . . the task of selling itself became bound up with the masculinity of the sellers' (p. 188). This meant that *internal* sales (in banks and building societies) became feminised, whereas the *external* sales force was predominantly male dominated. A similar finding emerged from research by Kate Boyer (2004) on the financial services industry in Canada.

These gender differences in the nature of service work, and in the ways in which particular roles are constructed according to gender ideologies, have also been studied in police work. Susan Martin (1999), in her study of police officers in the USA found that police work involves high levels of emotional interaction, and that officers must control their own emotional displays and also the emotions of members of the public with whom they come into contact who may be injured, upset, angry or under suspicion. She argues that police work is often viewed as masculine work involving fighting crime, but that it also involves a more caring aspect, which officers often disdain as 'the feminine side of the job'. Her analysis emphasises the ways in which gender is in part constructed through work and through the cultures of particular occupations and work organisations.

Robin Leidner (1993) reaches a similar conclusion in her neo-Weberian study of the routinisation of service work in Combined Insurance and McDonald's, *Fast Food, Fast Talk*. She argues that with regard to gender and interactive service work, one of the most striking aspects of gender construction is that its accomplishment creates the impression that gender differences in 'personality, interests, character, appearance, manner and competence' are somehow natural. Hence, 'gender segregation of work reinforces the appearance of naturalness' (p. 194). Rather, she maintains, gender is constructed in part through work, yet

> For the public, as well as for workers, gender segregation in service jobs contributes to the general perception that differences in men's and women's social positions are straightforward reflections of differences in their natures and capabilities.
>
> (Leidner, 1993, p. 211)

Many female jobs in the service sector are clearly regarded as using the abilities women are thought to deploy in the private sphere: caring, preparing and serving food, nursing, anticipating and responding to the needs of others, and so on. In short, much of this work is thought to involve what US sociologist Arlie Russell Hochschild (1983) described in her book *The Managed Heart* as 'emotional labour' – work involving the commodification of emotion, and associated largely with women's capacity to provide service and care.

Men doing 'women's work'

Feminist studies have also emphasised that underpinning occupational segmentation and the gendered *structure* of the labour market is a *culture* of 'men's work' and 'women's work'. As Joan Evans has noted in her research on male nurses:

Men's participation in nursing reveals that prevailing definitions of masculinity have acted as a powerful barrier to men crossing the gender divide and entering the profession. At extraordinary times such as war and acute nursing shortages, gender boundaries are negotiable. For those men who have crossed over into nursing, a gendered division of labour is evidenced by men nurses' long-standing association with mental health nursing and, more recently, with their disproportionate attainment of masculine-congruent leadership and speciality positions.

(Evans, 2004, p. 321)

Women's work, as we have already noted, is associated with low pay, low status and less autonomy than men's work, in part because of the interrelationship between the structure and culture of work and of the attribution of the skills involved to women's nature or gender. Most ethnographic studies have focused either on women's exclusion from areas of work traditionally dominated by men, or sectors of the labour in which women are concentrated. Men in non-traditional occupations have been relatively neglected until relatively recently. However, over the past twenty years or so, the proportion of women entering male-dominated occupations has begun to increase, but not vice versa. In her book, *Doing 'Women's Work'*, Christine Williams (1993) explores why men tend not to work in areas of the labour market associated with female employment, and also what happens to those men who do carry out 'women's work' in terms of their experiences of the workplace. Her research was undertaken in four settings: an elementary (primary) school, secretarial work, unpaid care work and a strip club. She found that men in women's work tend to either withdraw (by emphasising their masculinity and disassociating from the predominantly feminine culture) or emphasise and parody prejudices (about their sexuality, for instance) and become 'hyper-feminine'. She argues that when women carry out 'men's work' they can either emphasise their femininity (and become devalued) or adopt masculine values (when they are more likely to do well at work, and be seen as promotable for instance). Both men and women, she concludes, tend to be rewarded for emphasising distance from femininity. Most women, therefore, are typically penalised. She argues that the culture of work and the devaluation of femininity explains, in part, the persistence of the gender pay gap, and also why men are able to sustain their advantage over women in the labour market, even when they 'cross over' into women's work.

In the same collection, Harriet Bradley (1993) argues that most men (even unemployed ones) are unwilling to enter women's work because of the low pay and low status attached to it. Her work examines patterns of men's entry into women's work and the factors which influence their exit. She identifies three strategies of men's entry into women's occupations: *takeover* (through which female work becomes male work – baking and brewing, dairy work and spinning are examples); *invasion* (through which men take over the more technical, high status aspects of the work – obstetrics, personnel and social work, for instance); and *infiltration* ('the hardest to trace, to quantify and analyse' (p. 21), this involves male employees having no particular interest in driving women out or in changing the nature of the occupation, but at the same time appearing to reject hegemonic masculinity). She concludes that three factors influence men's 'cross over' into women's work: economic issues (high levels of unemployment, for instance), changes in masculinity and technological change.

Similar findings emerged from Simon Cross and Barbara Bagilhole's (2002) ethnographic study of ten men working in a range of women's jobs, which emphasised the challenges to their masculinity experienced by men from various sources and in various ways. They found that men attempted either to maintain a traditional masculinity by distancing themselves from female colleagues, and/or partially reconstructed an alternative masculine identity by aligning themselves closely with their non-traditional occupation. They conclude that these responses maintain masculinity as the dominant gender, even amongst men working in traditionally female jobs.

Other research has emphasised that when men enter women's work they often do so on a relatively temporary or transitional basis. England and Herbert (1993) for instance have argued that men enter women's work through a 'revolving door', and that the culture of masculinity ensures that they rarely stay long because 'men employed in female dominated occupations suffer a prestige penalty' (p. 50). Williams and Villemel (1993) have argued similarly that some men enter through a 'trap door', meaning that they intend to pursue more traditional male occupations, but end up (temporarily) in women's work. The metaphor of the trap door is intended to convey that men work in women's jobs 'only briefly and are likely to move upwards as they exit' (p. 72). Allan's (1993) study of male primary schoolteachers emphasises that men in women's work often have to renegotiate their masculinity and consciously perform their gender identity in order to overcome apparent contradictions. This gender performance, Allan argues, is 'a kind of unacknowledged work in itself' (p. 115). Developing this approach further, Rosemary Pringle (1993), in her study of male secretaries, adopts a Foucaldian approach that focuses on the gendered nature of occupational discourse (the language used to define the 'reality' of a particular occupation, and that shapes how that occupation is perceived and experienced). She argues that 'neither occupational titles nor gender labels merely describe a pre-given reality, but exist in discourses that actively constitute that reality' (p. 130). Hence, she concludes that men perceive and experience women's work differently to women. As we noted above, this is not only because of structural patterns of (horizontal and vertical) occupational segmentation, but also because of cultural segmentation, according to which men and women experience (and are perceived in) the same occupation differently, so that the culture of the job changes, depending on whether it is performed by a man or a woman. Therefore, men who do secretarial work are not perceived as secretaries, because of their gender, but often as 'personal assistants'. The significance of occupational discourse means that our perception of secretarial work is shaped not by what a secretary *does* but by what or rather who a secretary *is*, and how this relates to and is embedded within gendered perceptions of the difference between men and women.

A similar point is made by Applegate and Kaye (1993) in their study of male care workers, which found that in unpaid caring work men become 'feminised' and begin to adopt skills and personality traits traditionally associated with women. However, patriarchal ideology and discourses of masculinity and femininity meant that, for the men in their study, caring work continued to be perceived as women's work. Their research, they conclude, indicates the resilience of gender ideology and discourses to the work that men and women actually perform.

Gender and the professions

Women tend to be concentrated in the 'female' semi-professional occupations rather than in the male-dominated professions. Semi-professional occupations have less autonomy than professional ones, as well as lower status and less pay. Women are often seen as 'naturally' suited to the caring work involved, for example, in primary schoolteaching, nursing and social work. However, even within these occupations, women tend to be concentrated in lower grades and are often supervised by men. Although there have been improvements in recent years, there is still considerable evidence that sex stereotyping and discrimination occurs in many professional occupations (EOC, 2004). By the end of the twentieth century, younger women's professional qualifications had increased to a similar level to men's, whereas older generations of women were generally less qualified than men. As a result, there have been substantial changes in the proportion of women entering certain professions, such as higher education and the law. However, women's share of senior jobs even within those occupations in which they are generally as well qualified as men remains relatively low (a pattern that is explained in part by age difference) (EOC, 2004).

Certain professional or associated professional occupations remain heavily gender segmented (Table 9.6). For example, men still hold over 90 per cent of engineering jobs, even in the field of software engineering. Women, however, constitute over 80 per cent of primary school and nursery teachers, but only 38 per cent of university lecturers, and just over half of college lecturers. Women are over-represented in the 'caring' professions such as nursing and social welfare, as well as personnel and industrial relations, whereas men dominate professions such as the law and finance. Men are also the majority of surveyors and architects. Amongst the associated professions, the two female-dominated occupations (health professionals and social welfare) also have the highest proportion of part-time employees (EOC, 2004).

As we noted above, in the established professions, there has been an increase in recent years in the number of women entering the professions, but not necessarily in their representation at the higher levels. Medicine is the profession that has the highest proportion of women in most societies. In the UK, for instance, in 1976 23 per cent of all doctors on the General Medical Council Register were women, and the proportion of women entering medical school had increased from between 22 and 25 per cent in the years between the Second World War to 1968, to 37.8 per cent in 1978 (Elston, 1980), to 46 per cent in 1985 (Allen, 1988), and over to 50 per cent by the 1990s (Hockey, 1993). However, despite being 25 per cent of medical graduates in the 1960s and almost half by the 1980s, women are still under-represented in the higher levels of the medical profession (in 2000, only 21 per cent of hospital consultants were women, and only 5 per cent of consultant surgeons). Women are also concentrated in certain areas of medicine – in general practice, in the school health service, in mental health and particularly in paediatrics (in which they made up the largest group of female consultants in 2000 – nearly 40 per cent). These tend to be specialisms that are socially constructed as 'feminine' areas of medicine, or in which women's real or potential conflict between home and work can be reduced. They are also the areas of medicine that are less popular amongst men (women also tend to be concentrated in the same areas of medicine as immigrant male doctors). Some 34 per cent of GPs

Table 9.6 Employment in selected professional and associated professional occupations, UK, 2000 (%)

	Women	Men	All
All professional occupations	*40*	*60*	*100*
Natural scientists	35	65	100
Engineers and technologists	6	94	100
software engineers	8	92	100
Health professionals	40	60	100
medical practitioners	38	62	100
pharmacists/pharmacologists	61	39	100
Teaching professionals	64	36	100
universities	38	62	100
HE and FE colleges	54	46	100
secondary schools	53	47	100
primary/nursery schools	86	14	100
Legal professionals	32	68	100
solicitors	33	67	100
Business and financial professionals	30	70	100
chartered and certified accountants	26	74	100
management consultants and business analysts	34	66	100
Architects, town planners and surveyors	13	87	100
All associated professional occupations	*51*	*49*	*100*
Scientific technicians	24	76	100
Draughtspersons, quantity and other surveyors	9	81	100
Computer analysts and programmers	21	79	100
Health associate professions	87	13	100
nurses	90	10	100
Business and financial associate professionals	37	63	100
underwriters, claim assessors, brokers, analysts	30	70	100
personnel and industrial relations officers	79	21	100
Social welfare associate professionals	76	24	100
welfare, community and youth workers	73	27	100
Literary, artistic and sports professionals	38	62	100

Source: Labour Force Survey, Spring 2000, cited in EOC, 2004.

in England in 2000 were women, compared with only 25 per cent in 1990. One reason for this increase is that part-time work and job sharing have become better established in general practice than in other areas of the medical profession; by 1999, 41 per cent of female GPs worked half-time or three-quarter time contracts or were job-sharing. In contrast, 93.5 per cent of male GPs were employed on full-time contracts (EOC, 2004). Interestingly, only a small percentage of women become obstetricians or gynaecologists (the figure of roughly 12–15 per cent has remained stable since the 1970s).

It is often argued that the reason for women's lack of career prospects is their domestic commitments, because they take time out of their professional careers to have children, seek part-time work when they return and are not 'really' committed to their work in the same way as men. It could be argued, however, that women are disadvantaged in the professions because the training and promotion opportunities offered to them are based on assumptions about continuous, full-time work, that few professional occupations could realistically be carried out on a part-time basis and that candidates for promotion are expected to have had certain experiences and achieved certain 'benchmarks' by a certain age. All of these criteria are of course difficult for a woman who has had a career-break or who needs to work part-time for a particular period.

Isobel Allen (1988) found that from the point of entry to medical school through to hospital consultant posts, women doctors face sexist attitudes, have to compete with an 'old boys' network' of patronage, are often asked discriminatory questions at interviews (for example, questions about childcare arrangements were asked of most women in her study, some of whom did not even have children). Barbara Lawrence (1987), in a study of female general practitioners, found similarly that many women had decided to set up their own practice to avoid being dominated by male partners. They had found that in mixed group practices they were paid less than their male colleagues, and were expected to see all of the women and children on the patient list.

A similar pattern can be identified in the law. Women currently make up some 35 per cent of solicitors holding practising certificates (PCs) in England and Wales. This compares with only 21 per cent in 1989. Each year women have formed the majority of those admitted to the solicitors' roll, and in 2000 they comprised 53 per cent of new entrants to the profession. However, women remain concentrated in the lowest levels of the profession. In 2000, 82 per cent of partners with a PC in private practice were male, while women formed the majority of assistant solicitors. Overall, over half of all male solicitors, but less than a quarter of female solicitors, were partners. One factor contributing to this is age – the average age of a female solicitor with a PC in 2000 was 36 (compared with a male average of 43), and women also comprised the majority of PC holders aged 30 and under. Of barristers practising in England and Wales in 2000, 26 per cent were women, compared with only 18 per cent in 1990. Women also comprised 46 per cent of those called to the Bar in 2000. However, they accounted for only 8 per cent of practising QCs (Queen's Counsels), the recognised leaders of the profession in England and Wales (EOC, 2004).

In contrast to the male-dominated professions, women occupy the majority in the more feminised, semi-professions. Jobs such as nursing and teaching are seen as suitable jobs for women because of the hours worked, the demands on interpersonal skills and the relatively steady employment prospects. However, these occupations lack the autonomy enjoyed by the established professions and women who work in them are often dominated by men: nurses by male hospital doctors and consultants, female teachers by male headmasters, for instance. In 2000, 70 per cent of secondary school heads in England and Wales were men (EOC, 2004). While the pay is relatively high in these occupations, compared with the pay of women in general, it is poor in comparison with the salaries enjoyed by those in the 'male' professions. In both nursing and teaching, women are under-represented in the top grades when account is taken of the ratio of men to women in the occupation as a whole (EOC, 2004).

Women are marginalised then in professional and semi-professional work in a range of ways. They occupy the lower-status, less well-remunerated levels within most professional and semi-professional occupations, and gendered assumptions about appropriate work for men and women, as well as the impact of women's domestic responsibilities, continue to shape the gendered division of professional work.

In her neo-Weberian analysis of gender and professional work, Davies (1996) emphasised two ways in which the professions engage in exclusionary 'closure': organisational cultures and informal networks that exclude women or make women 'uncomfortable', and the social construction of skill. In her discussion of professional work in medicine and in professions allied to medicine, she develops this latter theme in particular, emphasising that the social construction of 'professionalism' is itself gendered in so far as it relies on values, such as impartiality, objectivity, that are traditionally associated with men rather than women, as well as on the unacknow-ledged emotional and support work of women (through which men are able to maintain the 'illusion' of detachment). Male doctors, for instance, are seen as professional (detached, scientific, and so on) in part because of the emotional support work of nurses that women are thought to be more suited to. From this, Davies concludes that a key sociological problem is not simply women's exclusion from professional work, but rather the nature of their inclusion in it. A similar point has been made about women's role in managerial work (Gherardi, 1995).

Managerial work

Since the mid-1990s women's representation amongst executives has doubled and amongst company directors it has tripled (Table 9.7). At the same time, there has been an overall increase in the number of women working in management jobs (although the overall number of managers increased considerably during the 1990s; and manage-ment still accounts for only 9 per cent of female employment, but 14 per cent of men's). The patterns of occupational segmentation that exist in other areas of work can also be identified in management, however. Women still comprise less than a quarter of executives, and only one in ten company directors; men outnumber women in most sectors of management, the exceptions being office managers (66 per cent), and health and social services (73 per cent). Men, in contrast, account for 79 per cent of corporate managers and 94 per cent of production managers (EOC, 2004). Women also account for a higher proportion of managers in the public than the private sector; their share of managerial employment also varies between industries. For example, women comprise two-thirds of managers in health and social work, but only one in ten of those

Table 9.7 Female share of managers, UK, 1990–2001 (%)

	1974	1990	1995	2000	2001
Director	0.6	1.6	3.0	9.6	9.9
Function head	0.4	4.2	5.8	15.0	15.8
Department head	2.1	7.2	9.7	19.0	25.5
Section leader	2.4	11.8	14.2	26.5	28.9
All managers	1.8	7.9	10.7	22.1	24.1

Source: National Management Salary Survey, cited in EOC, 2004.

in construction. Although, as we noted above, women are over-represented in personnel and industrial relations, they comprise only 57 per cent of personnel and HR managers (the majority being employed at 'officer' level).

What some management writers refer to as the 'glass ceiling' (Davidson and Cooper, 1992) – the situation where women can see but not reach or break through seemingly invisible barriers to high-level jobs and so are prevented from progressing their careers – appears still to exist in many organisations. Several explanations for women's continuing low representation in management have been put forward. First, like most occupations, there is a tendency for some types of management jobs to be associated with either men or women; in other words, to be constructed in gendered terms. For example, while women are comparatively well represented in personnel management and the public sector, men still dominate in production management and in information and communication technology management. Second, opportunities to work part-time are relatively limited in management jobs, in which a 'long hours' culture prevails – in the UK, only 6 per cent of managers and senior officials (three-quarters of whom are female) work part-time (EOC, 2004). Similarly, there are few (formal) opportunities for flexible working at senior levels in organisations. The EOC (2004) reports that no other occupational group has a lower proportion of part-time workers. A higher proportion of managers (22 per cent in 2001) than employees in any other occupational group usually work more than 50 hours per week. Male managers (27 per cent) are twice as likely as females (10 per cent) to do so (EOC, 2004). Also, a higher proportion of female managers than male managers are single or divorced. Women managers are also much less likely than male managers to have dependent children, particularly very young children.

A study of 220 managers in a banking organisation found, for instance, that women managers are significantly less likely to be married or to have children, concluding that 'women still have to make choices that men do not in order to further their careers'. The same study found that men reported higher levels of pressure stemming from the work environment and managerial relationships with subordinates and superiors than women, whereas women reported considerably higher pressures stemming from perceived gender inequalities at work, and concerns about balancing their work and domestic commitments (Granleese, 2004, p. 219).

The long hours culture, which pervades many organisations and management occupations, means that those women with family responsibilities are at a particular disadvantage. This is compounded by their exclusion also from the (largely male-dominated) informal networks within organisations and within which power relations (and promotion opportunities, for instance) are often negotiated. Even where women have broken through the 'glass ceiling' into management positions, their pay is often lower than that of men.

Much of the academic literature on managerial work has focused on the barriers women face in organisations, particularly with regard to the effects of the 'glass ceiling'. While early (mainly liberal) feminist texts such as Rosabeth Moss Kanter's (1977) *Men and Women of the Corporation* provided a comprehensive review of these barriers, advocating solutions (such as equal opportunities policies and legislation), more recent managerially oriented texts have tended to focus on the benefits to an organisation of employing women in management positions. Reflecting the gendered assumptions underpinning women's concentration in caring and service work, what has come to be known as the 'women in management' literature focuses on gender differences in management styles, arguing that women's ways of managing are particularly appropriate to contemporary work organisations, and that women's skills in multitasking and in interpersonal communication are ideally suited to management. A key management writer in this area is Judy Rosener whose (1990) article in the *Harvard Business Review* focused on the differences between male and female management styles, arguing that the latter is increasingly suited to the turbulence and uncertainty of the contemporary workplace. Women she argued, adopt a 'transformational' style of management based on nurturing, enabling and empowering, whereas men prefer a 'transactional' approach which associates leadership with direction and control. A similar article by Nanette Fondas (1997) advocated a feminisation of management, making the point that 'qualities that are culturally associated with females are appearing in descriptions of managerial work in the texts of contemporary writers, and these texts function as carriers of a feminine ethos to practicing managers' (p. 257). She associates the feminisation of managerial work with three developing themes that, she argues, are espoused by contemporary management writers and which are associated with feminine qualities. These are: surrendering control in favour of shared responsibility, helping and developing others through a nurturing rather than a controlling approach to management, and building a connected network of relationships.

Emphasising themes such as these, the 'women in management' literature has placed women at the centre of analyses of managerial work, and has attempted to highlight the value to organisations of the skills associated with women's role in the domestic sphere. Various studies have examined the difficulties women face in organisations from work/family conflicts and caring responsibilities (Davidson and Cooper, 1992), from the 'old boys' network' (Coe, 1992; Ibarra, 1993) and from patriarchal assumptions about gender differences in work orientations and commitment (Sturges, 1999). Many such analyses, however, are dependent upon universal and essentialist assumptions about men's and women's 'natures' or roles. They are also managerial in so far as they are concerned largely with the organisational benefits of women's attributed natures or skills, rather than with advancing women's rights. Hence, they are primarily concerned with the commodification and management of sexual difference, rather than advancing a feminist agenda concerned with alleviating inequalities experienced by women as a group.

Less managerial approaches have argued that many work organisations support a competitive, hegemonic masculinity that sustains and reproduces a variety of controlling, instrumental and goal-oriented behaviours that serve to exclude women and femininity (Calas and Smircich, 1991), or to undermine women managers (Kerfoot and Knights, 1998). Silvia Gherardi (1995) has drawn attention to the exclusion of women through organisational symbolism and cultures. Gender difference, she argues, is both an organising principle, and an outcome of the organisation of work. As she puts it, 'gender is an organising principle and an organisational outcome. Gender characteristics are presupposed, imposed on people and exploited for productive ends, and there are organisational dynamics which create them' (p. 185).

In her study of women managers in five multinational companies, Judy Wajcman (2002) focused on the ways in which gender relations in the private sphere are adapted to accommodate a managerial career. Her analysis reveals that 'the domestic arrangements necessary to sustain the life of a senior manager are very different for men and women' (p. 609). Her conclusion is that for all the organisational initiatives designed to promote equal opportunities, the managerial career is still 'largely dependent upon the services of a wife at home, or a housewife substitute in the form of paid domestic services' (p. 609).

Other studies, such as Fiona Wilson's (1995) have drawn attention to the ways in which women managers are controlled and marginalised, in part through their experiences of sexual harassment and sexual power relations in the workplace.

Sexuality and work

As well as sexualised labour (see above), feminist studies of the workplace have highlighted that masculine power and sexuality are evident in work organisations in a number of ways. Sexual harassment, for instance, is one of the ways in which men subordinate and control women at work (Collinson and Collinson, 1996; MacKinnon, 1987; Stanko, 1988; Ramazanoglu, 1987) and sexual power relations permeate organisational cultures in a range of ways (Brewis and Linstead, 2000). Indeed, feminists such as Cockburn (1990) have argued that men actively employ a number of tactics, including sexual harassment, to offer active resistance to moves towards sexual equality in work organisations. Sexuality, and particularly an ideology of 'compulsory heterosexuality' (see Chapter 8) is also deeply embedded within the culture of many work organisations (Hall, 1989). This affects women's position in the labour market and their experiences of the workplace in a number of ways that cross-cut other aspects of identity, such as age. Women are frequently judged on the basis of their looks, and often have to dress and behave in ways different from men in the same occupation. Research by Tyler and Abbott (1998) found that female flight attendants were subject to a more stringent regime of appearance norms than their male colleagues, for instance. Women's sexuality is often commodified in order to make their employing organisation, or its products or services, more marketable. Clara Greed (1994) points to a comment frequently made by the male surveyors she interviewed: 'attractive women make unattractive property more attractive.' Gherardi (1995) has similarly highlighted how the sexualisation of the employment relationship is particularly evident in 'boundary roles' where workers interact with environments external to the organisation. She emphasises how women are often used to control these relationships, to inhibit hostility and ensure social control.

While socialist and liberal feminists have argued that sexual relations are determined by the unequal power between men and women, radical and poststructuralist feminists argue that they do not reflect but also determine unequal power relations. Boys and young men are socialised to see heterosexuality as an integral aspect of being masculine, of being a 'real man' with all its associated privileges, status and rewards. They are often socialised to believe that men have sexual access to women as of right, and to see women's bodies primarily in sexual terms. Thus women's bodies in a whole range of occupational settings are objectified (in advertising and in pornography, for instance, as well as in prostitution). Conversely, girls and young women are often socialised to see women as providing service and pleasure for men in the private and public spheres; they are socialised into service roles and largely into servicing men. However, gender relations in the labour market – in patterns of participation and segmentation, for instance, as well as in men's and women's experiences of work – have been explained largely with reference to a combination of supply and demand factors, as well as in terms of gendered and sexual ideologies. Both the search for profit in the capitalist mode of production, and the power of men and masculinity have been seen as central.

Explaining the gendered labour market

Like many other areas of sociology, feminists have developed a critique of malestream theories of work and its organisation. As Peta Tancred (1995) notes, feminist research on domestic labour, homeworking, the link between production and reproduction, sexuality in organisations, the gendered nature of skill, and gendered service work has problematised malestream definitions of work and skill, as well as theories about the organisation of work. As she puts it, 'in subjecting the sociology of work . . . to feminist binoculars, the essential point is that the basic categories of analysis were not thought through in gendered terms' (p. 12). What this means is that the ability of sociology to deal 'not only with women's work, but also with the changing contours of men's work' remains problematic (p. 11).

Most malestream theories of work and organisation derive from Marxist or Weberian ideas and focus either on the nature of capitalism and the labour process, or on bureaucratic modes of organisation, power relations and the labour market. More recently, postmodern and poststructuralist ideas, particularly associated with the influence of Foucault, Lyotard and Derrida (see Hancock and Tyler, 2001), as well as post-colonial theories, have begun to shape organisation theory. It is only relatively recently, as we noted in Chapter 1, that feminist writing has begun to have a significant impact on sociological theories of work and organisation.

However, within organisation studies the focus on work tends to be limited to waged work, and mainly to the realm of formal organisations, thereby neglecting much of the work that women do, both in the 'informal' economy and in the performance of domestic labour and caring work. Similarly, the assumed separation of the productive and reproductive spheres has been accorded limited critical attention. As Tancred puts it, 'an investigation of the changing relations between the two spheres would be far more illuminating' (p. 13). Yet, the sociology of work and organisation continues to focus its critical attention largely on waged labour and the formal realm of the work organisation. Equally, and despite giving critical attention to the deskilling debate, triggered largely by Braverman's (1974) highly influential consideration of what he called the 'degradation of work' in *Labour and Monopoly Capital*, the sociology of work has tended to neglect the ways in which the definition of skill is gendered. Feminist and pro-feminist contributions have emphasised the socially constructed nature of skill and argued that whether or not work is defined as skilled depends more on the gender of the worker than on the nature of the work itself (Phillips and Taylor, 1980). Feminist research, particularly on women's caring and service work, has highlighted the 'tacit' or 'invisible' skills involved in occupations in which women are over-represented, and has also argued that the attribution of these skills to gender or to women's 'nature' has provided ideological justification for the persistence of patterns of occupational segmentation, for women's concentration in part-time, low-status work, and for the gender pay gap.

In order to explain men's and women's position in the labour market and many of the issues neglected by malestream theories of work, many feminists have argued that we need to understand the ways in which patriarchy and capitalism articulate together to subordinate and exploit women. Put simply, feminists such as Sylvia Walby (1990) in her book *Theorizing Patriarchy* have argued that patriarchy is concerned with the subordination of women to serve the needs of men, including their sexual needs, and capitalism with securing a flexible, cheap labour force in which women's supposedly 'innate' skills can be commodified and exploited in the pursuit of profit. While it may be in the interests of patriarchy for women to stay at home, it is in the interests of capitalism for women to engage in (low) paid work. One of the ways in which these interests reach a mutual accommodation is in the concentration of women in part-time work, for instance.

According to Walby (1990), there has been a move in many Western societies away from the 'private patriarchy' of the nineteenth and early twentieth centuries (involving the non-admission of women to the public sphere), to a system of 'public patriarchy' whereby women are not excluded from the public sphere but are disadvantaged, marginalised and exploited within it. In terms of employment, this has meant a move away from strategies designed to exclude women from paid work (through 'protective' legislation, for example) to segregationist and subordinating strategies (manifest in occupational segmentation and in women's under-representation in trade unions and professional bodies, for instance). This means that many women are exploited and dominated by men in the private sphere (as wives, mothers and daughters), and in the public sphere, as well as meeting the needs of capitalism for a cheap, flexible labour force. The relationship between capitalism and patriarchy is thought to be dynamic so that changes in one aspect of it will cause changes elsewhere, and it is thought to vary in its impact on different groups and in different societies.

Feminists have argued then, that patriarchy and capitalism have competing interests but reach mutual accommodations; thus men (as fathers, partners and husbands) benefit from the additional income generated by women who work – especially as research suggests that many women continue to retain the major responsibility for childcare and domestic labour (especially given their relatively lower wages than men). Employers are able to sell goods and services by exploiting the caring 'nature' attributed to women, their ascribed interpersonal skills, and their sexuality.

Other explanations for the gendered nature of work and its organisation have drawn on poststructuralism, and have emphasised particularly the role of power relations and discourse. A notable example of this approach is Silvia Gherardi's (1996) account of women in organisations as 'travellers in a male world'. This 'travel' discourse, she argues, presumes the existence of a territory marked out as male which is trespassed upon by women who are formally members of the same organisation or occupation, but who must 'stake out' their positions in the field. This process – that she terms gender positioning – involves transitional work. Gender relations in work organisations and in the labour market, she argues, can therefore be viewed as 'cultural performances learned and enacted on appropriate occasions both by men and women' (p. 187).

The changing nature of work

In their account of key transformations in the nature of work and its organisation, Macionis and Plummer (2002) describe five notable changes to the economies of Western societies brought about by the industrial revolution beginning in the mid-eighteenth century. These are: new forms of energy, the centralisation of work in factories, the expansion of manufacturing and mass production, the establishment of a division of labour and of specialisation, and the establishment of wage labour. By the mid-twentieth century, the nature of production had changed considerably, however, and many Western societies were being transformed once again by what many writers have described as an 'information revolution' and the development of 'post-industrial society'. As Macionis and Plummer (2002, p. 349) note, 'automated machinery reduced the role of human labour in production, while bureaucracy simultaneously expanded the ranks of clerical workers and managers'. Service industries such as public relations, health care, travel and tourism, education, the mass media, advertising, banking and sales, began to dominate the economies both in financial and in employment terms. Commentators such as Daniel Bell (see Bell, 1999) began to argue in the 1970s that a post-industrial era could be distinguished by a shift from industrial labour to service jobs. Alongside this process of structural reconfiguration has been the expansion of media and communications technologies – most obviously, the computer – and the emergence of what sociologist Manuel Castells (1989, 1996) has termed 'the network society'. Much of this has changed the nature and experience of work just as the emergence of factory-based production did over two centuries ago. Macionis and Plummer (2002) outline three key changes unleashed by the information revolution and the alleged shift towards a post-industrial society. These are:

1 *A shift from tangible products to ideas* – whereas the industrial era was defined by the production of goods, in post-industrial society economies are shaped by the exchange of ideas and services, so that work increasingly revolves around the creation and manipulation of symbols or experiences (advertising executives, architects, design consultants, and so on).
2 *A shift from mechanical skills to literacy skills* – whereas the industrial revolution required mechanical and technical skill of its workforce, the post-industrial labour market demands that workers have the ability to speak, write and communicate effectively, and increasingly to be computer literate also.
3 *Decentralisation of work* – just as industrial technology resulted in a process of urbanisation that drew workers and their families into towns and cities, computer and mobile telecommunications technology now means that this trend is in many ways reversing. It is also (as we noted above with reference to managerial work) perpetuating a long hours culture in which there is little 'escape' from work.

Capitalism is clearly a dynamic system, and keeps changing its form. One of the major changes that has come about in recent years has been characterised as a shift in the flexibility of production from Fordism to post-Fordism. Fordism is associated with the car manufacturer Henry Ford who, at the beginning of the twentieth century, developed assembly line production techniques to manufacture cheap cars that could be purchased by the masses. This system of production, and its link to mass consumption of standard products, has come to be described as Fordism. It depends on dedicated machinery and tools; centralised unskilled or semi-skilled labour organised according to highly specialised task divisions, and low-cost production of vast quantities of uniform goods. As Huw Beynon's (1973) study of a Ford factory in Liverpool in the late 1960s documented, the work is tedious yet the conveyor-belt production line creates relentless pressure, and the mode of organisation is particularly inflexible.

Whilst Fordist production techniques continued throughout most of the twentieth century, other modes of organisation began to develop (especially in Japan and Southeast Asia), involving more flexible systems of production; more flexible use of time (use of temporary and self-employed workers, for instance); decentralisation of labour into small units; the 'casualisation of labour' with less stability and job security; 'just-in-time' rapid production and distribution; movement from production to market-led production (and proliferation of consumer choice); a gradual replacement of mass marketing and advertising with 'niche marketing'; and globalisation, with a new international division of labour. This global division of labour means that each region of the world specialises in particular kinds of economic activity. Agriculture occupies more than 70 per cent of the workforce in low-income countries. Industrial production is concentrated in the middle- to high-income nations, and the richest economies, including those in Europe, now largely specialise in service provision, many having 'outsourced' their more polluting, industrial production and manufacturing to poorer countries, at a lower cost. This latter trend had led many writers to argue that the global division of labour signals a form of neo-colonialism.

Contemporary trends in the organisation of work are likely to impact on women in a number of ways, particularly in relation to the gender pay gap (EOC, 2001). First, the trend towards more fragmented organisations may continue to undermine legislation on equal pay, which in most countries is based on comparable work for the same employer. There are an increasing number of situations in which there is no single employer and in these cases (when work is subcontracted, franchises are operated, in joint ventures or partnerships, or when employment agency staff are used), the scope for direct comparison in pay and working conditions is restricted. The further fragmentation of the public sector in the UK and elsewhere, through the contracting out of services, may widen the pay gap further and exacerbate women's already disadvantaged working conditions. Second, the dismantling of traditional career paths within organisations may widen the gap between the lifetime earnings of men and women. It may also mean that the ability and willingness of employees to fund skills and training development for lower level employees is further restricted. A greater emphasis on career mobility across organisations may also penalise women, particularly those with children or other caring responsibilities. Third, as payment systems in many work organisations shift away from collective bargaining coverage towards greater use of individualised performance awards and personal contracts, women may become further disadvantaged. The increased emphasis on individual competencies may lead to greater attention being paid to leadership skills, which (as we noted above) are often culturally associated with masculinity, and may also result in increased pressure to work longer hours (EOC, 2004).

The global division of labour

Such significant changes in the world economy, such as rapid globalisation and technological developments, have shaped the economic realities experienced by men and women in various ways. Many global organisations or TNEs (transnational enterprises) operate according to a global division of labour that involves 'outsourcing' some of their functions (such as garment manufacturing, or more recently call-centre operations) to relatively poor regions of the world in which wages are low and working conditions are relatively unregulated.

Women comprise an increasing share of the labour force in almost all regions of the world, and in many countries this has translated, as many early feminists anticipated, into a more equitable relationship between men and women in terms of the distribution of social, political and economic resources. However, even in these societies (as elsewhere) women generally still suffer worse economic conditions than men, although this is to a varying degree within and between different countries and regions. In most countries, men and women are concentrated in different sectors of the labour market, often due to the impact of their (actual or assumed) domestic responsibilities, and as a result of gender ideologies about what work is most appropriate for women – usually in the lowest status, lowest paid sectors of the labour market. In most countries of the world, men are more likely to be employers or self-employed than women; men dominate in crafts and trade, whereas women are concentrated in service and caring occupations (www.unece.org). Women are more often unpaid family workers, in temporary or part-time jobs, or in the informal sector without job security. Men generally have more status and are more often employed at senior, managerial or professional levels than women. This impacts on the economic and social security of individual women and their families, usually to the detriment of women. Women are often the first to be affected when job opportunities are lacking, and often find it more difficult to find work than men do when they are unemployed.

As we noted in Chapter 3, economic development in some of the poorest regions of the world can both alleviate and exacerbate women's disadvantage relative to men and in some areas, such as sub-Saharan and West Africa, in which there has been considerable internal migration in recent decades, many women and their children have been left without any means of sustaining a living and hence their vulnerability to poverty has increased considerably. In other parts of the world, in Southeast Asia for example, economic development has occurred alongside the expansion of the sex industry, in which large numbers of women (and children) are exploited (see Chapter 8).

Conclusions

With the process of industrialisation, clear boundaries between work and home were established and women became concentrated largely in the latter on the assumption that caring for the domestic sphere was women's 'natural' role. As well as the bifurcation of spheres, industrialisation also resulted in the establishment of patterns of labour market segmentation. Although many of the early liberal and socialist feminists fought for the right for women to engage in paid work, on the assumption that it would lead to liberation, and many latter-day Marxists – including those in the former Soviet Union – have done the same, we can see that work is not necessarily a source of liberation for women. The work that women do in the labour market often reinforces their traditional roles within the family and, many feminists have argued, is often determined by those roles. Hence, women tend to be over-represented in a narrow range of occupations, and within those in the lowest levels of the occupational hierarchies; women are also over-represented in part-time work and in service sector work. These patterns are reflected in the gendering of professional and managerial work, and in the control and commodification of women's sexuality in the workplace. Indeed, many of the recent changes that have taken place in the labour markets of Western societies have served to compound women's relatively disadvantaged position in paid work, by further commodifying the skills attributed to women. Feminists have explained women's marginalisation and exploitation in paid work largely with reference to the dynamic relationship between patriarchy and capitalism, and some feminists such as Walby (1990) have argued that a move from 'private' to 'public patriarchy' has taken place during the last century or so, so that rather than being excluded from paid work, many women are exploited within it.

SUMMARY

1 Feminists have developed a critique of malestream sociological definitions of 'work' and 'leisure' arguing that this distinction does not reflect many women's experiences of work, primarily because it ignores the role of domestic labour.

2 Whereas before the industrial revolution there was no clear separation of work and home, industrialisation bifurcated these spheres and established patterns of labour market segmentation. Domestic ideology and protective legislation, as well as the idea of the 'family wage', gradually excluded most women from paid work.

3 Even though women are increasingly engaging in paid work, they tend to remain responsible for domestic labour (including childcare) and are concentrated in a narrow range of relatively low-paid, low-status jobs and in part-time work.

4 Feminists have undertaken a range of workplace studies, involving research on factory work, care work, clerical work, work in the service

sector, professional and managerial work, and have argued that occupations in each of these sectors are gendered in a range of ways. Feminists have also emphasised that women's sexuality is controlled and commodified in paid work.

5 Feminists have argued that 'skill' is used to justify women's relatively low pay and that certain occupations are essentialised, some are feminised and others are sexualised.

6 Recent changes in the labour markets of Western societies, such as the expansion of the service sector, have reinforced women's roles.

FURTHER READING

Alvesson, M. and Due Billing, Y. (1997) *Understanding Gender and Organizations.* London: Sage. This pro-feminist text explores a range of theoretical and empirical themes relating to gender and work and avoids equating gender solely with women. It focuses on gendered processes in work organisations, and also warns against the dangers of gender 'over-sensitivity' (i.e. privileging gender as an analytical category over all issues within work and organisations). The writing style is quite 'dense' however, and it would perhaps be useful to start with a more introductory overview.

Blackwell (2003) *The Blackwell Reader in Gender, Work and Organization.* Oxford: Blackwell. As the title suggests, this is a collection of articles which explore some of the central themes which have emerged from the sociological analysis of gender and work in recent years. It is thematically comprehensive, and incorporates papers from a range of feminist (and pro-feminist) perspectives.

CHAPTER TEN

Crime, violence and criminal justice

We are all concerned to explain or make sense of criminal behaviour – to make sense of actions that appear to us as unnatural or strange. Of course, some behaviours may seem more problematic than others: for example, we may find it relatively easy to understand why a lone-parent mother on supplementary benefit stole food from the local supermarket, but much more difficult to understand why our next-door neighbour beat his wife. When we try to explain criminal behaviour, we tend nonetheless to use a few single-factor motivational or trait categories – sickness, jealousy, hate, greed, over-permissiveness and lack of social (especially parental) control. We tend to assume that the behaviour can be explained by characteristics of the individual or her life experiences. Sociologists and other criminologists tend to argue that lay explanations or common-sense theories are simplistic and inadequate. Despite this, there are close parallels between common-sense and social science explanations.

Explaining crime – women as criminals

Much crime seems to us inexplicable; we cannot understand how any human being could have committed it. We hear the details of the behaviour with incredulity and see the perpetrator as less than human, as an animal. Theories of crime that see criminal behaviour as innate (genetic/biological) were developed at the end of the nineteenth century by the Italian criminologist Lombroso and other degeneration theorists. Criminal conduct was seen as caused by biological or physiological characteristics of the individual. The biological factors were said to project the individual into a life of crime. Lombroso argued that criminals were atavistic – that is, genetic throwbacks to an earlier form of man (*sic*). While Lombrosian theories of crime are no longer given wide credence, biological theories continue to have some influence. The psychologist Hans Eysenck (1971), for example, argues that extraverts are more likely to commit crime than other types for ultimately biological reasons – differences in neural organisation with behavioural consequences – and Katarina Dalton (1961) has suggested that some female crime can be explained by hormonal changes during the menstrual cycle (for instance, by premenstrual tension).

Another way in which we try to account for what appears to be totally incomprehensible behaviour is by seeing the perpetrator as mentally sick and suggesting that he or she is mad and therefore not responsible for his or her actions. Some criminological theories have suggested that criminal behaviour is caused by serious mental pathology or at least is the result of some emotional disturbance. These types of explanation have been especially prevalent in explaining female criminality, and we discuss them more fully below. Here we shall note only that while it must be acknowledged that some lawbreakers may suffer from mental disturbance, the same can be said of many non-offenders.

A further way in which criminal behaviour is explained is by suggesting that it is a result of the social conditions in which the offender lives or of life experiences of individuals. Two sets of explanations are frequently encountered: those that 'blame' the socialisation of the individual and the family, and those that see the immediate 'bad' social environment as the cause. Thus wife-beating is frequently explained by reference to the socialisation of the offender in a home in which he either saw his mother beaten or was beaten himself. Child abuse is sometimes similarly explained, or sometimes explained by reference to the current living conditions of the family – for example, living in poverty in one room.

In the 1960s some sociologists began to challenge the idea that it was possible to establish the causes of social behaviour in the same way that it was possible to establish causes in the natural sciences, as the theories described above have done. The positivistic mode of analysis had argued that it was possible to discover the causes of criminal behaviour in the same way that it is possible to establish laws in physics, and that it was possible to be value-free and objective about the social world (see Chapter 13). The 'new' criminologists, as they became known, argued that in the guise of value-freedom sociologists had studied things from the perspective of those with power in society and had ignored the perspectives of the powerless. Furthermore, they pointed out that by paying attention to violations of law, criminology had ignored the legal system and devalued the place of human consciousness and the meaning that criminal activities had for those engaged in them.

The new criminologists were concerned to examine the relationship between law and crime, the purpose and function of the legal system and the relatively autonomous role of individual meaning, choice and volition. Labelling theorists suggested that if criminals do differ from non-criminals in social characteristics, this is not the cause of their lawbreaking but because these very characteristics are used by society to label some people as criminal and ignore others. Maureen Cain (1973) and Steven Box (1971), for example, suggest that the police are more likely to suspect and arrest a working-class man than a middle-class one, or a Black young man than a white one (Hall *et al.*, 1978, and see also the *Stephen Lawrence Inquiry* – Macpherson Report, 1999). Furthermore, it was suggested that the only way that criminals differed from non-criminals was that the former had been involved in the criminal justice system. Sociologists, then, became concerned to identify the key mechanisms by which crime is socially constructed through law creation, law enforcement and societal reaction.

Subsequently some sociologists, from what is called a left realist position (see, for example, Matthews and Young, 1986), have argued that the new criminology was idealistic and romanticised the criminal. They point out that the people who suffer most from criminal acts are working-class people. We can also add that the new criminology, like most of the old, neglected women and crime. Women are relatively powerless, yet these sociologists rarely considered them. Furthermore, women frequently are the victims of abuse from men, both in the domestic sphere and in public. While the new deviancy theorists were challenging the view that it is possible to establish the causes of men's lawbreaking, their failure to include women in their analysis meant that biological and pathological explanations continued to be accepted as explaining female lawbreaking.

Men, women and crime

One of the reasons that 'women and crime' has been a neglected area in sociology is that women appear to be remarkably non-criminal. With the possible exceptions of shoplifters and prostitutes, women convicted of crime are seen as exceptions and extreme deviants both from the law and from femininity – that is, acceptable female behaviour. This is probably, at least in part, because so few women compared with men are convicted of crimes, but it also relates to what is seen as acceptable behaviour for women as compared with men. Much male deviance is associated with what it means to be 'a man' – theft using force, fighting in gangs, football violence, and so on.

The British Crime Statistics (published annually for the Home Office) provide information on convictions for criminal offences. These are broken down by age, sex and type of offence but not by social class or ethnicity. We can ask three questions of the statistics which will enable us to begin to determine whether women are less criminal than men and how female criminality differs from male:

1 Are there differences in the amount of crime committed by men and women?
2 Are there differences in the kinds of crime committed by men and women? and
3 Are there any recent changes in the amount or kind of crime committed by men and women?

The crime statistics for England and Wales for 2002 (Home Office, 2003) suggest that women are considerably less criminal than men. This appears to be as true for the more serious (indictable) offences as for the less serious (summary) ones. (Indictable offences are those for which an offender has the right to have, or must have, a trial before a jury in a Crown Court; summary offences are triable only in a Magistrate's Court.) Table 10.1 shows that in 2002, 85 per cent of those convicted of indictable offences were men, and only 15 per cent were women; the proportion of women would be a little higher (18.5 per cent) if we included cautions as well as convictions, as women are more likely than men to be cautioned rather than prosecuted, but men would still form the vast majority. The available evidence suggests that the gender difference in criminal behaviour is universal – that women are both less likely to be convicted of crime and likely in general to be convicted of less serious crime than men, across jurisdictions (Walklate, 2004). (Walklate also points out that men are more likely to be repeat offenders than women.) The pattern appears to hold true for all age groups in England and Wales in 2002. Women and girls are more likely than boys and men to receive only a caution if apprehended by the police, and the difference increases with age.

Table 10.1 Persons sentenced or cautioned for indictable offences by sex and age, in England and Wales, 2002

Age	Offences no. (000)			Cautioned %		Sentenced (%)	
	Males	Females	Total	Males	Females	Males	Females
10 and under 14	25.5	9.9	35.4	65	85	85	15
14 and under 17	56.9	13.4	70.3	49	62	85	15
17 and under 21	65.1	11.7	76.8	29	41	87	13
21+ years	242.5	53.4	295.9	19	32	84	16
Total	390.0	88.4	478.4			85	15

Source: Home Office, 2003.

Women are convicted of all categories of crime, but men commit a far higher number of crimes in all categories (Table 10.2). There are only two categories of crime, 'Theft and handling stolen goods' and 'Fraud and forgery', where less than 85 per cent of those convicted were men. Theft and handling stolen goods is the offence for which both men and women had the highest conviction rates. However, the category accounted for 53 per cent of all females convicted and only 35 per cent of all men convicted; 79 per cent of the people convicted in this category were men and 21 per cent women. Furthermore, other evidence shows that women are mainly convicted of shoplifting in this category, but that even here men predominate; far more men are convicted of shoplifting than women.

The statistics on sentencing also suggest that there are differences in the types of crime committed by men and women. Women/girls are more likely to be given a

Table 10.2 Offenders found guilty of indictable offences at all courts by type of offence, in England and Wales, 2002 (% by sex)

Offence	Males		Females	
	No. (000)	%	No. (000)	%
Violence against the person	33.9	89.9	3.8	10.1
Sexual offences	4.3	97.7	0.1	2.3
Burglary	25.4	95.1	1.3	4.9
Robbery	6.9	89.6	0.8	10.4
Theft and handling stolen goods	100.7	79.1	26.6	20.9
Fraud and forgery	12.9	70.9	5.3	29.1
Criminal damage	9.8	89.1	1.2	10.9
Drug offences	44.3	90.4	4.7	9.6
Other (excluding motoring)	42.1	87.7	5.9	12.3
Motoring offences	7.8	95.1	0.4	4.9
Total	288.1	85.2	50.1	12.8

Source: Home Office, 2003.

caution by the police than men/boys – 44 per cent of all persons sentenced or cautioned in 2002, compared with 28 per cent for men – or if brought to court for an indictable offence then given an absolute or conditional discharge – 23 per cent of women compared with 13 per cent of men (though the figures even out if we include all offences) – and substantially less likely to be given immediate custody (Table 10.3). Men are also likely to receive longer prison sentences than women (Table 10.4). Proportions committed and average sentence length increased over the ten years since 1992, with a tendency towards greater increase for women than men, although the figures for women remain lower than the men's.

The final question concerns changes in women's behaviour – Has the number of women convicted of criminal offences changed in recent years, and how does this compare with men? Numbers convicted fluctuate from year to year, and trends are therefore difficult to determine. However, between 1977 and 1986 the number of women found guilty of crime in England and Wales increased steadily from 207 thousands in 1977 to 277 thousands in 1986 but has since declined to about 251 thousands in 1993 and has remained reasonably stable since then (Walklate, 2004);

Table 10.3 Selected sentences awarded by sex, 2002 (%)

Sentence	Indictable offences		All offences	
	Males (%)	Females (%)	Males (%)	Females (%)
Absolute or conditional discharge	13.2	22.9	9.6	9.6
Fine	24.2	17.9	67.3	74.2
Community sentence	31.8	39.2	13.6	11.0
Suspended custody	0.5	1.0	0.2	0.2
Immediate custody	27.0	15.7	8.9	3.4
Total (000)	286.9	49.8	1161.0	258.6

Source: Home Office, 2003.

Table 10.4 Proportion sentenced to immediate custody and average term awarded, by sex and court, 2002

	Males		Females	
Proportion awarded immediate custody				
Type of court				
Magistrates	18	(5)	12	(2)
Crown Court	66	(47)	44	(24)
Average sentence awarded (months)				
Type of court				
Magistrates	2.5	(2.7)	2.3	(2.2)
Crown Court	27.8	(21.1)	24.7	(17.7)

Source: Home Office, 2003.

Note: bracketed figures are for 1992.

Table 10.5 Offenders found guilty at all courts by sex and type of offence, in England and Wales, 1977–2001

	1977	1981	1985	1989	1993	1997	2001
Males (figures are numbers of offences, in **tens** of thousands)							
Violence	3.9	4.7	4.4	5.1	3.6	3.1	3.2
Sexual offences	0.7	0.7	0.6	0.7	0.4	0.4	0.4
Burglary	6.8	7.4	6.4	4.2	3.9	2.8	2.4
Robbery	0.3	0.4	0.4	0.4	0.5	0.5	0.6
Theft and handling	18.0	18.4	17.4	10.8	10.0	10.5	10.1
Fraud and forgery	1.6	2.0	2.0	1.8	1.4	1.5	1.3
Criminal damage	0.8	1.1	1.1	0.9	0.9	1.0	1.0
Drugs	*	1.3	1.7	2.0	2.0	4.4	4.1
Other (excl. motoring)	1.4	1.2	1.7	2.6	3.6	4.2	3.9
Motoring	2.3	2.7	2.8	1.1	1.0	0.8	0.7
Total indictable	35.8	39.9	38.5	30.0	27.0	29.3	27.7
Total summary	138.6	146.6	127.8	101.6	90.4	89.6	87.4
All offences	174.4	186.4	166.2	131.0	117.4	118.8	116.2
Females (figures are numbers of offences, in *thousands*)							
Violence	3.5	4.0	3.6	4.4	3.4	3.6	3.4
Sexual offences	<0.1	0.1	0.1	0.1	0.1	0.1	0.0
Burglary	2.4	2.6	2.2	1.3	1.0	1.1	1.1
Robbery	0.2	0.2	0.2	0.2	0.3	0.4	0.6
Theft and handling	54.0	48.2	42.2	26.6	22.1	26.1	25.8
Fraud and forgery	4.5	5.5	5.4	4.7	3.9	5.6	5.2
Criminal damage	0.6	0.8	0.8	0.7	0.8	1.0	1.0
Drugs	*	1.9	2.3	2.4	2.0	5.2	4.5
Other (excl. motoring)	1.7	1.3	1.1	2.1	3.6	5.5	5.3
Motoring	0.8	0.9	0.9	0.4	0.5	0.5	0.4
Total indictable	67.7	65.5	59.0	43.0	37.8	49.0	47.4
Total summary	139.7	175.6	189.3	179.2	213.3	171.0	208.7
All offences	207.4	241.0	248.4	222.2	251.1	220.0	258.8

Source: Home Office, 1987, 1994, 2003.

Note: * figures not available.

put another way, the ratio of male to female offenders fell between 1955 and 1975 from 7.1:1 to 5.2:1 but has remained stable since (Tarling, 1993). See also Table 10.5 for trends and fluctuations since 1977.

A major problem with the official statistics on convictions is that they tell us only the numbers arrested and convicted for crimes. There is a large amount of unsolved crime, and we know nothing about those who perpetrate it. Much of the crime recorded by the police is never 'cleared up' – that is, no one is ever convicted of it. Furthermore, self-report and victim surveys suggest that there is a large amount of crime that is never reported to the police. The problem is that we do not know the size or distribution of this hidden crime. Known crime is like the tip of an iceberg, that which is visible; research suggests that some crimes, visible ones, are more likely to be reported to and recorded by the police than hidden crimes, those that take place in private. A mugging is much more likely to be reported than an assault on a wife, for example. The police and public are more likely to suspect some people of crimes than others – working-class men and ethnic minority men are more likely to be suspected and arrested than middle-class white men (Box, 1971; Chapman, 1968). The crime statistics do not, then, represent the 'real' amount of crime, nor are those convicted of crime necessarily representative of all lawbreakers.

We can ask, then, if the differences between the conviction rates of men and women represent a 'real' difference in the lawbreaking of men and women, or just reflect the fact that women are better at hiding their crimes and less likely to be suspected of crimes – that is, that they do not fit the stereotype of the criminal. Pollack (1950) argued that women were not less criminal than men. He argued that women were naturally good at concealing their actions and naturally secretive because they had to hide the fact of menstruation. Women commit large amounts of crime that remain hidden, he argued, especially child abuse and murder of spouses. However, even if this were the case it seems unlikely that the amount would be sufficient to increase women's incidence of lawbreaking to that of men, especially as there is also hidden male crime, for example male middle-class crime, wife and child abuse, and other domestic crimes. Self-report studies suggest that women are indeed less criminal than men (Naffine, 1987). Mawby (1980) found that both young men and young women in Sheffield admitted to more crime than would seem to be indicated by the official statistics, but that the ratio of male to female crime seemed about right. Feminists conclude that on balance the available evidence does indicate that women commit less, and less serious, crime than men. Also, while there was a period when it was true that more women became involved in crime, this seems to have been mainly petty crime, and male crime also increased during the same period (Box and Hale, 1983). Thus there is no evidence to support the claim that as women become more liberated they increasingly develop the same patterns of criminality as men.

The need for feminist theory

Feminists have suggested that to understand the issues surrounding women and crime two key questions need to be considered:

1 Why do so few women commit crimes? and
2 Why do those women who do commit crimes do so?

They suggest that malestream theories have either failed to tackle these questions or provided inadequate answers.

Thus psycho-positivistic (biological/psychological) theories of female criminality have stereotyped women and do not provide an adequate explanation. However, they continue to hold a dominant place in the explanation of female crime long after they have been seriously challenged as adequate explanations for male criminality. Thus Hilary Allen (1987) argued that women accused of serious violent crimes are much more likely than men charged with comparable crimes to be portrayed in court reports as suffering from psychological problems that suggest they are not responsible for their actions. Furthermore, women are more likely to be found insane or of diminished responsibility and, if convicted, are more likely to be given psychiatric treatment in place of a penal sentence than are men. Another example is premenstrual tension (PMT): women have successfully defended themselves against criminal charges by (being advised to state) a plea of diminished responsibility on the grounds that they were suffering from PMT at the time they committed the crime. The success of these pleas, feminists argue, depends not only on the evidence of expert witnesses, but also on the courts' preparedness to believe this evidence because it fits their stereotype of female criminals. This stereotype has itself been informed, at least in part, by psycho-positivistic theories of crime, theories which argue that female lawbreakers are either biologically different from those who do not break the law or that they are out of their minds – mentally ill – and therefore not responsible for their actions.

Traditional (malestream) sociological theories, on the other hand, have with few exceptions ignored women. They have not seen gender as an important explanatory variable and have assumed that theories based on male samples and a male view of the world can be generalised to women. In some cases they have implicitly or explicitly accepted biological theories, as for example Durkheim (1897) did in his study of suicide, when he agreed that women were less likely to commit suicide than men because they were biologically at a lower stage of development than men and therefore less influenced by the social forces that resulted in people committing suicide. Even major critics of conventional criminology failed to raise the issue of women and crime (e.g. Taylor *et al.*, 1975).

Feminist theories of crime

Feminists have argued that a paradigm shift is essential so that gender can be seen as an important explanatory variable in understanding why some women are lawbreakers; women have their experiences mediated by gender, race, class relationships, and so on. They are also agreed that patriarchal relationships, ideologies of femininity and women's assigned role in the family all play key roles. While the individual must be seen as free to shape her own actions, destiny and consciousness, this happens in an economic, ideological and political environment which she does not control. Furthermore, it is recognised that empirical studies of women who have engaged in lawbreaking are essential so that it is possible to determine under what circumstances women do break the law. An analysis which makes connections between women's lawbreaking and how women are handled in the criminal justice system is also essential. Finally, while the multiple control of women in the class, race and gender system may explain why most women do not break the law, theories need to be developed that explain why some women do break it.

The ideology of femininity constructs girls and women in a particular way. The natural role for women is seen as that of a wife and mother. Girls and women are seen as needing protection and care. Consequently, young girls tend to be controlled more than their brothers and given less freedom. Of special concern is the protection of girls' virginity (particularly in societies outside of the West – see Therborn, 2004; United Nations, 2003). While boys are expected to 'sow their wild oats', girls are expected to remain virgins until they marry – or at least to have a 'steady' relationship. While young men who come before the courts and are handled in the juvenile justice system have generally committed criminal offences, girls are more likely to come before the courts for being in need of care and protection, including from their own promiscuity – what are referred to as 'status offences', coming within the ambit of the law only because of the age of the 'offender'. This seems to remain true even when the girls have in fact committed criminal offences.

This alerts us to the important fact that the boundary between normality and abnormality is elastic – that is, what is seen as normal for men may be seen as abnormal for women, not to mention class and ethnic variations as well. Crime and deviance are not immutable but historically and culturally variable. Whether or not behaviour is seen as criminal/deviant depends both on the context and on the individual doing the behaviour. The stereotype of the criminal as working class and male, and of female criminals as being psychologically inadequate, influences not only sociological theories, but also the people involved in the administration of the criminal justice system on the one hand and our common-sense view of the nature of women on the other.

However, studies of women who have been convicted of criminal offences and who have been imprisoned (e.g. Dobash *et al.*, 1986; Carlen, 1983; Carlen *et al.*, 1985; Mandaraka-Sheppard, 1986) have confirmed the main feminist criticisms of traditional criminology. Four major characteristics of female offenders have been highlighted:

1 that women who engage in property crime are motivated by economic factors – that is, they steal because they need or want the goods they steal;
2 that women commit all types of offences;
3 that women do fear and feel the impact of the stigma of the 'criminal' label; and
4 that women are seen as *doubly deviant* – deviant for breaking social rules, and also 'unfeminine' and 'unnatural' because they have offended against rules of feminine behaviour.

Feminists argue that what is necessary is to develop theories that are adequate for explaining and understanding the lawbreaking of both men and women. This does not mean that feminists are looking for a universal theory that will explain all criminal behaviour in all circumstances. There is no reason to assume that all criminal behaviour can be explained in the same way. What is necessary is theories of crime that take account of gender, ethnic and class divisions and studies that are situated in the wider moral, political, economic and sexual spheres which influence women's and men's status and position in society. As Carol Smart (1976) argues, it is necessary to carry out research on women, in order to make women visible and to find alternative ways of conceptualising the social world so that the interests and concerns of women are adduced and included rather than subsumed or ignored.

However, some feminists have argued that existing theories of crime can be developed to the point where they can account adequately for women. There is no reason, they suggest, why explanations for female crime should be different from those for male crime. Morris (1987), for example, argues that disorganisation theory and differential association can both be extended to account for female crime. Leonard (1978) has suggested that a reformulated labelling theory with elements of critical theory can be developed, and Shaklady Smith (1978) has used labelling theory to explain female juvenile delinquency.

More recently (see Walklate, 2004) some feminists have indicated a number of difficulties associated with a position that focuses on women and crime, suggesting that biological essentialism (sex) is being replaced by a sociological essentialism (gender). They suggest that it is necessary to problematise masculinity and crime and develop a *gendered* understanding of crime and criminal behaviour, rather than one that focuses either on men or women.

Disorganisation theory

Cloward and Ohlin (1961) argued that crime occurs because not everyone is able to achieve the accepted goal of society (economic success) by the legitimated means (hard work), especially via the gaining of educational qualifications. Cloward and Ohlin suggested that crime happens because, just when working-class adolescents have been encouraged to adopt a set of economic and material aspirations of which the larger society approves, the means of achieving these goals is locked off from them – that is, they do not gain the necessary qualifications to embark on a career that will enable them to achieve economic success by legitimated means. In reaction to this, adolescents most at risk of becoming criminals develop an alternative authority to that of the state – the delinquent gang.

Given that women experience unequal opportunities even more than men, then this would seem to be a possible explanation for female crime. Indeed, given that opportunities are more restricted for women than for men, we might expect women to exhibit a higher rate of crime than men. The fact that they do not can be explained, however, by their limited access to illegitimate opportunities.

There are major problems with this theory, however. It assumes that there is universal agreement on societal goals and accepted means of achieving them, and that crime is committed mainly by working-class men and women. While it is recognised that there may be differential access to the goals, based on gender as well as class, it fails to recognise differential access to the means. More important, however, it fails to take account of the key fact that social goals are different for men and women. Girls are often socialised into a world that sees marriage, childcare and domesticity as the main goal (see Chapters 4–6). Indeed, girls who reject the societal view of appropriate feminine behaviour and who consequently endanger their chances of achieving these goals are seen as deviant (Lees, 1986).

Differential association

Sutherland (see Sutherland and Cressey, 1966) developed differential association as a theory of crime as a result of his criticisms of sociological theories of crime which regarded crime as a male working-class phenomenon. He argued that the official statistics under-represented middle-class criminals because their crimes were often dealt with by the civil rather than the criminal courts – or out of court altogether, by the 'private justice' of employers, clubs and private institutions. Sutherland argued that criminal behaviour was a result not of poverty or inadequate socialisation, but of the people with whom one associates. Behaviours, values and justifications were picked up by association with others. Sutherland argued that people who committed crime have more contact with those who condoned criminal behaviour than with those who opposed it. He also suggested that this approach applied equally to women and men. However, his theory fails to explain why more men than women become criminals; it does not explain why brothers and not sisters commit crimes, why the wives of criminal men do not become criminals, and so on.

Critical (Marxist) criminology

Critical criminology has sought to understand the basis of social inequality and power relationships within capitalist societies. It has explored the class dimension of crime and has illustrated the ways in which the criminal law is selectively enforced against the powerless. However, women are not easily accommodated within these accounts, as women are relatively powerless in capitalist societies and also rarely commit crime. Thus despite the relatively subordinate social and economic position of women and their exploitation and domination by men, women appear in the crime statistics much less frequently than men.

Leonard (1978) and Gregory (1986) argued that Marxist theory needs to be reformulated so that the considerable impact of gender as well as class position on crime is taken into account. What is needed, they suggest, is a 'dual-systems' theory (see Chapter 2) that can understand women and crime adequately. A theory is needed that enables us to understand why women are relatively uninvolved in crime and what structural factors influence the particular pattern of the crimes in which women do participate. It is necessary to understand the way that legitimate and illegitimate means to socially valued goals are different for women than for men and how women's associates affect them as compared with men's. It is necessary to take into account the ways in which the distribution of wealth and power affect women in capitalist societies and how this influences their criminality. It is necessary to consider why women who are relatively powerless are nonetheless infrequently labelled criminal. Finally, it is necessary to consider what role women play in a class society, the difference in the oppression of working-class women and working-class men, and the way in which women are controlled and handled in the legal system and in society generally.

Using a dual-systems perspective, Dee Cook (1987) has studied women who committed fraud against the supplementary benefit system. She argued that the majority of women claiming supplementary benefit are single-parent mothers. They are seen as deviant because they are not living in families that conform to ideas of a normal family in capitalist societies (see Chapter 6). The major reason for these women fiddling supplementary benefit, she argues, is economic necessity. When they are caught for fiddling they provoke a negative reaction because of their deviant personal status as well as because of their criminal acts. Social security fiddling for women is seen within a framework that takes into account their class situation and patriarchal ideology.

Labelling theory

Leonard (1978) argued that labelling theory is potentially valuable for understanding female crime. Using labelling theory it is possible to look at the inherent bias in the law, its relativity, and the different ways in which it is enforced. Within such a framework it would also be possible to examine social reaction to female criminals and how this influenced their self-definitions.

Labelling theory developed in the 1960s as one response to positivistic criminology. It was argued that crime was caused by a number of factors, that it was impossible to obtain a representative sample of people who commit crimes from which to generalise, and that deviancy theorists should concentrate on studying societal reaction to crimes and criminals and how labelling as an outsider resulted in changes in self-identity. Labelling theorists also argued that crime and deviance were relative and not universal categories. Finally, they rejected the view that value-free research was possible in the social sciences and argued that it was important to look at things from the perspective of the underdog.

Labelling theorists have been criticised for ignoring female deviance and crime. Milkman (1976) suggested that while labelling theorists presented sympathetic accounts of male deviants, they failed to do so for female ones. She points out that labelling theorists have portrayed prostitutes, for example, in a stereotypical way and through the eyes of 'punters and pimps' rather than through their own self-perceptions.

However, labelling theory has been used by feminists carrying out research on young people. Sue Lees, in her study of teenage girls (1986), argued that the ways in which young men and young women label young women act as a powerful mechanism of social control (see Chapters 4 and 5). Shaklady Smith (1978), in a small ethnographic study of teenage girls, argues that labelling theory can be used to understand the pattern of female delinquent activities. Using open-ended interviews she studied three groups of young women in the Bristol area in 1970 – 30 girls on probation orders, 15 girl members of gangs and 30 girls who had never been referred to any agency dealing with juvenile delinquency, as similar as possible to the first group. She found that girls committed all the kinds of offences with which young men, but not girls, are usually associated; for example, 67 per cent of the probation group and 73 per cent of the gang sample had deliberately damaged property (see Table 10.6). An analysis of the responses of the gang and probation samples demonstrated that many of them had committed most of the offences for which male juveniles are usually taken to the courts. However, an analysis of court records suggests that girls are much more likely to be brought before the court as in need of care and protection than as charged with offences, but if charged are more likely to be given a custodial sentence.

Her data also suggest that girls tend either to be conformist or very delinquent. Girl delinquents were labelled, she argues, by parents, teachers and non-delinquent girls alike as unfeminine and to be disapproved of. However, the labelling of them by others as unfeminine did not result in further status loss, nor did they become promiscuous. Rather, they responded with aggressive behaviour and remained popular among their peers. Nonetheless they did suffer a double rejection; they were rejected both on account of their violation of the law and because they rejected femininity. The girls saw themselves as tough, dominant and tomboyish.

Table 10.6 Self-report of delinquent acts and offences committed by girls in research by Shaklady Smith (1978)

Type of offence	Control sample	Probation sample	Gang sample
	Total numbers: 30	30	15
	%	%	%
Skipped school	63.3	90.0	93.3
Shoplifting	36.7	90.0	80.0
Breaking and entering	10.0	33.3	26.7
In car without owner's permission	16.7	60.0	60.0
Deliberate property damage	26.7	66.7	73.3
Running away from home	3.3	76.0	53.3
Sex under age of consent	13.3	70.0	73.3
Taken drugs	3.3	10.0	33.2
Taken part in a fight	23.3	63.3	73.3

Source: Shaklady Smith, 1978.

Once labelled, these girls became isolated from their normal peers; parents of non-delinquent girls forbade their daughters to mix with the girl juvenile delinquents. The girls became more and more dependent on the delinquent group:

> social definitions of female delinquency lead not so much to a total rejection of femininity in that a male role is aspired to, as a rejection of certain elements of the culturally stereotyped female role which is perceived by the girls as too constraining.
>
> (Shaklady Smith, 1978, p. 84)

Labelling propelled them into more extreme forms of delinquency. Shaklady Smith suggests that the protective attitudes of probation officers, social workers and other agencies paradoxically resulted in the same labelling of behaviour as 'common' or 'sluttish'. Long before they reached court girl juvenile delinquents had 'experienced a continued defining process which classified them as unfeminine'.

Carlen *et al.* (1985) have also shown the ways in which labelling influences the patterns of female crime and the ways in which female criminals are labelled un-feminine. However, labelling theory does not explain why people become criminal in the first place, nor does it take full account of power relations between various social groups and in different social contexts.

Social control theory

Heidensohn (1986) has suggested that the question we should be asking is not why some women commit crime, but why women are so non-criminal. In other words, we should be explaining why women do not become criminal. She suggests that the reason is because of the ways in which women are controlled. She argues that women are controlled within the family and within society generally. She suggests that there are two types of theory of social control. Some theories emphasise the ways in which societies are cemented together by a shared value system. These values or ideologies are transmitted via the media, the educational system, the family, courts, police, and so on. A second type of theory emphasises bonding in relationship to the family, the peer group and the school, whereby people are bound into society's norms and values. Thus women are controlled by ideologies of appropriate behaviour for women and by their role in the family.

However, Pat Carlen (in Carlen and Worrall, 1987) has suggested that the problem with control theory is that it does not explain why some women *do* become criminal. She attempts to develop feminist control theory so that it can do this. She suggests that:

1 Women generally conform while they perceive it to be worth while to do so. Such calculation takes into account the costs and benefits of criminal behaviour.
2 Working-class women are controlled within two areas, the workplace and the family – that is, they are doubly controlled. They thus have to make a 'class deal' – to accept a wage for work; and a 'gender deal' – to take on feminine behaviour.
3 Most working-class women make the class deal and the gender deal because the exploitative nature of these two deals is obscured by the ideology of familialism and community working together in women to engender an attraction to the (imaginary) norm of respectable working-class womanhood.
4 A commitment to the norms of respectable working-class womanhood is most likely to happen where girls are brought up in families where there is a male bread-winner and a female carer – although girls can learn appropriate behaviour from the mass media, especially women's magazines and pop songs which report marriage coupled with a wage-earning job as a deal to which young women should aspire. Thus the woman most likely to become criminal is one brought up in care or taken into care in adolescence.
5 The majority of women are not criminalised even when caught breaking the law. While they remain in the family as a daughter or wife they are seen as having made the gender deal. It is unassimilated women, women who have been in care or rejected 'normal' family life, who are likely to be seen as recidivist lawbreakers.
6 Women who see themselves as marginalised and consequently have nothing to lose may turn to lawbreaking and see it as preferable to poverty and social isolation.

Social control theory emphasises the ways in which girls and women are controlled within both the public and the private spheres and how they are therefore likely to be more conformist than men. The stereotype of women and a woman's role plays an important part in explaining the ways in which the control of women is achieved. These assumptions underlie the law governing sexual behaviour, the social benefit system, the interventions of health visitors and the ways in which the criminal justice system handles and disposes of female offenders. The normal woman is seen as a wife and mother who is in need of protection, while the deviant woman is seen as needing to be trained to perform domestic tasks and childcare. However, it is evident that more research needs to be carried out before we can answer the key questions that have been raised concerning women and crime: explanations for the patterning of crime;

explanations for why women's crime differs so much from men's; and assessment of how far and in what ways gender differences in crime are linked to class, age and race.

However, it is clear that explanations which see female crime as a result of a failure of individual women to adapt themselves to their supposedly natural biological role are inadequate and misleading. Women's behaviour, criminal and non-criminal, needs to be explained by reference to a social formation which imposes restrictive and exploitative roles on women. Furthermore, it must be recognised that in certain economic and ideological circumstances crime may be a rational and coherent response to women's awareness of the social constraints imposed on them by their social roles and identities.

Radical feminist perspectives on crime

Radical feminists have paid more attention to analysing crimes of which women are victims rather than looking at female criminality – that is, to manifestations of male power, and especially to domestic violence, rape, pornography and prostitution. However, a radical feminist account would emphasise patriarchal power relationships and women's exploitation and subordinate position in examining female crime, emphasising that the locus of male power is sexuality.

Sue Edwards (1987) carried out research into women and prostitution. She argues that explanations for why women become prostitutes are an extension of explanations of the oppression and exploitation of women in patriarchal society; she suggests that girls and young women enter prostitution because of women's low earning potential, a decline in job opportunities for women and the erosion of welfare benefits. Prostitutes, she argues, are harassed by the police if they walk the streets and are controlled by pimps if they work off-street. While women prostitutes face high risks of prosecution or exploitation, their pimps and clients and others benefiting from prostitution remain relatively free to exploit prostitute women, as they are placed in an increasingly vulnerable position in both the law and the economy.

In sum, most theories of deviance have been developed to account for male crime and deviance. Women appear less often in official statistics of crime, and the evidence suggests that they do in fact commit fewer crimes. The pattern and nature of their crimes are likewise different from men's. Feminists have tried to extend malestream theories of deviance – such as the labelling perspective – to fit female crime. However, they have also highlighted the importance of taking other factors into account – such as the economic position of women, and their role in the family – in understanding women's crimes.

Violence, fear and social control

Research on victims of crime and fear of crime indicates that while those most at risk of being victims are young men, those who have the greatest fear of crime are young women. Women of all ages express more fear of crime than men (Tables 10.7–10.9). Criminologists have argued that while women have an exaggerated fear of crime, young men either ignore or do not recognise their risk. However, feminists have argued that what women fear is sexual crime and that they do so with good reason. Women are at risk of sexual crimes from both strangers and those they know, in public and private space. Women are at risk of sexual harassment, stranger rape, date rape, partner rape, domestic violence, wife murder and mugging. They are aware of the consequences of their behaviour in public and private and they act to minimise the possibility of violent/sexual attack. They police their own behaviour – where they go, what they wear, how they behave and how they interact with men (Walklate, 2004).

Table 10.7 Fear of crime[1]: sex, age and type of crime

	Males				Females			
	16–29	30–59	60+	All	16–29	30–59	60+	All
Theft of car[2]	22	18	10	10	27	21	21	22
Theft from car	19	16	15	16	18	15	15	16
Burglary	17	16	15	16	23	21	22	22
Mugging	12	19	12	11	24	21	25	23
Physical attack	11	8	8	9	33	26	23	27
Rape	12	7	4	7	37	29	24	29

Source: British Crime Survey, 2000.

Notes:
1 Describing self as 'very worried'.
2 Car owners only.

Table 10.8 Feeling unsafe at night (%) by country

	Alone at home		Walking alone	
	Males	Females	Males	Females
England	—	2	5	21
Wales	1	2	3	17
Scotland	—	2	4	16
Northern Ireland	—	2	5	16

Source: British Crime Survey, 2002/3.

Table 10.9 Objective risk of violent crime – selected age ranges

Age range	Males	Females
16–24	15.1	6.9
45–64	2.7	2.0
75+	0.4	0.6

Source: British Crime Survey, 2002/3.

Crimes against women

Women are likely to be victims of all forms of crime, but they are especially vulnerable to violent attacks by men, both sexual and physical and by the men with whom they live as well as men not previously known to them. It is not just that women are the victims of violent men, but that fear of violent crime is a powerful control over women's lives. Research has consistently suggested that violence against women is the most pervasive human rights violation in the world.

Women experience three types of violence from men: gender harassment (sexist and derogatory comments and jokes about women – on the street, at work, and so on); unwanted sexual attention (unsolicited sexual remarks and/or sexual touching, and so on) and sexual compulsion (including all forms of forced sex or other physical attack – rape, murder, forced prostitution, clitoridectomy, and so on).

It is estimated that 130 million women and girls have undergone clitoridectomy – a practice designed to enable a man to know that his new bride is a virgin. In a trade estimated to be worth $76 million annually, between 700,000 and 4 million women are trafficked for commercial sex work (UN, 2003; see also Therborn, 2004). In the Rwandan genocide of 1994, women and girls were raped, often by men who knew they were HIV positive. In India and China sex selection and the killing of baby girls occurs because of preference for boys, and in India women are killed by their husbands because their families are unable to meet continuing demands for dowries (Therborn, 2004). In 48 surveys from around the world between 10 and 69 per cent of women reported being physically assaulted by male partners at some point in their lives (www.who.org).

In the UK, 25 per cent of all violent crime is 'wife assault' (Home Office, 1999). Stanko *et al.* (1997) found in their survey that one in nine women had experienced domestic violence in the previous year, and the British Crime Survey estimates that 25 per cent of women will be assaulted by a male partner at some point during their lives. Of all female murder victims in the UK, 45 per cent are killed by a current (or former) male partner; the figure for men is 8 per cent. Contrary to popular views, women do not invite violence; indeed, they often shape their behaviour to reduce the possibility. Also, women are likely to blame themselves; for example, less than two-thirds of female rape victims are prepared to classify their experience as rape (Myhill and Allen, 2002), preferring to classify it as 'pressured sex' rather than 'coerced sex' (Walklate, 2004). Men continue to believe that it is acceptable for women to be chattels; research in the UK, for example, found that half of young men aged 14–21 thought that in some circumstances it was acceptable to hit a woman or force her to have sex (ESRC, 2002).

Feminists have been interested not only in explaining why men are violent towards women, but in exposing the ways in which women who have been attacked by men are treated in the criminal justice system and by welfare agencies. Frequently, it is argued, women who have been assaulted, whether physically or sexually, end up feeling that they themselves are to blame. Indeed, attacks on women are frequently explained by saying that 'she deserved it' – for example, rape victims are blamed because they went out late at night alone, or wives who have been beaten by their husbands are blamed because they failed in their wifely duties, or daughters who are the victims of incest are said to have tempted their fathers or brothers with their flirtatious behaviour.

Sue Lees (1989) has analysed cases in which men have pleaded provocation as a mitigating circumstance when they are being tried for killing a wife, lover or former lover. (A successful plea of provocation means that the jury returns a verdict of manslaughter rather than murder. Murder carries a mandatory life sentence, but for manslaughter a judge can give any sentence from a conditional – or even in theory an absolute – discharge to life imprisonment.) Lees quotes a number of cases in which male killers who have used the plea of provocation have been given relatively light prison sentences on being found guilty of manslaughter. She argues that the evidence for provocation is often based on the uncorroborated assertion of the accused and his friends, and that verdicts of manslaughter (unpremeditated killing) are often brought in even when there is evidence of premeditation. She points out that if a man kills his wife on finding her in bed with another man he can successfully plead provocation and be found guilty of manslaughter. She suggests that:

> The concept of provocation is based on three very questionable assumptions. Firstly, that a reasonable man can be provoked into murder by insubordinate behaviour – infidelity, bad housekeeping, withdrawal of sexual services and even nagging . . . The law provides for a legitimation for men to behave violently in the face of insubordination or marriage breakdown. . . . If it can be successfully alleged that the victim was unrespectable, negligent in her wifely duties, then provocation is usually accepted. Secondly, the idea that women can be similarly provoked even when they have been beaten up or raped is seldom entertained. This would be a 'licence to kill' rapists or wife batterers. Thirdly, although the main distinction between murder and manslaughter revolves around whether the killing is premeditated or not ('malice aforethought', or intention to kill, is murder, but if someone kills by accident or through negligence, or is provoked, it is manslaughter) a defence of provocation on the basis of 'loss of self-control' in practice . . . often over-rides evidence of premeditation.
>
> (Lees, 1989, pp. 2–3)

Three major forms of explanation of violence towards women have been developed – the first two within malestream theory, and the third (by feminists) as a critique of the malestream theories and an alternative, feminist account:

1 From a *traditional* perspective crimes such as rape and assault on wives are seen as infrequent. While not all women are seen as the cause of the violent behaviour, many are. Thus rape victims are said to have enticed the rapist and 'caused' him to have uncontrollable sexual urges. This can be either because of their behaviour in public places or by 'leading on' the man with whom they have been out, encouraging him to expect that he will be given sex. It is accepted that some victims are innocent, but they are expected to demonstrate this by resisting the attack and showing considerable evidence of physical injury.

   Assaults on wives are also seen as being deserved by the wife for failing in her duties, and men are assumed to have responsibility for controlling their wives.

Indeed, until the nineteenth century in England the debate concerned not *whether* a man could beat his wife but *how much* he could beat her. It was not until the end of the nineteenth century that assaults on wives became illegal. In the traditionalist perspective, as with rape, it is accepted that some men beat their wives without just cause, but this is thought to be a relatively small proportion.

2 *Liberal/psychiatric* perspectives accept that violence towards women is a social problem, but see it again as a relatively minor problem. In this view either the male perpetrator is seen as sick or disturbed or the female victim is seen as seeking out violence. Thus for rape, the rapist is seen as mentally ill or socially inadequate, or female victims are said to be masochistic. Similarly, men who beat their wives are said either to have been brought up in a home where they were battered as children or to beat their wives as a result of being drunk, or the wives are said to want to be beaten. In this perspective men who are violent to women are seen as sick and as needing treatment, or to be the 'victims' of women who invite violence.

3 *Feminist perspectives* locate violence to women by men within the broader context of women's position as subordinate to men. In the 1970s feminists tended to try to explain rape and assaults on wives as serious indications of men's violence towards women. However, more recently feminists have broadened this view and suggest that anything that frightens or intimidates women must be seen in the context of men's control of women's behaviour. Thus women's fear of violence acts to control their behaviour, so that they restrict and limit their activities, and if they do go out at night they place themselves in the protection of a man. Furthermore, the advice to women is always not to go out when another woman has been raped in an area; it is never suggested that men should stay in so that it is safe for women to go out. Feminists have also become more concerned with doing research that explores how women experience male violence and power and how fear of rape and attacks from men restrict their behaviour, rather than in developing explanations for male violence. Feminist research has also demonstrated the limited value of legal reforms aimed at helping women who are the victims of male violence and the failure of the police and the courts to deal adequately with such men.

Until the 1970s the victimisation of women by men remained relatively hidden. (See Chapter 11, however, for the nineteenth-century feminist campaigns around these issues.) With the rise of second wave feminism, the extent of assaults on wives, of rape and of child sexual abuse became more evident. Women have become more prepared to report men who commit violence against them and, more importantly, welfare agencies, the police and the courts have become more prepared to believe women and children. However, feminists argue that the extent of these crimes is still grossly underestimated and that the criminal justice system is still reluctant to accept how widespread violence against women and children is and to deal with the offenders. Feminists argue that rape and assaults on wives are serious crimes and should be treated as such. The perpetrators of these crimes should be charged and punished in the same way as they would be for any other serious violent crime.

Rape

Feminists argue that:

> the fear of rape affects all women. It inhibits their actions and limits their freedom, influencing the way they dress, the hours they keep, the routes they walk. The fear is well founded, because no woman is immune from rape.
>
> (Clarke and Lewis, 1977, p. 23)

In Britain until 1994 rape was defined in law as unlawful sexual intercourse, which in turn meant that the penis had to penetrate the vagina and therefore that only women could be raped. However, the Criminal Justice and Public Order Act 1994 widened the definition to include non-consensual penetration of the anus by the penis, so that a man committed rape if:

1 he had sexual intercourse with a person (whether vaginally or anally) who at the time of intercourse did not consent to it; and
2 at the time he knew that the person did not consent to the intercourse or he was reckless as to whether the person consented to it.

The Sexual Offences Act 2003 further widened the definition of what constitutes rape. This Act states that a person (A) commits an offence if

a) he intentionally penetrates the vagina, anus or mouth of another person (B) with his penis,
b) B does not consent to that penetration, and
c) A does not 'reasonably believe' that B consents.

Whether a belief is 'reasonable' is to be determined having regard to all the circumstances, including any steps A has taken to ascertain whether B consents.

In Britain until 1990 a man could not be charged with raping his wife, as the law assumed that the marriage contract gave him the right to have sexual intercourse with her. (Although the law has not been changed to make it a criminal offence, it has now become established in case law through convictions in the courts.)

Feminists have been concerned to examine three issues: first, to ask why rape occurs and what attitudes and beliefs support it, second to examine the social and legal constraints which prevent women obtaining their legal rights, and third, to understand the experience of rape victims.

Rape is commonly viewed as the outcome of the male sex drive – that men have uncontrollable sexual urges. However, Barbara Toner (1977) suggests that the anthropological evidence shows that the strength of the male sex drive depends on cultural attitudes and values. She points out that amongst the Arapesh of New Guinea rape is virtually unknown, while amongst the Gusii of Kenya it is a major form of social control of women by men.

Feminists argue that rape is an act of violence and domination which devalues and dehumanises the victim. Susan Brownmiller (1976), a radical feminist, argues that men are natural predators and women their natural prey. Men have the ability to rape women, but women cannot easily retaliate in kind. Rape, she argues, is used by men to generate fear in all women, and this is a conscious process of intimidation. Women, she argues, continue to be subordinated by men through the threat of rape. Women will be able to overcome their subordination only when they are fully integrated into the state apparatus for legislating against rape and for enforcing that legislation. The state will then be able to protect women from rape. In this view the cause of rape is male sexuality itself, and the solution sometimes advocated is political lesbianism (for a discussion of feminist debates on political lesbianism and resistance to male sexual violence see Jackson and Scott, 1996).

Many feminists, however, reject biological explanations for rape and argue that rape is sustained and justified by patriarchal ideology and patriarchal relations. Lynne Segal (1987), for example, suggests that the problem is masculinity – that male sexual violence is about social roles and gender, not essential biological characteristics such as innate violence and/or uncontrollable sexual urges. Convicted rapists have been found to exhibit a range of motivations, from wanting to control women to excitement from impersonal sex (Scully and Marolla, 1993), revealing the cultural roots of attitudes towards sex and aggression embedded in masculinity. Feminists argue that patriarchal ideology defines women as either mothers who are respected or sexual objects for men's pleasure. Men want to gain sexual possession of women, and men control women's sexuality for their own purposes. They argue that while patriarchal ideology overtly condemns rape, it covertly legitimates it by viewing it as normal. In courts of law rapists often use the excuse, successfully, that the victim 'asked for it'. Furthermore, feminists argue that the rape law is concerned to protect the interests of men as much as the honour of women. Rape is viewed as a crime against property – daughters and wives; the father's/husband's property is damaged. Rape, they argue, is a political act that takes away a woman's autonomy to decide what to do with her own body. It is an act of aggression which carries with it the threat of death. Rape victims are chosen indiscriminately, in that no woman is immune from rape. Rape teaches all women that they are subordinate to men and it keeps women in a state of fear. It is thus an effective way of controlling women and restricting their freedom.

However, Joni Lovenduski and Vicky Randall (1993) point to the ways in which women in Leeds actually rejected the attempts by police and others to control their behaviour as a result of the 'Yorkshire Ripper' murders. They argue that while 'a lot of women were controlled by the "Ripper" murders: they gave up jobs and evening classes, women students left university and returned to homes in other parts of the country', other women acted differently and 'organised life for each other and lent each other their guard dogs. Instead of a siege mentality, there was the development of a sense of collective strength, a sense of shared experience' (pp. 331–332).

Feminists argue that the victims of rape are frequently 'put on trial' by the court procedures and blamed for the crime themselves. This is especially the case if the woman leads a sexually active life or her behaviour is seen as having 'caused' the rape by, for example, hitching a lift at night. Recent changes in the law so that a woman's sex life could not automatically be examined in court have not protected women from this, as most judges have in practice given permission for the woman to be questioned about her sexual history (Edwards, 1984). Helen Kennedy QC has pointed out that:

> In rape trials women are asked all sorts of irrelevant and inappropriate questions which have nothing to do with the crime – and which are never put to men. Barristers home-in on their lifestyle to show that they encourage rape.
>
> (quoted in Bouquet, 1995, p. 46)

Sue Lees has argued in this respect that: 'Women who are brave enough to take their cases to court go through a form of judicial rape. They are subjected to ruthless character assassination and humiliation' (quoted in Bouquet, 1995, p. 46).

Carol Smart (1995) has argued that actors in rape trials share a view of sexuality which emphasises the pleasure of penetration and intercourse. The assumption, then, is that rape must be pleasurable for women because it involves penetration. Rape trials often centre on the meaning of the word 'no'. The court, Smart argues, shares an understanding that women are capricious about sex and may say 'no' when they mean 'yes'. The key issue becomes whether a woman's 'no' meant 'no'. Clearly this issue is central to what has become known as 'date' as opposed to 'stranger' rape. In the former case it is frequently argued that the woman 'really' wanted sex, that she has clearly indicated this despite the fact that she said 'no'.

Also, in rape trials the rules of corroboration play a key role. Until the Criminal Justice Act 1994 juries were warned by the judge that it was dangerous to convict on the uncorroborated evidence of the complainant, but that they might do so if they were satisfied that it was true. The dangers of convicting on the basis of uncorroborated evidence are present in all trials, but the law required the jury to be warned of this only in rape trials, treason trials and when the evidence has been given by children or accomplices. In rape trials the implied insult, that rape victims were no more reliable as witnesses than children or accomplices, was compounded by the jury being told that the experience of the courts was that women accuse men of rape for totally malicious reasons and innocent men must be protected from such allegations. Given that there are rarely witnesses to rape, and often the victim's and accused's accounts differ only as to whether she consented to sexual intercourse, rape convictions are difficult to obtain unless there is corroborative evidence – for example, if the victim received injuries. Indeed, Home Office research has indicated that rapists are rarely convicted and imprisoned unless the victim is sexually inexperienced, was raped by a stranger *and* sustained injuries (Bouquet, 1995).

Indeed, long before the crime comes to trial women are often degraded and disbelieved. Women are reluctant to report rape in the first place because of the ways in which rape victims are questioned by the police and the ways in which medical examinations are carried out. The police are less likely to believe the rape allegation of some women than others. For example, Ann Burgess and Linda Holmstrom (1979) studied the cases of 146 women and girls who reported to a hospital emergency room (casualty reception) in the US as having been raped. They suggest that the responses of the police and the decision as to whether to prosecute or not were based on stereotypes of rape. The woman was believed and the police carried out an investigation if the woman was previously a virgin, if she was judged emotionally stable, if the rapist was a stranger and if the rapist used or threatened to use a weapon. The case was dropped if the victim had gone willingly, if she was unmarried and sexually experienced, if she had emotional problems, if she was calm when she was making the report and if the rapist was known to her.

Barbara Toner (1977) found that the police in Britain held similar stereotypes of rape. Women reporting rape are more likely to be taken seriously if they report the offence immediately, are upset, did not know the rapist and showed signs of having put up a struggle. (However, feminists have suggested that women do not want to be beaten, and victims of rape have often said that they were too frightened to resist and that they were afraid they would be killed if they did.) Toner found that women who reported rape often felt they were treated unsympathetically by the police and found the medical inspection conducted in an insultingly matter-of-fact way. Research carried out for Thames Valley Police by Oxford Brookes University in 1994 found that only a fifth of rape victims reported the crime to the police. Over half of the victims thought they were unlikely to be treated fairly by the courts (Bouquet, 1995). Catharine MacKinnon (1987) has suggested that women do not report rape or at least do not proceed with allegations because of the type of evidence that they will be required to give in court.

Feminists have challenged a number of myths about rape:

1 Rape is widely believed to be impossible. It is argued that women can always avoid being raped by running away or resisting and fighting back. This ignores the aspect of fear, that women are too frightened to run away and are scared of the consequences if they resist.
2 It is believed that women enjoy rape. However, studies of women who have been raped suggest that they felt humiliated and frightened. Also, men benefit from the belief that women want intercourse.
3 It is believed that rape is a rare act. However, victim studies and the experience of Rape Crisis centres suggests that only a small number of rapes are reported to the police. Ruth Hall (1985), in the only published UK incidence report, found prevalence figures of 17 per cent for rape and 20 per cent for attempted rape.
4 It is believed that rape is committed by strangers. Statistics show that the rapist is as likely to be known to the victim as to be a stranger. Also, rapes are as likely to happen indoors as in the open. For example, Amir (1971) found that 57 per cent of rapists were known to their victims.
5 It is believed that rape is committed only by psychopaths. However, studies suggest that few convicted rapists are mentally abnormal. Carol and Barry Smart (1978) point out that rapists are not treated differently from other offenders by the legal system and generally receive short sentences, and that few are dealt with under the mental health legislation. Furthermore, the criminal records of convicted rapists often include non-sexual as well as sexual crimes.
6 It is believed that rape is an impulsive act, the result of uncontrollable sexual urges and unplanned. Women are said to 'cause' the urges which men cannot control. However, research has demonstrated that most rapes are planned. For example, Amir (1971) found that 70 per cent were planned, 11 per cent partially planned and only 16 per cent what he called 'explosive'.

7 It is believed that rape is a problem of the lower classes. However, men of all ages, all social classes and all ethnic groups attack and rape women.

Assaults on wives and partners

The extent to which wives are violently assaulted became evident in the early 1970s when women's liberation groups began to respond to the obvious need for refuges for women who wanted to leave violent men (see Chapter 6). As Dobash and Dobash observe:

> In 1971 almost no one had heard of battered women, except of course the legions of women who were being battered and the relatives, friends, ministers, social workers, doctors and lawyers in whom some of them confided. Many people did not believe that such behaviour actually existed, and even most of those who were aware of it did not think that it affected sufficient numbers of women or was of sufficient severity to warrant wide-scale concern.
>
> (Dobash and Dobash, 1980, p. 2)

Domestic violence occurs across all social classes, all kinds of family circumstances and all localities (Mirrlees-Black, 1999). The UK police receive the equivalent of one call a minute asking for assistance with domestic violence, only 5 per cent of which include a male victim (ESRC, 2002).

The women who come to refuges – about 12,000 in any one year in the UK (Lovenduski and Randall, 1993) – have often been living with men who have beaten them violently for years. Many have tried unsuccessfully to leave their husbands or partners on a number of occasions, but the problem of finding accommodation and supporting themselves and their children has frequently driven them back to the violent home. Welfare agencies, the police and the courts were seen as at best unhelpful and at worst likely to advise them to 'make the best of it'.

This comes about at least in part because violence in the family often continues to be seen as a private affair, something to be sorted out by the husband and wife themselves, rather than something needing intervention by welfare agencies, the police and the courts. The police frequently refer to such incidents as 'domestic' rather than regarding them as serious cases of assault. Furthermore, calling them domestic shifts the blame for the violence from the husband to the husband-and-wife and normalises it as part of family life. Police reluctance to take assaults on wives seriously is also evidenced by their reluctance to charge husbands with assault and take them to court. They argue that this is because wives usually refuse to testify and forgive their husbands. However, evidence from states in the US where police are required to charge husbands who assault wives does not support this contention, and nor does research in Britain that has examined this 'attrition rate'. In Britain the practice of 'no criming' domestic disputes is gradually being abandoned (Edwards, 1989; Bourlet, 1990). (In practice, however, the change had to be underpinned by training in consistent practice (Walklate, 2004).) A series of Home Office memos to police forces between 1983 and 1990 instructed them to take domestic violence more seriously, and in 1991 the Home Office instructed police forces to set up data-banks of women at risk. The response of police forces, organised regionally, has been mixed, with a few forces having very good practices and others having apparently made no changes. In some forces there are *no* Police Domestic Violence Units, while in others not only are there such Units, but domestic assault on women is treated as seriously as assaults on strangers (Lovenduski and Randall, 1993; Walklate, 2004).

In the US it is estimated that between two and four million and possibly as many as eight million women are battered every year by the men with whom they live (Sassetti, 1993). It is likely that it is the single greatest cause of serious injury to women, accounting for more injuries than car accidents, muggings and rape combined. Domestic violence also accounts for between 30 and 40 per cent of female murder victims in the US every year (see Chapter 6). Some 25 per cent of all violent assaults in Britain are domestic assaults on women, over a *thousand* women a week in London alone telephone the police with a domestic violence complaint (Lovenduski and Randall, 1993), and one in five murder victims is a woman killed by her partner or ex-partner (Smith, 1989). Research into domestic violence indicates that in the overwhelming majority of cases men are the perpetrators and women the victims (Smith, 1989), and this holds true for different ethnic and cultural groups. Mama (1989) has indicated that 'the prevalence of violence against women in Black communities illustrates the full meaning of triple oppression along the dimensions of race, class and gender' (p. vii). Mama, like the Southall Black Sisters (Sahgal, 1989), has been critical of pressures put on Black women to keep quiet about their experiences of male violence. Indeed, she argues that because of the focus on fighting against *police* violence it took 'a long time to address a reality in which black women are more likely to be assaulted by their male partners than to be attacked by racists' (p. 16).

Most research into assaults on wives has been carried out by interviewing women in refuges. In the main the research has been carried out by academics. Indeed, the Department of Health and Social Security has been criticised for commissioning research on wife-assault from academics rather than involving the women in the refuge movement, it being suggested that the DHSS spent large sums of money on research that could better have been spent helping the victims of abuse (Hanmer and Leonard, 1984). The findings of research, they suggest, have added little that the women in the refuges did not know already.

Feminist researchers have rejected individualistic explanations for domestic violence. The largest single feminist study of wife-beating was carried out by Rebecca and Russell Dobash (1980) in Scotland. They argued that the problem of violence against women is a deep-rooted societal one arising out of the patriarchal family system, a system in which the husband's authority over the wife creates a particular marriage power relationship and a subordinate position for wives and mothers. They argued that men are more powerful than women and exploit the labour of women in marriage – that is, women are expected to serve their husbands by providing domestic services for them. They argue that one of the major factors precipitating male violence to their wives is husbands' perceptions that a wife is not performing her wifely duties satisfactorily – for example, a house not cleaned properly, a meal not prepared promptly, or a wife suspected of not being sexually faithful. Jan Pahl (1985), in her research, also found that men who beat their wives had frequently tried to control their behaviour and expected them to stay at home and not go out alone. Henrietta Moore (1995) has suggested that interpersonal violence can always be seen as evidence of the struggle for the maintenance of power – in this case, the power of men to control women.

Feminist researchers have also explored why women find it so difficult to leave violent men. They argue that there are economic, social, ideological and legal factors which all interact to make it difficult for women to leave violent men. In economic terms it is difficult for a woman to support herself and her children, but more urgent is the problem of finding housing (Walklate, 2004). Indeed, Jan Pahl found that the women she interviewed were frequently surprised to discover that they were financially better off on supplementary benefit than they had been when living with their husbands (Pahl, 1985). Housing was a major problem; in the past the women had left home but had been forced back because of their inability to find suitable accommodation. The refuge provided a warm and friendly environment that battered wives could turn to, but it was not suitable for the long term.

In social terms wives who have been assaulted often feel that they cannot admit that their marriage has failed. They blame themselves and see it as an individual problem. Also, a woman's relatives and friends may well tell her that she has herself to blame for being in the situation and that she must put up with it (Homer *et al.*, 1984).

Mama (1989) and Maguire (1988) have pointed to the additional problems of Black women leaving violent partners. Mama, for example, documents incidents where the collective pressures of the extended family make it difficult to leave, and Maguire points to the problems that women who have come to Britain to marry confront – of deportation, of stigma and of their family's response if they have to return to their own countries.

Patriarchal and familial ideology also influence the response of welfare agencies to wives who have been assaulted. Johnson (1985) argues that social workers have often not been trained to deal with assaults on wives, that they lack the resources to help women victims and at best they can refer women to a hostel. A large proportion of assaulted women seek medical help – for example, 80 per cent of the Dobash and Dobash (1980) sample had been to the doctor, and 64 per cent of the women Jan Pahl (1985) interviewed – although they rarely mentioned that they were beaten by their husbands. Doctors do not see marital problems as part of their concern; this is not the kind of problem that 'real' medicine is concerned with (see Chapter 7). In a number of studies women have been critical of the response of doctors to their attempt to seek help, and especially of the medical practice of prescribing tranquillisers (Dobash and Dobash, 1980; Pahl, 1985). Non-medical advice, when it was offered, was generally to leave the man, but no account was taken of practical problems. The police were also frequently criticised in these studies and by the women who had been assaulted. Police, it is argued, are reluctant to intervene in what they regard as domestic disputes and will rarely take the men to court (Dobash and Dobash, 1980; Edwards, 1989; Bourlet, 1990). This is a problem because women frequently turn to the police for help, and while (as we noted above) the police response is improving, this is probably happening only slowly and patchily in Britain (Johnson, 1995).

In the 1970s the one major response of the government to the problem of assaults on wives was a set of legal reforms designed to give women greater protection from violent men and to make it easier for women to leave them. An analysis of how the legal reforms have worked in practice demonstrates, feminists argue, both the limitations of reform and the ways in which patriarchal ideology influences judicial decisions.

Three Acts were passed in the late 1970s, all designed to assist women assaulted by their husbands: the Domestic Violence and Matrimonial Proceedings Act 1976, the Domestic Proceedings and Magistrates' Courts Act 1978 and the Housing (Homeless Persons) Act 1977. The 1977 Housing Act made it the responsibility of local authorities to rehouse certain categories of people – mainly families – providing they had not intentionally made themselves homeless. The Act explicitly stated that women who had left a violent man should not be seen as having intentionally made themselves homeless and should be rehoused if they had dependent children. However, many local authorities have not rehoused women and their children. Furthermore, even if they are prepared to accept the woman as homeless the problem is not solved. The woman and her children will have to live in accommodation designated for homeless persons for some time and then to accept the first offer of permanent accommodation, however unsatisfactory the woman may find it. Also, while she is in temporary accommodation the husband may be able to gain custody of the children; still living in the matrimonial home, he may be able to convince the court that he can better provide for his children than can his wife. If the wife no longer has custody of the children, she is no longer entitled to be rehoused by the local authority.

The Domestic Violence and Matrimonial Proceedings Act (DVMPA) and the Domestic Proceedings and Magistrates Act (DPMA) were both designed to give battered women greater protection. The DVMPA applied in the County Courts and permitted courts to issue non-molestation and exclusion injunctions independently of any other proceedings before the court. Injunctions were to be available in an emergency, could have powers of arrest attached, and men could be sent to prison for breach of an injunction. Relief was available to married and cohabiting women equally. The DPMA extends similar powers to Magistrates' Courts. This meant that women had a local, inexpensive, simple and quick access to relief if they were assaulted. However, the provisions applied only to married women, magistrates had no powers to exclude men from certain localities, and husbands could be arrested only if they inflicted actual physical injury on their wives.

In practice these Acts have not extended much greater protection to wives. Case law has established legal precedents which demonstrate judges' and magistrates' reluctance to prevent a man entering his property. It has been made evident that the courts see the protection of children as the most important factor. There has been a reluctance to use the emergency powers, and injunctions are frequently issued without powers of arrest attached, which means the police argue that they cannot enforce the injunction. Over and above this, the police have been reluctant to intervene even when powers of arrest have been attached.

We can conclude, then, that the current state of English law on domestic violence is one of a legal system which provides all the necessary remedies, but which in its operation fails to protect women as fully as it should and leaves them vulnerable. What we must bear in mind however is that abused women are not just victims but also survivors – Hoff (1990) describes them in her study as 'crisis managers rather than helpless victims' (p. 56), and Dobash and Dobash (1992) reject the view that abused women become the victims of learned helplessness.

Women, violence and male power

Some feminists have argued that by concentrating on rape and assaults on wives the real extent of male violence against women is obscured. They argue that all women are affected by male violence and that the crime statistics and official victim and self-report studies seriously underestimate the extent of violence towards women by men. Violence is a powerful mechanism of social control; women's movements are severely restricted by the actual violence they experience and by fear of male violence. Violence, it is argued, encompasses more than actual physical assault and includes all behaviour designed to control and intimidate women carried out by men. The extent to which men control and intimidate women only becomes evident when we include sexual harassment, obscene telephone calls, flashing and other behaviour by men designed to control women. Liz Kelly has offered the following definition of sexual violence:

> [Sexual violence] includes any physical, visual, verbal or sexual act that is experi-enced by the woman or girl, at the time or later, as a threat, menace or assault, that has the effect of hurting her or degrading her and/or takes away her ability to control intimate contact.
>
> (Kelly, 1988, p. 4)

Research by Jalna Hanmer and Susan Saunders (1984) and by Jill Radford (1987) has found that women's behaviour is very much restricted by their fear of men – both in the domestic sphere and in the public. Women do not go out at night, or to certain places, not only because they fear attack, but also because the men with whom they live try to prevent them going out alone. They also found that women experience considerable amounts of violent behaviour from men, but that much of this is hidden – it is not reported to the police, nor do women reveal their experience of violence in response to surveys such as the British Crime Survey. They suggest that this is because women are reluctant to reveal the extent to which men are violent and there is no reason to suppose that the women who have not reported the violence to the police are more likely to reveal it to a survey. In their research they acknowledged the reasons why they were doing the research in advance and left the women to define violence themselves. They argue, therefore, that their findings reflect more accurately the experiences of the women and their perceptions of violence.

Jacqui Halson (1989) argues that her research among 14-year-old girls in a co-educational school confirms that sexual harassment is a form of sexual violence commonly experienced by young women both in school and outside. The young women experienced sexual harassment from both male teachers and male pupils, and she argues that the school sanctioned it by not intervening and therefore reproduced the existing imbalances of power between women and men. The girls felt uncomfortable and threatened by the behaviour of one male teacher, who was referred to as 'a right Casanova'. The boys leered at the girls, verbally harassed them and physically assaulted them, although the behaviour usually stopped short of rape. Often one girl was sexually harassed by a gang of boys, and this increased a sense of powerlessness and meant that the girls policed their own behaviour so that they were not likely to meet a group of boys when on their own. The girls did not find the boys' behaviour flattering, but offensive and humiliating, and in no way could it be said to be experienced as 'friendly', 'inoffensive' or 'just teasing'. Nor was it mutual, and it could not be dismissed as banter or mutual flattery. The girls were not empowered to challenge the boys because the school's attitude was that such behaviour was harmless, not a serious problem, and there were no school rules forbidding it.

Halson suggests that one incident reveals the lack of understanding by the school authorities of how seriously the girls viewed sexual harassment. Some graffiti was put up in the school – 'Mary is a slag'. The young woman concerned was extremely upset, and her mother came to the school and threatened to take action. However, a senior member of the staff suggested that the mother was making a lot of fuss over nothing and that 'slag' was a common term of abuse used to refer to girls – precisely missing the key point, that terms like 'slag' are used to diminish women, to humiliate them and to enable men to control them.

Carol Ramazanoglu (1987) has pointed out how difficult it is for female academics to challenge sexual harassment from male colleagues, and in other situations women do not have the physical strength to fight men. Other researchers have argued that the response of women to other forms of violence is eminently rational when seen from their perspective. Women who are raped or flashed at say that they are scared of being killed and this conditions their response. Women do not report incidents of violence to the police because they are aware of the patriarchal response that they will elicit. Women who are the victims of male violence are likely to see themselves as blamed for it. Feminists are aware that neither changes in legislation nor asking men to change their behaviour are likely to make much difference, although both are important. They therefore argue that women should organise to help themselves, arguing for more refuges to be run and controlled by women, for rape crisis centres, and for women to be taught self-defence techniques.

What is vital also is to challenge the view that assaults on wives and rape are in some sense different from other violent crimes. They are, of course, in that they are examples of the ways in which men use violence to maintain or reassert their power over women and control women, but they are not less serious. Indeed, it could be argued that they are more serious. What must be challenged is the common-sense view that crimes in the domestic sphere are a private matter and not the concern of the police and the criminal justice system, and that rape is a sexual crime, the result of men's innate sexual urges.

Conclusions

In this chapter we have dealt with two aspects of feminist work on crime. In the first half we discussed feminist work on women and crime, and in the second half work on male violence towards women. The two halves reflect very different feminist approaches. The work on women and crime is heavily academic in orientation and concerned with either incorporating women into existing theories of crime or arguing for the need to reformulate sociological approaches to crime in order that they can adequately explain both why women are so non-criminal and the behaviour of the women who do break the law.

The work on women and violence has to a large extent been carried out by radical feminists (see Chapter 2 for more details) who are concerned not only with researching the problem of men's violence to women but also with developing strategies for dealing with it. They argue that male violence affects all women, irrespective of age, race or social class, and that it is one of the major ways in which men control women in patriarchal societies. We have included such material in this chapter on women and crime because we want to demonstrate not only the ways in which malestream sociology has ignored or marginalised the crimes that are committed by men against women; but also the ways in which the legal system marginalises, trivialises and belies women's victimisation, and how it often blames violence on the victim. Men who are attacked on the street are not told that they should not have been out there; women often are. Men who are beaten up are not told it was because of the way they behaved; women often are. Men are not advised not to go out at night alone or not to visit certain places; women often are. Men control women's behaviour and this control is reinforced not only by the media, the police and the courts but also by other women. Control of women is a key aspect of understanding women's behaviour – why women break the law and why they do not, and why they are attacked, beaten and abused by men.

SUMMARY

1 Feminists have highlighted aspects of crime hitherto ignored or considered 'normal' – for example, rape, assault on wives and sexual harassment.
2 Feminists have argued that these need to be explained in the context of male power and the fact that violence is considered 'normal' behaviour for men in our society but not for women.

FURTHER READING

Heidensohn, F. (2000) *Sexual Politics and Social Control*. Buckingham: Open University Press. This is an interesting and accessible book that focuses on the relationship between gender and social control, taking account of issues such as globalisation and the gendered politics of risk, and how these issues shape men's and women's behaviour.

Lees, S. (1997) *Ruling Passions: Sexual Violence, Reputation and the Law*. Buckingham: Open University Press. This interesting and thought-provoking book explores the disciplinary processes that constrict women's lives with particular reference to sexuality. It places particular emphasis on the ways in which gendered and sexualised discourses mean that women subject themselves and each other to self-surveillance. It also explores some of the ways in which institutional and social practices relating to criminal justice are gendered.

Naffine, N. (1996) *Feminism and Criminology*. Cambridge: Polity. This engaging and accessible book reviews feminist criticisms and contributions to criminology from a range of perspectives.

CHAPTER ELEVEN

Politics

Women are notably absent from what is conventionally seen as 'politics' in most societies including Britain. When the Labour Government was elected in 1997, much was made of 'Blair's babes' – the newly elected female Labour MPs. However, British politics remains dominated by men at national level. Most Cabinet Ministers are male, and most MPs are male. Despite the fact that the former Conservative Party leader, Mrs Thatcher, was Prime Minister from 1979 to 1991, there are and have been few other women in key positions of political power in Britain, few women trade union leaders and few Members of Parliament (though the number of women local government councillors has increased). Women are assumed to be less able at carrying out political tasks than men and less interested in politics. Interestingly, the collapse of communism in the former USSR has resulted in a reduction in the number of women engaged in positions of political power as social institutions have begun to resemble those of the West more closely. In some countries such as Rwanda, meanwhile, 50 per cent female membership of Parliament has been achieved – through a quota system designed to ensure this.

Political sociology has tended in the past to accept this common-sense view of women's relationship to politics and to give it 'scientific' authority. In malestream political sociology, women have tended to be seen as irrelevant to politics or, when mentioned, have been seen as behaving in less authentically political ways than men. Feminist criticisms have been raised of the ways in which women have been distorted in political sociology and especially in voting studies, and there have been feminist studies of women's political activity, as well as analyses of gendered politics, examining not only women's political activity but also patriarchal resistance – that is, the power struggle between feminism and patriarchy. Analysis has also been undertaken of the role of the state in creating and maintaining the nuclear family and the role of women as wives and mothers. In this chapter we shall examine feminist criticisms of malestream political sociology and feminist research on women's politics, considering each of these various issues.

Men, women and voting studies

Malestream research has suggested that women's participation in politics is less than men's and that women's concerns and demands are a reflection of moral or familial commitments rather than an authentic political stance. For example, men are said to be concerned about pay and hours of work while women are more concerned with working conditions. However, this literature has exaggerated the differences between men and women in political behaviour, and while suggesting that women's political behaviour is influenced by the private sphere it has discounted the influence of the private sphere on the political behaviour of men. In terms of voting behaviour, male-stream researchers have claimed that women vote less than men, that women are naturally more conservative than men, that women are more fickle than men, and that women are more influenced by personalities. However, a re-examination of the literature and research findings by feminists suggests that the evidence on which these conclusions are based is very flimsy indeed.

Susan Bourque and Jean Grosshaltz (1974) have argued that malestream researchers have often interpreted data and made assumptions that 'fit in' with their preconceived ideas of women's political behaviour. First, Bourque and Grosshaltz point to the 'fudging of the footnotes' which enables statements to be made about women's political orientations which are either unsupported by the references or misleading simplifications of the original. Second, they argue there is a tendency to assume that men (especially husbands) influence women's political opinions and behaviour, but not vice versa – especially in terms of voting. Third, there is the un-questioned assumption that the political attitudes, preferences and style of participation characteristic of men define mature political behaviour. Women's behaviour is seen as immature by definition, if it differs from this. Fourth, it is assumed that women's political concerns are located in their role as mothers, and this results in a constrained view of women's political potential. Similarly, references to the fact that women are more conservative than men are often supported by data which in fact show at most very small differences.

We can mount a similar challenge to the view that women's political participation demonstrates that they are less politically aware than men, or less interested. The evidence indicates the degree to which political parties, trade unions and the norms of political participation often do not resonate with the concerns, needs and oppor-tunities of many women. The timing of trade union and political party meetings often makes it difficult for women with domestic commitments to attend and participate. Men often argue that issues of central concern to women are less important or some-how 'less political' than the issues which concern men. Indeed, some issues of critical concern to women are seen as tied in with their natural role and not something that should be on the political agenda at all. Political matters which have been interpreted in this light include workplace issues such as paid maternity leave, demands for the provision of workplace nurseries, school holiday play-schemes and paid time off from work to care for sick children. At a national level, 'the endowment of motherhood' – the idea that women should be paid to bring up children on behalf of the nation – has been viewed similarly, and it took a ruling by the European Commission for married women caring for a sick or disabled husband to be allowed to claim a carer's allowance (an allowance paid to someone who cares for a severely incapacitated adult or child). Women have had to fight to get issues such as abortion rights, contraception, equal pay, and so on to be seen as important political issues. Given this, plus the fact that so few women are candidates in national or union elections, it is perhaps not surprising that women's political participation is not identical to men's.

However, careful research has suggested that gender differences are not a major factor in voting behaviour and that other issues such as social class and age are more important predictors. For example, it has been suggested that women are less likely to cast their vote than men, and this has been used to argue that women are less interested in politics. However, older people are less likely, statistically, to vote than younger people, and there are more old women than old men; when allowance is made for age, the apparent difference virtually disappears. It is often argued that women are influenced in how they vote by the preferences of their husbands (see e.g. Lazarsfeld *et al.*, 1968). However, the best conclusion from the evidence is that the influence is mutual (Weiner, 1978; Prandy, 1986).

Political scientists have not in general been much concerned with women's political behaviour, and it has generally been assumed that women are less interested in political issues because their main interest lies in the domestic sphere. However, this division between a public and a private or domestic sphere is itself a political issue, and to say that a concern with working conditions, the education of children, the availability of abortion, and so on is the mark of a moral rather than a political concern is to make a definite and in many ways contemptuous value judgement. It is indeed possible – likely, even – that women's experiences differ from men's and therefore determine their voting behaviour differently. Women may well be more affected than men by cuts in public expenditure in education, health and the implementation of community care, or at least more aware of the results of such policies. As Dorothy Smith (1979) argued, women's lives are cast by their circumstances less in the 'abstract mode' of conceptual argument and more in the concrete reality in which such arguments are grounded; men may have theories on education or health care, but it is the women who take the children to school and to the doctor. Issues such as working hours, the provision of nurseries, antenatal care, and the like may therefore loom larger for women than for men. They are political issues, however, and to ignore them or relegate them to the domestic sphere is to ignore the basis on which many women make their political choices. Finally, one may argue that if women were less interested in public politics than men – a proposition for which the empirical evidence is not strong – it would be because they felt, realistically, that they had little chance of influencing events because the political agenda and the processes of politics are dominated by men.

Thus some feminists have concluded that malestream assumptions about gender differences in political sociology are inappropriate. Such assumptions have a number of consequences:

1 By emphasising the characteristics that are seen as 'male' or 'female', studies treat men and women as if they were homogeneous social groups, and the variations amongst men and amongst women are played down. Thus, for example, the 'job model' – the view that a man's political attitudes and behaviour are determined by work experiences – is applied to men, and a 'gender model' to women.
2 Roles in the domestic sphere are seen as shaping women's and only women's voting behaviour. It is suggested that women vote for candidates because of their personal qualities, though it has not been suggested that men voted for Mrs Thatcher because of her charms or wifely qualities.

3 The assumption that political parties, trade unions, etc. are gender-fair, and that women's lack of active participation is due to their lack of interest, ignores the male domination and control of such organisations. Indeed, the difference in trade union membership between men and women has narrowed in recent years – mainly as a result of industrial restructuring and the concentration of women in unionised occupations such as teaching, nursing and social work (CSO, 1995).

Feminists have not been concerned, however, to argue that women's political action is identical to men's. They have argued that malestream research and male-dominated trade unions and political parties have a taken-for-granted definition of what is to count as political. However, this definition excludes much of women's expertise and political concerns. Feminists offer an alternative interpretation of women's relationship to public life. They demonstrate the extent to which the 'male as the norm' principle operates in political and social analysis – emphasising the way in which a demarcation between the 'political' and the 'social' or 'moral' is based on arbitrary but sex-linked criteria. For example, Greenstein (1965) found that girls scored more highly than boys on measures of 'citizen duty' and 'political efficacy' but relabel these attributes as moral rather than political. Feminists suggest that it is necessary to attribute new meanings to women's political activities. For example, refraining from voting may actually be a reflection of the low efficacy of voting. Given that women's political concerns are not reflected in politics, the question should be why women should vote rather than why they should not. Finally, it is argued that what are seen as women's skills need to be revalued and seen to be of relevance to political life. It is suggested that the priorities, skills and issues that women bring with them from the domestic sphere are valuable additions to politics. Women's struggle for better working conditions, for instance, might be an example of this.

Defining feminist politics

Feminists have argued that women do engage in political activities as conventionally defined. As we have seen above, women's voting behaviour is very similar to men's. Women do belong to trade unions. There are women who are active members of trade unions and political parties, women local councillors, women Members of Parliament, women general secretaries of trade unions, and so on. Women *are* active in politics, even if the number of women so engaged is much smaller than the number of men. Feminists have also suggested that women are often alienated from politics and excluded by the control and domination of organisations by men. However, feminists have also argued that women's political activities and concerns have been marginalised and 'hidden from history'. What is seen as political needs to be redefined feminists have argued. Thus they have maintained that feminism is itself political and is concerned with the struggle for women's liberation and emancipation. Feminists, for example, have had to rediscover the political activities of first wave feminists, a movement often portrayed as just a group of middle-class women fighting for the vote. The other activities they engaged in and the writings of nineteenth-century feminists are often ignored or reinterpreted as concerned with moral/personal issues. However, the major argument of feminists has been that 'the personal is the political' – that is, that politics is concerned with the dynamics of power relationships in society and must therefore be concerned with the power relationships between men and women. Thus in the public sphere the power that men exercise over women is often ignored while their domination in the domestic sphere is even less often considered.

Kate Millett (1977), in *Sexual Politics*, defines politics as 'power-structured relationships, arrangements whereby one group of persons is controlled by another' (p. 23). The feminist definition of politics puts on the agenda not only power relationships between men and women at the personal level, but also the importance of patriarchal ideology in controlling women's lives. Thus the orthodox idea, for example, that women have a free choice in deciding whether to do housework is challenged. Furthermore, feminists argue that the very division between public and private is a patriarchal idea used to exclude women and women's concerns from politics. They argue that women have been excluded from participation in politics and public life and that the state has construed the family as private – as an institution outside of state intervention. In this way, in the name of personal freedom and privacy, one of the arenas in which women are most exploited and subordinated, in the family, is exempt from political intervention. The separation between the public and the private has made possible the legislation of female equality in the former while ignoring the real differences that exist in the latter. Furthermore, the public/private split makes it possible to keep women's values out of the public sphere. Some radical feminists (see Chapter 2) argue that because of their roles as mothers women have a deeper sense of humility, caring and community, of belonging and selflessness, than men. Also, women are prevented from participating on equal terms with men in the public sphere because of the responsibilities they have or are attributed in the domestic sphere, and men are often prevented from taking on caring roles in the home.

Feminists have pointed out that this conceptual split between the public and the private does not even necessarily accord with men's and women's lived experiences of social and political life. Indeed, it has been argued that the state has actually 'created' and sustained the family as an institution, and women's subordination within it. Legislation on matters such as social security and income maintenance has assumed that women do and should live with a man on whom they are financially dependent. On the other hand, matters arising in the public sphere are said to be private: for example sexual harassment, legislation on contraception and abortion have all been said to be private/moral issues rather than political ones.

Feminist political activism

The rediscovery of women's history has been a major achievement of feminist scholarship in recent years. As part of the reclaiming of 'herstory', first wave feminism as a political movement (in the West at least), has been uncovered. Writing by post-colonial feminists has also been brought to the fore.

Women, and especially married women, had few rights in the nineteenth century, and throughout the century women struggled to achieve the same rights as men. Many of these women were white, middle-class, and so on and sought to have the same rights to education, to voting, to work, etc. as middle-class men, but few were concerned about the plight of working-class women or of Black women, or women in other parts of the world, who were often forced to work long hours and had even fewer rights than their middle-class sisters. Nevertheless, working-class and Black women were politically active, especially towards the end of the century, when women founded their own trade unions and participated in the suffrage movement.

The situation of Caroline Norton provides a graphic illustration of the lack of rights which married women experienced. She was married to a man who assaulted her physically and lived off her earnings as a writer. When she eventually decided she could take no more and left him, she found she had no right of access to her own children, no right to control her own property, including even her jewellery and clothing, and no right to her own earnings. It would have been impossible for her to remain separated from her husband if she had not had relatives who were prepared to keep her. In the nineteenth century women were a legally inferior class; they were not regarded as persons under the law. Women in the UK did not gain the right to custody of infant children until 1839, nor to control their own property until 1882, nor to vote on the same basis as men until 1928, nor to get a divorce on the same grounds as men until 1934.

Juliet Mitchell (1986) traces the origins of the feminist movement to the concept of equality and equal rights that was first introduced during the English Revolution in the seventeenth century and was further developed in the eighteenth-century Enlightenment and the French Revolution. The first expressions of feminism were based on the concept of equality – that men and women should be treated equally. This was demanded by women who saw themselves as a social group completely excluded from the tenets and principles of the 'new' society that had developed after the English Revolution. Eighteenth-century feminists were middle-class women who argued their case in relation to the economic changes that were taking place. The emerging bourgeois class was seeking freedom and equality in society, and the feminists argued that these new freedoms and equalities should be extended to middle-class women as well as men. Writing on marriage in 1700, Mary Astell asked:

> If all men are born free, how is it that all women are born slaves? As they must be if their being subjected to the inconsistent, uncertain, unknown, arbitrary will of men be the perfect condition of slavery.
>
> (quoted in Mitchell, 1986, p. 71)

Eighteenth-century feminists rejected the view that women were naturally different from men. They argued against the social power of men and the ways in which men used that power to exclude women and prevent their being equal.

Arguably the main influence on first wave feminism, however, was Mary Wollstonecraft, who published *A Vindication of the Rights of Women* in 1792. She maintained that inequalities between men and women were not the outcome of natural (biological) differences but due to the influence of the environment, and especially the fact that women were excluded from education. She argued that both women and society in general were damaged by conditioning women into an inferior social status. What was necessary was both to educate women and to change society so that men and women were seen and treated as equal. Another major influence on the first wave feminist movement was *The Subjection of Women*, published in 1869 by John Stuart Mill and Harriet Taylor Mill. This was written at the height of the Victorian repression of women and put forward a coherent equal-rights argument – that men and women should have the same rights under the law.

Nineteenth-century feminism was mainly concerned with women having the same legal rights as men. The campaigns that were fought on issues connected with sexuality and sexual politics have been ignored or seen as right-wing because the women concerned were opposed to sexual liberation (Jeffreys, 1985). However, they argued that sexual liberation was for men and that it exploited women. They argued, for example, to raise the age of sexual consent from 13 to 16 for girls, which happened in 1885. Another issue that feminists campaigned around was the repeal of the Contagious Diseases Acts which were introduced in the 1860s in an attempt to reduce the spread of venereal diseases among men in the armed forces. The Acts, which applied to a number of garrison towns, enabled the police to stop any women they suspected of being a common prostitute and have her examined for venereal disease. If the woman was found to have a venereal disease she was taken to a 'lock hospital' for compulsory treatment (Walkowitz, 1980).

During the nineteenth century it was believed that women had no interest in sex themselves and that sexual relations were purely for men's pleasure. Male homosexuality was against the law, but there was no law against lesbianism because it was not thought to exist. Women were seen as a moral force in the home and in society precisely because they were resistant to the pleasures of the body, such as sexual relations, drinking, and so on. The view of the early feminists was therefore to protect women from being exploited for men's pleasure.

> They were particularly outraged at the way in which the exercise of male sexuality created a division of women into 'the pure' and 'the fallen' and prevented the unity of a 'sisterhood of women'. They insisted that men were responsible for prostitution and that the way to end such abuse of women was to curb the demand for prostitutes by enforcing chastity upon men rather than by punishing those who provided the supply. They employed the same arguments in their fight against other aspects of male sexual behaviour which they regarded as damaging to women, such as sexual abuse of children, incest, rape and sexual harassment in the street.
>
> (Jeffreys, 1985, p. 8)

They successfully campaigned against incest, legislation being passed in 1908, but were less successful in their attempt to get the law on 'rape in marriage' changed – the right of men to have sex with their wives was embodied in English common law. However, the Matrimonial Causes Act 1884 ended the power of husbands to imprison a wife who refused conjugal rights, and legal decisions in the late twentieth century made rape in marriage a criminal offence under common law (see Chapter 10).

In other words, some feminists of the late nineteenth and early twentieth century argued that men were able to exploit and abuse women sexually and that this was an abuse of power by adult men. Feminists in the late twentieth century, and especially radical feminists, made very similar points and campaigned about the ways men use sexuality as a tool for controlling and subordinating women. In taking on these issues the early feminists exposed themselves to both ridicule and detestation. Sexuality was a 'taboo' subject and the feminists who campaigned around issues to do with sexuality destroyed their reputations by making public issues which were not discussed (Walkowitz, 1980).

While women did not achieve equality with men in the nineteenth century, or even the early twentieth century, most of the rights have been won in the UK with the passage of the Sex Discrimination and Equal Pay legislation implemented in the 1970s. However, contemporary feminists have argued that the provision of formally equal rights is insufficient; while women are subordinated by the gender order and subject to patriarchal power and ideology, they cannot be equal (either to men, or to each other – Irigaray, 1993).

The second wave feminist movement has been concerned to make women aware of the shared female condition that controls and constrains all women regardless of individual circumstances. A major element of the movement has been consciousness-raising – women meeting together in small groups to share their common experiences as women. The movement has rejected conventional political organisation and has sought to establish itself as a movement with no leaders, no spokespersons or privileged analysis – a key concept particularly in the 1970s has been 'sisterhood'. While the movement has been accused of being comprised predominantly of middle-class, young, educated, white women, it has nevertheless campaigned successfully and worked on a number of important issues, notably in relation to sexuality. The Women's Movement was primarily responsible for bringing to light the large number of women who are physically assaulted by their husbands, and the inadequacies of state services for these women. Women's groups have established hostels for abused women and their children around the country. Rape has been another issue about which women have campaigned. Not only has there been pressure for changes in attitudes and in the law, but also research that suggests that most women who are raped do not go to the police. Women's groups have also established confidential rape crisis lines to help women who have been raped or sexually abused. The Women's Movement has campaigned actively against sexual harassment in the workplace and raised awareness in trade unions and political organisations about the problems that women experience in relation to men. Women have also campaigned actively around contraception issues and abortion. Initially the Movement argued for free access to abortion on demand, but more recently it has argued for the woman's right to choose whether or not to have an abortion. The change came about as middle-class white women were made aware that some others, especially Black and working-class women, were pressured into having abortions. Also feminists are concerned that the choice should be made a realistic one – that is, women who choose to have the baby should have the financial and other necessary support to be able to provide for it adequately. Initially the fight was for abortion law reform, but more recently the fight has been to prevent the law being reformed so that women's access to abortions becomes very limited.

Globally, women have fought against female circumcision and arranged marriage and for legislation to intervene in the case of dowry deaths and child marriage. Women have been politically active in a range of ways, fighting for women's rights and challenging laws and institutions that keep women in a subordinate role. Women have also been central to political campaigns and activities (at Greenham Common in the UK for instance – see Roseneil, 1995), have organised and taken part in political demonstrations and have been involved in a range of movements such as campaigns for animal rights and environmental politics. Women have also played a major role in the disability movement, and have highlighted the important areas of overlap between feminism and disability politics – in challenging patriarchal perspectives on the body, for instance (Hughes, 2000). Contemporary feminism has recognised that legislation is necessary but not sufficient for women's emancipation and that (despite the claims of post-feminists – see Chapter 2) feminism is an ongoing political struggle. The law has limited power to change attitudes and to transform an essentially masculine social order (particularly in societies, such as in Southeast Asia or parts of India and Africa, in which an 'equal rights' discourse is entirely alien to the masculine cultural hegemony). As we saw in Chapter 2, feminists differ in their aims and primary concerns (sexual difference, class, race, disability, age, global power relations, and so on), but all feminists want to emancipate women.

Women and the state

Some feminists have argued that the state has played an important role in constructing and maintaining the bourgeois nuclear family and the ideologies that suggest that this type of family is normal and natural (e.g. Abbott and Wallace, 1992). They identify the 'welfare' aspect of the state as particularly instrumental in this respect. Here we are using 'the state' to refer to the government and all the other institutions involved in regulating society: the civil service, local government, the courts, the police, and so on. The state is not just a set of institutions, but rather institutions that all exercise power and control in society and have the backing of physical force if necessary. In theory the power of the state is limitless, but in practice it is limited by ideas of non-intervention in civil society and in the domestic sphere. What we and many other feminists would argue is that the state does in fact play an important role in constructing and maintaining the private/domestic sphere and consequently is central to the continuing subordination and exploitation of women. It is important to remember that women's role in the domestic sphere limits the role they can and are assumed to be able to play in the public sphere. As we suggested in Chapter 9, feminists have demonstrated the ways in which jobs are 'created' for married women and that women's employment opportunities are limited by assumptions about their roles as wives and mothers. The UK welfare state was built on a 'male breadwinner' model – the assumption that men engaged in paid employment; married women, it was assumed, provided care in the domestic sphere and were mainly or wholly dependent on their husbands.

Women, family and caring

In Chapters 6 and 9 we saw that feminists have shown how an alliance between the male craft trade unions and the state resulted in the acceptance of the idea that a man should earn 'a family wage' – a wage sufficient to maintain a non-employed wife and children. This ideology was reinforced by protective legislation that limited the hours and types of work that women and children would be employed to do. This effectively resulted in wives becoming excluded from paid employment and the acceptance of the idea that women should care for their husbands and children in the domestic sphere. Similarly, compulsory schooling assumes that a parent (the mother) is available to take and collect children: school hours are not compatible with full-time employment for both parents. Similarly again, the lack of state provision of adequate nurseries, holiday childcare provision, and the like makes it difficult for mothers to take on employment.

However, it is the interaction of ideologies about motherhood and the role of women, reinforced by state policies, that confines women to their domestic sphere or at least makes it difficult for women, and especially married women, to participate with men in the labour market and in political organisations. This is why legislation for equal opportunities has failed to result in women actually being able to compete on equal terms with men in the public sphere and why it has been equally difficult for men to take on responsibilities in the domestic sphere. The general assumption is that it is women's responsibility to care for their husbands and children, and men's to provide economic support for the family. Welfare state policies have been developed on the assumption that this is how people do and should live.

Ideologies of the role of women as mothers, especially working-class women, developed in the UK in the late nineteenth century. The debates surrounding concern about the health of the working class at the time of the Boer War were used to reinforce the idea that women with children should not work but should care for them full-time in the home, that women (but not men) should be taught domestic skills, and that state intervention in the family was legitimate to ensure that mothers were adequately performing their role (see Sapsford, 1993, for a discussion of the later intrusion of psychologists into the control of mothers.)

Welfare provision exercises control over its recipients, and is underpinned by ideologies emphasising that a particular family form is not just how people *do* live but how they *should* live – thus privileging one way of life and disadvantaging alternative patterns of social organisation. The welfare state legislation introduced in the UK in the 1940s clearly and explicitly made these assumptions in terms of providing, for example, for income maintenance during unemployment, sickness and old age with the assumption that women would be dependent on men and therefore did not need to pay full contributions in order to be entitled to these benefits.

In the 1970s and 1980s, partly as a result of pressure from the European Court of Human Rights, there were some changes in welfare and taxation policies that removed some aspects of discrimination. More recently, European legislation has forced the UK Government to introduce family-friendly policies, such as the right to ask for flexible working hours when caring for young children and the availability of paternity leave. Most women, including married women, now pay full National

Insurance contributions when in employment and can have contributions credited for periods when they are caring for dependent children or relatives. Married women are now entitled to claim the care allowance and are taxed separately from their husbands. However, few social policy measures have been implemented that would make it easier for married women to take paid employment – although the policies of the Labour Government are to support dual-earner families through the National Children Strategy announced in 1998. However, the reality for many women is that they are now expected to take on the double burden of domestic and paid labour and often the triple burden of providing care for elderly or dependent relatives as well (see Chapters 6 and 7).

The ideological proposition that a woman's place is in the home caring for her children and husband continues to be a widely accepted and unquestioned one. Indeed, in the former Soviet Union and Eastern Europe there was a resurgence of familial ideology following the collapse of communism in 1991, when the view began to emerge again that women should not be in paid employment and should not engage in political activity. Interestingly, even under communism, with all its stress on equality of the right to work, women were seen as responsible for the domestic sphere and expected to care for their husband, children and other dependent relatives. The state did provide support, however, especially in the provision of nurseries – and these have now virtually disappeared.

The Thatcher government in Britain attempted in speeches and publications to reinforce the familial ideology that assumes the economic dependency of married women in the family. Policies such as community care (further emphasised in the 1990 National Health Service and Community Care Act) which assume that women are ready, able and willing to care for dependent and elderly relatives are an important aspect of this, assuming as they do that women are available to take on this burden and are naturally able to provide care. The government were concerned to argue that negligent mothers and mothers who work are a major cause of many contemporary social problems. The Labour Government from 1997 has moved the debate forward by introducing measures to support working parents, but the assumption that women provide care has not been seriously challenged. Women are expected to take on the double shift and in some cases this becomes a *triple* shift.

Women and poverty

State welfare policies and familial ideology also mean that women are more likely to be in poverty than men. An analysis of the groups most likely to be in poverty in contemporary Britain and of income distribution within households enables us to see that women are much more likely to be poor than men. Analysis by household also conceals the ways in which women's low-paid employment can keep households out of poverty or mitigate against the full impact of poverty being felt by other members of a household. The assumption that most women can depend on a man's wages to keep them out of poverty conceals the low pay among women workers and the low resources over which women have command, because some women are seen as financially dependent. Indeed, official statistics now talk about 'households on low incomes'. The gender pay gap remains at about 19 per cent and has changed little in the thirty years since the implementation of the Equal Pay Act (see Chapter 9).

The main groups in poverty in contemporary Britain are:

- those on low wages,
- the unemployed,
- the long-term sick or disabled,
- single parents, and
- those over retirement age.

However, none of these factors is a cause of poverty in itself. Most of these groups are dependent on state benefits; poverty ensues because state benefits are too low to lift the recipients above the poverty threshold. Governments have been explicit that benefits are designed as income maintenance, to provide a basic subsistence level. Women are over-represented in all of the groups listed above. There are in addition two further reasons why women are likely to be in poverty:

- as unpaid carers of sick, disabled or elderly relatives, or
- as dependants of a male wage earner – either because that wage is at the poverty level or because the man does not share his resources equitably within the household.

Caroline Glendinning and Jane Millar (1992) found that two household types are the most likely to be poor (i.e. living on 140 per cent or less of the supplementary benefit level) – elderly women living alone (of whom 60 per cent were in poverty) and lone mothers (of whom 61 per cent were in poverty). Together the two types account for 32 per cent of households in poverty but constitute only 15 per cent of all households.

Feminists have argued that women's poverty has to be seen in the context of women's marginal position in the labour market and the assumed dependency of women on men for financial support. This latter assumption is employed both in the income support system (despite minor changes in recent years) and in the ideology of the 'family wage'. The assumption is not only that there is a sexual division of labour such that men are the economic providers and women the carers, but the ideology also carries over and influences the economic position of women who do not live with a man, whether because single, divorced or widowed. Women's position in the labour market means that they are less likely than men to earn a living wage and are concentrated in low-paid jobs (see Chapter 9). It is this assumed dependence of women on men that has been used, historically, to justify the higher pay of men (the 'family wage') and is reflected in welfare state legislation. The disadvantages that women in the labour market experience also contribute to the poverty of lone-parent mothers. Even when a woman bringing up children on her own feels that she can manage to take on paid employment as well, she may find that there is no economic advantage in doing so. The kind of low-paid work she is likely to be able to find, coupled with the expenses of work and childminding fees, mean that most lone mothers will not be better off than when drawing benefit.

Finally, women are expected to be primarily responsible for children, the elderly and other dependents, although if they take on these roles they will be in danger of

falling into poverty. For many married women with children or other caring responsibilities, poverty will be the major problem.

Women's low pay, interrupted labour-market participation and tendency to take
on part-time employment for a period of time also affects their entitlement to income
maintenance when they are not economically active. Women are assumed to be
dependent on the men with whom they live, whether married or not, and it is assumed
that these men will make provision for income maintenance for themselves and their
wives in old age. This assumption has been reflected in legislation, and while there have
been some changes in social security legislation in recent years this has not markedly
changed the situation. Under social security regulations current in the UK at the time
of writing, a woman whose male friend stays more than three nights per week is
deemed to be supported by him, and her benefit is cut. The case for this is particularly
strong if she also does his washing or cooks him meals. It is clear that in social security
regulations economic support should be provided in return for sexual and domestic
services. While the 'cohabitation rule', as it is known, can also be applied to female
visitors of men, in practice this is rare.

Women who are caring for children receive no income maintenance, although
those caring for an adult dependent are entitled to a care allowance. However, this
does not compensate for loss of wages, being paid in any case at a lower rate than
contributory benefits such as unemployment or sick pay. Women who become unemployed are entitled to unemployment pay only if they have made sufficient
contributions and can fulfil the criteria for registering as unemployed (i.e. they are
available for work). Women may not be entitled to unemployment pay because they
have not been working for long enough or because they were working too few hours
to pay contributions. They may not be able to register because they cannot demonstrate satisfactorily their availability for full-time work (because they have young
children) or because they will not state that they are prepared to travel anywhere
in the country. Similarly, many married women are not entitled to claim contributory
invalidity benefits, and the 'housework test' of the non-contributory benefit is extremely
difficult to satisfy. Income support (the replacement for supplementary benefit) is
paid to a household, and the principle of assessment is household need. Feminists
have also pointed out that household income is often not equally shared and that
women can be in poverty even within a relatively affluent household if benefits and
wages all go to the man (Graham, 1984).

Feminists have therefore concluded that women's poverty can be understood
only in the context of gender inequalities that persist throughout the life course.
Ideologies of women's 'natural' abilities and 'natural' roles structure women's opportunities to take on paid work and the type of jobs that are offered to them. The realities
of women's lives, structured by these ideologies and state policies, also limit their
opportunities to take on employment and the range and types of employment they can
take on. Furthermore, the assumption that men support their wives means that much
female poverty is hidden. Women are expected to manage on the money, to be wise
spenders and to make the money stretch. They are also likely to be the ones to have
to refuse their children the treats, clothes, outings and activities that many children
take for granted and to have continually to disappoint their children. Women also
disproportionately have to suffer the stress, the lack of opportunities for fulfilment and

the feelings of insecurity that go with being poor. Also, women's health as well as their general well-being suffers as a result of being poor, especially if they lack an adequate diet because they put the needs of other family members before their own.

Conclusions

Thus the idea of the public and private and the exclusion of women from the public sphere have been created by political processes – government legislation and state policies. Familial ideologies that place women in the domestic sphere as wives and mothers are reinforced both by legislation and by the speeches and manifestos of political parties. In contemporary societies and historically, women have (collectively and individually) resisted these in a number of ways, however, including the first and second wave feminist movements (in the West), as well as taking part in a variety of pressure group campaigns, and modes of political activism and resistance movements.

SUMMARY

1 Women have been stereotyped in conventional accounts of political behaviour as being uninterested in politics, politically conservative and influenced by their husbands. All these stereotypes have been shown not to hold.
2 Conventional politics reflects male concerns and has effectively excluded women. Hence women are under-represented in public political life.
3 The welfare state and welfare policies have constructed and reinforced women's traditional position as wives and mothers.
4 Feminists have struggled over issues affecting women – specifically their rights to property and custody of their children in the nineteenth century, and their rights to abortion, equal pay and nursery provision in the twentieth century. Furthermore, feminists have redefined the notion of politics around personal struggle as well as public campaign.

FURTHER READING

Colgan, F. and Ledwith, S. (2003) *Negotiating Gender Democracy: New Trade Union Agendas.* London: Palgrave. Issues of gender are at the heart of this study of trade union politics, which considers themes such as race, ethnicity and representation, leadership, social movement activities and disability politics – neglected themes in much malestream research on trade unions.

Nash, K. (1999) *Contemporary Political Sociology: Globalization, Politics and Power.* Oxford: Blackwell. This book thoroughly reviews recent work in political sociology, taking account of feminist criticisms and contributions. It also considers themes such as globalisation, new social movements and citizenship, particularly in the light of postmodern debates within sociology.

Roseneil, S. (1995) *Disarming Patriarchy: Feminism and Political Action at Greenham.* Buckingham: Open University Press. This book is an engaging account of women's political activism at Greenham Common, and of women's contribution to campaigns for disarmament outside of malestream political institutions.

Waylen, G. (1996) *Gender in Third World Politics.* Buckingham: Open University Press. This book develops a feminist analysis of third world politics, and focuses particularly on the relationship between gender and development. It examines organised politics and political institutions, as well as 'grassroots' social movements, focusing particularly on women's organisations.

CHAPTER TWELVE

Mass media and popular culture

Culture is a central concept in sociological analysis, providing an important link between the individual and society. It has been a key concern of feminist sociology. As Michele Barrett pointed out, 'cultural politics are crucially important to feminism because they involve struggles over meaning' (1982, p. 37). Although the cultures found in all parts of the world and even within the same societies and social settings differ in many ways, what sociologists think of as 'cultures' seem, as Macionis and Plummer (2002, pp. 100–107) outline, to be built on five major components. These are:

1 *symbols* (anything that carries a particular meaning recognised by people who share the same culture);
2 *language* (a system of symbols that allows members of a society to communicate with one another);
3 *values* (the beliefs that people have about what is good and bad);
4 *norms* (social rules and expectations which guide behaviour); and
5 *material culture* (the tangible objects that sociologists term *artefacts*).

In this chapter we focus on feminist and sociological debates about the role of culture in shaping gender relations and, particularly, in reproducing gender inequalities. If we accept, as most feminist sociologists argue, that gender is socially constructed, that is, a learned and negotiated aspect of our identity, then we need to give consideration to where gender comes from, to how we acquire it and to why it takes the various forms that it does. Important, in this respect, is to consider the role of culture and particularly the mass media as an agent of gender socialisation throughout our lives.

The relationship between gender and media culture has been the subject of considerable debate for feminists. Feminists continue to be divided for instance over the extent to which pornographic representations of women are linked to sexual violence (see Chapter 8). Broadly speaking, feminist perspectives on gender, the mass media and popular culture can be divided into two distinct approaches. Whilst most would agree that the media is a powerful source of identity, some feminists have argued that the media actually dictates gender identity to us allowing women to perform or identify with only a relatively narrow range of roles. Those feminists who adopt this approach tend to emphasise what has been termed the 'symbolic annihilation of women' (Tuchman, 1981). Marshment (1993), who adopts this perspective, argues that representation is a highly political issue and that the apparent 'naturalness' of media representations of men and women is evidence of the power of patriarchal ideology. As she puts it,

> From primary school reading schemes to Hollywood films, from advertising to opera, from game shows to art galleries, women are depicted in ways that define what it means to be a woman in this society: what women are like (naturally), what they ought to be like, what they are capable of, and incapable of, what roles they play in society, and how they differ from men.
>
> (Marshment, 1993, p. 124)

In her book *The Beauty Myth*, Naomi Wolf (1990) has similarly argued that capitalism, patriarchy and compulsory heterosexuality interact to produce a crude ideology manifest in representations such as the film *Pretty Woman*, characterised by the message 'be pretty, get a man, be complete, escape poverty and misery'. What she calls the 'beauty myth' (drawing on Betty Friedan's earlier work on the 'feminine mystique' – the idea that women can find self-satisfaction in housework, see Chapter 2) is a media ideology that perpetuates the idea that if women buy enough products they will be able to conform to patriarchal ideals of beauty and sexual attractiveness. Wolf goes on to argue that the beauty myth defines women visually in two ways. First, it defines an ideal 'look' for women. Although this varies culturally and historically, it usually involves – in Western societies at least – being tall, slim and white. So women are defined or measured against an ideal standard of beauty. Second, the beauty myth emphasises that femininity itself is an aesthetic phenomena – in other words, to be feminine is defined largely in terms of looking feminine. This means that both men and women learn to think of femininity primarily as a visual identity. Wolf argues that this is evidenced in the enormity of the beauty and cosmetics industries, in women's magazines, in film and music videos, in sport and leisure, and also in gender disparities in eating disorders. She likens the impact of the beauty myth on women's lives to the Iron Maiden, a sarcophagus-like medieval instrument of torture that enclosed women in a spiked interior while the exterior featured beautifully painted women's (often smiling) faces. Wolf emphasises that as women have made political and economic gains, images of female beauty have become more rigid and have reinforced patriarchal ideology, disguising it (like the Iron Maiden) as something women enjoy. Magazines, she argues, now concentrate on 'beauty work' rather than housework. As she puts it,

> The more legal and material hindrances women have broken through, the more strictly and heavily and cruelly images of female beauty have come to weigh upon us. . . . As women released themselves from the feminine mystique of domesticity, the beauty myth took over its lost ground, expanding as it wanted to carry on its work of social control.
>
> (Wolf, 1990, p. 10)

Wolf's perspective echoes earlier work on media culture by feminists such as Laura Mulvey (1975), in her essay 'Visual Pleasure and Narrative Cinema'. Writing in the 1970s, the height of the soft-focus close-up, Mulvey proposes that in classic Hollywood cinema women are constructed as passive objects to be looked at by men for voyeuristic pleasure. She argues that the 'male gaze' operates in three ways, involving:

1   the gaze of the *camera* on the female (often sexualised) body, which is often from the male point of view;
2   male *characters* and identities, that gaze upon female bodies in the narrative; and
3   male *spectators* who gaze at the female bodies on the screen.

However, Mulvey (1981) herself has since expressed some reservations about the overly deterministic nature of this position, and it has been criticised more generally for ignoring both how women may subvert or negotiate the male gaze, and how popular culture offers opportunities for women to gaze (at both men and women) as well. Moreover, such a deterministic approach has also been criticised for reducing all power relations to gender, and thus neglecting other aspects of power which affect patriarchal relations, such as class, race, disability and sexuality, and which other feminists have sought to integrate into their frameworks of analysis.

Other feminists have adopted a different perspective emphasising instead of the power of media culture the pleasures women derive from the escapism and iden-tification it offers. Instead of concurring with Mulvey's 'active/looking/masculine' and 'passive/looked at/feminine' formula, such approaches have focused on women as active readers and consumers of media culture. Yet, much of this work has begun with the question: 'Why do out of date myths of femininity still continue to exert a magnetic pull over us, and why is it easier to criticize those media that target us than to explain their fascination?' (Macdonald, 1995, p. 11).

Feminists emphasising the pleasures women derive from various media cultural forms – magazines and soap operas, for instance – have tended to focus not on the media as dictating gender identity to us, but instead have highlighted its role in negotiating a range of available identities. Writers such as Ros Coward, Jackie Stacey and Angela McRobbie have all emphasised that media culture provides women with a range of options from which to choose. In particular, their work has emphasised that we don't have to accept what the media offers us at face value but rather, can consume media representations selectively, ironically and cynically. In her book *Star Gazing* for instance, Jackie Stacey (1994) emphasises that the mass media is a site of negotiated meanings, of resistances, and of challenges to patriarchal ideologies. She argues that the media provides: escapism, identification and opportunities for consumption, which can be empowering as well as exploitative. In doing so, she rejects the universalism and textual determinism of much feminist work on mass culture. Her account empha-sises that images of Hollywood stars can be role models, and that the relationship between media representations and the lived realities of gender is more complex than simply the passive reception of stereotypes.

At the heart of the distinction between these two approaches is a debate over the extent to which many of the media forms in which gender is represented are ways simply of maintaining patriarchal ideology. This argument seems to write off millions of women (and men) who take pleasure in reading women's magazines, or in watching soap operas, as cultural dupes who collude in their own oppression. Both feminist and non-feminist women take pleasure in fashion, romance, horoscopes, soap operas, cooking programmes, magazines, and so on. An alternative position adopted by feminists such as Modleski (1982) has argued that we should not condemn these cultural forms themselves, or the men and women who engage with them (thereby dismissing their genuine pleasure), but the conditions that have made them both possible and necessary (e.g. watching soap operas or reading magazines as an 'escape'), and as the only 'choice' within a relatively narrow range of leisure options for women (see Chapter 9). As she puts it, the contradictions in women's lives are more responsible for the existence of mass cultural forms that appeal to women than the forms are for the contradictions (p. 57).

Black feminists such as bell hooks (1992) have been particularly critical of the ways in which white, ethnocentric media have reproduced racist stereotypes originating in slavery and in colonial societies. In particular, hooks is critical of white women media 'stars' like Madonna for their 'appropriation of Black culture as yet another sign of their radical chic' (p. 157). She goes on, 'fascinated yet envious of black style, Madonna appropriates black culture in ways that mock and undermine, making her presentation one that upstages' (p. 161). Black and Asian feminists have also drawn attention to the narrow ways in which racialised women are represented, even in feminist art and cultural criticism. A.S. Larkin (1988), for instance, highlights the issue of ethnocentrism in both verbal and visual forms of culture, and in anthropology (the scientific study of culture):

In a feminist art project dealing with heroines at the Women's Building in Los Angeles, a white woman chose the prehistoric 'Lucy' as her heroine. 'Lucy' is a tiny lady three feet tall, sixty pounds light and 3.5 million years old. Lucy is the oldest, most complete skeleton of any erect-walking human ancestor ever found. I pose the following questions: Why is it that the remains of a prehistoric Ethiopian woman are called 'Lucy'? Did it ever occur to the white world that Lucy is not an African name? The Ethiopians did not call her Lucy. . . .

The Public Broadcasting System screened a documentary on the discovery of 'Lucy'. The audience was introduced to the anthropologists at the site in Africa. The programme included an animated segment which brought the ancient people to life. They were not Black people; the artist had whitened them. They did not look like the Ethiopians at the site; they looked like the white anthropologist.

As a Black woman film-maker I would have featured visuals of contemporary Ethiopian women as part of the documentary. I would have let Ethiopian men and women talk about 'Lucy'. Most importantly, I would not have called her, as did the documentary, by the name the Western anthropologist, Donald Johnson, gave her from a pop song out of his culture: 'Lucy in the Sky with Diamonds' by the Beatles. I would have mentioned this, but I would have called her what her Ethiopian children call her: 'Wonderful'.

(Larkin, 1988, pp. 167–168)

Many of these debates over the role and impact of media culture, and over the contested ways in which culture is constructed and represented, are also shaped by different definitions of culture. Indeed, the meaning of culture and the way in which it is used in academic studies has changed considerably over time.

'Culture': a brief history of the concept

As Raymond Williams (1968) noted, culture is one of the most difficult words in the English language to define. Used to refer to a range of different yet related phenomena, its meaning has changed considerably over time. In Western societies, in the fifteenth century, culture was used as a verb to refer to the tending of crops and animals (in the process of cultivation), as it is still used in agriculture today. It was also used as a noun to refer to an entity which is natural in origin yet which has been grown or developed artificially. By the sixteenth century, its use had been expanded to refer to human life and the term culture tended to be used to describe the highest levels of civilisation. By the mid-eighteenth century, culture came to be associated with social class, in so far as what was thought to be 'cultured' was associated with the activities and tastes of a cultivated social elite – those who had an appreciation for great litera-ture, classical music or fine art, for instance. This is what sociologists now call 'high culture' – the highest expressions of human civilisation and artistic sensibility. As Macionis and Plummer (2002, p. 109) note, the term 'high' culture is a shorthand one used to refer to 'cultural patterns that distinguish a society's elite'. In his work on the relationship between high culture and the ways in which certain privileged social groups maintain their 'distinction' from others, French sociologist Pierre Bourdieu (1984) used the term 'cultural capital' to describe not the material wealth (although the two are of course related), but the power and status accorded to particular social groups because of their educational credentials, cultural awareness and aesthetic sensibilities. Hence, cultural capital reproduces class and other distinctions by setting apart those who are thought to be more 'cultured' than others (and who are therefore able to perpetuate the idea that their tastes and lifestyles are superior).

As Macionis and Plummer (2002, p. 109) also point out, the phrase 'high culture' is thought to derive from the more everyday term 'highbrow'. Influenced by phrenology (the idea – popular in the nineteenth century – that personality types could be discerned by the shape of a person's skull), it originally referred to the view that those with 'highbrows' had more refined personalities and tastes than 'lowbrows'.

In the eighteenth century, the term culture also came to be used to refer to a 'way of life' and the values, attitudes, needs and expectations binding people together as a community (in the form of national or regional cultures, for instance). This is how cultural anthropologists and historians such as Williams (1968) tend to define culture, and is what sociologists refer to as 'lived' or 'popular culture' (literally, the culture of the people). This understanding of culture became the central concern of emerging academic disciplines such as anthropology and sociology.

By the beginning of the twentieth century, culture began to be used to describe the symbolic expression of such characteristics – the ways in which they came to be represented in language, printed texts, sound, visual images, and so on. These are what we now tend to refer to as cultural forms, or material culture. Some of these cul-tural forms are what we would call cultural artefacts – material manifestations or signifiers of culture. Many sociologists have argued that because in contemporary societies these cultural forms are primarily mass-produced and disseminated to wide, undifferentiated audiences, they are best described as 'mass culture'. Most of these are produced, marketed and distributed by global corporations that have been described as the 'culture industries' (Adorno, 1991) and produce most of what we would call mass media – cultural forms that are produced and consumed on a mass, undifferentiated scale. Some sociologists have argued that because most of the cultural forms that we encounter in our everyday lives are produced or at least strongly influenced by the mass media, and that because most of our social interactions are so highly mediated, that the distinction between society and the mass media is increasingly difficult to discern, Western societies, at least, are best understood as 'media cultures'. Douglas Kellner (1995) for instance argues that we live in a media culture to the extent that the only culture deemed to exist is that produced and disseminated by the mass media:

> A media culture has emerged in which images, sounds and spectacles help produce the fabric of everyday life, dominating leisure time, shaping political views and social behaviour and providing the materials out of which people forge their very identities.
>
> (Kellner, 1995, p. 1)

Other sociologists and cultural theorists such as Dominic Strinati (1995) have similarly argued that the growth of mass culture means that there is less room for any culture which cannot make money, which cannot be mass produced for a mass market, like art and folk culture. This view has been refuted by (more optimistic) commentators such as John Fiske (1989) who, while accepting the argument that the mass media is increasingly powerful, argues that popular culture does still exist as an expression of people's everyday lives and experiences and, as such, holds the potential for resistance to the massive influence of the media.

The sociology of culture and the emergence of cultural studies

What we now term 'cultural studies' emerged as an academic discipline in Britain during the 1950s, inspired largely by the literary criticism of F.R. Leavis and the writings of Matthew Arnold. Both writers believed that high culture (especially in the form of literature) had a civilising effect on people that was threatened by the rise of mass culture. Arnold summed up this view when he argued that culture is 'the best that has been thought and said'. His perception is of culture as expressing the highest values of human sensibility. This distinction between high culture and mass culture informed education in the UK in the 1950s and 1960s, when it was deemed that only classic literature should be taught in schools as a means of improving and civilising working people and their children.

An alternative way of conceptualising culture could be found in the work of Richard Hoggart (1957) whose book *The Uses of Literacy* developed a more radical perspective on culture. Hoggart argued that while high culture was important and should be preserved as such, of equal significance were the cultural practices and traditions of working-class communities. Both types of culture – high culture and popular or folk culture – he argued, should be protected from the rise of commercially driven, mass-produced culture which was merely concerned with maximum profit and not education or cultural expression.

Hoggart thus made a sociologically important distinction between high culture, popular culture and mass culture. Following Hoggart, most sociologists define popular culture as the values and practices that emerge from the everyday lived experiences of ordinary people. It is not homogenous, but is based on diverse local and regional traditions, and ways of life. Mass culture, on the other hand, is considered to represent values and ideas which are imposed on people through various primarily commercial avenues (public sector broadcasting is perhaps the most obvious exception to this latter point), most notably the mass media. Clearly, there is a political (critical) dimension to this distinction. For Hoggart, high culture is elitist because it imposes middle-class values and tastes onto other groups. Popular or folk culture is something that must be preserved in the face of mass-produced culture which serves only the interests of capital accumulation, and is essentially alien to those people who consume it en masse.

As these various definitions of culture indicate, the study of culture and the mass media draws on a range of theoretical perspectives and traditions. These include Marxism, linguistics, structuralism, postmodernism and feminism. What each of these otherwise diverse ways of thinking about culture share in common is the view that to understand culture in contemporary societies, we must consider its production, transmission, dissemination and reception. In each of these stages, the mass media plays an increasingly important role, but so too do other forms of communication technology such as the internet, for instance, which many people use to bypass or undermine the accumulation imperatives of global media corporations. Websites that facilitate the exchange of music files are one notable example of this. Groups such as Adbusters have also used the internet to challenge the hegemonic power of global branding and advertising.

Broadly speaking, the term mass media refers to technologies of communication that are able to broadcast to a mass audience. Mass media include newspapers (tabloids and broadsheets), radio, magazines, books, websites, and so on. The information transmitted can be designed to induce sales, to inform or to entertain (although it is often hard to distinguish between these aims). Increasingly, in magazines for instance, so-called 'advertorials' provide guidance and advice – on skincare, for example, at the same time as trying to sell us a particular product. This social significance of the mass media is indicated by the way in which the use of the term has changed. It is technically a plural term ('media' implying a range of communication forms and mechanisms), but now tends to be used in the singular (*the* mass media) denoting its emergence as a relatively homogenous social institution.

What is perhaps of most sociological interest, however, is the term 'mass', which refers to the ability of these various communication technologies to reach a mass audience. This capacity has contributed significantly to the idea that the world has 'shrunk'. Perhaps one of the most obvious examples of this is that words such as 'Coca-Cola' and 'McDonald's' have not only become global brands but also universally recognised forms of communication understood in every language throughout the world. This suggests that the mass media has resulted in a process of cultural homogenisation, and has led some commentators to argue that a process of McDonalization has occurred in recent decades. The 'McDonaldization thesis', as it has come to be known, asserts that local, popular cultures have begun to be swamped by a McDonaldized, global, mass culture (Ritzer, 1996).

Cultural studies then, has been concerned with the history of culture and its social significance. The distinction in cultural studies between high culture, popular culture and mass culture, the role of the mass media and the emergence of what has been termed 'media culture' have all been the focus of key debates in cultural studies. These debates have been based largely on the distinction between mass culture and popular culture, with some sociologists and cultural theorists arguing that popular culture has become obsolete or excluded from the age of the mass media, while others have argued that there is still room and, indeed, critical potential for a range of cultural forms and expressions.

Cultural studies as ideology studies

The idea that popular culture has been taken over by media culture which generates and transmits values and beliefs rather than reflects cultural practices and traditions of everyday life draws heavily on a Marxist perspective. This approach emphasises that society (including the culture industries that produce the mass media) is run in the interests of a minority social class who own most of society's wealth and so exercise power over society as a whole. This idea, while challenged by other perspectives, remains perhaps the most influential in cultural studies.

As noted in Chapter 1, there are two main ways in which the term ideology is used in the social sciences. A standard, dictionary definition describes ideology as a body of ideas and beliefs used as the basis for social or political action. The term is also used to refer to the scientific study of those ideas. In the common-sense definition, the emphasis is largely on ideology as *ideas*. A more radical, Marxist-derived definition is of ideology as the presentation of the interests of a particular group or individual as those of the whole of society (e.g. patriarchal ideology). This definition assumes asymmetrical power relations and a system of social stratification (see Chapter 3). This is the version of ideology that we most commonly encounter in the social sciences, and particularly in sociology and cultural studies. Here the focus is on the *interests* served by particular ideas, rather than simply the ideas themselves.

A Marxist theory of ideology

For Marx, those who own and control the means of material production (the ruling class) also own and control the production and dissemination of ideas. Dominant ideas, for Marx, help to maintain the economic system (the capitalist mode of production). Ideology represents a distorted form of knowledge. It is not simply lies, but refers to those ideas generated to conceal what Marx believed were contradictions in the way social and economic life was organised within capitalism. Ideology helped to maintain the dominant position of those who owned and controlled the means of production. As we have suggested, this usually takes the form of portraying the interests of this

325

particular group as those of society as a whole. This is summed up in Marx's assertion: 'The ideas of the ruling class are, in every epoch, the ruling ideas: the class which is the ruling material force of society, is at the same time its ruling intellectual force.' When Marx was writing, principles of hard work, loyalty, honesty and punctuality were propagated as universal human values, often backed – as Weber emphasised – by religious ideology, to ensure that working people were kept in their place.

Gramsci and hegemony

A Marxist theory of ideology is based on the idea that ordinary people believe what they are told by their superiors. This tends to result in a very monolithic view of power, one that denies the ability of people to 'see through' ideology. This problem was addressed in the work of Italian Marxist Antonio Gramsci, writing in the 1920s and 1930s. Gramsci focused on the role of the individual in maintaining social inequality. He argued that ideology only works if it resonates in some way with people's everyday lived experiences. In this way, it does not present what appears to be a false vision of the world, but one that seeks to explain life with a particular slant.

Gramsci maintained that ideology is effective because it is not simply imposed but is negotiated. Dominant groups maintain their powerful position by achieving moral and intellectual leadership, not simply by imposing their will on others by force. Adopting Gramsci's perspective, it could be argued that the mass media has become a prime site on which such 'negotiations' take place. This intellectual and moral leadership, achieved through dominant ideas, is what Gramsci termed 'hegemony'. This describes a type of power that is achieved and maintained through dominant ideas engendering negotiation and consent, rather than by force.

Structuralism and ideology

While Gramsci was concerned with the role of the individual in maintaining social inequality, the work of the French philosopher Louis Althusser in the 1950s and 1960s, while influenced by Gramsci, essentially developed Marx's theory of ideology in precisely the opposite direction. Althusser focused largely on the role of social structures in maintaining ideology and hence, social inequality. Ideology is transmitted, Althusser argued, through what he termed ideological state apparatuses (ISAs).

Althusser makes a distinction between two dimensions of the capitalist state: repressive state apparatuses (RSAs) which include the police, government, the armed forces, and so on (those that rely on the use of force to maintain control) and ideological state apparatuses (ISAs). The latter include religion, education, the family and the mass media; those institutions that we would identify as agents of socialisation, and which rely on the use of ideas to persuade and coerce rather than force compliance. ISAs are those institutions that are deemed to equip us with the kind of consciousness we need to function within the relations of production as these are organised within capitalism. Education, for example, teaches us to be punctual and compliant, advertising teaches us that we should work hard to achieve more and that we should be judged by our material worth, and so on.

Ideology has been understood in various ways in the social sciences, then, and in cultural studies has tended to be conceptualised according to a Marxist theory of ideology, particularly as this has been developed in Gramsci's concept of hegemony and in Althusser's concern with ideological state apparatuses. The function of ideology from a Marxist perspective is to serve the interests of the powerful by mystifying their power. In other words, by making their relatively powerful position and their unequal share of society's wealth seem natural or immutable, and by inducing us to desire (at least some aspects of) the status quo, even though it disempowers most people. As the basis for a critical approach to the sociology of culture, what Marxist perspectives emphasise is the importance of being aware that media images may not be neutral or disinterested but rather, serve particular interests and communicate particular messages. Sociologists have been particularly concerned to devise ways of uncovering these often hidden or 'coded' meanings and messages.

Studying media culture

There are two main methods that sociologists have used to analyse media and cultural representations, namely content analysis and semiotics. While this sounds relatively straightforward, the choice of research methods in sociology is often complex (see Chapter 13). Rather than delving too deeply into philosophical debates on method-ology, which we consider in more detail in Chapter 13, our focus here is specifically on how sociologists have devised ways of studying cultural forms.

Content analysis

One of the most popular methods of analysing media texts – content analysis – is a largely quantitative method of data collection. This means that content analyses of media culture are concerned primarily with the collection of data that can be subject to statistical analysis. Content analysis is a research technique that involves counting the number of times an item (an image or word, for instance) appears in a particular text. Its main strength is its ability to produce quantitative data that is often relatively easy to analyse, although large-scale or longitudinal content analyses often involve very complex systems of data collection and analysis. Content analysis proceeds from the assumption that there is a relationship between the frequency with which a certain item (e.g. a woman washing up) appears in a media text (e.g. a television soap opera) and the impact it has on society more generally, through its audience.

Content analysis therefore involves a concern with the frequency with which certain items (events, words, images, relationships) appear in a given media text, with the significance or prominence of these items within the text, and with how many times the item is expressed in conjunction with positive or negative connotations (e.g. how many times a Black man is shown as the 'bad guy' and a white person as the 'hero' in a film). Content analysis is concerned not simply with the content of media texts, but also with their context. It was employed in a number of relatively early studies of media representations, particularly of representations of gender in magazines, romantic fiction and in advertising.

Its strengths are that it provides a useful means of substantiating general observations, it generates easily quantifiable data, and is relatively cheap and easy to undertake. However, sociological studies that rely solely on content analysis have been criticised because they only recognise the obvious or immediate meanings (and hence tend to ignore the symbolic nature of much media imagery, particularly in advertising for instance). Content analysis, like many other sociological research methods, is also highly subjective in so far as it is dependent upon the researcher's interpretation of what is important and what is not. Most crucially, content analysis neglects wider structures of economic, political and cultural power, and the absence of explanatory theories which can account for say, sex-role stereotyping, has also been identified as a major weakness (Strinati, 1995). While content analysis has been a useful method of analysing media representations (it is still one of the most popular methods in sociology) it has some notable limitations, therefore. A more in-depth, analytical approach – semiotics – is also a popular method of studying media culture, and one that has also been used extensively by feminists.

Semiotics

Semiotics or semiology is the study of signs. These include: 'images, gestures, musical sounds, objects and the complex associations of all these, which form the content of ritual, convention or public entertainment' (Barthes, 1967, p. 9). Semiologists argue that signs have no intrinsic or fixed meanings. Instead, their meaning is arbitrary and is derived from the way they relate to other words and signs; in other words, to their cultural reference points. Both semiology (and the structuralism from which it derives) have had an important influence on the study of mass media and popular culture.

Semiotics derives from the work of the late nineteenth and early twentieth-century Swiss linguist Ferdinand de Saussure. In his *Course in General Linguistics* (1974; originally published in English in 1959), he made a crucial distinction between two components of a sign – the signifier and the signified. According to Saussure, any linguistic sign such as a word or phrase can be broken down into these two elements of which it is composed. In the linguistic sign, the signifier is the 'sound image' (the word as it is actually written down or said), and the signified is the concept – the object or idea which is being referred to. Saussure maintained that because the meanings of particular linguistic signs are not externally determined but derive from their place in the overall structure of language (what he calls *langue*), it follows that the relationship between the signifier and the signified is a purely arbitrary one. This is because there is no intrinsic, natural or essential reason why a particular concept should be linked with one sound or written image rather than another. What we think of as a 'table' for instance (the signified or idea of a table) could just as easily be signified by the word (or signifier) 'dog' for instance, as long as it became part of the 'langue' or structure of language within which the sign operates. Hence, signs cease to be arbitrary and assume relatively stable meanings once they are located within the general structure of language.

Saussure's work emphasised that language can be studied as a semiological system of signs which express ideas. This approach has come to be known as 'structural linguistics' and, as Strinati (1995) notes, laid the foundations for more recent attempts to extend the analytical potential of structuralism and semiology to other systems of meaning, such as media and popular culture.

Applied to the mass media and popular culture, semiotics is concerned with analysing the content of a media form or text as a system of signs. This often involves mapping out the broader cultural meanings – or connotations – of particular signs in relation to each other, in order to discern underlying patterns of meaning not just within language (as in structural linguistics) but in culture more generally. The French social anthropologist Lévi-Strauss is well known for introducing the concepts and methods of structuralism into the sociological study of culture, and for using semiology to study the myths circulating in pre-industrial societies.

As Strinati (1995) also notes, however, the semiological study of popular culture probably owes most to Roland Barthes, and in particular his book *Mythologies* (originally published in 1957). Here Barthes develops the idea that the function of a myth is 'to transform history into nature' (1973, p. 140). 'Myth' for Barthes is a system of communication, or a mode of signification, that is grounded in social relations. Hence, while retaining the analytical value of the distinctions made by structural linguistics, Barthes suggests that for studying myths it is more appropriate to think of the signifier as a *cultural form*, the signified as a *concept*, and the sign as a system of *cultural signification*. Using these concepts, Barthes argues that myth works through the particular relationships between form, concept and signification. Some signs (their forms and concepts) are iconic (that is, their meanings are relatively universal), whereas others are culturally specific and are dependent upon a range of cultural connotations for their cultural associations to be conveyed, he argued.

Despite its significance as a method of cultural analysis – Judith Williamson's *Decoding Advertisements* (1978) is a notable example of a semiotic approach to media studies – one of the main problems associated with semiological analysis is that there is no way of 'objectively' discerning the meanings in a particular text. Semiology is always likely to give rise to arbitrary opinions. As Strinati (1995) notes, one of the biggest problems is that of 'empirical validation' – 'how do we discriminate between these interpretations?' (p. 123).

One response to this criticism has been to suggest that texts contain a number of different messages; they are polysemic. Semiology from this perspective is not intended to be scientific in claiming to uncover *the* hidden meaning but rather to tease out a range of otherwise hidden ways of interpreting a particular text. However, as Strinati (1995) has also pointed out, this might be seen to undermine the credibility of semiology as a method. In his view, scientific criteria still need to be established in order to determine the limits which can be set on meanings and interpretations.

Sociological perspectives on media culture

Sociologists have developed various concepts and methods for considering the mass media and popular culture. They have drawn attention, for instance, to the 'political economy' of the mass media, emphasising how the ownership and control of the major means of communication have come to be concentrated in the hands of a few global corporations. Sociologists have argued that these powerful economic interests work to consistently exclude those groups lacking economic or cultural power (Murdock and Golding, 1977). This is just one view however; sociologists have devised a range of theoretical perspectives that attempt to make sense of the relationship between the various aspects of culture considered above, namely high culture, popular or folk culture, and media culture, as well as the impact of contemporary media culture on social relations and identities. The term 'contemporary' is slightly misleading in this respect because one of the most influential approaches is based on material written between the 1930s and the 1960s. Nevertheless, much of this work, many sociologists and cultural theorists have argued, remains deeply influential and highly relevant to a sociological analysis of media culture.

The Frankfurt School and the critique of mass culture

What has come to be known as the Frankfurt School describes a school of thought associated with the work of a group of intellectuals and scholars who were all members of, or associated with, the Institute for Social Research at the University of Frankfurt, which was set up in 1923. Known collectively as the Frankfurt School, key members were Max Horkheimer, Herbert Marcuse, Theodor Adorno, Walter Benjamin and Leo Lowenthal. It is important to stress that not all of the individuals associated with this group agreed with each other. Indeed, many of their most important insights grew out of their disagreements. Nevertheless, they shared a number of concerns and came from a common intellectual heritage. They were all essentially concerned with why Marx's revolutionary predictions had never come to fruition; with why, despite the continual instability of capitalism as an economic system, and the misery it caused to millions of people, a Marxist revolution had never come about. Instead, Europe had witnessed the rise of a totalitarian regime in Stalinist Russia, and of Nazism in Germany and Fascism in Italy. As a group of Marxist, Jewish intellectuals, living in Germany in the 1920s and 1930s, they were particularly concerned to understand why fascism had succeeded where socialism seemed to have failed. In particular they were concerned to understand the role of culture, and particularly the rapidly expanding mass media, in keeping the masses docile and compliant.

Perhaps the most important analysis of culture produced by the Frankfurt School was written by two of its leading members, Adorno and Horkheimer, in an essay entitled 'The Culture Industry' (originally published in 1944). In this essay, they argued that popular culture is in fact produced by industrial capitalism in order to maintain the repressive social relations upon which it is dependent. Comprised of cinema, publishers, advertising agencies, record companies, and the like, what they termed the 'culture industry' had one primary function according to Adorno and Horkheimer: mass deception. As such, the culture industry, they argued, turns people into passive, consuming vessels incapable of discriminating between what they really need and what they are told they want (and should have) – namely standardised, homogenised, mass-produced cultural products that people are led to believe are original and individual.

Adorno and Horkheimer were particularly critical of the way in which the culture industry produces and promotes goods and services that purport to promote individuality, novelty and cultural expression. In their view, this is an illusion and the products of the culture industry are actually standardised, predictable and highly regulated. They stifle rather than encourage creativity. This ensures that their consumption remains stable and unquestioned.

This view is particularly evident in Adorno's work on popular jazz music of the 1930s and 1940s which, he argued, was incredibly standardised and formulaic (much like the boy/girl band or the Pop Idol/Popstars genre today, pieces of music were the same in their core structure but different enough at a superficial level to maintain the idea that each one was novel and original). Adorno argued that, in this sense, jazz could be distinguished from classical music, which had resisted incorporation into mass culture.

Yet the Frankfurt School's position was not simply one of cultural elitism (although they have been accused of this) – their critique was a fundamentally political one. For Adorno, the basic problem with the products of the culture industry was that they promoted passivity and conformity. With reference to jazz and popular music, Adorno referred to this as 'regressive listening', producing a state in which the listener remains almost childlike and unable to face up to anything that challenges his or her sense of order and predictability. As Adorno (1991, p. 9) said of the culture industry, 'by craftily sanctioning the demand for rubbish it inaugurates total harmony'.

Herbert Marcuse also explored the role of media culture in capitalist societies in his book *One Dimensional Man* (1986; originally published in 1964). Marcuse agreed with Adorno that the culture industry was little more than a tool of mass repression, giving the illusion of free choice while at the same time closing down opportunities for genuinely free thought and action. Marcuse distinguished between what he termed 'true needs' and 'false needs'. True needs are those that are essential human needs such as autonomy, creativity and liberty. False needs are those defined as essential by the culture industry and refer largely to consumer goods such as cars, TVs, and so on – those that we sell our labour power to buy, in order to achieve what Marcuse saw as a false sense of fulfilment. False needs are thus defined as true needs by the culture industry, Marcuse argued. In another book, *Eros and Civilization* (1972 [1955]), he argued that even the most intimate aspects of our lives – sexual relations – have become commodified and commercialised. As we noted in Chapter 8, sex is used to sell a range of products from tyres to ice cream. Because of the expansion of mass culture, for Marcuse, society has become one-dimensional. Unlike Adorno, however, Marcuse did not see high culture as our 'salvation', but as increasingly commercialised as well. Rather, he hoped a revolutionary movement would develop amongst those who rejected material culture – most notably, students.

The ideas associated with the Frankfurt School have been subject to a number of criticisms by sociologists and cultural theorists. Dominic Strinati (1995) for instance argues that their analyses lack empirical evidence, that their work is grounded in a cultural elitism and is expressed in terms that are highly intellectually demanding. Also Marcuse's designation of 'true' and 'false' needs is problematic – who defines which are which? If a person needs cosmetic surgery to improve his or her psychological well-being is this a 'true' or a 'false' need? If a family need a washing machine to keep their children's clothes clean, is this 'true' or 'false'?

The work of the Frankfurt School has had a massive impact on sociological perspectives on culture, particularly in relation to debates about mass and popular culture, about the mass production and dissemination of culture, and its effects on the way we think and act. Their work effectively laid the foundation for a critical approach to mass culture within sociology, one that has been subsequently developed in a number of ways, one of which is George Ritzer's McDonaldization thesis.

The McDonaldization thesis

The origins of George Ritzer's McDonaldization thesis can be found in Weber's critique of rationalisation. Writing in the nineteenth century (an era of rapid modernisation), Weber argued that a process of rationalisation was a defining feature of modern societies. Rationalisation, in his work, refers to the increasing centrality of rational calculation and the pursuit of efficiency in all aspects of economic, social and cultural life. Rationalisation means that everything must be done in accordance with the most efficient and effective means possible. Efficiency and effectiveness become the overriding, instrumental concerns. This idea forms the basis of Ritzer's thesis.

Originally published in 1992, *The McDonaldization of Society* presents Ritzer's somewhat pessimistic vision of an increasingly disenchanted world; one in which the straitjacket of rules and regulations feared by Weber has become a reality. The victory of instrumental rationality is epitomised, for Ritzer, by the practices and procedures of the McDonald's fast food chain. Effectively, the contemporary version of what Weber terms rationalisation, Ritzer terms McDonaldization.

For Ritzer, McDonaldization is based on four key principles:

1 *efficiency* (food is prepared off site, there is minimum choice);
2 *calculability* (the exact time it should take to prepare and serve is specified);
3 *predictability* (no matter where you are in the world, a Happy Meal or a Big Mac should be the same);
4 *control* (non-human technologies dictate production and consumption rhythms).

The concept of McDonaldization is more than simply a metaphorical device, however. Ritzer argues that the instrumental logic that has made McDonald's such a profitable organisation can be identified in every dimension of contemporary capitalist societies, facilitated particularly through the continual introduction of what he terms 'new means of consumption'.

Ritzer argues that the continual emergence of new means of consumption is having a major impact on the ways in which people spend their leisure time and money. By new means of consumption, he means the technologically driven modes of standardised consumption including fast food restaurants, home shopping channels, online shopping websites, credit and store card spending, and so on. Related to this is the explosion of consumption as a means of entertainment. For instance, Disneyland and Disneyworld, while ostensibly amusement parks are, at the same time, giant shopping malls for Disney products. In this sense, Ritzer argues, McDonaldization represents a process that impacts upon every aspect of our lives, particularly in terms of the way in which we consume culture. In many ways, this perspective is similar to the approach taken by the Frankfurt School (whose work Ritzer draws on) in that it suggests that cultural products, such as music, films, books, package holidays, and so on, are available to us primarily in a sterile, standardised form (produced according to commercially successful formulae).

Why should we be concerned about McDonaldization, though, if it provides us with what we want? Following Weber, and also the work of the Frankfurt School, Ritzer's position on this is that the various dimensions of McDonaldization outlined above are fundamentally detrimental, in the long term, to human society. He argues that at the heart of what professes to be a process of rationalisation lies something essentially irrational – the denial of humanity's creativity, imagination and autonomy (what many would argue are the very qualities that make us 'human'). Human beings are effectively reduced to little more than cogs in huge machines that are essentially producing nothing of any real value to humanity, critics of mass culture argue. From this perspective, popular culture has become an obsolete term, because McDonaldization has swallowed up opportunities for us to devise our own cultural forms and practices so that everything is commercially produced, derived or driven.

The McDonaldization thesis, then, is a contemporary version of a much older dimension of sociological theory, derived largely from Weber's critique of rationalisation and, with regard to the critique of mass culture at least, developed in the Frankfurt School's work on the culture industry (itself grounded in a Marxist theory of ideology). To what extent we should take this dystopian vision seriously, of course, depends on our acceptance or otherwise of a number of propositions upon which Ritzer's thesis, and critical theories of mass culture more generally, rest.

Most fundamentally, such approaches tend to emphasise the idea that the media does something to us – it indoctrinates us with ideologically driven ideas and attitudes. Yet they focus primarily on the production of cultural texts, rather than their consumption and reception. In doing so, these largely structuralist approaches tend to underplay the role of agency – the ability of human beings as thinking, speaking and acting subjects to make sense of (and influence) their social environment. In contrast to the work of the Frankfurt School and to Ritzer's McDonaldization thesis, an emphasis on reception and consumption and on agency (on the way in which we make sense of, and respond to, media culture) has underpinned the work of two other important approaches to the study of mass media and popular culture, namely the Centre for Contemporary Cultural Studies (CCCS) at the University of Birmingham, and the Glasgow University Media Research Group's audience reception studies.

Both groups have drawn heavily on Gramsci's concept of hegemony outlined above, in their focus on the ways in which individuals and groups negotiate media representations and forms. In particular, they have emphasised not simply the significance of production, but also transmission, dissemination and reception in understanding media culture. They argue that we need to give more attention than the Frankfurt School did to the part we all play in keeping particular ideologies alive, but also in challenging and resisting them.

CCCS and counter-hegemony

To recap, Gramsci (writing in the 1920s and 1930s) argued that ideology is maintained because it is not simply imposed but is negotiated. Dominant groups maintain their powerful position by achieving moral and intellectual leadership – by dominating through ideas, rather than force. The term derives from the Italian *egemonia* meaning dominant or powerful ideas. Gramsci suggests that ideologies are not simply imposed, then, but are the outcome of negotiation. The mass media, it could be argued, has become a prime site on which such negotiations take place.

Both the Birmingham CCCS and the Glasgow Media Research Group drew attention to the potential for counter-hegemony in Gramsci's writing. This refers to the ability of individuals and groups to challenge, resist, renegotiate and reappropriate dominant ideas and representations, and places the emphasis on culture as a site of struggle and contestation, rather than mass deception.

The Birmingham CCCS focused on what they termed the 'circuits of production, circulation and consumption' (Johnson, 1986) of cultural texts. They argued that it follows that if we are located at one particular point in a circuit, we cannot 'see' the whole or other parts of it, and seeing the whole or the totality is the task of cultural studies. CCCS were critical of the Frankfurt School (and Adorno in particular) for focusing too closely on the production of cultural forms and so giving insufficient attention to reception and consumption. They argued that this focus on production creates two particular problems. First, it infers that cultural forms are consumed as they are produced, instead of being rejected or reappropriated. Second, they argued, mass culture theories tend to ignore the elements of production in reception – of popular culture as a site of creativity and resistance. CCCS tended to concentrate, instead of on standardisation and homogenisation, on the potential for creativity in the ways in which certain cultural products and forms are consumed. Their work highlighted, for instance, the ways in which people customise mass produced goods, reappropriate cultural images or subvert dominant ideologies by imbuing them with counter-hegemonic meanings.

Audience reception studies

One of the main analytical categories used by CCCS and the Glasgow Media Research Group to consider how people receive and respond to the messages transmitted by the mass media is 'audience'. This term refers to 'the groups and individuals addressed and often partly "constructed" by the media industries' (Branston and Stafford, 1996, p. 309). An important term to consider here is 'constructed'. This suggests that audiences are defined, at least in part, by the media in their targeting of certain demographic groups with products they are seeking to market. Thus, identifiable audiences are actually 'created' by products that draw people into a relationship of production and consumption.

Take, for example, the rise of the so-called 'New Man' in the 1990s. This particular media and marketing construction coincided with developments in advertising that were moving from product- to lifestyle-based campaigns. More sophisticated techniques of market research were uncovering changes in male and female roles and expectations. Men were more likely to be single well into adulthood (see Chapter 6), and also carrying out a range of household tasks including food shopping. Women were also increasingly working outside of the home, many on a full-time basis (see Chapter 9). The 'New Man' therefore became an effective advertising theme (Athena's *L'Enfant* poster, a black and white image featuring a man who is naked from the waist up and holding a newborn baby, was supposedly their best-selling poster).

One of the founder members of the Birmingham CCCS who has studied the influence of the mass media is Stuart Hall. Hall's analysis of audience reception was based largely on the semiotic insights of Saussure and Barthes considered above. He argued that media images often have ideological messages embedded or hidden within them; he termed this 'encoding' – the process of loading particular cultural forms (such as advertisements) with hidden meanings. Hall also emphasised that audiences are often able to identify this ideological content – to 'see through' the encoded meanings, and so resist the ideological effects of the media. He referred to this as 'decoding' (Hall, 1980). Hence, the mass media is deemed to involve:

PRODUCTION ↔ Encoding ↔ MEDIA TEXT/CODE ↔ *Decoding* ↔ CONSUMPTION

Hall argued that processes of encoding and decoding result in three types of audience reception:

1 *dominant* (where the reader agrees with the preferred reading offered by the text);
2 *oppositional* (where the preferred reading is recognised but rejected);
3 *negotiated* (where the reader subjects elements of the text to acceptance; others to rejection or refinement).

This raises the questions: What factors influence reception? What shapes how audiences decode or interpret symbolic messages in the media? Hall argued that we have to understand not only the production of cultural products but also the conditions of their reception and consumption.

The work of the Glasgow Media Group has also focused on audience perceptions of media coverage. In a similar way to the Birmingham CCCS, their work has concluded that what we understand and believe about media messages is based on both power structures *within* the text (encoded or preferred meanings), and power structures *outside* of the text (those shaped by social class, gender, race and ethnicity, global power relations, and so on).

Youth culture and rebellion

Another key aspect of media culture that sociologists have been concerned with is the role of youth cultures, and particularly what they have termed sub- or countercultures. The study of youth subcultures has, for around forty years or so, been an important focal point for the sociological analysis of mass media and popular culture. Yet the term youth culture has lost much of its sociological pertinence. Until recently, the appearance and disappearance of youth subcultures, marked by their own particular styles of dress, music, language and cultural codes, was a major feature of urban life.

Today, however, there seems to be a considerable fragmentation of styles and, at the same time, a decline in the idea of youth rebellion and dissatisfaction. Sociologists have recently tried to reflect on why this might be the case.

The idea of a youth subculture really only emerged after the Second World War, initially in the US, and slightly later in the UK and Europe and other Western societies. The term implied that young people had come to share a similar social and economic position and thereby had similar interests and concerns. The term also suggested that young people were involved in some kind of rebellion against previous generations. This latter emphasis became particularly prominent in sociology and cultural studies in the 1960s and 1970s, and was a recurring theme in the work of the Birmingham CCCS. They argued that the development of youth subcultures must be understood within its socio-economic context, and effectively analysed young people as if they constituted a social class.

In many Western societies, and particularly so in Britain, the 1950s were a period of post-war prosperity, economic expansion and relatively full employment and, particularly, of relative working-class affluence. The Conservative Government, under the prime-ministership of Harold Macmillan, declared that the majority of the population in the UK had 'never had it so good'. As we noted in Chapter 5, the implementation of the 1944 Butler Education Act and the establishment of the NHS and the welfare state had given young people greater access to education and cultural resources, and had eradicated many of the fears associated with unemployment and ill health. Within this context, age began to emerge as a new social divider, whereas class seemed to be becoming less important (see Chapter 4). People began to refer to 'the generation gap'.

Armed with their new financial independence and the opportunity to be in education for longer, young people began to have not only the inclination but also the means to express their own interests, ideas and values. They began to constitute a new audience and a distinct market for the products of the culture industry, one that did not go unexploited.

Yet, to an extent, the 'never had it so good' culture was something of a political myth. Of course, not everybody was well off. The work of sociologist Peter Townsend in the 1960s emphasised the continued existence of widespread poverty in the UK. It also became clear that credit was beginning to play an increasing role in the development of consumer culture. This meant that the idea of a homogenous youth culture began to be perceived as problematic. Sociologists such as Stuart Hall also pointed out that youth cultures were also shaped by racial and ethnic inequalities, which needed to be understood within the context of post-war patterns of immigration.

Many sociologists writing in the 1960s and 1970s began to perceive youth subcultures as expressions of struggle between young people and the dominant values of society. Sociologists such as Paul Willis in his (1977) book *Learning to Labour* began to argue that it is through youth subcultures that resistance takes place, but that this resistance is rarely consciously political. Rather, it is a form of resistance that takes place at the level of style, or appearance.

Phil Cohen (1980) examined the situation of working-class young men in London's East End and argued that they were caught in a tension between traditional working-class values and middle-class affluence. Subcultures were therefore an expression of this tension between traditional (popular) culture and mass-produced, consumer culture. Skinheads, for instance, could be seen as developing a style based on a very (albeit stereotypical and exaggerated) traditional working-class masculinity. Their tendency towards nationalism and racism could also be understood as an ill-conceived attempt to restore some notion of 'community' during an era of rapid social change. Similar arguments have been made about Mods in the 1960s, and in relation to the 1980s Mod revival. Namely, that their style was an expression both of traditional working-class identity and of (aspirational) middle-class consumer culture.

A more complex analysis of this tension in youth subcultures was developed by Dick Hebdige (1979) who drew on Gramsci's concept of hegemony (considered above), and also on French anthropologist Roland Barthes's work on semiology, to argue that youth cultures appropriate certain objects, artefacts and symbols from mainstream culture and ascribe them with new and different meanings. Hebdige uses certain concepts in his analysis of youth culture that are important to consider in this respect. In particular, he uses the term 'homology' which refers to the study of particular styles, attitudes and symbols (cultural forms) that reflect the concerns of particular groups (e.g. a study of the cultural differences between those who ride motorbikes and those who ride scooters would focus on the homology of each group – on the cultural beliefs, practices and forms that bind them together as a group). In this context, Hebdige's work also emphasises the importance of 're-articulation'. By this he means the practice of attributing a particular (often political) meaning to certain cultural forms (words, images, and so on) that is different from, but related to, their accepted or dominant (hegemonic) meaning. Examples might include gay men calling each other 'queers', Black men and women calling each other 'niggers', or women calling each other 'girls'. A related term, developed initially by Lévi-Strauss and adopted by Hebdige in his work on youth subcultures, is 'bricolage'. Deriving from the French term for DIY, meaning literally 'to rearrange', bricolage refers to the process of re-ordering and recontextualising objects in order to communicate new meanings. Examples might include feminists wearing Doc Martin boots (traditionally signifiers of masculine power), Goths wearing crucifixes or (as one of us saw in a busy shopping area recently) a mobility scooter used by a disabled woman adorned with Harley Davidson badges. Often bricolage also involves the use of space, with particular groups appropriating spaces in coffee shops and shopping centres in which they are otherwise relatively marginalised or disempowered. In the case of Mods, for instance, sea fronts also became important spaces for bricolage.

In his book *Subculture: The Meaning of Style*, Hebdige (1979) focused on youth subcultures among young African–Caribbean people who had been born in the UK. The symbols associated with Rastafarianism were, he argued, used as symbols of resistance to a dominant white culture. In a similar vein, he termed punk a form of 'semiological guerilla warfare', in which symbols such as the Union Jack, the Queen, the national anthem, and so on were used (perhaps most famously by the London-based punk group, the Sex Pistols) to signify a sense of alienation from the dominant culture of the 1970s. Through this technique of 'bricolage', punks asserted their identity as different from, and crucially as a rejection of, mainstream society. What this research raises is an important conceptual difference between what sociologists call 'subcultures' and 'countercultures'.

Subcultures are groups whose members identify themselves as sharing a cultural identity and belonging together that sets them apart from mainstream culture, but who also identify themselves as being part of the mainstream. Such groups often share languages, practices, beliefs, traditions and styles that reflect the dominant group or culture, rather than reject it, but which also set them apart from it. This means that members of a subculture may be aware of their separate identity, but also feel conscious of the need to conform to the norms and values of the larger group in which the subculture is embedded.

Subcultures are important sociologically because they are a source of social and cultural diversity, but also because they can be important sites of social conflict and negotiation. (This is partly why the Birmingham CCCS was so interested in youth sub-cultures – because they can be regarded as key sites on which hegemonic struggle takes place). This is especially the case in relation to countercultures.

Countercultures are cultural groups whose beliefs, practices, norms and values derive from, but are at odds with and often strongly oppose or reject, those widely accepted in society (in effect, a 'contraculture' – Macionis and Plummer, 2002, p. 109). Countercultures are therefore understood to exist specifically as a site of conflict and resistance; of counter-hegemony or what Stuart Hall and the Birmingham CCCS more generally referred to as 'oppositional readings'. Countercultures are often based on the frustrations of marginalised groups; on varying degrees of non-conformity and rebellion against mainstream culture.

Several points of critique can be made about the sociological focus on youth subcultures and countercultures, and particularly the work of the Birmingham CCCS. First, it is questionable whether youth cultures were ever really that radical (many of the most influential people behind the punk movement in Britain were middle-class musicians and designers, for instance). Angela McRobbie has argued that few youth subcultures have ever been genuinely radical because most are highly patriarchal. Most aspects of youth subcultures are also highly commodified, commercial and apolitical. However, some commentators have argued recently that the impact of new communication technologies, facilitating a whole range of mediated forms of interaction, have given the concept of youth culture a new lease of life. Internet chat rooms, mobile phones, computer games and websites designed for exchanging music files might be thought of as new forms of culture around which oppositional (e.g. anti-corporate capitalist) or at least distinct youth identities and styles can emerge and flourish. Some sociologists have argued that many of the new media can be understood as postmodern cultural forms.

Postmodern cultural forms

Over the past two decades or so, a group of postmodern social and cultural theorists – perhaps the most notable being Jean Baudrillard – have begun to highlight the centrality of the mass media in our lives. They have argued that media messages are a new form of reality, one characterised by a range of postmodern cultural forms. Baudrillard sees contemporary societies as concerned primarily with the consumption of signs, and as characterised by what he calls 'simulacra'. Simulacra are worlds of media-generated signs and images (the term is derived from Plato, and describes 'a copy which has no original'). Examples of simulacra might include Disney theme parks or theme pubs that purport to replicate a 'bygone' era that historians argue never actually existed in the form in which it is 'represented' here. Similarly, so-called 'reality TV' shows such as *Big Brother* and *Survivor* collapse the distinction between reality and representation; no longer does the media provide us with a copy of real life, it is a reality of its own.

The idea that certain forms of media and popular culture are postmodern is based on the premise that postmodernism is manifest in the world around us in particular types of culture. Examples, according to Strinati (1995), might include cinema, music, advertising or television. Modernist films tend to be realist (that is, claim to represent or somehow relate to an external, objective reality – see Chapter 2). They tend to be linear and logical in the way in which their plot, narrative and character development proceeds. Films such as *Blade Runner*, *Pulp Fiction* or *Mulholland Drive* tend to be described as postmodern because they question reality, contain critical or ironic images of progressive modernity, are dominated by information technologies, and have plots or narratives that problematise the idea that an external, objective reality exists (Lyon, 1994). In *Blade Runner*, for instance, the action is set against a post-industrial, urban wasteland teaming with roaming gangs. The respectable inhabitants don't leave their dehumanised enclaves, but instead communicate by means of the omnipresent video screens. So-called postmodernism films are also described as 'inter-textual'. This means that they take many of their cultural reference points from other media forms. The Austin Powers or Shrek films, for instance, make many intertextual references to other films.

In music, postmodernism implies a conflation of the distinction between the 'high' and 'popular' or 'mass' forms of culture that we discussed above. In the 1980s, one of the key figures associated with the punk movement in Britain, Malcolm MacLaren released a single called *Madame Butterfly* that interspersed opera singing with rap vocals and mingled Puccini's original (translated) lyrics with new ones. Similarly, the performance of opera music at the opening ceremonies of football matches also signals a conflation of cultural forms, many would argue. Also apparent within contemporary music, postmodernists would argue, is the idea of the 'death of the author' – rather than performing cover versions of songs by 'original' artists, many musicians now sample fragments of previously released pieces of music, integrating them into something new to the extent that it is no longer possible (or meaningful) to designate certain forms of music as 'original' and others as copies or 'cover versions'. Postmodern musical styles are therefore thought to be eclectic, fragmented and defined by constant intertextuality, or references to other cultural forms and products (Strinati, 1995). They might be thought of in terms of what Frederic Jameson (1991) has described as 'pastiche' – cultural forms that are pieced together from a range of different sources, none of which are thought to be 'original'. Clearly, the impact of technological developments, not least the expansion of the internet, has changed the nature of music and of music production dramatically, particularly in terms of the integration of computer-generated sounds into musical forms. Similarly, mechanisms through which the products of the culture industry are disseminated have begun to conflate – in the form of music television, for instance, which conflates a range of media forms and products (Kellner, 1995).

Similarly, dramatic changes that, many commentators argue, signal the emergence of a postmodern era have also occurred in advertising. Much contemporary advertising, for instance, makes no direct or even indirect reference to the product itself, but instead focuses largely on what marketers describe as 'lifestyle factors'. Contemporary adverts also tend to rely heavily on intertextuality, parody and irony. As Strinati puts it, advertisements nowadays

> say less about the product directly, and are more concerned with sending up or parodying advertising itself by citing other adverts, by using references drawn from popular culture and by self-consciously making clear their status as advertisements.
>
> (Strinati, 1995, p. 232)

In his book *America*, Jean Baudrillard (1988) argued that 'all we consume is signs' and by this he means that the act of consuming and being seen to have consumed a particular product or brand, or even the packaging of the product, is often more important than having the product itself.

One of the criticisms that is often made of the idea that certain cultural forms are somehow postmodern is that many of the observations made by theorists of postmodernity were anticipated by the Frankfurt School (the conflation of high and mass or popular culture, for instance). However, whereas the criticisms of this process made by Adorno, Marcuse, and the like were fundamentally of the mass deception engendered by the culture industry, postmodern theorists tend not to share these political concerns and instead emphasise the proliferation of choice and styles that postmodernism has brought about. Instead of defining those who consume mass culture as 'dupes' in the way the Frankfurt School arguably did, they highlight the potential for creativity, irony and resistance, as well as for political opposition and challenge in and through consumer culture – in the form of slogan T-shirts, for instance, or practices of bricolage and reappropriation. In this sense, postmodern theorists adopt and echo some of the insights of the earlier work of the Birmingham CCCS.

The feminist critique of cultural studies

The legacy feminists inherited from cultural studies must be understood in the context of the history of cultural studies as a discipline, and stems from two distinct ideological and institutional sources. The first derives from the historical and ethnographic work on working-class popular culture, associated initially with writers such as Richard Hoggart and Raymond Williams. Such work eventually, as we considered above, informed the studies produced by the Birmingham CCCS. But their work, as we have outlined so far, focused largely on issues such as class (and to a lesser extent race – see CCCS, 1982) and youth subcultures. Feminists have highlighted the neglect of sexual difference (the difference between men and women) in these studies.

The second aspect of the legacy feminists inherited from cultural studies involved rescuing cultural forms associated with women's everyday lives – soap operas, popular fiction and magazines, and so on – from the realm of mass culture to which they had been assigned by malestream sociologists. Feminists tended to reject both the cultural pessimism and intellectual elitism thought to be inherent in the Frankfurt School's ideas about mass culture. According to some feminists, cultural forms such as romantic fiction, soap operas and magazines rather than being guilty of ideological manipulation spoke to the 'very real problems and tensions in women's lives' (Modleski, 1982, p. 14). Others argued that the ideological messages inherent in these media forms were fundamentally patriarchal, so that rather than casting them aside as sociologically insignificant, feminists needed to develop a sustained critique of the ways in which women were constructed and represented in them.

Since the 1970s, feminists have therefore developed a sustained critique of the role of the mass media in perpetuating patriarchal ideologies, and in sustaining gender oppression. Of course, this critique has in no sense been homogenous but has developed several strands and opposing ideas.

One of the major points of critique made by feminists was to challenge the focus on class in cultural studies which was inherited mainly from Marxist sociologists. Feminists criticised their mode of theorising cultural forms. They argued that this mode of theorisation excluded or marginalised gender analytically and women empirically; it placed too much emphasis on men and, in particular, on male working-class and youth cultures. They pointed out, for instance, that the theoretical models and methodologies of the Birmingham CCCS, particularly in the text *Resistance Through Rituals*, demonstrated this focus on men and class, and thereby neglected women. The Centre's ethnographic studies of Teds, Skinheads and Mods, for instance, were undertaken in the context of a class analysis and with reference to a discussion of class-based hegemony derived from Gramsci (see above). In each case, the interest was in seeing ways in which subcultural groups negotiated and resisted the dominant cultural hegemony. Thus it was argued by feminists that the choice of these subcultures led to the effective exclusion of the cultural practices and political identities of working-class girls and women.

Angela McRobbie and Jenny Garber (1976) were among the first writers to focus on the role of girls in youth subcultures, in an attempt to correct what they say as the male bias of previous studies. They argued that girls are present in subcultures but are invisible in sociological studies of them. This is because they play different roles to boys in subcultures and organise themselves differently; what can be discerned by feminist research, they argued, is the existence of distinct, feminine subcultures. Moreover, girls in their research had less spending power than boys; they were meant to be more focused on the home and marriage, and were less visible on the streets.

McRobbie and Garber's work was consistent with 1970s Marxist feminism in that it argued that girls' marginality in youth subcultures was related to the assumption that women's primary role was defined by the family and the household; by the private sphere of reproduction. In effect they argued that consequently women and girls were engaged in much less publicly observable activities than men or boys. However, they pointed out that even when girls did participate in youth subcultures, their roles and status tended to reflect their subordinate position in society generally. McRobbie suggested that it would be more appropriate for sociologists for look for girls' subcultural activities in sites other than the streets. In her view, girls have a different way of organising their cultural life. In explaining this she introduced the concept of 'bedroom culture', arguing that most girls' social lives take place in their bedrooms because these are private spaces, inaccessible to teachers, boys or parents. McRobbie and Garber (1976) also argued, however, that girls' bedroom cultures cannot be defined as resistant to the dominant cultures, in the way that some male-dominated youth cultures are; rather, they concluded, most are highly dependent on manufactured, standardised cultural forms such as boy band formulas.

In her (1978) book, *Feminism and Youth Culture*, McRobbie carried out an ethnographic study of working-class girls, similar to the one undertaken by Paul Willis in *Learning to Labour*. In this study, she explored in more depth the degree to which young girls 'resist' the dominant culture. She observed and interviewed a group of girls aged 14–15 in a Birmingham youth club and found that although the girls accepted their future roles as wives and mothers, and were immersed in a traditional 'feminine' culture, many expressed broader interests in social activities such as dancing, and particularly in their friendship groups. Talk of marriage, the family, romance, fashion and beauty were all part of their feminine, anti-school culture. Much like the 'lads' in Willis's study, McRobbie concludes that the girls she studied were not really oppositional in any meaningful way. Rather than resisting cultural hegemony and patriarchal ideology, they 'gently undermined' it, she argued. McRobbie induced from this that subcultures can function as effective agents of social control as the girls that took part in her study effectively ended up doing exactly what was expected of them, namely complying with the requirements of their gender role in a capitalist society – aspiring to romance, marriage and motherhood.

These early studies carried out in the 1970s led feminists subsequently to analyse the importance of femininity in relation to the mass media and popular culture, and also to consider the construction of gendered subjectivity in a variety of cultural forms. Ideas about class identity and resistance gave way to a more explicit focus on femininity in a range of studies that also drew on the insights of earlier work in cultural studies. A notable example is McRobbie's (1991) work on *Jackie* (the best-selling magazine for girls in the UK in the 1970s) and other girls' magazines, which attempted to trace the hidden meanings or 'ideologies of femininity' that such texts convey.

McRobbie argued that *Jackie* magazine mapped out every stage of the life course for women, from childhood through womanhood to old age, in terms of a patriarchal ideology of femininity. Drawing on Gramsci's concept of hegemony, she argued that girls' magazines are an explicit attempt to win girls' consent to the dominant social and cultural order. In attempting to reveal how this is achieved, McRobbie adopted a semiological mode of analysis which identified four 'subcodes' or strategies through which *Jackie* appeals to its readership. These are: romance, domestic life, fashion and beauty, and pop music.

In sum, McRobbie argued that magazines such as *Jackie* limit and shape femininity in so far as they instruct girls on how to act, and convey what significant others (friends, boyfriends, parents) expect of them. In McRobbie's view, such magazines cannot be dismissed as harmless nonsense because they function as powerful ideological forces – in the case of young girls – in the 1970s, each week for several years. They are part of the dominant ideology which is predicated upon girls' future roles as wives and mothers. The implication, according to McRobbie's analysis, is that all readers will inevitably succumb to the power of gendered ideology in this respect.

In her later work, however, McRobbie (1994, 1996) revised her earlier reading of magazines such as *Jackie*, and particularly her views on the ideologies of femininity contained within their pages. Her underlying message was the same – that magazines are an important part of the socialisation of girls and young women into their future roles in a patriarchal–capitalist society. As she put it, magazines are 'possibly the most concentrated and uninterrupted media-scape for the construction of normative femininity' (McRobbie, 1996, p. 172). She also argued, however, that the content of these magazines had changed considerably over time (see also McRobbie, 2000).

During the 1980s, she argued, there was a significant shift in both the form and content of girls' magazines. In terms of content, there was a shift away from the traditional terrain of femininity towards a more liberated version. She also argued that the ways in which young women read magazines changed; no longer uncritically regarding them as informative or instructive, girls had begun to engage 'knowingly' and ironically with their content. More generally, McRobbie argued, the emphasis on romance dominant in *Jackie* had been replaced in magazines such as *Just Seventeen* and *More!* by a greater emphasis on fashion, music, travel and careers, and this was true of a range of girls' and women's magazines. Most strikingly, she argued, 'there is love and there is sex and there are boys, but the conventionally coded meta-narratives of romance which . . . could only create a neurotically dependent female subject, have gone for good' (1994, p. 164).

According to McRobbie, this shift occurred as a result of a number of factors. First, a greater awareness of sexual equality meant that girls began to reject notions of female passivity and traditional sex-role stereotyping. It was recognised by magazine editors, advertisers and writers that readers were more self-confident and found romantic narratives irrelevant and old-fashioned. Second, developments in media and cultural studies, and also in sociology, began (as we noted above) to focus more on readership, and less on the production of cultural forms such as magazines, and hence began to draw attention to the extent to which readers 'negotiated meanings'. Third, such approaches also emphasised the extent to which individuals were beginning to be increasingly exposed to a diverse variety of media forms and hence, were more likely to be read in fragments. In other words, magazines were more likely than previously to be read 'at a glance', rather than from cover to cover.

McRobbie concluded that in the 1980s the new emphasis on individuality and a display of personalised style was in marked contrast to the traditional ideologies of femininity, and particularly of romance, that dominated magazines such as *Jackie* in the 1970s. Ideologies of femininity remained prevalent, she argued, but were both produced and consumed with a more confident, ironic edge than previously. But the cost of this equality, according to McRobbie, is that girls were more caught up than ever in a hectic cycle of consumerism, or what she has described as 'an endless series of imperatives to buy' (McRobbie, 1996, p. 172).

Crucially, however, making the case for 'a reappraisal of the pleasures of femininity' (1996, p. 175), McRobbie also argued that women's enjoyment of magazines should be taken seriously, particularly as a critique of malestream analyses of media culture. In this respect, she emphasised that the millions of men and women who enjoy lifestyle magazines, soap operas, and so on, should not be dismissed as passive dupes of the culture industry or simply as the 'victims' of patriarchal ideology. Instead, she argued, sociological analysis should focus on the consumption of media texts and the lived experience of popular culture.

McRobbie's work has been subject to a number of criticisms, however, not least because her initial analysis was largely semiological and, as we noted above, semiotics has been subject to methodological criticism (see Strinati, 1995). McRobbie's use of the term 'ideology' has also been subject to critique. Frazer (1987), for instance, has argued that McRobbie's analysis tends to presume that only dominant ideas influence the way people think and act; it neglects other factors, material ones for instance, which shape the course of people's lives. Frazer concludes that McRobbie's analysis is therefore too simplistic and overly deterministic. In particular, Frazer points out that if texts are polysemic, that is open to multiple interpretation, then this must limit their ideological effects. What McRobbie's work, and subsequent criticisms of it (as well as McRobbie's reflections on these criticisms – see McRobbie, 2000), emphasise is that cultural forms such as magazines are key sites where gendered meanings are contested, and where dominant ideologies can be both disseminated and disturbed. Other feminist sociologists have drawn attention to a wide range of media forms in which gender ideology is both reinforced and challenged.

Feminist studies of media culture

A range of feminist approaches have examined the ways in which gender is constructed or represented in diverse forms of media such as advertising, women's magazines, films and soap operas. Early feminist work on media representations tended to adopt a content analysis approach and examined gender stereotypes evident in the mass media. These studies involved, for instance, noting the different roles adopted by men and women in advertisements and counting the number of times these occurred in a given sample. In relation to advertising, Dyer (1982) found women to be routinely portrayed as stereotypically feminine, as sex objects, or as housewives and mothers, whereas men are shown in positions of dominance and authority over women, and in a much broader range of social roles.

Much of the impetus for early feminist critiques of media representations of men and women came from the feeling that available images of women were inadequate, generating the complaint that 'women are not really like that'. Hence, it was suggested that the media was guilty of sex-role stereotyping which was thus reinforced in wider society. In other words, in the way it represented women, the media was thought to be guilty of distorting the reality of women's lives, portraying a fantasy world rather than the one women actually live in. Although content analyses were useful in providing a static picture of how women are represented in the media, some feminists began to argue that these studies were merely descriptive, not explanatory. Content analysis does not tell us anything, for instance, about where stereotypical representations come from in the first place, or about who has the power to define the so-called 'objective reality' that the media is purported to represent. Some feminists attempted to study the role of the media itself in actively constructing 'reality'. This shift in feminist media analysis reflects what is often referred to as the 'cultural turn' in the social sciences, and humanities more generally, and is marked by a shift from the dominance of realist perspectives on the social world, to a more social constructionist approach (see Chapter 2). Hence, feminist analyses shifted away from the idea that the mass media either represents or distorts an objective reality in which 'real' women live, towards an emphasis on the belief that reality itself, including gender identities and relations, is socially constructed and that the mass media plays a central role in this.

Gender in advertising

Almost from the beginning of the feminist movement, feminists responded critically to images of women portrayed in advertising (much of it aimed at women, as the main household consumers). Based primarily on content analyses of advertisements, feminists such as Betty Friedan (1963) in her book *The Feminine Mystique* argued that women were routinely portrayed either as housewives and mothers, or as sex objects. Women are encouraged by adverts to view their bodies as objects, and thus as separate from and more important than their subjective selves, and in need of constant alteration and improvement. The implication is, as Naomi Wolf (1990) has pointed out in *The Beauty Myth*, that the required level of bodily perfection can be achieved through the purchasing and application of appropriate products. Feminists have also pointed out that advertising frequently 'symbolically dismembers' women so that their bodies are fragmented into various parts – women's faces, legs, breasts, eyes, hair, and so on all become the focus of consumption. This reduction of women to their body parts, it is suggested, dehumanises and degrades women so that they are seen as less than fully human, rather than as thinking, speaking, acting 'whole' subjects.

In her work on advertising (which adopted a content analysis approach), Gillian Dyer (1982) argued that men are more likely to be depicted as independent; women as dependent, and men are generally shown as having expertise and authority (for example, as being objective and knowledgeable about particular products), whereas women are often shown merely as consumers. She also found that in adverts focusing on the home, the majority featured images of women but with male voice-overs. This was the case in the majority of adverts for home products, for food products and also for beauty products. Dyer concludes from this that the treatment of women in adverts amounts to what Tuchman (1981) has described as the 'symbolic annihilation' of women. In other words, adverts reflect the dominant belief that 'women are not important, except in the home, and even there, men know best', as the male voice-over suggests (Dyer, 1982, p. 109).

These findings can be compared with those of a more recent study carried out by Cumberbatch (1990) for the Broadcasting Standards Council in the UK. This study found that there were twice as many men as women in adverts, by far the majority (89 per cent) of which used male voice-overs even when the advert predominantly featured a woman. Women in adverts were younger and more physically attractive than the men. Men were twice as likely to be depicted in paid employment as women, and work was shown as being crucial to men's lives whereas relationships were shown to be more important for women, even those at work. Only 7 per cent of adverts studied showed women doing housework, but women were twice as likely as men to be shown washing up or cleaning. Men were more likely than women to be shown cooking for a special occasion or where special skills were seen to be necessary. Women were more likely than men to be shown doing 'everyday' cooking. Women were twice as likely to be depicted as married, and as receiving sexual advances (though usually not in the same advert!) as men.

Drawing on Gramsci's concept of hegemony, Myra Macdonald (1995) in her book *Representing Women* has identified three constructions of feminine identity that, she argues, dominated advertising discourse throughout the course of the twentieth century. These are: the capable household manager, the guilty mother and, more recently, the new woman – 'playful, indulgent, sexually aware, and adventurous' (p. 85). The latter, she argues, has flattered rather than coerced women into purchasing consumer goods, particularly beauty products. In the advertising discourse of the 'New Woman', Macdonald identifies three forms of co-option of feminist ideas and ideology that, she argues, emerged in consumer discourses in the 1980s and 1990s. These are: the appropriation of quasi-feminist concepts; the redrafting of caring to make it compatible with self-fulfilment, and the acknowledgement of female fantasies.

Feminist studies have suggested, then, that there has been a shift in the construction of gender in adverts in recent years, a shift that requires a more in-depth treatment than content analysis of stereotypical representations allows for. Some feminists have pointed out that the most marked transition in the representation of women has been from the portrayal of the domestically oriented woman to a woman who seeks to please herself (see in particular adverts for beauty and hair products). This has led some commentators such as Macdonald (1995) and also Goldman (1992) to argue that a 'new woman' has emerged in advertising in recent years. She is generally presented as a 'Superwoman' – a woman who manages to be successful in her career, to have a clean and shiny home, to be a good mother and wife, to produce delicious home-cooked meals and, of course, to be sexually attractive, and so on. In seeking to explain the emergence of Superwomen in advertising, Goldman (and others) have focused not on the content of the adverts themselves, but on their broader social context. Goldman for instance argues that advertisers, forced to recognise the greater participation of women in the labour force, as well as changes in gender relations, began to exploit this new market and target a specific type of consumer, the 'career woman'. Hence, in Goldman's view, marketing strategies sought to co-opt and commodify the very notion of women's liberation. Goldman's account emphasises, then, that advertisers sought to incorporate feminist ideas and thereby remove their critical power with respect to advertising.

Drawing on semiology and also a Marxist theory of consumption, Goldman describes this co-option of feminism as 'commodity feminism' (playing on the Marxist conception of 'commodity fetishism' – the idea that commodity relations turn the relations of acting subjects into relations between objects). This means that, from the point of view of advertisers, feminism is not so much a social movement with a particular politics and ideology that might threaten to undermine the power of advertising, but rather a 'style' that can be achieved by consuming particular products. Feminism then is redefined and re-packaged so that certain objects are professed to signify a feminist lifestyle. Feminists are therefore constructed, Goldman argues, as just another consumer category amongst many others. In advertising, feminism is supposedly signified by assembling a range of signs which connote independence, participation in paid work, individual freedom and self-control. In 'commodity feminist' adverts, Goldman suggests, women are depicted not as needing a man to be complete, but rather a particular product. The implication is that social change occurs not through protest, strikes or challenges to the legal system (see Chapter 11), but through individualised commodity consumption. Hence, this particular aspect of consumer culture has often been associated with post-feminism (see Chapter 2).

In sum, feminists have pointed out that content analyses of advertising have been useful to the extent that they can give us a description of the sexism inherent in much advertising, and of the extent to which the range of roles on offer to women in advertising has remained surprisingly stagnant (Macdonald, 1995). But content analysis cannot explain where these images come from in the first instance. Nor can it account for sex-role stereotyping, and why this might change alongside other social changes – in women's political and economic circumstances, for instance. Content analysis cannot account, for example, for why traditional images of women in advertising have apparently evolved into more 'liberated' or 'ironic' portrayals. Gill (1988) has argued, for instance, that an advert which used a demand raised by feminists in abortion campaigns, 'a woman's right to choose', as a slogan for a holiday for young people, would have been judged to be 'feminist' on the basis of a study merely of its content. A content analysis approach would have registered words such as 'freedom' or 'rights' or 'express herself' as affirmative of feminist ideas. Hence, more recent analyses have drawn on concepts derived from Marxism and also from semiology to argue that advertisements are *made* to mean something as a result of the ways in which the ideologies contained within them resonate with their broader social context.

Women's magazines

Feminists who have studied women's magazines have adopted a more qualitative approach than merely counting types of images and, in short, have placed their analyses of the content of magazines within a broader critique of patriarchal society. Such magazines have a long history. Indeed Janice Winship (1987) has argued that women's magazines provide an unparalleled popular or mass documentation of women's changing roles and lifestyles.

Historically, women's magazines have had a domestic focus. This is reflected for instance in titles in the UK such as *Woman and Home* and *Good Housekeeping*. Whilst in the nineteenth century, publications such as these addressed women as an undifferentiated mass, increasingly the category 'woman' has been fractured into a more complex collection of status categories as the market has expanded throughout particularly the latter part of the twentieth century. That is, more individual types of women are constructed by these magazine titles. Hence, several titles see the female subject as caught up in traditional arenas such as the family and marriage, as signified by the abundance of magazines on weddings and parenting, for instance. A range of specialist magazines is also devoted to particular themes such as fashion and dieting. At the same time, however, the more general category of 'lifestyle' magazines has expanded considerably, evolving for instance into a burgeoning teenage market. As

Lisa Duke and Peggy Kreshel (1998) emphasise in their research on young women and magazines, these play an important role in reinforcing patriarchal standards of femininity (see also Winship, 1987 and McRobbie, 1991, 1994, 1996).

Despite the expansion of women's magazines and the apparent fracturing of women's roles and identities, feminist studies have emphasised that particular themes remain relatively constant in the ways in which women are constructed and portrayed. Writing in the 1980s, Janice Winship (1987), for instance, suggested that themes of domestic work and beauty, as well as personal relationships, dominated women's magazines throughout the course of the twentieth century. Across a range of magazine genres, Winship argues, women have been defined as emotional workers in the realm of relationships with men, children, family and friends. Thus readers tend to be addressed as wives, mothers and as emotional workers more generally.

More recently magazines such as *New Woman* and *She*, as feminists such as Ien Ang (1989) have pointed out, have tended to draw on feminist repertoires in emphasising women's independence. However, Ang argues that in doing so they have failed to take account of feminist diversity and therefore tend to exclude all but the most affluent, urban, white, middle-class women. In particular, contradictory fantasies such as being an 'independent mother' are presented; yet, she points out, rarely are issues such as how to be 'independent' with 'dependent' children addressed.

The relationship between patriarchal ideology, social change and women's magazines has been considered by Glasser (1997) in her research on women's magazine fiction in China before and after the implementation of the Four Modernisation Policies in the late 1970s. Her study focuses on the relationship between representations of women and the shifting ideological landscape, revealing an important irony. As China moves towards relative political openness and economic modernisation, traditional stereotypes of women as homemakers and caregivers increasingly re-emerge. Glasser argues that such representations have to be interpreted contextually. The image of the public-minded model worker in the 1960s masked a 'repression of personal aspiration in the name of the collective' so that 'the image of the family orientated homemaker, mother, or nurturer from the late 1970s onward, is a dialectic response to the re-emphasis of personal desires' (p. 85).

Women and soap operas

As we noted above, feminist content analyses initially sought to demonstrate that media representations of women were unrealistic. In her work on women in soap operas, Christine Geraghty (1996) pointed out a number of problems with this approach. First, she argued, it implied that an important function of the media is to make 'realistic' representations. Second, it suggested that representations should therefore more accurately reflect what women are 'really' like. Third, it implied that accurate representations are important to those being represented, because media representations affect how men and women see themselves, and how others see them. However, Geraghty and others have argued that this emphasis on the need for realism fails to recognise the socially constructed nature of reality. As Macdonald (1995) has pointed out, such an approach assumes that reality is directly 'knowable' and accessible, unfiltered by our own perceptions and beliefs, and is capable of being presented in an unadulterated, unmediated form.

More social constructionist feminist studies of media and cultural forms turned their attention to programmes such as soap operas and narrative forms such as romantic fiction with a view to examining the way in which they actually constituted femininity, rather than simply represented 'real' women's lives, accurately or otherwise. Crucially, they looked at why women might enjoy them, focusing on what they offered women. To elaborate, this focus on the pleasure and the cultural forms mainly consumed by women was a clear reaction to the ideas of the Frankfurt School considered above, and, particularly, their denigration of such media forms as examples of 'mass' as opposed to 'high' culture, and therefore of no value. Feminists objected to this, arguing that it was an outcome of the masculinist bias by which men were associated with 'high' cultural forms and women with 'mass' culture; with emotion, passivity and consumption. As Tania Modleski (1982) has pointed out, it was these categorisations and the hierarchy they implied that needed to be challenged, not the pleasure women derived from engaging with particular cultural forms that were different from those associated with (and valued by) men. In her view, the terms in which such cultural forms were assessed were derived from, and refer back to, patriarchal ideology. They merely evaluate the masculine at the expense of the feminine.

Focusing specifically on the 1980s US soap opera *Dallas*, Ien Ang (1989) suggests that despite surface glamour and its distance from the everyday life of viewers, women still identified with the emotional problems of the main female characters (in particular Sue Ellen). Indeed, *Dallas* allowed for the expression of emotions in a more direct and forceful way than the restrictions of realism allowed.

Similarly, Geraghty (1996) points out that soap operas portrayed women as wives, mothers, daughters and girlfriends and that many of the stories revolved around the emotional problems generated by these relationships. What was important, however, and what gave women viewers pleasure was the care and intensity with which the problems in these relationships were played out, and the value they gave to women's roles in maintaining them. Hence, Geraghty argues, they rendered visible women's emotional work in a way not previously acknowledged in malestream cultural forms. Soap operas therefore gave women a space in which emotional relationships could be discussed in terms of gender and power, and the subordinated position of women could be acknowledged, and discussed, by women viewers.

A similar point has been made by Modleski (1982) in her book *Loving with a Vengeance*. She suggests that soap operas allow for the representation of strong and transgressive women. The fact that they are often punished and/or contained within the home does not, she insists, detract from the importance of their articulation of anger, ambition and contempt for those who try to control them. Soaps therefore allow viewers to recognise not so much real (individual) women, but the reality of women's (collective) social position. This puts them potentially in a position in which they can begin to recognise and hence resist male domination, and oppressive modes of representation, Modleski argues.

Feminist work on soap operas therefore opened up sociological analysis of media presentations, by drawing attention to the otherwise neglected theme of the pleasures women derive from mass culture. It drew attention to the constructions of masculinity and femininity which frame the ways in which we make sense of media representations. This was assisted by developments in semiotics which challenged the notion that meanings were transparent and argued instead that we need to examine how meanings are signified; how things are *made* to mean. Work on soap operas also showed that media products were not simply imposed on women but were part of popular culture; feminists claimed them from 'below' because they could support women's resistance to male domination, or at least provide women with a common ground on which to discuss their position. The meaning and importance of media products can lie with the audience, this research emphasised, not merely with the producers of representations.

Reading romantic fiction

In a similar vein to her analysis of soap operas, Modleski (1982) refused to see romantic fiction as some form of ideological manipulation. Instead, she suggested that reading romantic fiction is a way of exploring contradictions – in the cultural representations of femininity and the family, and women's experiences of domestic labour in the home, for instance. The very impossibility of becoming a romantic heroine experienced in each reading of a romantic novel, Modleski argues, is a way of negotiating identity and the tensions between aspiration and reality.

In her book *Female Desire*, Ros Coward (1984) similarly explored a range of cultural forms concerned with 'feminine' pleasures and pursuits – horoscopes, soap operas, cooking programmes, fashion, popular music, women's magazines and also romantic fiction. In particular, she writes about the material not from the perspective of a 'distant critic' but from the standpoint of her own pleasure and guilt about enjoying these particular cultural forms. A similar tone characterises Janice Winship's (1987, p. xiii) *Inside Women's Magazines* in which she confesses to being a 'closet' reader. Coward's (like Winship's) is an approach therefore that is in marked contrast to say Adorno's critique of the culture industry in that mass and popular forms of culture are not denigrated from a 'great height' as the disappointing culture of others. Rather, Coward writes about magazines, soap operas and romantic fiction as 'our' (women's) culture.

In particular, she explores the cultural representations of women in romantic fiction not as limiting stereotypes that are imposed on women, but as promoting pleasure and desire. According to Coward, media representations of women produce and sustain particular feminine positions or subjectivities. They inform how we see ourselves and represent ourselves to each other. She points out that, ironically, the growth of feminism has been paralleled by an increase in the popularity of romance novels; and it is this she seeks to explain. Coward suggests that romantic fiction is popular because it satisfies some basic need in women; it offers evidence of and contributes to a powerful fantasy that promises women safety and security, rather than oppression and exploitation.

Coward's analysis is echoed by Janice Radway's (1987) study of romantic fiction, *Reading the Romance*. Radway interviewed 42 readers of romantic novels and asked them how they selected and rejected certain titles. According to her readers, the ideal romance is one in which the intelligent, independent heroine, with a good sense of humour, is overwhelmed by the love of an intelligent, tender, good humoured man but only after much distrust and some cruelty has been overcome. The man is transformed during the relationship from an emotional pre-literate to someone who can care for her and nurture her. She suggests therefore that romantic fiction expresses not the desire for a uniquely interesting partner, but the wish to be cared for. It is a 'fantasy of reciprocation', Radway argued, that sustains women's interest in romantic fiction, involving the wish to believe that men can bestow on women the care and attention women are expected regularly to bestow on men.

In her view, the romantic fantasy offers more than this; it recalls a time when the reader was the recipient of intense maternal care. Drawing on the work of Nancy Chodorow (see Tong, 1998), Radway argued that romantic fantasy is a form of regression in which the reader is transported to a time when she was the centre of her mother's attention. Romance reading is a means by which women can experience the emotional security they are expected to provide to others without adequate reciprocation. In a somewhat essentialist vein, Radway argues that in order to experience regressive emotional fulfilment, women have three options: lesbianism, a relationship with a man or to seek fulfilment by other means. Homophobia and the nature of masculinity mitigate against the first two, so that romance reading might be an example of women pursuing the third option, she argues. The resolution to the ideal romance provides perfect triangular satisfaction, Radway concludes: paternal protection, maternal care and passionate adult love.

Radway also looked at the act of reading itself and found that this was both important and pleasurable to women because it offered them a means of escape in two senses. First, reading was a way of claiming time for themselves away from the demands of family and domesticity; for the women in her research, time spent reading was a gift to themselves. Second, it contributed to the emotional reproduction of women themselves; it helped to sustain them emotionally. Although the experience (as outlined above) was vicarious, the pleasure it induced was nonetheless real. Thus Radway's research led her to make two (apparently contradictory) conclusions. On the one hand, reading romantic fiction could be seen as an act of resistance by women, in so far as it allowed them to refuse (albeit momentarily) their self-sacrificing role as caregivers. But, if the focus was on the text itself, on the content rather than the context of romantic fiction, Radway's research emphasises the ways in which women find pleasure in patriarchal ideologies, for as she concludes, romantic fiction often implies that male indifference or violence are really expressions of love, or of the 'nature' of masculinity, merely waiting to be decoded by the right woman.

Masculinity and media culture

Until relatively recently, men appear to have paid little attention to their status as men; masculinity is something that most men take for granted, but do not find easy to articulate, feminists have argued. As we noted in Chapter 1, a burgeoning literature that has now come to be associated with Men's Studies has begun to reflect on the meaning of masculinity. In the main, this has been a consequence of three sets of factors. First, feminists have put relations between men and women on the political agenda and have argued that sexual difference (the difference between men and women as social subjects – see Chapters 1 and 2) is socially constructed. Feminist theories of patriarchy in effect 'problematised' masculinity and have been relatively success-ful (in Western cultures at least) in requiring men to reflect on their role in maintaining women's oppression. Second, broad social changes such as structural reconfiguration involving, particularly, the expansion of the service sector in many societies has resulted in increasingly large numbers of women entering the labour force (see Chapter 9) and in the contraction of many areas of traditional male employment. This, combined with the changing nature of family life (see Chapter 6) has resulted in what some sociologists have described as a 'crisis of masculinity' requiring some degree of reflection on the changing nature of what it means to be a man (see Connell, 1995, 2002). Third, activities by the gay rights movement have challenged a con-ventional understanding of what it means to be a 'real' man, and of what counts as socially acceptable expressions of masculinity. Hence, there is now a wealth of literature from diverse disciplines and media that takes masculinity as its object of interest.

Some of the earliest considerations of masculinity associated with Men's Studies, however, tended to replicate hegemonic conceptions and to provide relatively unitary or one-dimensional views of men and masculinity. As Frank Mort (1988) has pointed out, in much of the early sociological work on male youth subcultures, referred to above, a relatively coherent and homogenous image of young working-class men was presented.

Recent work has insisted that masculinity is socially constructed, and varies over time and place, emphasising that various versions of masculinity can coexist. These approaches have highlighted changing modes of masculinity, and the diverse ways in which masculinity is constructed in a range of cultural forms such as film, magazines and advertising. They have also highlighted the role of the media in shaping the relationship between masculinity and other aspects of identity such as sexuality, race and ethnicity. Julien and Mercer (1988) have drawn attention to the ways in which media images are both racist and ethnocentric in their construction of Black and Asian masculinities, for instance, by arguing that

> As black men we are implicated in the same landscape of stereotypes which is dominated and organized around the needs, demands and desires of white males. Blacks 'fit' into this terrain by being confined to a narrow repertoire of 'types' – the supersexual stud and the sexual 'savage' on the one hand or the delicate, fragile and exotic 'oriental' on the other. . . . The hegemonic repertoire of images of black masculinity, from docile 'Uncle Tom', the shuffling minstrel entertainer, the threatening native to 'Superspade' figures like *Shaft*, has been forged in and through the histories of slavery, colonialism and imperialism . . . a central strand in this history is the way black men have incorporated a code of 'macho' behaviour in order to recuperate some degree of power over the condition of powerlessness and dependency in relation to the white slave-master.
>
> (Julien and Mercer, 1988, pp. 133–136)

Rutherford (in Chapman and Rutherford, 1988) suggested that one of the main recurring images of masculinity in films of the 1980s, and which is still in evidence in Hollywood cinema today, is what he calls 'Retributive Man'. In his view, the classic figure here is Rambo. Retributive Man represents the struggle to assert what might be described as traditional masculinity – a tough, independent authority – and has entered popular culture as an enduring myth. What this image implies is that a destructive and forceful machismo is the solution to men's (and society's) problems. According to Rutherford, this figure is also epitomised by John Wayne, wildly lashing out at everything that threatens him. He confronts a world full of traitors, cowards and 'feminised men' in which he has only himself to rely on. Rutherford emphasises that many of the images of masculinity in the 'action hero' films of the 1980s sat comfortably alongside Thatcherite ideology in Britain that emphasised values of individualism and heroism.

A similar approach to Rutherford's can be seen in work by Susan Jefford (1994) in the USA, in her book *Hard Bodies: Hollywood Masculinity in the Reagan Era*. Here she makes links between cinematic representations of 'hard bodies' and the prevailing ideologies of the Reagan administration. In brief, she maintains that after the Vietnam War and the resignation of Nixon, the US experienced a crisis of purpose, followed by a period of malaise and uncertainty. The perceived weakness came to an end at the advent of the Reagan era, and a cinematic culture dominated by action films featuring tough, aggressive masculinities began to prevail. Rutherford argues that such films reflected shared presuppositions about what a 'man' and a 'state' should be like – assertive, tough and, when necessary, violent; in short, a 'hard body'.

Frank Mort (1988) and others have argued that this type of film waned in popularity in the 1990s because of the evolution of a new male identity, the 'New Man'. As Mort argued, this discourse of masculinity emerged from the late 1980s onwards and occurred repeatedly in a range of media forms, but particularly in film and advertising. The rise of the so-called New Man, he suggests, coincided with developments in consumerism and advertising and (as we noted above) broader social and demographic changes in the labour market, the family and the household. In developing the New Man as a new market, advertisers were greatly assisted, Mort notes, by the burgeoning 'style press' (see also Nixon, 1996), and particularly the launch of men's lifestyle magazines. These magazines provided new but socially acceptable images of masculinity, focusing on fashion through the lenses of work and travel or music, for instance, and hence made it easier to target men as consumers.

As Chapman (1988) pointed out, consumer culture was instrumental in 'feminising' men. The New Man was constructed as family-oriented and was linked to more progressive and nurturing versions of fatherhood and emotional expression. Chapman wryly described the New Man thus:

> If the old man was characterized by his abhorrence of all things female, the new man was invigorated by his enthusiastic embrace of female roles and qualities. He knew his Borsch from his Brioche, he could dangle junior on his knee while discussing the internecine convolutions of 'our relationship'. Tough but tender, he knew his way 'round a futon and could do more than just spell clitoris. Not for him the wham-bam-thank-you-man thrust of the quick fuck. He was all cuddles and

protracted arousal, post-penis man incarnate, the doyen of non-penetrative sex. He abandoned a lifetime's belief in the myth of the loo fairy, did his share of the household chores, ironed tramlines in his own shirts, and could rustle up a chicken chasseur, with an extra portion for that 'surprise' guest, when 'she' brought the Boss home.

(Chapman, 1988, pp. 227–228)

The New Man, however, is not merely the caring-sharing man; he is also a sex object. In other words, codes of narcissism have been added to those of nurturing, Chapman goes on to argue. In advertising campaigns such as those for Levi's 501s, and in posters produced by the Athena chain (referred to above), the male body is sexualised and commodified. According to Mort (1996), these male bodies openly invite a desiring look from women or other men. This eroticisation of the male body in magazines, fashion photography, advertisements, and so on has meant, he argues, that men have been able to articulate their sexuality and identity in ways which would have been impossible twenty years ago. Thus, masculinity is now defined, he argues, not by a single dominant message but by a self-conscious assemblage of styles.

Perhaps, somewhat ironically, evidence for this latter point might also include a reaction against the trend towards more egalitarian, feminine modes of masculinity, namely the contemporary figure of the Lad. So-called 'Lad culture' has seemingly rejected and reacted against liberal sexual politics, and has retreated in chauvinism and male social exclusivity. In contrast to the New Man, Lad culture involves a display of masculinity, in media and popular culture, that supposedly involves a parody of sexism. In *Loaded* magazine (launched in Britain in 1994) and in TV series such as *Men Behaving Badly* and *Fantasy Football* stereotypes of masculinity are presented, and male pastimes such as drinking, watching football (see King, 1997) and regarding women as sex objects dominate in a supposedly ironic, 'knowing' way (*Loaded*'s masthead is 'for the man who knows better'). Much of the humour that shapes this culture relates to reclaiming, in a supposedly ironic way, language that has traditionally been used to oppress and objectify women, and hence, it is a culture with which most contemporary feminists have a particularly problematic relationship. This is not least because one of the central concerns of feminist politics has been to highlight the significance of language both in perpetuating, and in challenging, gender oppression.

Feminist perspectives on language

Sociologists often make a distinction between cultural practices (fashion, dance, and so on) and cultural representations (media images of 'new men', for instance). Language, however (and particularly feminist work on the relationship between gender, language and power), highlights that this distinction is somewhat problematic because language is *both* a cultural practice and a representation. Think of when a couple are pronounced 'man and wife' in a heterosexual marriage ceremony – this is both a representation (of gender relations in language) and a practice (that takes places through language).

Language has been of particular significance to feminist theory and politics, not least because what Deborah Cameron (1998) describes as 'the power to name and define' can be understood in two ways. First, it can refer to the power of dominant groups (men, the middle- and upper-classes, white people, Western cultures, able-bodied people, and so on) to name and define reality for everyone else. But it can also refer, second, to the capacity of marginalised and oppressed groups to rename and redefine their own realities. As she puts it,

> Since our lives and relationships are carried on to a large extent through language, since our knowledge of the world is mediated through language, the power to name and define is an important arena for reproducing or challenging oppressive social relations.
>
> (Cameron, 1998, p. 148)

Robin Lackoff (1975), in her book *Language and Women's Place*, was one of the first to explore gender and language from a feminist perspective. She argued that women often lack authority and seriousness, conviction and confidence in their use of language. Men, she argued, are more forceful and effective in using language, and tend to speak more purposefully than women. Women, by contrast, are more tentative, hesitant and are therefore 'deficient' as she described it, in their use of language. Crucially, she argued this is not because of biological sex differences; women are not innately deficient in their speech patterns, she emphasised. Rather, it is an outcome of gender socialisation; of gender roles and power relations rather than some essential deficiency in women.

Although Lackoff's was an influential study, it was constrained by what Dale Spender (1990) has described as its 'sexist assumptions about speech roles'. Spender argues that Lackoff takes male language use as the norm and identifies women's speech, by definition, as a deviation from that norm. Spender points out that 'in a society where women are devalued, it is not surprising that their language should be devalued' (1990, p. 10). She argues that the problem is not that women don't speak like men, but that women's ways of communicating are devalued, because women themselves are devalued and because language is essentially 'man-made'.

Language as 'man-made'

Perhaps the most important contribution to the analysis of gender and language has been made by Dale Spender (1990), who argued that 'the English language has been literally man made and . . . is still primarily under male control' (p. 12). Her account emphasised that language supports patriarchy and is inherently sexist because both *semantics* (the meaning of words) and also *syntax* (sentence structure, or the form in which meanings are expressed) are male dominated. Both aspects of language, she argued, are patriarchal in so far as they are biased in favour of men.

Spender identifies three main ways in which language is male dominated. These are:

1 *linguistic sexism* (including *androcentrism in syntax* and the *semantic derogation of women*);

2 *the male line* (women's and children's adoption of men's surnames); and
3 *gender differences in speech patterns.*

What she calls *linguistic sexism* operates on two levels. *Androcentrism in syntax* involves the use of 'man' as a generic term and 'he' as a universal pronoun to refer both to men and women. Spender argues that there are more words for men and masculine things in most languages. (In romantic European languages particularly, in which nouns are masculine or feminine, there tend to be more masculine words.) She also points out that generic terms often require a deviation when applied specifically to women (e.g. chairwoman, stewardess, waitress, mayoress, and so on). This, she argues, reinforces the male version as the norm.

Deborah Cameron (1995) developed this idea of linguistic sexism and of andro-centrism in syntax by arguing that gender divisions are not merely 'lexicalised' (encoded in words) but are also 'grammaticised', that is 'built into the rules for constructing well-formed sentences' (p. 151). This often involves giving words and phrases with masculine connotations priority within the construction of sentences, she argues.

In her discussion of linguistic sexism, Spender (1990) also notes that language tends to be structured around a series of dualisms and that there are more negative words for women (especially those with sexual connotations), yet there is no linguistic reason why this should be the case. In contrast, words associated with men and masculinity tend to be more positive in their associations. She terms this the *semantic derogation of women*, and illustrates this point with reference to the ways in which words used to designate the same condition have different (positive and negative) connotations for men and women. Compare the terms 'stud' and 'slag' for instance; both refer to sexually active males and females, respectively, but the former is almost complimentary whereas the latter is particularly derogatory (see Lees, 1986, 1993). A similar point could be made about the terms 'bachelor' and 'spinster', and a whole range of gendered oppositions in language that serve to position women negatively relative to men and to limit the ways in which women, especially, perform gender. The same words applied to women often have different (frequently negative) asso-ciations – e.g. 'she's a tramp' has a sexual connotation that tends not to apply when the same term is used to describe a man. Rosemary Pringle developed this latter point in her book *Secretaries Talk* in which she argued that

It is no more possible to label [heterosexual] men bitches than it is to label them sluts or tarts – though, of course, gay men have appropriated all three terms. It may be acknowledged that 'men bitch too', and we do not have to look very far to find men indulging in manipulation, back-stabbing, whingeing and gossiping. But the term is not easily applied to them. This disguises the extent to which men do bitch and, perhaps more significantly, the extent to which they are bitched about. The apparent absence of men from the bitching discourse facilitates the presentation of masculinity as rational, abstract and autonomous; women by contrast are locked into the petty and the concrete.

(Pringle, 1989, p. 235)

Second, Spender (1990) argues that the use of surnames is male dominated in what she calls *the male line* and that a surname functions as a signifier of patriarchy, which often makes it difficult to trace women's genealogies. It also reinforces the idea that women are men's property, particularly in the use of formal titles such as Mrs John Smith, presenting a married woman as a female variant of her husband, and not as a person in her own right.

Similar to Lackoff, Spender also emphasises *gender differences in speech patterns*, noting gender differences in access to, and in the use of, language as a form of cultural expression. She argues that women tend to be more tentative in their use of speech, as a consequence of their subordinate social status, and tend to be relatively silent, particularly in public or in mixed sex groups. Research (see David Graddol and Joan Swann's *Gender Voices*, 1989) has found that men tend to dominate mixed sex conversation in several ways:

1 they tend to *set the agenda* (determine the topic and its development);
2 they tend to *speak more*, and to *speak louder* than women;
3 they tend to *interrupt and contradict* more than women; and
4 they tend to *close conversations* more so than women do.

Spender argues that mainstream linguistic research has often served to reinforce these gender differences by implying that men's use of language is more 'serious' than women's (that women 'chatter' and 'gossip' – using derogatory terms for women's ways of speaking) and perpetuating the idea that women's voices are too high pitched to listen to for any length of time, or to be taken seriously (hence, until recently, relatively few women were employed as newsreaders or hosts of current affairs programmes).

Deborah Cameron (1990) develops this approach in her book *The Feminist Critique of Language*, as well as in more recent work (Cameron, 1995), arguing that women are 'silenced' and excluded from dominant forms of language use, especially in the public sphere, and in formal contexts such as meetings. As we noted in Chapter 8, research on language use amongst young women with reference to their apparent reluctance to articulate their own sexual desires and expectations (around condom use, for instance), has similarly highlighted a 'gendered division of linguistic labour' that serves to entrap young people into the gendered language of heterosexuality and to reinforce women's responsibility for the emotional aspects of sexual relationships (Holland *et al.*, 1998).

Feminist criticisms of man-made language

Not all feminists are convinced by Spender's argument that language is man-made, however, and her analysis has been subject to two main criticisms. First, it suggests that language is a fixed rather than evolving system. Second, and related to this, it makes language users sound passive rather than actively engaged in the production, dissemination and consumption of language.

Janet Holmes (1997) is one such commentator, who argues that whilst language can be oppressive, it can also be an important mechanism for challenging oppression.

357

Her analysis emphasises that groups of people who are marginalised, in part at least, in and through language can reappropriate derogatory terms, and that the relationship between language and power is more complex and contested than Spender suggests. Holmes argues that not only does the argument that language is 'man-made' privilege (and also homogenise) women over other groups who are subject to 'linguistic oppression', but also underestimates the critical potential of language to challenge and undermine established power relations. Holmes cites women's use of the term 'girl' as an example of the ways in which language can be reclaimed. As Russell and Tyler (2002) have recently noted, 'The term "girl" is clearly a marker of status, denoting both a positioning within childhood but also a relatively passive designation within a gender hierarchy; one that the . . . theme of "girl power" attempted to re-articulate' (p. 620).

Gender and the linguistic turn

Developing this perspective further, and following the so-called 'linguistic turn' in the social sciences (see Chapter 2), some feminists (particularly those influenced by poststructuralism) have recently highlighted the ways in which language does not simply reflect a pre-existing social reality but actively constructs that reality. This approach is premised on the assumption that, as sociologist Stuart Hall has put it, the very concept of

> identity is not as transparent or unproblematic as we might think. Perhaps instead of thinking of identity as an already accomplished fact, which cultural practices then represent, we should think, instead, of identity as a 'production', which is never complete, always in process, and always constituted within, not outside representation.
>
> (Hall, 1990, p. 222)

Hence, gender is understood to be shaped not just by social structures but by dominant discourses – forms of language that construct what it means to be a man or a woman. Feminists who adopt this perspective emphasise that, in their engagement with dominant discourses, men and women actively reconstruct gender relations in a way that enables male power to be perpetuated. This means that men and women subject themselves and each other to what, paraphrasing Foucault, might be understood as a form of gender surveillance – subjecting each other to forms of discipline and control, particularly in terms of patriarchal norms on feminine appearance, for instance. As Sandra Lee Bartky (1990, p. 72) has put it in this respect: 'In contemporary patriarchal culture a pan-optical [all seeing] male connoisseur resides within the consciousness of most women; they stand perpetually, before his gaze and under his judgement.'

Echoing earlier work by Mulvey (considered above), feminists such as Bartky have argued, then, that gendered discourses play a powerful role in controlling and regulating particularly female behaviour, for example by perpetuating sexual double standards through discourse. In contrast to Mulvey's earlier work however, they have also emphasised that language is the site of contested and negotiated gendered meanings. One interesting example of this complexity is the gendered culture of cheerleading in the US, in which over 3.5 million girls and young women are thought to participate (Adams and Bettis, 2003). In their feminist poststructuralist reading of cheerleading, Adam and Bettis situate cheerleading as 'a discursive practice that has changed significantly in the past 150 years or so to accommodate the shifting and often contradictory meanings of normative femininity' (p. 73). They argue that cheerleading is

> a gendered activity representing in some ways a liberatory shift in reconstituting normative femininity, while simultaneously perpetuating a norm of femininity that does not threaten dominant social values and expectations about the role of girls and women in society.
>
> (Adam and Bettis, 2003, p. 73)

Other recent studies have emphasised the extent to which various media forms have begun to incorporate feminist ideas in a more progressive way than its co-option in advertising imagery considered above. Banet-weiser (2004) has argued, for instance, that the cable television network Nickelodeon has been recognised by both industry professionals and media scholars for its representation of girls and young women as strong, intelligent lead characters. One of the most notable examples of strong female TV characters in recent years is Buffy the Vampire Slayer who manages to overpower her enemies, and is often cited by young girls as a positive role model (Russell and Tyler, 2002). Wilcox and Williams (1996) have also argued that the relationship between agents Mulder and Scully in *The X Files* represents a reversal of traditional gender roles in so far as 'Scully represents the rationalistic world view usually associated with men, while Mulder regularly advocates supernatural explanations and a reliance on intuition usually associated with women' (p. 99).

The role of the media in challenging and subverting dominant racial ideologies of gender has also been highlighted, with reference to the role of Bollywood cinema and new music television, for example (Aftab, 2002; Kumar and Curtin, 2002; Srinivas, 2002). Some feminists have argued that the role of the media in challenging and inverting traditional gender roles has become even more important given recent developments in media and communication technologies.

New media technologies and cyberfeminism

The relationship between women and technology, as Liza Tsaliki (2001) notes, has always been an uneasy one, since the traditional perception of technology is heavily weighted against women. As she puts it, 'in many cases, the symbolic representation of technology reproduces the stereotype of women as technologically ignorant and inept' (p. 80). This means that recent developments in media, information and communication technologies are both a challenge and a potential opportunity for feminists. On the one hand, in increasingly technologically driven and highly IT-skilled societies there is a considerable risk that women can become further marginalised and disempowered (the majority of IT graduates and professionals are men, for instance – see Chapter 9). On the other hand, the evolution of so-called 'cyberfeminism' emphasises the radical potential of what Tsaliki describes as 'technology as empowerment'. Such dilemmas are not entirely new, however. As Myra Macdonald (1995) points out in her discussion of domestic technology in post-war Britain, developments such as the advent of automatic washing machines and cookers potentially freed women from much of the burden of domestic labour (particularly its more physical aspects) – a theme that dominated advertising discourses at the time. Yet, such developments also increased (patriarchal and commercial) expectations and, in many ways, merely served to intensify women's domestic role (everyday became 'wash-day' for instance). A similar concern about there being no 'escape' has characterised sociological responses to developments in media and communication technologies in recent years – mobile phones and email, for instance, mean that people are rarely unobtainable by employers, families and other social networks.

So-called 'cyberspace' (the social spaces we inhabit when we go 'online' and visit various web sites, including discussion lists and chat rooms or MUDS – multi-user domains) is becoming an increasingly important arena for communication between people who have never met in person. Other forms of communication technology such as mobile phones and text-messaging have also begun to play an increasingly significant role in social relations. Some cultural theorists, such as Sadie Plant (1993), see this as an exciting opportunity for experimentation with gender identities; with men adopting female personae and vice versa. In her view: 'Cyberfeminism is information technology as a fluid attack. . . . Its flows breach the boundaries between man and machine. . . . Cyberfeminism is simply the acknowledgement that patriarchy is doomed' (p. 14).

For Plant, cyberfeminism is a computer culture in which inequalities are eradicated, and traditional gender relations and stereotypes are defied. Others are more pessimistic, and argue that structural inequalities (not only those between men and women), transfer from 'real' social life into the 'virtual reality' we encounter online. As Tsaliki puts it,

> Very often, debates on globalisation, electronic democracy and telematics-based social networks seem to imply a (utopian) degree of uniformity in social access to information technology. The truth is, though, that given the ever-increasing complexity of digital technology, power in cyberspace is based on expertise, and is available to technologically-adept users – in itself leading towards the creation of a cyber-elite which is, nevertheless, primarily male-dominated.
>
> (Tsaliki, 2001, p. 88)

By far the majority of 'traffic' on the internet is thought to be pornographic, for instance, and there is some evidence to suggest that women are often subject to harassment and what has (not unproblematically) been described as 'cyber-rape'. As we noted in Chapter 8, it is easy to forget in the discussion of cyberfeminism and 'cyber-sex' that internet-based pornography often involves real women whose participation remains grounded in material inequalities. Clearly, the issues are complex and evolving. As Mark Poster notes, for instance,

> One must admit that the mere fact of communicating under the conditions of the new technology does not cancel the marks of power constituted under the

conditions of face-to-face, print and electronic broadcasting modes of intercourse. Nonetheless, the structural conditions of communicating in Internet communities do introduce resistances to and breaks with these gender determinations. The fact of having to decide on one's gender [for example, participation in MUDs, or on-line game-playing, often requires the assumption of a character identity with a 'username'] itself raises the issue of individual identity in a novel and compelling manner.

(Poster, 1997, p. 212)

In sum, socio-linguists and feminist sociologists such as Lackoff, Spender and Cameron have all argued that language not only reflects (represents), but perpetuates and maintains gender inequalities. Whilst acknowledging that merely changing our language would not automatically liberate women (and men) from patriarchy, feminists such as Dale Spender have argued that the coinage of new words and meanings could be a way of challenging male domination. Other feminists have criticised this approach, emphasising instead the extent to which language is always negotiated and evolving. Recent developments in various modes of communication technologies may begin to facilitate this and, at the very least, heighten our awareness of the relationship between gender and communication.

The World Bank (cited in Macionis and Plummer, 2002, p. 560) have commented that 'the global economy is undergoing an Information Revolution that will be as significant in its effect as the Industrial Revolution of the nineteenth century'. Whether this will be, in part at least, a feminist revolution remains to be seen. Indeed, the full implications of recent developments in information and communication technologies, and in global processes of 'mediatisation' have yet to become clear. Macionis and Plummer (2002, p. 565) argue that we need to begin asking ourselves at least three questions. First, once the full implications of home multimedia start to be realised, will we spend less and less time in public spaces and in social exchanges (what sociologists have traditionally thought of as 'society'), and more and more time in virtual space (as Baudrillard suggests, we will all move into 'hyper-reality')? Second, the media world seems set to become an increasingly commercialised global one dominated by huge transnational corporations. Will this mean an increasing McDonaldization of culture, as Ritzer has argued? Third, the countries with the highest internet accessibility are overwhelmingly Western and at least 80 per cent of the world's 200 or so nations still lack substantial communication technologies. Is this a process that will have serious consequences for wider global inequalities, and particularly for the world's women?

Conclusions

Sociologists have emphasised that culture is a central concept of analysis; crucial to understanding the relationship between the individual and society. One of the reasons why the term is so difficult to define, however, is its intricate historical development; and also the way in which it has come to be used in several different ways by distinct and often incompatible schools of thought within sociology. In the twentieth century, culture came to refer both to 'high' culture – to the highest expressions of human civilisation in art, literature and music, for instance; as well as to 'popular' or lived culture – the ways of life that bind groups of people together as a community – and media culture – mass-produced and disseminated by the culture industries.

In studying culture, sociologists have drawn on a range of concepts derived largely from Marx's theory of ideology. In particular, Gramsci's concept of hegemony and Althusser's analysis of 'ideological state apparatuses' (ISAs) have been central. Critics of mass culture, associated largely with the Frankfurt School and, more recently, Ritzer's McDonaldization thesis, have argued that mass culture is culture that is consumed as a product like any other, and that as a result, traditional distinctions in taste, quality and value are dissolved into a homogenous culture which is passively consumed by individuals organised into demographic groups by market researchers. Critics of mass culture such as Adorno and Marcuse have also emphasised that technological developments in broadcast media have allowed unprecedented access to individuals, creating 'false needs' which are, in turn, satisfied by the products of the culture industry. The scope for political resistance and change, and the expression of individual identity are negated by conformist consumer culture.

Others, for example Fiske, have insisted on the resilience of popular culture, and on the capacity of individuals to 'read' dominant cultural forms in a variety of ways other than those intended by those who produce and disseminate cultural forms. As Fiske has put it,

> Despite the cultural pessimism of the Frankfurt School, despite the power of ideology to reproduce itself in its subjects, despite the hegemonic force of the dominant classes, the people still manage to make their own meanings and to construct their own culture within, and often against, that which the industry provides for them.
>
> (Fiske, 1987, p. 286)

Feminist debates have tended to parallel this 'mass culture/production' versus 'popular culture/consumption' split within sociology more generally. Feminist approaches have drawn attention to the ways in which cultural studies has tended to exclude, marginalise or denigrate women, and have highlighted the ways in which media culture misrepresents women, or constructs femininity only according to a relatively narrow range of roles and identities. Feminists have also highlighted the relative absence of women in cultural production, as well as the importance of understanding the social context within which women both seek and derive pleasure from consuming a range of mass cultural forms. Feminist sociologists and cultural theorists have studied a range of media forms, including advertising, film, television (especially soap operas), romantic fiction, magazines and, most recently, new forms of media and communication technologies.

SUMMARY

1 The term culture is central to sociological analysis, although its meaning has changed historically, and has been contested by different schools of thought within cultural studies. Sociologists tend to distinguish between high culture, popular culture and mass culture. Some sociologists have argued that we now live in a McDonaldized, 'media culture'.

2 Cultural studies has been largely concerned with the ideological effects of the mass media, and has drawn variously on Marx's theory of ideology, Gramsci's concept of hegemony and Althusser's structuralism in understanding the role of the mass media. Two of the main schools of (malestream) thought include the Frankfurt School and the Birmingham Centre for Contemporary Cultural Studies (CCCS).

3 Two main methodologies have dominated sociological analyses of media culture: content analysis and semiotics.

4 Until relatively recently, most studies of youth subcultures were concerned primarily with white, male working-class cultures.

5 Feminists have undertaken studies of a range of media forms and have focused variously on the representation and construction of gender within these. Feminists have studied advertising, women's magazines, soap operas, romantic fiction and also language.

6 While some feminists are excited by the radical potential of 'cyberfeminism', others are more cautious.

FURTHER READING

Cameron, D. (ed.) (1998) *The Feminist Critique of Language: A Reader.* Second edition. London: Routledge. This is an excellent text that incorporates a range of feminist contributions to understanding the relationship between gender and language. It incorporates 'classic' contributions, as well as more contemporary perspectives.

Strinati, D. (1995) *An Introduction to Theories of Popular Culture.* London: Routledge. This introductory text covers a range of perspectives central to cultural studies, and reviews a range of feminist contributions.

CHAPTER THIRTEEN

Feminist knowledge

A central argument of this book has been that sociology has tended to ignore, distort or marginalise women and femininity. We have also suggested that this is a result of the systematic biases and inadequacies in malestream theories, not just an omission of women from empirical research. Sociology has tended not to ask questions or do research in areas of concern to women, and frequently women have been excluded from samples; when they have been included they have tended to be viewed from a position that sees men and masculinity as the norm. As we pointed out in Chapter 1, malestream sociological theories such as Marxism and functionalism have often taken for granted, rather than challenged, the view that the biological differences between men and women are sufficient to explain and justify social divisions and inequalities. This explains, for instance, the startled response of one feminist writer when told by a young Sudanese student that she had written a structural functionalist dissertation on clitoridectomy (Spivak, 1987).

Rather than unproblematically adopting malestream theories and 'adding gender on', feminist sociologists have argued that it is necessary to develop feminist theories: theories that explain the world from the position of women, and that enable us to conceptualise reality in a way that reflects women's interests and values, drawing on women's own interpretations of their own experiences. In recent decades (and primarily as a result of these efforts), sociology has begun to take the feminist challenge seriously and to acknowledge women both as the subjects of sociological research, and as the bearers of knowledge.

Thus feminist theories criticise the abstraction and over-inclusiveness of male-generated categories that conceal women's oppression. Theories should enable us to make sense of our lives, feminists argue. Furthermore, they should enable us to relate our experiences to the ways in which the society in which we live is structured. Individual men may be the agents of oppression, but patriarchal relationships also exist in the institutions and social practices of society. Feminist theories must also enable us to understand how we come to see ourselves as individuals – how we come to accept that a woman's role is in the home, that women are capable only of certain jobs, that girls are worse at mathematics and sciences than boys, that only women who have had and cared for children are fully developed women, and so on. They must enable us to understand how we become both subjects (housewives, mothers, nurses, secretaries) and also subject to the idea that it is natural that women should take on these roles.

However, it is important to recognise that different women have different experiences of reality; the way in which they are subordinated varies. Feminist theory has tended to be developed by white, middle-class women who work in institutions of higher education. While all women may share a subordinate position, not all women experience it in the same way; theories developed by white, middle-class, Western women have been correctly criticised for marginalising the experiences of working-class and racialised women, or women subject to global power relations, or marginalised because of disability or age, and so on. To represent reality adequately from the standpoints of women, feminist theory must draw on a variety of women's experiences. To do this it is necessary to find ways in which all groups of women can participate in theory-building – to ensure that feminist theories adequately incorporate the experiences of all women.

As we also noted in Chapter 2, feminist theories are also political: they set out not just to explain society but to transform it. Feminist theories are concerned to analyse how women can transform society so that they are no longer subordinated by understanding how patriarchal relations control and constrict them. Consequently the adequacy of feminist theories is tested at least in part by their usefulness, that is the extent to which they provide useful and usable knowledge for women. Feminist sociology is concerned, then, to build what Dorothy Smith (1987) has called a sociology for women – a sociology that relates to women, with which women can identify, in which women recognise themselves as the subject of what is being said, and which helps us to understand our everyday lives as well as the ways in which they are structured and established within a male-dominated society.

A sociology for women would empower women because, as feminists have long since noted, knowledge *is* power (see Smith, 2004). Women have inhabited a cultural, political and intellectual world from whose making they have been excluded and in which they have often been recognised as of no more than marginal relevance. Malestream scientific knowledge, including sociology, has been used to justify the exclusion of women from positions of power and authority in cultural, political and intellectual institutions. Feminist knowledge, including sociology, challenges the objectivity and truth of that knowledge (which is presented as gender neutral) and seeks to replace it with more adequate knowledge – more adequate because it arises from the position of the oppressed and seeks to understand that oppression.

Some radical feminists would argue that we should not seek to develop new, feminist theories because the theoretical approach is an essentially masculine way of working. Theorising is seen as a task undertaken by an elite that devalues, or even ignores, the experiences of women not included in that elite. Feminist sociologists, they argue, are trying to replace one 'truth' with another and in doing so fail to recognise the validity of the experience of all women. The feminist task, they suggest, is to use the experiences of all women in making sense of women's lives and fighting oppression.

However, we would argue that all explanation and research is an essentially theoretical activity, whether the theory is made explicit or remains implicit. 'Facts' – our experiences and our observations – do not speak for themselves; we have to explain them – that is, to theorise them. Feminist theories have enabled women to do this – to make sense of their lives and the cultural, political and intellectual worlds that they inhabit. Experience itself is a product of our theories; we *interpret* and *make sense of* what is happening in our lives. In the past women have had to use malestream theories; but as we outlined in Chapter 2, have begun to replace them with a range of feminist alternatives.

It could be argued that attempts to develop feminist sociology are themselves a contradiction (in much the same way as it has been argued that a Marxist sociology is a contradiction): that the Women's Movement and feminism are themselves concerned with understanding women's lives and developing strategies that will enable women to liberate themselves from oppression. Feminists have sought to break down artificial – man-made – barriers between disciplines and to develop interdisciplinary studies that recognise that we cannot compartmentalise knowledge or women's lives into discrete areas. A Women's Studies syllabus would include, for example, women's literature, women's art, women's history and feminist biology as well as feminist social science. The subjects would not necessarily be taught as disciplines, but as they are lived. Likewise, feminist theories are not bound by discipline. The theories that we have used in this book and the epistemological stances which we examine in more detail in this chapter are not restricted to sociology – they are not *sociological* theories and epistemological positions, but *feminist* ones. Nevertheless, feminists have been interested in many areas that concern sociologists, and many female sociologists would regard themselves and the work they do as feminist. Feminists have never claimed to be scientific observers of the world, however, and would argue that no knowledge is neutral; malestream knowledge has been used to control women, and feminist knowledge is an aid to the emancipation of women.

Doing feminist research

Theories are world views that enable us to make sense of the world. They guide us in terms of what is important and relevant to question and help us to interpret what is going on. However, to understand the world it is also necessary to collect evidence – to carry out research. Research methods are the means by which sociologists gather material about society. The main research methods used in sociology are usually divided into 'quantitative' methods, most notably the survey and the statistical analysis of secondary-source data; and ethnographic or 'qualitative' methods, most notably participant observation, in-depth interviewing and the qualitative analysis of secondary sources of data. One could argue that no research method is explicitly feminist or anti-feminist; it is the ways in which research is carried out and the theoretical framework within which the results are interpreted that determine if research is feminist or not. However, many feminists have rejected quantitative methods of data collection and analysis because they argue these assume a scientific status that sociology cannot and should not strive to attain, and because they treat people as objects, as natural scientists treat chemicals or rocks, rather than as human subjects. Indeed, as Porter (1995) has pointed out, quantitative methods of data collection and analysis, in particular the survey method, were developed largely as technologies of distance that became the preferred vehicle for studying social groups such as the insane, the unemployed, criminals, factory workers and prostitutes (so that a degree of physical and moral distance could be maintained). However, Ann Oakley (1998) has argued in favour of rehabilitating quantitative methodology and integrating a range of methods into a feminist social science. Her analysis is grounded in the contention that

> The case against quantitative ways of knowing is based on a rejection of reason and science as masculine and an embracing of experience as feminine; but this is essentialist thinking which buys into the very paradox that it protests about.
>
> (Oakley, 1998, p. 725)

Feminist research has generally been concerned to move away from the positivistic view of sociology as a science and to argue that research should involve a commitment to the emancipation of women. While some feminists have suggested that feminist research should be research by women, for women and with women, others have argued that it should include both men and women in its 'subject-matter', explicitly recognising and investigating the sex–gender system that exists in the society being researched.

Harding (1987) has suggested that it is not the *method* of research that makes feminist research significantly different from malestream research, but:

1 *the alternative origin of problems* – raising problems and issues that are of concern to women rather than to men;
2 *the alternative explanatory hypotheses* that are developed and the evidence that is used;
3 *the purpose of the enquiry* – to facilitate an understanding of women's views of the world and to play a role in female emancipation; and
4 *the nature of the relationship* between the researcher and the 'subjects' of her enquiry.

She points to the need to distinguish between methods, methodologies and epistemologies. Methods are techniques for gathering evidence. Methodologies are theories of how research should proceed; they are usually qualitative or quantitative. Epistemologies define what counts as an adequate theory and how research findings can be judged: what makes the findings of one piece of research more adequate than the findings of other research in the same area. The question of epistemology raises the issue of who the knower (researcher) can be, what tests of belief something must pass to count as legitimate knowledge, and what class of things can be known.

What is distinctive about feminist research is the methodology and epistemology that underpins it. However, feminists are not in total agreement; there are competing theories and arguments about the ways in which feminists should undertake research. There is, however, some measure of agreement about the reasons for rejecting malestream research:

1 In the name of science, malestream sociologists have helped to sustain an ideology that supports the continuing subordination of women.
2 Women, and women's concerns, have not been seen as a major aspect of the research project. When women are included in research they are often seen as marginal and viewed from the perspective of men. There has also been a tendency to present men and masculinity as the norm, and when women do not conform to this norm to present them as deviant.

3 Those who have been researched have been treated as objects to be worked on. Researchers have also used those studied to serve the researchers' purposes rather than to meet the needs and aspirations of the researched. Feminists have referred to this as the 'research as rape' model. Shulamit Reinharz (1983) captures this criticism well:

> conducted on a rape model, the researchers take, hit and run. They intrude into their subjects' privacy, disrupt their perceptions, utilise false pretences, manipulate the relationships, and give little or nothing in return. When the needs of the researchers are satisfied, they break off contact with the subjects.
>
> (Reinharz, 1983, p. 80)

Feminists are concerned to develop research strategies to incorporate women and not to treat the researched as objects to be used by the researcher. There are differences among feminists as to how this is to be done – as to what exactly feminist research is and how to go about doing it. Initially much feminist scholarship and research involved a form of deconstruction – that is, it was concerned to expose the male-centred nature of existing sociological research, and to point out that it ignored the experiences and perceptions of women. A second stage was research on women by women. This research asked new questions and was concerned to provide knowledge from the perspective of women. It was recognised that it was necessary to develop theories to provide an understanding of women's experience. Many feminists see this as the main objective of feminist research – especially radical feminists. A third stage has been the development of the argument that feminists can develop a feminist sociology only if they research men as well as women, but with the proviso that the research is from a feminist perspective, providing a fuller and more adequate knowledge.

The logic of the feminist position on research seems to demand non-individual co-research, where the researcher helps the women involved to undertake their own research, so that researcher and researched decide together on the object of the research, how the research is to be conducted and how the findings are to be used. In practice, few feminists have adopted this method. This is partly because it is not possible for the researcher to share her knowledge and expertise, and to imply that she is doing so conceals a power relationship rather than overcoming it. Furthermore, most researchers are middle-class women with a university education, and many of those who are researched lack this privileged background. Most feminists have argued, however, that rather than concealing, exploiting or pretending to overcome this power relationship, (academic) feminist researchers should use their relatively privileged background and position in a way that benefits women as a group and not merely their individual careers. As Alcoff and Potter (1993, p. 14) put it, many feminists argue that 'feminist epistemologies must be tested by their effects on the practical political struggles occurring in a wider frame of reference that the academy'.

As we noted above, many feminists have argued that feminist researchers in sociology must adopt a qualitative methodology, so that the women (and men) who are the subjects of research can be 'heard' and so that it becomes possible to see and understand the world from the position of the research subjects. They have also rejected the view that feminist researchers can be objective in the sense of being uninvolved, because as researchers they are part of what is being researched. Involvement is seen as necessary and inevitable; necessary because the researcher must and does identify with the women she is researching, and inevitable because she is a part of what is being researched – she is involved. This means that what sociologists call 'reflexivity' is essential – the researcher must be constantly aware of how her values, attitudes and perceptions influence the research process, from the formulation of the research questions, through the data-collection stage, to the ways in which the data are analysed, explained and disseminated.

Clearly a dilemma for feminist researchers is how to balance reflexivity with representation. Gayle Letherby (2002), in her account of researching the social, emotional and medical experiences of women who are 'infertile' or 'involuntarily childless', argues that feminist research must aim both to represent and interpret the experiences of respondents, at the same time as theorising and making sense of those experiences within the context of a broader totality of knowledge and understanding, not least because (unlike individual respondents), researchers have access not only to their intellectual knowledge base but also the experiences and reflections of all respondents involved in the research. On this basis she distinguishes between 'descriptive reflexivity' (in which respondents engage) and 'analytical reflexivity' (which is the responsibility of the researcher).

In practice, feminist sociologists have found it difficult to carry out research that lives up to the demands of the methodology that has been set out above. This is because of the sheer difficulty of doing research at all, because the training (and funding) of most female researchers has taken place within malestream assumptions, because there are inevitably power relationships involved in research, because the funders of research have certain views about what constitutes 'good' research practice, and because feminist sociologists are part of a wider academic community to which they have to justify their research practices and findings. Yet, one of the main traps into which they fall is to take on a neutral stance, so that the research is on women, asks questions of interest to women and uses qualitative methods, but the researcher tries to stand back and remain detached from what is going on rather than being a part of the research process and making explicit her involvement as a woman. In her early work, Ann Oakley (1982) suggests that she was often aware of how much of a danger this was when she was interviewing women about the events surrounding maternity and childbirth – a subject of central interest to the women being researched and to Oakley herself as a woman and mother. For this reason, she describes interviewing women as a 'contradiction in terms' because the interviews she carried out were more like conversations than interrogations or 'scientific' observations.

Feminist sociologists also frequently use the research findings for publications that are as much for their career advancement as to help the women (and men) who were the subjects of research – although, of course, the publication of research findings can influence policy-makers and social perceptions more generally, and could result in changes in women's lives that meet their needs. The danger here is that the researcher does not have control over how others interpret and use the research findings.

Most feminists would argue against the view that the researcher/scientist is not responsible for how the findings of research are used, but once research is published the researcher effectively loses control. Janet Finch's research finding (1983) that working-class mothers find it difficult to organise pre-school playgroups for their children could as easily be used to argue that this means that they are responsible for their children not having pre-school education as to argue that the state should organise and run pre-school facilities for working-class children. This does not mean that we reject feminist research or that we do not publish our findings. It means that we have to be constantly aware of the dangers of appearing to be a neutral scientist and of the ways in which research findings can be distorted by an anti-feminist interpretation.

Feminist epistemologies

One of the main problems for feminists in sociology is having their research findings taken seriously. On what basis are their findings better than, more true than, those of malestream sociologists? Indeed, why should we believe the findings of *any* sociological research? Truth claims are generally based on a particular epistemological perspective, that is a theory of what constitutes knowledge and a justification of particular criteria for discerning between competing truth claims. In the social sciences the dominant basis for truth claims is that the research was scientific – that is, the researcher was objective and value-free and followed certain agreed procedures for carrying out the research – the Scientific Method. This epistemology is generally referred to as 'positivism'. Although sociologists other than feminists have been critical of positivistic social science, feminists have made a significant contribution to understanding the connection between power and knowledge. In particular, they have pointed out that the recognition of knowledge claims is intrinsically tied to relations of domination and exclusion.

A major problem is that feminist research can be accused of being 'subjective' and therefore of no value. If it is seen as subjective then there is no way of showing how feminist conclusions are any better than those reached by anyone else, and why the findings of feminist research are better than those of malestream research and should be taken seriously. There are a number of feminist epistemological stances which have been adopted to provide the basis for feminist truth claims. However, we must be aware, as Liz Stanley and Sue Wise (1993) point out, that:

> Marking out the attributes of different although related feminist epistemologies, such as feminist empiricism, feminist standpoint and postmodernism feminism, is useful as long as it is recognised that this produces *a model*, and is thus necessarily a simplified (not a literal/representational) account of the epistemological possibilities that exist.
>
> (Stanley and Wise, 1993, p. 190)

They go on to argue that feminists typically encompass, in their actual work, elements of a number of epistemological stances. They suggest (p. 191) that five broad principles should be adopted in considering feminist epistemologies:

1   While there is a range of feminist epistemologies, in practice these shade into each other in people's research.
2   Different feminist epistemological positions sometimes disagree over the basis of knowledge, who generates it and under what conditions.
3   Feminist sociologists often combine elements of a number of epistemological positions within their work, and this indicates not only that we can work within contradictions, but that either we do not think carefully through the basis of what we do and what we claim for it, or alternatively that we do think it through but choose to work with 'contradictory' elements because this is what social reality is like.
4   There is no 'true' feminist epistemology – each can be seen to be sensible and plausible given the purposes and project of those who hold it.
5   We can challenge and question other positions, but that we should have mutual respect for different feminisms and recognise the value of diversity.

Feminist empiricism

A position adopted by many liberal feminists, feminist empiricism is critical of male-stream research because it has been male-centred. Feminist empiricists suggest that feminists are more likely to produce adequate knowledge because they include women and women's experiences in their research as central and normal rather than as marginal and deviant. In terms of the accumulation of knowledge, feminist empiricists are concerned primarily to correct bias in our knowledge of men and women (and in relations of sexual difference), and do so largely through trying to ensure that our understanding of the world is more scientific, and thus more accurately reflects what is believed to be the reality of men's and women's lives. This approach is therefore underpinned by a realist ontology (the belief that there is an external, objective reality) and the view that the role of research is to produce accurate – scientific – knowledge of that reality (see Chapter 2).

The logical goal of this perspective is the development of non-sexist research. Magrit Eichler (1988) has produced guidelines for such research. She argues that non-sexist research should eliminate:

1   *sexism in titles*: titles should be explicit (for example, 'The Affluent Worker' study should be retitled 'The Male Affluent Worker');
2   *sexism in language*: language should be used that makes it clear whether men or women or both are being addressed or referred to;
3   *sexist concepts* (for example defining class by reference to the occupation of the head of household);
4   *sexism in research designs* (so that men and women are both included in the research where this is relevant);
5   *sexism in methods*;
6   *sexism in data interpretation* – the interpretation of data from the perspective just of men or just of women;
7   *sexism in policy evaluation* (so that policies that serve the needs of both men and women are advocated).

371

Most feminists would agree with Eichler but argue that what she says is insufficient. They would reject the positivistic research stance that underlies her preoccupation with non-sexist methods, arguing that given the power relations that exist in society such research practices would continue to be male-dominated and meet the needs of men rather than of women. This is because such research does not challenge the underlying assumptions inherent in malestream research, which are presented as truths.

The main critique of this approach focuses on the extent to which it leaves established values and dualisms intact (the idea that the social world exists independently of our knowledge of it has been criticised particularly by feminists whose epistemological position has been influenced by social constructivism and postmodernism). These feminists have criticised a continued faith in the ability (or rather viability) of a neutral scientist (researcher) to represent an objective reality. Feminists have also criticised a continued faith in the ability of metanarratives such as science to emancipate women, when they have traditionally provided a framework for the production of knowledge that has served to oppress and marginalise women, and to trivialise women's lived experiences. Further, feminist empiricism has been criticised for its tendency to position human beings as objects of research. Many feminists working from alternative epistemological perspectives have claimed that this is unethical, and is counter to the emancipatory principles of feminist research.

In their critique of feminist empiricism, Liz Stanley and Sue Wise (1983) argue that research carried out in the traditional sociological framework, whether 'positivistic' or 'anti-sexist', draws on a pre-chosen framework – the findings are abstracted from reality and presented as if given research logics had been followed. Material is organised for the reader, and information is not given about what happened, when it happened, how it happened and how the people involved (including the researchers) felt about it. They argue that it is essential to recognise that malestream sociological research is written up as if a formal pattern of procedures were carried out, but that in practice this is rarely what happens. We would argue that non-sexist research as advocated by Eichler would fall into the same trap. This type of research account fails to examine the relationships between experience, consciousness and theory because it acts as if they are unimportant or do not exist. The researcher is presented as an objective, neutral and value-free technician who is following set procedures. All that Eichler does is to replace what she and many other feminists would agree are sexist practices with practices which attempt to overcome only the sexism, rather than the structural or cultural inequalities by which they are underpinned. Most feminists would argue that following such a set of procedures would not produce feminist knowledge because they reject the view that the researcher can be neutral. Feminists challenge the assumption that knowledge exists not only independently of the person(s) who produce it, but also that those who produce knowledge can do so without their values and attitudes influencing the knowledge they produce. That is, even if there is a reality independent of our understanding, we cannot reproduce that reality uncontaminated. However, it is important to keep in mind that while feminist empiricists do subscribe to the idea of an objective, knowable world (a realist ontology), they are also committed to carrying out research for women and providing empirical knowledge to be used in feminist politics and campaigns (see e.g. Riley, 1992). Ann Oakley (1998), as we noted above, has recently advocated dissolving the dualism between quantitative and qualitative methods, and adopting a feminist empiricist approach which, she argues, 'is more likely to promote policy-relevant research "for" women' than other approaches (p. 708). As Sara Delamont (2003, p. 71) notes, however, 'this assumes a rationality among policy researchers that those who are not liberal feminists with a faith in the Enlightenment project do not share'.

Feminist standpoint epistemology

As Sandra Harding (2004a, p. 1) puts it in her introduction to *The Standpoint Theory Reader*, 'standpoint theory has continued to attract both enthusiasts and critics during the three decades of its recent history'; it has also begun to evolve into a range of perspectives and has certainly not responded stubbornly to its critics. Since it was introduced in the 1970s, it has influenced a number of feminist thinkers, and has been the focus of ongoing debates within academic feminism (Harding, 2004b). Standpoint feminists seek to justify their research findings as better, more adequate, than those produced by the malestream or other feminist researchers. Standpoint epistemology is a position most closely associated with materialist perspectives (including Marxist feminism, dual-systems theory and critical feminist theory – see Chapter 2) and takes a realist stance – that is it believes that there is an underlying material reality that structures the social world. As one of its main advocates, Nancy Hartsock (1998, p. 400) has argued, in standpoint epistemology 'the understanding of the relation between knowledge and power present in Marx's work provides important criteria for what can count as better, or more privileged, knowledges'. In Hartsock's work particularly, standpoint epistemology involves the adoption of what Marxists describe as 'the dialectical method'; a way of thinking about the social world that involves replacing the idea that the world is composed of 'things' with an emphasis on the importance of 'processes', and of understanding these processes within the context of the social totality. Malestream theory, it is argued by feminists who adopt this position, has a distorted or partial view of this reality, and has ignored the social processes that shape women's lives, but feminist research is able to provide a better, less partial account of these processes (like the ways in which certain types of work come to be gendered, for instance).

The concept of a 'standpoint' is based on the view that what we do (our social position, determined primarily for Marxist feminists by the sexual division of labour) shapes what we know (our view of the social world). A standpoint is therefore a perspective or viewpoint based on our social position, and the concept of a standpoint epistemology is derived from the Marxist proposition, associated largely with the work of Georg Lukacs, that there is a discernible 'standpoint of the proletariat'. This idea takes as its starting point the Marxist view that human activity (material life) shapes our consciousness (our subjective perception of the world, and how we experience it). As Hartsock (1998, p. 402) notes: 'Both Marx and Lukacs recognized that truth and power are intimately connected: what is to count as truth, methods for obtaining it, criteria for evaluation – all are profoundly influenced by extant power relations.'

This position shares with positivism a realist ontology and the view that trained or well-educated experts have a greater degree of knowledge and understanding of how to access and explain that reality than others. However, unlike positivists, stand-point epistemologists also emphasise that the production of knowledge is a politically engaged activity. Malestream researchers have often refused to acknowledge this, but it is a problem which feminist researchers have confronted. They want to reject the view that all knowledge is equally valid (relativism) and to argue that it is essential to be able to justify some research findings and theoretical explanations as more adequate than others. If this is not possible then it is difficult to see why feminist research find-ings and explanations should be seen as better or more true than malestream ones. It is necessary to be able to demonstrate that some statements are better accounts of social reality than others, while recognising their inevitable partiality.

All knowledge is based on experience, and standpoint theorists claim their research is scientifically preferable because it originates in and is tested against a more complete and less distorted kind of experience than malestream research. Human activity, it is suggested, structures and sets limits to human understanding, as what we do shapes and constrains what we can know. However, human activity is structured for and experienced differently by men and women because the latter are subordinated; feminist sociologists have a privileged access to *real* social reality because the oppressed can see people and events as they really are. In the words of Dorothy Smith (1987), they have 'a wider angle of view because they can see things from the perspective of not only the privileged (men) but also the oppressed women' (p. 99). There is an important claim to power here – the power of knowledge and the power to claim true knowledge. Knowledge production is seen as a political process, with some knowledge claims being seen as superior to others.

Standpoint theorists argue that men's knowledge can never be complete. It is not just that the oppressed can see more, but also that their knowledge emerges through their struggle against oppression – women's knowledge emerges from a struggle against men and the attempt to replace the distorted knowledge produced by men, which is used to control and subordinate women, with feminist knowledge. The feminist standpoint is an achievement – it is the portrayal of social life from the viewpoint of the activity which produces women's social experience, not from the partial and perverse perspective available from the 'ruling gender' experiences of men.

Standpoint feminists argue that their accounts of the social world are less partial and less distorted than malestream ones. Feminist science is better able to reflect the world as it is and is able to replace the distorted and distorting accounts produced by malestream sociology and consequently to advance sociological knowledge. It is based on the view that there is a real world, but that our accounts of it are always and inevitably partial, and that feminist accounts are less partial and less distorted than malestream ones. They emphasise particularly the subjective implications of the sexual division of labour for women's knowledge of the social world. For feminists such as Nancy Hartsock, men's and women's different experiences of work shape their different views of social reality.

Where standpoint epistemology becomes slightly complex, and for many feminists particularly problematic, is in the claim that the standpoint of the oppressed offers a clearer vision – a more accurate, or objective perception of reality that is, ultimately, more emancipatory. This is what Hartsock (drawing on Marx) calls an 'oppositional consciousness' – a view of the social world that is not driven by the maintenance of ideology, but by the desire to uncover the 'truth' of an objective reality. Undistorted by a political interest in maintaining a relatively powerful position, feminist knowledge (knowledge produced by the oppressed) is thus believed to be less ideological, and more truthful. In terms of this latter point, however, some standpoint epistemologists (particularly those who might more accurately be described as feminist critical theorists than Marxist feminists) tend to reject the concept of absolute, objective truth in favour of 'certitude'. Their concern is with the accumulation of knowledge that is credible; that is, 'good enough' to act upon (Benhabib, 1992). For standpoint feminists, then, the imperatives for producing feminist knowledge are not simply epistemological, but political.

However, standpoint feminists have been criticised for ignoring differences *between* women and for assuming an unproblematic commonality. Standpoint epistemology tends to assume that oppression is somehow unitary, or that women identify primarily as women rather than as members of other oppressed or privileged groups in society. The 'adding on' of difference – race, age, sexuality, etc. – is done in an unproblematic way that assumes that middle-class white feminist theory can be used to theorise the experience of all women. The same criticism can probably be made of the inclusion of women as a category in malestream research – it does not take account of differences that are the outcome of processes of racism, ageism, heterosexism that result in super- and subordination.

Some Black feminists, for example Patricia Hill Collins, have argued that as a more oppressed group Black women's standpoint is not only different from but has a wider angle of vision than white women's standpoint. Subsequently (1990), however, she has questioned this earlier argument that the more oppressed you are the more 'correct' your analysis of the social origins of oppression. Instead she has argued that Black women's accounts of the social world are different from but not necessarily better than white women's. Arguably this raises the question of how we choose the 'best' accounts of reality. Alternatively, it can be argued that all knowledge is partial and that accounts from different standpoints will add to our knowledge and understanding of social reality, a point to which we return towards the end of this chapter.

Feminist constructivism

Feminist constructivism challenges the foundationalism of both positivistic and standpoint epistemologies and argues for a social constructionist approach to knowledge. Foundationalism is the view that reality is singular and exists 'out there' independently of our understanding of it, available for experts to probe and discover – for example that capitalism and patriarchy have an independent objective reality discoverable by experts. Constructivism argues that the social world is constructed and shaped by members of society – they reject the claim that there is a 'true' knowledge which certifies some feminist knowledge as better than, superior to, other feminist or non-feminist knowledges.

In rejecting the standpoint position, they argue that there cannot be a feminist science and that academic feminists who advocate the standpoint position are only trying to set up a new truth. These feminists are deeply sceptical about claims to universal knowledge and argue that there is no social world or set of social structures 'out there' waiting to be known, but only many subjective experiences. 'All that feminist (or indeed any) researchers can do is to uncover the many stories that different women tell and reveal the different knowledges that they have' (see Stanley and Wise, 1983, pp. 145–148). In a later book (1993), Liz Stanley and Sue Wise argue that all knowledge is a product of human social experience: 'Thus there is no way of moving outside of experience to validate theories 'objectively' – nothing exists other than social life, our place within it and our understandings of all this' (p. 193). In this later work, they argue for a position which they describe as 'fractured foundationalism'; a position that does not dispute the existence of truth and a material reality, but acknowledges that judgements about them are always relative to the context within which such knowledge is produced. This perspective emphasises that researchers are not intellectually superior to their respondents, and that they have the responsibility to produce reflexive accounts of both their research process and of the findings, so that readers can have access to the procedures which underlie the way that knowledge is presented and constructed by the researcher.

Feminists such as these are critical of malestream research because of its claims to objectivity, and the claim that the researcher is not involved in the research process. They reject the view that the sociologist can be a dispassionate and uncritical 'scientific' observer and argue that the experiences and feelings of the subject should be at the centre of the production of all social knowledge. In their early work, Stanley and Wise (1983) argued that in presenting accounts of their research researchers often 'do not tell it as it happened' but present a reconstructed account of how the research was undertaken that accords with textbook prescriptions. Not only are these accounts false, but they fail to reveal the ways in which the researcher was involved in the research process. Consequently they argue that feminist research must be genuinely reflexive – that is, the accounts of the research must make available to the reader the procedures which underlie the way the knowledge which is presented was produced, and draw on the 'intellectual autobiography' of the researchers. (Letherby's (2002) account of researching childless women, which draws on Stanley and Wise, is a notable example of autobiography in feminist research.) It is also essential not to deny one's experiences and feelings as a feminist, they argue, but to use them as part of the process of validating one's research rather than vice versa – that is we should accept the validity of our own experiences as women as the basis for feminist knowledge. The adequacy of feminism is based on the extent to which it enables us to understand better our situation as women and gives us the resources with which to emancipate ourselves.

This position rejects the idea of feminist grand theory but argues that women do have a unity of experience in the same way that racialised groups, lesbian women, disabled people, and so on do. These social/political constructions, it argues, are fundamental to the systematic assignment of positions of super- and subordination. However, it is also necessary for feminist theorisation to take account of the multiple fragmentation of women's experiences of oppression, based on age, sexuality, race, disability, and so on. It argues for the valid existence of varieties of feminist epistemology, together with the acknowledgment of the contextual specificity of feminist as of other knowledge. The recognition that who a researcher is, in terms of their sex, race, class and sexuality, affects what they 'find' in research is as true of feminists as any other researchers.

(Stanley and Wise, 1993, p. 228)

The major problem with this position is its relativism. While we agree that researchers must be reflexive, that women must speak for themselves and that research findings should help the oppressed, we are sceptical of the view that all women's accounts are equally valid and that there is no way of selecting between them. If all women's accounts are equally valid, how can a feminist researcher claim that her version is more 'true' than those of others? One way of responding to this question is to adopt Letherby's (2002) position that, while researchers may not necessarily be intellectually superior to respondents, they do nevertheless occupy an intellectually privileged position that provides a basis for their claims both to be able to interpret and contextualise the views or experiences of their respondents, at the same time as claiming that these interpretations constitute knowledge of the social world. Hence, Letherby's position (one with which we would agree) is that convincing claims to feminist knowledge are based not necessarily on intellectual superiority but on 'epistemic privilege'. This issue becomes particularly significant for feminist researchers who undertake research on non- or anti-feminist women, for whom claims to know 'better' than other women can become especially problematic.

In her discussion of some of the methodological and epistemological issues involved in doing feminist research on non-feminist women scientists in the UK, Millen (1997) argues that we need to define feminist research 'in terms of values which it might uphold rather than techniques it might use'. A key issue, she notes, is the conflict between the researcher and the participants' construction of the meaning of gendered experience. Like Letherby, Millen attempts to resolve some of the epistemological dilemmas involved in the conflict between respondents' and researchers' meanings by drawing on both feminist standpoint epistemology and insights derived from postmodernism feminism. Again, in a similar vein to Letherby, she argues that the role of the researcher is to make sense of experiences and to locate individuals within historical and social contexts. For her,

it is neither possible (nor, to my mind, even desirable) that the researcher should disclaim her privilege with respect to participants, in terms of her greater knowledge of the issues raised and of the theoretical framework of the research and of social life generally.

(Millen, 1997, para. 3.4)

Clearly there are some complex issues here that need to be disentangled, and Millen goes on to substantiate the notion of epistemic privilege, by arguing that

Firstly, it is facile to assume that the analysis of experience necessarily means the exploitation of experience to the detriment of the participant, or that the researcher's reinterpretation of that experience will change its fundamental meaning to the participant. The participant will always own the construction of meaning she has ascribed to experience, regardless of the interpretation placed upon this by the researcher within the publication of his or her work. Secondly, the researcher is the one who has been motivated to explore the theoretical ideas before conducting research, and to try to construct knowledge from experience: it is a practical necessity that some individuals should do it, if we are ever to have any knowledge at all.

(Millen, 1997, para. 3.4)

A key issue for both Letherby and Millen, then, in their attempts to address some of the problems associated with Stanley and Wise's 'fragmented foundationalist' approach, is the relationship between representation and reflexivity, as well as between knowledge and power in shaping epistemic privilege. This latter theme in particular has been of central concern to those feminists whose epistemological perspective is allied most closely with the theoretical ideas associated with postmodernism and poststructuralism.

Postmodern feminist epistemologies

Postmodern perspectives on knowledge tend to vary between an extreme position maintaining that all knowledge is relative and a more moderated version of post-modernism (not unlike Stanley and Wise's 'fragmented foundationalism') characterised by the contention that all knowledge is socially situated and contextual. This latter approach (one with which we are more sympathetic than the former) has been easier for feminists to develop alliances with (particularly Black and post-colonial feminists) because it emphasises that what becomes accepted as 'the truth' and what is thought of as a viable claim to knowledge is disproportionately associated with powerful social groups. Hence, this approach derives largely from Foucault (1980) the idea that power and knowledge are inseparable.

In epistemological terms, syntheses of feminism and postmodernism have placed a considerable emphasis on plurality, the contextual basis of knowledge and the con-tingent nature of reality. Much of the postmodern feminist approach has been based largely on a critique of the realist ontology that underpins both feminist empiricism and standpoint epistemology. Instead, postmodern feminists emphasise that reality is socially constructed and is shaped by the existence of multiple truths that, they argue, cannot be explained with reference to any single metanarrative. For those feminists influenced particularly by the poststructuralist insights of Foucault and Derrida (see Chapter 2), what we come to think of as 'reality' is largely the outcome of discourse, and is shaped by the interrelationship between power, knowledge and language. For these feminists, competing epistemological or 'truth' claims merely add layer upon layer to these discursive constructions of reality.

In complete contrast to the attempt to construct a non-sexist approach to feminist research, or a feminist standpoint, postmodern feminists have proposed theories which discard entirely the possibility of accessing a single, objective 'truth' whether it is done by non-sexist, empirical research methods, or by privileging women's experiences or everyday lives. Postmodern feminism involves a critique both of the idea of a standpoint, and of the notion of a stable subject as the focus of standpoint research. McLennan (1995, p. 392) sums this position up when she argues that 'the search for a unitary notion of "truth" about the world is impossible, a relic of the sterile Enlightenment: knowledge is partial, profane and fragmented'. Rather than seeking out a unifying epistemology, albeit one that incorporates sexual difference, we should be developing ways of thinking about the social world that enable us to accept the existence of multiple truths. In this sense, as Millen put it, postmodernism feminism

> Exposes the tension at the heart of feminist research most acutely. On the one hand, it embodies and empowers feminism as a tool for critical examination of epistemology and praxis, and provides additional critical tools for the examination of power and knowledge. It points out that power is not unitary, and that some forms of power are situated and concentrated. . . . However, in the act of so doing it may seriously undermine the political role of feminist research, of incorporating women's lives and gendered experience into the corpus of knowledge. . . . On a practical level, do postmodernist ideas about the status of theory and of methods of inquiry rule out many ways of gathering knowledge which might have some political utility for the feminist project?
>
> (Millen, 1997, para. 7.8)

What the variety of disparate approaches to knowledge, truth and reality that could broadly be termed postmodernist or poststructuralist seem to share in common is the conviction that there are multiple truths, and that all knowledge is relative to the social context and position of the knowing subject. This is both potentially valuable and problematic for feminists. On the one hand, the relativism that this implies could, in this sense, perhaps be understood as an anti-epistemology. Elizabeth Grosz (1995), for instance, has argued that knowledges are merely perspectives produced from a multiplicity of vantage points. This has led some feminists (notably those advocating a standpoint approach) to argue that postmodernism is politically disabling for feminism, because it negates the possibility of the feminist claim to 'know' that the social world as it is currently organised serves to oppress women as a social group.

On the other hand, in taking philosophy and theories of knowledge as its critical object, feminist theory influenced by postmodernism has tended to regard deconstruction as a political activity in itself. In this sense, feminist research involving deconstruction has tended to focus on the ways in which what we term knowledge or truth is the outcome of a series of binary oppositions and power relations. Hence, postmodern feminists argue that supposedly neutral, sexually indifferent or universal 'truths' merely conceal masculine interests and perceptions of reality.

One particular feminist writer associated with this approach is Susan Hekman. Like many contemporary thinkers, Hekman sees modern Western thought as structured according to a series of dualisms. The three she focuses on are rational/irrational, subject/object and culture/nature. In her book *Gender and Knowledge* (1990) she discusses masculinity and femininity in relation to each of these three dualisms claiming that, in each case, feminists have responded to them by arguing that either women participate in the masculine, privileged side (e.g. the rational) as much as men do (e.g.

as liberal feminists who advocate an empiricist epistemology), or that the feminine side is really superior to the privileged side (e.g. as standpoint epistemologists). Hekman's general objection to these approaches is that they accept the dichotomies and simply take one side or the other. Because the dichotomies are rooted in gender dualisms, which are inherently hierarchical, any theory of knowledge that adopts them merely perpetuates (however unwittingly), rather than deconstructs, male domination.

In her critique of the social construction of knowledge, French feminist writer Luce Irigaray (1993) argues, similarly, that men conceal and rationalise their domination by claiming that their interests and views are universal and neutral. She argues that this is possible only because universal claims to truth are grounded in cultural processes that correlate men's ways of knowing with the mind and women's with the body and 'instinct' or 'intuition' (and hence, as natural, irrational, unreasonable and subjective). She argues that within a philosophical tradition that has consistently equated women with the body and men with the mind (and which has prized the latter over the former), men have been able to establish and maintain their position as disembodied, universal and 'perspectiveless' knowing subjects.

The role of feminist epistemology from this perspective is to reveal the ways in which men have defined and described the social world as they see and experience it – from their point of view, while claiming that this is an absolute truth (de Beauvoir, 1988 [1949]). As well as emphasising the social construction of knowledge and the discursive nature of reality, a postmodernist approach to feminism also emphasises the importance of highlighting the existence of multiple truths (rather than simply men's and women's standpoints). Anna Yeatman (1994) sums this up when she argues that a postmodernist epistemology involves:

1 *a deconstructive approach* to understanding the discursive nature of the social world;
2 *a critique of metanarratives*, and of claims to universal knowledge of the social world as an objective reality;
3 a relational, contextual theory of knowledge and *truth as plural*;
4 an emphasis on the *embodied nature of knowledge*; and
5 a conception of *language* as a material, active, productive system.

Postmodernists therefore reject the 'will to truth' that they associate with Enlightenment thought, and the view that there can be true knowledge – that feminist knowledge is better than, truer than malestream knowledge. For this reason they argue that standpoint feminism, which does not challenge the idea of a valid or universal truth, cannot handle the concept of multiple realities or deconstructionist ideas.

Carol Smart's account of the relationship between power, knowledge and the law is a notable example of feminist deconstruction underpinned by a postmodernist epistemology. As she argues,

I want to attempt to analyse law in a way which recognises the power of law to disqualify or silence, yet does not seek to posit an alternative truth as the main strategy to resist legal discourse.

(Smart, 1995, p. 78)

Using rape as the main example, she goes on to suggest that acknowledging the existence of multiple truths could be an important political strategy for feminism: 'My point is that there may be other accounts of rape [than legal ones] which could become forms of resistance rather than sources of victimisation' (p. 86). However, she refuses to privilege any account as more 'true', or more accurate than others, and indeed parenthetically indicates that if women did take up an account that enabled them to resist the ways in which rape victims are characterised within legal discourse they might lose the existing protection from the law. This means that we are left with the view that all sociology can do is 'construct subversive knowledge' (p. 230).

Whilst many of the conceptual insights of postmodernism have made a significant contribution to feminist ideas, its epistemological implications have been subject to several criticisms. These include claims that:

1   The position is self-defeating in philosophical terms – it elevates the principle of 'no truth except within a discourse' to a general principle which is true outside of discourse (and, indeed, it is impossible to enunciate a general principle which others are to believe and not do so).
2   It effectively abolishes both sociology and feminism as academic modes of research – if there are no general categories, then there can be no study of structured inequalities or power relations and no attempt to understand women's oppression. We sympathise with and are much influenced by postmodernism's insistence on the specific, the detailed, and the difference between elements which 'grand theory' may wish to combine. Nonetheless we still see the need for grand theory, however tentative it may have to be and however necessary it may be to remember that what is true of a collective does not necessarily explain the actions and experiences of any individual member of it. (See also Rattansi (1995), who makes the case for avoiding a polarisation into 'the postmodern' and 'the rest'.)
3   Postmodernism appears to abolish politics: if, for example, the category 'woman' is meaningless, then the notion of women (or other groups) fighting their oppressors is equally meaningless.
4   Finally, postmodernism strongly suggests that the subject is fragmented and that it makes little sense to talk about it as a coherent bounded whole which acts and takes decisions. Again we understand the force of this position. If taken to the extreme, however, it negates ethics, because there is no self to take responsibility for actions.

Nevertheless, as many feminists have recently argued, postmodernist insights can be used to continually reflect on the role of feminist research, and on the gendered aspects of malestream research. There is an argument, for instance, for drawing on postmodernist concepts of discourse and plurality in this respect, as well as the idea, developed particularly by Donna Haraway (1991, 2004), that all knowledge is 'situated'.

Epistemic communities

Bringing together elements of both standpoint epistemology and postmodernist feminism, some feminists, such as Alison Assiter (1996), have developed the idea that there is not one standpoint, but many. Drawing on critical theorist Jurgen Habermas, Assiter develops the idea that what locates feminist women in a shared epistemological standpoint is not a homogenous social identity or position, but a shared political interest (in emancipation). She describes not a woman's standpoint, then, but a feminist one, as an 'epistemic community'. As she puts it,

> An epistemic community . . . will be a group of individuals who share certain fundamental interests, values and beliefs in common, for example, that sexism is wrong, that racism is wrong, and who work on consequences of these presup-positions. . . . Thus, feminists world-wide, despite our numerous disagreements, share a commitment to modifying and helping to eliminate power differentials based on gender. . . . Feminists may argue about what 'gender' means and what 'power' means, and how these differentials have come about. Yet there is a broad commitment to a set of values, and it is this commitment, I am suggesting that makes feminists as a group, world-wide, an epistemic community.
>
> (Assiter, 1996, pp. 82–83)

This leads her to develop the idea of epistemic communities defined not according to universal experience or homogenous identity (in the more traditional Marxist sense), but as contextually specific. Unlike the concept of a standpoint, therefore, an epistemic community is believed to be contingent and contextual, yet bound together by shared political interests. As Assiter puts it, 'its boundaries are constantly shifting, and it may go in and out of existence' (p. 95).

Although realist in its orientation, the concept of an epistemic community does not assume an Enlightenment 'view from nowhere' from which the truth is revealed. Rather, it is 'historically located, its beliefs and its experiences are inflected by the values it holds' (p. 95). However,

> The nature of the values upheld by any one community are such as to undermine the claims to 'truth' made by other communities. The claims of any one community are not true for all times and in all places; rather they are open to constant revision by other communities.
>
> (Assiter, 1996, p. 95)

In a sense, the idea of an epistemic community vindicates both realism and relativism, albeit in a mediated, situated form.

A not dissimilar approach has been developed by Sandra Harding (2004a, b) in her work on standpoint epistemology, in which she attempts to defend standpoint theory from postmodernist criticism by articulating a version adequate not only for a postmodern context, but also a post-colonial era. In this sense, she draws on work by bell hooks (1990) on the epistemological 'politics of location', by Chela Sandoval (1991) on a 'differential oppositional consciousness' amongst women in developing countries, and also Uma Narayan (1989) on the epistemological implications of global power relations.

Although a useful attempt to draw together two apparently conflicting theories of knowledge within feminism (standpoint epistemology and postmodernism), approaches such as these nevertheless remain problematic not least because (from a postmodernist perspective) they continue to assume a degree of unity and, particularly in the case of Assiter's concept of a feminist 'epistemic community', a shared goal of emancipation amongst feminists. At the other extreme, a more materialist approach would argue that an element of relativism remains in these 'multiple standpoint' approaches, in so far as the question 'Who is the final arbiter of truth?' remains unaddressed.

Conclusions

We are not suggesting that one feminist epistemology is correct and that others are wrong. (While attacking postmodernism as an epistemological stance, for example, we are nonetheless very much influenced by it.) We have tried to point out some of the inadequacies of epistemological positions, and we see this as constructive rather than destructive; it is by recognising what an epistemology cannot explain that we can develop more sophisticated ones. Our major contention in this book has been that mainstream sociology is inadequate because it ignores, distorts or marginalises women. It is inadequate not only because it does not fully incorporate women, but because the knowledge it produces is at best partial because it does not take account of over half of the population. Women have often found that the knowledge provided by conventional sociology does not relate to their lives or their concerns.

Feminism does seek to speak to the experiences of women, to understand reality from the viewpoint of women, to ask questions that relate to women's lives and to uncover the systematic biases and distortions in malestream knowledge. In this book we have tried to show the ways in which feminist scholarship has made a contribution to sociology. We have argued that this does not mean that we can just add one more perspective to the list of sociological topics. What is necessary is a total rethinking of sociological knowledge and the ways in which that knowledge is produced. This is because it is not accidental or the result of an oversight that women have been ignored, marginalised or distorted in sociology, but the outcome of the theoretical and historical underpinning of the discipline. Until relatively recently, malestream sociology failed to confront the assumption that women are naturally determined and that women's role is the outcome of biological imperatives. Consequently the concepts developed to carry out sociological research, and the issues deemed worthy of being researched, often ignored women. To produce adequate sociological knowledge it is necessary to reformulate these concepts and questions so that women become central to the concerns of the discipline.

A key question, however, is whether feminists have epistemological privilege – whether they can provide more adequate, better theoretical understanding than malestream theorists. Standpoint feminists argue that women as an oppressed group do provide more adequate, better accounts than malestream theorists. In other words, they are suggesting that feminist epistemology is privileged. In opposition to this, Liz

Stanley and Sue Wise (1993) argue that feminist epistemologies provide a *different* view on what is taken for 'reality' and that it may indeed be a preferable view. They suggest that it is an authentic position because it posits the oppressed as superior. However, they reject the view of the hierarchical relationship and indicate the problem of how we determine whose work to privilege as 'the oppressed', when we consider race and ethnicity, sexuality, disability, global power relations, and so on. They ask how claims to superior knowledge are to be adjudicated. Rejecting the argument that the category 'woman' is oppressed and that suffering is used to calculate whose knowledge is to be privileged, they argue that there are:

> no foundational grounds for judging the *a priori* superiority of the epistemologies of the oppressed, nor of any one group of the oppressed, in the production of knowledge and the settling of its problems . . . there are, however, moral and political grounds for finding one of them *preferable* . . . the grounds of preference are . . . that it better fits with proponents' experiences of living or being or understanding.
>
> (Stanley and Wise, 1993, p. 228)

For us, the turn to feminist theory was to enable us to make sense of women's lives, and the ways in which society is shaped by sexual difference (the differences between men and women as social subjects) – something which malestream theories did not. However, we accept that feminist theories have themselves been partial and inadequate, that they were constructed largely from the point of view of white, Western, middle-class, able-bodied, heterosexual women and therefore are seen as inadequate from the position of many women. Nevertheless, we do believe that all women share the experience of being exploited and subordinated because of sexual difference and that this provides the basis for commonality, while recognising that there are also important differences between women. Furthermore, we see the construction of theory as dynamic, developing both in response to critique and to the complex task of explaining changing 'realities' (however we conceptualise those realities). The relationship between theories and the social world they are trying to make sense of is dynamic, not static. Theories are modified and changed as part of the continuing development of sociology as a discipline and, indeed – as we indicated in the Introduction – sociology has finally begun to take account of feminist criticisms and contributions, although the sociological imagination is still some way from being as gendered as the social world it seeks to understand.

SUMMARY

1   Research methods are not just 'tools of the trade': what gives meaning to the research is the underlying theory and epistemology used. The methods at the more quantified 'positivistic' end of the spectrum claim to be more scientific and neutral and for this reason feminists have

attacked them, arguing that they in fact represent a malestream view of the world under the guise of science.

2 Feminists have tended to espouse qualitative methods as the better means for carrying out feminist research because they imply more equality between researcher and researched; they allow the viewpoint of the researched to be taken into account, and they do not turn the researched into fragmented objects.

3 Four feminist positions on epistemology have been described – empiricist, standpoint, constructivist and postmodern.

4 More recently, feminists have developed the concept of 'epistemic communities' and have highlighted the epistemological politics of post-colonialism.

FURTHER READING

Delamont, S. (2003) *Feminist Sociology*. London: Sage. More sociological than the other texts listed here, this is an excellent starting point for a consideration of the feminist critique of sociology, and of the production of feminist knowledge. It focuses particularly on methodological debates within sociology, but also engages with epistemological issues and includes a (brief) consideration of standpoint epistemology and postmodernism. It also explores malestream responses to feminist debates on methodology and epistemology (see Chapter 1).

Harding, S. (ed.) (2004) *The Feminist Standpoint Theory Reader: Intellectual and Political Controversies*. London: Routledge. This is the first anthology to collect some of the most important essays on feminist epistemology into a single volume. It includes a range of 'classic' contributions from the 1970s and 1980s, as well as a series of critical engagements and more recent contributions from well-known theorists, and relatively neglected works by post-colonial writers.

Kemp, S. and Squires, J. (1997) *Feminisms*. Oxford: Oxford University Press. Part of the Oxford Reader series, this collection includes two large sections on 'Academies' and 'Epistemologies' which address many of the issues considered in this chapter. Again, it incorporates a broad range of ideas and is not limited to white, Western academic feminism.

References

Abberley, P. (1997) 'The Limits of Classical Social Theory in the Analysis and Transformation of Disablement', in L. Barton and M. Oliver (eds) *Disability Studies: Past, Present and Future*. Leeds: The Disability Press.

Abbott, P. (1995) 'Conflict over the Grey Areas: District Nurses and Home Helps Providing Community Care', *Journal of Gender Studies*. 3: 299–306.

Abbott, P. (2000) 'Gender' in G. Payne (ed.) *Social Divisions*. London: Macmillan.

Abbott, P. (2004) 'Place, Control and Health in Post-Soviet Societies', paper presented to the World Congress of the International Institute of Sociology, Beijing, July.

Abbott, P. and Sapsford, R. (1987) *Women and Social Class*. London: Tavistock.

Abbott, P. and Tyler, M. (1995) 'Ethnic Variation in the Female Labour Force: A Research Note', *British Journal of Sociology*. 46: 339–353.

Abbott, P. and Wallace, C. (1992) *The Family and the New Right*. London: Pluto.

Abel-Smith, B. (1960) *A History of the Nursing Profession*. London: Heinemann.

Abrahams, J. (1995) *Divide and School: Gender and Class Dynamics in Comprehensive Education*. London: Falmer.

Abu-Habib, L. (1997) *Gender and Disability: Women's Experiences in the Middle East*. Oxford: Oxfam Publications.

Acker, J. (1973) 'Women and Stratification', *American Journal of Sociology*. 78: 2–48.

Acker, S. (1994) *Gendered Education*. Buckingham: Open University Press.

Ackers, L. and Abbott, P. (1996) *Social Policy for Nurses and the Caring Professions*. Buckingham: Open University Press.

Adams, N. and Bettis, P. (2003) 'Commanding the Room in Short Skirts: Cheering as the Embodiment of Ideal Girlhood', *Gender and Society*. 19(1): 73–91.

Adamson, J., Ben-Schlomo, Y., Chaturvedi, N. and Donovan, J. (2003) 'Ethnicity, Socioeconomic Position and Gender – Do They Affect Reported Health-Care Seeking Behaviour?', *Social Science and Medicine*. 57: 895–904.

Adkins, L. (1995) *Gendered Work: Sexuality, Family and the Labour Market*. Buckingham: Open University Press.

Adkins, L. (1997) 'Review Essay: Sex (Ad)dressed: Empiricism, Periodisations and Fetish', *Sociology*. 31(2): 353–360.

Adkins, L. (2000) 'Mobile Desire: Aesthetics, Sexuality and the "Lesbian" at Work', *Sexualities*. 3(2): 201–218.

Adorno, T. (1991) *The Culture Industry*. London: Routledge.

Aftab, K. (2002) 'Brown: The New Black! Bollywood in Britain', *Critical Quarterly*. 44(3): 88–98.

Alam, S. (1985) 'Women and Poverty in Bangladesh', *Women's Studies International Forum*. 8(4): 361–371.

Alcock, P., Erskine, A. and May, M. (eds) (2003) *The Student's Companion to Social Policy*. Oxford: Blackwell.

Alcoff, L. and Potter, E. (1993) 'Introduction: When Feminisms Intersect Epistemology', in L. Alcoff and E. Potter (eds) *Feminist Epistemologies*. London: Routledge, pp. 1–14.

Alexander, P. (1988) 'Prostitution: A Difficult Issue for Feminists', in S. Jackson and S. Scott (eds) (1996) *Feminism and Sexuality: A Reader*. Edinburgh: Edinburgh University Press.

Allan, J. (1993) 'Male Elementary Teachers: Experiences and Perspectives', in C. Williams (ed.) *Doing 'Women's Work'*. London: Sage.

Allen, H. (1987) *Justice Unbalanced*. Milton Keynes: Open University Press.

Allen, I. (1988) *Any Room at the Top? A Study of Doctors and their Careers*. London: Policy Studies Institute.

Allen, S. (1982) 'Gender Inequality and Class Formation', in A. Giddens and G. Mackenzie (eds) *Social Class and the Division of Labour*. Cambridge: Cambridge University Press.

Allen, S. and Walkowitz, C. (1987) *Homeworking: Myths and Realities*. London: Macmillan.

Amir, M. (1971) *Patterns in Forcible Rape*. Chicago: University of Chicago Press.

Amnesty International (2001) *Crimes of Hate, Conspiracy of Silence*. London: Amnesty International.

Amnesty International (2002) *Equal Rights: A Brief to the UN Committee on the Elimination of Discrimination Against Women*. Ottawa: Amnesty International Canada.

Amos, V. and Parmar, P. (1981) 'Resistance and Responses: The Experiences of Black Girls in Britain', in A. McRobbie and T. McCabe (eds) *Feminism for Girls: An Adventure Story*. London: Routledge and Kegan Paul.

Anderson, B. (2000) *Doing the Dirty Work: The Global Politics of Domestic Labour*. London: Zed Books.

Ang, I. (1989) *Watching Dallas*. London: Routledge.

Ankomah, A. (1999) 'Sex, Love, Money and AIDS: The Dynamics of Premarital Sexual Relationships in Ghana', *Sexualities*. 2(3): 291–308.

Anthias, F. and Yuval-Davis, N. (1993) *Racialised Boundaries*. London: Routledge.

Applegate, J. and Kaye, L. (1993) 'Male Elder Caregivers', in C. Williams (ed.) *Doing 'Women's Work'*. London: Sage.

Arber, S. (1997) 'Comparing Inequalities in Women's and Men's Health in Britain in the 1990s', *Social Science and Medicine*. 48: 773–787.

Arber, S. and Ginn, J. (1991) *Gender and Later Life: A Sociological Analysis of Resources and Constraints*. London: Sage.

Arber, S. and Ginn, J. (eds) (1995) *Connecting Gender and Ageing: A Sociological Approach*. Buckingham: Open University Press.

Arber, S., Gilbert, N. and Dale, A. (1985) 'Paid Employment and Women's Health: A Benefit or a Source of Role Strain?', *Sociology of Health and Illness*. 7: 375–400.

Arnot, M. (1989) 'Crisis or Challenge: Equal Opportunities and the National Curriculum', *NUT Education Review of Equal Opportunities in the NEW ERA 3*. Autumn.

ASE Educational Research Committee (1990) *Gender Issues in Science Education*. Hatfield: ASE.

Ashton, H. (1991) 'Psychotropic Drug Prescribing for Women', *British Journal of Psychiatry*. 158 (Supplement 10): 30–35.

Assiter, A. (1996) *Enlightened Women: Modernist Feminism in a Postmodern Age*. London: Routledge.

Atchley, R. (1982) 'Retirement as a Social Institution', *Annual Review of Sociology, Volume 8*. Palo Alto, CA: Annual Reviews. pp. 263–287.

Baldock, J. (2003) 'The Personal Social Services and Community Care', in P. Alcock *et al.* (eds) *The Student's Companion to Social Policy*. Oxford: Blackwell.

Baldwin, S. and Twigg, J. (1991) 'Women and Community Care: Reflections on a Debate', in M. Maclean and D. Groves (eds) *Women's Issues in Social Policy*. London: Routledge.

Ball, S. (1988) 'A Comprehensive School in a Pluralist World: Divisions and Inequalities', in B. O'Keeffe (ed.) *School for Tomorrow*. Lewes: Falmer.

Banet-weiser, S. (2004) 'Girls Rule! Gender, Feminism and Nickelodeon', *Critical Studies in Media Communication*. 21(2): 119–140.

Barkhatov, D., Boukharov, A., Vlasova, Y., Ivanov, S., Kotov, Y., Snopova, S. and Shmeleva, Y. (2002) *In-Depth Analysis of the Situation of Working Street Children in Moscow*. ILO/IPEC working paper, Moscow: International Labour Office.

Barnes, C., Mercer, G. and Shakespeare, T. (1999) *Exploring Disability: A Sociological Introduction*. Cambridge: Polity.

Barrett, M. (1980) *Women's Oppression Today*. London: Verso.

Barrett, M. (1982) 'Feminism and the Definition of Cultural Politics', in R. Brunt and C. Rowan (eds) *Feminism, Culture and Politics*. London: Lawrence and Wishart.

Barrett, M. and McIntosh, M. (1980) *The Antisocial Family*. London: Verso.

Barry, K. (1995) *The Prostitution of Sexuality*. New York: New York University Press.

Barthes, R. (1967) *Writing Degree Zero*. First published 1953. London: Cape.

Barthes, R. (1973) *Mythologies*. First published 1957. London: Paladin.

Bartky, S.L. (1990) *Feminism and Domination: Studies in the Phenomenology of Oppression*. London: Routledge.

Bates, I. (1993) 'A Job Which is Right For Me?', in I. Bates and G. Risborough (eds) *Youth and Inequality*. Buckingham: Open University Press.

Baudrillard, J. (1988) *America*. London: Verso.

Bauman, Z. (1998) 'On Postmodern Uses of Sex', *Theory, Culture and Society*. 15(3/4): 19–33.

Beasley, C. (1999) *What is Feminism? An Introduction to Feminist Theory*. London: Sage.

Beck, U. and Beck-Gernsheim, E. (1995) *The Normal Chaos of Love*. Cambridge: Polity.

Beechey, V. (1986) 'Familial Ideology', in V. Beechey and J. Donald (eds) *Subjectivity and Social Relations*. Buckingham: Open University Press.

Beechey, V. (1987) *Unequal Work*. London: Verso.

Begum, N. (1992) 'Disabled Women and the Feminist Agenda', *Feminist Review*. 40: 70–84.

Bell, D. (1999) *The Coming of Post-Industrial Society*. Second edition (first published 1973). New York: Basic Books.

Benhabib, S. (1992) *Situating the Self: Gender, Community and Postmodernism in Contemporary Ethics*. Cambridge: Polity.

Benhabib, S. (1995) 'Feminism and Postmodernism: An Uneasy Alliance', in S. Benhabib, J. Butler, D. Cornell and N. Fraser (eds) *Feminist Contentions: A Philosophical Exchange*. London: Routledge, pp. 17–34.

Benhabib, S. and Cornell, D. (1987) *Feminism as Critique: Essays on the Politics of Gender in Late Capitalist Societies*. Cambridge: Polity.

Bernard, J. (1973) *The Future of Marriage*. London: Souvenir Press.

Beynon, H. (1973) *Working for Ford*. Harmondsworth: Penguin.

Beyres, T., Crown, B. and Wan Ho, M. (1983) *The Green Revolution in India*. Buckingham: Open University Press.

Bhavnani, K-K. (1993) 'Talking Racism and the Reality of Women's Studies', in D. Richardson and V. Robinson (eds) *Introducing Women's Studies: Feminist Theory and Practice*. London: Macmillan, pp. 27–48.

Black Report, The (1978) *Report of a Royal Commission on Health Inequalities*. London: HMSO.

Blaikie, A. (1999) *Ageing and Popular Culture*. Cambridge: Cambridge University Press.

Blaxter, M. (1985) 'Self-Definition of Health Status and Consulting Notes in Primary Health Care', *Quarterly Journal of Social Affairs*. 1: 131–171.

Blumberg, R.L. (1981) 'Rural Women in Development', in N. Black and A.B. Cottrell (eds) *Women and World Change*. Beverly Hills, CA: Sage.

Bordo, S. (1990) 'Feminism, Postmodernism and Gender-Scepticism', in L. Nicholson (ed.) *Feminism/Postmodernism*. London: Routledge, pp. 133–156.

Bordo, S. (1993) 'Feminism, Foucault and the Politics of the Body', in C. Ramazanoglu (ed.) *Up Against Foucault*. London: Routledge.

Bouquet, T. (1995) 'Rape Trials: A Second Violation', *Reader's Digest*. May: 45–50.

Bourdieu, P. (1984) *Distinction*. London: Routledge.

Bourlet, A. (1990) *Police Intervention in Marital Violence*. Milton Keynes: Open University Press.

Bourque, S. and Grosshaltz, J. (1974) 'Politics and Unnatural Practice: Political Science Looks at Female Participation', *Politics and Society*. 4: 225–266.

Bowles, S. and Gintis, H. (1976) *Schooling in Capitalist America: Education Reform and Contradictions of Economic Life*. London: Routledge and Kegan Paul.

Box, S. (1971) *Deviance, Reality and Society*. London: Holt, Reinhart and Winston.

Box, S. and Hale, C. (1983) 'Liberation of Female Criminality in England and Wales', *British Journal of Criminology*. 23: 35–49.

Boyer, K. (2004) 'Miss Remington Goes to Work: Gender, Space and Technology at the Dawn of the Information Age', *Gender and Society*. 56(2): 201–212.

Bradley, H. (1993) 'Across the Great Divide: The Entry of Men into Women's Jobs', in C. Williams (ed.) *Doing 'Women's Work'*. London: Sage.

Bradshaw, J. (2003) 'Lone Parents', in P. Alcock *et al.* (eds) *The Student's Companion to Social Policy*. Oxford: Blackwell.

Bradshaw, J., Clegg, S. and Trayhorn, D. (1995) 'An Investigation into Gender Bias in Educational Software used in English Primary Schools', *Gender and Education*. 72: 167–174.

Brah, A. (1986) 'Unemployment and Racism: Asian Youth on the Dole', in S. Allen, K. Purcell, A. Waton and S. Wood (eds) *The Experience of Unemployment*. London: Macmillan.

Braham, P., Rattansi, A. and Skellington, R. (eds) (1992) *Racism/Antiracism*. Buckingham: Open University Press.

Branston, G. and Stafford, R. (1996) *The Media Student's Book*. London: Routledge.

Braverman, H. (1974) *Labour and Monopoly Capital*. New York: Monthly Review Press.

Brewis, J. and Linstead, S. (2000) *Sex, Work and Sex Work: Eroticizing Organization*. London: Routledge.

Brooks, A. (1997) *Postfeminisms: Feminism, Cultural Theory and Cultural Forms*. London: Routledge.

Brown, G. and Harris, T. (1978) *Social Origins of Depression: A Study of Psychiatric Disorder in Women*. London: Tavistock.

Brownmiller, S. (1976) *Against our Will: Men, Women and Rape*. Harmondsworth: Penguin.

Bruce, J. (1987) 'Users Perspectives on Contraceptive Technology and Delivery Systems: Highlighting Some Feminist Issues', *Technology in Society*. 9: 359–383.

Bryan, B., Dadzie, S. and Scafe, S. (1985) *The Heart of the Race: Black Women's Lives in Britain*. London: Virago.

Burgess, A. and Holmstrom, L. (1979) *Rape, Crisis and Recovery*. Bowie, MD: Robert J. Brady.

Burgess, H. (1990) 'Co-Education – The Disadvantages for Schoolgirls', *Gender and Education*. 2(1).

Butler, J. (1990) *Gender Trouble*. London: Routledge.

Butler, J. (1993) *Bodies That Matter: On The Discursive Limits of 'Sex'*. London: Routledge.

Butler, J. (2000) *Gender Trouble*. Tenth anniversary edition. London: Routledge.

Buurman, G. (1997) 'Erotic Bodies: Images of the Disabled', in K. Davis (ed.) *Embodied Practices: Feminist Perspectives on the Body*. London: Sage, pp. 131–134.

Cain, M. (1973) *Society and the Policeman's Role*. London: Routledge and Kegan Paul.

Calas, M. and Smircich, L. (1991) 'Voicing Seduction to Silence Leadership', *Organization Studies*. 12(4): 567–601.

Calvert, P. and Calvert, S. (2001) *Politics and Society in the Third World*. Second edition. London: Longman.

Cameron, D. (1990) *The Feminist Critique of Language*. London: Routledge.

Cameron, D. (1995) *Verbal Hygiene*. London: Routledge.

Cameron, D. (1998) 'Lost in Translation: Non-Sexist Language', in D. Cameron (ed.) *The Feminist Critique of Language*. Second edition. London: Routledge.

Campbell, B. (2004) 'Village People', *The Guardian Weekend*, 7 August 2004, pp. 30–33.

Caplan, P. (ed.) (1987) *The Cultural Construction of Sexuality*. London: Routledge.

Carabine, J. (1992) 'Constructing Women: Women's Sexuality and Social Policy', *Critical Social Policy*. 34: 23–37.

Carby, H. (1982) 'White Women Listen! Black Feminism and the Boundaries of Sisterhood', in CCCS *The Empire Strikes Back*. London: Heinemann.

Carlen, P. (1983) *Women's Imprisonment*. London: Routledge and Kegan Paul.

Carlen, P. and Worrall, A. (eds) (1987) *Gender, Crime and Justice*. Milton Keynes: Open University Press.

Carlen, P., Hicks, J., O'Dwyer, J., Christina, D. and Tchaikovsky, C. (1985) *Criminal Women*. Cambridge: Polity.

Carter, J. (2003) *Ethnicity, Exclusion and the Workplace*. London: Palgrave.

Castells, M. (1989) *The Information City*. Oxford: Blackwell.

Castells, M. (1996) *The Information Age: Volume One*. Oxford: Blackwell.

Cavendish, R. (1982) *Women on the Line*. London: Routledge and Kegan Paul.

CCCS (Centre for Contemporary Cultural Studies) (1982) *The Empire Strikes Back: Race and Racism in 70s Britain*. London: Heinemann.

CEC (Commission of the European Community) (1993) *Employment in Europe*. Brussels: CEC.

Chapkis, W. (1997) *Live Sex Acts: Women Performing Erotic Labour*. New York: Routledge.

Chapman, D. (1968) *Sociology and the Stereotype of the Criminal*. London: Tavistock.

Chapman, R. (1988) 'The Great Pretender: Variations on the New Man Theme', in R. Chapman and J. Rutherford (eds) *Male Order*. London: Lawrence and Wishart.

Chapman, R. and Rutherford, J. (eds) (1988) *Male Order: Unwrapping Masculinity*. London: Lawrence and Wishart.

Chapman, T. (2003) *Gender and Domestic Life*. London: Palgrave.

Clark, A. (1982 [1919]) *Working Life of Women in the Seventeenth Century*. London: Routledge.

Clarke, L. and Lewis, D. (1977) *Rape: The Price of Coercive Sexuality*. Toronto: The Women's Press.

Clarricoates, K. (1980) 'The Importance of Being Earnest – Emma . . . ture: Reperception and Categorisation of Gender Conformity and Gender Deviation in Schools', in R. Deem (ed.) *Schooling for Women's Work*. London: Routledge and Kegan Paul.

Cloward, R. and Ohlin, L. (1961) *Delinquency and Opportunity: A Theory of Delinquent Gangs*. London: Routledge and Kegan Paul.

Coats, M. (1994) *Women's Education*. Buckingham: Open University Press.

Cockburn, C. (1990) *In the Way of Women: Men's Resistance to Sex Equality in Organisations*. London: Macmillan.

Coe, T. (1992) *The Key to the Men's Club*. Corby: Institute of Management.

Cohen, P. (1980) *Folk Devils and Moral Panics: The Creation of the Mods and the Rockers*. Second edition. Oxford: Martin Robertson.

Collinson, M. and Collinson, D. (1996) 'It's only Dick: The Sexual Harassment of Women Managers in Insurance Sales', *Work, Employment and Society*. 10(1): 29–56.

Commeyras, M. and Alvermann, D. (1996) 'Reading about Women in World History Textbooks from one Feminist Perspective', *Gender and Education*. 8: 31–48.

Connell, R.W. (1995) *Masculinities*. Cambridge: Polity.

Connell, R.W. (2002) *Gender.* Cambridge: Polity.

Cook, D. (1987) 'Women on Welfare', in P. Carlen and A. Worrall (eds) *Gender, Crime and Justice.* Milton Keynes: Open University Press.

Cornwell, J. (1984) *Hard-Earned Lives.* London: Tavistock.

Coward, R. (1984) *Female Desire: Women's Sexuality Today.* London: Paladin.

Coward, R. (1987) 'Sex after AIDS', in S. Jackson and S. Scott (eds) *Feminism and Sexuality: A Reader.* Edinburgh: Edinburgh University Press, pp. 245–247.

Cowie, C. and Lees, S. (1985) 'Slags and Drags', *Feminist Review.* 9.

Coyle, A. (1984) *Redundant Women.* London: The Women's Press.

Crompton, R. (1986) 'Women and the Service Class', in R. Crompton and M. Mann (eds) *Gender and Stratification.* Cambridge: Polity.

Crompton, R. (1993) *Class and Stratification.* Cambridge: Polity.

Crompton, R. and Jones, G. (1984) *White-Collar Proletariat: Deskilling and Gender in Manual Work.* London: Macmillan.

Crompton, R. and Mann, M. (eds) (1986) *Gender and Stratification.* Cambridge: Polity.

Crompton, R. and Sanderson, K. (1990) 'Credentials and Careers', in G. Payne and P. Abbott (eds) *The Social Mobility of Women: Beyond Male Mobility Models.* Basingstoke: Falmer.

Crompton, R. and Le Feuvre, N. (1996) 'Paid Employment and the Changing System of Gender Relations: A Cross-national Comparison', *Sociology.* 30(3): 427–445.

Cross, S. and Bagilhole, B. (2002) 'Girls' Jobs for the Boys? Men, Masculinity and Non-Traditional Occupations', *Gender, Work and Organization.* 9(2): 204–226.

Crow, L. (1996) 'Including All Our Lives: Renewing the Social Model of Disability', in J. Morris (ed.) *Encounters with Strangers.* London: The Women's Press.

CSO (Central Statistics Office) (1995) *Social Trends 25.* London: HMSO.

Cumberbatch, G. (1990) *Television Advertising and Sex Role Stereotyping.* London: Broadcasting Standards Council.

Cumming, E. and Henry, W. (1961) *Growing Old: The Process of Disengagement.* New York: Basic Books.

Dalley, G. (1988) *Ideologies of Caring: Rethinking Community and Collectivism.* London: Macmillan.

Dalton, K. (1961) 'Menstruation and Crime', *British Medical Journal.* 2: 1,972.

Daly, M. (1978) *Gyn/Ecology: The Metaethics of Radical Feminism.* Boston: Beacon Press.

Darwin, C. (1871) *The Descent of Man and Selection in Relation to Sex.* London: John Money.

David, M. (1985) 'Motherhood and Social Policy – A Matter of Education?', *Critical Social Policy.* 12: 28–43.

David, M. and Woodward, D. (1998) *Negotiating the Glass Ceiling.* London: Falmer.

Davidoff, L., L'Esperance, J. and Newby, H. (1976) 'Landscape with Figures: Home and Community in English Society', in J. Mitchell and A. Oakley (eds) *The Rights and Wrongs of Women.* Harmondsworth: Penguin.

Davidson, M. and Cooper, C. (1992) *Shattering the Glass Ceiling.* London: Paul Chapman.

Davies, C. (1996) 'The Sociology of Professions and the Profession of Gender', *Sociology.* 30(4): 661–678.

Davin, A. (1979) 'Mind that You Do as You are Told: Reading Books for Board School Girls 1870–1902', *Feminist Review.* 3: 89–98.

Davis, K. (1995) *Reshaping the Female Body: The Dilemma of Cosmetic Surgery.* London: Routledge.

De Beauvoir, S. (1988) *The Second Sex.* First published 1949. London: Jonathan Cape.

Delamont, S. (2003) *Feminist Sociology.* London: Sage.

Delphy, C. (1984) *Close to Home: A Materialist Analysis of Women's Oppression.* London: Hutchinson.

Delphy, C. and Leonard, D. (1992) *Familiar Exploitation: A New Analysis of Marriage in Contemporary Western Societies.* Cambridge: Polity.

Denfeld, R. (1995) *The New Victorians: A Young Woman's Challenge to the Old Feminist Order.* New York: Warner Books.

Deshormes LaValle, F. (ed.) (1987) *Women and Men of Europe.* Women of Europe Supplements No. 26, Brussels: CEC.

Dobash, R.E. and Dobash, R.P. (1992) *Women, Violence and Social Change.* London: Routledge.

Dobash, R.P. and Dobash, R.E. (1980) *Violence Against Wives: A Case Against the Patriarchy.* Shepton Mallet: Open Books.

Dobash, R.P., Dobash, R.E. and Gutteridge, S. (1986) *The Imprisonment of Women.* Oxford: Blackwell.

Doezema, J. (2002) 'Who Gets to Choose? Coercion, Consent and the UN Trafficking Protocol', *Gender and Development.* 10(1): 20–27.

Doucet, A. (2001) 'You See the Need Perhaps More Clearly than I Have: Exploring Gendered Processes of Domestic Responsibility', *Journal of Family Issues.* 22(3): 328–357.

Downe, P. (1999) 'Laughing When it Hurts: Humour and Violence in the Lives of Costa-Rican Prostitutes', *Women's Studies International Forum.* 22: 63–78.

Doyal, L. (1987) 'Women and the National Health Service: The Carers and the Careless', in E. Lewin and V. Olsen (eds) *Women, Health and Healing.* London: Tavistock.

Doyal, L. (1995) *What Makes Women Sick.* London: Macmillan.

Doyal, L. (2000) 'Gender Equity in Health: Debates and Dilemmas', *Social Science and Medicine.* 51: 931–939.

Duke, L. and Kreshel, P. (1998) 'Negotiating Femininity: Girls in Early Adolescence Read Teen Magazines', *Journal of Communication Inquiry.* 22(1): 48–71.

Duncombe, J. and Marsden, D. (1995) 'Workaholics and Whingeing Women: Theorizing Intimacy and Emotion Work – The Last Frontier of Gender Inequality?', *Sociological Review.* 151–169.

Durkheim, E. (1952 [1897]) *Suicide: A Study in Sociology.* London: Routledge and Kegan Paul.

Dworkin, A. (1981) *Pornography: Men Possessing Women.* London: The Women's Press.

Dwyer, C. (1999) 'Negotiations of Femininity and Identity for Young British Muslim Women', in N. Laurie, C. Dwyer, S. Holloway and F. Smith (eds) *Geographies of New Femininities.* Harlow: Longman.

Dyer, G. (1982) *Advertising as Communication.* London: Methuen.

Dyer, R. (1992) *Only Entertainment.* London: Routledge.

Dyhouse, C. (1981) *Girls Growing up in Late Victorian and Edwardian England.* London: Routledge and Kegan Paul.

Edgell, S. (1980) *Middle-Class Couples.* London: Allen and Unwin.

Edwards, S. (1984) *Women in Trial.* Manchester: Manchester University Press.

Edwards, S. (1987) 'Prostitutes: Victims of Law, Social Policy and Organised Crime', in P. Carlen and A. Worrall (eds) *Gender, Crime and Justice.* Milton Keynes: Open University Press.

Edwards, S. (1989) *Policing Domestic Violence.* London: Sage.

Ehrenreich, B. and English, D. (1979) *For Her Own Good: 100 Years of the Experts' Advice to Women.* London: Pluto Press.

Ehrenreich, B. and Hochschild, A.R. (2003) *The Global Woman: Nannies, Maids and Sex Workers in the New Economy.* New York: Grant Books.

Eichler, M. (1988) *Non-Sexist Research Methods.* London: Allen and Unwin.

Einhorn, B. (1993) *Cinderella Goes to Market.* London: Verso.

Eisner, M. (1986) 'A Feminist Approach to General Practice', in C. Webb (ed.) *Feminist Practice in Women's Health Care.* Chichester: Wiley.

Elkind, D. (1981) *The Hurried Child: Growing Up Too Fast Too Soon.* Reading, MA: Addison-Wesley.

Elliott, A. and Turner, B.S. (2001) *Profiles in Contemporary Social Theory.* London: Sage.

Elston, M.A. (1980) 'Medicine' in R. Silverstone and A. Ward (eds) *Careers of Professional Women*. Beckenham: Croom Helm.

Engels, F. (1972) *The Origin of the Family, Private Property and the State*. First published 1884. Harmondsworth: Penguin.

England, P. and Herbert, M. (1993) 'The Pay of Men in Female Occupations: Is Comparable Worth only for Women?', in C. Williams (ed.) *Doing 'Women's Work'*. London: Sage.

EOC (Equal Opportunities Commission) (2001) *Sex Stereotyping: From School to Work*. Manchester: EOC.

EOC (2004) *Men and Women in Britain*. Manchester: EOC. (www.eoc.org)

ESRC Violence Research Programme (2002) *Taking Stock*. London: Royal Holloway College/Home Office.

Ettore, E. (2002) 'Reproductive Genetics, Gender and the Body: "Please, Doctor, may I have a normal baby?"', in S. Nettleton and V. Gustaffson (eds) *The Sociology of Health and Illness Reader*. Cambridge: Polity.

Evans, D. (1993) *Sexual Citizenship: The Material Construction of Sexualities*. London: Routledge.

Evans, J. (1995) *Feminist Theory Today: An Introduction to Second Wave Feminism*. London: Sage.

Evans, J. (2004) 'Men Nurses: A Historical and Feminist Perspective', *Journal of Advanced Nursing*. 47(3): 321–328.

Evetts, J. (1990) *Women in Primary Teaching*. London: Unwin Hyman.

Eysenck, H. (1971) *The IQ Argument: Race, Intelligence and Education*. New York: Library Press.

Falk, P. and Campbell, C. (1997) *The Shopping Experience*. London: Sage.

Faludi, S. (1991) *Backlash: The Undeclared War Against Women*. London: Vintage.

Fawcett, B. (2000) *Feminist Perspectives on Disability*. London: Prentice Hall.

Filby, M. (1992) 'The Figures, the Personality and the Bums: Service Work and Sexuality', *Work, Employment and Society*. 6(1): 23–42.

Finch, J. (1983) *Married to the Job: Wives' Incorporation in Men's Work*. London: Allen and Unwin.

Finch, J. and Groves, D. (1980) 'Community Care and the Family: A Case for Equal Opportunities?', *Journal of Social Policy*. 9: 437–451.

Finkelstein, V. (1993) 'The Commonality of Disability', in J. Sawin, V. Finkelstein, S. French and M. Oliver (eds) *Disabling Barriers – Enabling Environments*. London: Sage, pp. 9–16.

Firestone, S. (1974) *The Dialectic of Sex: The Case For Feminist Revolution*. New York: Morrow.

Fiske, J. (1987) *Television Culture*. London: Methuen.

Fiske, J. (1989) *Understanding Popular Culture*. London: Unwin Hyman.

Flax, J. (1997) 'Postmodernism and Gender Relations in Feminist Theory', in S. Kemp and J. Squires (eds) *Feminisms*. Oxford: Oxford University Press, pp. 170–178.

Flitcraft, A.H., Hadley, S.M., Hendricks-Mathews, M.K., McLeer, S.W. and Warshaw, C. (1992) 'American Medical Association Diagnostic and Treatment Guidelines of Domestic Violence', *Archive of Family Medicine*. 1: 39–47.

Fondas, N. (1997) 'Feminism Unveiled: Management Qualities in Contemporary Writings', *Academy of Management Review*. 22(1): 257–282.

Ford, J. (1969) *Social Class and the Comprehensive School*. London: Routledge and Kegan Paul.

Foster, P. (1995) *Women and the Health Care Industry*. Buckingham: Open University Press.

Foucault, M. (1979) *The History of Sexuality Volume One: An Introduction*. Harmondsworth: Penguin.

Foucault, M. (1980) 'Questions of Method', *Ideology and Consciousness*. 8: 3–14.

Francis, B. (2000) *Boys, Girls and Achievement: Addressing the Classroom Issues*. London: Falmer.

Francis, B. and Skelton, C. (eds) (2002) *Investigating Gender: Contemporary Perspectives in Education*. Buckingham: Open University Press.

Frazer, E. (1987) 'Teenage Girls Reading *Jackie*', *Media Culture and Society*. 9.

Freedman, L.P. and Maine, D. (1993) *Women's Mortality: A Legacy of Neglect*. Boulder, CO: Westview Press.

Friedan, B. (1963) *The Feminine Mystique*. Harmondsworth: Penguin.

Friedan, B. (1993) *The Fountain of Age*. New York: Simon and Schuster.

Fuller, M. (1980) 'Black Girls in a London Comprehensive School', in R. Deem (ed.) *Schooling for Women's Work*. London: Routledge and Kegan Paul.

Furlong, A. and Cartmel, F. (1997) *Young People and Social Change: Individualism and Risk in the Age of High Modernity*. Buckingham: Open University Press.

Gagnon, J. and Simon, W. (1973) *Sexual Conduct: The Social Sources of Human Sexuality*. Chicago: Aldine.

Gamarnikow, E. (1978) 'Sexual Division of Labour: The Case of Nursing', in A. Kuhn and A-M. Wolpe (eds) *Feminism and Materialism*. London: Routledge.

Gamble, S. (ed.) (2001) *The Routledge Companion to Feminism and Postfeminism*. Second edition. First published 1998. London: Routledge.

Ganetz, H. (1995) 'The Shop, the Home and Femininity as Masquerade', in J. Fornas and G. Bolin (eds) *Youth Culture in Late Modernity*. London: Sage, pp. 72–99.

Garber, L. (ed.) (1994) *Tilting the Tower*. London: Routledge.

Garnsey, E. (1978) 'Women's Work and Theories of Class Stratification', *Sociology*. 12: 223–243.

Gavron, H. (1966) *The Captive Wife: Conflicts of Housebound Wives*. Harmondsworth: Penguin.

Gedalof, I. (1999) *Against Purity*. London: Routledge.

Geraghty, C. (1996) *Women and Soap Operas*. Cambridge: Polity.

Gerami, S. and Lehnerer, M. (2001) 'Women's Agency and Household Diplomacy: Negotiating Fundamentalism', *Gender and Society*. 15(4): 556–573.

Gherardi, S. (1995) *Gender, Symbolism and Organizational Cultures*. London: Sage.

Gherardi, S. (1996) 'Gendered Organizational Cultures: Narratives of Women Travellers in a Male World', *Gender, Work and Organization*. 3(4): 187–201.

Giarchi, G.G. (2000) *Older People in Europe*. London: Longman Higher Education.

Giddens, A. (1991) *Modernity and Self-Identity: Self and Society in the Late Modern Age*. Cambridge: Polity.

Giddens, A. (1992) *The Transformation of Intimacy: Sexuality, Love and Eroticism in Modern Societies*. Cambridge: Polity.

Gilbourn, D. (1995) *Racism and Antiracism in Real Schools*. Buckingham: Open University Press.

Gilbourn, D. and Mirza, H. (2000) *Educational Inequality: Mapping Race, Class and Gender – A Synthesis of Evidence*. London: OFSTED.

Gill, R. (1988) 'Altered Images? Women in the Media', *Social Studies Review*. 4(1).

Gilligan, C. (1982) *In a Different Voice: Psychological Theory and Women's Development*. Cambridge, MA: Harvard University Press.

Gittens, D. (1985) *The Family in Question: Changing Households and Familial Ideologies*. London: Macmillan.

Gittens, D. (1992) 'What is the Family? Is it Universal?', in L. MacDowell and R. Pringle (eds) *Defining Women: Social Institutions and Gender Divisions*. Cambridge: Polity.

Glasser, C. (1997) 'Patriarchy, Mediated Desire and Chinese Magazine Fiction', *Journal of Communication*. 47(1): 85–108.

Glendinning, C. and Millar, J. (eds) (1992) *Women and Poverty in Britain in the 1990s*. Hemel Hempstead: Harvester Wheatsheaf.

Goddard-Spear, M. (1989) 'Differences Between the Written Work of Boys and Girls', *British Educational Research Journal*. 15: 271–277.

Goffee, R. and Scase, R. (1985) *Women in Charge: The Experiences of Female Entrepreneurs*. London: Allen and Unwin.

Gold, K. (1990) 'Get Thee to a Laboratory', *New Scientist.* 14 April, pp. 42–46.

Goldman, R. (1992) *Reading Ads Socially.* London: Routledge.

Goldthorpe, J. (1983) 'Women and Class Analysis: In Defence of the Conventional View', *Sociology.* 17: 465–488.

Goldthorpe, J. (1984) 'Women and Class Analysis: A Reply to the Replies', *Sociology.* 18: 491–499.

Goldthorpe, J., Llewlyn, C. and Payne, C. (1980) *Social Mobility and Class Structure in Modern Britain.* Oxford: Oxford University Press.

Goldthorpe, J., Lockwood, D., Bechhofer, F. and Platt, J. (1969) *The Affluent Worker in the Class Structure.* Oxford: Oxford University Press.

Graddol, D. and Swann, J. (1989) *Gender Voices.* Oxford: Blackwell.

Graham, H. (1984) *Women, Health and the Family.* Brighton: Wheatsheaf.

Graham, H. (1987) 'Providers, Negotiators and Mediators: Women as Hidden Carers', in E. Lewin and V. Olsen (eds) *Women, Health and Healing.* London: Tavistock.

Graham, H. (1991) 'The Concept of Care in Feminist Research: The Case of Domestic Service', *Sociology.* 25: 61–78.

Graham, H. (1993) *Hardship and Health in Women's Lives.* Hemel Hempstead: Harvester Wheatsheaf.

Graham, H. (2002) 'Building an Interdisciplinary Science of Health Inequalities: The Example of Lifecourse Research', *Social Science and Medicine.* 55: 2,005–2,016.

Graham, H. and Oakley, A. (1981) 'Competing Ideologies of Reproduction: Medical and Maternal Perspectives on Pregnancy', in H. Roberts (ed.) *Women, Health and Reproduction.* London: Routledge and Kegan Paul.

Granleese, J. (2004) 'Occupational Pressures in Banking: Gender Differences', *Women in Management Review.* 19(4): 219–226.

Greed, C. (1994) 'Women Surveyors: Constructing Careers', in J. Evetts (ed.) *Women and Career: Themes and Issues in Advanced Industrial Societies.* London: Longman.

Greenstein, F. (1965) *Children and Politics.* New Haven, CT: Yale University Press.

Greer, G. (1999) *The Whole Woman.* London: Anchor.

Gregory, J. (1986) 'Sex, Class and Crime: Towards a Non-Sexist Criminology', in R. Matthews and J. Young (eds) *Confronting Crime.* Beverley Hills, CA: Sage.

Griffin, C. (1985) *Typical Girls?* London: Routledge and Kegan Paul.

Griffin, C. (1997) 'Troubled Teens: Managing Disorders of Transition and Consumption', *Feminist Review.* 55: 4–21.

Grosz, E. (1995) *Space, Time and Perversion: Essays on the Politics of Bodies.* London: Routledge.

Groves, D. (1992) 'Occupational Pension Provision and Women's Poverty in Old Age', in C. Glendinning and J. Millar (eds) *Women and Poverty in Britain in the 1990s.* Hemel Hempstead: Harvester Wheatsheaf.

Guillaumin, C. (1995) *Racism, Sexism, Power and Ideology.* London: Routledge.

Guillebaud, J. and Low, B. (1987) 'Contraception', in A. McPherson (ed.) *Women's Problems in General Practice.* Oxford: Oxford University Press.

Hakim, C. (1995) 'Five Feminist Myths about Women's Employment', *British Journal of Sociology.* 46(3): 429–455.

Hakim, C. (1996) *Key Issues in Women's Work.* London: Athlone.

Hall, E. (1993a) 'Waitering/Waitressing: Engendering the Work of Table Servers', *Gender and Society.* 17(3): 329–346.

Hall, E. (1993b) 'Smiling, Deferring, and Flirting: Doing Gender by Giving "Good Service"', *Work and Occupations.* 20(4): 452–471.

Hall, E.J. and Rodriguez, M.S. (2003) 'The Myth of Postfeminism', *Gender and Society.* 17(6): 878–902.

Hall, L. (2000) 'Eyes Tightly Shut, Lying Rigidly Still, and Thinking of England? British Women and Sex from Marie Stopes to Hite 2000', plenary lecture presented to a Wellcome Library conference on 'Aspects of Gender in Contemporary British History', London, July 2000.

Hall, M. (1989) 'Private Experiences in the Public Domain: Lesbians in Organizations', in J. Hearn, D. Sheppard, P. Tancred-Sheriff and G. Burrell (eds) *The Sexuality of Organization*. London: Sage. pp. 125–138.

Hall, R. (1985) *Ask any Woman*. Bristol: Falling Wall Press.

Hall, S. (1980) 'Encoding/Decoding', in S. Hall, D. Hobson, A. Lowe and P. Willis (eds) *Culture, Media, Language*. London: Hutchinson.

Hall, S. (1990) 'Cultural Identity and the Disapora', in J. Rutherford (ed.) *Identity: Community, Culture, Difference*. London: Lawrence and Wishart.

Hall, S. (1992a) 'The West and the Rest: Discourse and Power', in S. Hall and B. Gieben (eds) *The Formations of Modernity*. Cambridge: Polity.

Hall, S. (1992b) 'Introduction', in S. Hall, D. Held and T. McGrew (eds) *Modernity and Its Futures*. Cambridge: Polity.

Hall, S. and Jefferson, T. (1976) *Resistance through Rituals*. London: Hutchinson.

Hall, S., Critcher, C., Jefferson, T., Clarke, J. and Roberts, B. (1978) *Policing the Crisis*. London: Macmillan.

Halsey, A.H., Heath, A. and Ridge, J.M. (1980) *Origins and Destinations*. Oxford: Clarendon Press.

Halson, J. (1989) 'The Sexual Harassment of Young Women', in L. Holly (ed.) *Sex in Schools*. Milton Keynes: Open University Press.

Halson, J. (1991) 'Young Women: Sexual Harassment and Mixed-Sex Schooling', in P. Abbott and C. Wallace (eds) *Gender, Power and Sexuality*. London: Macmillan.

Hancock, P. and Tyler, M. (2001) *Work, Postmodernism and Organization: A Critical Introduction*. London: Sage.

Hanmer, J. (1990) 'Men, Power and the Exploitation of Women', in J. Hearn and D. Morgan (eds) *Men, Masculinities and Social Theory*. London: Unwin Hyman.

Hanmer, J. (2003) 'Lesbian Subtext Talk: Experiences of the Internet Chat', *International Journal of Sociology and Social Policy*. 23(1–2): 80–106.

Hanmer, J. and Leonard, D. (1984) 'Negotiating the Problem: The DHSS and Research on Violence in Marriage', in C. Bell and H. Roberts (eds) *Social Researching: Politics, Problems, Practice*. London: Routledge and Kegan Paul.

Hanmer, J. and Saunders, S. (1984) *Well-Founded Fear*. London: Hutchinson.

Haraway, D. (1991) *Simians, Cyborgs and Women: The Reinvention of Nature*. London: Free Association Books.

Haraway, D. (2004) 'Situated Knowledges: The Science Question in Feminism and the Privilege of Partial Perspective', in S. Harding (ed.) *The Feminist Standpoint Theory Reader*. London: Routledge.

Harding, J. (1980) 'Sex Differences in Performances in Science Examinations', in R. Deem (ed.) *Schooling for Women's Work*. London: Routledge and Kegan Paul.

Harding, S. (1987) *Feminism and Methodology*. Milton Keynes: Open University Press.

Harding, S. (2004a) 'Introduction: Standpoint Theory as a Site of Political, Philosophic, and Scientific Debate', in S. Harding (ed.) *The Feminist Standpoint Theory Reader*. London: Routledge.

Harding, S. (ed.) (2004b) *The Feminist Standpoint Theory Reader: Intellectual and Political Controversies*. London: Routledge.

Hargreaves, A. (1996) Contribution to Review Symposium of J. Abraham (1995) *Divide and School: Gender and Class Dynamics in Comprehensive Education*. London: Falmer, *British Journal of Sociology of Education*. 17(1): 95–97.

Hartmann, H. (1978) 'The Unhappy Marriage of Marxism and Feminism: Towards a More Progressive Union', *Capital and Class.* 8: 1–33.

Hartsock, N. (1990) 'Foucault on Power', in L. Nicholson (ed.) *Feminism/Postmodernism.* London: Routledge.

Hartsock, N. (1998) 'Marxist Feminist Dialectics for the 21st Century', *Science and Society.* 62(3): 400–413.

Hawkes, G. (1995) 'Responsibility and Irresponsibility: Young Women and Family Planning', *Sociology.* 29(2): 257–273.

Hawkes, G. (1996) *A Sociology of Sex and Sexuality.* Buckingham: Open University Press.

Hearn, J. (1982) 'Notes on Patriarchy, Professionalisation and the Semi-Professions', *Sociology.* 26: 184–202.

Heath, A. and Britten, N. (1984) 'Women's Jobs Do Make a Difference', *Sociology.* 18: 475–495.

Hebdige, D. (1979) *Subculture: The Meaning of Style.* London: Methuen.

Heidensohn, F. (1986) *Women and Crime.* London: Macmillan.

Hekman, S. (1990) *Gender and Knowledge: Elements of a Postmodern Feminism.* Cambridge: Polity.

Hey, V. (1997) *The Company She Keeps: An Ethnography of Girls' Friendship.* Buckingham: Open University Press.

Heywood, C. (2001) *A History of Childhood: Children and Childhood in the West from Medieval to Modern Times.* Cambridge: Polity.

Hill Collins, P. (1986) 'Learning from the Outsider Within: The Sociological Significance of Black Feminist Thought', *Social Problems.* 33(6): 14–32, reprinted in S. Harding (ed.) (2004) *The Feminist Standpoint Theory Reader.* London: Routledge.

Hill Collins, P. (1990) *Black Feminist Thought.* London: Harper Collins.

Hite, S. (1976) *The Hite Report.* London: Hamlyn.

Hite, S. (2000) *The New Hite Report: The Revolutionary Report on Female Sexuality Updated.* London: Hamlyn.

Hochschild, A.R. (1983) *The Managed Heart.* Berkeley, CA: University of California Press.

Hockey, J. (1993) 'Women and Health', in D. Richardson and V. Robinson (eds) *Introducing Women's Studies.* London: Macmillan.

Hockey, J. and James, A. (1993) *Growing Up and Growing Old: Age and Dependency in The Life Course.* London: Sage.

Hockey, J. and James, A. (2002) *Social Identities Across the Life Course.* London: Palgrave.

Hoff, L.A. (1990) *Battered Women as Survivors.* London: Routledge.

Hoggart, R. (1957) *The Uses of Literacy.* Harmondsworth: Penguin.

Holland, J., Ramazanoglu, C., Scott, S., Sharpe, S. and Thomson, R. (1990) *'"Don't Die Of Ignorance" – I Nearly Died of Embarrassment': Condoms in Context.* London: The Tuffnell Press.

Holland, J., Ramazanoglu, C., Sharpe, S. and Thomson, R. (1994) 'Power and Desire: The Embodiment of Female Sexuality', *Feminist Review.* 46.

Holland, J., Ramazanoglu, C., Sharpe, S., and Thomson, R. (1998) *The Male in the Head: Young People, Heterosexuality and Power.* London: The Tuffnell Press.

Hollibaugh, A. (1989) 'Desire for the Future: Radical Hope in Passion and Pleasure', in S. Jackson and S. Scott (eds) (1996) *Feminism and Sexuality: A Reader.* Edinburgh: Edinburgh University Press.

Holmes, J. (1997) 'Gendered Discourse', in R. Wodak (ed.) *Discourse and Gender.* London: Sage.

Home Office (1999) *Statistics on Women and the Criminal Justice System.* London: HMSO.

Home Office (2003) *Criminal Statistics for England and Wales 2002.* London: HMSO.

Homer, M., Leonard, A. and Taylor, P. (1984) *Private Violence and Public Shame.* Middlesbrough: Cleveland Refuge and Aid for Women and Children.

hooks, b. (1982) *Ain't I a Woman? Black Women and Feminism.* Boston: South End Press.

hooks, b. (1984) *Feminist Theory: From Margin to Centre.* Boston: South End Press.

hooks, b. (1990) 'Choosing the Margin as a Space of Radical Openness', in *Yearning: Race, Gender and Cultural Politics*. Boston: South End Press. Reprinted in S. Harding (ed.) (2004) *The Feminist Standpoint Theory Reader*. London: Routledge.

hooks, b. (1992) *Black Looks: Race and Representation*. London: Turnaround.

Hughes, B. (2000) 'Medicine and the Aesthetic Invalidation of Disabled People', *Disability and Society*. 15(4): 555–568.

Hunt, P. (1980) *Gender and Class Consciousness*. London: Macmillan.

Huntley, R. (2000) 'Sexing the Belly: An Exploration of Sex and the Pregnant Body', *Sexualities*. 3(3): 347–362.

Ibarra, H. (1993) 'Personal Networks of Women and Minorities in Management: A Conceptual Framework', *Academy of Management Review*. 18(1): 56–87.

Ilkkaracan, P. (2002) 'Women, Sexuality, and Social Change in the Middle East and the Maghreb', *Social Research*. 69(3): 753–779.

Irigaray, L. (1993) *Je, Tu, Nous: Toward a Culture of Difference*. London: Routledge.

Jackson, M. (1987) 'Facts of Life or the Eroticization of Women's Oppression? Sexology and the Social Construction of Heterosexuality', in P. Caplan (ed.) *The Cultural Construction of Sexuality*. London: Tavistock, pp. 52–81.

Jackson, P. and Salisbury, J. (1996) 'Why Should Secondary Schools Take Working with Boys Seriously', *Gender and Education*. 8: 103–116.

Jackson, S. and Cram, F. (2003) 'Disrupting the Sexual Double Standard: Young Women's Talk about Heterosexuality', *British Journal of Social Psychology*. 42(1): 113–127.

Jackson, S. and Scott, S. (1996) 'Sexual Skirmishes and Feminist Factions: Twenty-Five Years of Debate on Women and Sexuality', in S. Jackson and S. Scott (eds) *Feminism and Sexuality: A Reader*. Edinburgh: Edinburgh University Press, pp. 1–31.

Jagger, A. (1983) *Feminist Politics and Human Nature*. Brighton: Harvester Wheatsheaf.

James, A. and Prout, A. (1997) *Constructing and Reconstructing Childhood*. Second edition. London: Falmer Press.

James, A., Jenks, C. and Prout, A. (1998) *Theorizing Childhood*. Cambridge: Polity.

James, N. (1989) 'Emotional Labour: Skill and Work in the Social Regulation of Feelings', *Sociological Review*. 37: 15–42.

Jameson, F. (1991) *Postmodernism*. London: Verso.

Jefford, S. (1994) *Hard Bodies: Hollywood Masculinity in the Reagan Era*. New York: Rutgers University Press.

Jeffreys, S. (1985) *The Spinster and Her Enemies*. Hammersmith: Harper Collins.

Jeffreys, S. (1990) *Anticlimax: A Feminist Perspective on the Sexual Revolution*. London: The Women's Press.

Jeffreys, S. (1997) *The Idea of Prostitution*. Melbourne: Spinifex.

Jeffreys, S. (1998) 'Child Versus Adult Prostitution: A False Distinction', paper presented at the First European Meeting of the Main Partners in the Fight Against Child Sex Tourism, *Participants' Speeches and Contributions*. Brussels: EC Tourism Directorate, pp. 64–71.

Jensen, A. (1973) *Educability and Group Differences*. New York: Harper Row.

Jezierski, M. (1992) 'Guidelines for Interventions by ER Nurses in Cases of Domestic Abuse', *Journal of Emergency Nursing*. 18: 298–300.

Johnson, N. (ed.) (1985) *Marital Violence*. London: Routledge and Kegan Paul.

Johnson, N. (1995) 'Domestic Violence: An Overview', in P. Kingston and B. Penhale (eds) *Family Violence and the Caring Professions*. London: Macmillan.

Johnson, R. (1986) 'What is Cultural Studies Anyway?', *Social Text*. 16: 38–80.

Johnson, T. (1972) *Professions and Power*. London: Macmillan.

Jordan, E. (1995) 'Fighting Boys and Fantasy Play: The Construction of Masculinity in the Early Years of School', *Gender and Education*. 7: 69–96.

Julien, I. and Mercer, K. (1988) 'Territories of the Body', in R. Chapman and J. Rutherford (eds) *Male Order*. London: Lawrence and Wishart.

Kahn, A. and Holt, L.H. (1989) *Menopause*. London: Bloomsbury.

Kane, P. (1991) *Women's Health: From Womb to Tomb*. London: Macmillan.

Kanter, R.M. (1977) *Men and Women of the Corporation*. New York: Basic Books.

Kehily, M.J. (2002) 'Issues of Gender and Sexuality in Schools', in B. Francis and C. Skelton (eds) *Investigating Gender*. Buckingham: Open University Press.

Kellner, D. (1995) *Media Culture*. London: Routledge.

Kelly, A. (1982) 'Gender Roles at Home and School', *British Journal of Sociology of Education*. 3: 281–296.

Kelly, A. (1987) *Science for Girls*. Buckingham: Open University Press.

Kelly, E. (1988) *Surviving Sexual Violence*. Cambridge: Polity.

Kempadoo, K. and Doezema, J. (1998) *Global Sex Workers: Rights, Resistance and Redefinition*. London: Routledge.

Kent, J. (2000) *Social Perspectives on Pregnancy and Childbirth for Midwives, Nurses and the Caring Professions*. Buckingham: Open University Press.

Kerfoot, D. and Knights, D. (1998) 'Managing Masculinity in Contemporary Organizational Life: A Managerial Project', *Organization*. 5(1): 7–26.

Khotkina, Z. (1994) 'Women in the Labour Market', in A. Posadskaya (ed.) *Women in Russia*. London: Verso.

King, A. (1997) 'The Lads: Masculinity and the New Consumption of Football', *Sociology*. 31(2): 329–346.

Kingsley Kent, S. (1993) *Making Peace: The Reconstruction of Gender in Inter-war Britain*. New York: Princeton University Press.

Kirkby, D. (1997) *Barmaids: A History of Women's Work in Pubs*. Cambridge: Cambridge University Press.

Koblinsky, M., Campbell, O. and Harlow, S. (1993) 'Mother and More: A Broader Perspective on Women's Health', in M. Koblinsky, T. Timyan, and J. Gray (eds) *The Health of Women: A Global Perspective*. Boulder, CO: Westview Press.

Koedt, A. (1972) 'The Myth of the Vaginal Orgasm', in S. Jackson and S. Scott (eds) (1996) *Sexuality and Feminism: A Reader*. Edinburgh: Edinburgh University Press, pp. 111–116.

Kosofsky Sedgwick, E. (1990) *Epistemology of the Closet*. Berkeley: University of California Press.

Kuhn, A. and Wolpe, A. (eds) (1978) *Feminism and Materialism: Women and Modes of Production*. London: Routledge.

Kumar, S. and Curtin, M. (2002) '"Made in India": In Between Music Television and Patriarchy', *Television and News Media*. 3(4): 345–366.

Kurian, A. (2001) 'Feminism and the Developing World', in S. Gamble (ed.) *The Routledge Companion to Feminism and Postfeminism*. London: Routledge.

Kushner, T. and Knox, K. (1999) *Refugees in an Age of Genocide*. London: Cass.

Lackoff, R. (1975) *Language and Women's Place*. New York: Harper and Row.

Lahelma, E., Arber, S., Kivela, K. and Roos, E. (2002) *Social Science and Medicine*. 6: 773–787.

Land, H. (2003) 'Altruism, Reciprocity and Obligation', in P. Alcock *et al.* (eds) *The Student's Companion to Social Policy*. Oxford: Blackwell.

Larkin, A.S. (1988) 'Black Women Film-Makers Defining Ourselves', in E. Pribram (ed.) *Female Spectators*. London: Verso.

Larkin, G. (1983) *Occupational Monopoly and Modern Medicine*. London: Tavistock.

Laurie, N., Dwyer, C., Holloway, S. and Smith, F. (eds) (1999) *Geographies of New Femininities*. Harlow: Longman.

Lawrence, B. (1987) 'The Fifth Dimension: Gender and General Practice', in A. Spencer and D. Podmore (eds) *In a Man's World*. London: Tavistock.

Lazarsfeld, P.F., Berelson, B. and Gaudet, H. (1968) *The People's Choice*. Second edition. Chicago: University of Chicago Press.

Lazzaro, M.V. and McFarlane, J. (1991) 'Establishing a Screening Program for Abused Women', *Journal of Nursing Administration*. 21: 24–29.

Leach, E. (1967) *A Runaway World?* London: BBC Publications.

Lee, N. (2001) *Childhood and Society: Growing Up in an Age of Uncertainty*. Buckingham: Open University Press.

Lees, S. (1986) *Losing Out: Sexuality and Adolescent Girls*. London: Hutchinson.

Lees, S. (1989) 'Naggers, Whores and Libbers: Provoking Men to Violence', paper presented at the annual conference of the British Sociological Association, Plymouth, April.

Lees, S. (1993) *Sugar and Spice: Sexuality and Adolescent Girls*. Harmondsworth: Penguin.

Lees, S. (1997) *Ruling Passions: Sexual Violence, Reputation and the Law*. Buckingham: Open University Press.

LeGrand, J. (1982) *The Strategy of Equality*. London: Allen and Unwin.

Leidner, R. (1993) *Fast Food, Fast Talk: Service Work and the Routinization of Everyday Life*. Berkeley: University of California Press.

Leonard, E.B. (1978) *Women, Crime and Society*. London: Longman.

Leonard, E.B. (1982) *Women, Crime and Society: A Critique of Theoretical Criminology*. New York: Longman.

Lesson, J. and Gray, J. (1978) *Women and Health*. London: Tavistock.

Letherby, G. (2002) 'Claims and Disclaimers: Knowledge, Reflexivity and Representation in Feminist Research', *Sociological Research Online*. 6(4): www.socresonline.org.uk/6/4/letherby.html

Lewin, E. and Olsen, V. (eds) (1987) *Women, Health and Healing: Towards a New Perspective*. London: Tavistock.

Lewis, A. and Lindsay, G. (eds) (1999) *Researching Children's Perspectives*. Buckingham: Open University Press.

Lewis, J. (1980) *The Politics of Motherhood: Child and Maternal Welfare in England 1900–1939*. London: Croom Helm.

Lewis, J. (2003) 'Feminist Perspectives', in P. Alcock *et al.* (eds) *The Student's Companion to Social Policy*. Oxford: Blackwell.

Lim, Lin L. (ed.) (1998) *The Sex Sector: The Economic and Social Bases of Prostitution in Southeast Asia*. Geneva: International Labour Organization.

Lincoln, R. and Kaeser, L. (1988) 'Whatever Happened to the Contraceptive Revolution?', *Family Planning Perspectives*. 20: 20–24.

Lindroos, M. (1995) 'The Problems of "Girls" in an Educational Setting', *Gender and Education*. 7: 175–184.

Livingston, S. and Bovill, M. (1999) *Children, Young People and the Changing Media Environment*. London: London School of Economics.

Lloyd, M. (2001) 'The Politics of Disability and Feminism: Discord or Synthesis?', *Sociology*. 35(3): 715–728.

Locker, D. (1981) *Symptoms and Illness*. London: Tavistock.

Lockwood, D. (1958) *The Black-Coated Worker*. London: Allen and Unwin.

Lockwood, D. (1986) 'Class, Status and Gender', in R. Crompton and M. Mann (eds) *Gender and Stratification*. Cambridge: Polity.

Lorber, J. and Moore, L.J. (2002) *Gender and the Social Construction of Illness*. Oxford: Alta Mira Press.

Loudon, N. (ed.) (1985) *Handbook of Family Planning*. Edinburgh: Churchill.

Lovenduski, J. and Randall, V. (1993) *Contemporary Feminist Politics: Women and Power*. Oxford: Oxford University Press.

Lucey, H. and Reay, D. (2000) 'Carrying the Beacon for Excellence: Pupil Performance, Gender and Social Class', paper presented at the British Educational Research Association annual conference, Cardiff, September.

Lury, C. (1995) *Consumer Culture*. Cambridge: Polity.

Lynott, P.P. and Logue, B. (1993) 'The "Hurried Child": The Myth of Lost Childhood in Contemporary American Society', *Sociological Forum*. 8(3): 471–491.

Lyon, D. (1994) *Postmodernity*. Buckingham: Open University Press.

Lyotard, J-F. (1984) *The Postmodern Condition: A Report on Knowledge*. Manchester: Manchester University Press.

Mac an Ghaill, M. (1994) *The Making of Men: Masculinist Sexualities and Schooling*. Buckingham: Open University Press.

Macdonald, M. (1995) *Representing Women: Myths of Femininity in the Popular Media*. London: Arnold.

McIntosh, M. (1992) 'Liberalism and the Contradictions of Oppression', in S. Jackson and S. Scott (eds) (1996) *Feminism and Sexuality: A Reader*. Edinburgh: Edinburgh University Press, pp. 333–341.

Macionis, J. and Plummer, K. (2002) *Sociology: A Global Introduction*. Second edition. London: Prentice Hall.

McKeganey, N. and Barnard, M. (1996) *Sex Work on the Streets*. Buckingham: Open University Press.

MacKinnon, C. (1982) 'Feminism, Marxism, Method and the State: An Agenda for Theory', *Signs*. 7(3): 515–545.

MacKinnon, C. (1987) *Feminism Unmodified: Discourses on Life and Law*. Cambridge, MA: Harvard University Press.

McLennan, G. (1995) 'Feminism, Epistemology and Postmodernism: Reflections on Current Ambivalence', *Sociology*. 29(3): 391–409.

Macpherson, Sir W. (1999) *The Stephen Lawrence Inquiry*. London: Stationery Office.

McRobbie, A. (1978) 'The Culture of Working-class Girls', in A. McRobbie (ed.) (1991) *Feminism and Youth Culture*. London: Macmillan.

McRobbie, A. (1991) *Feminism and Youth Culture: From Jackie to Just Seventeen*. London: Macmillan.

McRobbie, A. (1994) *Postmodernism and Popular Culture*. London: Routledge.

McRobbie, A. (1996) '*More!* New Sexualities in Girls' and Women's Magazines', in J. Curran, D. Morley and V. Walkerdine (eds) *Cultural Studies and Communications*. London: Arnold, pp. 172–194.

McRobbie, A. (2000) *Feminism and Youth Culture*. Second edition. Basingstoke: Macmillan.

McRobbie, A. and Garber, J. (1976) 'Girls and Subcultures: An Exploration', in S. Hall and T. Jefferson (eds) *Resistance through Rituals*. London: Hutchinson.

Madigan, R. and Munro, M. (1996) 'House Beautiful: Style and Consumption in the Home', *Sociology*. 30(1): 41–57.

Maguire, S. (1988) 'Sorry Love – Violence against Women in the Home and the State Response', *Critical Social Policy*. 23: 34–46.

Mama, A. (1989) 'Violence against Black Women: Gender, Race and State Responses', *Feminist Review*. 28: 16–55.

Mandaraka-Sheppard, K. (1986) *The Dynamics of Aggression in Women's Prisons in England*. London: Gower.

Marcuse, H. (1972) *Eros and Civilization*. First published 1955. London: Abacus.

Marcuse, H. (1986) *One Dimensional Man*. First published 1964. London: Ark.

Marshment, M. (1993) 'The Picture is Political: Representation of Women in Contemporary Popular Culture', in D. Richardson and V. Robinson (eds) *Introducing Women's Studies*. London: Macmillan.

Martin, E. (1987) *The Woman in the Body*. Buckingham: Open University Press.

Martin, J. and Roberts, C. (1984) *Women and Employment: A Lifetime Perspective*. London: HMSO.

Martin, S. (1999) 'Police Force or Police Service? Gender and Emotional Labour', *Annals of the American Academy of Political and Social Science*. 561: 111–126.

Maruani, M. (1992) *The Position of Women in the Labour Market*. Brussels: CEC.

Matthews, R. and Young, J. (eds) (1986) *Confronting Crime*. Beverley Hills, CA: Sage.

Mawby, R. (1980) 'Sex and Crime: The Results of a Self-Report Study', *British Journal of Sociology*. 31: 525.

Mayall, B. (2002) *Towards a Sociology For Childhood: Thinking From Children's Lives*. Buckingham: Open University Press.

Measor, L. and Sikes, P. (1992) *Gender and Schools*. London: Cassell.

Meyer, M. (1994) 'Reclaiming the Discourse of Camp', in M. Meyer (ed.) *The Politics and Poetics of Camp*. London: Routledge, pp. 1–22.

Mickelson, R.A. (1992) 'Why Does Jane Read and Write So Well? The Anomaly of Women's Achievement', in J. Wrigley (ed.) *Education and Gender Inequality*. Basingstoke: Falmer.

Miles, S. (2000) *Youth Lifestyles in a Changing World*. Buckingham: Open University Press.

Miles, S. and Middleton, C. (1990) 'Girls' Education in the Balance: The ERA and Inequality', in M. Hammer (ed.) *The Education Reform Act 1988: Its Origins and Implications*. Lewes: Falmer.

Milkman, R. (1976) 'Women's Work and Economic Crises', *Review of Radical Political Economy*. 9: 29–36.

Millen, D. (1997) 'Some Methodological and Epistemological Issues Raised by Doing Feminist Research on Non-Feminist Women', *Sociological Research Online*. 2(3): www.soc.resonline.org.uk/2/3/3.html

Millett, K. (1977) *Sexual Politics*. London: Virago.

Mills, C. Wright (1954) *The Sociological Imagination*. Harmondsworth: Penguin.

Minturn, L. (1993) *Sita's Daughters*. Oxford: Oxford University Press.

Mirrlees-Black, C. (1999) *Domestic Violence: Findings From the 1992 British Crime Survey*. London: HMSO.

Mirza, H. (1992) *Young, Female and Black*. London: Routledge.

Mitchell, J. (1986) 'Women and Equality', in J. Donald and S. Hall (eds) *Politics and Ideology*. Milton Keynes: Open University Press.

Modleski, T. (1982) *Loving with a Vengeance: Mass Produced Fantasies for Women*. Hamden, CT: Archon Books.

Modleski, T. (1991) *Feminism Without Women: Culture and Criticism in a 'Postfeminist' Age*. London: Routledge.

Moir, A. and Moir, B. (1999) *Why Men Don't Learn*. London: Harper Collins.

Moore, H. (1995) *A Passion for Difference*. Cambridge: Polity.

Moore, S. (1988) 'Getting a Bit of the Other – the Pimps of Postmodernism', in R. Chapman and J. Rutherford (eds) *Male Order*. London: Lawrence and Wishart, pp. 165–192.

Morgan, D. (1999) 'Risk and Family Practices', in E. Silva and C. Smart (eds) *The New Family?* London: Sage.

Morgan, G. and Knights, D. (1991) 'Gendering Jobs: Corporate Strategy, Managerial Control and the Dynamics of Job Segregation', *Work, Employment and Society*. 5(2): 181–200.

Morris, A. (1987) *Women, Crime and Criminal Justice*. Oxford: Blackwell.

Morris, J. (1991) *Pride Against Prejudice: Transforming Attitudes to Disability*. London: The Women's Press.

Morris, J. (ed.) (1996) *Encounters with Strangers: Feminism and Disability*. London: The Women's Press.

Morris, J. (1997) *Conundrum*. London: Penguin.

Mort, F. (1988) 'Boys Own? Masculinity, Style and Popular Culture', in R. Chapman and J. Rutherford (eds) *Male Order*. London: Lawrence and Wishart.

Mulvey, L. (1975) 'Visual Pleasure and Narrative Cinema', *Screen*. 16(3): 6.

Mulvey, L. (1981) 'Afterthoughts on "Visual Pleasure and Narrative Cinema" Inspired by *Duel in the Sun*', *Framework* Summer Issue; reprinted in L. Mulvey *Visual and Other Pleasures*. Basingstoke: Macmillan.

Muncie, J. (1984) *The Trouble With Kids Today: Youth Culture and Post-war Britain*. London: Hutchinson.

Murdock, G. and Golding, P. (1977) 'Capitalism, Communication and Class Relations', in J. Curran, M. Gurevitch and J. Woollacott (eds) *Mass Communication and Society*. London: Edward Arnold.

Murphy, R. (1984) 'The Structure of Closure: A Critique and Development of the Theories of Weber, Collins and Parkin', *British Journal of Sociology*. 35: 574–602.

Myhill, A. and Allen, J. (2002) *Rape and Sexual Assault: The Extent and Nature of the Problem*. Home Office Research Study No. 237. London: HMSO.

Naffine, N. (1987) *Female Crime*. Sydney: Allen and Unwin.

Narayan, U. (1989) 'The Project of a Feminist Epistemology: Perspectives from a Nonwestern Feminist', in *Gender/Body/Knowledge: Feminist Reconstructions of Being and Knowing*, reprinted in S. Harding (ed.) (2004) *The Feminist Standpoint Theory Reader*. London: Routledge.

Nava, M. (1992) *Changing Cultures: Feminism, Youth and Consumerism*. London: Sage.

Nayak, A. (1997) 'Frozen Bodies: Disclosing Whiteness in Haagen-Dazs Advertising', *Body and Society*. 3(3): 51–71.

Nicholson, L. (ed.) (1990) *Feminism/Postmodernism*. London: Routledge.

Nixon, S. (1996) *Hard Looks: Masculinities, Spectatorship and Contemporary Consumption*. London: UCL Press.

NUT (National Union of Teachers) (1980) *Promotion and the Woman Teacher*. London and Manchester: National Union of Teachers/Equal Opportunities Commission.

O'Connell Davidson, J. (1995) 'The Anatomy of "Free Choice" Prostitution', *Gender, Work and Organization*. 2: 1–10.

O'Connell Davidson, J. (1997) 'Extended Review: Sex Work – Current Research Agendas', *Work, Employment and Society*. 11(4): 777–779.

O'Connell Davidson, J. (1998) 'Macho Lads in Pornutopia', paper presented at the First European Meeting of the Main Partners in the Fight Against Child Sex Tourism, *Participants' Speeches and Contributions*. Brussels: EC Tourism Directorate.

O'Reilly, K. (2004) 'Developing Contradictions: Women's Participation as a Site of Struggle Within an Indian NGO', *Professional Geographer*. 56(2): 174–184.

Oakley, A. (1972) *Sex, Gender and Society*. London: Temple Smith.

Oakley, A. (1974a) *Housewife*. London: Allen Lane.

Oakley, A. (1974b) *The Sociology of Housework*. London: Martin Robertson.

Oakley, A. (1980) *Women Confined: Towards a Sociology of Childbirth*. Oxford: Martin Robertson.

Oakley, A. (1982) *Subject Women*. London: Fontana.

Oakley, A. (1984a) *The Captured Womb*. Oxford: Blackwell.

Oakley, A. (1984b) 'The Importance of Being a Nurse', *Nursing Times*. 12 (December): 24–27.

Oakley, A. (1987) 'From Walking Wombs to Test-Tube Babies', in M. Stanworth (ed.) *Reproductive Technologies*. Cambridge: Polity.

Oakley, A. (1998) 'Gender, Methodology and People's Ways of Knowing: Some Problems with Feminism and the Paradigm Debate in Social Science', *Sociology*. 32(4): 707–731.

Oakley, A. and Oakley, R. (1979) 'Sexism in Official Statistics', in J. Irvine, I. Miles and J. Evans (eds) *Demystifying Social Statistics*. London: Pluto Press.

Oliver, M. (1983) *Social Work with Disabled People*. London: Macmillan.

Oliver, M. (1990) *The Politics of Disablement*. London: Macmillan.

Oudshoorn, N. (1994) *Beyond the Natural Body: An Archaeology of Sex Hormones*. London: Routledge.

Paechter, C. (1998) *Educating the Other: Gender, Power and Schooling*. London: Falmer.

Pahl, J. (1980) 'Patterns of Money Management within Marriage', *Journal of Social Policy*. 19: 313–335.

Pahl, J. (1983) 'The Allocation of Money and the Structuring of Inequality Within Marriage', *Sociological Review*. 31: 237–262.

Pahl, J. (ed.) (1985) *Private Violence and Public Policy*. London: Routledge and Kegan Paul.

Pahl, J. (1995) 'Health Professionals and Violence Against Women', in P. Kingston and B. Penhale (eds) *Family Violence and the Caring Professions*. London: Macmillan.

Parkin, F. (1979) *Marxism and Class Theory: A Bourgeois Critique*. London: Tavistock.

Parsons, T. and Bales, R. (eds) (1955) *Family, Socialization and Interaction Process*. New York: Free Press.

Pateman, C. (1988) *The Sexual Contract*. Cambridge: Polity.

Paterson, K. and Hughes, B. (2000) 'Disabled Bodies', in P. Hancock, B. Hughes, E. Jagger, K. Paterson, R. Russell, E. Tulle-Winton and M. Tyler (eds) *The Body, Culture and Society: An Introduction*. Buckingham: Open University Press, pp. 29–44.

Penfold, P.S. and Walker, G. (1984) *Women and the Psychiatric Paradox*. Milton Keynes: Open University Press.

Petchesky, R.P. (1987) 'Foetal Images: The Power of Visual Culture in the Politics of Reproduction', in M. Stanworth (ed.) *Reproductive Technologies*. Cambridge: Polity.

Peterson, P.B. and Lach, M.A. (1990) 'Gender Stereotypes in Children's Books: Their Prevalence and Influence in Cognitive and Effective Development', *Gender and Education*. 2: 185–197.

Phillips, A. and Taylor, B. (1980) 'Sex and Skill: Notes Towards a Feminist Economics', *Feminist Review*. 6: 79–88.

Phillipson, C. (1982) *Capitalism and the Construction of Old Age*. London: Macmillan.

Phizacklea, A. (1983) *One Way Ticket: Migration and Female Labour*. London: Routledge.

Phoenix, A. (2002) 'Radicalisation and Gendering in the (Re)production of Educational Inequalities', in B. Francis and C. Skelton (eds) *Investigating Gender*. Buckingham: Open University Press.

Pill, D. and Stott, N. (1986) 'Concepts of Illness Causation and Responsibility: Some Preliminary Data from a Sample of Working Class Mothers', in C. Currer and M. Stacey (eds) *Concepts of Health, Illness and Disease: A Comparative Perspective*. Leamington Spa: Berg.

Plant, S. (1993) 'Beyond the Screens: Film, Cyberpunk and Cyberfeminism', *Variant*. 13–17., reprinted in S. Kemp and J. Squires (eds) (1996) *Feminisms*. Oxford: Oxford University Press, pp. 503–508.

Plant, S. (1997) *Zeroes and Ones: Digital Women and the New Technoculture*. New York: Doubleday.

Plummer, K. (1996) 'Foreword: Symbols of Change', in W. Simon *Postmodern Sexualities*. London: Routledge, pp. ix–xvi.

Pollack, O. (1950) *The Criminality of Women*. Philadelphia: University of Pennsylvania Press.

Pollack, S. (1985) 'Sex and the Contraceptive Act', in H. Holmans (ed.) *The Sexual Politics of Reproduction*. Aldershot: Gower.

Pollert, A. (1981) *Girls, Wives, Factory Lives*. London: Macmillan.

Pollert, A. (1996) 'Gender and Class Revisited; or, The Poverty of Patriarchy', *Sociology*. 30(4): 639–659.

Poovey, M. (1989) 'Scenes of an Indelicate Character: The Medical Treatment of Victorian Women', in S. Jackson and S. Scott (eds) (1996) *Feminism and Sexuality: A Reader*. Edinburgh: Edinburgh University Press, pp. 40–45.

Popay, J. and Jones, J. (1990) 'Patterns of Health and Illness among Lone Parents', *Journal of Social Policy*. 19: 499–534.

Porter, T. (1995) *Trust in Numbers: The Pursuit of Objectivity in Science and Public Life*. Princeton, NJ: Princeton University Press.

Poster, M. (1997) 'Cyberdemocracy: Internet and the Public Sphere', in D. Porter (ed.) *Internet Culture*. New York: Routledge, pp. 201–218.

Prandy, K. (1986) 'Similarities of Lifestyle and Occupations of Women', in R. Crompton and M. Mann (eds) *Gender and Stratification*. Cambride Polity.

Pringle, R. (1989) *Secretaries Talk: Sexuality, Power and Work*. London: Verso.

Pringle, R. (1993) 'Male Secretaries', in C. Williams (ed.) *Doing 'Women's Work'*. London: Sage.

Quart, A. (2003) *Branding: The Buying and Selling of Teenagers*. London: Random House.

Radford, J. (1987) 'Policing Male Violence – Policing Women', in J. Hanmer and M. Maynard (eds) *Women, Violence and Social Control*. London: Macmillan.

Radner, H. (1995) *Shopping Around: Feminist Culture and the Pursuit of Pleasure*. London: Routledge.

Radway, J. (1987) *Reading the Romance: Women, Patriarchy and Popular Literature*. London: Verso.

Ramazanoglu, C. (1987) 'Sex and Violence in Academic Life, or You Can Keep a Good Woman Down', in J. Hanmer and M. Maynard (eds) *Women, Violence and Social Control*. London: Macmillan.

Rattansi, A. (1995) 'Forgetful Postmodernism? Notes from de Bunker', *Sociology*. 29: 339–350.

Reay, D. (2002) 'The Paradox of Contemporary Femininities in Education: Combining Fluidity with Flexibility', in B. Francis and C. Skelton (eds) *Investigating Gender*. Buckingham: Open University Press.

Reid, K. (1985) 'Choice of Method', in N. Loudon (ed.) *Handbook of Family Planning*. Edinburgh: Churchill.

Reinharz, S. (1983) 'Experiential Analysis: A Contribution to Feminist Research', in G. Bowles and R.D. Klein (eds) *Theories of Women's Studies*. London: Routledge and Kegan Paul.

Rich, A. (1980) 'Compulsory Heterosexuality and Lesbian Existence', in A. Rich *Blood, Bread and Poetry*. London: Virago.

Richardson, D. (1998) 'Sexuality and Citizenship', *Sociology*. 32(1): 83–100.

Richardson, D. and Robinson, V. (1994) 'Theorising Women's Studies, Gender Studies and Masculinity: The Politics of Naming', *European Journal of Women's Studies*. 1(1): 11–27.

Riley, D. (1992) 'A Short History of Some Preoccupations', in J. Butler and J. Scott (eds) *Feminists Theorise the Political*. London: Routledge.

Ritzer, G. (1996) *The McDonaldization of Society: An Investigation into the Changing Character of Contemporary Social Life*. Revised edition. Thousand Oaks, CA: Pine Forge Press.

Roberts, E. (1982) 'Working Class Wives and their Families', in J. Barker and M. Drake (eds) *Population and Society in Britain 1850–1980*. London: Batsford.

Roberts, H. (ed.) (1981) *Women, Health and Reproduction*. London: Routledge and Kegan Paul.

Roberts, H. (1985) *The Patient Patients: Women and their Doctors*. London: Pandora.

Robinson, V. (1993) 'Introducing Women's Studies', in D. Richardson and V. Robinson (eds) *Introducing Women's Studies: Feminist Theory and Practice*. London: Macmillan, pp. 1–26.

Roiphe, K. (1993) *The Morning After: Sex, Fear and Feminism*. London: Hamish Hamilton.

Rose, J. (1992) *Marie Stopes and the Sexual Revolution*. London: Faber and Faber.

Roseneil, S. (1995) *Disarming Patriarchy: Feminism and Political Action at Greenham*. Buckingham: Open University Press.

Rosener, J. (1990) 'Ways Women Lead', *Harvard Business Review*. November–December: 119–125.

Rowbotham, S. (1981) 'The Trouble with "Patriarchy"', in R. Samuel (ed.) *People's History and Socialist Theory*. London: Routledge.

Royal College of General Practitioners (1990) *Mortality Statistics from General Practice 1981–1982, Third National Study*. London: HMSO.

Rubin, G. (1984) 'Thinking Sex', in C. Vance (ed.) *Pleasure and Danger*. London: Routledge.

Ruddock, J., Wallace, G. and Chaplin, R. (1996) *School Improvement: What Can Pupils Tell*. London: David Fulton.

Russell, R. and Tyler, M. (2002) 'Thank Heaven For Little Girls: "Girl Heaven" and the Commercial Context of Feminine Childhood', *Sociology*. 36(3): 619–637.

Sahgal, G. (1989) 'Fundamentalism and the Multiculturalist Fallacy', in Southall Black Sisters (eds) *Against the Grain: Southall Black Sisters 1979–1989*. Southall: Southall Black Sisters.

Sanders, T. (2004) 'Controllable Laughter: Managing Sex Work Through Humour', *Sociology*. 38(2): 273–291.

Sandoval, C. (1991) 'US Third World Feminism: The Theory and Method of Oppositional Consciousness in the Postmodern World', *Genders*. 10: 1–14, reprinted in S. Harding (ed.) (2004) *The Feminist Standpoint Theory Reader*. London: Routledge.

Sapsford, R. (1993) 'Understanding People: The Growth of an Expertise', in J. Clarke (ed.) *A Crisis in Care? Challenges to Social Work*. London: Sage.

Sassetti, M.R. (1993) 'Domestic Violence', *Primary Care*. 20(2): 289–306.

Saul, J. (2003) *Feminism: Issues and Arguments*. Oxford: Oxford University Press.

Saussure, F. de (1974) *Course in General Linguistics*. First published 1959. London: Fontana.

Savage, M. (2000) *Class Analysis and Social Transformation*. Buckingham: Open University Press.

Savage, W. (1986) *A Savage Enquiry*. London: Virago.

Sayers, J. (1986) *Sexual Contradictions: Psychology, Psychoanalysis and Feminism*. London: Tavistock.

Scambler, G. and Scambler, A. (1984) 'The Illness Iceberg and Aspects of Consulting Behaviour', in R. Fitzpatrick, T. Hilton, S. Newman, G. Scambler and T. Thompson (eds) *The Experience of Illness*. London: Tavistock.

Scambler, G. and Scambler, A. (1997) *Rethinking Prostitution: Purchasing Sex in the 1990s*. London: Routledge.

Scott, J. (1995) *Sociological Theory: Contemporary Debates*. Aldershot: Edward Elgar.

Scully, D. and Bart, P. (1978) 'A Funny Thing Happened on the Way to the Orifice: Women in Gynaecology Textbooks', in J. Ehrenreich (ed.) *Cultural Crisis of Modern Medicine*. New York: Monthly Review Press.

Scully, D. and Marolla, J. (1993) 'Riding the Bull at Gilleys: Convicted Rapists Describe the Rewards of Rape', in P.B. Bart and E.G. Moran (eds) *Violence against Women: The Bloody Footprints*. London: Sage.

Seabrook, J. (1996) *Travels in the Skin Trade: Tourism and the Sex Industry*. London: Pluto Press.

Seager, J. and Olsen, A. (1986) *Women in the World: An International Atlas*. London: Pluto Press.

Segal, L. (1987) *Is The Future Female?* London: Virago.

Seidler, V. (1994) *Rediscovering Masculinity: Reason, Language and Sexuality*. London: Routledge.

Shaklady Smith, L. (1978) 'Sexist Assumptions and Female Delinquency', in C. Smart and B. Smart (eds) *Women, Sexuality and Social Control*. London: Routledge and Kegan Paul.

Shapiro, R. (1987) *Contraception: A Practical and Political Guide*. London: Virago.

Sharpe, K. (1998) *Red Light, Blue Light: Prostitutes, Punters and the Police*. Aldershot: Ashgate.

Sharpe, S. (1995) *Just Like a Girl*. Second edition. Harmondsworth: Penguin.

Shaw, J. (1976) 'Finishing School: Some Implications of Sex Segregated Education', in D. Barker and S. Allen (eds) *Sexual Divisions and Society: Process and Change*. London: Tavistock.

Sillaste, G. (2004) 'Women's Day in Russia', *The Russia Journal*. 7 April, p. 2.

Simon, W. (1996) *Postmodern Sexualities*. London: Routledge.

Skeggs, B. (1995) 'Introduction' in B. Skeggs (ed.) *Feminist Cultural Theory: Process and Production*. Manchester: Manchester University Press.

Skeggs, B. (1997) *Formations of Class and Gender*. London: Sage.

Additional web-based resources

http://www.eserver.org/feminism/index.html
A US based website with very useful links to women's studies programmes at various universities as well as to women's libraries. This site also includes useful sections on feminist activism and history.

http://www.sociologyonline.co.uk
A useful introductory site that makes links between topical issues and sociological concepts. Ideal for A level students.

http://www.un.org
This is the home page for the United Nations, with a wide range of links to material on gender related topics.

http://www.amnesty.org
An excellent site for material on human rights and inequalities. It also has a vast number of links to research reports and to other relevant sites.

http://www.eoc.org.uk
The home page of the Equal Opportunities Commission in the UK. A very useful source of research material, with excellent links to publications and research reports.

http://www.cre.gov.uk
Similar to the EOC site and very user-friendly, this is a useful source of material on issues relating to race and ethnicity.

http://www.who.org
This is the homepage of the World Health Organization, and contains many useful links as well as downloadable publications and research reports on a range of gender related topics.

http://www.unicef.org
This is the homepage of UNICEF, which provides information and a range of downloadable publications on children across the world.

Author index

Subject index

Abortion 127, 167, 177, 182, 187, 191, 201, 215, 304, 310, 347
Activism: see Politics
Adolescence 126–132: see also Sexual double standard, Sexuality
Adulthood 132–5
Advertising: see Mass media
Age 3, 59
  as socially constructed 117,
Ageing
  and sexuality 134–5,
  ageing populations 117, 137–141, 247,
  ageing and poverty: see Poverty
  feminist perspectives on 137,
  sociological perspectives on 135–6,
  retirement 140–1,
Ageism 141
Agency 8, 20, 21, 145, 214, 217, 248
Androgyny 32, 34
Anthropology 321–2
Anti-feminism 370
Apprenticeships 105, 232
Assaults on wives and partners: see Family
Assisted reproduction: see Pregnancy and childbirth

Backlash xi, 51, 173
'Bedroom culture': see 'Culture of femininity'
Biological determinism 8, 21, 63, 135, 218: see also Sexuality
Birth control: see Pregnancy and childbirth
Body, the 5, 34, 46, 131–5, 168, 211–2, 217–9, 226, 252, 264, 309, 311, 354, 380
'Bricolage' 337
Buffy the Vampire Slayer 6, 160, 359

Camp 222–4
Capitalism 21–3, 28, 44–5, 73, 136, 146–7,

151, 158, 174, 224, 265–6, 268, 270, 282, 319, 325–6, 330–2
Caring: see also Disability, Family, Work
  Caring professions: see Work
  Caring work: see Work
  Informal health care 171, 190, 195–6, 314–5,
Caste xii, 58
Cheerleading 358–9
Child abuse 123–4, 273, 278, 290, 309
Child care 64, 156, 196, 238–9, 246: see also Work
Childbirth: see Pregnancy and childbirth
Childhood 117–126, 200
  child labour 118,
  global experiences of 118–121, 125,
  mortality 120,
  sociological perspectives on 125–6,
  spending 125–6,
Class: see Social class
Clerical work: see Work
Clitoridectomy 34, 49, 198, 288, 310, 364
Cohabitation: see Marriage and cohabitation
Commercial surrogate motherhood: see Motherhood
Compulsory heterosexuality 91, 198, 212, 222, 264, 319
Cosmetic surgery 131, 220
Crime: see also Sexual violence
  committed against women 288–299,
  committed by women 274–9,
  degeneration theories of 272,
  differential association theories of 280–2,
  disorganisation theories of 280–1,
  feminist theories of 278–286,
  'hidden' 277–8,
  labelling theory of 273, 280–1, 283–4,
  Marxist theories of 282,
  positivist theories of

home-based 74,
managerial work 261–4,
men doing 'women's work' 255–7,
part-time 64, 91, 232, 234, 242–3,
    245, 247–8, 259–260, 262, 266,
    315,

professional work 67, 190–5, 204,
    258–261,
racial and ethnic inequalities in 239, 250,
semi-professional work 94,
sexuality at 223, 241, 254, 264–5,
women's orientations to 248–9,

ROUTLEDGE SOCIOLOGY